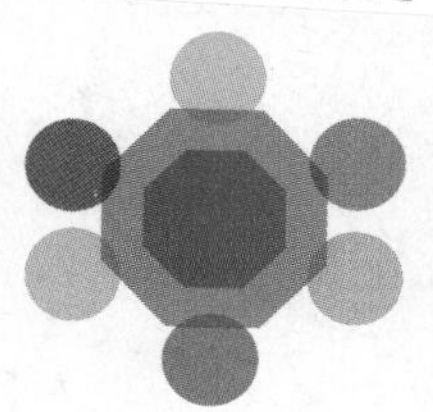

Your Guide to

College Success

Your Guide to College Success

Strategies for Achieving Your Goals

FIFTH EDITION

John W. Santrock
University of Texas, Dallas

Jane S. Halonen
James Madison University

Australia • Brazil • Canada • Mexico • Singapore • Spain • United Kingdom • United States

Your Guide to College Success: Strategies for Achieving Your Goals, **Fifth Edition**
John W. Santrock and Jane S. Halonen

Publisher: Lyn Uhl
Acquisitions Editor: Annie Todd
Development Editor: Elisa Adams
Editorial Assistant: Daniel DeBonis
Senior Technology Project Manager: Stephanie Gregoire
Marketing Manager: Stacy Best
Marketing Communications Manager: Darlene Amidon-Brent
Content Project Manager: Sarah Sherman
Senior Art Director: Cate Rickard Barr

Printed in the United States of America
1 2 3 4 5 6 7 09 08 07 06

Print Buyer: Betsy Donaghey
Permissions Manager: Ronald Montgomery
Production Service/Compositor: Pre-Press Company, Inc.
Text Designer: Rara Avis Graphic Design
Senior Permissions Account Manager, Images: Sheri Blaney
Photo Researcher: Cheri Throop
Cover Designer: Dutton and Sherman Design
Cover Photo: © Kevin Radford/Superstock
Text and Cover Printer: Courier Kendallville

Library of Congress Control Number: 2006907504

ISBN-10: 1-4130-3192-7
ISBN-13: 978-1-4130-3192-8

Thomson Higher Education
25 Thomson Place
Boston, MA 02210-1202
USA

For more information about our products, contact us at:
Thomson Learning Academic Resource Center
1-800-423-0563

For permission to use material from this text or product, submit a request online at **http://www.thomsonrights.com**
Any additional questions about permissions can be submitted by e-mail to **thomsonrights@thomson.com**

Credits appear on pages 359–362, which constitute a continuation of the copyright page.

Brief Contents

Commit to College Success xxi

1 Making Connections 1

2 Master Communication Skills and Build Relationships 31

3 Be a Great Time Manager 61

4 Diversify Your Learning Style 89

5 Expand Your Thinking Skills 119

6 Take It In: Notes and Reading 149

7 Enhance Your Study Skills and Memory 185

8 Succeed on Tests 213

9 Express Yourself 241

10 Take Charge of Your Physical and Mental Health 273

11 Be a Great Money Manager 301

12 Explore Careers 331

Contents

Preface xv

PROLOGUE
Commit to College Success xxi

IMAGES OF COLLEGE SUCCESS xxii
Marian Wright Edelman xxii

Effectively Make the College Transition xxiii
The High School–College Transition xxiii
Strengths of Returning Students xxiv

Clarify Values xxv
Connect Your Values with College Success xxv
Forge Academic Values xxvi

Build Competence xxvi
Set Goals and Work to Reach Them xxvii
Think and Learn xxviii

Manage Life xxviii
Take Responsibility for Your Successes and Failures xxix
Persist Until You Succeed xxix
Get Involved and Tackle Boredom xxix
Manage Your Time xxx

Expand Your Resources xxx

Know Yourself xxx

Create Your Future xxxi
Connect College and Careers xxxi
Master Content and Develop Work and People Skills xxxii

Your Learning Portfolio xxxiii
Self-Assessments xxxiii
Your Journal xxxiii

SUMMARY STRATEGIES FOR MASTERING COLLEGE xxxiv

Review Questions xxxv

Self-Assessment
1 What Are My Values? xxxvi

Your Journal xxxvii
Reflect xxxvii

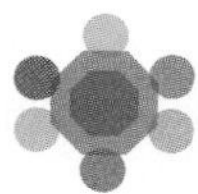

CHAPTER 1
Making Connections 1

IMAGES OF COLLEGE SUCCESS 2
Meg Whitman 2

Explore Your New Environment 3
Get Help from Advisers, Acadamic Support Services, and Counselors 3
Learn about Academic Support Services 4
Delve into the Library 4
Stay Healthy 5
Practice Safety 5
Pursue Extracurricular Activities 6
Connect with Your Community 7
Enrich Your Cultural Life 7
Overcome Limitations 7

Map Your Academic Path with Your Adviser 8
Get to Know Your College Catalog 9
Get the Right Courses 10
Choosing Your Major 10
Explore a Certificate or AA Degree 12
Create a Four- or Five-Year Plan 15
Transfer Credits 15

Connect with Computers 16
Get Up to Speed 16
Explore the Internet 16
Use a Word-Processing Program 17
Online Education 18
Use Computers in Other Ways to Reach Your Goals 19
Avoid Computer Addiction 20

SUMMARY STRATEGIES FOR MASTERING COLLEGE 22

Review Questions 23

Self-Assessments
1 Campus Resources to Meet My Needs 24
2 What Are My Interests? 25
3 A Four- or Five-Year Academic Plan 26
4 Is Online Coursework for Me? 27

Your Journal 28
Reflect / Do / Think Critically / Create 28

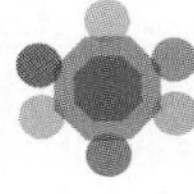

CHAPTER 2
Master Communication Skills and Build Relationships 31

IMAGES OF COLLEGE SUCCESS 32
Oprah Winfrey 32

Communicate Effectively 33
Develop Good Listening Skills 34
Avoid Barriers to Effective Verbal Communication 34
Tune in to Nonverbal Communication 36
Use Communication to Resolve Conflict with Others 36

Develop Good Relationships 38
Recognize Attachment Styles 38
Assess The Social Scene 39
Avoid Sexual Threat 40
Deal with Loneliness 41

Maintain Specific Positive Relationships 42
Connect with Parents at the Right Level 42
Make Room for Partners and Family 43
Relate to Instructors 45
Get Along with Roommates 45
Build Professional Networks 46

Appreciate Diversity 46
Explore Individual and Cultural Differences 47
Gain Insights into Gender Influences 49
Respect Sexual Orientation 51
Improve Your Relationships with Diverse Others 52

SUMMARY STRATEGIES FOR MASTERING COLLEGE 54

REVIEW QUESTIONS 55

Self-Assessments
1 Do You Blow Up, Get Down and Dirty, or Speak Up? 56
2 Loneliness 57

Your Journal 58
Reflect / Do / Think Critically / Create 58

CHAPTER 3
Be a Great Time Manager 61

IMAGES OF COLLEGE SUCCESS 62
Mark Zuckerberg 62

Take Charge of Your Life by Managing Your Time 63
Counter Time-Management Misconceptions 63
Tackle Time Wasters 64
Put the 80–20 Principle into Action 64
Reap the Benefits of Managing Your Time Effectively 65

Connect Values, Goals, and Time 66
Revisit Your Values 66
Revisit Your Goals 66
Develop an Action Plan 67

Plan for the Term, Week, and Day 67
Choose the Right Planning Tools 67
Create a Term Planner 69
Create, Monitor, and Evaluate a Weekly Plan 71
Develop and Adhere to a Daily Plan 74

Never Procrastinate Again (Much) 76
Know What It Means to Procrastinate 77
Conquer Procrastination 78

Balance College, Work, Family, and Commuting 78
Balance College and Work 78
Save Time for Relationships 79
Use Commuting Time Effectively 80

SUMMARY STRATEGIES FOR MASTERING COLLEGE 82

REVIEW QUESTIONS 83

Self-Assessments
1 Evaluating My Week of Time Management 84
2 Are You a Procrastinator? 85

Your Journal 86
Reflect / Do / Think Critically / Create 86

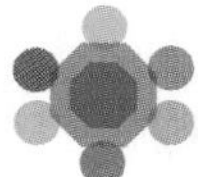

CHAPTER 4

Diversify Your Learning Style 89

IMAGES OF COLLEGE SUCCESS 90
Mia Hamm 90

How You Learn 91
Your Intelligence Profile 91
Sensory Preferences 92
Experiential Learning Preferences 93
Personality Factors 95
Technological Facility 98

Think Strategically about Your Learning 98
Understand How Effort Relates to Learning Style 99

Build Positive Relationships with Instructors 101
Reconcile Your Learning Style with Your Instructor's Teaching Style 101
Create a Good First Impression 102
Maintain the Connection 103
Solve Problems with Instructors 104

Choose a Major That Fits Your Learning Style 107
Target an Intelligent Career 108
Find the Right Mix 109
Keep a Flexible Outlook 111

SUMMARY STRATEGIES FOR MASTERING COLLEGE 112

REVIEW QUESTIONS 113

Self-Assessments
1 Your Intelligence Profile 114
2 Sensory Preference Inventory 115
3 Experiential Learning Preferences 116

Your Journal 117
Reflect / Do / Think Critically / Create 117

CHAPTER 5

Expand Your Thinking Skills 119

IMAGES OF COLLEGE SUCCESS 120
Anne Swift 120

Think Critically 121
Ask Questions 122
Offer Criticism 123
Critical Thinking and the Internet 124

Reason 126
Make the Right Inferences 126
Learn How to Handle Claims 127
Refine Your Reasoning 129

Solve Problems 132
Find the IDEAL Solution 132
Problem-Solver Characteristics 133
Practice Mindfulness 134

Make Good Decisions 135
Avoid Snap Decisions 135

Expand Narrow Thinking 135
Contain Sprawling Thinking 135
Clarify Fuzzy Thinking 135
Recognize Factors in Good Decision Making 136

Think Creatively 136
Break the Locks 136
Foster Creativity 137
Discover "Flow" 138

SUMMARY STRATEGIES FOR MASTERING COLLEGE 140

REVIEW QUESTIONS 141

Self-Assessments
1 The Critical Difference 142
2 How Systematically Do I Solve Problems? 144
3 My Creative Profile 145

Your Journal 146
Reflect / Do / Think Critically / Create 146

CHAPTER 6
Take It In: Notes and Reading 149

IMAGES OF COLLEGE SUCCESS 150
Condoleezza Rice 150

Commit, Concentrate, Capture, Connect 151

Take Charge of Lectures 151
Commit to Class 151
Concentrate 152
Capture Key Ideas 154
Connect Ideas 156

Take Great Lecture Notes 157
Develop Your Style 157
Choose the Best Method 157
Master Note-Taking Strategies 160

Take Charge of Your Reading 163
Commit to Reading Goals 163
Plan Time and Space to Concentrate 165
Capture and Connect 166
Levels of Reading Effort 166
Pick Up the Pace 169
Know How to Read Primary and Secondary Sources 169

Master Reading in Different Disciplines 170

Take Great Reading Notes 172
Choose the Best Method 172
Other Note-Taking Tips 173
Take What You Need from the Internet 176

Process Information Professionally 177

SUMMARY STRATEGIES FOR MASTERING COLLEGE 178

REVIEW QUESTIONS 179

Self-Assessments
1 Auditing Your Note-Taking Style for Lectures 180
2 What's Your Reader Profile? 181
3 How Fast Do You Read? 182

Your Journal 183
Reflect / Do / Think Critically / Create 183

CHAPTER 7
Enhance Your Study Skills and Memory 185

IMAGES OF COLLEGE SUCCESS 186
Janeane Garofalo 186

Plan Your Attack 187
Where to Study 187
When to Study 188
What to Study 189

Master the Disciplines 191
The Humanities 191
Natural Science and Math 192
Social Science 193
Foreign Languages 194

Join a Study Group 195
Making Study Groups Work 195
Overcoming Group-Work Obstacles 196

Overcome Learning Disabilities 196
Evaluate Your Issues 197

Know Your Rights 198
Compensate 199

Improve Your Memory 199
How Memory Works 199
How to Memorize 201
Additional Memory Strategies 202
Evaluate Your Progress 206

SUMMARY STRATEGIES FOR MASTERING COLLEGE 206

REVIEW QUESTIONS 207

Self-Assessments
1 Early Bird or Night Owl? 208
2 Could I Have a Learning Disability? 209
3 Am I Ready to Learn and Remember? 210

Your Journal 211
Reflect / Do / Think Critically / Create 211

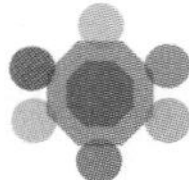

CHAPTER 8
Succeed on Tests 213

IMAGES OF COLLEGE SUCCESS 213
Albert Einstein 214

Get on with It! 215

Get in Gear 215
Plan for the Long Term 216
Plan for the Short Term 216
If You Must, Cram Strategically 219
Set the Stage for Test-Taking Success 220
Control Your Test Anxiety 221
Handle Emergencies Honestly 222

Meet the Challenge 223
Use General Test-Taking Strategies 223
Master Multiple-Choice Strategies 224
Master True/False Strategies 225
Master Fill-in-the-Blank Strategies 225
Master Short-Answer Strategies 226
Master Essay-Question Strategies 226

Make the Grade 228
Recover Your Balance 228
Review Your Work 228
Know When to Challenge 229
Understand Grading Systems 229

Build Your Character 230
Understand Cheating 231
Show Integrity and Resist the Impulse 232

SUMMARY STRATEGIES FOR MASTERING COLLEGE 234

REVIEW QUESTIONS 235

Self-Assessments
1 How Serious Is My Test Anxiety? 236
2 How Well Do I Test? 237
3 Your Personal Honor Code 238

Your Journal 239
Reflect / Do / Think Critically / Create 239

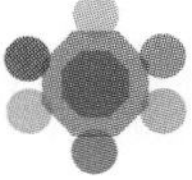

CHAPTER 9
Express Yourself 241

IMAGES OF COLLEGE SUCCESS 242
J. K. Rowling 242

Express Yourself! 243

Prepare Before You Write 243
Clarify Your Goal 244
Define Your Purpose 244
Select a Topic 245
Narrow Your Topic 246
Develop a Working Thesis 247

Do Your Research 248
Gather Sources 248
Master the Library 248
Use the Internet 249

Get Organized 249
Establish Your Writing Routine 249
Develop Your Writing Plan 250
Prepare Outlines 250

Write with Impact 250
Prepare Your First Draft 250
Revise and Revise Again 252
Edit 253
Finish in Style 255

Solve Writing Problems 257
Learn from Feedback 257
Find Your Unique Voice 257
Stop Procrastinating 258
Unlock Writer's Block 258
Build Your Integrity 258

Speak! 261
Pursue the Spotlight 261
Write a Good Speech 261
Deliver a Good Speech 262
Improve Your Speaking Skills 264

SUMMARY STRATEGIES FOR MASTERING COLLEGE 266

REVIEW QUESTIONS 267

Self-Assessments
1 What Are My Writing Strengths and Weaknesses? 268
2 Are You at Risk for Plagiarism? 269
3 What Are My Speaking Strengths and Weaknesses? 270

Your Journal 271
Reflect / Do / Think Critically / Create 271

CHAPTER 10
Take Charge of Your Physical and Mental Health 273

IMAGES OF COLLEGE SUCCESS 274
Brooke Ellison 274

Value Health and Adopt a Healthy Lifestyle 275
Value Your Health 275
Risks to College Students 276

Pursue and Maintain Physical Health 276
Develop Healthy Behaviors and Address Problems 276
Exercise Regularly 277
Get Enough Sleep 277
Eat Right 278
Don't Smoke 280
Avoid Drugs 280
Make the Right Sexual Decisions 284

Safeguard Your Mental Health 287
Cope with Stress 288
Tackle Depression 290
Understand Suicide 291
Seek Help for Mental Health Problems 292

SUMMARY STRATEGIES FOR MASTERING COLLEGE 294

REVIEW QUESTIONS 295

Self-Assessments
1 Is Your Lifestyle Good for Your Health? 296
2 Do I Abuse Drugs? 297
3 My Sexual Attitudes 298

Your Journal 299
Reflect / Do / Think Critically / Create 299

CHAPTER 11
Be a Great Money Manager 301

IMAGES OF COLLEGE SUCCESS 302
Reed Hastings 302

Take Control of Your Finances 303
Look to the Future 303
Recognize Income and Acknowledge Expenses 304
Budget for Success 305
Plan to Save 306

Find the Right Place for Your Money 308
Open a Bank Account 309
Manage Your Accounts 310

Explore Financial Resources 312
Get a Job 312
Pursue Financial Aid 314

Understand Credit 317
Know the Basics 317
Know the Myths 318
Avoid Problems with Credit Cards 318

Say Good-Bye to Debt 321
Reduce Your Expenses 321
Pay It Off Sooner 322
Consider Friends and Family 322
Recognize the Incredible Value of School 322

SUMMARY STRATEGIES FOR MASTERING COLLEGE 324

REVIEW QUESTIONS 325

Self-Assessments
1 Where Does Money Rank? 326
2 Are You a Compulsive Spender? 327
3 Your Money and You 328

Your Journal 329
Reflect / Do / Think Critically / Create 329

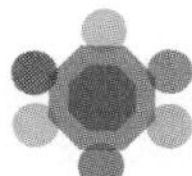

CHAPTER 12

Explore Careers 331

IMAGES OF COLLEGE SUCCESS 331
Giselle Fernandez 332

Evaluate Yourself 333
Choose Career Options That Match Your Values 333
Assess Your Skills 333
Link Your Personality and Career Choice 336

Acquire Positive Work Experiences During College 337
Explore Relevant Part-Time and Summer Jobs 337
Do an Internship or a Co-op 338
Engage in Service Learning 338

Become Knowledgeable about Careers 339
Explore the Occupational Outlook Handbook 339
Select Several Careers, Not Just One 340
Network 340
See a Career Counselor 340
Scope Out Internet Resources 340

Set Career Goals 341

Land a Great Job 341
Know What Employers Want 342
Research the Job 342
Network Some More 343
Create a Résumé and Write Letters 343
Knock 'Em Dead in a Job Interview 345

SUMMARY STRATEGIES FOR MASTERING COLLEGE 346

REVIEW QUESTIONS 347

Self-Assessments
1 My Values and My Career Pursuits 348
2 My Self-Management Skills 349

Your Journal 350
Reflect / Do / Think Critically / Create 350

References 353
Credits 359
Index 363

PREFACE

Your Guide to College Success is a practical, experiential textbook that develops six themes to help students master their college experience by focusing on reachable goals:

- clarify values
- manage life
- create your future
- know yourself
- build competence
- expand your resources

These themes are woven throughout all the chapters and are consistently applied to practical topics like goal setting, learning styles, time management, thinking and study skills, communication, relationships, money management, physical and mental health, and career planning.

Features of the Text

To help students build the skills they need to succeed in the college environment, *Your Guide to College Success* addresses real and pressing student needs for information and guidance on current topics like plagiarism, Internet research, online communities, sexual behavior and birth control, substance abuse, test-taking strategies, efficient reading and memory aids, credit card debt, diet and exercise, and work-life balance.

Each chapter is structured around the following special features:

- **six-strategies model**—a visual map of the book's six themes (clarify values, build competence, etc.)
- **Know Yourself**—a quick prechapter diagnostic to assess the student's current skills, knowledge, and values in relationship to the chapter
- **Images of College Success**—an insightful profile of the formative years in the lives of figures like Netflix founder Reed Hastings, soccer star Mia Hamm, author J. K. Rowling, entrepreneur Anne Swift, and Facebook.com creator Mark Zuckerberg, along with Oprah Winfrey, Condoleezza Rice, Janeane Garofalo, Albert Einstein, and others
- **boxes** that briefly set out tried-and-true tips, examples, strategies, and real-life stories to prominently apply the chapter's content to each of the six themes
- **photos** that make chapter situations come to life
- **marginal quotes** from the famous and not-so-famous throughout history that focus attention on the chapter's relevance in memorable words
- **review questions** to assess learning and ensure mastery
- **self-assessment instruments** to help students personalize their learning and make it concrete
- **journal activities** that take learning a step further into the realm of experience

Other Points of Distinction

The authors' content priorities are focused on the college success course's main goals—to give students practical skills support for each academic discipline, to reinforce personal values for achieving success, and to answer perennial student questions about health, relationships, and money management. The six-theme focus is retained (with new themes more tightly integrated to the chapter content), and the text concludes with a practical look at assessing career options.

The widely acclaimed self-assessment exercises/activities that follow each chapter have been retained, along with popular chapter topics like editing and grammar violations, building a support network, learning styles, stress management, procrastination, eating habits, and a chapter-long discussion of money management, credit card debt, and strategies for reducing spending.

New to This Edition

- The table of contents includes twelve chapters, condensed from thirteen.
- New Chapter 2 covers relationships and diversity more prominently than before.
- New Chapter 9 brings together all coverage of written and spoken communication.
- A brief new Preface to the Student stresses student commitment to success.
- Six new themes, including "Know Yourself," "Manage Life," and "Create Your Future" help students focus on a set of achievable goals.
- Nearly all the Images of College Success are new and introduce people relevant to students' lives and experiences.
- Increased attention to diversity and nontraditional students is given throughout the text, the examples, and the illustrations.
- Coverage of plagiarism and responsible use of the Internet has been increased.
- Discussions of computer topics, including privacy, online communities, online learning, and blogging, have been expanded and updated.
- Coverage of birth control has been updated.

For Instructors

Instructor's Manual/Test Bank for *Your Guide to College Success: Strategies for Achieving Your Goals,* Fifth Edition (1-4130-3261-3). This is a comprehensive guide for teaching the freshman seminar course. It includes sections on using popular culture in the freshman seminar classroom, advice for first-time instructors, and hints on integrating technology resources in the classroom. Each chapter contains additional activities, collaborative learning suggestions, alternative teaching strategies, and quiz questions, including essays to be used for discussion, testing, or journal writing.

MultiMedia Manager for College Success 2007 (1-4130-2791-1). This easy-to-use tool helps you assemble, edit, and present custom multimedia lectures for your college success course. Organized into thirteen common college success topics, the MultiMedia Manager contains PowerPoint® slides, digitized CNN® video clips, full-color images from our textbooks and other sources, and live web links. The MultiMedia Manager is available free to adopters of this text.

WebTutor™ on WebCT for *Your Guide to College Success: Strategies for Achieving Your Goals,* Fifth Edition (1-4282-9978-5), or WebTutor™ on Blackboard for *Your Guide to College Success: Strategies for Achieving your Goals,* Fifth Edition (1-4282-9979-3). This is a content-rich, web-based teaching and learning tool. Use WebTutor to post syllabi, set up threaded discussions, track student progress on quizzes, and hold virtual office hours. WebTutor is easily customizable to specific course needs. In addition to course management capabilities, WebTutor contains an array of exercises, activities, an electronic journal, and additional resources.

ExamView® Computerized Test Bank for *Your Guide to College Success: Strategies for Achieving your Goals,* Fifth Edition (1-4130-3264-8). ExamView is a premiere test-building program that allows instructors to quickly create tests and quizzes customized to individual courses. ExamView's Quick Test Wizard guides you step by step through the process of creating and printing a test in minutes. Tests can contain up to 250 questions using 12 unique types of questions.

Videos. See your Thomson Wadsworth representative for more information.

ABC Video for College Success 2008 (1-4130-3300-8). An exclusive series of video clips has been selected by Wadsworth and the ABC television network, specifically for use in college success courses.

***10 Things Every Student Needs to Know to Study* (1-4130-1533-6).** This 60-minute video covers such practical skills as note-taking, test-taking, and listening.

***10 Things Every Student Needs to Succeed in College* (1-4130-2907-8).** This concise video illustrates ten highly effective practices that every student needs to master to ensure a successful college experience.

Custom Publishing Options. Faculty can select chapters from this and other Wadsworth College Success titles to bind with your own materials into a fully customized book. For more information, contact your Wadsworth/Thomson Learning representative or visit www.thomsonedu.com/success/.

College Success Workshops. Wadsworth offers on-campus regional training designed to focus on the demands of teaching college success courses as well as web e-seminars. These workshops and e-seminars provide active learning exercises you can use to enhance your course, and they provide an opportunity for instructors and administrators to exchange ideas. See www.thomsonedu.com/success/ for more details regarding the locations of the live workshops and the schedule for the e-seminars.

For Students

A **single Sign-On Card (1-4130-3285-0)** is available with a new textbook. Students open the card, create an account at www.thomsonedu.com/login/, and can access the following free resources:

- **ThomsonNOW™ College Success.** This is an integrated testing, tutorial, and class management system that is as powerful as it is easy to use. For instructors, it provides assignable exercises, with students' test results flowing automatically to a grade book. For students, it offers a Pre-test, Personalized Study Plan, and Post-test for each of the book's chapters, helping students improve their performance in the classroom. This dynamic web-based teaching and learning tool replaces the CD-ROM that accompanied previous editions of this book.
- **College Success Factors Index.** This unique online assessment tool measures eight indices that can affect student adjustment to college life. An excellent pre-

and post-test for incoming freshmen, this online assessment provides a way for individual instructors to tailor their course topics to the needs of the students. The data collected can also be applied to longitudinal studies of college success and freshman seminars on a schoolwide level. For more information about the CSFI, visit www.thomsonedu.com/success.

- **Companion website.** A free companion website is available at www.thomsonedu.com/success/santrock5. Containing many useful assessment exercises, practice quizzes, and other useful tools, the site is organized by chapter so that students can use it in conjunction with the book to make the most of their learning opportunities.

Premiere College Success Academic Planner (1-4130-2905-1). Thomson Wadsworth is pleased to offer a spiral-bound calendar designed for first-year college students. Featuring eighteen-month coverage, a unique design, and plenty of room for students to record their academic and personal commitments and schedule, the planner is a great way to encourage time management skills. For a minimal extra charge, the planner can be offered as a bundle with the textbook.

Acknowledgments

We are fortunate to have worked with three remarkable people—Annie Todd, Carolyn Merrill, and Elisa Adams—whose expertise, passion, and commitment have made the fifth edition of this book far better than its predecessors.

College Success Director Annie Todd and Executive Editor Carolyn Merrill provided insights and enthusiasm that helped to improve dramatically the fifth edition of this book. Development Editor Elisa Adams put her mind and heart into this positive revision with the result of a much-improved book. We also appreciate the superb support of this project by Editor-in-Chief P. J. Boardman and Thomson Higher Education CEO Susan Badger. We thank our spouses—Mary Jo Santrock and Brian Halonen—for their enthusiastic support of our work, patient tolerance of our work habits, and good-humored companionship.

We also would like to extend our appreciation to the reviewers, whose time, opinions, and suggestions helped to make this fifth edition a better book:

Yvonne Fry, *Community College of Denver*
Laurie Grimes, *Lorain Community College*
Elizabeth Kennedy, *Florida Atlantic University*
Susan Landgraf, *Highline Community College*
Judy Lynch, *University of Kansas*
Donna Musselman, *Santa Fe Community College*
Ricardo Romero, *University of New Mexico*
Kimberly Shaw, *Boise State University*
Susan Sparling, *California Polytechnic State University*
Lester Tanaka, *Community College of Southern Nevada*
Brenda Winn, *Texas Technical University*

In addition, we thank the reviewers of previous editions:

Anne Aiken-Kush, *University of Nebraska, Omaha*
Alicia Andrade-Owens, *California State University, Fresno*

Frank Ardaiolo, *Winthrop University*
Diane D. Ashe, *Valencia Community College*
Clarence Balch, *Clemson University*
Marilyn Berrill, *Joliet Junior College*
Nate Bock, *University of Nebraska, Omaha*
Phyllis Braxton, *Pierce College, Los Angeles*
Cynthia Bryant, *Tennessee Technical University*
Tricia Bugajski, *University of Northeast Oklahoma*
Bev Cavanaugh, *Joliet Junior College*
Diana Ciesko, *Valencia Community College*
Dorothy R. Clark, *Montgomery Community College*
Carol A. Copenhefer, *Central Ohio Technical College*
Dr. Kara Craig, *University of Southern Mississippi*
Anne Daly, *Cumberland County College*
Susann B. Deason, *Aiken Community College*
Cynthia Desrochers, *California State University, Northridge*
Anthony R. Easley, *Valencia Community College*
Susan Epstein, *Drexel University*
Barbara Foltz, *Clemson University*
Stephen Ford, *Anne Arundel Community College*
Cheryl Fortner-Wood, *Winthrop University*
D. Allen Goedeke, *High Point University*
Lorraine Gregory, *Duquesne University*
M. Katherine Grimes, *Ferrum College*
Erica Henningsen, *Colorado School of Mines*
Hollace Hubbard, *Lander University*
Lucky Huber, *University of South Dakota*
Cynthia Jenkins, *University of Texas, Dallas*
Elvira Johnson, *Central Piedmont Community College*
Laura Kauffman, *Indian River Community College*
Christine Landrum, *Mineral Area College*
Alice Lanning, *University of Oklahoma*
Judy Lynch, *Kansas State University*
Jeannie Manning, *University of Nebraska, Kearney*
Maritza Martinez, *State University of New York, Albany*
Kathleen McGough, *Broward Community College*
Alison Murray, *Indiana University/Purdue University, Columbus*
Christina Norman, *University of Oklahoma*
Jean Oppel, *Oklahoma State University*
David M. Parry, *Pennsylvania State, Altoona*
Jori Beth Psencik, *University of Texas, Dallas*
Glen Ricci, *Lake Sumter Community College*
Marti Rosen-Atherton, *University of Nebraska, Omaha*
Diane Savoca, *St. Louis Community College*
Regina C. Schmidt, *Texas Women's University*
Karen Siska, *Columbia State Community College*
Kathleen Speed, *Texas A&M University*
Sarah Spreda, *University of Texas, Dallas*
Nancy Taylor, *Radford University*
Karen Valencia, *South Texas Community College*
Vivian Van Donk, *Joliet Junior College*

Kimberly Vitchkoski, *University of Massachusetts, Lowell*
Mary Walz-Chojnacki, *University of Wisconsin, Milwaukee*
Vicki White, *Emmanuel College*
Donald Williams, *Grand Valley State University*
Kathi Williams, *College of the Siskiyous*
Kaye Young, *Jamestown Community College*

Prologue

© Royalty-Free/CORBIS

KNOW YOURSELF

BY ENTERING COLLEGE, you've embarked on an important journey. What is life like as you make this transition? To evaluate where you stand right now, place a check next to only those items that apply to you, leaving the others blank.

- I know what my values are and how they will connect with my success in college.
- I am highly motivated to be a competent person.
- I effectively manage my life.
- I have good resources.
- I know myself well and I have high self-esteem.
- I am confident about my ability to create a positive future for myself.

As you read about Marian Wright Edelman on the next page, think about what her values are and how motivated she is.

CHAPTER OUTLINE

Effectively Make the College Transition

The High School–College Transition
Strengths of Returning Students

Clarify Values

Connect Your Values with College Success
Forge Academic Values

Build Competence

Set Goals and Work to Reach Them
Think and Learn

Manage Life

Take Responsibility for Your Successes and Failures
Persist Until You Succeed
Get Involved and Tackle Boredom
Manage Your Time

Expand Your Resources

Know Yourself

Create Your Future

Connect College and Careers
Master Content, and Develop Work and People Skills

Your Learning Portfolio

Self-Assessments
Your Journal

Images of College Success

Marian Wright Edelman

Marian Wright Edelman is the head of the Children's Defense Fund, an advocacy group for poor, minority, and handicapped children. For more than two decades she has worked to advance the health and well-being of children in the United States. When she was fourteen, her father died. The last thing he told her was to let nothing get in the way of her education. Four years later she entered Spelman College in Atlanta. Challenged by college, Edelman responded by working hard. Beginning in her junior year, she won scholarships to study in Paris and Moscow.

Edelman later commented that the experiences abroad showed her that she could navigate the world and do just about anything. She later graduated from Yale Law School and became the first African-American woman to pass the bar and practice law in the state of Mississippi.

In her book *The Measure of Our Success* (1992), Edelman highlighted several lessons about life for college-aged students, including:

Create opportunities. Don't think that you are entitled to anything you don't sweat and struggle for. Take the initiative to create opportunities. Don't wait around for favors. Don't assume a door is closed. Push on it until you get it open.

Challenge yourself to do things right. Everyone makes mistakes. Don't be afraid of taking risks or being criticized. It's the way you learn to do things right. It doesn't matter how many times you fall down. What matters is how many times you get up.

Don't ever stop learning and improving your mind. College is a great investment. But you can't just park your mind there as if everything you need to know will be poured into it. Be an active learner. Be curious and ask questions. Explore every new horizon you can.

© Theo Westenberger

MARION WRIGHT EDELMAN (center) mastered the college experience and went on to become a powerful advocate for improving the lives of children.

Success in college? It is not enough to just want to be successful. By taking an active role in mastering specific skills and strategies, you can actually shape your own success. The Six Strategies for Success listed to the left will help form the foundation of your success . . . not just in college, but in life. As you read each chapter, you will begin to see how much you can accomplish by clarifying values, building competence, managing life, expanding your resources, knowing yourself, and creating your future.

Effectively Make the College Transition

Life is change and college is change. Whether you have entered college right out of high school or as a returning student, you'll need to adapt to this new place. What unexpected things are going on around you? What's different? What changes are you going through as you make this transition? In this and every chapter, you'll be able to assess where you are now, what you need to change, and how to change. Consider these issues in the Journal activity "Your New Life" on page xxxvii.

The High School–College Transition

One first-year student said that a difference between high school and college is that in high school you can't go off campus for lunch because you aren't allowed, but in college you can't because you can't afford it. Here are some more important differences; you'll probably be able to add your own observations:

- *College classes are much larger, more complex, and more impersonal.* Your teachers in high school probably knew your name and maybe even your family. In college, however, your instructors may not know your name or recognize your face outside class.
- *In college, attendance may be up to you.* Although some of your instructors will require attendance, many won't. If you miss class, it's your responsibility to find out what you missed. Most instructors do not allow makeup work without a reasonable, well-documented explanation.
- *College instructors give fewer tests.* They may hold you responsible for more than what they say in class. Some won't let you make up tests.
- *In college, nobody treats you like a kid anymore.* You have more independence, choices, and responsibility. You are more on your own about how you use your time than you were in high school.
- *You have to do much more reading in college.* More of your work will need to be done outside class. You may be expected to make your own decisions about what information from your reading is most important for you to remember.

- *Good grades are harder to get in college.* In many colleges, there is more competition for grades than in high school, and instructors set the bar higher for an A or B.
- *Your college classmates may be more diverse in age and backgrounds.* Look around. You'll probably see more older individuals and more people from different cultures than you did in your high school.

> ***Life is change.***
> ***Growth is optional.***
> ***Choose wisely.***
> Karen Kaiser Clark
> *Twentieth-century American author*

Strengths of Returning Students

An increasing number of students start or finish college at an older age (Pryor and others 2005). Today more than one out of five full-time students and two-thirds of part-time students are returning students. Some work full-time, are married, have children or grandchildren, are divorced, retired, or changing careers. Some have attended college before, while others have not.

If you have entered or returned to college at an older age, you may experience college differently from recent high school graduates. You may have to balance your class work with commitments to a partner, children, a job, and community responsibilities. This means you may have less flexibility about when you can attend classes. You may need child care or have special transportation needs. As an older student, you may lack confidence in your skill and abilities or undervalue your knowledge and experience.

Despite such challenges, as a returning student you bring specific strengths to campus. These include a wide range of life experiences that you can apply to issues and problems in class.

Your multiple commitments may stimulate you to be more skilled than younger students in managing your time. You may have greater maturity in work habits and more experience participating in discussions. You may also face setbacks more easily. Failing a pop quiz, for instance, is not likely to feel devastating for those who have experienced greater disappointments in life.

What are some strengths of returning students?

See "Expand Your Resources: Returning-Student Strategies" for some helpful guidelines.

Returning-Student Strategies

Evaluate your support system. A strong and varied support system can help you adapt to college. If you have a partner or family, their encouragement and understanding can help a lot. Your friends also can lend support.

Make new friends. As you seek out friends of different ages, focus on meeting other older students. You'll find they also juggle responsibilities and are anxious about their classes.

Get involved in campus life. The campus is not just for younger students. Check out the organizations and groups at your college. Join one or more that interest you.

Don't be afraid to ask for help. Learn about the services your college offers. Health and counseling services can help you with the special concerns of older students. These include parenting and child care, divorce, and time management. If you have any doubts about your academic skills, get some help from the study skills professionals on your campus.

© Bill Aron/PhotoEdit

What are some strengths of returning students?

Clarify Values

Just what are "values"? Values are our beliefs and attitudes about the way we think things *should* be. They involve what is important to us. We attach values to all sorts of things: politics, religion, money, sex, education, helping others, family, friends, self-discipline, career, cheating, taking risks, self-respect, and so on. As the contemporary U.S. columnist Ellen Goodman commented, "Values are not trendy items that can be traded in."

Connect Your Values with College Success

One of the most important benefits of college is that it gives you the opportunity to explore and clarify your values. Why is this so critical? Our values represent what matters most to us, so they should guide our decisions. Without seriously reflecting on what your values are, you may spend too much time in your life on things that really aren't that important to you. Clarifying your values will help you determine which goals you really want to go after and where to direct your motivation. Clarify Values is one of the most important Strategies for Success listed on page xxiii and explored throughout this book.

Sometimes we're not aware of our values until we find ourselves in situations that expose them. For example, you might be surprised to find yourself reacting strongly when you discuss religion or politics with other students. Spend some time thinking about and clarifying your values. This will help you determine what things in life are most important to you. Self-Assessment 1, "What Are My Values," on page xxxvi will help you with this process. One of the values listed in this self-assessment is "happiness." What makes college students happy? A recent study compared very happy college students with their counterparts who were average in happiness or unhappy (Diener and Seligman 2002). Very happy college students were more likely to be socially connected with positive romantic and/or social relationships.

Many students place family relationships high on their list of values. Positive, supportive family relationships can help you through some difficult times as you go through college. One self-assessment that you can take to discover the extent of your family's involvement in your values is called the *College Success Factors Index* (Halberg, Halberg, and Sauer 2000). You can complete this self-assessment at the Wadsworth College Success website: http://www.thomsonedu.com/success

Stephen Covey, author of the highly successful book *The Seven Habits of Highly Effective People: Powerful Lessons in Personal Change* (1989), has helped many individuals clarify their values. He stresses that each of us needs to identify the underlying principles that are important in our lives and then evaluate whether we are living up to those standards. Covey asks you to imagine that you are attending your own funeral and are looking down at yourself in the casket. You then take a seat, and four speakers (a family member, a friend, someone from your work, and someone from your church or community organization) are about to give their impressions of you. What would you want them to say about your life? This reflective thinking exercise helps you to look into the social mirror and visualize how other people see you. See "Clarify Values: Matching Your Dreams and Your Values" for some other helpful tips from Covey.

Matching Your Dreams and Your Values

Stephen Covey and his colleagues (Covey, Merrill, and Merrill 1994) recommend the following to help you clarify your values (use your watch to go through the timed exercises):

1. Take one minute and answer this question: *If I had unlimited time and resources, what would I do?* It's okay to dream. Write down everything that comes into your mind.
2. Return to Self-Assessment 1 on page xxxvi and review the list of five values that are the most important to you.
3. Take several minutes to compare this list with your dreams. You may be living with unconscious dreams that don't mesh with your values. If you don't get your dreams out in the open, you may spend years living with illusions and the feeling that you somehow are settling for second best. Work on the two lists until you feel that your dreams match up with your values.
4. Take one minute to see how your values relate to four fundamental areas of human fulfillment: physical needs, social needs, mental needs, and spiritual needs. Do your values reflect these four needs? Work on your list until they do.

Forge Academic Values

Throughout your college career, you will be making many choices that reflect your values (Narvaez 2006). Although your primary goal in seeking a college education may be learning about new ideas, your journey through college can also help to build your character.

Participate Fully College involves a higher level of personal responsibility than most students experienced in high school. This freedom can be alluring, even intoxicating. Especially when instructors do not require attendance, you may be tempted to skip classes. What's wrong with skipping class?

- It's expensive. See Figure P.1 to calculate how much a skipped class will cost.
- It harms your learning.
- It hurts your grades.
- It annoys those who end up lending you their notes to copy. (If you must miss a class, be sure to borrow notes from someone who is doing well in the course!)

Throughout college you will frequently have opportunities to clarify your academic values. For example, when you make a choice to linger over a computer game rather than get to class on time, you make a statement about what really matters to you. The frivolous minutes you spend in short-term pleasures may cost you some points on the next exam. Deciding early to do your best, even if it requires sacrifice, will have the best long-term payoff.

Participate with Integrity Most campuses publish in their college handbooks their expectations about appropriate academic conduct. Many colleges have adopted an honor code to promote academic integrity.

This represents your formal agreement to abide by rules of conduct that promote trust and high ethical standards. Typically, codes address such problems as cheating, plagiarism (submitting someone else's work for your own), or other forms of dishonest performance. When a student violates the campus honor code, it dictates how severe the consequences might be. These may include something as mild as "censure," formal recognition of wrongdoing, to expulsion from school.

Why do some students make choices that put them at risk for expulsion? They cheat or plagiarize based on faulty conclusions:

1. The risk of getting caught is small.
2. There is no other way to be "successful."
3. The penalty for getting caught won't be severe.

Why should you embrace academic integrity and commit to doing your best?

1. *Practicing academic integrity builds moral character.* Doing the right thing often means doing the hard thing.
2. *Choosing moral actions builds others' trust in you.*
3. *Making fraudulent grades keeps you from learning important things that will benefit you in the future.*

By clarifying your values, you gain a better idea of how to build competence and where to direct your energy and motivation.

FIGURE P-1 The Cost of Cutting Class

How much tuition did you pay for this term?
How many credits must you take on your campus to be considered full-time?
Divide the full-time hours into your tuition dollars (cost per credit hour):
How many credit hours does the course youre most tempted to avoid have?
Multiply the course credit hours by the cost per credit hour (cost of the course):
How many classes meet in this course over the term?
Divide the cost of the course by the number of classes:
The final calculation represents the financial loss that happens every time you cut this class.

Build Competence

An extremely important aspect of your college years is to build your competence. Among the ways to do this are to set goals and put forth considerable effort to reach them; you must also think and learn effectively.

Set Goals and Work To Reach Them

For every goal you set, ask yourself, "Is it challenging? Is it reasonable? Is it specific?" Be realistic, but stretch yourself to achieve something meaningful. Also be concrete and precise.

Instead of, "I want to be successful," commit to a goal like, "I want to achieve a 3.5 average this term." One study found that individuals who construct their goals in concrete terms were 50 percent more likely to be confident that they would attain them and 32 percent more likely to feel in control of their lives than those who created abstract goals (Howatt 1999).

Make a Personal Plan A goal is nothing without a means of achieving it. Good planning means getting organized mentally, which often requires writing things down. It means getting your life in order and controlling your time and your life, instead of letting your world and time control you.

> ***A goal is a dream with a deadline.***
> Napoleon Hill
> *Contemporary American author*

Set Completion Dates for Your Goals Set completion dates for your goals and work out schedules to meet them. If you want to obtain a college degree, you might want to set a goal of four to six years from now as your completion date, depending on how much time each year you can devote to college. If your goal is to make one good friend, you might want to set a time of six weeks from now for achieving it. If your goal is to become the funniest person on campus, set a date for that as well.

Create Subgoals In *Even Eagles Need a Push* (1990), David McNally suggests that as you set goals and plan, you should think in terms of intermediate steps or subgoals. McNally recommends living your life one day at a time and making your commitments in daily, bite-sized chunks. Don't let long periods of time slip by when you aren't working on something that will help you reach your goals.

You don't need to do everything today, but you should do something every day. Researchers have found that people who do not feel they are taking steps toward their goals are five times more likely to give up and three times less likely to feel satisfied with their lives (Elliott 1999).

One of your life goals is obtaining a college degree. You can break this down into either four subgoals (if you're in a four-year degree program) or two subgoals (if you're in a community college). Each subgoal can be the successful completion of a year in your degree program. You can break these subgoals down into getting successful grades on exams, quizzes, and term papers, and so on. Also set aside the amount of time you plan to study each week. Figure P.2 illustrates this strategy.

Commit and Get Started Now Commit yourself today to setting goals and reaching them. A true commitment is a heartfelt promise to yourself that you will not back down. Your goals should engage you. If your goals do not move you, if they don't inspire you to action, then you need to re-evaluate them and come up with goals that do challenge and excite you.

Monitor Your Progress Effective monitoring lets you know whether you are spending too little time on the tasks you need to complete to accomplish your goal. Make daily lists of things you need to do to stay on track toward your goal. Place the list where you can easily see it, such as on a calendar or taped to the inside of your personal planner or address book. Check each day to be sure you've done what you need

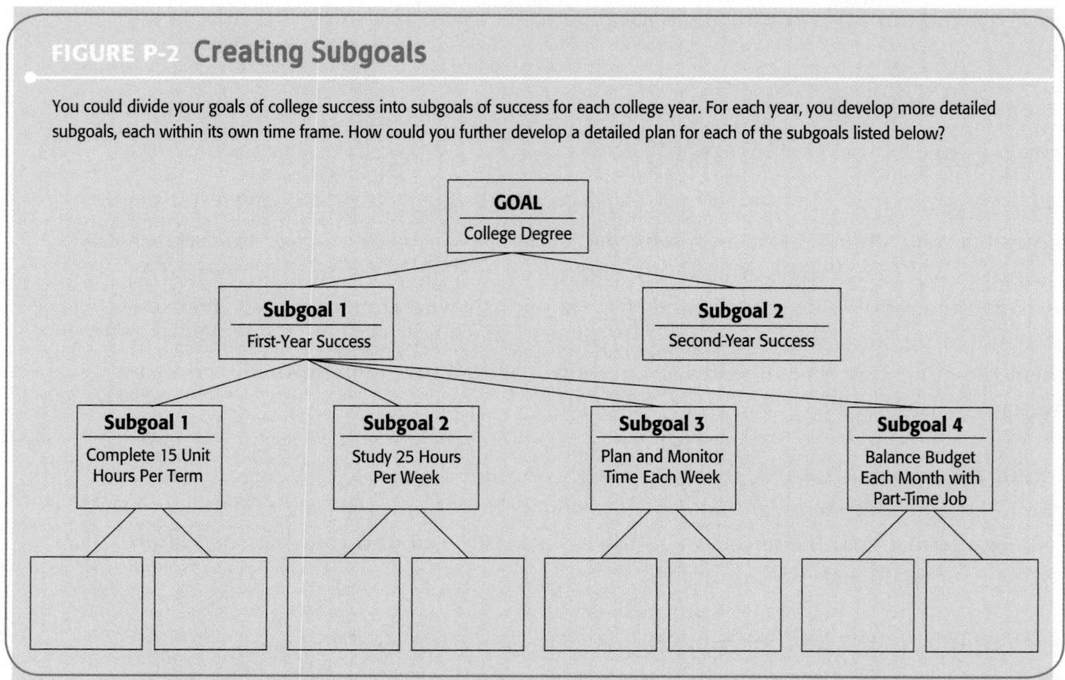

FIGURE P-2 **Creating Subgoals**

You could divide your goals of college success into subgoals of success for each college year. For each year, you develop more detailed subgoals, each within its own time frame. How could you further develop a detailed plan for each of the subgoals listed below?

to. Chapter 3 discusses such strategies in more depth. If after a week or month you find that you are falling behind, evaluate what you can do to get back on track.

Look at the setbacks you experience as opportunities to learn. Not only can you learn what you might have done wrong but also you can learn what led you to choices you have made. Are you seeking the goals you truly want?

Think and Learn

Building competence involves putting a great deal of effort into thinking and learning. College is a place to think and learn; practice thinking reflectively, critically, and productively. Keep an open mind about different ideas and decide for yourself what you believe. Evaluate, analyze, create, solve problems, and poke holes in arguments. Be prepared to show "why" and back up your assertions with solid evidence. Don't just stay on the surface of problems. Stretch your mind.

Some courses may put you to sleep because they don't tie in well with your needs and current interests. Others may spark new interests and even make you passionate about a subject. Where you "catch fire" and become highly motivated to learn will point you to a successful future. Remember that not all learning takes place in the classroom. If a topic in class seems interesting to you, explore it more deeply. Scan books and journals and do online searches on the topic, picking out several articles to read more closely.

To succeed in college you need many work skills, such as knowing how to take good notes, participate in class, collaborate with other students, and interact with instructors.

You also need good study and test-taking strategies and good reading, writing, and speaking skills. The following chapters will provide you with a solid foundation and extensive strategies for improving these skills.

Manage Life

Managing your life effectively is going to equate to college success for you. Especially important is to take responsibility for your behavior.

Take Responsibility for Your Successes and Failures

If you take responsibility for your successes and failures, you have an internal locus of control. If you don't take such personal responsibility and let others, or luck, be responsible for what happens to you, you have an external locus of control. Being internally controlled means seeing yourself as responsible for your achievement, believing that your own effort is what gets you to your goals, and being self-motivated. Being internally controlled can help you succeed in college (Wigfield, Byrnes, and Eccles 2006).

M. Scott Peck (1978, 1997) made some insightful comments in his book *The Road Less Traveled* about internal control and self-responsibility. He says that life is difficult and that each of us will experience pain and disappointment.

Peck believes that we might be right that some of our problems are caused by other people, including our parents. However, you are not going to succeed in college and life thereafter by continually blaming others. Peck urges you to take responsibility for yourself. For ways to increase your internal control, see "Manage Life: Becoming More Internally Controlled."

Becoming More Internally Controlled

These are some good strategies for becoming more internally controlled:

Take self-responsibility. Don't blame others or bad luck for your problems and failures. Recognize how important self-motivation is for college success.

Maximize your effort. Understand that the more effort you put forth, the more you are likely to feel that you are responsible for your achievement outcomes.

Engage in positive self-talk. When you face a challenging task in a course, tell yourself, "I can do it" rather than "I cannot do it." Positive self-talk is especially important when you are feeling stressed out.

Examine your skills and resources. Take a careful look at your skills and evaluate which ones are strengths and which ones are weaknesses.

Also assess the resources (such as study skills instructors, counselors, and tutors) that could help you improve skills critical for college success. Engaging in this type of reflective self-evaluation is an indication that you are on the road to self-responsibility and a stronger internal locus of control.

Being internally motivated, though, does not mean doing everything in isolation. Surround yourself with other motivated people. Ask individuals who are successful how they motivate themselves. Find a mentor, such as an experienced student, an instructor, or a teaching assistant you respect, and ask for advice on motivation.

Some first-year college students lack motivation because they have not separated their parents' "shoulds" from their own, sometimes opposite, interests and motivations. Examine your motivations and interests. Are they yours, or are you currently acting as a clone to fulfill your parents' or someone else's motivations and interests? Your motivation will catch fire when you are doing what YOU want to do. To think further about the importance of internal control, see "Manage Life: Becoming More Internally Controlled."

Persist Until You Succeed

Being motivated also involves persistence. Getting through college is a marathon, not a hundred-yard dash. Studying a little here and a little there won't work. To be successful you have to study often, almost every day for weeks and months at a time. You'll often need to make small sacrifices to gain long-term rewards. College is not all work and no play, but if you mainly play you will pay for it by the end of the term. Remember, from the beginning of the chapter, Marian Wright Edelman's advice not to feel entitled to anything for which you don't sweat and struggle.

Get Involved and Tackle Boredom

Successful college students are often involved in college activities. This can be accomplished in many ways—through socializing and studying with friends, engaging in extracurricular activities, living on campus, having a part-time campus job, and interacting with faculty. Students who are not involved in college activities frequently feel socially isolated and unhappy with their college experience.

If you want to become more involved, think about the values you listed in Self-Assessment 1, "What Are My Values?" What interests do these values suggest?

To explore them, you can get to know new people, seek out new situations, ask new questions, read new books, and re-examine your school's catalog for new ideas and possibilities that turn on your mind.

Manage Your Time

Learning takes a lot of time. Your life as a college student will benefit enormously if you become a great time manager. If you waste too much time, you'll find yourself poorly prepared the night before an important exam, for instance. If you manage time well, you can relax before exams and other deadlines. Time management will help you be more productive and less stressed, with a better balance between work and play. Chapter 3 is all about managing time. Among other things, it will explain how to set priorities, eliminate procrastination, and monitor your time.

Expand Your Resources

An important aspect of learning is figuring out what resources are available to you and the best ways to use them. Family members and friends can be important resources. Your college also has many resources that can support your college success, including academic advisers, physicians, mental health counselors, and many others. Become acquainted with these resources early in your college transition, and don't hesitate to use them when you think that you need help. In the next chapter, we will extensively explore your connection to campus and ways to use college resources.

To get the most out of your college education, you need to be familiar with computers. We encourage you to take every opportunity to effectively use the computer and applications such as word processing, e-mail, and the World Wide Web. If you don't already have good computer skills, developing them will make your college life much easier and improve your chances of landing a good job later. From the humanities to the sciences, we now are squarely in the middle of the information age and the technological revolution.

Throughout the book, you'll find strategies for using technology to your advantage in both college and your career. Chapter 1 offers many strategies for effectively using a computer, and Chapter 3 presents the benefits of electronic planners. On the website for this book, http://www.thomsonedu.com/success/santrock5 you can connect with many other sites that have information to help you master college.

Know Yourself

> ***As long as you keep searching, the answers will come.***
> Joan Baez
> *American folksinger*

Knowing yourself is an important aspect of college success. For example, if you don't know yourself well, you may end up with a major and ultimately a career that you don't enjoy. Knowing yourself involves exploring your identity and asking yourself questions such as: Who am I? What am I all about? What do I want to do with my life? (Kroger 2006).

At the beginning of this chapter, you read a section titled, "Know Yourself." Each chapter begins with the feature, and asks you to reflect about various aspects of yourself related to the key topics of a chapter.

The college years represent one of the most important, if not the most important, time(s) in your entire life for forging your identity (Arnett 2006). Take advantage of your college years to explore what you want to do with your life and to understand yourself better.

Self-esteem is an important part of your identity. Self-esteem is your general evaluation of yourself—how you feel about you, the image you have of yourself. Self-esteem will give you the confidence to tackle difficult tasks and create a positive vision of the future. It will help you reach your goals and give you the confidence to act on your values. If you have low self-esteem, commit to raising it. Here are some good strategies for increasing self-esteem, based on a number of research studies:

- Above all else, have confidence in yourself. Believe in your ability to succeed and do well in life. Believing that you can make changes in your life is a key aspect of improving your self-esteem. Psychologists call this ability to believe that one can make effective changes in their lives *self-efficacy* (Bandura 2006). Individuals who don't think they can make such changes often never even take the first step to improve themselves.
- *Monitor what you do and say to yourself.* Putting yourself down will only lower your self-esteem.
- *Take responsibility for yourself and believe in your abilities.* Remember, though, if you have legitimate weaknesses in skill areas, such as math or English, just thinking positive thoughts won't be enough.
- *Work hard to improve your skills.* This may require obtaining support through tutoring, study skills workshops, and the like.
- *Experience emotional support and social approval.* When people say nice things to us, are warm and friendly, and approve of what we say and do, our self-esteem improves. Sources of emotional support and social approval include friends, family, classmates, and counselors. Seek out supportive people and find ways to give support back.
- *Achieve.* Learning new skills can increase both achievement and self-esteem. For example, learning better study skills can improve your GPA. This, in turn, might do wonders for how you feel about yourself this term and will also pay off in the long run.
- *Cope.* Self-esteem also increases when we tackle a problem instead of fleeing. Coping makes us feel good about ourselves. When we avoid coping with problems, they mount up and lower our self-esteem. See the Journal activity "Conscious Coping" and think about some stressful situations and how you managed them.

"It took a long time before I could look myself in the mirror and say, 'I'm Frosty the Snowman, and I like me.'"

Create Your Future

Exploring careers now will help you link your short-term and college goals with some of your long-term life goals and be motivated by your long-term prospects. What do you plan to make your life's work? Is there a specific career or several careers that you want to pursue? If you have a career in mind, how certain are you that it is the best one for you?

An important aspect of college is training for a career. Each of us wants to find a rewarding career and enjoy the work we do. If you're a typical first-year student, you may not have any idea yet of which particular career you would like to pursue. That's okay for right now, especially if you're currently taking a lot of general education courses. But as you move further along in college, it becomes ever more important to develop such ideas about your future. The sixth and final point in the Six Strategies for Success model on page xxiii is Create Your Future. This strategy links back to the first point, Clarify Values, demonstrating the interconnectedness of strategies for success.

Connect College and Careers

Choosing a career based on a college education will likely bring you a higher income and a longer, happier life. College graduates can have careers that will earn them considerably more money in their lifetimes than the careers of those who do not go to college (*Occupational Outlook Handbook* 2006–2007). In the United States, individuals with a bachelor's degree make, on average, more than a thousand dollars a month more than those with only a high school diploma. Individuals with two years of college and an associate degree make more than five hundred dollars a month more than those who only graduated from high school. Over a lifetime, a college graduate will make, on average, approximately six hundred thousand dollars more than a high school graduate will! College graduates also report being happier with their work and having more continuous work records than those who don't attend or don't finish college.

How would you like to give yourself several more years of life? One of the least known ways to do this is to graduate from college. If you do, you will likely live longer than your less-educated counterparts. How much longer? At least one year longer. And if you go to college for five years or more, you are expected to live three years longer than you would if you had only finished high school.

Master Content and Develop Work and People Skills

A successful career often involves three things:

1. gaining specialized knowledge of the content of a particular field (like electrical engineering or English)
2. having good work skills, especially for those involved in communication and computers
3. having good personal skills, including being able to get along with people, having high self-esteem, and working from one's own values, motivations, and goals

Your college experiences will give you plenty of opportunities to develop your talents in these three areas. In addition, every chapter contains a special feature titled "Create Your Future," which demonstrates how important skills and strategies are implemented in the workplace, as shown in "Create Your Future: Establishing Career Connections in College." And in Chapter 12, "Explore Careers," you will get many opportunities to learn the best strategies for figuring out the best career for you.

© Christine Kennedy/DK Stock/Getty

Exploring careers is a key aspect of your college experience. Take advantage of the career counseling opportunities at your college.

Your Learning Portfolio

We have included a Learning Portfolio section at the end of each chapter to help you practice different types of learning and apply various strategies to help increase your chance of success in college and beyond. This section has two parts:

1. Self-Assessments
2. Your Journal

Self-Assessments

At the end of each chapter are one or more self-assessments related to the chapter topics, which provide the opportunity to evaluate yourself in a number of areas related to your college success. At the end of each self-assessment, we give you information about how to score it or evaluate your responses. In addition, the website for this book, located at http://www.thomsonedu.com/success/santrock5, contains these self-assessments in electronic format and a number of others, with customized scoring. Completing these assessments will provide you with important information about your strengths and weaknesses in a variety of areas.

Your Journal

There are four types of journal exercises at the end of each chapter (except for this Prologue) that will help improve your self-understanding, enhance your writing skills, and give you the other benefits of keeping a journal. For example, James Pennebaker (1997), a professor at the University of Texas at Austin, found that first-year students who write in a journal cope more effectively with stress and are healthier than those who don't. Another study revealed that individuals who regularly kept a journal that focused on their aspirations were 32 percent more likely to believe that they were making progress in their lives than those who did not (Howatt 1999). The four types of exercises include:

Reflect These items ask you to reflect on the topics of the chapter. You will be encouraged to expand your thinking and consider issues in more depth.

Do These exercises involve action projects such as conducting interviews, participating in discussions, taking field trips, and putting together presentations. These projects help you to solve problems, practice report writing, and collaborate with others.

Think Critically These exercises help you to practice thinking more deeply, productively, and logically. In some, you will evaluate evidence. In others, you may criticize an idea. Your critical insights may be expressed in critiques, memos, reports on group discussions, and so forth.

Create These exercises will help you pursue new insights alone and with other students. You may be asked to write creatively or to try your hand at drawing images, inventing quotations, or crafting posters. Some exercises will encourage you to brainstorm with others.

Establishing Career Connections in College

As a single mother of two, Simone entered Portland Community College determined to graduate in two years with the skills and background knowledge to secure a good job, something with better pay and benefits than her current position as a part-time sales clerk. She was a good salesperson, known for her upbeat personality and strong social skills. She selected the field of alcohol and drug counseling because of her interest in working with people, the value she placed on helping others, and her goal of completing a career program in two years (this particular program offered lots of evening courses).

Additionally, the campus career counselor recommended it as a growing field with a strong demand for qualified counselors, driving her motivation to secure a good job immediately upon graduation. This type of program allowed her to gain specialized knowledge that she could immediately apply in a job setting, utilizing her strong work ethic and personal skills.

Jorgé also was determined to complete a career-oriented program in two years and was interested in helping others, but he had always been interested in medicine and hoped to go to medical school some day. First, he needed to expand his experience and his savings account! The emergency medical technician (EMT) program was just the ticket. It offered career training in an emergency medical setting, allowing him to expand his knowledge base and prepare for state certificate exams.

Once he became a certified EMT, Jorgé secured a job with a local ambulance company, providing immediate medical care and transportation and even helping with emergency childbirth on a few occasions. This foundation in emergency prehospital care was a good first step toward his long-term goal of becoming a doctor.

Summary Strategies for Mastering College

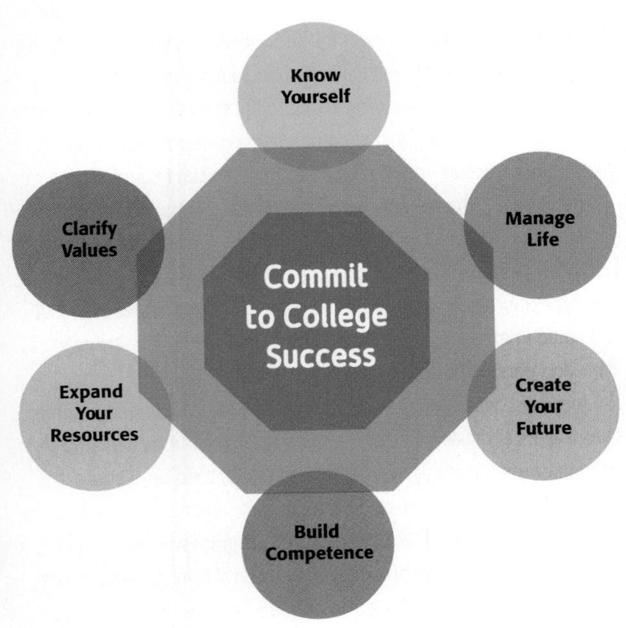

1 Effectively Make the College Transition

- If you're making the transition from high school to college, think about the ways that college differs from high school. Remind yourself that change can be challenging and requires you to adapt. Let go of some old ties. Get some new friends.
- If you're a returning student, evaluate your support system, make new friends, get involved in campus life, and don't be afraid to ask for help. Evaluate how you may need to balance your class work with commitments to partners, children, jobs, and the community.
- Realize that you bring strengths to campus.
- Explore your motivation for being in college.

2 Clarify Values

- Examine how your values relate to college success.
- Forge positive academic values.

3 Build Competence

- Set goals that are challenging, reasonable, and specific; plan how to reach these goals.
- Make a plan that includes completion dates and divides goals into subgoals. Commit and get started now. Monitor your progress toward your goals.
- Think and learn. Focus your talents and master work skills.

4 Manage Life

- Take responsibility for your successes and failures. Learn how to develop an internal locus of control.
- Persist until you succeed.
- Get involved and tackle boredom by exploring new avenues and tuning into inspiration.
- Manage your time effectively.

5 Expand Your Resources

6 Know Yourself

7 Create Your Future

- Connect college and careers.
- Master content and develop work and people skills.

8 Your Learning Portfolio

- Complete Self-Assessments to learn about your strengths and weaknesses.
- Do the different types of Journal activities to improve self-understanding and writing skills.

Review Questions

1. Consider your roommate or another student you have met recently. How do the challenges you both face making the transition to college differ? How are they similar?

2. How will your values help determine your success in college? Did you learn anything in this chapter that changed your opinion of what values are most important to you?

3. Imagine talking to a friend who is still in high school about the importance of setting goals, planning, and monitoring progress in college. What would you tell him or her? What would you tell an older, returning student?

4. How good are you at taking responsibility for your successes and failures? What aspect of your life could you take more responsibility for that might improve your chances of being very successful in college? Explain.

5. Do you know anyone who suffers from low self-esteem? How would you recommend tackling this problem? Why is it important to address now?

SELF-ASSESSMENT 1

What Are My Values?

This list presents a wide variety of values. Place a checkmark in the spaces next to the ten values that are the most important to you. Then go back over these ten values and rank the top five.

____ having good friendships and getting along well with people
____ having a positive relationship with a spouse or a romantic partner
____ self-respect
____ being well-off financially
____ having a good spiritual life
____ being competent at my work
____ having the respect of others
____ making an important contribution to humankind
____ being a moral person
____ feeling secure
____ being a great athlete
____ being physically attractive
____ being creative
____ having freedom and independence
____ being well educated
____ contributing to the welfare of others
____ having peace of mind
____ getting recognition or becoming famous
____ being happy
____ enjoying leisure time
____ being a good citizen and showing loyalty to my country
____ living a healthy lifestyle
____ being intelligent
____ family relationships
____ honesty and integrity
____ dedication and commitment
____ having personal responsibility
____ other values

List any values important to you
____
____

My five most important personal values are

1. ______________________________

2. ______________________________

3. ______________________________

4. ______________________________

5. ______________________________

As you review your selections, think about how you got these values. Did you learn them from your parents, teachers, or friends? Or did you gain them from personal experiences? How deeply have you thought about each of these values and what they mean to you? Think about whether your actions support your values. Are you truly living up to them? Do they truly reflect who you are?

Your Journal

REFLECT

1. Your New Life

Think about the changes that have taken place in your life since you started college.

- What is different?

____

____

- What excites you the most about your life and opportunities in college?

____

____

2. Conscious Coping

- Describe the most stressful experience you have had so far in college.

____

- What made it so stressful?

____

- How did you cope with it?

____

- Were you successful?

____

- If the problem still bothers you, how do you plan to cope with it in the future?

____

1 Making Connections

© Chuck Savage/CORBIS

KNOW YOURSELF

YOU WANT TO BE INDEPENDENT, but even the most successful college students don't do it all on their own. They get connected to find the resources that will help them master college. They pursue the best resources on campus for what they need in and out of classes. They navigate skillfully in the community to enhance their learning. They are comfortable in cyberspace.

To evaluate your skill in making connections, place a check mark next to only those items that apply to you.

- I know what campus resources are available to meet my needs.
- I know how to use library services efficiently.
- I plan to participate in one or more extracurricular activities.
- I can describe how contributing to the community can enhance my learning.
- I have spent adequate time with my academic adviser.
- I have studied my college catalog and use it as a resource.
- I know what I want my major to be.
- I have made a coursework plan toward a degree or certificate.
- I have selected a mentor.
- I use the Internet appropriately to search for information and stay connected.
- I use a word-processing program for most of what I write.

As you read about Meg Whitman, think about the importance of her college experiences in her career success.

CHAPTER OUTLINE

Explore Your New Environment

Get Help from Advisers
Delve into the Library
Stay Healthy
Practice Safety
Pursue Extracurricular Activities
Connect with Your Community
Enrich Your Cultural Life
Overcome Limitations

Map Your Academic Path with Your Adviser

Get to Know Your College Catalog
Get the Right Courses
Choose Your Major
Explore a Certificate or AA Degree
Create a Four- or Five-Year Plan
Transfer Credits

Connect with Computers

Get Up to Speed
Explore the Internet
Use a Word-Processing Program
Access Online Education
Electronic Text and Supplements
Online Courses
Use Computers in Other Ways to Reach Your Goals
Avoid Computer Addiction

Images of College Success

Meg Whitman

Today, only two Fortune 500 companies have women as CEOs or presidents. One of those women is Meg Whitman, the President and CEO of the highly successful online auction company eBay.

She initially majored in premed as a freshman at Princeton University and took courses such as chemistry, calculus, and physics. She continued to major in premed during her sophomore year, taking a very difficult organic chemistry course. By the time she completed the organic chemistry course, she realized that premed wasn't for her and that she probably wasn't cut out to be a doctor.

A summer job between her sophomore and junior years helped to clarify what she wanted to pursue further in college and in a career. She took a summer job selling *Business Today,* an undergraduate college magazine. Meg enjoyed the business orientation of the job and changed her major to economics.

Meg was a well-rounded college student. In addition to doing very well in her courses, she managed to find time to be a member of the university's lacrosse and squash teams.

In reflecting on her college experiences, Meg said, "The university inspired me to think in ways that have guided me throughout my life" (Horvitz 2006, p.10). In gratitude for what she learned and experienced during college, she donated thirty million dollars to Princeton, the largest gift ever by a Princeton alumna. The money is being used to construct an undergraduate dormitory, dining, educational, and recreational complex for approximately five hundred students.

MEG WHITMAN, CEO of eBay. How did Meg Whitman's college experiences contribute to her career success?

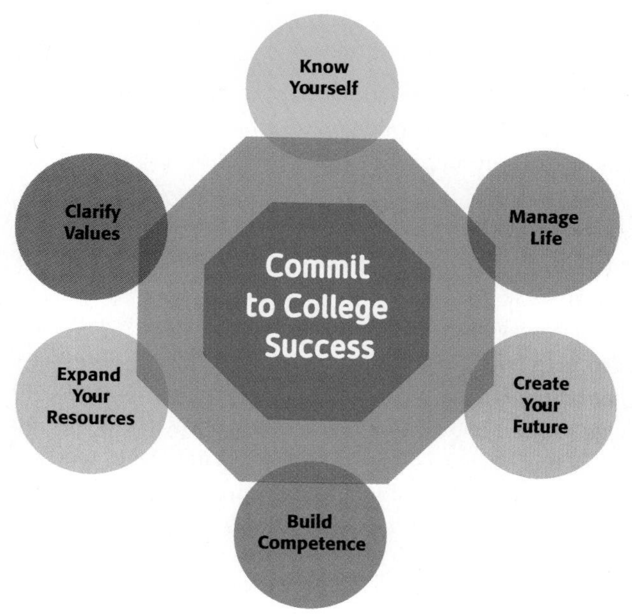

As you read this chapter, think about the Six Strategies for Success listed to the left and how this chapter can help you maximize success in these important areas. For example, to master college and reach your goals, you need skills in matching available resources to your needs. Important resources include knowledgeable and helpful people on campus, such as academic advisers, more-advanced students, and mentors. If you connect effectively, your college life will be easier, less stressful, and more productive.

Explore Your New Environment

It costs you nothing to connect with your campus, yet nothing will help you be more successful in college than knowing and wisely using your campus resources. You probably have visited some of them already—the bookstore for textbooks and supplies, the student center to check out bulletin boards, and the business office to make financial arrangements. However, most college campuses are very complex places that may take some time to get to know (see "Expand Your Resources: Box Head to Come"). Also, complete "Do: Explore Campus Jobs" on page 28.

An important goal in college is learning how to solve your personal problems and to get your needs met. You can learn a great deal about the best campus resources to assist you if you make this an important goal and aren't afraid to ask questions.

Complete Know Yourself: Self-Assessment 1, "Campus Resources to Meet My Needs," on page 24 to get started. The Journal exercise "Only the Best" on page 29 will also help you locate such places as the best cheap, hot breakfast, live music, free or cheap movies, and so on. Furthermore, the Journal activity "Your Cognitive College Map" on page 29 encourages you to draw your own campus map, emphasizing the places that you need to know about the most.

> EXPAND YOUR RESOURCES
>
> **Get To Know Your Campus**
>
> As you start to know the campus, begin your journey by studying the campus telephone directory. Most directories have compact listings of the offices and services that comprise the campus. You may be surprised at the array of options you have. For example, the campus child care center may give you some alternatives for helping with family obligations. The tutoring center may be just the right spot to visit during the downtime between your morning and your afternoon class on Wednesday. Perhaps the campus provides a service to assist you in identifying carpooling partners. There might even be a Spanish club that will help you sharpen your language skills. Scan the entries and think about how these services can help you meet your special needs.

Get Help from Advisers, Academic Support Services, and Counselors

Most people on campus will be eager to help you in your quest to master college. Whether you want information or training, here are some things you can do to get the help you need (Canfield and Hansen 1995):

- *Ask as though you expect to get help.* Your tuition dollars pay for assistance in the classroom, the library, and even the cafeteria line. Most campus employees—whether faculty or staff—strive to provide good customer service to their students. Act confidently to mobilize that assistance.

- *Ask someone who is in a position to help you.* You may have to do some homework to find out who can help you best. If someone you approach can't deliver, ask whether that person knows of someone else who might be able to help you. Form a network of resources.
- *Ask clear and specific questions.* Even those who enjoy helping students don't like to have their time wasted. Think ahead about what you need and what level of detail will satisfy you. Take notes so you won't have to ask twice.
- *Ask with passion, civility, humor, and creativity.* Enthusiasm goes a long way toward engaging others to want to help you. A polite request is easier to accommodate than a loud, demanding, or whiny one. Sometimes problems yield more readily to a playful question. A clever request is just plain hard to turn down. But size up whether a humorous approach is likely to be well received. If not, your good intentions and creativity may backfire. To explore getting optimal help with your college needs, complete the Journal activity "My Best Helpers" on page 28.

Learn about Academic Support Services Perhaps the most important helper on campus will be your academic adviser, but your campus offers access to other specialists who can assist you with academic problems.

For example, many study skills specialists can conduct diagnostic testing to determine the nature of your learning difficulties, if any, or they can refer you to specialists who provide this service. They can suggest compensating strategies for your assignments and may be able to give you some directions about taking courses with instructors who are more sympathetic to your struggle to learn. They also can set up and monitor additional study supports, including tutoring and study groups, to get you accustomed to the demands of college-level work.

Seek Counseling for Personal Concerns College life is often challenging on a personal level. Talking to a counselor or therapist may provide the relief you need. Large campuses have mental health departments or psychology clinics, but even small colleges are likely to provide some access to mental health services. They may have therapists and counselors on site who will give you support on a one-on-one or a group basis. The fee for such services will be on a sliding scale (meaning that the cost is proportional to your income), covered by your health insurance policy, or covered by your tuition.

Some student services offer topic-specific support groups, such as a group for single parents returning to college or for students struggling with English as a second language. In support groups you can meet others who have problems similar to yours and who may have developed helpful solutions. Ask the counseling center or dean's office about support groups on campus.

If you do not find a group that addresses your concern, consider creating one. Most support groups start from the concerns of one or two students. The student services office can usually assist you with the advertising and the room arrangements to help your group get off the ground.

Delve into the Library

Libraries may not seem a likely site for adventure. But think about it. Each visit to the library can be a treasure hunt. The treasure might be a bit of information, an opportunity to go online, or a chance to check out a new book by your favorite author. The sooner you get a feel for how the library works, the more useful it will be to you.

One of your classes may arrange a library tour. If not, ask a librarian for help in getting oriented. Librarians can give you a schedule of library tours or provide you with maps or pamphlets to help you search independently. Although librarians may look busy when you approach them, step up and ask for help. They expect to be interrupted. Most of them enjoy teaching others how to use the library. If you find an especially friendly librarian, cultivate the relationship.

A librarian friend can be a lifesaver.

What do you need to know in order to use the library effectively? The following questions may help you organize your first tour:

- How can I check out materials?
- What are the penalties for late returns?
- Do instructors place materials on reserve? How does this work?
- What interesting or helpful journals does the library have? Are they available online?
- Can I access the library's resources electronically?
- How long does it take to get through interlibrary loan?
- What kinds of reference materials are available?
- What is the most efficient way to access abstracts of published research?
- Where are "the stacks" and when can I use them?
- What technological resources does the library have that will help me succeed in college?

The Journal activity "My Library Needs" on page 29 will help you to think further about library services that might benefit you.

> ***We don't receive wisdom; we must discover it for ourselves after a journey that not one can take for us or spare us.***
>
> Marcel Proust
>
> *Nineteenth-century French writer*

Stay Healthy

Many campuses have fully equipped medical centers for students. Health care services may offer blood testing, health screenings, pregnancy tests, flu shots, and educational programs, as well as regular physicians' care. Smaller campuses may offer access to a nurse or health specialists trained in emergency care. Find out the phone numbers for these services. Carry them with you. When health emergencies arise, contact an employee of the campus or call the campus switchboard to explain the situation and request urgent help. Call 911 in serious emergencies.

Practice Safety

Personal safety is an important concern on all campuses. Security personnel monitor the campus for outsiders and sometimes provide escorts after dark. If you feel unsafe or spot activities that you think may threaten the well-being or property of others, do not hesitate to call the campus switchboard or security and report your suspicions or concerns.

Most campuses teem with activity. Unfortunately, that level of activity also attracts people who know a campus is an opportune context for stealing. No matter what the size of your campus, possessions that can be converted to cash can disappear. Keep your personal belongings locked up when you are not around. Consider insuring valuable property.

Exercise good judgment about the risks you take. You'll be meeting many people who will enrich your life, but some may try to take advantage of you. Be careful about lending money or equipment, especially to people you've just met. Exercise your street smarts on campus to avoid potential exploitation.

You may sometimes feel pressured by friends to take safety risks, such as drinking inappropriately, taking drugs, or hanging out in places that don't feel safe. Don't succumb to friendly pressures to do things that make you uncomfortable or place you at risk. True friends have your best interests at heart. If you feel pressure to take risks, it's time to re-evaluate your friendships.

Pursue Extracurricular Activities

> ***Either I will find a way or I will make one.***
> Sir Philip Sidney
> *Sixteenth-century English poet and soldier*

Participating in extracurricular activities not only improves your chances of meeting people who share your interests; research demonstrates that such activities appear to enhance your academic success (Astin 1983). People who pursue extracurricular activities tend to have higher grade-point averages and higher rates of degree completion.

Activities may be listed in the campus handbook or advertised in the student newspaper. Many majors sponsor clubs that allow you to explore careers through field trips or special speakers. If you're interested in journalism, you can work on the college newspaper or yearbook. Prospective drama students can audition for plays. Students interested in business can join an entrepreneurs' group to examine how business people manage their lives and work. Intramural and campus sports also are available.

It may seem like your study life is too full to accommodate extracurricular activity, especially if you are a commuting student and have pressing responsibilities at home. However, leisure activities are important for balance in your life. Extracurricular activities can help you develop leadership skills, promote effective management of multiple commitments, and give you an opportunity to get to know your professors informally. If campus participation creates too great a strain at home, investigate activities that might welcome your partner, children, and friends who predated your college involvement. Concerts, festivals, and other events can help you reconnect with your loved ones while you relax and have the fun that will help you manage your life. If your income is limited, look for activities that don't wipe out your cash.

One decision that many first-year students face is whether to join a sorority or a fraternity, which are known as "Greek" organizations after the Greek alphabet used to name most organizations. They were originally established not only to enhance academic achievement but also to encourage social participation outside the classroom. Membership in a fraternity or sorority takes place through what is known as "rush," a process of mutual selection that matches students interested in joining a Greek organization and the individual sorority or fraternity. Rush usually begins at the start of the fall or spring term. The organizations invite students to "pledge" when they think there is a good match between students' interests, values, and talents and those of the organization.

Joining a sorority or fraternity can have advantages and disadvantages. The advantages can include becoming closely connected with a group of people who share similar interests with you. You are a part of not only a sorority or fraternity at your particular college but also of a national organization with many chapters and a network of people. These contacts may be beneficial after college for social and business opportunities. Many sororities and fraternities also participate in worthwhile service activities.

The disadvantages can include the extensive amount of time and money involved in pledging and membership. Although many Greek organizations have embraced initiatives to reduce alcohol abuse and hazing, some Greek organizations have not. Consequently, affiliating with poor-quality groups can be hazardous to your academic standing, physical health, and self-esteem.

Sometimes you can get too involved in campus life. Before you know it, you may have more commitments than you can manage and too little time to study. Have fun, but keep your larger goals in mind (see "Manage Life: Choose Your Commitments Wisely"). Also, complete "Do: Explore Extracurricular Activities" on page 28.

Choose Your Commitments Wisely

David loved to multitask but quickly found that the exciting extracurricular options available in his first semester left him feeling scattered and ill-prepared for class. He also noticed that his eating habits were not in control as he developed a little paunch for the first time in his life. He complained more regularly about headaches, which he thought were linked to the stress of too many deadlines. His lab partner Tyler proposed a regular racquetball commitment following their shared biology lab. David examined his commitments and withdrew from two of the extracurricular options that added to his time pressures to create space for racquetball after class. The racquetball games also gave David and Tyler an opportunity to discuss fuzzy points from their class. As a consequence, David did better in class, improved his focus, lost weight, had fewer headaches, and developed a substantial friendship in the bargain.

Connect with Your Community

Some first-year programs create interesting ways to get to know the surrounding community through participation in "service learning" activities. Service learning opportunities may involve a commitment to build a Habitat for Humanity home, clean up litter on a stretch of highway, or distribute educational leaflets, among other worthy projects. Such projects have multiple goals. You can get to know the community and its needs in a new way as you exercise your leadership muscles and refine your teamwork skills. Typically, such programs are geared to help you embrace civic responsibilities. Initially students required to contribute time to a community project may feel some aggravation because they may not see how the activity clearly contributes to their personal learning goals; however, their objections generally recede based on the success of the projects and the new connections and relationships such projects encourage. Service learning activities can provide a major boost to self-esteem and clarify the degree to which civic engagement could become a central personal value.

> ***Never doubt that a small group of thoughtful, committed citizens can change the world. Indeed, it is the only thing that ever has.***
>
> Margaret Mead
> *Twentieth-century American anthropologist*

Enrich Your Cultural Life

Your campus and community may offer unique opportunities for cultural enrichment. Because most campuses are training grounds for artists and performers, they often operate an art gallery for display of student work or for work of invited artists. They host live performances in music, dance, and theater to showcase student and faculty talent, as well as talent of outside professional performers. In the community, museums, galleries, theaters, the symphony, and political gatherings can all enrich your learning.

To address spiritual concerns, campus ministries usually coordinate religious activities for various denominations. These may be formal religious services or social groups where you can simply get together with others who share your faith. You not only can practice your faith but also expand your network of friends with common values. Of course, religious services also are available off campus. To further about enriching our campus life, see "Clarify Values: Make Time for Your Faith."

CLARIFY VALUES

Make Time for Your Faith

The crush of homework assignments and deadlines can sometimes threaten the practice of long-standing religious practices. How important will it be for you to set aside time to exercise your religious and spiritual concerns? How will you build in this important element to ensure your balance? What kind of commitments should be in your schedule to help you address this life-sustaining activity?

Overcome Limitations

In the last decade, the number of college students with a disability has increased dramatically. Today more than 10 percent of college students have some form of physical or mental impairment that substantially limits their major life activities. Federal regulations require colleges to make reasonable accommodations to allow students with a disability to perform up to their capacity. Accommodations can be made for motor and mobility impairments, visual and hearing deficits, physical and mental health problems, and learning disabilities.

If you have a disability, determine what support you need to succeed in college. The level of service a college provides can be classified as follows:

- *Minimal support.* Students generally adapt to the college and advocate for their own services and accommodations.
- *Moderate support.* The campus offers a service office or special staff to help students with advocacy and accommodations.
- *Intense support.* The campus provides specific programs and instructional services for students with disabilities.

Many individuals overcome physical disabilities and other limitations to become successful college students. What are some services that colleges provide for individuals with physical limitations?

Among the academic services that may be available on your campus are:

- *Referrals for testing, diagnosis, and rehabilitation.* Specialists who can help in this area may be located on or off campus.
- *Registration assistance.* This involves consideration regarding the location of classrooms, scheduling, and in some cases waivers of course requirements.
- *Accommodations for taking tests.* Instructors may allow expanded or unlimited time to complete tests and you may be able to use a word processor or other support resources during the exam.
- *Classroom assistance.* Someone may be assigned to take notes for you or translate lectures into sign language. Instructors may allow their lectures to be taped for students with impaired vision or other disabilities.
- *Special computing services and library skills.* Support services on campus are finding inventive new ways to interpret written texts to overcome reading and visual limitations.

CREATE YOUR FUTURE

Contacting Your Adviser

Think strategically about developing a strong connection to your academic adviser given your particular constraints. In addition to great advice for the best tailoring of courses to your needs, a good relationship lays a solid foundation for a future letter of reference. If you are on campus during the day, drop in during office hours for a short visit to strengthen the connection. To maximize your effectiveness and efficiency when you have a serious problem, call or e-mail your academic adviser for an appointment before dropping by. Be sure to include your telephone number, e-mail address, and good times to reach you in case a change in scheduling is necessary. If you are on campus more regularly for evening classes when your adviser may not be available, call your adviser and inquire how best to pursue assistance. Many advisers use e-mail as electronic office hours. Some prefer phone calls during the regular work hours. Some may not mind being called at home, but it is best to clarify your adviser's preference. Discussing your options and agreeing on the best course of action will impress your adviser and enhance your profile when it comes time for him to write your reference letter.

Memo
To: Dr. Charles
From: Tyrell Wilkins
Re: Changing majors
Date: 9/27

I would like to meet with you during your 11 a.m. office hour on Monday, 10/5. I am thinking about changing majors, but I want to find out whether this could delay my graduation. Please e-mail me or call me any weekday evening after 7 p.m. if the proposed time doesn't work for you.

Thank you!
Tyrell Wilkins
Phone: 555–3300
E-mail: tykins@omninet.edu

Map Your Academic Path with Your Adviser

Navigating academic life by yourself is not a good idea. Get to know your academic adviser. Contact your adviser whenever you have any questions about your academic life. Your adviser has important information about your course requirements that can help you realize your plans. Advisers can explain why certain courses are required and can identify instructors who will offer the right level of challenge. Confer with your adviser regularly. When it's time to register for next term's courses, schedule a meeting with your adviser early in the registration period. Collaborate with your adviser to develop a longer-term plan. To read about strategies for developing a good relationship with an adviser, see "Create Your Future: Contacting Your Adviser."

Bring a tentative plan of the courses that you think will satisfy your requirements. Be open to suggestions if the adviser offers you compelling reasons for taking other courses. For example, your adviser may suggest that by taking some harder courses than you had planned, you can prepare yourself better for the career you have chosen.

If the chemistry between you and your academic adviser isn't good, confront that problem by discussing what behaviors make you feel uncomfortable. Recognize that your own actions may have something to do with the problem. You need an adviser you can trust. If you can't work out a compromise, request a change to find an adviser who is right for you. To think further about the importance of an academic adviser, complete the Journal activity "Ask the Right Questions" on page 29.

In addition to your academic adviser, a mentor also can enhance your opportunity for college success. Read "Expand Your Resources: Find a Mentor," and start putting together a list of individuals who might meet your needs.

Get to Know Your College Catalog

A college catalog is a valuable resource. If you don't have one, check with your adviser or the admissions office to obtain one, or browse the campus website to locate the information you need. College catalogs usually are revised every one or two years. Be sure to save the catalog that is in effect when you enroll for the first time. Why? Because requirements for specific programs sometimes change, and you usually will be held to the degree plan that was in place when you enrolled. It will help if you familiarize yourself with curriculum terminology to help you plan efficiently.

General Education Especially in your first several semesters, you'll probably have to take a number of general education courses. Typically, you will select a set of courses that distribute your study across the social and natural sciences, humanities, and the arts. Some colleges include special requirements to develop writing and math skills or knowledge about diversity.

Many students are so eager to get to the specialized courses in their major that they resent liberal arts requirements, particularly when they must take courses in areas that strain their comfort levels. However, exposure to a broad liberal arts base not only provides a strong foundation, but it can sometimes engender experiences that prompt students to rethink their original majors. It is usually not a good idea to postpone general education requirements in favor of courses in your major because you will feel out of sync if you are taking introductory courses just prior to graduation.

Core Courses *Core courses* are the central courses that students must take for any program they select. The catalog should tell you what the core requirements are for the degree program you are considering, whether there are any *prerequisites* (courses you must take first to be prepared properly for other harder courses), and whether there is a specific sequence of courses you should follow.

Many courses have prerequisites and other enrollment requirements, such as "consent of instructor," "enrollment limited to majors," "seniors only," "honor students," and so on.

You may be tempted to ask for a waiver of prerequisites, but it is in your best interest not to do so. Prerequisite courses provide building blocks that will facilitate your learning in the next course.

Electives In addition to core courses, you will be able to take *electives,* courses that are not required but count toward graduation requirements. You likely will take some of these in your major, others outside your major. Electives provide you with an opportunity to explore your interests and expand your education. In some cases, students take an elective that interests them so much that it becomes a springboard for taking more courses in the area, establishing a major, or sometimes even changing majors.

EXPAND YOUR RESOURCES

Find A Mentor

A *mentor* is an adviser, coach, and confidant who can help you become successful and master many of life's challenges. Mentors can advise you on career pursuits, suggest ways to cope with problem situations, and listen to what's on your mind. A mentor might be: a student who has successfully navigated the first-year experience, a graduate student, an instructor, and/or someone in the community you respect and trust. If you don't have a mentor, think about the people you've met in college so far. Are there people whom you admire whose advice might benefit you? If you don't have anyone in mind right now, start looking around for someone. As you talk with various people and get to know them better, one person's competence and motivation can start to rub off on you. This is the type of person who can be a good mentor. Explicitly ask your preferred candidates to serve as your mentors. They will probably be flattered and will have a framework to understand why you want to capture some special time with them.

Get the Right Courses

With a little effort, you can learn how to select courses that both fulfill your requirements and are enjoyable. Here are some strategies for making sound selections:

- *List your constraints.* You might have child-care responsibilities, an inflexible work schedule, or commuting issues. If so, block out the times you can't take classes before you begin your selection.
- *Examine your interests.* In many ways, college provides an almost endless array of interests that you can explore by taking electives, participating in extracurricular activities, and signing up for internship experiences. You may find that your interests fluctuate a great deal over the course of your college experience. That's okay, but keep monitoring what interests you the most. To evaluate your interests, complete Know Yourself Self-Assessment 2, "What Are My Interests?" on page 25.
- *Study your options.* Colleges have lists of classes required for various specialty diplomas or majors. Examine the college catalog to determine which courses are required for general education requirements and specific courses in the specialty or major that you want to pursue.
- *Register for a reasonable course load.* Many colleges do not charge for additional courses beyond those needed for full-time status. You might be tempted to pile on extra courses to save time and money. But think again. By taking too many courses, you may spread yourself too thin.
- *Take the right mix of courses.* Don't load up with too many really tough courses in the same term. Check into how much reading and other time is required for specific courses. If you can't find anyone else who can tell you this, make appointments with instructors. Ask them what the course requirements are, how much reading they expect, and so on.
- *Ask the pros.* The pros in this case are students who are already in your preferred program. Ask their advice about which courses and instructors to take. On many campuses, academic departments have undergraduate organizations that you can join. If you want to be a biology major, consider joining something like the Student Biology Association. These associations are good places to get connected with students more advanced than you are in a major.
- *Check the web.* Many students find it helpful to check out specific professors' informal reviews on a national website (www.ratemyprofessors.com). There is no guarantee that you will react to a professor in the same manner as those voluntarily posting reports, but the comments may help you to prepare mentally for the challenges ahead. "Build Competence: Get What You Want," provides more tips on getting the right courses.

Get What You Want

1. **Register as soon as you can.** Early registration improves your chances of getting the courses you want.
2. **Use computer registration.** Many campuses encourage students to register directly by using the campus computer system. This gives you immediate feedback about your scheduling. It may even suggest alternatives if you run into closed courses.
3. **Have a backup plan.** Anticipate the courses that might close out (for example, preferred times or popular instructors). Have alternatives in mind to meet your requirements.
4. **Explore the waiting list option.** If you want to get into a closed class, find out your chances for getting into a class if you agree to be put on the waiting list. If the odds aren't good, explore other options.
5. **Plead your case.** If you get closed out of a class you really want, go directly to the instructor and ask for an exception. To improve your success, base your request on your intellectual curiosity for the course content, not on scheduling convenience. Some instructors may reject your request, but others will listen and try to help you.

Choosing Your Major

One of the most frequent questions that you will get asked on campus is, "What is your major?" A college *major*, or field of concentration, is a series of courses that provides a foundation of learning in an academic discipline. Majors vary in the number of courses required. For example, engineering typically requires more major courses than does history or psychology, which allow you to choose more electives.

The major you select is also something that your parents or partner might show a special interest in, because they want you to major in something that will promote a successful career after college or enhance the career you've begun. The major or specialization that you select should match up with your career goals and values, which we discuss extensively in Chapter 12. Your academic adviser will be essential for efficient planning. For example, if you want to be an English teacher in a public school setting, you need to get good advice about the blend of English and education courses you must take to satisfy certification in your state. Also, your college counseling or career center can help you learn more about your interests, skills, and abilities, and how these might link up with certain majors and careers. It is never too early to start planning ahead.

"Well, we've finally done it. We've listed two courses, each of which is a prerequisite for taking the other."

If you're not sure what you want to focus on, you're not alone. More than two-thirds of first-year college students change their intended majors in the first year. Don't panic. When college administrators have you fill out forms during your first year, most let you write "undecided" or "exploring" in the column for a college major. It is perfectly appropriate not to decide on a major before you do some exploring. In fact, some colleges won't let you declare a major until you have sampled many disciplines through general education requirements. However, if you're in a four-year program and aren't sure about a major after two years, you may end up taking extra courses that you don't need for graduation, and you might have trouble fitting in all the classes you do need to complete your major.

Some institutions offer more creative degree options through interdisciplinary combinations or individualized majors where you will have greater latitude in designing your academic path. Even individualized majors, though, usually require one or two concentrations of courses to keep the coursework somewhat unified, not totally disconnected.

Some students also choose a double major when two areas are equally appealing. However, when you choose this option, you must plan even more carefully if you expect to graduate in the same timeframe as a single major. In addition, you can expect the workload to be more intense since two disciplines will be demanding advanced skill development to complete their majors at the same time.

If you hope to pursue graduate education, you need to know that graduate programs vary in their expectations for your undergraduate preparation. For example, law schools admit students from many different undergraduate majors. In contrast, graduate schools in physics usually require a physics undergraduate degree or a large concentration of physics classes. Your adviser can help you pace your preparation for the process of applying to graduate school, including scheduling specialized testing and the pursuit of strong letters of recommendation.

How Do You Know Whether a Major Is Right for You? Before choosing a major, make a realistic assessment of your interests, skills, and abilities. Chapter 4 allows you to explore intellectual and personality strengths and weaknesses that can influence your choice of major. Are you getting Cs and Ds in biology and chemistry, although you've honestly put your full effort into those courses? Then premed or a science area may not be the best major for you. On the other hand, if you love the math or computer science class you're taking, you may be destined for a career that will thrive based on that background.

But be patient. The first year of college, especially the first term, is a time of exploration and learning how to succeed. Many first-year students who don't do well at first in courses related to a possible major adapt, meet the challenge, and go on to do extremely well in that area. A year or two into your college experience, you should have a good idea of whether the major you've chosen is a good fit. At that point, you will have had enough courses and opportunities to know whether you're in the right place.

Seek out students who are more advanced in the field you're considering. Ask them what it's like to specialize in that particular area, and ask them about various courses and instructors.

Unfortunately, too many students choose majors for the wrong reasons: to please their parents, to follow their friends, or to have a light course load. What really interests you? You have the right to choose what you want to do with your life. Reconsider your values and review the long-term goals listed in the Preface to Students. You should be enthusiastic about the major and motivated to learn more about the field. To examine some possible links between majors, skills, and careers, see Figure 1.1.

Explore a Certificate or AA Degree

Some students enter a community college with a clear idea of what they want to major or specialize in, but many enter with no clear idea. Some students plan to obtain an associate degree, others intend to pursue a certificate in a specialty field.

The associate of arts (AA) degree includes general academic courses that allow students to transfer to a four-year institution. If you plan to transfer, you'll need to select a college and study its degree requirements as soon as possible. You should consult regularly with an adviser at your community college and the four-year institution to ensure that you're enrolling in courses appropriate to your major at the new institution.

In addition to a core of general education courses, obtaining an AA degree means taking either a concentration of courses in a major (or area of emphasis) such as history, English, psychology, and so on or taking a required number of electives. In most community colleges, a minimum of 60 or more credit hours is required for an AA degree.

A typical breakdown might be 45 credits in general education and 15 in your major, area of emphasis, or electives. Some community colleges also offer an associate of science (AS) degree that requires a heavy science concentration.

Many community colleges also offer certificate programs designed to help people re-enter the job market or upgrade their skills. There are many specializations: food and hospitality, graphic communication, press operation, medical record coding, word

FIGURE 1.1 Choose the Best Major and Career for Your Skills

Skills	Major	Potential Occupations/Careers
Research information Analyze numerical options Perform mathematical functions and apply formulas Communicate information through written and oral presentations	Accounting	Accountant Commercial/Consumer Loan Officer Compensation & Benefits Specialist Investment Analyst
Make three-dimensional models from plans and drawings Use computer-aided design and drafting software Research codes, laws, and regulations Prepare and give presentations	Architecture	Architect Building Construction Inspector Drafter Estimator

(continued)

FIGURE 1.1 Choose the Best Major and Career for Your Skills (Continued)

Skills	Major	Potential Occupations/Careers
Use lab equipment and instruments to test materials Write articles, papers, and reports describing research Evaluate written and statistical data Develop and conduct scientific experiments	Biology	Epidemiologist Quality Control Soil Conservationist Pharmaceutical Sales
Enjoy working in team environments Focus on goals and results Analyze numerical data Lead and facilitate discussions	Business Administration	Retail Store Buyer Advertising Account Executive Production Manager Logistics Coordinator
Interpret systems analystís program specifications Plan program logic for software applications Collaborate with team of programmers, analysts, and end users Program, test, and correct errors	Business Computer Information Systems	Programmer Systems Analyst Database Administrator Website Specialist
Evaluate written and statistical data Develop and conduct scientific experiments Use sensitive lab equipment to test materials Read journals and articles	Chemistry	Science Lab Scientist Chemist Toxicologist Forensic Scientist
Design integrated hardware/software system Prepare engineering specifications for performance and design Conduct research regarding various materials and components Prepare schematics of components for a computer	Computer Engineer	Computer Programmer Systems Analyst Operations Research Analyst Computer Network Analyst
Coordinate movements and choreography with others Listen to and follow director's/producer's instructions Create and develop character roles Practice complex dance patterns	Dance	Choreographer Dance Instructor Dance Therapist Arts Manager
Prepare and write reports Analyze statistical and numerical information Construct mathematical models Explain, interpret, and present information	Economics	Economist Underwriter Financial Analyst International Trade Specialist
Use computers to research databases for information Develop graphics using creative software Meet with other writers, editors, photographers, and graphic artists Pay attention to detail and style while writing	English	Continuity Writer Editor Journalist Screenwriter
Perform mathematical functions and apply formulas Analyze numerical data Use computer software to track information Present information to supervisor and committees	Finance	Treasury Management Specialist Financial Analyst Trust Officer International Trade Specialist
Use computer software to simulate three-dimensional models Analyze minerals using lab equipment Describe results in written reports and presentations Compile data from logs, articles, and research	Geology	Parks and Natural Resources Manager Hydrogeologist Park Ranger Oil Drilling Analyst

(continued)

FIGURE 1.1 Choose the Best Major and Career for Your Skills (Continued)

Skills	Major	Potential Occupations/Careers
Use a variety of resources and databases to research information Collaborate with various departments and people Research and prepare reports summarizing plans and projects Use computer software to develop models for projects	Government	Congressional Aide Public Administrator Urban/Regional Planner Lobbyist
Apply investigative and research skills to solving problems Synthesize data from a variety of resources Analyze and interpret data Write and present reports	History	Curator Lobbyist Paralegal Public Administrator
Coordinate with editors, graphics artists, and photographers Establish rapport with people as a part of the interview process Write and review articles Use computer databases to assist with research	Journalism	Public Relations Specialist Newspaper/Magazine Journalist Proofreader Editorial Assistant
Analyze statistical information Present information to groups of people Write papers to reinforce ideas Coordinate plans with team	Marketing	Advertising Copywriter Advertising Account Executive Distribution Manager Merchandiser
Design computer simulation models Analyze, interpret, and evaluate data Formulate and solve equations in order to explain concepts Compute and calculate applied mathematical formulas	Math	Actuary Inventory Control Specialist Investment Analyst Statistician
Make drawings using computer-aided design software Write reports outlining results of tests performed Conduct research and study effects Compare options and make recommendations to committees	Mechanical Engineering	Manufacturing Engineer Field Service Engineer Sales Engineer Industrial Designer
Follow director's instructions and composer's notations Concentrate on quality of sound during rehearsals and practices Develop new interpretation of musical compositions Collaborate with other musicians, directors, and producers	Music	Music Instructor Music Therapist Artist and Repertoire Manager Booking Manager
Observe, analyze, and interpret Resolve or mediate conflicts Listen effectively and establish rapport with people Evaluate various programs	Psychology	Human Resources Interviewer Case Worker Psychological Assistant Job Development Specialist
Interact well with diverse cultures Have insight into group dynamics Understand and improve relationships	Sociology	Demographer Market Research Analyst Nonprofit Administrator Case Worker
Establish rapport easily with people Assist people with the identification of appropriate services Consult with interdisciplinary treatment team Prepare and present reports	Social Work	Probation/Parole Officer Medical Social Worker Community Worker Training Specialist
Collaborate with directors, producers, and other actors Perform before audiences Research customs, social attitudes, and time periods Develop new ways to express character's emotions	Theatre	Set Designer Theatre Manager Television/Film Producer Stage Director

processing, property management, travel management, vocational nursing, and others. The course work in certificate programs does not include general education requirements like associate of arts and associate of science programs do. Certificate programs focus specifically on the job skills needed in a particular occupation. The number of credits required varies but is usually fewer than the number required for an associate's degree.

If you're a community college student, whether you're enrolled in an associate's or a certificate program, it's a good idea to map out a plan that lists each of your courses until graduation. Study your college's catalog and become familiar with the requirements for your degree.

Create a Four- or Five-Year Plan

Even though many first-year students don't know what to major in, or find themselves changing majors in their first year, it's still a good idea to map out a four- or five-year plan for your intended major that lists each of your courses every term until graduation. In this way, you can take control of your academic planning and give yourself the most flexibility toward the end of your four or five years of college.

The risk in not doing so is that you'll end up in your junior or senior year with too many courses in one area and not enough in another, which will extend the time needed to get your bachelor's degree. The four- or five-year plan also lets you see which terms will be light and which will be heavy, as well as whether you'll need to take summer courses. Of course, it's unlikely that you'll carry out your plan exactly. As you make changes, the plan will allow you to see the consequences of your moves and what you have to do to stay on track to complete your degree.

The four- or five-year plan is an excellent starting point for sessions with your academic adviser. The plan can be a springboard for questions you might have about which courses to take this term, next term, and so on. If you're considering several different majors, make a four- or five-year plan for each one and use the plans to help you decide which courses to take and when. If you're in a four-year institution, begin your planning with Self-Assessment 3, "A Four- or Five-Year Academic Plan," on page 26.

Transfer Credits

If you decide to transfer to another college, you'll want to know whether the credits you've earned will transfer to the new school. How well your credits will transfer depends on the school's standards and on your major. Check the catalog of the new college and see how its requirements match up with those of your current college. The catalog also will describe transfer requirements. Next, be sure to talk with an adviser at the new college about which of your courses will transfer. Here are some questions you might ask the admissions adviser (Harbin 1995):

> What are the minimum admission criteria that I have to meet in order to transfer to your college?
> Do I need a minimum grade-point average for admission? If so, what is it?
> What are the application deadlines for transfer admissions?
> Where can I get a transfer application?
> What else can you tell me about transferring to your college?

If you want to change colleges but aren't sure where you want to go, consult some general guides to colleges such as Peterson's National College Data Bank (http://www.petersons.com) or Barron's Profiles of American Colleges (http://www.baronseduc.com). Try to visit several campuses that might meet your needs. Talk with students there, as well as an academic adviser. Walk around and get a feel for how you like it. Be clear about what aspects of your current life are unsatisfying and why the new school will be better.

Connect with Computers

Computers can make your college life easier. They can support your efforts to think and learn, help you reach many of your college goals, provide a foundation for building important career skills, and help you stay connected to the people who are important to you.

Get Up to Speed

Technology has transformed how we do our work. Most instructors will assume you have basic computer skills and expect you to participate in class electronically through e-mail, Listservs, or electronic homework submission. Check with your computer center for special classes that can improve your ability to use the computer fluidly. Although most campuses provide free computer lab access, consider investing early in a laptop that can make your work portable and efficient. Some campuses offer special purchase or rental programs to expand your resources.

Explore the Internet

World Wide Web (WWW) The World Wide Web is both the most exciting and the most frustrating development on the Internet. The excitement comes from the impressive variety of information presented in pictures, sounds, and dazzling graphics available to anyone with a browser. The web lets you move easily from one piece of information to other related information by clicking "buttons" on a website. When you find a site that you especially like and wish to revisit, you can create bookmarks that let you return there directly.

Students routinely turn to the Internet to solve academic problems. "Googling" a concept or topic on the World Wide Web is a great way to get inspiration for assignments. Many organizations and businesses offer information on the web that pertains to college subjects. For example, a class studying AIDS may find facts on the web about AIDS, including current research on medication, legal concerns, and support groups. Because many web pages are updated frequently, this information may be among the most current professional research available.

However, sometimes the Internet can create problems. First, students encounter frustration from the sheer quantity of information available on the web (Haag's Perry 2003). Entering a key word on the search engine of a browser may result in the browser listing thousands of possible resources, or "hits." You may have no easy way to separate the valuable ones from the junk. Visiting every site takes too long. Some students report that they spend hours on the web but still can't find answers to the questions that prompted their search.

Second, some websites are seriously out-of-date. The web does not have the same quality control procedures that you would find in the academic journals in your college library. Get in the habit of examining the information about the maintenance of the website. It will help you judge the currency and value of the information posted. "Build Competence: Critically Evaluate Web Information," will help you judge what you read on the web.

Third, it can be tempting to conduct research by what is easy to access rather than identify more appropriate sources. For example, you may be tempted to cite a definition from the Wikipedia, the communal electronic encyclopedia, when writing a paper. Unfortunately, your professors may deem that citation unacceptable. In fact, some professors may specify how many references are acceptable from the Internet; most will want you to use the library databases and resources to develop academically rigorous work.

© Stewart Cohen/Index Stock Imagery

Not all computer time has to be spent in physical isolation. If you're spending too much time alone on a computer, start collaborating with others at least some of the time when using the computer.

Fourth, term papers can be downloaded and submitted for assignments. Not only does this practice short-circuit your learning, but professors have developed a variety of electronic strategies to identify when your work is not original. Don't shop for the best bargain. Use the opportunity to sharpen your skills.

Fifth, use the web for social purposes with caution. Sites such as Facebook.com, MySpace.com, or online dating services, can provide a way to meet people, but you should recognize that postings may not be truthful. Develop some additional strategies for screening before making commitments. In addition, remember what you post on the web is available for the world to see, including parents and your future employers. Think carefully before you hit the send button.

Finally, surfing the web can sometimes be too wonderful. Most users report that hours can slip away while they're online. Be prepared to invest some time if you choose to use this helpful tool, and monitor your habits so you don't get swept away.

E-mail E-mail and instant messaging allow ongoing Internet conversations to help you stay connected to people who are important to you, but increasingly faculty rely on cyberspace strategies as well. For example, technologically oriented faculty will incorporate electronic class participation through class Listservs to help you practice using the concepts of the course to improve your understanding. Some instructors welcome questions via e-mail because it's often more convenient than office hours for both parties. Many instructors are often remarkably open to developing online relationships with their students. Some may be even more open to online chats than face-to-face discussions.

Your campus may provide you with a free e-mail account. Most campuses that have not yet provided this service are hard at work raising funds to do so. If your campus does not offer such accounts, you can join a full-range commercial service for twenty dollars per month or less.

E-mail has its hazards, too. Install spam blockers and antivirus protection or you can lose time and money in trying to manage your queue. Never send out personal data in response to requests over the Internet, especially your Social Security number. It is unlikely that you have won a lottery, a luxury cruise, or have a fortune waiting offshore, so don't fall for the scams that may find their way onto your screen.

Use a Word-Processing Program

Computer word-processing programs can make the process of writing and rewriting papers easier because you can edit without having to retype most of your work. You also can select different print types, called *fonts,* and use other features to highlight or underline key sections of your work. With most word-processing programs, you can incorporate headers (standard headings at the top of each page), page numbers, and footnotes easily. Many programs will also develop your reference list, placing it in the conventional format for the discipline in which you're writing. Perhaps most helpful of all are the features that allow you to check spelling, grammar, and word count when you complete your paper. Of all the tips for success in this book, one of the most important is: *Learn to use a word-processing program and write all your papers with it.*

Critically Evaluate Web Information

1. **How Accurate Is the Information?** Do you have any way of checking the accuracy of the content?
2. **How Authoritative Is the Information?** What authority or expertise do the creators of the website have? How knowledgeable are they about the subject matter? For example, there is a big difference between the information about space launches that is provided by an armchair amateur and which is provided by NASA.
3. **How Objective Is the Information?** Is the information presented with a minimum of bias? To what extent is the site trying to push a particular idea and sway opinions versus presenting facts?
4. **How Current Is the Information?** Is the content of the site up-to-date? When was the website last updated?
5. **How Thorough Is the Coverage?** Are topics covered in sufficient depth? What is the overall value of the content?

CREATE YOUR FUTURE

Learn New Skills

When Joleen took the summer job as an office assistant, she assumed she would spend lots of time filing and answering the phones, but she thought it would still look good on her résumé to have office experience. She was surprised to find herself spending most of the day on the computer. The insurance company had computerized all of its files, so the first place she looked for any information was their online database. When calls came in on the computerized switchboard, she would download the appropriate client information and later update the database with the newest developments on each case. She was expected to learn how to navigate the computer systems and have strong word-processing skills to keep up with the workload. Although it was more challenging than she expected, it certainly was more interesting than filing, and gave her real experience for an even better job after college.

Dion's job as a graphic designer also involved spending most of the day on the computer, a far cry from what he expected when deciding to major in art his first year in college. His designs were mainly computer-generated on complex systems and then sent to clients over the Internet for their feedback. He used a spreadsheet program to track his costs versus his budget for each project and was required to produce electronic weekly reports on his progress. Occasionally he even helped produce client presentations, integrating his designs into elaborate PowerPoint presentations to demonstrate their impact and help win new business for the company. These skills made him an even more valued employee than simply someone with strong design skills. One day he hoped to manage other designers, and he was well on his way.

Word processing also involves some hazards. If you don't make a habit of saving your work often, you can end up with nothing to print. Also, spell-checkers do not substitute for good proofreading, because they will identify words that are misspelled but not words that are misused. For example, most won't catch the difference between *there* and *their* or *to, too,* and *two.* The worst problem associated with word processing is that it might encourage you to procrastinate and therefore lose revision time, because your first draft can look very professional even if it isn't.

Better papers are better because the writer allowed some time to think again and revise.

Online Education

Technology advances have spawned new learning opportunities for students, such as electronic texts and supplements, online courses, and even online degree programs.

Electronic Text and Supplements

Increasingly, learning materials are provided to students through an online website or a CD-ROM. For example, this book has a companion website at http://www.thomsonedu.com/success/santrock5. Electronic text supplements usually include review sections, practice tests with various types of items (such as multiple-choice and essay questions), and opportunities to expand your learning beyond the information found in the textbook. Take advantage of these electronic supplements to make learning more effective for you.

Online Courses

A key benefit of taking some of your courses online is convenience. This arrangement is especially helpful for students who travel or have other time or geographic constraints that make on-campus classes more challenging to complete.

In a typical online course, you will find the syllabus posted and each week's assignments and activities fully explained. However, in some cases, online courses are self-paced, with all assignments due by the end of the term. You probably will be required to read a textbook and take quizzes or exams online, and in some cases participate in online discussions. An instructor will monitor your work, and in most cases you will be able to contact him or her via e-mail. You will need a computer camera to participate in some of the online technologies instructors are now using that facilitate face-to-face contact.

Online education may not be for everybody. Many students want and need the personal interaction that a traditional classroom provides. Examine the Know Yourself: Self-Assessment 4, "Is Online Coursework for Me?" at the end of the chapter to evaluate whether this approach is a good match for your learning characteristics.

Online Degree Programs Many institutions offer complete degree programs online or host "blended programs" that involve a mix of face-to-face and online activity. Some programs involve participation in a "cohort" of students. In this arrangement, a specific group of students commits to pursuing a degree together over a predetermined timeframe. These offerings greatly increase opportunities for degree completion. However, students need to be careful to evaluate the academic standing of the program before signing on the dotted line. Legitimate programs should be accredited by appropriate agencies. Also, before you make your decision, check the reputation of the program to find out how graduates with that specific degree fare in the job market.

Use Computers in Other Ways to Reach Your Goals

Using e-mail, the World Wide Web, and word-processing programs regularly will help you succeed in college and thereafter. You may also want to consider developing expertise in using other tools—research databases, spreadsheets, and graphics and presentation software—that can help you enormously if the task at hand is appropriate for their use. (See "Create Your Future: Learn New Skills.")

TABLE 1.1 Helpful Library Research Databases

Research Coverage	Title
Behavioral sciences	PsychInfo/PsychLit Sociological Abstracts
Business	PROMT ABI/INFORM
Education	ERIC
Humanities	Economic Literature Index Historical Abstracts Humanities Abstracts Philosopher's Index
Natural science	BIOSIS MEDLINE
News reports	Associated Press NEXUS Reuters
Reference	Books in Print Dissertation Abstracts Academic Index Britannica Online

Mick O'Leary. *The Online 100*, 1995.

Research Databases Your campus library houses electronic databases that you can use for research assignments. Each database uses key words, years, or authors to direct you to specific articles in the professional literature. Table 1.1 lists some of the most frequently used academic databases.

You may encounter other databases as well. For example, business classes may explore how to keep track of inventory or potential customers. If you get a part-time job at the college, you may be working with databases of alumni addresses or bookstore inventories. Knowing how to navigate Excel or Access, popular database programs, may help you land a good job.

Database programs that allow you to perform calculations on numerical data are called *spreadsheets*. For example, you can enter data from a chemistry experiment into the columns of a spreadsheet and set up the spreadsheet program to calculate and summarize the results.

Students who major in business are likely to use spreadsheets in marketing analyses, business plans, and financial projections. Your instructors will probably tell you which spreadsheet programs will best suit your needs.

Graphics and Presentation Software Graphics packages let you express yourself visually. They allow you to copy and design images, create animations, develop charts and graphs, and make impressive computer-driven presentations. Some of your courses may have graphics requirements. In other classes, graphics can improve the content and aesthetic appeal of your work.

When used properly, PowerPoint can be an especially powerful presentation software tool. If you have to prepare a class presentation, PowerPoint can help you organize it

> ***Home computers are being called upon to perform many new functions, including the consumption of homework formerly eaten by the dog.***
>
> Doug Larson
> *American cartoonist*

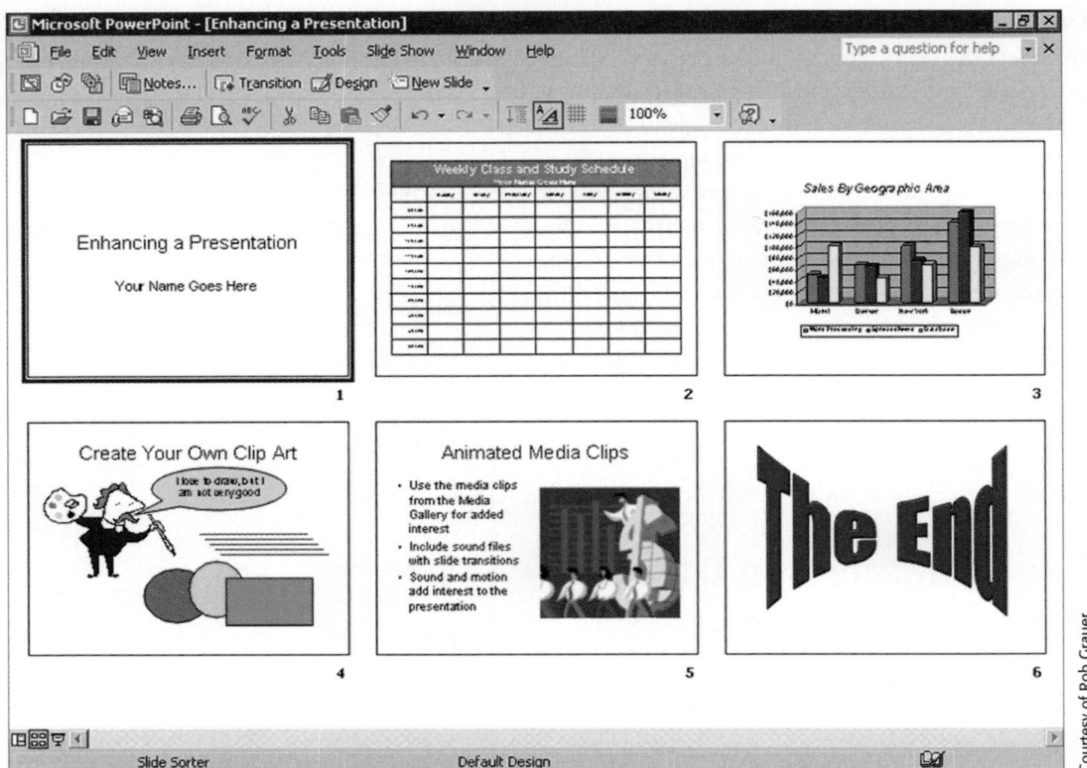

PowerPoint enables you to include a variety of visual elements that add impact to a presentation.

and create a dynamic, visually attractive format for it. Many successful individuals in a wide range of careers use PowerPoint, saying that it has made the art of giving presentations easier and more professional and that it makes presentations much more interesting for the audience. PowerPoint enables you to include a variety of visual elements that add impact to a presentation.

Used improperly, Powerpoint can be deadly. Whiz-bang graphics are no substitution for a well-rehearsed presentation. Text presented on the screens should support material presented orally. It should be telegraphic or "bulleted" rather than consisting of massive paragraphs that will make it hard for the reader to pay attention to what you are saying. Excessive use of animations and sound effects generally detract from the quality of the thinking you are trying to showcase.

Avoid Computer Addiction

It's hard to pry some people away from their computers. Some computer technology fans are so dedicated to their computers that they neglect their work or studies. How can a computer be so addictive? Here's how:

- *The compelling opportunity to explore the world.* Casual surfing of the Internet can take you in many directions. Anyone with a healthy curiosity can find it hard to stay away from the vast and varied sources of information that computers can reach.
- *The obsessive attraction of computer games.* The thrill of good performance is rewarding. It's easy to keep playing "just one more time" to see whether you can better your score. Hours slip by as you gradually refine your game skill and lose your real social connections.
- *The seduction of electronic relationships.* An electronic relationship between two people can feel profound, because the absence of physical cues may allow you to

connect to another person in a novel way. Without the other elements of real life intruding, such exchanges can lead to deeper emotional involvement and reward than a user may currently experience in face-to-face relationships. However, this sense of intimacy can be based on half-truths, or even lies, because you have no real way of knowing who the other person is. In any case, such relationships can be compelling and time-consuming. If you find yourself favoring "e-friends" over "real friends," think twice!

To read about one student's computer addiction, see "Manage Life: When Computer Games Stop Being Fun." Completing the Journal activity "Dealing with Computers" on page 28 will also help you to think further about how you are doing in the computing world.

When Computer Games Stop Being Fun

Dennis Bennett was failing all of his college classes, his marriage was in trouble, and he wasn't being much of a father to his one-year-old son. However, he had progressed to level 58 as Madrid, the Great Shaman of the North, his character in the online role-playing game, EverQuest, and that was all that mattered at the time.

Bennett's grades and family life have improved recently, because he quit playing the game. He considers himself a recovered EverQuest addict, now able to control his desire to immerse himself in the game's rich fantasy world. He says that the game almost ruined his life. "It was my life. I ceased being me; I was Madrid, the Great Shaman of the North. Thinking of it now, I almost cringe" (CNET Tech 2002).

How can you get unplugged?

- Audit your online patterns. Estimate the number of hours per day you are in cyberspace and distinguish what is necessary (related to school demands) and what is voluntary.
- Seek expert opinion. Candidly discuss your concerns with those who share your living space. Find out whether they support the view that you may have a problem.
- Identify what you have lost. What advantages or rewards from other leisure pursuits have you lost by obsessive devotion to the Internet?
- Schedule commitments with noncyber companions. They will welcome you back into the flesh-and-blood world. Explore other activities that will make this option more rewarding.
- Add some constraints. Commit yourself to computer-free time zones during your week. Do your academic or pleasure reading. Call your friends. Do some yoga. Just don't return to the keyboard.

Summary Strategies for Mastering College

To Master College and Reach Your Goals, You Need Good Resources

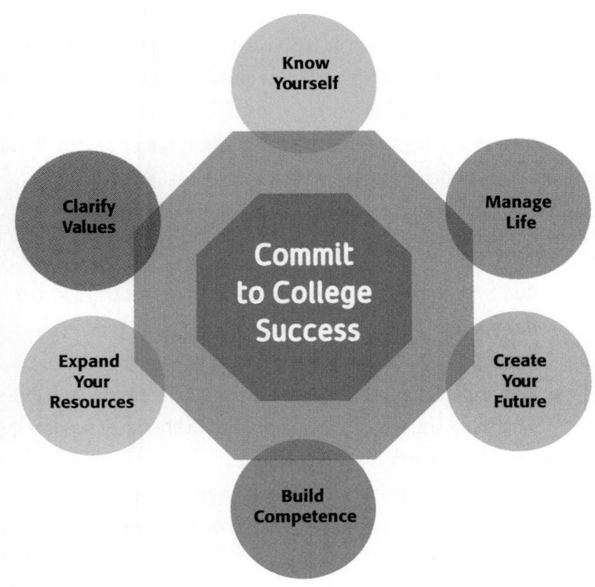

Focus on the Six Strategies for Success shown in the hexagon as you read each chapter to learn how to apply these strategies to your own success.

1 Explore Your New Environment

- Know which campus resources you need now or might need in the future. Find out their locations, hours, e-mail addresses, and phone numbers.
- Learn about academic support services, such as help for writing and math. Find out whether tutoring and study groups are available.
- Seek counseling if you have personal concerns.
- Take extra steps to connect with your adviser if you aren't on campus during business hours.
- Investigate library resources and learn to use the library effectively.
- Stay healthy and use your campus health services when needed.
- Keep safe and know how to contact the campus security personnel when you need them.
- Participate in one or more extracurricular activities, but don't spend too much time on those that interfere with your academic work.
- Connect with your community and become culturally enriched by learning about and going to some cultural activities at your college and in the community.
- If you're a student with a physical limitation, learn about and use available campus resources.

2 Map Your Academic Path with Your Adviser

- Get to know your college catalog. Study it and use it as a resource. Know what is required for various coursework, including prerequisites and core courses.
- Get the right courses through such strategies as listing your constraints, examining your interests, and studying your options.
- Choose the right major for you. Realistically assessing your interests, skills, and abilities will help you.
- If you are a community college student, explore the requirements for a certificate program or AA degree.
- If you are attending a four-year college or university, create a plan to ensure that you take all the classes you need in a reasonable time period. Use this as a guide for regular discussions with your adviser.
- Know some good strategies for transferring to another college, if this is on your mind.

3 Connect with Computers

- Get up to speed and become computer literate. If you don't own a computer, use campus labs. Consider taking a computer class.
- Use e-mail and instant messaging to keep in touch with friends, classmates, and instructors, but don't let your social network interfere with your work. Learn to use the World Wide Web to support your success in college. Be sure to evaluate the accuracy and quality of information on the web when using it for academic purposes.
- Use a word-processing program for most or all of your writing. If you can't yet, learn how as soon as possible.
- Explore potential online courses and utilize electronic and web-based supplements to enhance your learning.
- Request help at the campus computing center. Take advantage of online education.
- Use computers in other ways to reach your goals. For example, learn to use research databases, graphics spreadsheet programs, and PowerPoint.
- Avoid computer addiction by limiting the time you spend surfing the net, playing computer games, and exploring online relationships.

Review Questions

1. What kinds of campus connections matter and why? Name at least three.

   Resource: ____________________

   Why is it important? ____________________

   Resource: ____________________

   Why is it important? ____________________

   Resource: ____________________

   Why is it important? ____________________

2. What are some key aspects of designing an academic career path? List three things you can do *now* to begin this process.

   A. ____________________

   B. ____________________

   C. ____________________

3. Why is your college catalog such a valuable resource? What are some of the most important facts you can learn from this guide?

4. What are some key considerations when selecting a major? How might you know if you made an inappropriate choice?

5. List at least three important computer skills that will help you succeed in college. Which one do you think will have the greatest impact on your immediate success?

SELF-ASSESSMENT 1

Campus Resources to Meet My Needs

First, cross off any items that you know you won't need. Add any other locations that you think you will need. Then answer yes or no after the items not crossed off. Next, write down the location of the campus resource and any notes you want to make about the resource, such as its hours, phone number, and e-mail address.

Does My Campus Have	Yes or No	Location/Notes
Career services center?		
Student testing center?		
Math laboratory?		
Performing arts center?		
Campus security?		
Financial aid office?		
ROTC service?		
TV or radio station?		
Work–study program?		
Writing lab?		
Health center?		
Travel agency?		
Mental health services?		
Language lab?		
Intramural sports office?		
Student government office?		
Post office?		
Lost and found?		
Printing service?		
Banking center?		
Computer labs?		
Multimedia and graphics lab?		
International students' center?		
College newspaper office?		
Religious services?		
Campus cinema?		
Lost and found?		
Other		
Other		
Other		

Compare your information with that of others in the class. How are you doing in discovering resources on your campus? Put the information about resources in the planner that you carry with you on campus. Note: This list is also on the website for this book, where you can easily tailor it to meet your own needs and print out a copy.

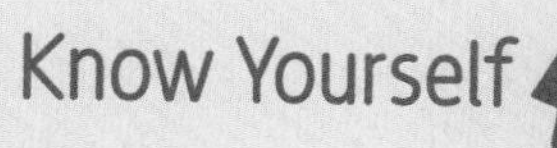

SELF-ASSESSMENT 2

What Are My Interests?

Answering these questions can help you pinpoint your interests.

What activities do you enjoy doing the most?

When you are doing what you want, what are you doing?

What do you do in your leisure time?

What are your hobbies?

Can you relate any of the activities, hobbies, or interests to possible academic majors? If so, which ones?

Can you link any of the activities, hobbies, or interests to possible careers? Is so, which ones?

After Weston Exploration, (2002). *The Model for Exploration.* Urbana-Champaign: Weston Exploration, University of Illinois.

SELF-ASSESSMENT 3

A Four- or Five-Year Academic Plan

Study your college catalog to find out what courses you need to graduate with a particular major. If you have not selected a major, examine the requirements for one you're considering. Then fill in the blanks with the courses you plan to take. Use this self-assessment to discuss your decisions with your academic adviser. The plan here is for schools on a semester schedule. If your school has a quarterly system, create your own plan by listing the quarters for each of the four or five years and then filling in the courses you plan to take.

Fall	**Spring**	**Summer**
	First Year	
	Second Year	
	Third Year	
	Fourth Year	
	Fifth Year	

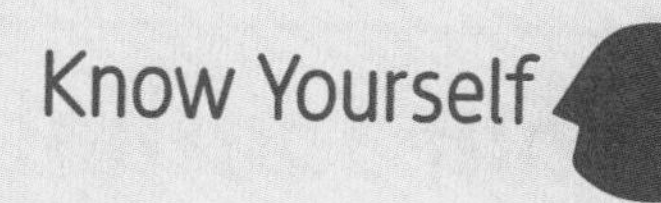

SELF-ASSESSMENT 4

Is Online Coursework for Me?

Which of the following characteristics that appear to predict successful adjustment to online education are consistent with your self-concept?

__________ I feel aggravated by the amount of time I waste in commuting to classes.

__________ I have keyboarding skills that allow me to communicate with reasonable efficiency.

__________ I am intrigued with Internet resources and like to explore the web in my spare time.

__________ I usually have good self-discipline about initiating and completing projects.

__________ I don't usually hesitate to express my opinion.

__________ I find it easier to write than to speak my opinions.

__________ I don't mind working on projects with others whom I have not met.

__________ I don't necessarily have to see people or be in their physical presence to develop a working relationship with them.

__________ I will be closer to some important career opportunities with each course I complete.

The more items you have checked, the greater your success is likely to be in an online course experience. If you have not developed good self-regulation skills, online coursework may not be for you.

Your Journal

REFLECT

1. My Best Helpers

- The names of the persons who have helped me the most on campus so far:
- How they have helped me:
- The aspect of college that I need the most help in right now is:
- The person on campus who most likely could help me in this area is:

2. Dealing with Computers

- What computer skills do you have?
- Do you have any fears or problems regarding computers? What are they?
- How can you address them? Write down a few specific resources to help you overcome these issues.

1. ______________________________
2. ______________________________
3. ______________________________

DO

1. Explore Campus Jobs

Perhaps the fastest way to find work is to go to the financial aid office on campus. Ask for a list of available part-time jobs. Do any of these jobs appeal to you? Will any help you develop skills toward a future career? Write down at least three jobs that best link up with future careers that interest you. Include a strategy for exploring each opportunity.

1. JOB: ______________________________

STRATEGY: ______________________________

2. JOB: ______________________________

STRATEGY: ______________________________

3. JOB: ______________________________

STRATEGY: ______________________________

2. Explore Extracurricular Activities

Locate or create a list of extracurricular events or meetings on your campus. Write down a few that appeal to you most, then attend one or two. Decide whether you want to make these activities a regular part of your college life by making a list of pros and cons for such involvement.

Interesting activities:

Pros for involvement

Cons for involvement

THINK CRITICALLY

1. My Library Needs

Libraries often provide many services that students are unaware of. What service does your library provide that you might need to use in the next year? If you can't answer this question, obtain a library brochure of services or talk with a librarian about the services. Describe them below, linked with the need they will help fulfill.

Library service: How will I use it?

2. Ask the Right Questions

Make an appointment to see your academic adviser. Create a set of questions to ask, such as:

- What classes should I take this term and next?
- What sequence of classes should I take?
- Am I taking too many difficult classes in one term?
- What electives do you recommend?
- What career opportunities are there if I study mainly ________ or ________?

Write about your conversation with your academic advisor.

CREATE

1. Only the Best

Ask students you trust and who have been on campus longer than you about where to locate at least five of the following.

- Best cheap, hot breakfast
- All-night food store
- Local businesses that give student discounts
- Best software
- Live music
- Best pizza
- Best coffee
- Free or cheap movies
- Best place for quiet conversation
- Best place to exercise
- Best bulletin board
- Best place to dance
- Discount bookstores
- Cheap photocopies
- Best place to view the stars

2. Your Cognitive College Map

You may have received a campus map as part of your orientation materials. Draw your own map as well. On it, emphasize the aspects of campus that are most important to you by drawing them larger and in a more stylized way. You might also try constructing the map using computer graphics.

2 Master Communication Skills and Build Relationships

© John Henley/CORBIS

KNOW YOURSELF

Success in college isn't just about grades. Total college success includes mastering communication and developing positive relationships with many different kinds of people. Being skilled in these areas will make your college years more enjoyable and productive. To see where you stand right now, place a checkmark next to only those items that apply to you.

- I am a good listener.
- I am a good communicator.
- I have strategies for resolving conflicts.
- I get along with my instructors.
- I have one or more good friends.
- If I get lonely, I can usually find ways to reduce those feelings.
- I have good relationships with my family.
- I get along well with people from other cultural and ethnic groups.
- I get along well with the opposite gender.

As you read about Oprah Winfrey, think about how good communication skills have been central to her life and career.

CHAPTER OUTLINE

Communicate Effectively

Develop Good Listening Skills
Avoid Barriers to Effective Verbal Communication
Tune in to Nonverbal Communication
Use Communication to Resolve Conflict with Others

Develop Good Relationships

Recognize Attachment Styles
Assess the Social Scene
Avoid Sexual Threat
Deal with Loneliness

Maintain Specific Positive Relationships

Connect with Parents at the Right Level
Make Room for Partners and Family
Relate to Instructors
Get Along with Roommates
Build Professional Networks

Appreciate Diversity

Explore Individual and Cultural Differences
Gain Insights into Gender Influences
Respect Sexual Orientation
Improve Your Relationships with Diverse Others

Images of College Success

Oprah Winfrey

Oprah Winfrey hosts one of the most-watched TV shows in America. She also received an Oscar for her role in *The Color Purple*, in which she played a proud, assertive woman. Oprah was born on a Mississippi farm and spent her early years there, reared by her grandmother. When Oprah was six, she was sent to live with her mother in a Milwaukee ghetto. From the age of nine, she was sexually abused by a series of men she had initially trusted. She began committing delinquent acts as a young adolescent, until her father had her come live with him in Nashville. At that point, her life improved dramatically.

As a high school senior, when raising money for charity, Oprah visited a local radio station and talked her way into a part-time job broadcasting the news. On a scholarship at Tennessee State University, she started a major in speech and drama. At age nineteen, she switched from radio to local television and became the youngest person and the first African-American woman to anchor the evening news at Nashville's WTVF-TV. Still, she continued college until a Baltimore TV station lured her away in her senior year. A few years later, she moved to Chicago to host a local talk show that eventually became *The Oprah Winfrey Show*, now the highest-rated talk show in television history.

The billions of dollars Oprah has earned have not decreased her motivation to achieve. She continues to seek new ways to use her tremendous energy and talent productively. As Oprah says, "I have been blessed, but I create the blessings." Success has not spoiled her. Oprah spends many nights lecturing, often for free, at churches, shelters, and youth organizations.

She established the Little Sisters program in a poverty-stricken area of Chicago. She continues to spend some of her Saturdays working with young girls to improve their lives. Her book club has been instrumental in a national increase in reading and promotion of literacy.

When she finally finished college, Oprah was a multimillionaire. In 1987, when invited to speak at TSU's commencement, she insisted on finishing the last bit of coursework for her degree. Then, because her father had always urged her to finish college, she endowed ten scholarships in his name.

What are some of Oprah Winfrey's effective communication skills?

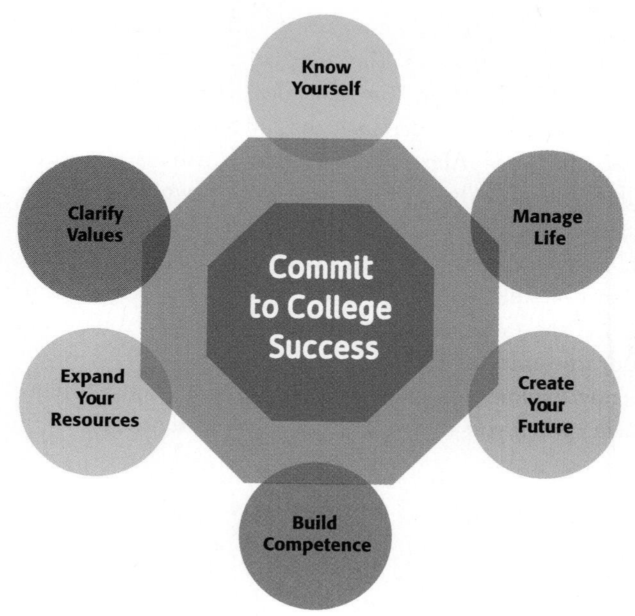

When employers describe what they seek most in college graduates, the consistent answer is "communication skills." Thus, mastering communication skills will benefit you not only in college but in future careers and many other aspects of your life. It is also beneficial to build good relationships with different kinds of people, accepting and appreciating their diversity. As you read, think about the Six Strategies for Success listed to the left and how this chapter can maximize your success in these important areas. For example, building effective communication skills and enriching your support will help you to manage your life more effectively, build competence, and expand your resources.

Communicate Effectively

Oprah Winfrey's communication skills are admirable. She listens attentively, shows interest, and asks appropriate questions. She is skilled at getting people to open up and talk about even their most troubling issues. Her magical touch also encourages people to feel good about themselves.

It's hard to do much in life without communicating. We communicate when we ask an instructor a question or listen to another student give an explanation of a concept. We communicate in the warmth of an intimate exchange, the heat of an intense conflict, even the chill of a faded relationship.

Communication skills are powerful. For example, asking good questions and listening carefully can stimulate thinking and advanced learning. When you ask questions, you prompt others to go to a deeper level in their consideration. When others ask you questions, you may be surprised by how more satisfying your ideas can become because you have been prompted to go review, reflect, or defend your position. Good communications skills tend to inspire trust and promote genuine positive regard.

Good communication skills also can help you reach your goals and attain career success. (See "Create Your Future: Practice Communication Skills.") Employers rate communication skills as the most important skills they look for in potential employees. In fact, when things turn foul in a job situation, chances are that poor communication skills will be at the heart of the trouble. Let's explore some of the characteristics of communication.

Communication consists of a *sender* who *encodes* and delivers a *message* to a *receiver* who attempts to understand or *decode* what he hears. Messages can be verbal or nonverbal and both channels can be in operation simultaneously. Few interpersonal communications are brief one-time interactions. In contrast, most interpersonal communication is an ongoing volley of verbal and nonverbal actions between the sender and receiver.

In the back-and-forth exchanges of communication, messages can easily become garbled and misunderstood. Consider the communication between two college students—Latisha and Alex. Latisha thinks Alex doesn't really listen to her; he keeps

BUILD COMPETENCE

Develop Active Listening Skills

- **Give complete attention to the speaker.** This focus shows you're interested in what the speaker has to say. Don't do your e-mail or try to keep an eye on a television show while the conversation unfolds if you want optimal results.
- **Show respect.** In U.S. culture, listeners show greatest respect for the speaker by maintaining good eye contact and a relaxed posture, leaning slightly toward the speaker. However, in some cultures, direct eye contact communicates hostility or disrespect. It helps to know what the norms for demonstrating respect are for any context in which you are trying to communicate effectively.
- **Paraphrase.** State in your own words what someone just said, such as "Let me see, what I hear you saying is . . . " or "Do you mean . . . ?" Paraphrasing is particularly useful when someone says something important or complex. A good paraphrase communicates that you cared enough to listen carefully and you understood the most critical elements.
- **Summarize central ideas.** Conversations can become strewn with bits and pieces of disconnected information. Active listeners pay attention to the key points covered by the speaker and may recount them ("Let's review the ground we've been covering so far. . . ."). Summarizing especially helps when the communication is complex or meanders.
- **Synthesize themes and patterns.** A slightly more challenging listening skill is synthesizing what you hear into the most prominent themes or patterns. At times the speaker may not be aware that a central idea undergirds complex, messy, or emotionally charged communication. Reflecting an integration of those ideas (e.g., "One theme you seem to be coming back to is. . . .") may produce important insights and increases your value as the listener.
- **Give accurate feedback.** Verbal or nonverbal feedback gives speakers an idea of how well they are getting their points across. Positive nonverbal feedback can include smiling and nodding, whereas a furrowed brow or frown communicate disagreement. Effective listeners give honest feedback quickly, clearly, and informatively ("I understand what you mean. . . ." or "That was awesome."). Most helpful is feedback that details specifics of what was pleasing or upsetting.
- **Use extra care when offering negative feedback.** If constructive feedback is necessary, good critics try to find some positive aspects to comment on before moving to the developmental ideas that will be harder for the speaker to hear ("It is clear to me that you have great passion for this topic, but. . . ."). Some good listeners ease into constructive suggestions by reporting their confusion about what the speaker intended ("I am confused by what you are trying to say. Would it be clearer if. . . ?").

asking her questions and then answering them himself, before she has a chance to respond. She complains that he talks *to* her rather than *with* her. When they get together with his friends, the conversation moves so fast, Latisha can hardly get a word in edgewise. Afterward, Alex concludes that Latisha is too quiet, although she is certainly not like that with her own friends. Alex assumes that she's quiet because she doesn't like his friends, whereas Latisha thinks that his friends ignore her perhaps because they don't like her very much. The poor communication between Latisha and Alex exemplifies how all too often messages are lost or misunderstood.

Let's now explore some ways you can become a better listener and speaker when you are communicating with someone.

Develop Good Listening Skills

In the third century BCE, the Greek philosopher Zeno of Citum said that the reason people have two ears and one mouth is so they can listen more and talk less. Listening is essential for building relationships, but many people fall into the bad habit of *pseudolistening*, in which the receiver goes through the motions of listening but doesn't really process any meaningful information. As one college student put it, "My friends *listen* but my parents only *hear* me talk."

Bad listeners can also hog conversations. They talk *to* rather than *with* someone. They show greater investment in what they plan to say next rather than in their conversation partners. Such tactics initially frustrate and eventually alienate, taking a huge toll on the quality of interpersonal relationships.

Good listening skills provide a lot of interpersonal traction. By listening actively rather than passively absorbing information, others will be drawn to you. "Build Competence: Develop Active Listening Skills" provides some good advice.

Avoid Barriers to Effective Verbal Communication

Messages are conveyed more effectively when you speak in a simple rather than a complex way, a concrete rather than an abstract way, and a specific rather than a general way. When you do need to convey ideas that are abstract, general, or complex, use appropriate examples to illustrate the ideas. Often the best examples are those that listeners can relate to their own personal experiences. For instance, suppose Margaret is trying to explain the concept of *elitism*. She might offer a definition, cite some examples in which she thought someone's superior attitude had a harsh outcome, and encourage others to identify similar examples to verify that the example has been communicated effectively.

Good speakers also make their verbal and nonverbal messages consistent. If you say one thing and nonverbally communicate the opposite, you are likely to create confusion and distrust. For example, if you are trying to explain to an instructor why

Reprinted by permission of United Feature Syndicate, Inc.

you didn't turn a paper in on time and you look down at the floor rather than maintaining eye contact, the teacher may be less likely to believe you, even if your excuse is legitimate.

Good speakers also avoid barriers to effective communication. Consider Ethan's dilemma. Ethan's lab partner, Brian, is performing in a lackluster manner by not getting his share of the work done on time, jeopardizing Ethan's grade in the course. The following (based on Gordon 1970) demonstrate many negative ways that Ethan's response could make the situation even worse:

- *Criticizing* (making negative evaluations): "You act like you don't know what you are doing in the lab."
- *Name-Calling* (putting down the other person): "You're such an idiot for not planning better."
- *Advising* (talking down to the other person while giving a solution to a problem): "You should really do a better job of time management."
- *Ordering* (commanding the other person to do what you want): "You have to make this your number-one priority!"
- *Threatening* (trying to control the other person): "If you don't listen to me, I'm going to ask the professor to let me change partners."
- *Moralizing* (preaching to the other person what she should do): "You know you shouldn't have gone out last night. You ought to be sorry."
- *One-upping* (pushing the other person's problems aside): "You think *you* have it bad? Let me tell you about how tough *my* schedule is."
- *Logical arguing* (trying to convince the other person with logical facts without considering the person's feelings): "Here are all the things you've done wrong that hurt our grade on our last lab report. You *know* I'm right." It's good to use logic to try to persuade, but if you lose sight of the person's feelings, no matter how right you are, the other person won't be persuaded and may be hurt.

Ethan would be better off stating simply that he thinks he and Brian need to talk about strategies for making their lab partnership work more effectively and then get ready to do some listening so a mutually satisfying solution can be found.

To evaluate some of your own barriers to good communication, complete the Journal activity "Overcome Your Barriers" on page 59.

Practice Communication Skills

Antoine felt fortunate to have landed his part-time campus job working in the admissions office. Although he spent a good deal of time filing applications and doing data entry, he also answered phones and helped greet parents and prospective students when they arrived for interviews. He needed to listen closely to help address their questions and communicate effectively about the strengths of the school. The campus had a diverse student body, providing him with the chance to meet different types of people. He did his best to establish relationships with prospective students from a variety of backgrounds to help them feel comfortable during their visit. Although he had always planned on becoming an accountant, the part-time campus job in admissions made him think more about ensuring that his future career included enough interpersonal interaction. He was surprised by how much he enjoyed it—and how much his communication skills had improved already.

Elise had majored in communications, so she was thrilled to land a job as an associate events planner her first year out of college. She assisted in the planning of corporate events that ranged from the negotiation of contracts with caterers and hotels to the ordering of food and flowers. It was important to listen to all of the client's needs and communicate effectively about the status of the event throughout the process. She also was working on building relationships with clients to help ensure repeat business in the future. It was a very challenging job, but she loved all of the interaction and felt that her communication skills were being utilized every day.

Tune in to Nonverbal Communication

> *What you are speaks so loudly I cannot hear what you say.*
> Ralph Waldo Emerson
> *Nineteenth-century American poet and essayist*

How do you behave when talking with others? Does the way you fold your arms, cast your eyes, move your mouth, cross your legs, or touch someone send a message? Communications experts believe it does. You might:

- lift an eyebrow for disbelief
- clasp your arms to isolate or protect yourself
- shrug your shoulders for indifference
- wink one eye for intimacy
- tap your fingers for impatience
- slap your forehead for forgetfulness

These are conscious, deliberate gestures people make in the course of communicating.

Are there also unconscious, nonverbal behaviors that offer clues about what a person is feeling? Hard-to-control facial muscles especially tend to reveal emotions that people are trying to conceal. Lifting only the inner part of your eyebrow may reveal stress and worry. Eyebrows raised together may signal fear. Fidgeting may reveal anxiety or boredom.

Many communications experts believe that most interpersonal communication is nonverbal. Even if you're sitting in a corner silently reading a book, your nonverbal behavior communicates something—perhaps that you want to be left alone. It might also communicate that you're intellectually oriented.

You'll have a hard time trying to mask or control your nonverbal messages. True feelings usually express themselves, no matter how hard we try to conceal them, so it's good to recognize the power of nonverbal behavior (DeFleur and others 2005). To think about how touch can communicate information, complete the Journal activity "What Does Touch Communicate?" on page 59.

MANAGE LIFE

Control Your Anger

Everyone gets angry at one time or another. These strategies can help you take responsibility for controlling your anger (American Psychological Association 2002, Tavris 1989):

- When your anger starts to boil and your body is getting aroused, work on lowering your arousal by waiting. Your anger will usually simmer down if you just wait long enough.
- Don't say the first thing that comes into your head when you get angry, but slow down and think carefully about what you want to communicate. At the same time, listen carefully to what the other person is saying and take your time before answering.
- Slowly repeat a calm word or phrase, such as "relax," or "take it easy." Repeat it to yourself while breathing deeply.
- Change the way you think. Angry people tend to curse, swear, or speak in highly colorful terms that reflect their inner thoughts. When you are angry, you can exaggerate and become rather dramatic. Replace these thoughts with more rational ones. For example, instead of telling yourself, "Oh, it's awful, it's terrible, everything is ruined," say something to yourself such as, "It's frustrating and it's understandable that I'm upset about it but it's not the end of the world."
- Work on not being chronically angry over every little bothersome annoyance. Also, avoid passively sulking, which simply reinforces your reasons for being angry.
- Take the perspective of others and think about how you look to them when you get angry. Is this how you want others to think of you?

Use Communication to Resolve Conflict with Others

Conflicts are inevitable in our everyday interactions, especially in an intense college environment. Developing skills to resolve these conflicts can make your life calmer and more enjoyable.

Deal Effectively with Conflict Strategies for reducing interpersonal conflict include assertiveness and effective negotiation. Four main ways to deal with conflict include:

- *Aggression.* People who respond aggressively to conflict run roughshod over others. They communicate in demanding, abrasive, and hostile ways often characterized by anger or entitlement. Aggressive people often are insensitive to the rights and feelings of others. As a consequence, aggressive people tend to alienate others by their bullying or obnoxious approach to solving problems. See "Manage Life: Control Your Anger" for some ideas about being more responsible for controlling your anger.
- *Manipulation.* Manipulative people try to get what they want by making others feel guilty or sorry for them. They don't take responsibility for meeting their own needs. Instead,

manipulative people play the role of the victim or martyr to get others to do things for them, working indirectly to get their needs met. Manipulators also alienate others who resent not being able to deal directly with the issues.

- *Passivity.* Passive people act in nonassertive, submissive ways. They let others run roughshod over them. Passive people don't express their feelings or let others know what they want or need. Extreme dependence drives away most other people unless they see the passive person as easy to exploit for their own purposes.
- *Assertion.* Of the four styles of dealing with conflict, acting assertively is clearly the most appropriate and the most helpful for building long-term solid relationships (Alberti and Emmons 1995). Assertive people act in their own best interests. They stand up for their legitimate rights and express their views openly and directly. Be assertive in any situation in which you need to express your feelings, ask for what you want, or say no to something you don't want.

To determine your dominant style of dealing with conflict, complete Self-Assessment 1, "Do You Blow Up, Get Down and Get Dirty, or Speak Up?" on page 56. In addition, some helpful strategies (based on Bourne 1995) are described in "Build Competence: Become More Assertive."

Negotiate Effectively Everybody negotiates. You negotiate when you apply for a job, dispute a grade with a teacher, buy a car, ask your landlord to paint your apartment, or try to get your roommate or partner to do something. Whenever you want something from someone whose interests are at odds with your own, you can choose to negotiate.

Some negotiation strategies are better than others. Negotiating effectively helps you to get what you want from others without alienating them. Negotiation experts often describe three main ways of solving problems with others: win–lose, lose–lose, and win–win.

- *Win–lose strategy.* In this type of negotiating, one party prevails and the other comes up short, such as: "Either I get my way or you get your way." For example, roommates may have pooled their resources for a spring break trip but totally disagree about where to go. Eventually one of the roommates gives in. Most of the time a win–lose strategy is not wise. Why? Because the loser may harbor bad feelings and always feel dissatisfied with the outcome.
- *Lose–lose strategy.* This situation usually unfolds when both parties initially try a win–lose strategy that does not work. As a result of the struggle, both end up unsatisfied with the outcome. For example, after several frustrating sessions of being unable to develop a satisfying spring break plan, both roommates may just give up rather than suffer protracted turmoil.
- *Win–win strategy.* The goal in this strategy is to find a solution that satisfies both parties and to avoid winning at the other person's expense. By working together,

BUILD COMPETENCE

Become More Assertive

Suppose the people with whom you live play music too loudly for you to concentrate on your studies. Examine the following steps that will help you resolve the problem assertively.

- **Evaluate your rights.** Determine your rights in the situation at hand. Act assertively if you think these rights are being violated. Is it reasonable for you to expect a quiet study environment? If so, proceed to the next step.
- **Enlist cooperation.** Approach your living partners positively, asking for their assistance in helping you solve a problem that is important for your academic success. For example, say, "I have a problem that I could use your help to solve. . . ."
- **Choose the right time.** Unless you need to be assertive on the spot, find a mutually convenient time to discuss the problem with the other person involved. Avoid this discussion if you are fuming from another interrupted study session.
- **Describe the problem and consequence in concrete terms.** Clearly outline what is bothering you ("When you do *X*, *Y* is the consequence for me"). Limit yourself to describing the specific problem situation as objectively as you can without judging or blaming. Outline your point of view even if it seems obvious to you. This tactic allows the other person to get a better sense of your position. For example, you might tell someone you live with, "When you play music so loud, I have a hard time concentrating. . . ."
- **Add your feelings to emphasize adverse impact.** When you express unhappy feelings, such as disappointment, sadness, or frustration, even others who completely disagree with you can tell how much the circumstance bothers you. "When you play music so loud," you could say, "I have a hard time concentrating and I feel *distracted* or *upset* about losing study time."
- **Follow through with your request.** Make sure to ask for what you want (or don't want) in a straightforward way. "It would really help me out if we could schedule some music-free time periods after dinner," you could suggest.
- **Ask for feedback.** The problem may turn out to be larger than you anticipated, especially if the conflict has been brewing for a while. Make your request, but ask for your partner's perspective on the problem or any possible solutions. With two people collaborating assertively to resolve the problem, the solution may be even more successful than what you originally hoped to achieve.

the parties can find a solution that satisfies everyone. For example, after considerable discussion and negotiation, each roommate agrees to some concessions and they arrive at an agreeable vacation plan.

Some compromises are often necessary in this win–win ideal. You and the seller settle on a price for a used car. The price is between what the seller was asking and what you wanted to pay. Neither of you got exactly what you wanted, but the outcome left each of you happy. Similarly, you and your companion each want to see a different movie. To spend the evening together, you might choose another movie that you both agree on.

The best solutions of all, though, are not compromises. Rather, they are solutions in which all parties get what they want. For example, Andrea and Carmen are roommates with different study habits. Andrea likes to study in the evening. This leaves most of her day free for other activities. Carmen thinks that evenings should be for relaxation and fun. They arrived at the following solution. On Monday through Wednesday, Andrea studies at her boyfriend's; Carmen does anything she wants. On Thursday and Sunday, Carmen agrees to keep things quiet where she and Andrea live. On Friday and Saturday they both have fun together.

The win–win strategy gives you a creative way of finding the best solution for a problem between two or more parties. You can use it to solve conflicts with others and make everyone involved feel better.

Develop Good Relationships

Relationships play a powerful role in college. College students who have positive, close relationships are much happier than those who do not. One recent study found that very happy college students rated their relationships with their friends, family, and romantic partners more positively than college students who were average in happiness or very unhappy (Diener and Seligman 2002). In this study, the very happy college students were more likely than the other two groups to spend more time with family, friends, and a romantic partner and considerably less time alone (see Figure 2.1).

Recognize Attachment Styles

As social creatures, human beings seek to bond or be attached to others and do so in different ways. These attachment styles develop in infancy and may affect the ease with which you make and maintain relationships with significant others in all settings, not just college. Three types of attachment that characterize adults are (Shaver, Belsky, and Brennan 2000):

- *Secure attachment.* Secure adults find it easy to get close to others and don't worry much about becoming too dependent or being abandoned. They tend to have satisfying and enduring close relationships.
- *Avoidant attachment.* Adults with this type of insecure attachment tend to avoid closeness, be less invested in close relationships, and more likely to leave them. They tend to be either *fearful* ("I'm uncomfortable getting close to others") or *dismissing* ("It is very important for me to feel independent and self-sufficient"). About 20 percent of adults have an avoidant attachment style.
- *Ambivalent attachment.* Adults with an ambivalent attachment style are less trusting and thus more possessive and jealous. They may break up repeatedly with the same person. When discussing conflicts, they tend to become very emotional and angry. About 10 percent of adults have an ambivalent attachment style.

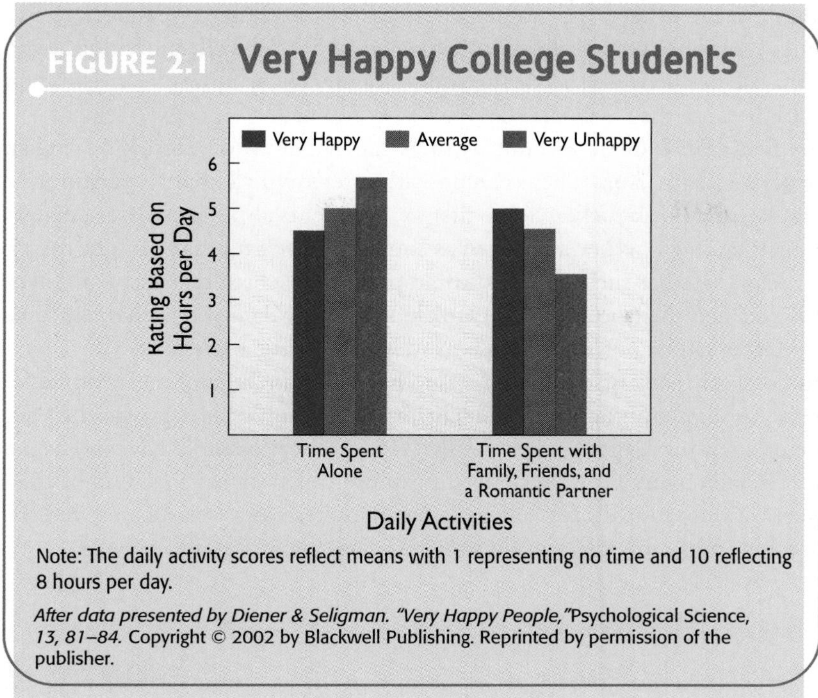

Note: The daily activity scores reflect means with 1 representing no time and 10 reflecting 8 hours per day.

After data presented by Diener & Seligman. "Very Happy People," Psychological Science, *13, 81–84.* Copyright © 2002 by Blackwell Publishing. Reprinted by permission of the publisher.

If your attachments tend to be avoidant or ambivalent, you may find that your relationships with friends and romantic partners are difficult and this is an area that you can work to improve. However, even if your secure attachment style predicts healthy relationships, you will have to choose wisely to provide the right balance between meeting your social and academic needs.

Having friends can reduce loneliness, be a source of self-esteem, and provide emotional support, especially in times of stress, both for women and men. However, women tend to have more close friends and their friendships involve more self-disclosure and exchange of mutual support than men's friendships. Women are more likely to listen at length to what a friend has to say and be sympathetic (Garner and Estep 2001).

Assess the Social Scene

College will provide many opportunities for you to design a satisfying social life. Hanging out and finding special people in your college life can involve wonderful, fulfilling times. Unfortunately, your social choices can also lead to unhappiness, anxiety, and even violence.

From the outset, mixers, student orientation sessions, and other social events at college will give you the chance to find and develop or expand your social circles. Many students prefer the security of navigating "in the pack." Others show some eagerness to date or spend their time with a significant other rather than hanging with the group. Students without partners may view dating as a way to find a spouse. Others see it as an important part of fitting into the social scene. Some students date for romantic reasons, others for friendship or companionship. Still other students, especially those who are attempting to combine work and school, may have very little discretionary time to take advantage of the social opportunities that college has to offer.

The quality of your social life can detract from or enhance your college success. For example, it's clearly not a good idea to get so head over heels in passionate love that all you can think about is your romantic partner. If that happens to you, you'll probably spend too little time studying. And nothing is harder on your GPA than a serious case of heartbreak. On the other hand, some people who date someone regularly or live with a partner feel more settled down and freer to work. As well, individuals who strike the right balance between socializing and studying may be more effective in their academic work because they feel relaxed and socially fulfilled.

Too many first-year students without partners get caught up in wanting to date an ideal rather than a real person. They search for the stereotypical jock, a person with movie-star looks, or a punk rocker. Some first-year students also look at every date as a potential girlfriend or boyfriend, or even as someone they eventually might marry. College counselors say that such students would probably be better adjusted and happier if they broadened their perspective. Don't look at every date as a potential Mr. or Mrs. Perfect. Dates can be potential friends as well as romantic partners.

It's not unusual for many first-year students to have a serious relationship with someone back home. Also, many commuter students have a romantic partner who does not go to college or attends college somewhere else. You do not necessarily have to give up this romance. In fact, many pre-existing relationships nicely weather this kind of challenge. However, it's not unusual for college to facilitate changes in personality, careers, and goals that may make it harder for old romances and relationships to survive.

Avoid Sexual Threats

Some social choices can put students at risk of rape or other unwanted sexual acts. For example, some people engage in unwanted sexual acts when not physically forced to do so. Why would they do this? They might be:

- turned on by their partner's actions but later regret it
- fearful that the relationship will end if they don't have sex
- intoxicated or high on drugs
- feeling obligated because of the time and money spent by a partner

Many college students participate in "hooking up," casual sexual relationships with partners selected from a group of their friends. Although such activity may not feel coercive since individuals participate of their own free will, there may be some not-so-subtle pressures to join in. Many report substantial regret about participating because it can negatively affect the relationship as well as produce pregnancy and sexually transmitted disease.

A special concern in college is date or acquaintance rape: forced sexual intercourse with someone who has at least a casual acquaintance with the victim. One-third to one-half of college men admit that they have forced sexual activity on women (Bachar and Koss 2001). Given this frequency, it pays to be vigilant about ways to avoid finding yourself in a compromising situation. See "Manage Life: Strategies for Avoiding Settings in Which Rape Most Often Occurs" for some safety precautions.

Rape is a violent crime and traumatizes victims, who initially feel shocked and numb. Once the shock wears away, victims of rape typically feel shame of such magnitude that they do not report the crime and attempt to manage their trauma without appropriate intervention. Recovery is easier with the support of parents and friends, and professional counseling also

"Of course I can accept you for who you are. You are someone I need to change."

can help. Reporting the crime and cooperating to secure appropriate punishment for the rapist can be an important part of recovery. In addition, successful prosecution reduces the likelihood that the acquaintance rapist will seek other victims.

In sum, monitor your sexual feelings and make good sexual decisions. Act assertively to meet your social needs and defend the kind of social life you genuinely wish to pursue. Sexual regret and academic achievement can be a difficult mix.

Strategies for Avoiding Settings in Which Rape Most Often Occurs

- Things to Do:
  - Go places with other people.
  - If you go alone, first tell someone your plans.
  - Walk briskly, with purpose.
  - Stay in well-lighted, populated areas.
  - Limit your drug and alcohol intake; these can make you vulnerable.
  - Exercise good judgment about sharing your private information.
  - Have your keys ready when going to your car or residence.
  - Lock all doors and windows in your car and residence.
  - Do not open doors for strangers.
  - Carry a whistle or other alarm.
  - If someone is following you or you feel threatened, go to a public place, call the police, run, scream, or blow a whistle.
- Things to Remember:
  - No one has the right to rape you.
  - Rape is never the fault of the victim.
  - Rape is a criminal act of violence for the purpose of power.
  - Date or acquaintance rape is still rape.
  - Rape is a sexual assault. Assault is a crime.

Women's Issues Network (WIN), *Dallas Working Against Rape* brochure.

Deal with Loneliness

Although college campuses teem with people, first-year students—whether resident or commuter—still report feeling lonely at times. Loneliness can be a dark cloud over your everyday life. Researchers have found that loneliness is linked with impaired physical and mental health (Cacioppo 2002).

Especially when students attend college away from home, they face the challenge of forming new social relationships. Many first-year students feel anxious about meeting new people and developing new social lives; first-year students rarely carry their high school popularity and social standing into college. In one study, two weeks after the college year began, 75 percent of the first-year students felt lonely at least part of the time after arriving on campus (Cutrona 1982).

Loneliness is not reserved for first-year students just out of high school. Older first-year students can be lonely as well. The demands of school, work, and family may leave little time to feel replenished through contacts with friends. Also, it is common for divorced adults and widows/widowers to return to college to further their education and develop skills. Because of the dissolution of their marital relationship, loneliness may penetrate their lives.

Are You Lonely? Time spent alone can be meaningful and satisfying. However, when we feel isolated and long to be with others, we need to do something to become more connected. If you think that you aren't in tune with the people around you and can't find companionship when you want it, you're probably lonely. If you've recently left an important relationship, you'll likely feel lonely until you rebuild your social network.

To evaluate the extent to which you are lonely, complete Self-Assessment 2, "Loneliness," on page 57.

Strategies for Reducing Loneliness How can you become better connected with others? Whether you are a traditional or nontraditional student, here are some good strategies:

- *Get involved.* Explore activities with others through college, work, community announcements, or religious organizations. Join and volunteer time with an organization you believe in. You'll probably meet others who share your views. One social gathering can lead to new social contacts, especially if you introduce yourself to others and start conversations.
- *Stretch yourself.* Join a new group at dinner, sit with new people in class, or find a study or exercise partner. Meeting new people and developing new social ties always involves risk, but the benefits are worth it.

- *Practice positive character.* Listen with complete attention. Be upbeat and constructive. Make a point to comment on something special about the other person. Be the kind of friend you would like to have.
- *Exercise caution about cyberspace relationships.* Although social websites such as Facebook.com have made it easier to find friends who share your interests, be especially careful about posting personal details. This will help you avoid financial or sexual predators.
- *Recognize the warning signs of loneliness.* People often become bored or alienated before loneliness sinks in. Take action to head it off. Planning new activities is easier than struggling to escape loneliness once it has set in.
- *Ask for help.* If you can't shed your loneliness and make friends on your own, contact the student counseling center at your college or a mental health professional in your community. A counselor or mental health professional can show you ways to connect with others and reduce your loneliness.

> ***Where you used to be, there is a hole in the world, which I find myself constantly walking around in the daytime, and falling into at night.***
> Edna St. Vincent Millay
> *Twentieth-century American poet*

To enhance connecting with new people, complete the Journal activity "Combat Loneliness" on page 58. Also, see the resources section on this book's website at http://www.thomsonedu.com/success/santrock5.

So far we have explored ways to communicate more effectively, make solid social choices, and reduce loneliness. As we'll see next, special care should be taken to build and protect the relationships that will facilitate your college success.

Maintain Specific Positive Relationships

College can be a transforming experience. The personal changes that you will undergo may be a surprise not just to you but to your loved ones as well. Nurturing these important relationships will help them stay vital even after you achieve your degree. Practicing good social strategies can also help you with the new relationships you may acquire during your college years.

Connect with Parents at the Right Level

Relationships between first-year college students and parents who provide financial and emotional support for them can vary considerably. Researchers have found that there is a link between college success and the right level of involvement in student–parent relationships (Halberg and others 2000). Some parent–child patterns become *enmeshed* when parents find it too challenging to let go. They believe their college-age children are seriously in need of their guidance, giving rise to the term "helicopter parents" (http://www.healthyplace.com/Communities/Parenting/news_2006/parenting.htm). As a consequence the parents may be too involved in their student's decisions, which encourages the student to remain dependent and avoid tackling new challenges. On the other hand, some parents have little contact with, and provide little support for, first-year students who have left home, just as some students break off communication with their parents as soon as they no longer share living space.

Let Your Parents Know You Haven't Fallen Off the Planet No matter how much independence you want, it is not a good idea to break off communication with your parents, even if you felt stifled by them before you departed. You'll likely need them at some point, possibly for money, a place to live, or emotional support.

Maintaining communication doesn't mean you have to write them a letter three times a week, e-mail daily, or call every night. You don't have to tell them everything you do. However, if they don't hear from you for a couple of weeks, they may fear that something really bad has happened to you. In most cases parents want to know regularly how you are getting along.

What is regular contact? If you're away from home, a phone or text conversation or informative e-mail once a week should do. One first-year student didn't want his roommates to kid him about calling home regularly, so he wrote a coded reminder on his calendar once a week, "E.T.," from the movie where E.T. phones home. E-mail is cheap, convenient, and easy—another great way to keep in touch.

If you're a young adult student in your first year, your parents are probably concerned about your increased independence. Without necessarily intending to crowd you, they may ask questions that seem intrusive: "How much are you studying?" "How come you didn't get an A on your English test?" "What's your roommate like?" "Are you dating anyone?" "Have you been going to religious services?" Try to listen politely to their questions. Realize that they probably have your best interests at heart. You don't have to tell them all the details of your life. They usually will accept your answers if you tell them a few general things and contact them on a predictable basis.

What Your Parents Can't Find Out without Your Approval Your parents should know only what you choose to tell them about your college experiences. According to the Family Education Responsibility and Privacy Act (FERPA), the college cannot release your records to anyone but you. Instructors can discuss your progress or problems only in your presence or with your permission. This legal constraint encourages your family members to let you resolve your own problems. It also should reinforce that you are responsible for your own circumstances. Don't ask your parents to step in and resolve personal or academic problems when you could do it yourself. Use your control of personal information responsibly and wisely.

Make Room for Partners and Family

Many nontraditional students face special challenges in their relationships as they attempt to succeed in college. Among these challenges are protecting relationships with a spouse or partner, and with children.

Relate to Spouse or Partner Some strategies for keeping relationships with a partner positive include (Sternberg 1988):

- *Don't take your relationship for granted.* The seeds of a relationship's destruction are planted when you or your partner take each other for granted. Nourish the relationship, giving it high priority along with your studies. Schedule time with your partner just as you do for classes and studying. Don't expect your partner to take over all of the household duties or pamper you.
- *Share your college life.* Let your partner know what you're doing in college. Discuss your schedule, what you're learning, and what your day is like. Look for campus activities or events—such as lectures, sporting events, and plays—that you can attend together. To avoid being too self-focused, remember to ask about your partner's activities.
- *Nurture positive esteem and confidence in the relationship.* Don't seek in your partner what you lack in yourself. Feel good about your pursuit of education—it will enhance your confidence. Actively look for opportunities that will build mutual good feeling. Test-drive your ideas with your partner if your partner is willing. When both partners have high self-esteem, their relationship benefits.
- *Be open with your partner.* Sometimes it seems easier in the short run to lie or hold back the painful truth. The problem is that once omissions, distortions,

"When you say I mean the world to you, which part of the world are you talking about?"

and flat-out lies start, they tend to spread and ultimately can destroy a relationship. Talk becomes empty because the relationship has lost its depth and trust.

- *See things from your partner's point of view.* Ask yourself how your partner perceives you. This helps you to develop the empathy and understanding that fuel a satisfying, successful relationship. Recognize that your intellectual changes may be taxing rather than exciting if your partner is not integrated into the process.
- *Be a friend.* Researchers have found that one of the most successful factors in a successful marriage is the extent to which the partners are good friends (Gottman and Silver 1999). Friendship acts as a powerful shield against conflict.
- *Understand differences in communication styles between men and women.* Men tend to view talk in a relationship as an opportunity to give information (Tannen 1990). By contrast, women are more likely to view it as a way of exploring a relationship. Understanding this difference in perception can help you conquer this gender communication gap. To think further about differences in males and females, complete the Journal activity "Are Men Really from Mars and Women Really from Venus?" on page 59.

Care for Children If you're a parent as well as a student, you also face special challenges. Depending on their ages, your children may not be particularly patient with your sacrificing family time to meet obscure academic deadlines. How can you use parenting time to best advantage? Some helpful strategies include:

- *Be authoritative.* Psychologist Diana Baumrind (1991) wanted to know whether one type of parenting style is linked with having a child who is well-adjusted and competent. She found that the best parenting style is authoritative, which involves being nurturing, engaging in verbal give-and-take with the child, and exercising some control but not in a punishing way. That is, authoritative parents give children feedback to help develop self-control but don't let them run wild. By contrast, being either permissive and uninvolved, or punitive and cold, are less effective parenting styles. Children reared by these types of parents often have trouble controlling their behavior.
- *Reinforce their value.* If your children are old enough, talk with them about how important they are to you as well as how important your education is. If possible, link your success in college with your hopes for a positive impact on your family. Each day set aside time to listen to your children, but be prepared to listen to complaints about their perceptions that you are no longer as accessible.
- *Manage time expertly.* At times, you may feel overwhelmed with juggling a family and school. Planning can be an important asset in your effort to balance your academic and family time. Check into child-care facilities and community agencies for services and activities for your children before and after school. Chapter 3 also offers many helpful time management strategies that will help you strike a better balance between family and school obligations.
- *Set aside time for your children and yourself.* It's not going to be easy, but be sure to block out at least some time each week for activities you enjoy or for

relaxation. You might have a hobby, like exercise or going to movies. Set aside time every day for your children's interests as well.

Relate to Instructors

An important, but often overlooked, aspect of relationships in college is being able to get along with instructors. Many students never talk with an instructor in or out of class. One student remarked that he had no idea what kind of people his instructors were, and for all he knew, they were all locked in a vault each evening and then unleashed on Monday to feed on poor students during the day. Of course, that's not so.

Instructors have personality styles and social relationships just as students do. Some are shy, others are gregarious. Some have great social relationships, others miserable ones. For the most part, to get along with instructors you are going to have to adjust to their styles because they are unlikely to adjust to yours. "Expand Your Resources: Getting Along with Instructors" provides some good suggestions.

Getting Along with Instructors

Here are some good strategies for developing a positive relationship with an instructor (www. academictips.org):

1. *Assume that all instructors are human.* This may sound a little ridiculous, but too many students see instructors as aloof or perhaps even an alien species. However, like you, they are human and they have families, learning and personality styles, likes and dislikes, and good and bad days. Understanding that they are human may help you to demystify beliefs that you won't be able to get along with them or get to know them no matter how hard you try.
2. *Evaluate your learning and personality styles and your instructor's.* In Chapter 4, "Diversify Your Learning Style," you will spend considerable time examining your learning and personality styles. You probably will like and get along better with an instructor whose learning and personality styles are similar to yours. Don't let this restrict your opportunity to get along with an instructor. Just being aware of such differences may help you to think about ways to interact more positively.
3. *Talk with other students who have previously taken classes from the instructor.* Interview them about what the instructor is like. Ask them about his style during an entire course, how easy or hard it was to get to know and get along with the instructor, and any strategies that might have worked in developing a positive relationship.
4. *Establish rapport with an instructor early in the term.* You can ask questions after class and/or visit an instructor during his office hours. It is a good idea to begin this process early so that you will feel more comfortable talking with the instructor later when you don't understand a topic or might be having difficulty in the course.

Get Along with Roommates

If you live on campus, you will find that the quality of relationships with roommates varies. In many cases, a first-year student's roommate is a total stranger. You're asked to live in close quarters for nine months with someone you know little or nothing about. That's enough to cause apprehension in anyone. If you are lucky, you might become best friends. Or you might be mutually indifferent and simply live parallel lives in the same space. If you are unlucky, you might grow to hate each other.

Some good strategies for getting along with this total stranger are described in "Manage Life: Fixing Problem Roommates." Then do the Journal activity "Reflect on Your Relationship with Your Roommate" on page 58 to explore how to deal with roommate problems.

But what if, after trying hard to reconcile problems, your roommate seems destined to ruin your adjustment to college life? What can you do?

If you live in a college dorm, you probably have a resident adviser (RA) with whom you can discuss your roommate problems. Take the initiative. Go to the RA and ask for advice about what to do. Try out the advice and give it a chance to work. Then, if things are still intolerable, go to the campus housing office. Courteously and clearly state your roommate problems and explore your options there. You are more likely to negotiate a different room assignment if your current situation is unacceptable to both you and your roommate.

"Please tell me you aren't my roommate."

MANAGE LIFE

Fixing Problem Roommates

Whenever two people live together, problems are bound to appear. You can learn a lot about the importance of give-and-take in important relationships by living with a roommate. What's the best way to build solid roommate relationships?

1. **Address problems early.** Don't let them fester. Detect and resolve them early.
2. **Use good communication skills.** Listen actively and avoid barriers to communication whenever you can. If you have a roommate problem, review the strategies presented on pages XXX and use them with your roommate.
3. **Show respect.** Take your roommate's perspective into account. For example, it's not a good idea to come in at 2 a.m., flip the lights on, and wake up your roommate. It's also not a good idea to rev up the CD or DVD player when your roommate is trying to study.
4. **Be assertive.** If you think that you're doing more than your fair share of the giving in your roommate relationship, be more assertive. Stand up for your rights. Use the strategies for being assertive outlined earlier in the chapter.
5. **Recognize your part.** Objectively review what aspects of your behavior might be challenging for your roommate. For example, you may have gotten into the habit of not keeping your room clean before you came to college. Old habits are hard to break. Keep your area clean and neat or at least try to match the level of tidiness exercised by your roommate to avoid problems. Chances are good that your "roommate problem" involves some problem behaviors of your own.

Build Professional Networks

During her first year away at college, Martina discovered to her delight that there was a highly respected dentist, Dr. Denton, who attended her synagogue. During a social hour, she introduced herself and explained that she had been thinking about a career in dentistry. Dr. Denton invited her to visit him at his practice. He was delighted to show Martina how he had built his business, and he became a special source of support for her as her undergraduate work unfolded.

Success in college not only is enhanced by good friendships but also by your ability to network effectively with people in general. Networking involves connecting with others to enhance your opportunities, but it is particularly time well spent in building connections that will help you professionally. Successful networking takes practice. Some strategies include (Mrosko 2002):

- *Be patient, and follow up.* In many instances, it takes time to develop a relationship. Effective networking doesn't happen overnight. Follow up initial contacts. Consistent, focused contacts build relationships. Martina had to call Dr. Denton a few times before the relationship got rolling, but once he saw how serious her commitment was, he made time in his schedule to help her.
- *Encourage mutual gains.* Both sides need to receive a benefit, either now or in the future. Martina was able to gain insights into her chosen profession; Dr. Denton, by the assistance he provided, was able to re-experience the fun of preparing for a career.
- *Listen carefully.* Take notes and really hear what others are saying. Recording details shows that you place great value on the information and may reduce the embarrassing need to ask that details that you can't remember be repeated.
- *Ask for help.* Be specific about what you need.
- *Become involved.* Become active in support groups and campus organizations. Volunteer to be on a committee. Identify if there are specific interest groups that can help you realize your goals.

Appreciate Diversity

"We live to have relationships with other people."
Albert Camus
Twentieth-century French-Algerian philosopher

Ana Bolado de Espino represents how successful students can be, even when they come from backgrounds that wouldn't seem the best for beating the odds. She came to Dallas, Texas, from Mexico in 1980. She did not speak a word of English, but she did have a dream. Ana wanted to become a medical doctor.

She worked as a maid, scrubbing floors and doing laundry for fifteen years to earn enough money to enter college as a nontraditional student. Divorced, she raised two children while attending college and working. She feared that she would never make it to medical school. She also hit a major snag. As a young teen, her daughter began to hang out with a gang, ran away, and became pregnant. Ana thought about dropping out of college to spend more time with her daughter, but her daughter told her to stay in college and, at age fifteen, started to turn her own life around.

Ana was thirty-eight years old when she obtained her college degree with a GPA of almost 4.0. She worked as an outreach AIDS counselor for a year after graduating from college and then was accepted into medical school.

Ana Bolado de Espino represents the increased diversity prevalent on most U.S. college campuses. Diversity can come into our lives in many ways, both in terms of our own characteristics and the diverse others we interact with. In some circumstances, diversity obviously offers the potential to enrich our experiences; in others, it may involve conflict and uneasy feelings. Let's explore some aspects of the diversity you may encounter in your college life and some strategies for improving relationships with diverse others.

Explore Individual and Cultural Differences

We should be accustomed to thinking of the United States as a country with many different cultures. Our population is diverse and originates from many different places, and college campuses are among the most diverse settings in this country. Some smaller colleges tend to be more homogeneous, with most students and faculty sharing a predominant ethnic or religious heritage, whereas larger campuses tend to be more diverse; most have international students and U.S. students, as well as faculty and staff, from many ethnic backgrounds.

Despite the opportunities to mix, people tend to seek out their "own kind." Think about where you eat lunch. Commuters often hang out with other commuters. Fraternity and sorority members sit off by themselves. Faculty and students tend not to mix. Associating with people whom we perceive to be similar to ourselves provides a comfort zone, preventing us from taking advantage of the rich opportunities on campus to meet and learn about people who differ from us. Next, we examine some factors that can help us understand cultural diversity better.

Ethnicity, Stereotypes, and Prejudice on Campus College campuses present many issues and concerns related to diversity. According to a survey of students at 390

> ***We need every human gift and cannot afford to neglect any gift because of artificial barriers of sex or race or class or national origin.***
>
> Margaret Mead
> *Twentieth-century American anthropologist*

An increasing number of college students are from ethnic minority groups. It's important to keep in mind that each ethnic group contains diverse individuals. Not taking this diversity and individual variation into account leads to stereotyping. A good strategy is to think of other students as individuals, not as members of a majority or minority group.

colleges and universities, ethnic conflict is common on many campuses (Hurtado, Dey, and Trevino 1994). For example, more than half the African-Americans and almost one-fourth the Asian-Americans said they felt excluded from college activities. In contrast, only 6 percent of Anglo-Americans said that they felt excluded. Other research continues to show that a higher percentage of minority students experience discrimination (Marcus and others 2003).

Many of us sincerely believe that we are not prejudiced. However, experts on prejudice have concluded that every person harbors some prejudices (Sears, Peplau, and Taylor 2003). Why? Because we are naturally disposed to identify with others who are like us. We tend to be *ethnocentric*, favoring the groups we belong to and tending to think of them as superior. We also tend to fear people who differ from us. All of these human inclinations contribute to prejudice, so we need to monitor ourselves in an effort to reduce such harmful attitudes.

Reduce Prejudice and Stereotyping What characteristics come to mind when you think about the following images: the blonde cheerleader, the computer nerd, the absent-minded professor, the Asian math whiz, the female basketball star, the class clown, the desperately lonely single adult, and the rigid or feeble-minded older adult? Notice that with merely a simple label we can conjure up a picture of what to expect about each individual.

Now imagine that you get to know these people. You discover that

- The "blonde" has a 4.0 average.
- The computer "nerd" plays in a hot new jazz band at a local club on weekends.
- The "absent-minded professor" never misses a class.
- The "Asian math whiz" is only an average math student but is a campus leader who is very popular with her peers.
- The "female basketball star" is dating a man in his second year of law school.
- The "class clown" recently organized a campus-wide initiative to decrease the pollution coming from a nearby chemical plant.
- The "desperately lonely single adult" has many friends.
- The "rigid or feeble-minded older adult" is an adaptive, nontraditional college student making good grades.

Clearly, stereotypes lead us to view others in limited and limiting ways. There's so much more to people than the social roles they play or the groups to which they belong (Jandt 2004).

Prejudice is ugly and socially damaging, and many people believe that college campuses should demonstrate leadership in prejudice and the disadvantages it causes. Recently, various diversity initiatives have been enacted to work toward this goal: on-campus celebrations of ethnic achievements, festivals that highlight different traditions or beliefs, required coursework to promote the explorations of traditions other than one's own, and inclusion of examples from a broader range of human experience in required readings. In spite of diversity initiatives, we still have a long way to go to reduce discrimination and prejudice. Examine your experiences with discrimination and prejudice by completing the Journal activity "Your Own Experience with Discrimination and Prejudice" on page 58.

> ***How unpleasing to the eye if all the flowers and plants, the leaves and blossoms, the fruits, the branches, and the trees were all the same shape and color. Diversity of hues, forms, and shape enriches and adorns the garden.***
>
> Allah Baha'
> *Nineteenth-century Persian founder of the Baha'i faith*

International Students Some colleges have students from a wide range of countries. These students bring with them customs, values, and behaviors that may be quite different from those of U.S. students. If you're a U.S.-born student, consider getting to know one or more international students. It will expand your education. If you're an international student, even if you were well-adjusted at home, adapting to college in the United States may bring confusion and problems. You now have to cope with a whole new set of customs and values. In some cases, you have to learn a new language and new rules for special conduct. "Expand Your Resources: International SOS" provides some advice.

Gain Insights into Gender Influences

Gender refers to our social and cultural experiences as a female or a male person. We live in a world in which gender roles are changing, and these changes have affected campus life. For example, first-year student Gina is the first woman in her family to attend college. Her grandmother did not go because it was not an option. Neither did her mother, who still believed that her place was in the home. However, her mother supported Gina's desire for a different kind of life and supported education as the best way to make that change.

Women now attend college and seek careers outside the home in greater numbers than ever before. In 1966, 57 percent of first-year college students agreed that a married woman should be confined to the home and family; in 2005, that figure had dropped to 20 percent (Pryor and others 2005). In fact, on many campuses female students outnumber males, sometimes dramatically so.

Overcoming Sexist Traditions Not too long ago, virtually all American boys were expected to grow up to be "masculine" and girls to be "feminine." The gender blueprints seemed clear-cut. The well-adjusted man should be independent, assertive, and dominant. The well-adjusted woman should be dependent, nurturing, and submissive. These beliefs and stereotypes led to *sexism*, the negative treatment of females and preferential treatment of males because of their sex. Some examples are as follows:

- thinking that women are not as smart as men
- not being equally comfortable with a woman or man as a boss
- thinking that a woman's only place is in the home
- choosing males over females as lab partners in science
- thinking that men can't be nurses
- expecting that men can't cook or nurture
- criticizing men for crying or expressing sentimental emotions

Although today's society is generally more flexible than before, this flexibility produces confusion and uncertainty for many people. Women have gained more opportunity in several professional spheres, but many still experience glass ceilings that limit their access to the most powerful positions. In contrast, women who choose more traditional roles sometimes think that other women criticize them unfairly for "selling out." Some women are angry at men in general for their historic abuse of privilege. The glass ceiling is still real. Despite changing attitudes, females' share of executive management positions dropped from 32 percent in 1998 to 19 percent in 2000 (U.S. Bureau of Labor Statistics 2003).

Improving the Lives of College Women In *The Mismeasure of Woman*, Carol Tavris (1992) wrote that no matter how hard women try, they may not be able to measure

EXPAND YOUR RESOURCES

International SOS

- **Be patient.** Give yourself time to adapt to your new life. Things may not be easy at the beginning. Over time, you will develop greater comfort with U.S. culture. What seems odd or challenging right now may be easier to understand with a little more experience.
- **Create or join a support system.** Most campuses have international student clubs where you can meet and get to know other international students. If your campus has none, this represents a great opportunity to make a contribution to campus life by founding a support system.
- **Make new friends outside your comfort zone.** Get the most out of your international experience by reaching out to others to learn about their cultures. Reach beyond relationships with students from your home or host country and make connections with other international students who may share your struggles.
- **Be an ambassador.** Look for opportunities to share your background so your teachers and classmates can learn about your culture. Many assignments or class projects lend themselves to your teaching others about your origins and culture.
- **Adopt a cultural mentor.** Identify someone who can provide social support and learning opportunities to make the most of your international adventure. Consider a faculty member or someone on the advising staff who seems especially interested in your background.
- **Keep your own goals in mind.** Don't let cultural obstacles interfere with getting a great education.

©Bill Losh/Getty Images

If you're a student from the United States, respect the differences between yourself and international students. Value diversity. If you're from another country, create a support system and get involved in campus life. Be patient in adjusting to this new culture.

up. They are criticized for being too female or not female enough. Tavris argues that women are judged by how well they fit into a man's world, which tends to fixate on the beauty of a woman's body. Tavris said that as a culture we need to emphasize the woman's *soul* as the key indicator of competence and worth.

In her study of women's lives, Jean Baker Miller (1986) concluded that a large part of what women do is active participation in the development of others. Women are inclined to help others emotionally, intellectually, and socially. College offers many opportunities for women to explore their lives and set out on a course to improve their opportunities while providing service to others. For example, nontraditional student Ana Bolado de Espino supported her daughter while pursuing her dream of going to medical school, and her daughter supported her. Miller argues that women need to retain their relationship skills but become more self-motivated as well by focusing more on themselves and their own needs.

The message to women is this. Women are certainly not inferior to men. Start evaluating yourself in terms of female competencies, not male ones. Women (and society) need to place a higher value on relationship skills. To be leaders, women do not need to stop caring for others but may be able to exercise distinctive leadership skills because of their relationship focus.

Sexual harassment in colleges and the workplace is also a major barrier to women's progress. Two million women currently enrolled in college will experience some form of sexual harassment in their student lives (Paludi 1998). This includes:

- *Gender harassment.* Sexist remarks and behavior that insult and degrade women, a problem apart from harassment for sex.
- *Seductive behavior.* Unwanted, inappropriate, and offensive advances toward women.
- *Sexual bribery.* Harassment for sex, with the threat of punishment for refusal. For example, a woman might be threatened with a lower or failing grade if she does not go along with a professor's advances, or if she reports him to the school authorities.

Every college is required by law to take action against sexual harassment, and many have resources to protect women from this harassment. If you are sexually harassed, report it to your school's administration.

Improving the Lives of College Men Some men are confused by the changes in gender expectations. They struggle to grasp what life is really like for women and are uncertain about how much they can stray from traditional masculine role characteristics before inviting criticism. However, college experiences can open up new horizons by encouraging a broader range of acceptable behavior.

One way to expand options, according to Goldberg (1980), is for men to adopt more emotionally expressive strategies. He argues that men need to become better attuned to their emotional makeup and relationships with others. Goldberg claims that a huge gulf separates the sexes: women sense and articulate feelings; men tend not to because of their masculine conditioning. Men's defensive armor causes them to act out or engage in other self-destructive patterns. They become effective work machines but suffer emotionally. As a result men live about eight fewer years than women and have higher hospitalization rates and more behavior problems. Goldberg believes that early mortality is a heavy price to pay for masculine "privilege" and power.

For more recommendations on how women and men can lead more competent lives, see "Clarify Values: Gender-Based Strategies for Self-Improvement."

Gender-Based Strategies for Self-Improvement

Women:

- Avoid using male standards to judge your competence.
- Retain strengths in building relationships and staying in touch with emotions. Be proud of them.
- Focus on knowing your own needs and meeting them. Go beyond the idea that this is selfish.
- Know what qualifies as sexual harassment. Don't hesitate to report it when it happens.

Men:

- Retain your strengths and take appropriate pride in your achievements.
- Strive to understand the emotional elements of the situation and give more consideration to the feelings of others.
- Think more about how you want others to perceive you and act accordingly.
- If you're aggressive and hostile, tone down your anger. Control how you express your negative emotions.
- Emphasize collaboration over competition. Academic situations and employers alike appreciate a good team player.

Respect Sexual Orientation

A large majority of people are heterosexual. Although for many years it was estimated that about 10 percent of the U.S. population are lesbians or gay males, more recent surveys put the figure at about 2–5 percent (Michael and others 1994). About 1 percent of the population is bisexual (attracted to both men and women).

Issues Related to Lesbians, Gay Males, and Bisexual Individuals In most ways, the college goals of lesbian, gay male, and bisexual students are similar to those of heterosexual students. However, their minority status does bring some difficulties. Many heterosexual students still consider them abnormal rather than simply different. Even the American Psychiatric Association once labeled homosexuality as abnormal behavior and a mental disorder. That is no longer the case, but the stigma remains, along with discrimination. Lesbian, gay male, and bisexual students often encounter physical abuse, hostile comments, and demeaning jokes. Heterosexuals may feel uncomfortable around them. For example, when he found out that one of his new fraternity brothers, Bob, was gay, Jim said he felt uncomfortable and consistently avoided him. Several years later, Jim had to work with Bob on a senior project and found him to be helpful, savvy, and funny. Jim regretted treating Bob the way he did. He realized that nothing prevented a heterosexual from being friends with a gay male. Explore your own attitudes by completing the Journal activity "Evaluate Your Own Attitudes Toward Sexual Diversity" on page 59.

Improving the Lives of Gay, Lesbian, and Bisexual College Students How can gay, lesbian, and bisexual students have a better college experience? What positive role can heterosexuals play in this improvement?

- Many campuses have organizations for gay, lesbian, and bisexual students that you may want to join. Some of them include friends and family, as well as other

© Jim Ruymen/Reuters/CORBIS

Be tolerant of others' sexual orientations.

students with questions, regardless of sexual orientation. These organizations provide a safe place for students to voice their thoughts and feelings about sexual orientation.

- If you are a lesbian, gay male, or bisexual student and your campus does not have a related organization, consider starting one. This action may require following procedures that your student activities office has established for creating a campus organization. If you feel uncomfortable on your own campus, consider joining an organization on a nearby campus or in the local community.
- Some good books written by and for lesbians, gay males, and bisexual individuals cover many practical issues. See the list in the resources on the website for this book at http://www.thomsonedu.com/success/santrock5.
- Be tolerant of the sexual orientation of others. If you are a heterosexual and harbor negative feelings toward lesbians, gay males, and bisexual individuals, consider taking a course on human sexuality. You'll learn not only about others who have a different sexual orientation than you but about yourself as well. Researchers have found that college students who take such a course gain positive views of lesbian, gay male, and bisexual individuals (Walters 1994).

Improve Your Relationships with Diverse Others

Regardless of the nature of the difference, how can you get along better with people who differ from you? Here are some helpful strategies:

Assess Your Attitudes One of the first steps is to understand your own attitudes better. Most of us sincerely think that we are not prejudiced. Are there people you don't like because of the group they belong to? Honestly evaluate your attitudes toward people who don't share your characteristics or background.

Take the Perspective of Others You can improve your attitude toward others by clarifying your perspective and trying to better understand that of others. Ask yourself:

- "What are these people feeling and thinking?"
- "What is it about their background and experiences that makes them different from me?"
- "In what ways might we be similar?"
- "What kinds of stress and obstacles are they facing?"
- "Is the fact that they are different reason enough for me to not like them or to be angry with them?"
- "How much do I really know about these other people? How can I learn more?"

Students can benefit from asking themselves these questions about gender, ethnic groups, and sexual orientation. They also can benefit by asking such questions about traditional and nontraditional students.

Seek Personal Contact Martin Luther King Jr. once said, "I have a dream that my four little children will one day live in a nation where they will not be judged by the color of their skin but by the content of their character." How can we reach the world Martin Luther King Jr. envisioned, a world beyond prejudice and discrimination? Mere contact with people from other ethnic groups won't do it. However, a particular type of contact—personal contact—often is effective in improving relations with others. *Personal contact* here means sharing one's worries, troubles, successes, failures, personal ambitions, and coping strategies. When we reveal information about ourselves, we are more likely to be perceived as individuals than as stereotyped members of a group. When we share personal information with people we used to regard as "them," we begin to see that they are more like "us" than we thought.

Respect Differences but Don't Overlook Similarities Think how boring our lives would be if we were all the same. Respecting others with different traditions, backgrounds, and abilities improves communication and cooperation. When we perceive people as different from us, we often do so on the basis of one or two limited characteristics such as skin color, sex, age, or a disability. When someone seems different, do you ever try to see how the two of you might be similar? Think about the many similarities between you and someone you regard as totally different:

- You might both be shy and anxious, fearful of speaking in public.
- You might both feel overwhelmed by all the demands you need to juggle.
- If you've both chosen the same campus to pursue your education, you might have similar achievement standards like making the dean's list.
- You may share an interest in a certain sport, type of movies, computer games, or food.

You probably have much more in common than you imagine. Complete the Journal activity "Seek Common Ground" on page 58 to explore similarities between you and someone from a different cultural or ethnic background.

Search for More Knowledge In many instances, the more you know about people who are different from you, the better you can interact with them. Learn more about the customs, values, interests, and historical background of such people. Take a course on cultures around the world, for example.

Treat People as Individuals In our culture, we want to be treated as individuals. We each want to be unique. You will get along much better with others who seem different if you keep in mind that they are individuals than if you think of them as members of a group. Talk with them about their concerns, interests, worries, hopes, and daily lives. Avoid stereotypes.

Summary Strategies for Mastering College

Master Communication Skills and Build Relationships

1 Communicate Effectively

- Develop active-listening skills. Pay attention to the person who is talking. Paraphrase.
- Speak in simple, concrete, and specific ways. Make your verbal and nonverbal messages consistent.
- Avoid barriers to effective verbal communication.
- Tune in to nonverbal communication and think about your own nonverbal messages.
- Resolve conflicts with others by being assertive and negotiating effectively rather than relying on aggression, manipulation, or passivity.

2 Develop Good Relationships

- Recognize how your personal attachment style may influence developing healthy relationships.
- Determine the optimal balance between meeting your social and academic needs.
- Avoid settings in which rape occurs most often, limit alcohol and drug use, and use good judgment. Make good sexual decisions.
- Friends reduce loneliness, are a source of self-esteem, and provide emotional support. Learn about strategies for making and keeping friends.

3 Maintain Specific Positive Relationships

- If you are a traditional student, keep in touch with your parents to ease any concerns about your independence.
- If you have a partner or spouse, use good communication skills to have a positive relationship with him or her during your college years.
- If you have children, be an authoritative parent, communicate well, and be a good time manager.
- Understand that instructors are human. Evaluate their learning and personality styles, and establish rapport with them.
- If you have a roommate, address any problems early and use good communication skills.
- Network to enhance your professional opportunities.

4 Appreciate Diversity

- Recognize and reduce any prejudice and stereotyping you might engage in or encounter.
- If you're an international student, be patient, create or join a support system, and make new friends.
- Appreciate the effects of gender. Strive to reduce the effects of sexism.
- Appreciate diversity in sexual orientation. Homosexual and bisexual individuals can join supportive campus organizations. Be tolerant of the sexual orientation of others.
- To improve your relationships with diverse others, assess your attitudes, take the perspective of others, seek personal contact, and share information.

Review Questions

1. List three basic strategies for improving your communication skills. Then list at least one situation in which you can practice each strategy.

   1. Strategy: ____________________ Situation: ____________________
   2. Strategy: ____________________ Situation: ____________________
   3. Strategy: ____________________ Situation: ____________________

2. Describe a conflict you are currently experiencing or anticipate facing in the near future. What are some strategies you can apply to this problem?

3. If you are a traditional student, list a few common problems with relationships among roommates or other individuals with whom you might live. If you are a nontraditional student and have a partner or spouse and/or children, describe some issues that might arise involving your close relationships as you pursue a college degree. What are some positive ways of addressing these issues?

4. Describe at least three strategies for combating loneliness. How can these strategies also help you build relationships and network on campus?

5. What types of diversity do you encounter on a regular basis? How can the strategies described in this chapter help you improve your relationships with diverse others?

Know Yourself

SELF-ASSESSMENT 1

Do You Blow Up, Get Down and Get Dirty, or Speak Up?

Think about each of the following situations. Check which style you tend to use in each.

	Assertive	Aggresive	Manipulative	Passive
You're being kept on the phone by a salesperson trying to sell you something you don't want.				
You want to break off a relationship that no longer works for you.				
You're sitting in a movie and the people behind you are talking.				
Your doctor keeps you waiting more than twenty minutes.				
You're standing in line and someone moves in front of you.				
Your friend has owed you money for a long time and it's money you could use.				
You receive food that is overcooked or undercooked at a restaurant.				
You want to ask your friend, romantic partner, or roommate for a major favor.				
Your friends ask you to do something that you don't feel like doing.				
You're at a large lecture. The instructor is speaking too softly, and you know other students are also having trouble hearing her.				
You're sitting next to someone who is smoking, and the smoke bothers you.				
You're talking to someone about something important to you, but she doesn't seem to be listening.				
You're speaking and someone interrupts you.				
You receive an unjust criticism from someone.				

Total up the number of your aggressive, manipulative, passive, and assertive marks. Whichever style has the most marks is your dominant personal style of interacting with others in conflicts. If you did not mark the assertive category ten or more times, you would benefit from working on your assertiveness.

After E. J. Bourne, *The Anxiety and Phobia Workbook,* revised second edition (Oakland, CA: New Harbinger Publications, 1995). http://www.newharbinger.com.

SELF-ASSESSMENT 2

Loneliness

Read each of the following statements and describe the extent to which they characterize you as:

1 = Never 2 = Rarely 3 = Sometimes 4 = Often

_______ 1. I feel in tune with the people around me.

_______ 2. I lack companionship.

_______ 3. There is no one I can turn to.

_______ 4. I do not feel alone.

_______ 5. I feel part of a group of friends.

_______ 6. I have a lot in common with the people around me.

_______ 7 I am no longer close to anyone.

_______ 8. My interests and ideas are not shared by those around me.

_______ 9. I am an outgoing person.

_______ 10. There are people I feel close to.

_______ 11. I feel left out.

_______ 12. My social relationships are superficial.

_______ 13. No one really knows me well.

_______ 14. I feel isolated from others.

_______ 15. I can find companionship when I want it.

_______ 16. There are people who really understand me.

_______ 17. I am unhappy being so withdrawn.

_______ 18. People are around me but not with me.

_______ 19. There are people I can talk to.

_______ 20. There are people I can turn to.

Total your score for these ten items: 1, 4, 5, 6, 9, 10, 15, 16, 19, 20. Next, reverse your score for items 2, 3, 7, 8, 11, 12, 13, 14, 17, and 18 (for example, if your score was a 1 on item 2, change it to a 4 for scoring purposes), and add up your total for these ten items. Add the two subtotals (subtotal 1 plus subtotal 2) to arrive at your overall loneliness score:

If you scored 70 or above, you likely have good social connections and experience little loneliness.

If you scored 60–69, you likely experience quite a bit of loneliness.

If you scored 59 or below, you likely experience a great deal of loneliness. If you are a lonely individual, a counselor at your college can likely help you develop some good strategies for reducing your loneliness and becoming more socially connected.

From D. Russell et al., "The revised UCLA Loneliness Scale: Concurrent and discriminant validity evidence," *Journal of Personality and Social Psychology* 39, 472–480.

Your Journal

REFLECT

1. Reflect on Your Relationship with Your Roommate

Think about your relationship with your roommate. Are there ways you could make it better? Write down everything that you don't like about your roommate. Cross out those issues you can live with. Then write down strategies for dealing with those behaviors you can't tolerate and plan a time to talk about these issues.

2. Your Own Experience with Discrimination and Prejudice

What life experiences have you had with discrimination and prejudice? The discrimination might have been directed at you, or someone else. What were the consequences? If the discrimination took place in school, did anyone do anything about it? The discrimination doesn't have to be about race or gender. You might have been discriminated against because of the part of the country you're from, the way you dress, or how you style your hair. If you were discriminated against, how did you feel? If someone else was, how did you respond?

DO

1. Seek Common Ground

Identify someone who comes from a different cultural and ethnic background from yours. It might be a classmate, someone who lives in your neighborhood, or someone in an interest group you attend. Ask the person to sit down and talk with you for fifteen minutes. Tell the person that this involves a requirement for a college class you're taking. Your conversation objective: Establish how similar you are in as many ways as you can. Describe the identity of the person and list these similarities below. Were you surprised by anything that you learned?

2. Combat Loneliness

Choose a club meeting or another social activity to attend. At this activity, strike up a conversation with one person in the room. Take some time to observe and listen, picking a person with whom you might like to have a relationship. Then come back to your room and write about the conversation. Write down other things that you would like to know about this person and make a plan for getting together again in the near future.

Your Journal

THINK CRITICALLY

1. What Does Touch Communicate?

Touch and posture can be important forms of communication. What are some different ways they can communicate information? How might the same touch or posture be interpreted differently depending on the identity of the person being touched—a friend, a romantic partner, a teacher, a person of a different age, or a stranger, for example?

2. Evaluate Your Own Attitudes Toward Sexual Diversity

No matter how well intentioned we are, life circumstances produce some negative attitudes toward others. Think about people with a sexual orientation different from yours.

- Do you have any negative attitudes toward these people? Explain.
- Did the attitude come from a bad encounter with someone you decided was representative of the group?
- Have you learned any prejudices by modeling the attitudes of others you admire?
- What will it take for you to eliminate your negative attitudes toward this group or person?

CREATE

1. Overcome Your Barriers

For one week, make a note of every situation in which you feel you could have communicated better with someone. This could be an instructor, friend, family member, or even your doctor or a store clerk. At the end of the week, revisit this list and write down some strategies for improving similar conversations in the future. What barriers do you think you encountered and how can you address them better next time?

2. Are Men Really from Mars and Women Really from Venus?

In the popular book, *Men Are from Mars, Women Are from Venus*, the differences between men and women are described as being so extensive that the two sexes are from different planets. Get together with three or four male and three or four female college students and brainstorm about whether men and women are as different as this book suggests or whether they actually have more in common. Write down some of your conclusions here.

3 Be a Great Time Manager

© PhotoDisk Red/Getty Images

KNOW YOURSELF

What you do with your time is critical to your success in college and beyond. Highly successful scientists, business people, and other professionals say that managing their time on a daily basis is crucial to reaching their goals. How strong is your current ability to manage time effectively? Place a checkmark next to only those items that apply to you.

- I am good at spending time on activities that are related to my most important values and goals.
- I use a paper or electronic planner to manage my time effectively.
- I have created a term planner and monitor it.
- I regularly set priorities in managing my time.
- I make weekly plans, monitor how I use my time each week, and evaluate what I need to do or change in order to reach my goals.
- I complete daily to-do lists.
- I treat my academic commitment as a serious job.
- The time I spend on academics equals or exceeds the time I spend on leisure, play, recreation, sports, and watching TV or surfing the Internet.
- I don't procrastinate much.
- I'm good at balancing my academic life with other demands.

As you read about Mark Zuckerberg, think about how his solutions for managing time have led to dramatic changes in social networking.

CHAPTER OUTLINE

Take Charge of Your Life by Managing Your Time

Counter Time-Management Misconceptions
Tackle Time Wasters
Put the 80–20 Principle into Action
Reap the Benefits of Managing Your Time Effectively

Connect Values, Goals, and Time

Revisit Your Values
Revisit Your Goals
Develop an Action Plan

Plan for the Term, Week, and Day

Choose the Right Planning Tools
Create a Term Planner
Create, Monitor, and Evaluate a Weekly Plan
Develop and Adhere to a Daily Plan

Never Procrastinate Again (Much)

Know What It Means to Procrastinate
Conquer Procrastination

Balance College, Work, Family, and Commuting

Balance College and Work
Save Time for Relationships
Use Commuting Time Effectively

Images of College Success

Mark Zuckerberg

It started out as a computer-based system to overcome the social inefficiency that students routinely complained about at Harvard. Despite the presence of so many people on campus, many students complained that they couldn't figure out an efficient way to meet new friends. Mark Zuckerberg's own social struggles resulted in his development in two short years of Facebook, the fastest growing social website in cyberspace history. Membership in the online social directory grows at an astonishing rate with estimates of well over 11 million subscribers representing two thousand universities.

Zuckerberg showed early promise in solving problems of all kinds with computers. In the sixth grade, he and a friend developed a system that could analyze and predict individual musical preferences from a playlist. His creativity surfaced in multiple projects at Harvard University where he coded a system that would allow students to compare their course schedules to others and another system that captured and displayed photos. However, Harvard shut down the latter system within four hours due to concerns for invasion of privacy.

Undaunted, Zuckerberg provided the leadership and programming to develop Facebook, a social networking website that displays personal postings, photos, and interests lists that put Zuckerberg in the public eye. Zuckerberg and his business partners have built and expanded Facebook with no venture capital to underwrite the operation. Ironically, the enormous popularity of the site, which generates revenue through its advertising, prompted Zuckerberg to drop out of Harvard so he could devote more time to managing the site. According to a recent profile in the Harvard Crimson (March 26, 2006), Zuckerberg anticipates returning to school when he gets bored with this project and the right financial offer comes along. In the meantime, he is enjoying coding in pajamas, learning to be a businessman, and "making something really cool." Another irony: Zuckerberg claims he doesn't have time to use his own website to meet people.

As you read, think about the Six Strategies for Success listed to the left and how this chapter can help you maximize success in these important areas. For example, to reach your goals and still be able to live a balanced life, you need to do two critical things: (1) Discipline yourself to plan and monitor your time with your values and goals in mind. (2) Take steps to minimize procrastination and distractions. Being a great time manager will help you to build competence, manage your life effectively, and create your future in positive ways.

Take Charge of Your Life by Managing Your Time

Many college students feel overwhelmed with all they have to do. Yet some of the busiest and most successful students get good grades *and* find enough leisure time. How do they do it? They control their life by controlling how they spend their time.

How often have you said or heard people say, "I just don't have enough time"? Tough luck! Each of us has the same amount of time—24 hours, or 1,440 minutes, a day—yet individuals vary enormously in how effectively they plan and use their hours and minutes. You can't really change the nature of time or buy more of it than you're given. What you can change is how you manage *yourself* in relation to time.

You alone control how *you* use it. Once you've wasted time, it's gone and can't be replaced. Students often have ingrained habits that they practice in managing time. To evaluate your good and bad time-management habits, complete the Journal activity "Change a Habit" on page 86.

Counter Time-Management Misconceptions

There are a number of myths about time management. See if any of the following misconceptions relate to your beliefs about time management (Mackenzie 1997):

- *Time management is nothing but common sense.* Time management is simple, but it is not necessarily common sense. What is not simple is the self-discipline to use time management strategies.
- *I do well in school and I'm happy, so I must be managing my time effectively.* It is more likely that you are successful in spite of the way you manage time. What if you could double your productivity with more effective time-management strategies? How much more successful do you think you could be?
- *I work better under pressure and time management would take away my edge.* Hardly anyone works best under substantial pressure. What really happens is people do the best they can under stressful circumstances. Usually, this kind of

thinking is nothing but a rationale for procrastinating. If you put off an important task until the last minute with the excuse that you work better under pressure, you leave yourself no time to carry out the planning that is necessary to produce outstanding results. You also leave no room for correcting mistakes or including better ideas that might come to you too late to be included. By not managing your time, you miss the opportunity to do your best.

- *Taking time management too seriously sucks all the fun out of life.* If constant stress, forgetting appointments, missing deadlines, and working feverishly through the night sound like fun, perhaps you should reconsider. Think of effective time management this way: If you had two more hours a day (good time-management strategies can achieve this), could you think of some enjoyable ways to spend those hours?
- *Time-management strategies take a great deal of work. I don't have time for that.* You don't have time *not* to. Once you learn how to use effective time management techniques, like writing a daily plan and keeping a time log, they are not that time-consuming in themselves. A few minutes spent taking these steps can save you hours.

While we are postponing, life speeds by.
Seneca
First-century Roman philosopher

Tackle Time Wasters

There are many ways to waste time, such as surfing the web, daydreaming, socializing, worrying, or procrastinating. Many students don't say no to a request for their time because of their desire for approval, fear of offending, or false sense of obligation. Their reluctance can lead to wasting a lot of time in low-priority rather than high-priority activities. For example, you change your plan to go to the library to study when a friend says, "Come on with us and shoot some pool. You can afford a couple of hours with your friends." Decide what you need to do and what you can realistically do. Say no to everything else. If this is difficult for you, write "NO" in large letters on a card and place it next to the phone, computer, or on your desk (Yager 1999). You might suggest someone else who could do what is asked, or offer to do it when you have more time.

Letting the telephone or e-mail interrupt you is another time waster. Instead of letting callers or instant messages control your time, try some of these strategies:

- Use an answering machine to screen incoming calls and return the calls at your convenience.
- Learn to say, "I can't talk right now. Can I call you back?" Set aside a time to return calls.
- When you leave a message, try to give a specific time for someone to return your call so that you avoid playing telephone tag.
- Set a specific window to check your e-mail every day or two rather than responding to each message as it is received.
- Resist the impulse to stay in constant contact with friends through text messaging. Although text messages produce brief interruptions, the constant stream of social demands can compromise your best intentions. Shut if off!
- Consider changing your computer settings so messages don't pop up in the middle of important projects such as writing a paper or doing homework online.

Put the 80–20 Principle into Action

You might think all your responsibilities are so important that you can't drop any of them completely or reduce the time they take (Davis, Eshelman, and McKay 2000). Vilfredo Pareto, an Italian economist, conceived of the *80–20 principle.* He observed that about 80 percent of what people do yields about 20 percent of the results they achieve, while about 20 percent of what people do produces about 80 percent of the results. For example, approximately 20 percent of a newspaper is worth your while to read. It is a good idea to skim the rest. At least 80 percent of people's mail (e-mail and postal mail) is junk and best not read at all.

Many people spend their time in a frenzy of activity but achieve little because they are not concentrating on the things that will produce positive results for them. Separating the important stuff from the junk will help you become a better time manager. The Journal activity "The 80–20 Principle in Your Academic Life" on page 86 will help you learn to apply this theory.

"Hey, I'll get to the meeting on time. It's those creative types you ought to be checking on."

Reap the Benefits of Managing Your Time Effectively

You can reap many benefits by managing your time effectively.

- *Be more productive.* Using your time more effectively will increase your productivity in college. You'll have the hours you need to write that long term paper. Effectively managing your time will help you get better grades.
- *Reduce your stress.* Managing your time poorly will increase your stress. Imagine the day before an exam when you suddenly realize that you have a massive amount of studying to do. Panic! Tension builds and stress escalates. Effectively managing your time will help you reduce the stress in your life.
- *Improve your self-esteem.* Learning to manage time effectively will increase your self-esteem by making you feel successful and ahead of the curve. Wasting a lot of time will make you feel crummy about yourself because you are constantly playing catch-up.
- *Achieve balance in your life.* Developing good time-management skills and actively using them will let you achieve a more balanced life. You'll miraculously have more time for school, work, home, family, and leisure.
- *Establish an important career skill.* College provides you with an opportunity to work on developing many skills that you can carry forward into a career. Being a great time manager is a crucial skill. In most careers, to be successful you'll need not only to complete many different tasks but also to complete them quickly and by a deadline.

Create a Self-Contract and Find a Support Person

Some college students benefit from writing a contract for themselves related to their goals and time management action plan (Davis, Eshelman, & McKay 2000). In the contract, spell out your goals, how you are going to use your time to achieve them, and how you plan to reward yourself for your self-discipline and staying on track. Sign and date your contract. To ensure that you follow through on your self-contract, choose a support person to sit down with you every other week for the next three months to evaluate your progress.

The following is a sample self-contract form:

I, ______________________________ am going to do
(your name)

____
(activity or goal)

for or by ____________________________________.
(how long, how often, when)

I will monitor my progress by ________________________.
(the method that you will use)

I will evaluate my progress every ____________________
(how often)

with my support person ____________________________.
(name)

If I stick with this plan and reach my goal, I will reward myself with

____.
(something that will motivate you)

- *Reach your goals.* The act of setting goals and planning how to reach them will help you live the life you want to live. You need time to reach your goals, so the better you can manage time, the bigger you can dream. You don't have to reach your goals all by yourself. In many instances, it helps to have one or more support persons around you. Examine "Expand Your Resources: Create a Self-Contract and Find a Support Person" to think further about reaching your goals.

Connect Values, Goals, and Time

In the Preface for Students, we underscored the importance of knowing what your values are and creating goals that align with them. This is a good strategy to engage in before you develop plans for managing time effectively. You don't want to spend extensive time in activities that don't coincide with the values you admire the most, or that don't mesh with your most important short-term and long-term goals. A key aspect of effective time management is to manage your time in accordance with your values and goals.

Revisit Your Values

In Self-Assessment 1, "What Are My Values?" on page xxxvi, you can evaluate what things in life are important to you. They include such values as being a moral person, being competent at your work, being well-educated, being well-off financially, living a healthy lifestyle, having a good spiritual life, and many others. This exercise is designed to help you clarify your values. Complete the exercise now before reading further, and then write down the five values that are most important to you in the space below.

The Five Values That Are Most Important to Me:

1. ____________________
2. ____________________
3. ____________________
4. ____________________
5. ____________________

If education is one of your highest values but you are spending the bulk of your time socializing with friends and participating in campus organizations, something is wrong. You might want to think about developing a time-management plan that devotes more hours to studying. Knowing what is most valuable to you gives direction to your life. Your energy should be oriented first toward your most important values, with other values taking a back seat. When choosing how to spend your time, examine your values to help you make a smart decision.

Revisit Your Goals

Goals express your values. Returning to the example of education as a high-priority value, you might set a goal of attaining a 3.5 grade point average this term. It then follows that in planning to manage your time effectively, you will need to spend many more hours studying than socializing. Here are some important ingredients of effective goal setting:

Design goals that are challenging, reasonable, and specific.
Focus on both long-term and short-term goals.

Set completion dates for your goals.
Create appropriate subgoals.
Anticipate and overcome obstacles.

Now complete the Journal activity "Be More Precise" on page 86 to practice making your time-management goals and plans more specific. Finally, write down one or more specific long-term goals (this term to more than a year) and short-term goals (from a week to a month) for each of your top five values:

	Value	Long-Term Goal	Short-Term Goal
1.	______________	______________	______________
2.	______________	______________	______________
3.	______________	______________	______________
4.	______________	______________	______________
5.	______________	______________	______________

Develop an Action Plan

Now that you have identified your most important values and related them to long- and short-term goals, the next step is to manage your time effectively so that you can reach these goals. Developing an action plan starts with evaluating how you spend your time. Let's see how this could change the way you live your life this term.

> ***Time moves slowly, but passes quickly.***
> Alice Walker
> *Contemporary American author*

Plan for the Term, Week, and Day

Break down your time by term, week, and day using the following term planner. As you create plans for coordinating within these three time frames, always keep in mind the importance of breaking your goals down into subgoals and intermediate steps. For example, you might have a major paper in English due in three weeks that counts for one-third of your grade. This week you could create the following subgoals related to the paper (Winston 1995):

First Day: Go to library and survey topics.
Second Day: Narrow topics.
Third Day: Select topic.
Fourth Day: Construct outline.
Fifth Day: Write first two pages.
And so on.

Many people find it helpful to work backward to reach a goal. For example, decide on an important goal that you want to reach in one year. First, think what you need to do each month between now and then to attain that goal. Then, think about what you need to do weekly to achieve it. Finally, think what you can do in the next twenty-four hours to get started. In this way, you can focus on a goal and work backward to outline the steps that will enable you to reach it.

Choose the Right Planning Tools

Three basic types of planning tools that will help you manage time more effectively are paper-and-pencil planners, electronic planners, and smart cell phones.

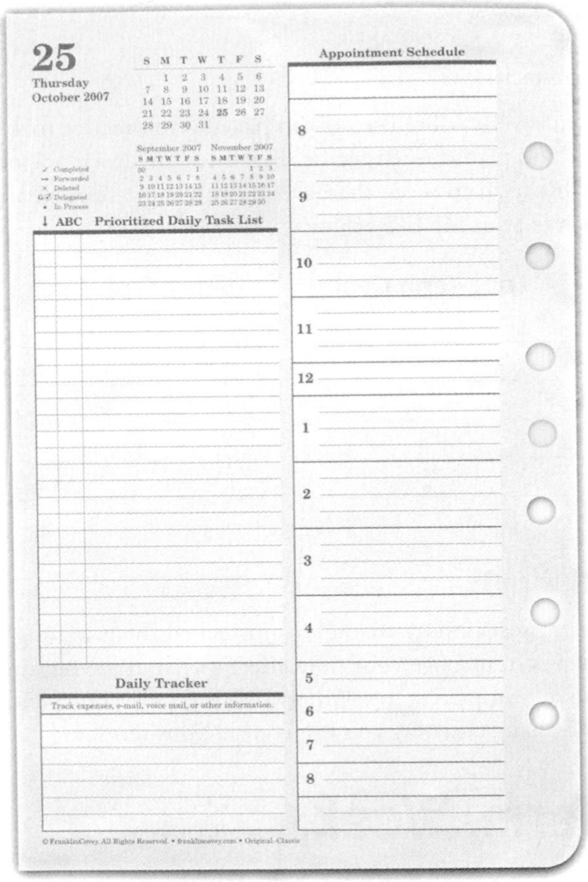

Franklin Covey Planner

© John Coletti Photography

Paper-and-Pencil Planners The traditional mode of planning uses a paper-and-pencil planner. Among the most effective and popular of these are the Franklin and Franklin Covey planners. The Franklin Covey planner especially encourages you to think about your goals and values as you set up your time-management program. For example, it asks you to set a long-range goal, write down the value of that goal or what its role is in your life, and then list the intermediate steps and their deadlines for reaching the goal. The Franklin Covey planner comes in a college version called the Franklin Covey Collegiate Planner.

Electronic Planners Several electronic time-management systems are available.

The Franklin Covey time-management program comes in an electronic form, as do others. These programs run on computers or handheld devices such as the Palm Pilot.

On the website for this book you can find links for exploring electronic planners to help determine what might work best for you. Advantages of electronic planners include:

- They are compact.
- They can sort, organize, and store information more efficiently.
- They can provide audible reminders of when to do things.
- They can easily exchange information between office and home computers.

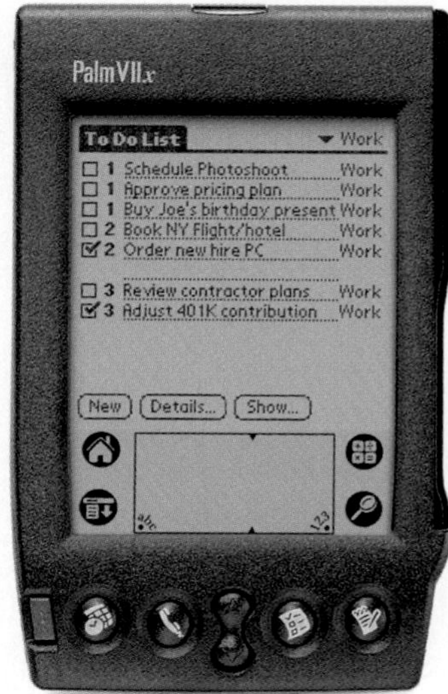

Palm Pilot

"Smart" Cell Phone

"Smart" Cell Phones Sophisticated cell phones are increasingly being used as time-management devices. Some users say that these so-called smart cell phones more easily handle the calendar and address chores than electronic planners such as the Palm Pilot. Blackberry, Treo, and other sophisticated cell phones integrate time-management chores in a handheld device. They include reminder functions, list makers, e-mail functions, and even electronic games to provide diversion during boring wait times.

Which should you use—a paper-and-pencil planner, an electronic planner, or a smart cell phone? If you are gadget-oriented, learn technology easily, and can afford them, you might want to consider an electronic planner or smart cell phone. If you are not, the paper-and-pencil planner is more than sufficient.

Create a Term Planner

Some of you may already own a planner or calendar of some type. For example, if you are a nontraditional student, you may use a planner or calendar to plan and keep track of family and/or job responsibilities. If so, you might want to integrate your college planning with those activities.

Whether you are a nontraditional or traditional college student, you will benefit enormously by mapping out a week-by-week plan for the entire term. Some colleges provide a term calendar that identifies breaks and holidays, or your college catalog may provide this information.

If you don't already have a calendar for the term, following is a grid of the days and weeks so you can create one. Notice that at the top of the page, it is important for you to once again list the five values that are the most important priorities of your life and then write down the five most important goals you want to attain this term.

Then, write in the weeks and number the days. Write in vacations and holidays.

Next, get out your course syllabi and write down dates and deadlines for exams, major homework assignments, and papers.

Consider coding your different courses by color. History might be in red, English in blue, biology in green, and so on. Using colored pencils allows you to revise schedules easily. Highlight exam dates with a marker or write them in large letters.

Term Planner

My Most Important Values Are	My Most Important Goals for This Term Are
1. ______	1. ______
2. ______	2. ______
3. ______	3. ______
4. ______	4. ______
5. ______	5. ______

Note: It is not necessary to have a goal for each value when listing your most important goals for the term. For example, if education is your most important value, you might have several important goals for this term related to education.

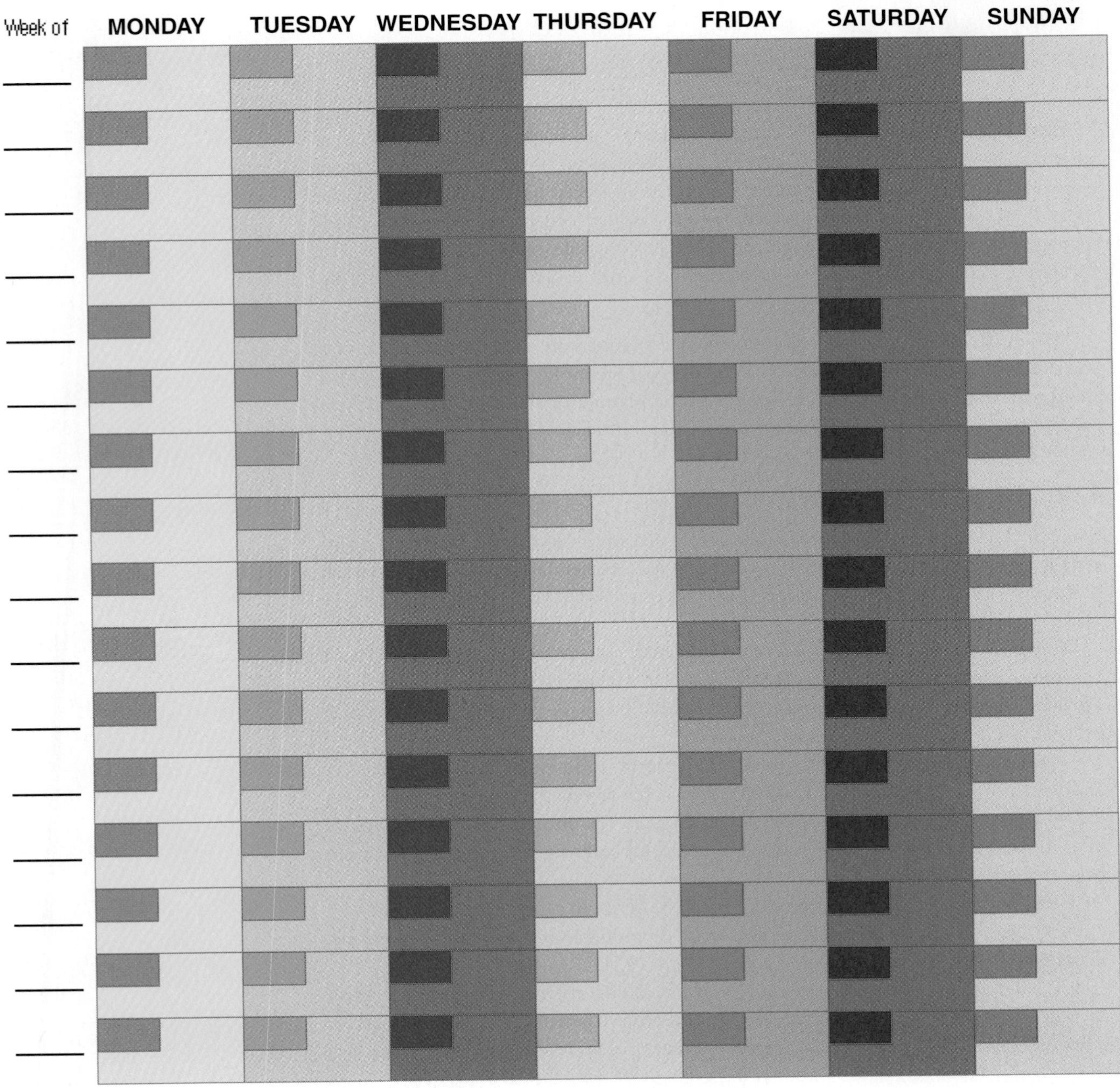

After you've written down your exam and other task dates on the calendar, look at the dates. Think about how many days or weeks you'll need to study for major exams and write major papers. Mark the days or weeks in which these tasks will be your main priorities. Refer often to the values and goals you listed at the top of the page when allocating your time for this term. Keep in mind important nonacademic responsibilities such as employment, family commitments, commuting time, and volunteer work and make sure to mark your calendar accordingly.

Keep a spare copy of your term planner in case you lose the original. You might want to carry a copy with you when you go to classes and place one on your bulletin board or in your desk. Consider posting an electronic version on your computer where you can access and edit it easily.

Your term calendar is not etched in stone. Check it regularly and decide when it needs modification. Your circumstances may change. An instructor might add another assignment or change a test date. You might find out that you need more study time than you originally predicted for a particular course, or your work schedule or family responsibilities may change during the term.

Create, Monitor, and Evaluate a Weekly Plan

In addition to your term plan, a weekly plan also will help you maximize your time. Former Chrysler Corporation CEO and President Lee Iacocca credited his weekly plan as the key to his success. Even if your life goal is not to run a mammoth corporation, weekly planning skills will serve you well long after college.

On pages 72 and 73 is a grid on which to map out your weekly plan. You might want to make copies or create an electronic version so that you will have one for each week of the term. You also can use the weekly planning grids in a commercial paper-and-pencil planner or an electronic planner, as discussed earlier.

Before you start filling in the grid, again write down your five most important values at the top of the page, followed by your five most important goals (priorities) for the week.

Next, ask yourself these questions about the next week:

- "What do I expect to accomplish?"
- "What will I have to do to reach these goals?"
- "What tasks are more important than others?"
- "How much time will each activity take?"
- "When will I do each activity?"
- "How flexible do I have to be to allow for unexpected things?"

In the *Plan* column on the grid, fill in your class hours, regular work commitments, family commitments, and other routine tasks. Then fill in the remainder of the things you plan to do next week.

A good strategy is to fill in the *Plan* column at the end of the preceding week. Put it together on Friday afternoon or Sunday evening at the latest. The plan takes no more than a half hour for most students to complete, yet it can save you at least an hour a day that week!

During the week, monitor your schedule closely to see whether you carried out your plans. A good strategy is to sit down at the end of each day and write in the *Actual* column what you actually did that day compared with what you planned to do. Analyze the comparison for problems, and plan some changes to solve them.

Use the weekly planner in concert with your term planner each week of the term.

Every weekend, pull out your term planner and see what your most important priorities are for the following week. Make any changes that are needed and then do the same thing with your weekly planner to help stay focused.

> ***Please. No crises next week. My schedule already is full.***
> Henry Kissinger
> *Twentieth-century secretary of state*

		MONDAY		TUESDAY		WEDNESDAY	
		Plan	Actual	Plan	Actual	Plan	Actual
AM	6:00						
	7:00						
	8:00						
	9:00						
	10:00						
	11:00						
	12:00						
PM	1:00						
	2:00						
	3:00						
	4:00						
	5:00						
	6:00						
	7:00						
	8:00						
	9:00						
	10:00						
	11:00						
	12:00						
AM	1:00						
	2:00						
	3:00						
	4:00						
	5:00						

Weekly Plan

My Most Important Values Are	My Most Important Goals for This Term Are
1. ______________________	1. ______________________
2. ______________________	2. ______________________
3. ______________________	3. ______________________
4. ______________________	4. ______________________
5. ______________________	5. ______________________

Note: It is not necessary to have a goal for each value when listing your most important goals for this week. For example, if education is your most important value, you might have several important goals for this week related to education.

THURSDAY		FRIDAY		SATURDAY		SUNDAY	
Plan	Actual	Plan	Actual	Plan	Actual	Plan	Actual

Allocate Time for Studying and Other Responsibilities As you construct your weekly plan, be sure to put enough time aside for doing assignments outside class. In a national survey, the more hours students spent studying or doing homework, the more they liked and stayed in college, improved their thinking skills, graduated with honors, and got into graduate school. Students who have higher grades and graduate with honors are less likely to watch TV or spend time partying (Astin 1993).

To find out how much time you actually spend studying each week and whether it's enough, complete the Journal activity "Link Goals with Time Spent in Activities" on page 87.

Swiss Cheese and Set Time Two strategies for getting the most out of your weekly plan are called *Swiss cheese* and *set time.* Time-management expert Alan Lakein (1973) describes the Swiss-cheese approach as poking holes in a bigger task by working on it in small bursts of time or at odd times. For example, if you have ten to fifteen minutes several times a day, you can work on a math problem or jot down some thoughts for an English paper. You'll be surprised at how much you can accomplish in a few minutes.

If you're not a cheese lover, the set-time approach may suit you better. In this approach, you set aside a fixed amount of time to work on a task. In mapping out your weekly plans, you may decide that you need to spend six hours a week reading your biology text and doing biology homework. You could then set aside 4–6 p.m. Monday, Wednesday, and Saturday for this work. To think further about getting the most out of your weekly plan, complete the Journal activities "Put Swiss Cheese into Action" on page 86 and "A New Kind of Cheese" on page 87.

A Week Later: How Did You Do? After you have planned what you will do with your time for a week and monitored yourself, a very helpful exercise is to complete Self-Assessment 1, "Evaluating My Week of Time Management," on page 84 to evaluate how effectively you stayed with your plan and to think about how you could better use your time.

Develop and Adhere to a Daily Plan

Great time managers figure out what the most important things are for each day and allocate enough time to get them done. Figuring out the most important things to do involves setting priorities.

An effective way to do this is to create a manageable to-do list. Your goal is at least to complete all the priority items on your list. A no-miss day is one on which you can cross off every item, having completed them all. If that turns out to be impossible, make sure you finish the most important tasks. For some good strategies, see "Manage Life: Setting Daily Priorities."

MANAGE LIFE

Setting Daily Priorities

1. Make up your daily to-do list before you go to bed at night. Or do the list first thing in the morning. Set priorities. Estimate how much time it will take to complete each task.
2. Identify the top-priority tasks and try to do these first. Do them in the morning if possible.
3. Raise your time consciousness. Periodically look at or think about your list. Maybe you have a few items that take only a little time. Knock them off in ten minutes here, fifteen minutes there. Keep your priorities in focus. Make sure you get your number-one priority done before it is too late in the day.
4. Toward the end of the day, examine your to-do list. Evaluate what you have accomplished. Challenge yourself to finish the few remaining tasks.

The ABC Method A to-do list identifies and sets priorities for daily tasks and activities. It can help you stay focused on what is important for you to accomplish that particular day and generally does not include your classes, which should be in your weekly plan. Time management expert Stephen Covey (1989) recommends prioritizing tasks by A, B, and C, determining whether they are:

A ***Vital.*** Extremely important tasks that affect your weekly goals and must be done today.

B ***Important.*** Tasks that need to be done soon, such as projects, class preparation, buying a birthday gift for a friend, and other time-driven activities or personal priorities.

C ***Optional.*** These also could be labeled "trivial." Examples include getting a haircut, going to a shopping mall, or rearranging your room. Do these activities when you have extra time and consider practicing the Swiss-cheese method here.

Figure 3.1 shows one student's to-do list. Notice that this student has chosen one A-level *vital* task and is planning on

FIGURE 3.1 Sample To-Do list

To Do

A. The Most Vital:

1. Study for Biology Test

B. Next Two Most Important:

2. Go to English and History Classes

3. Make Appointment to See Adviser

C. Task	Time	Done
Study for biology test	Early morning, night	
Call home	Morning	
Buy test book	Morning	
Call Ann about test	Morning	
Make adviser appt.	Afternoon	
Do exercise workout	Afternoon	

devoting the most time to it. The student also has allotted time for two B-level *important* tasks.

Commercial planning tools—especially electronic planners, such as the Palm Pilot—often are good for making to-do lists. Or you might just take a notepad and create a to-do list to be updated each day.

The Time Matrix Stephen Covey (1989) created a time matrix that is another way you can set and monitor priorities. This time matrix of four quadrants helps prioritize your most important and urgent activities. *Important* activities include those linked to your goals and values. *Urgent* activities require immediate attention but might not reflect those things most important to you. Following are some examples of activities that might be placed in the four quadrants.

1. IMPORTANT URGENT	2. IMPORTANT NOT URGENT
—Math test tomorrow —Make bank deposit today —Science project due today —Take back library book due today	—Date with friend —English paper due in thirty days —Call home —Visit with academic adviser today
3. NOT IMPORTANT	**4. NOT IMPORTANT NOT URGENT**
—Ringing phone —Unnecessary work —Trivial questions —Interruptions	—Hanging out at the student union —Watching TV —Playing computer games —Reading comic strips

Guidelines for using this matrix to manage your time include:

1. Spending time on important, nonurgent things (quadrant 2) before they become urgent (quadrant 1).
2. Not letting yourself be ruled by urgency.
3. Never avoiding important work because of tasks that are just urgent.
4. Doing important activities early. If you wait until they are urgent, you will just increase your stress level.
5. Identifying the most important work that needs to be completed after each class.
6. Setting priorities for your tasks and completing them in order.

College Success Planner (Wadsworth, 2000).

Get in the habit of using the time matrix on a regular basis. It is a great organizing tool for setting priorities.

Do successful people really use strategies like the time matrix and to-do lists in their everyday lives? For the most part, yes. These strategies help them keep track of the tasks they want to complete and let them monitor their progress.

Tune in to Your Biological Rhythms It has been said that people will accept an idea better if they're told that Benjamin Franklin said it first. Indeed, Benjamin Franklin did say, "Early to bed, early to rise, makes a man healthy, wealthy, and wise."

Some of us are "morning people." However, others are "night people." That is, some students work more effectively in the morning, while others are at their best in the afternoon or evening.

Evaluate yourself. What time of day are you the most alert and focused? For example, do you have trouble getting up in the morning for early classes? Do you love getting up early but feel drowsy in the afternoon or evening?

Many traditional-age college students in their late teens and twenties are "evening people," while nontraditional students in their forties and older are often "morning people." A recent study assessed the memory of traditional-age college students and older adults in the morning and in the late afternoon (Hasher and others 2001). The results: The memory of the traditional-age college students was better in the evening, the memory of the older adults better in the morning.

If you're a night person, take afternoon classes. Conduct your study sessions at night. If you're a morning person, choose morning classes. Get most of your studying done by early evening.

What can you do if you hate getting up early but are stuck with early morning classes? Start your day off properly. Many students begin their day with too little sleep and a junk-food breakfast or less. Does this description fit you?

Try getting a good night's sleep and eating a good breakfast before you tackle your morning classes. You may even discover that you're not a "night person" after all. Exercise is also a great way to get some energy and be more alert when you need to be—and is often more effective than caffeine.

Never Procrastinate Again (Much)

Procrastination often hurts many students' efforts to become good time managers. Do you tend to put off until tomorrow what you need to do today?

Know What It Means to Procrastinate

Procrastination can take many forms (University of Illinois Counseling Center 1984):

- *Ignoring the task, hoping it will go away.* A midterm test in math is not going to evaporate, no matter how much you ignore it.
- *Underestimating the work involved in the task or overestimating your abilities and resources.* Do you tell yourself that you're such a great writer that you can grind out a twenty-page paper overnight?
- *Spending endless hours on computer games and surfing the Internet.* You might have fun while you're doing this, but will you have to pay a price?
- *Deceiving yourself that a mediocre or bad performance is acceptable.* You may tell yourself that a 2.8 grade point average (GPA) will get you into graduate school or a great job after graduation. This mindset may prevent you from working hard enough to get the GPA you really need to succeed after college.
- *Substituting a worthy but lower-priority, nonacademic activity.* You might clean your room instead of studying for a test. Some people say, "Cleanliness is next to godliness," but if it becomes important only when you need to study for a test, you are procrastinating.
- *Believing that repeated "minor" delays won't hurt you.* You might put off writing a paper so you can watch *Desperate Housewives* or the World Wrestling Federation. Once the one-eyed monster has grabbed your attention, you may not be able to escape its clutches.
- *Dramatizing a commitment to a task rather than doing it.* You take your books along on a weekend trip but never open them.
- *Persevering on only one part of the task.* You write and rewrite the first paragraph of a paper, but you never get to the body of it.
- *Becoming paralyzed when having to choose between two alternatives.* You agonize over whether to do your math or English homework first, and neither gets done.

To evaluate whether you are a procrastinator, complete Self-Assessment 2, "Are You a Procrastinator?" on page 85.

Conquer Procrastination

Here are some good strategies for overcoming procrastination:

- *Put a deadline on your calendar.* This creates a sense of urgency. You might put deadline Post-its on the mirror and in other places you can see them at strategic times during the day. Think about other ways that you might create urgent reminders for yourself.
- *Get organized.* Some procrastinators don't organize things effectively. Develop an organized strategy for tackling the work you need to do. Your term planner, weekly planner, and to-do list will come in handy here.
- *Divide the task into smaller jobs.* Sometimes we procrastinate because the task seems so complex and overwhelming. Divide a larger task into smaller parts. Set subgoals of finishing one part at a time. This strategy often can make what seemed to be a completely unmanageable task into an achievable one. For example, imagine that it's Thursday and you have fifteen math problems due on Monday. Set subgoals of doing five by Friday evening, five more by Saturday evening, and the final five by Sunday evening. Reward yourself for completion.
- *Take a stand.* Commit yourself to doing the task. One of the best ways to do this is to write yourself a "contract" and sign it, like the self-contract we discussed earlier in the chapter. Or, tell a friend or partner about your plans.
- *Use positive self-statements.* Pump yourself up. Tell yourself things that will get you going, such as the following (Keller and Heyman 1987): "There is no time like the present." "The sooner I get done, the sooner I can play." "It's less painful if I do it right now. If I wait, it will get worse."
- *Build in a reward for yourself.* This gives you an incentive to complete all or part of the task. For example, if you get all your math problems done, treat yourself tonight to a movie you've been wanting to see. What other types of rewards can you give yourself for completing an important task?

Better three hours too early than a minute too late.
William Shakespeare
Sixteenth-to-seventeenth-century English playwright and poet

To reflect further on your procrastination tendencies, complete the Journal activity "Jump Starts" on page 87.

Balance College, Work, Family, and Commuting

Time management is particularly challenging for college students who also hold a job, have a partner or children, or commute. If you face these challenges, for the next term you can schedule your classes at the earliest possible time during registration. This will get you the classes you want at the times you want. You also can talk with other students who share similar challenges. Here are some additional time-management strategies for students with these special needs.

Balance College and Work

Managing time can be hard if you work to pay for college. (See "Manage Life: Working, Going to College, and Managing Time Effectively.") Students who work full-time are less likely than those working part-time or not at all to complete college, have high grade point averages, graduate with honors, or go on to graduate school (Astin 1993). If you need to work, here are some suggestions:

Limit Work if Possible It's best not to work more than ten to twenty hours in a week. Full-time students who work more than twenty hours a week get lower grades than students who work fewer hours. They are also much more likely to drop out of college.

Work on Campus if Possible Whether part-time work is positive or negative for college students depends on where they work. In general, a part-time job off campus is an academic minus (Astin 1993). However, a part-time job on campus is an academic plus. Why does it matter where you work? The answer has to do with involvement. Students who work part-time on campus will likely be connected with other students and faculty, which more than compensates for the time they devote to the part-time job.

Investigate Work–Study Options Some jobs can help you develop your skills for future careers. Others are good just for the money. Some companies pay for the courses of their student employees. Look for jobs and programs that suit your needs and goals.

Evaluate Your Course Load Carefully consider how many classes you are taking and how much work each one requires. You might want to take a reduced class load to give you more time for studying and work.

Working, Going to College, and Managing Time Effectively

Theo never thought his part-time job as a waiter at Pizza Hut would be such a challenge to his time-management skills. In just one shift he had to take and deliver drink orders, make sure food arrived promptly from the kitchen, clear tables, and deliver dessert and the check, all while juggling similar needs for multiple tables and squeezing in some study time in the back when things were slow. He also had to make sure his shifts fit into his weekly schedule of classes and study time. Falling behind meant lost tips, something he could not afford–his long-term goal of graduating on time depended on it.

In contrast, Nancy's job as an advertising executive involved client presentations planned up to a month in advance. She had to balance all aspects of the presentation and make sure the art, slogan, and visual aids were developed simultaneously by different teams, all completed on time without procrastination. She found working backward from the due date helped her create a good time-management plan, as well as prioritizing and monitoring tasks on a daily basis. While her business management major had helped her land the job, it was her time-management skills that helped get the job done.

Good time-management skills are essential for any job and will help make you a more valuable and successful employee now and in the future.

Explore Financial Aid Options You may quality for state or federal financial aid to help you afford tuition while working fewer hours. Visit your campus financial aid office or ask your adviser for more information.

Save Time for Relationships

Time is especially precious if you have a spouse, partner, or children. Communicating and planning are important assets in balancing your family time and academic time.

Talk with Your Partner Communicate with your partner about his or her importance in your life. Set time aside for your partner. Plan ahead for tasks that require extra study time. Inform your partner about test dates and other deadlines. After you've created your weekly and term calendars, let your partner see how you plan to use your time and consider posting a copy of your calendars on the refrigerator or another prominent place. If your partner is also a student, you may be able to coordinate your schedules so you can spend free time together. If one person works and another is in school, perhaps work-related activities can be coordinated with school/ study time, and vice versa.

Build in Study Time at School If you have a partner or child, try to do some studying while you're still at school. Use time between classes, for example. Possibly

Commute Boosters

- Save time by consistently using to-do lists and weekly plans.
- Audiotape your instructors' lectures if allowed. Play them back on the way home or on the way to school.
- Rehearse what you learned in class each day on your way to work, school, or home.
- If you carpool with classmates, use the commuting time to discuss class material with them.
- Use a backpack or briefcase to carry books and papers that you use each day. Organize these materials the night before to make sure you have everything you need.
- Exchange phone numbers and e-mail addresses with other students in your classes early in the semester. Call them if you need to discuss class issues or their notes for a class you missed.
- Create a personal commuter telephone and/or e-mail directory. Important phone numbers and addresses might include your instructors and their secretaries or teaching assistants, the library, student services, study partners, and other campus resources.

arrive at school thirty minutes before your first class and stay thirty minutes after your last class to squeeze in uninterrupted study time.

Be Creative in How You Manage Time with Children
If your child has homework, do yours at the same time. Take a break for ten minutes or so for each hour you study at home, and play or talk with your child. Then go back to your studying. If your children are old enough to understand, tell them what your study routine is and ask for their cooperation.

Consider having your children play with neighboring children during your study hours. If your children are young, this might be arranged under another parent's supervision. Or try to swap child care with other student parents. Also check into child care and community agencies that may provide service and activities for your children in the before-school and after-school hours.

Use Commuting Time Effectively

If you commute to class, you already know how much time disappears on the road. Commuting students also tend to have family and work commitments that cut into study time. Courses may be available only at inconvenient times. Conflicts in schedules can make it difficult for commuters to take part in study sessions and other learning opportunities.

"Anyone with a car."

Solving such scheduling problems requires good time management. "Manage Life: Commute Boosters" describes some good commuting strategies.

At this point, you have explored many aspects of being an effective time manager. To examine your time-management strengths and weaknesses, complete the Journal activity "Who's in Charge?" on page 86.

Summary Strategies for Mastering College

1 Take Charge of Your Life by Managing Your Time

- Manage yourself to manage your time effectively.
- Counter time-management misconceptions.
- Tackle time wasters like unnecessary phone calls, e-mail, or social obligations.
- Put the 80–20 principle into action to concentrate on what is most important to produce results.
- Reap the benefits of managing your time effectively: Be more productive and reduce your stress; improve your self-esteem; achieve balance in your life and conquer multitasking; find career success and reach your goals.

2 Connect Values, Goals, and Time

- Clarify your values and focus on the five values that are most important. Use these values to establish your goals.
- Create goals and establish five long- and short-term goals based on your most important values.
- Develop an action plan based on your values and driven by your goals.

3 Plan for the Term, Week, and Day

- Break down your time by term, week, and day, breaking goals into subgoals and intermediate steps. Consider working backward to help reach your goals.
- Choose from the right planning tools, including paper-and-pencil planners, electronic planners, and smart cell phones.
- Create a term calendar planner and monitor it. Make sure it is driven by your most important values and goals and includes all of your important responsibilities.
- Create, monitor, and evaluate a weekly plan. Allocate enough time for studying and other activities. Remember how many hours a week you need to study outside class to make good grades. Monitor this closely. Make sure it is driven by your most important values and goals.
- Use the Swiss-cheese and set-time strategies to get the most out of your weekly plan.
- Make a daily plan by setting priorities and managing to-do lists. Consider establishing a time matrix of responsibilities. Make sure you get the most vital priority done. In deciding when to carry out tasks, examine your daily biological rhythms.

4 Never Procrastinate Again (Much)

- Know what it means to procrastinate and avoid common traps.
- Conquer procrastination by engaging in such strategies as putting a deadline on your calendar, getting organized, dividing the task into smaller jobs, taking a stand, using positive self-statements, and building in rewards for accomplishments.

5 Balance College, Work, Family, and Commuting

- Balance college and work by limiting work and working on campus if possible. Evaluate your course load. Manage your time.
- Balance college and time with partners and children by practicing good communication, planning study time at school, and being creative in how you manage time with children.
- Use commuting time effectively.

Review Questions

1. How can becoming a great time manager help you control your life?
   What benefits does someone who effectively manages time enjoy?

2. What are some good strategies for staying on time to reach your goals?

3. What advice would you give someone who wants to create a term planner? A weekly planner? A to-do list?

4. What are some good strategies for tackling procrastination?

5. Describe ways to balance your academic responsibilities with all of the other demands in your life.

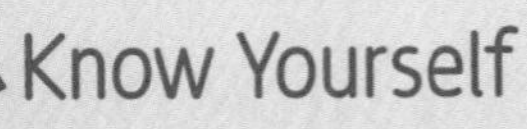

SELF-ASSESSMENT 1

Evaluating My Week of Time Management

Earlier in this chapter you planned how to use your time for a week and then monitored what you actually did during that time period. After one week of monitoring your time, what did you learn?

I spent too much time on:

1. ______________________________

2. ______________________________

3. ______________________________

I spent too little time on:

1. ______________________________

2. ______________________________

3. ______________________________

Next week, I will spend more time on:

1. ______________________________

2. ______________________________

3. ______________________________

Next week, I will spend less time on:

1. ______________________________

2. ______________________________

3. ______________________________

After a week of managing, monitoring, and evaluating my use of time, these are the most important things I have to work on to be a great time manager:

1. ______________________________

2. ______________________________

3. ______________________________

SELF-ASSESSMENT 2

Are You a Procrastinator?

	Strongly Agree	Mildly Agree	Mildly Disagree	Strongly Disagree
1. I usually find reasons for not acting immediately on a difficult assignment.				
2. I know what I have to do but frequently find that I have done something else.				
3. I carry my books/work assignments with me to various places but do not open them.				
4. I work best at the last minute, when the pressure is really on.				
5. There are too many interruptions that interfere with my accomplishing my top priorities.				
6. I avoid forthright answers when pressed for an unpleasant or difficult decision.				
7. I take half measures which will avoid or delay unpleasant or difficult action.				
8. I have been too tired, nervous, or upset to do the difficult task that faces me.				
9. I like to get my room in order before starting a difficult task.				
10. I find myself waiting for inspiration before becoming involved in important study/work tasks.				

Give yourself four points for each item you checked strongly agree, three points for each item you checked mildly agree, two points for each item you checked mildly disagree, and one point for each item you checked strongly disagree. Total your points: If you scored above thirty, you likely are a severe procrastinator; twenty-one to thirty, a chronic procrastinator; and twenty or below an occasional procrastinator. If your score is twenty-one or above, seriously consider going to the college counseling center for some guidance in conquering your procrastination.

University of Texas at Austin Learning Center.

Your Journal

REFLECT

1. Who's in Charge?

We discussed many different ideas about managing time, such as developing a term plan, creating a weekly plan, setting priorities, consistently creating to-do lists, and tackling procrastination.

- What are your current strengths and weaknesses with regard to managing time?
- What do you plan to do to address your weaknesses?

2. The 80–20 Principle in Your Academic Life

Recall our description of the 80–20 principle earlier in this chapter, which stated that approximately 80 percent of what people do produces about 20 percent of the results they achieve, and vice versa. Think about the courses you are taking this term. How might you apply the 80–20 principle to work more efficiently?

DO

1. Change a Habit

Select a bad habit that is hurting your ability to effectively manage time. The bad habit I'm going to get rid of is:

Many people find that in managing time, it helps to replace a bad habit with a new, more positive habit. Instead of spending time on my old bad habit, I will commit to spending more time on this good habit:

2. Put Swiss Cheese into Action

The Swiss cheese approach involves poking holes in bigger tasks by working on them in small bursts or at odd times. List your biggest task for next week. You should have some set time to work on it. However, also try to work on it in small bursts when you have a little time here, a little time there. At the end of next week, come back to this activity and write down how much more time you were able to sneak in on the big task by taking the Swiss-cheese approach.

THINK CRITICALLY

1. Be More Precise

Following are some vague plans. Make them more specific.
Vague: I'm going to start getting to school on time.
Precise:

Vague: I plan to watch TV less and study more.
Precise:

Vague: I'm going to quit wasting my time.
Precise:

2. Link Goals with Time Spent in Activities

- In what waking activities do you spend more than three hours a week?
- How does each of these activities relate to your goals?
- Examine your reasons for participating in activities that are unrelated to your goals.

CREATE

1. A New Kind of Cheese

We describe the Swiss-cheese and set-time approaches to using your time more productively. Come up with a catchy title for a time-management approach that works for you. Write down its title and briefly describe it.
Title of approach:

Description of approach:

2. Jump Starts

In this chapter we described some strategies for reducing procrastination. Get together with some other students and brainstorm about strategies for reducing procrastination. Summarize these strategies below.

4 Diversify Your Learning Style

KNOW YOURSELF

YOUR SUCCESS IN THE CLASSROOM will depend on several factors: how well you know your learning strengths and weaknesses, how fully you embrace personal responsibility for your actions, how effectively you relate to your instructors and classmates, and how actively you link current performance to your future plans and dreams.

To evaluate where you stand right now, place a check next to only those items that apply to you.

- I know my greatest strengths and weaknesses as a learner.
- I know whether I favor visual, auditory, or tactile sensory modes of learning.
- I can describe types of learning experiences that are easiest for me.
- I know how my personality influences my classroom success.
- I make specific choices about when to study at a deep versus a shallow level.
- I have started out my classes on the right foot.
- I deal well with different teaching styles.
- I get along well with my instructors and I know how to solve problems I may have with them.
- I can describe career options that fit with my learning style.

Consider what soccer star Mia Hamm's distinctive range of skills tell us about intelligence.

CHAPTER OUTLINE

How You Learn

Your Intelligence Profile
Sensory Preferences
Experiential Learning Preferences
Personality Factors
Technological Facility

Think Strategically about Your Learning

Understand How Effort Relates to Learning Style

Build Positive Relationships with Instructors

Reconcile Your Learning Style with Your Instructor's Teaching Style
Create a Good First Impression
Maintain the Connection
Solve Problems with Instructors

Choose a Major that Fits Your Learning Style

Target an Intelligent Career
Find the Right Mix
Keep a Flexible Outlook

Images of College Success

Mia Hamm

Easily the most recognizable female athlete in the world, Mia Hamm represents an unusual convergence of very different and highly developed abilities and intelligences. A skilled soccer athlete, a generous teammate, and a successful graduate majoring in political science at North Carolina at Chapel Hill, Mia also was voted one of *People* magazine's most beautiful people in the world in 1997.

Mia was born Mariel Margaret Hamm, the fourth of six children in an Air Force family, in Selma, Alabama in 1972. At birth, life threw a surprising and painful curve at Mia. She was born with a partial clubfoot that had to be corrected with casts and orthopedic shoes. However, once the casts came off, her talent for soccer was apparent to everyone.

At fifteen, Mia established herself as the youngest player ever to win a spot on a U.S. national Olympic team. In the 1996 Atlanta Olympics, Mia earned a gold medal, returning to play even after she sprained her ankle in an early match against Sweden. In 1998 Mia's team triumphed at the Women's World Cup in a match with China that turned out to be the most watched women's event in sports history.

Mia's soccer career flourished, based not just on her skill in the athletic challenge of the game but also on her gracious conduct as a team member. She is fond of saying "There is no 'me' in Mia." She retired from competitive soccer after carrying the flag for the United States in the 2004 Athens Olympics.

Mia provides a good model for the argument that human beings possess multiple kinds of intelligence. For example, her array of soccer awards, kudos, and accomplishments attests to superb kinesthetic and interpersonal intelligence. She has excelled in establishing sports and charitable organizations, highlighting her creativity and problem-solving skills.

MIA HAMM'S diverse skill sets support the theory that intelligence comes in multiple forms.

All of us learn a little differently, according to individual abilities, preferences, and characteristics. To reach your goals, it's important to understand how you learn and to look for ways to become more versatile. As you read, think about the Six Strategies for Success listed to the left and how this chapter can help you maximize success in these important areas, particularly as you build competence to take advantage of the areas where you show talent and to take risks to develop new abilities.

How You Learn

How you learn best is sometimes called your learning *style.* People differ in how easily they learn, but describing the differences isn't easy. Many things can simultaneously influence how well you acquire new information and skills.

This chapter will help you explore several different dimensions of your learning style to maximize your success in college and beyond. For example, your basic intellectual skill in specific areas can influence your success and even your career direction. How teachers present information also will determine how easy it is for you to learn. Your learning preferences will affect how you use that information to promote long-term learning. Your personality can also contribute to your success in the classroom. In combination, these dimensions influence how well you succeed in academic and other areas of college life. Let's start with the basic intelligence that you bring to college.

Your Intelligence Profile

Perhaps at some point in your past, someone measured your intelligence. On the basis of your intelligence quotient (IQ) score, you may have been able to skip a grade or qualify for special help in school. Recently, psychologists have begun to question the notion that we can capture individual intelligence with a single number.

Psychologist Howard Gardner (1989, 1999b) proposed that we would be wiser to consider several types of abilities rather than a single measure of intelligence. He formulated his theory of "multiple intelligence" based on patterns we observe in different sets of skills. For example, brain-damaged individuals sometimes show serious losses in certain skill sets. Child prodigies and others with exceptional talents possess or can develop superior skill sets in other specific areas.

Gardner suggested that these sorts of abilities cluster in nine different areas, or *domains:*

1. *Verbal-Linguistic Skills:* sensitivity to and appreciation of word meanings and the function of language
2. *Logical-Mathematical Skills:* orderly use of reasoning, logic, and mathematics to understand and explain abstract ideas

3. *Musical Abilities:* appreciating, performing, or creating music or the elements of music, such as rhythm or pitch
4. *Bodily-Kinesthetic Awareness:* coordinated and skilled use of objects in the environment, involving both gross and fine motor skills
5. *Spatial Skills:* accurate perception and reproduction of spatial images, including strong navigation and artistic skills
6. *Intrapersonal Abilities:* meaningful discrimination and interpretation of the behavior and moods of others
7. *Interpersonal Abilities:* accurate self-perception, including a refined capacity to identify and represent complex personal emotions and motives
8. *Naturalist Abilities:* understanding, relating to, classifying, and explaining aspects of the natural world
9. *Spiritual/Existential Abilities:* considering cosmic experiences that are not easily understood but are nonetheless important to understanding the deeper truths of human experience

Gardner argued that these domains are independent of one another, so humans can be highly developed in one area but not others. According to Gardner, most college courses tend to emphasize verbal-linguistic and logical-mathematic intelligences at the expense of other important skill areas.

You may be naturally more gifted in some areas than in others. Learning in those areas is simply easier for you. You may even resist taking required courses that don't fall within those easy areas. However, most college programs focus on developing a broad base of skills. So, for example, even if you don't have strengths in logical-mathematical skills, you'll probably have to take some basic courses that require those skills to earn your chosen degree.

Take a moment to complete Self-Assessment 1, "Your Intelligence Profile," on page 114 to help identify your intellectual strengths. It also can help you predict which courses will be relatively easy or difficult for you. For example, if your strengths lie in spatial skills, then taking an art history course may be a surprisingly happy learning experience. If the area of interpersonal abilities is your main strength, then you'll likely do well in courses that focus on group work.

By contrast, if algebra is "Greek" to you, you'll have to work much harder to grasp the concepts than will the mathematically gifted person seated next to you. You may struggle in courses that involve examination of the meaning of life if you have limitations in the spiritual/existential domain. You may want to get help right away before you get too far behind in a course that doesn't match your talents. Find a study partner who demonstrates the intelligence that you need to develop, or work with your study skills center on campus to help you take advantage of your learning strengths and style. If you cannot easily take advantage of campus resources to help you cope, consider doing some research ahead of registration to determine which professors might provide a student-friendly approach that will give you a greater comfort zone when you tackle disciplines that are more challenging for you.

Sensory Preferences

A second dimension that contributes to your learning style is your sensory preference for receiving information. Do you prefer to get input about the world through your ears, eyes, or sense of touch? The sensory mode you prefer will influence how easily you can learn in different academic situations.

Auditory Learning The majority of your course experiences will likely be lectures. Typically, the professor talks . . . and talks . . . and talks . . . while you try to take notes on the most important ideas. This traditional approach assumes that you have skills in auditory learning.

Some lucky people are good *auditory learners.* They absorb a lecture without much effort. They may not even need to take careful notes but learn just by listening. Auditory learners may avoid making eye contact with anyone in the class so they can concentrate on catching every word and nuance.

As smart as he was, Albert Einstein could not figure out how to handle those tricky bounces at third base.

Visual Learning Many of us have an easier time learning from lectures with visual components such as pictures, diagrams, cartoons, or demonstrations. *Visual learners* make images of words and concepts. Then they capture these images on paper for a quick review. Visual learners benefit from the use of charts, maps, notes, and flash cards when they study.

Visual learners may become distracted when professors provide no visual anchors in their lectures. They get overwhelmed when professors use slides with dense terminology and lecture at the same time. In this situation, visual learners need to tune out the auditory information and focus on what they can see for the most efficient processing.

Tactile or Kinesthetic Learning Some people are *tactile* or *kinesthetic learners.* They prefer touch as their primary mode for taking in information. Unfortunately, very few college classes provide an opportunity for tactile learners to use their preferred sensory mode. Art, recreation, and technical classes related to careers involving manual procedures are among the most prominent examples. Chances are that Mia Hamm's soccer expertise reflects natural strengths in kinesthetic learning abilities.

> ***Half of being smart is knowing what you are dumb about.***
> David Gerrold
> *Contemporary science fiction writer*

Tactile learners faced with auditory learning situations should write out important facts and perhaps trace the words that they have written with their fingers to give them extra sensory feedback. They can make up study sheets that connect to vivid examples. In some cases, role-playing can help tactile learners learn and remember important ideas.

Self-Assessment 2, "Sensory Preference Inventory," on page 115 provides an opportunity to identify your preferred sensory mode for learning. However, psychologist Robert Bjork (2005) suggests that it is not a good idea to pursue only learning contexts that are a good match for your learning style; greater long-term gains may occur in your flexibility as a learner when you are challenged in contexts that don't match your learning preferences. When you review "Build Competence: The Mismatch Game," you should be able to identify strategies that can help you learn more effectively, particularly if you find yourself in situations that aren't a good fit for your learning style.

Experiential Learning Preferences

Besides differing in intelligence domains and sensory preferences, people also differ in how they like to learn and think about ideas. Here are four distinctive ways based on

David Kolb's (1984) work on experiential learning. We also will explore how your experiential preferences relate to your intelligence profile and sensory preferences.

Learn by Doing Although some people can learn passively simply by listening, watching, or reading, those with active learning preferences fare better when they learn by doing through problems or games and simulations, for example. They like to apply principles through fieldwork, lab activities, projects, or discussions.

Many kinds of classes are ideal for learning by doing. These include science and math classes as well as career-oriented classes, such as business and nursing. Visual and tactile learners benefit from active learning strategies. Active learning strategies also tend to appeal to people with refined intelligence in spatial skills and bodily awareness.

Learn by Reflecting Reflecting here means having an opportunity to compare incoming information to personal experience. Reflective learners prefer classes such as the humanities that tend to be rich in emotional content. Reflective learners often show preferences for learning through auditory sensory channels, because these situations provide a manageable mode of sensory input which can then be enriched and made more memorable through the personal examples the learner produces through reflection.

Reflective learners often demonstrate strengths in intrapersonal and spiritual/existential intelligences as well. Because they look carefully at a situation and think about its meaning, they often set reasonable goals and achieve them. They enjoy grappling with life's larger questions. Reflective students take time to respond to and reflect on the quality and accuracy of their answers (Kagan 1965). Because they're good at problem solving and decision making, they like to set their own goals for learning (Jonassen and Grabowski 1993). Whether or not you are primarily a reflective learner, you can probably improve your learning by noticing connections between what you're studying and your own experience, and by staying aware of your learning goals.

Reflective students tend to enjoy journal or blog writing, project logs, film critiques, and essay questions, and prefer intimate discussions of content to group discussions. Learners who reflect carefully about ideas may not be the quickest to answer questions in class, because a question may provoke a great deal of thinking and remembering before the learner can arrive at a conclusion.

Learn by Critical Thinking Critical thinkers like learning situations that encourage them to grapple with ideas in ways that push beyond memorizing facts. They enjoy manipulating symbols, figuring out unknowns, and making predictions. They like to analyze relationships, create and defend arguments, and make judgments. Critical thinkers often are good with abstract ideas, even in the absence of concrete examples or applications. Classes that are theoretical in nature or that emphasize logical reasoning, model building, and well-organized ideas are especially appealing to critical thinkers.

Good critical thinkers perform especially well in courses that appeal to verbal-linguistic, logical-mathematical, and naturalist intelligences. They are comfortable in lecture-based classes that primarily rely on auditory sensory channels, although they also

BUILD COMPETENCE

The Mismatch Game

How can you adapt your skills when your instructor isn't a good match for your sensory learning style?

- If you are an **auditory** learner your best match will be instructors who LECTURE.

When your instructor doesn't lecture:

1. Concentrate on the spoken words.
2. Rehearse key ideas in your head.
3. Identify key concepts in your notes.
4. Summarize the key themes of the class out loud to a study partner.
5. Pay less attention to visual supports that may distract you.

- If you are a **visual** learner, your best match will be instructors who LECTURE WITH IMAGES.

When your instructor doesn't use visual supports:

1. Draw your own related pictures and graphs in your notes.
2. Use arrows in your notes to highlight connections.
3. Seek out related media that support or review key concepts.
4. Try to visualize imagery that will help you remember.
5. Create two or three images that capture the essence of the class.

- If you are a **tactile** learner, your best match will be instructors who use ACTIVE LEARNING.

When your instructor doesn't use active learning:

1. Make notes that highlight how the content is connected to you.
2. Form a study group to give you a chance to discuss key ideas.
3. Imagine how the information will have practical value for you.
4. Record class information on index cards that you can handle.
5. Select the two or three cards that represent the key ideas for each session.

can exercise critical-thinking strategies in other learning situations to make course ideas more engaging. Debates and other opportunities to exchange ideas appeal especially to critical thinkers.

Learn by Creative Thinking In contrast, creative thinkers thrive in learning situations that offer opportunities for unique personal expression. Although humanities and arts classes particularly develop creative thinking, creative opportunities can be found in other courses, too. Creative thinkers prefer to write stories, brainstorm, solve problems in original ways, design research, and so forth. They think more holistically, meaning that they try to consider a broad range of information in their problem solving. They may even enjoy violating the rules if it helps them come up with a unique solution or viewpoint.

Creative thinking is the hallmark of artists who demonstrate musical and spatial intelligence, respectively relying on auditory and visual sensory processing. Creativity also underlies the development of new theories, research strategies, novels, and computer games. That is, creative thinking can be expressed in all domains of multiple intelligence.

What learning processes do you prefer? Complete Self-Assessment 3, "Experiential Learning Preferences," on page 116 to identify your preferences among these experiential learning processes.

Put It All Together Now that you have examined a variety of learning styles and evaluated your own preferences, you may be wondering how this all relates and what it means for *your* success in college. Table 4.1 links the intelligence profiles, sensory preferences, and experiential learning preferences discussed earlier. It also lists some majors that might be appropriate for each learning style. First, go to Assessments 1, 2, and 3 to revisit your learning style preferences and circle them in the last three columns of Table 4.1. Then look in the first column to see what majors might be the best fit for you.

Personality Factors

Personality, which is comprised of enduring personal characteristics, also influences learning effectiveness. Your personality style can facilitate or hinder your success in the classroom. We'll examine two popular approaches to understanding how personality affects learning: the Five Factor Personality Model and the Myers-Briggs Type Inventory.

Five Factor Personality Model Many psychologists today believe that there are five basic dimensions of personality that people consistently demonstrate across cultures (Costa and McRae 1995). Each dimension represents a continuum and is described next, along with an overview of how these dimensions can affect success in college. The mnemonic to remember all five dimensions is OCEAN:

O = Open to experience
High O people are adventurous, imaginative, and unconventional. They tend to enjoy classes where they can experiment with new ideas.
Low O people are conventional, conservative, and rigid in their thinking, preferring more highly structured learning situations.
C = Conscientiousness
High C people are hardworking, ambitious, and driven. They tend to have developed work habits likely to place them on the dean's list.
Low C people are pleasure seeking, negligent, and irresponsible, making them more vulnerable to being placed on probation or being suspended.

TABLE 4.1 Linking Choice of Major with Learning Style Dimensions

Are there some majors that seem to be a particularly good match for specific dimensions of the various learning styles? See how the following majors might logically be linked with learning style characteristics. Do your preferences relate to the majors that you think you would find most satisfying?

Major	Intelligence Profile	Sensory Preference	Experiential Learning
Anthropology	Naturalistic	Auditory	Reflecting/Critical thinking
Archeology	Naturalistic	Tactile	Doing/Critical thinking
Art	Spatial	Visual	Doing/Creating
Biology	Naturalistic	Visual	Doing/Critical thinking
Business	Logical-math	Auditory	Doing/Creating
Chemistry	Naturalistic	Visual	Doing/Critical thinking
Criminal Justice	Intrapersonal	Auditory	Critical thinking/Doing
Dance	Bodily-kinesthetic	Tactile	Doing/Creating
Education	Interpersonal	Mixed	Reflecting/Doing
Engineering	Logical-math; Spatial	Tactile	Doing/Creating
English	Verbal-linguisitic	Auditory	Reflecting/Creating
Film Studies	Verbal-linguistic; Spatial	Visual	Creating/Doing
Foreign Languages	Verbal linguistic	Auditory	Reflecting/Doing
Health Studies	Bodily-kinesthetic	Tactile	Reflecting/Doing
History	Verbal-linguistic	Auditory	Reflecting/Critical thinking
Journalism	Verbal-linguistic	Auditory	Doing/Reflecting
Mathematics	Logical-math	Visual	Critical thinking/Reflecting
Medical Technology	Logical-math	Tactile	Doing/Critical thinking
Music	Musical	Auditory	Doing/Creating
Nursing	Interpersonal	Tactile	Doing/Reflecting
Philosophy	Verbal-linguistic	Auditory	Reflecting/Critical thinking
Pharmacy	Interpersonal; Logical-math	Visual	Doing/Reflecting
Physics	Logical-math	Tactile	Doing/Critical thinking
Political Science	Verbal-linguistic	Auditory	Critical thinking/Reflecting
Pre-Law	Verbal-linguistic	Auditory	Critical thinking/Reflecting
Pre-Med/Pre-Vet	Naturalistic	Tactile	Doing/Critical thinking
Psychology	Intrapersonal; Naturalistic	Mixed	Doing/Critical thinking
Religion	Interpersonal	Auditory	Reflecting/Doing
Social Work	Interpersonal	Auditory	Reflecting/Doing
Sociology	Verbal-linguistic	Auditory	Critical thinking/Reflecting
Theatre	Bodily-kinesthetic	Tactile	Doing/Creating

E = Extraversion

High E individuals (extroverts) are high-spirited and energetic, thriving on the continuous opportunity that college provides to meet and work with different people.

Low E individuals (introverts) are reserved and passive, tending to seek less social stimulation to do their best work.

A = Agreeableness

High A people are good-natured, trusting, and helpful. They tend to be well liked and respected and may have an easier time negotiating positive outcomes to conflicts.

Low A people are irritable, suspicious, and vengeful. They are less likely to get any breaks when negotiating because they tend to approach conflict with a hostile attitude and low expectations of others.

N = Neuroticism

High N individuals suffer a variety of problems related to emotional instability, such as anger, depression, and impulsiveness, which can create constant chaotic conditions that can threaten academic survival.

Low N individuals adapt well, tolerate frustration, and maintain more realistic perspectives. They tend to have developed personal resources that can help them garner success and rebound from failure.

Complete the Journal activity "Your Learning Metaphor" on page 118 to capture the essence of your personality style.

Myers-Briggs Type Inventory (MBTI) Another popular approach to understanding the role of personality in academic success is the Myers-Briggs Type Inventory (MBTI) (Myers 1962). The MBTI measures four dimensions of personality functioning by measuring responses to a series of questions that ask for a preference between two alternatives:

1. *Extraversion/Introversion (E/I)* measures social orientation. Extroverts (E) like talking with others and taking action. Introverts (I) prefer to have others do the talking. (This is similar to the "open to experience" dimension addressed in the Five Factor Model.)
2. *Sensing/Intuiting (S/N)* explores how students process information. Sensers (S) are most at home with facts and examples; they are drawn to realistic, practical applications. Intuiters (N) prefer concepts and theories, which can give greater play to imagination and inspiration.
3. *Thinking/Feeling (T/F)* emphasizes how students make decisions. Thinkers (T) like to take an objective approach and emphasize logic and analysis in their decisions. Feelers (F) prefer emotion to logic; they give greater weight to the impact of relationships in their decisions.
4. *Judging/Perceiving (J/P)* taps how students achieve their goals. Judgers (J) prefer clearly defined strategies to achieve their goals and may jump to closure too quickly. Perceivers (P) like to consider all sides to a problem and may be at some risk for not completing their work. (This also taps characteristics similar to the "openness to experience" dimension in the Five Factor Model.)

> ***I am an intermittent site-specific extrovert.***
>
> Mike Myers
> *Contemporary actor*

Your personality profile can be configured from your preferences on the four dimensions of the MBTI. The test captures your style using a four-letter code that communicates your preferences on each dimension. For example, the ENTJ code reveals an extrovert with a preference for an orderly pursuit of concrete details but a reliance on intuitive decision making. In contrast, the ISFP represents the style of someone who is drawn to solitary activities, relying on facts and emotions.

As you can imagine, students with these contrasting styles are unlikely to be equally happy in any class. For example, consider how students with different personality styles might relate to a highly structured classroom. Structure would be much more appealing to the introvert, who relies more on orderly process, than to the extrovert, who prefers spontaneity; the extrovert would have to do much more work to adapt to the highly structured classroom. See Figure 4.1,"MBTI Styles in the Classroom," for more examples.

Find out about your MBTI profile from the campus counseling or career center.

The inventory should be administered and interpreted by trained MBTI examiners, although an online version of this inventory, the Keirsey Temperament scale, can be found at http://Keirsey.com/frame.html. However, beware of relying on the results of personality tests in a way that restricts your options or limits your horizons. Instead,

FIGURE 4.1 MBTI Styles in the Classroom

This Style . . .	Prefers classes that emphasize . . .	But can adapt best to unfavorable conditions by . . .
Extraverts	active learning, group projects	forming a study group to meet their social needs
Introverts	lectures, structured tasks	setting manageable social goals (for example, contribute to discussions once every two weeks)
Sensers	memorizable facts, concrete questions	identifying key abstract ideas and theories along with their practical implications
Intuiters	interpretation, imagination	identifying the most important facts and figures
Thinkers	objective feedback, pressure to succeed	seeking extra feedback from instructor to create feeling of external pressure
Feelers	positive feedback, individual recognition	seeking extra time from instructor to create personal connection
Judgers	orderliness, structure, and deadlines	setting own deadlines and structure
Perceivers	spontaneity, flexibility	assuming a temporary role of a student who must be rigidly organized to be successful

use personality test results to help you avoid blind spots in your thinking and increase your adaptability. To pull together insights from all the self-assessments in this chapter, complete the Journal activity "A Matter of Style" on page 117.

Technological Facility

One final difference in learning style is becoming increasingly important for success in college: the relative comfort you have with the variety of technological challenges you will face. You have probably always experienced computers as a meaningful part of your life. However, not everyone is completely comfortable with computer technology. If you enjoy the challenge of learning new technology, you will have a definite advantage in enhancing your learning. For example, skilled use of technology can save time, expand your access to ideas, and open whole new worlds for you to explore from your keyboard. However, it is not enough to be skilled at shopping for information. You must be selective in the information you take from Internet resources and present that information in a manner that is consistent with standards for intellectual property. You cannot cut and paste your way to a degree. If you are not enamored of technology, you may end up doing many things in college the hard way. You will learn more about the role that technology plays in college and why it is so important to develop a technological comfort zone throughout this book.

Think Strategically about Your Learning

As you meet each challenge that college classes offer, your learning resources will expand and so will your self-confidence. You may discover abilities you never thought you had. Working harder on skills that don't come easily can improve your academic success.

Understand How Effort Relates to Learning Style

Success in college depends on more than your natural talents and preferences. You must take responsibility for your learning, and that requires making some important decisions and choices about how and when to apply yourself. Depending on your learning style, some of the following questions might be on your mind.

How hard do I want to work? Some college courses will be so intriguing that you'll naturally be drawn in deeply. It will be easy to learn because the content and instructor's approach match your interests, learning style, and abilities, making the material a breeze to learn. It's easy to be conscientious when your interests are such a good match to the class. However, you may find yourself wanting to devote just enough time and energy to get by. This choice will be tempting in courses that have little bearing on your ultimate career goals or when you're short on time.

Surface Learning Surface learning means studying the minimum amount you need to learn. Surface learners rely primarily on rote memory, often exercised at the last minute, thus generating learning that can be characterized as "shallow." They tend to be motivated by grades or feedback from the teacher rather than intrinsic interest in the course.

Surface learning can be risky. Surface learners are much less likely than deep learners to do well in college. Ultimately, surface learners may have serious problems in their chosen majors if they need to remember what they learned at a shallow level in prior courses. Still, you may choose to be a surface learner in some courses so that you can devote more time to deep learning in other courses.

Deep Learning Deep learners accept personal responsibility for truly understanding the course ideas. They construct their learning experiences actively. They enjoy the process of learning for its own sake and use a lot of thinking skills. Deep learners remember what they learn longer. If your interests parallel those of the course, deep learning may not be much effort. It might even be fun. The Journal activity "The Deep End of the Pool" on page 117 asks you to think about the courses you are taking and the type of learning you are doing in each.

Every time you're confronted with a learning opportunity, you must decide how deeply you wish to learn in order to succeed in college overall. Do you need to work hard in this particular course, or do you need merely to break the surface? Keep your level of effort and motivation in line with your broader goals and values.

If I have to miss class or have other questions about the university, whom should I ask for help? Your first impulse may be to ask for help from a good friend or nearby student (Clark 2005), but that is not always a good idea. Other new students may face the same knowledge limitations that you have but may be unwilling to admit what they don't know. Go to the university official (teacher, advisor, registrar) whose job it is to have the right answer.

I can already tell I won't have enough time to do well in my classes. How should I choose where to work hardest? It's a bad idea to do poorly in many classes when you can improve your standing by dropping a class or two. If you find that you're spreading yourself too thin, consult with your adviser about dropping a course to save your time and produce the most positive impact your self-esteem. Give priority to courses that overlap your natural talents.

I have trouble jumping into class discussions, because they seem to take off before I'm ready! Is there such a thing as being too reflective? Students process information at various speeds. This style can create some interesting class conditions. Some people respond quickly and are accurate and insightful in their contributions. Sometimes rapid responding is impulsive, producing ill-formed, off-target ideas.

In general, impulsive students tend to make more mistakes than students who carefully reflect on their experiences (Jonassen and Grabowski 1993). However, some reflective individuals, especially those with more introverted social styles, may think forever about a problem and not ever speak.

If the course rewards contributions other than class discussion, participating in class may not be required for success. However, if you don't routinely participate in class, here is an area where you can expand your skills. Make a note of the kinds of questions the instructor presents for discussion. Prepare answers based on what you think your instructor will ask. By carefully reflecting ahead of time, you should be able to cut your processing time in class and give voice to your good ideas. Success in the classroom can make it easier to join in the conversation in other settings, giving you more social options as well.

I am often annoyed by my classmates because they refuse to get involved in class. It seems like I'm the only one who ever volunteers to answer any questions. What's wrong with them? Probably nothing. Many of your classmates may have reflective style that requires a longer warm-up. However, they also may have learned already that your willingness to carry the burden relieves them of sharing the load. If you are a fast-responding extrovert, your pursuit of the spotlight may seem like "sucking up" to your less-involved classmates.

Rethink your role. You may want to sit on your hands and practice a longer reaction time. That will give your classmates a better chance to get involved and also may help your own ideas to be more fully developed and useful when you do volunteer.

Group work makes me crazy. How will I survive classes that require group projects? In almost every career domain, working with people is a requirement. This is a skill that is worth developing but a challenge for students who are introverted or who tend to have difficulties getting along with others. Think of your peers as additional resource people who can help you learn. In groups, volunteer to do tasks that allow you to contribute from your areas of strength.

For example, you may show great attention to detail, so you can volunteer to summarize the action of the group. Monitor each group situation for what doesn't work and engage the members to address the quality of the process.

Recipe for success: Study while others are sleeping; work while others are loafing; prepare while others are playing; and dream while others are wishing.

William A. Ward
Nineteenth-century English educator

I feel stifled by detailed assignments. Can I get away with being creative? Intuitive thinkers crave creative experience, but that can create problems for you in some classes. If you stray in a way that enhances the point of the assignment, the instructor may be pleased with your initiative. If you exceed the minimum criteria, most instructors will think of you as hardworking and creative. However, if you drift from the intended purpose, the instructor will see your work as deficient and possibly defiant. Check with your instructor ahead of time to make sure that your creative approach will get the right reception.

How do I decide when to stay safe and when to take a risk? What will happen if I fail? Many students just starting out in college feel like imposters. They worry that giving the wrong answer in class will forever brand them as stupid and alienate them from the other students. It's normal to feel a little anxiety about your performance, but you can't let neurotic behavior keep you from doing your best.

Going to college isn't just about acquiring knowledge; it's about personal change. The impact of a single failure can be a more powerful lesson than a string of successes. College should be a safe place in which to take thoughtful risks as you learn and change from both success and failure.

Should I take an online class? Many new opportunities are available for learning electronically, but it may not always be the best option. Common factors for success in completing online courses include reasonable technical expertise, good time-management skills, compatibility of the class with your work schedule, and strategies for dealing with obstacles along the way (Packam and others 2004).

Other questions may have occurred to you as you strategize to get the most from your college classes. See the Journal activity "Everything I Need to Know I Plan to Learn in College" on page 118 to help you latch on to some simple but enduring strategies to help you succeed.

Build Positive Relationships with Instructors

Now that you know more about how to assess your personality and learning preferences, you will be much better equipped to deal with your instructors. Knowledge of your own learning preferences should provide you with a greater sense of control, and that can help build your confidence. Take responsibility for relating to your instructors, to engage them in your pursuit of what they have to offer you. Instructors tend to be most responsive to students who are active or enthusiastic in the classroom. The quality of interactions with your professors will have a major impact on your overall success in college.

Reconcile Your Learning Style with Your Instructor's Teaching Style

The next time you register for class, invest your time in identifying which instructors have a teaching style that suits your learning style. Interview seasoned students. Go beyond questions about whether the instructor is "good." You can guess by now that "good instructor" means different things to people with different learning styles. Ask *how* the instructor teaches. For example, does he

- lecture the entire period
- involve the class in discussion
- use active learning strategies
- offer any note-taking supports such as outlines
- show enthusiasm for students

Teaching styles are every bit as diverse as learning styles. Teachers will vary not only in their disciplines but also in their enthusiasm, competence, warmth, eccentricities, and humor. Although you probably won't have access to your instructors' MBTI profiles, invest some time to maximize the match between their teaching styles and your learning needs. What about your teachers will matter the most to you? How do variations among your instructors relate to your learning style?

The Student-Centered Teacher Some instructors focus more on developing students' intellectual growth. They run their classes with a variety of activities chosen to motivate student interest and heighten learning. They might use small-group discussions, film clips, technology, and student performance as part of their teaching.

Finally, such instructors often depart from their original plans because they believe that a new direction serves the students' learning better; in these cases, class can be spontaneous. The student-centered teacher tends to appeal to individuals who are open to experience, like hands-on activities, and have energetic, extroverted approaches to learning.

If you learn best when you have the opportunity to apply course concepts to practical examples, then student-centered approaches probably will appeal to you. Your obligation to learn in such classes is simple: Work at as deep a level as you can manage. Because the instructor will include activities that appeal to your learning preferences, chances are good that you will succeed in the course.

However, you might prefer the structure and efficiency of a well-designed lecture, particularly if you're a good auditory learner, you like to memorize "the facts," or you tend to be introverted. If so, what can you do to survive the student-centered class?

- Outline your reading.
- Try to anticipate what the course will cover.
- Talk with the instructor about the course and how it's working for you.
- Form a study group to work more systematically on the key ideas.

The Content-Centered Teacher Content-centered teachers typically use lectures as their primary teaching method. The learning climate in lecture-based courses is highly structured, paced by the lecturer's strategy for covering material in a meaningful way. Instructors expect students to take careful notes to prepare for tests. Most college classes are lectures. Thankfully, there are good lecturers who tell stories and use humor to get their information across in an interesting way.

Some learning preferences fit well with lecturing. The content-centered approach tends to appeal to auditory learners who prefer classes that minimize involvement with peers. In fact, students who thrive in these environments might well consider college teaching as a potential career.

Visual and tactile learners or learners who prefer active or more social learning experiences simply have to work harder to adapt their learning style to the demands of content-centered courses. If you face this challenge, what can you do to succeed in a content-centered class?

- Learn to make systematic, creative notes or at least work with the notes creatively when you study.
- Generate practical examples that help you form concrete connections with the course material.
- Form a study group that can help you discuss course concepts in a manner that encourages deeper learning.

Create a Good First Impression

College instructors expect you to have academic common sense. Knowing how to develop relationships with your instructors is an important part of that common sense. Here are some guidelines that can help you get off on the right foot:

- *Buy the right stuff.* You won't look like a serious student if you don't have the required books.

- *Be prepared.* If you read assignments *before* class, you'll ask better questions and impress your instructors with your motivation to learn. You'll also get more out of the lecture or discussion.
- *Make contact.* Is it possible to get acquainted with your instructors in large classes? The answer is yes, although it may be challenging. By asking intelligent questions during class or visiting during office hours, you can stand out even in very large classes. Interviewing an instructor for this course can help you practice getting to know your instructors on an informal basis.

Complete the Journal activity "Connect with a Special Teacher" on page 117 to get some guidance on how to get acquainted with an instructor. Seeking contact with faculty outside the classroom is associated with staying in college and graduating with honors (Astin, 1993). How can you get your instructors to take a special interest in you? "Expand Your Resources: Become a Distinctive Student" gives some sound advice.

Maintain the Connection

Instructors respond most positively to students who show interest and enthusiasm for their courses. Later in the term, instructors have an easier time cutting some slack for students who have been responsive and responsible in the earlier weeks. When test scores fall between two grades, those students who seem to care about their work are often the ones who get bumped up instead of down.

What are some other strategies that will help you develop a stronger connection to your instructors?

- *Stay on task.* It is easy to get distracted and disengage, but it is just as easy for the instructor to notice and take offense. Concentrate on keeping the connection between you and the instructor personal and lively.
- *Do the work on time.* Coping with deadlines is serious business in college. Many students are surprised when they learn that college deadlines are not as flexible as they were in high school. If you miss a deadline, you may not be able to negotiate an extension. Most instructors do not extend deadlines to individuals without justification. Many believe that doing so isn't fair to students who do their work on time.
- *Use the syllabus.* A course syllabus comprehensively describes how the instructor expects the course to proceed. The syllabus can include the course objectives, reading list, grading policies, and other information that applies throughout the term. The syllabus also can give hints about the instructor's teaching style. It may contain helpful hints on how to study for tests. Some instructors hold students responsible for reading all materials listed in the syllabus. This can be a surprise at test time if you thought that your class notes would be enough. The Journal activity "Review a Syllabus" on page 118 will

EXPAND YOUR RESOURCES

Become a Distinctive Student

- **Sit in the front.** The most motivated and interested students often sit close to the instructor to minimize distractions and create the opportunity for informal discussion before or after class.
- **Bring articles or clippings related to the course to class.** Instructors like to see you make independent connections between what you're learning and your life outside the classroom. They may incorporate your ideas into the class and remember you for making the contribution.
- **Take advantage of existing opportunities to get to know your instructors informally.** On some campuses, faculty sponsor informal gatherings to help you network with others. You also can join student clubs with faculty sponsors. These are great opportunities to get to know the faculty as people.
- **Visit during your instructor's office hours.** Most instructors identify their office hours when the course begins. Check in with your instructor about something you found interesting or were confused about from class discussion. Ask the instructor to review your notes to see whether your note-taking skills are on target
- **Use e-mail to connect, if that is an option.** Many instructors like to communicate with their students via e-mail. This is a great option if you're shy or the instructor seems hard to approach. But remember, your e-mail represents you to the professor. Be polite, specific, and patient. Instructors don't respond well to overlong, whiny, or frivolous communications in their e-mail queues, and they may be unable to turn around a response quickly. Both your e-mail address and your sign-off should demonstrate maturity. Instructors may not get a favorable impression when they are responding to "hotbabe14." Be sure to provide sufficient lead time to get the help you need.

help you reflect carefully on how to use a syllabus profitably even in your most challenging courses.

- *Ask it this way.* When you can't attend a class, don't ask your instructor, "Did I miss anything important?" Although it may be innocent, your question implies that your instructor regularly spends time on unimportant information. Instead, ask, "Can I make up any of the work I missed?" Or you can talk with a classmate or borrow notes to help you get caught up.
- *Actively seek a mentor.* A mentor is someone who can give you guidance beyond the classroom and help you find other opportunities to develop. Mentors can be any individual who is willing to make an investment of time and energy in you and your plans. Faculty can serve as mentors. If you think an instructor has taken a personal interest in you, find out about the instructor's availability and willingness to serve as your mentor. This can be the most meaningful connection you make in college. See "Create Your Future: A Helping Hand" to consider who else might fulfill this important role.
- *Stay straight.* Even when instructors don't explicitly mention their expectations about your ethical performance, they will assume that you have read, understood, and will abide by the campus academic integrity code.

  Nothing ruins relationships with both your current and future professors more than the cloud of suspicion that develops around questionable integrity. Plan your work so that you aren't tempted to take short cuts that could cut short your reputation.

  To help you resist such temptations, refer to "Clarify Values: Develop Your Academic Integrity Pledge," which will help you clarify your personal commitment to staying straight.
- *Stay cool.* The best classes run on respectful and civil behavior. Respect does *not* mean that you can't challenge or ask questions. In fact, many instructors (but not all) regard student questions as an essential part of classroom learning. However, all instructors expect participation to be civil (calm, polite, and efficient rather than prolonged, pointless, or profane). Figure 4.2, "How to Get on the Wrong Side of an Instructor," describes other behaviors that can get in the way of a smoothly running class.

It takes a lot of courage to show your dreams to someone else.

Erma Bombeck
American humorist

CREATE YOUR FUTURE

A Helping Hand

It is never too early to get a start in developing a professional network to help you realize your dreams about what can happen after graduation. A seasoned professional can be invaluable in providing feedback about the courses and other experiences that will prepare you best for the job market or graduate or professional applications. Think about the following candidates as possible mentors:

- Your friendliest professor. You may want to stay in contact with those teachers who foster your enthusiasm for learning. Even if that teacher is not in your selected major, she may be able to offer some great general guidance about professional development.
- The least popular teacher in your major. This faculty member may have the greatest time available to devote to your cause and might appreciate some attention.
- A willing alumnus. Ask the head of the department in your major to connect you to someone who has already been through the major and has had some success after graduation. Alumni usually enjoy contact with undergraduates and may take special pains to help with sound advice.
- A student leader. Check with your adviser about identifying a student who really seems to have it altogether, contact that student, and make a pitch that you are seeking expert mentorship. The student may be flattered and will have extensive social networks on campus to assist with nonacademic needs as well.
- An experienced relative. Sometimes your choice of major can overlap with the experience of a cherished relative. Don't overlook this helpful resource.
- An adviser's nominee. Clearly communicate your desire for a strong mentor to your academic adviser. Enlist some suggestions that link to your desired career goals. The adviser may have just the right off-campus supporter whose expertise can be invaluable.

Solve Problems with Instructors

If you're lucky, you may not have to solve relationship problems with your instructors. However, four problems may prompt you to take action:

1. Your abilities are mismatched to the course.
2. You feel challenged by the instructor's professional boundary—or lack of it.
3. You and your instructor disagree about the completion status of your work.
4. You need to make a complaint about an instructor's actions. It can be surprising when professors themselves are irresponsible or disrespectful, but it does happen. When it interferes with your learning, you should take responsibility to get the problem resolved.

© Dennis McDonald/PhotoEdit

Just when you think you can speak in a private conversation in the middle of class, you are likely to be wrong. This photograph illustrates why. Off-task students tend to stand out against the sea of faces paying attention.

Develop Your Academic Integrity Pledge

Track down the rules that govern academic integrity on your campus. Read the rules carefully. Do you agree with the position taken by your campus regarding the consequences for academic dishonesty? In what ways do you think the rules could be improved? If possible, arrange to talk with a student who serves in the capacity of hearing complaints regarding integrity violations. Compare that student's experience to your own speculations about the effectiveness of the rules. Then formulate your own personal pledge based on your study. You may want to print the pledge and hang it near your primary study area to help keep you on course.

Resolve a Mismatch Courses are unsatisfying when the instructor does not teach at a level the students can handle. In some of these courses, students feel overwhelmed by an instructor who talks over their heads. In other cases, instructors offer too little challenge and students feel cheated.

FIGURE 4.2 How to Get on the Wrong Side of an Instructor

Behaviors That Show Questionable Maturity
Talking during lectures
Chewing gum, eating, or drinking noisily
Being late and leaving early
Creating disturbances
Wearing hats
Putting feet on desks or tables
Being insincere or "brownnosing"
Complaining about workload
Acting like a know-it-all
Wearing headphones
Making fun of others

Behaviors That Show Inattention
Sleeping during class
Cutting class
Acting bored or apathetic
Not paying attention
Being unprepared
Packing up books and materials before class is over
Asking already answered questions
Sitting in the back rows when there are empty seats in front
Yawning obviously
Slouching in seat
Asking "Did we do anything important?" after missing class
Not asking questions
Doing work for other classes in class
Reading the newspaper in class
Cruising the net
Text-messaging friends

Miscellaneous Irritating Behaviors
Cheating
Asking "Will this be on the test?"
Being more interested in grades than in learning
Pretending to understand
Blaming teachers for poor grades
Giving unbelievable excuses
Wearing tasteless T-shirts
Using foul language
Chatting off-task
Disclosing too much personal information
Answering every question

Drew C. Appleby, "Faculty and staff perceptions of irritating behaviors in the college classroom," from *Journal of Staff, Program, and Organizational Development,* 8, pp. 41–46. Copyright © 1990. Reprinted with permission of New Forum Press.

To resolve either problem, first talk with your classmates to verify that others are struggling too. Then, preferably with one or two other concerned students, request an appointment with the instructor and present your concerns directly. Many instructors will be pleased with your initiative and grateful for the feedback. Others will be less enthusiastic but can give you suggestions about how to cope with their demands. If you can't resolve the mismatch through talking with the instructor, consider withdrawing from the course. If necessary, you can take it again later with a different instructor.

Manage Boundaries Most instructors give clear signals about how and when they can be contacted. Instructors usually have office hours. They can and should respond to student questions or concerns during those periods as part of their professional responsibilities. Instructors differ in their enthusiasm about being contacted outside class or office hours. Some provide home phone numbers and encourage you to call whenever you have questions.

Others request not to be disturbed at home, because they want to separate their professional and personal lives. It is easy to see how students get confused about how and when to contact their instructors. If your instructors have not specified that they can be reached at home, use memos, voice mail, e-mail, office-hour visits, or the time just after class to ask questions or maintain contact, but strive to learn and honor the boundaries drawn by your instructors.

Friendships between instructors and students pose an especially complex boundary problem. Many instructors don't think it is a good idea to be friends with students. They do not want to do anything that could compromise their objectivity. Other instructors believe that they can be objective in grading the work of a student–friend so they aren't as rigorous about observing that boundary.

Keep Copies of Your Work When an instructor and student disagree about whether work has been completed, the burden of proof falls on the student. Get in the habit of making copies of your papers. Then, if a paper gets lost or misplaced, you can easily replace it. Keep returned projects in a safe place so you can retrieve them if the instructor has failed to record them.

When the term is over and your instructor has filed your grades, retain your best work for your academic portfolio. This habit will help you track your progress over time and will give you samples that may help in future job applications.

"Is the homework fresh?"

Know Your Rights As a student, you are guaranteed certain rights. The Family Educational Right to Privacy Act, also known as the Buckley Amendment, ensures your right to privacy. How you perform in class should remain a private matter.

Most campuses foster an atmosphere of respect for and equitable treatment of students to promote their taking responsibility. However, you may experience circumstances in which

© Bill Aron/PhotoEdit

If you have a complaint about a class, start by talking directly with your instructor. By describing the problem and offering your interpretation, you may be able to solve the problem quickly and fairly.

you believe your rights have been violated. You have several options when an instructor's conduct upsets you. First, recognize that the instructor is the authority in the class. Weigh carefully how upset you are against the possible consequences of confronting an instructor who holds greater power and probably more credibility than you do.

If you decide to complain, explain your concerns directly to the instructor. Ask for an appointment. Present your concerns and offer evidence to support it. If unsuccessful, appeal in writing to the instructor's immediate supervisor. In most cases, this supervisor is the department head or coordinator, who will hear you out and determine what steps to take. If the supervisor fails to take action and you still need further resolution, ask for an appointment with that person's supervisor, most likely the academic dean. At each stage of the chain of command, the person will review what attempts you already have made to resolve the problem before she does anything about it.

As one cautionary note, you're unlikely to have much luck appealing a final grade unless you can identify discriminatory treatment or a specific error in the instructor's judgment. Most college officials regard instructors as the final authority in grading and rarely overturn their grades.

Choose a Major That Fits Your Learning Style

A college degree can be a passport to a professional career, but a well-chosen major can also produce a great number of opportunities that are linked to your interests and skills. Your learning style should influence which career you pursue and the major you choose to help you get there.

Target an Intelligent Career

One way to start planning your future is to link your natural intellectual talents to possible career options. Gardner's theory of multiple intelligences has been used to explore the relationship between intellectual ability and career choice. See Figure 4.3, "Intelligent Career Choices," for some typical and creative career choices

FIGURE 4.3 Intelligent Career Choices

The theory of multiple intelligences suggests that intellectual strengths predict career choices. Review some traditional and less-conventional careers linked to different domains of intelligence.

Intelligence Domain	Traditional Careers	Less-Conventional Careers
Verbal-Linguistic	author reporter teacher librarian attorney advertising specialist politician	talk-show host poet childrens book writer crossword puzzle maker campaign manager
Logical-Mathematical	engineer scientist mathematician statistician insurance specialist computer expert claims adjuster	physicist astronomer astronaut
Intrapersonal	novelist psychologist philosopher	advice columnist feature writer
Interpersonal	politician social worker sales manager psychologist public relations specialist nurse, doctor, or other health-care provider	religious leader
Musical	performer singer music teacher	composer conductor sound effects specialist
Spatial	engineer architect surgeon painter sailor web designer fashion designer	mapmaker sculptor billboard designer
Bodily-Kinesthetic	artisan actor athlete dancer coach	professional juggler professional skater health writer
Naturalist	conservationist agricultural specialist floral designer museum curator librarian botanist	safari director antique specialist baseball card expert game-show winner

based on the multiple intelligence model. Revisit your intelligence profile in Self-Assessment 1 on page 114 and think about how well your profile matches up with these choices.

Find the Right Mix

Every college major tends to emphasize certain intellectual strengths, learning preferences, and personality styles more than others. Consider these examples:

- Marcia has a particular talent for music. She prefers hands-on learning in her music classes over courses where she passively takes notes on concepts. Her auditory skills are especially well developed. Because she is also effective at working with others, her major of music education represents a natural outgrowth of her interests and talents. *(auditory sensory preferences + active-learning preferences + extroversion/agreeableness personality style).*
- Darnell enjoys classes where he can sit, listen, and think carefully about the issues. He especially enjoys writing assignments that allow him to reflect on the significance of ideas, particularly if he has to take apart an issue and form some judgments. He enjoys learning new and complex words. He is thinking about opting for a journalism major *(verbal-linguistic, spiritual/existential, and intrapersonal skills + auditory sensory preference + reflecting and critical-thinking preferences + thinking/perceptive personality style).*
- Carra enjoys taking risks. She likes to combine her strengths in mathematics and her growing ability to deal effectively with others in action-oriented projects. She learns best when she can apply principles in hands-on situations. Carra believes a business major will complement her entrepreneurial style *(logical-mathematical and interpersonal intelligences + tactile sensory preference + active-learning preference + open to experience personality style).*
- Bruce has never been a big fan of reading or writing, but he keenly appreciates courses that allow him to be physically active. He likes the hands-on activities that his kinesiology classes offer and is considering a career in recreation management *(bodily awareness intelligence + tactile sensory preference + active-learning preference + extroversion/sensing personality style).*
- Portia has a vivid visual imagination. She prefers classes where she can express her creative impulses. She is thinking about a career in graphic design but knows she has some work to do to develop her interaction skills for business success *(spatial intelligence + visual sensory preference + creative-thinking preference + intuitive/disagreeable personality style).*

Earlier in the chapter, you learned about the Myers-Briggs Type Indicator. Career counselors have used the MBTI to provide some direction to career selection. See Figure 4.4, "The Myers-Briggs Type Indicator and Potential Career Links," to learn how MBTI codes and personality factors predict professional styles that seem to be well suited to different occupational profiles.

Review the results of your self-assessments in this chapter one final time. What career directions and majors does your learning style suggest? If no obvious directions appear, consider consulting with a career-counseling specialist on campus who can help you make more concrete links between your learning style and possible majors and careers. Now complete the Journal activity "The Stylish Major" on page 118 to further assess your best potential major.

The university is not engaged in making ideas safe for students. It is engaged in making students safe for ideas.

Clark Kerr
Former president of Stanford University

FIGURE 4.4 The Myers-Briggs Type Indicator and Potential Career Links

Myers-Briggs Code	Description	Possible Career Matches
ISTJ	Quiet, serious, responsible, sensible, patient, conservative, and loyal	police and protective services, administrators and managers, engineers, military personnel, scientists, physicians
ISTP	Factual, sensible, logical, and reflective	farming, mechanics, military personnel, engineering and science technicians, optometrists
ISFP	Quiet, practical, sensitive, and spontaneous	Nursing, secretarial, health service workers, clerical, technicians, forestry
ISFJ	Private, faithful, sensible, and sensitive	Nursing, clerical, teachers, librarians, physicians, health service workers
INFJ	Intuitive, caring, quiet, and peace-loving	Consultants, clergy, teachers, media specialists, physicians, social workers, marketing personnel, psychologists
INFP	Quiet, creative, sensitive, and perceptive	Physicians, editors and reporters, writers, journalists, psychologists
INTJ	Independent, innovative, logical, and driven by the inner world of ideas	Lawyers, scientists, research workers, engineers, computer systems analysts
INTP	Private, intellectual, impersonal, analytical, and reflective	Lawyers, scientists, research workers, engineers, computer programmers and analysts
ESTP	Outgoing, practical thinkers who are masters of experience and observation. They don't rely on their emotions to make decisions.	Marketing personnel, sales, police and detectives, public service and community workers, computer specialists and programmers
ESTJ	Assertive, practical, rational, loyal, opinionated, and decisive	Teachers, managerial and administration, sales, insurance and banking, military personnel, computer analyst, public relations
ESFP	Warm, outgoing, optimistic, and caring	Receptionist, hospitality and catering, designers, teachers, sales, artists and entertainers
ESFJ	Outgoing, sociable, practical, and organized	Receptionists, restaurant workers, sales, teachers, health service workers
ENFJ	Sociable, intuitive, sensitive, and organized	Teachers, actors, musicians, artists, counselors, writers, nurses, marketing personnel
ENTP	Enthusiastic, outgoing, analytical, multitalented, independent	Marketing personnel, sales, journalists, actors, computer systems analysts, public relations
ENTJ	Outgoing, logical, decisive	Managerial and administrative, marketing personnel, sales
ENFP	Open-minded, imaginative, caring, and outgoing	Journalists, counselors, teachers, writers, social scientists

Note: The characteristics described and the occupations listed are provided to stimulate your thinking about your personality and possible links with careers. They are not intended as a formal testing of your personality and career interests.

Adapted from Looking at Type and Careers *by Charles R. Martin. Used by permission of the Center for Applications of Psychological Type, Inc.*

Keep a Flexible Outlook

You may be fortunate to have natural talents in many areas. You may discover many new abilities through your college experiences.

Don't close off your options by locking yourself into a career path too soon. After you commit to a specific major, stay flexible about what the future may bring. The career you ultimately pursue may not even have emerged yet as a viable option. Versatility as a learner will give you more choices about where you want to go in your major and your career. Consider the Journal activity "Career Cruising on the Web" on page 118 to assist you in thinking through some new options based on your learning profile.

Don't measure yourself by what you have accomplished, but by what you should have accomplished with your ability.

John Wooden

Retired UCLA basketball coach

CREATE YOUR FUTURE

Keep Your Options Open

Sandra's story offers a good example about why it is so important to stay flexible about your options. Both of her parents and her older brothers were lawyers. Like them, she was especially skilled in verbal-linguistic intelligence and enjoyed a good debate. But she was surprised to discover how much she enjoyed the community service work that she was required to do in her sociology class. By her junior year, she abandoned her prelaw major in favor of social work. Eventually she found great career satisfaction in managing a residential home for delinquent teenagers.

Seth wasn't too sure he would like college. He had always nurtured fantasies of being a cartoonist, but drawing was not something for which Seth ever earned positive feedback. After a few frustrating semesters in art classes, he sought some career counseling to figure out other alternatives. Career testing demonstrated that Seth had a knack for business and solid social skills.

He recognized that these abilities, honed by a major in business, would help him develop into being an entrepreneur. In college, he started putting together a business plan that would help him establish a string of successful hobby shops where he would have the opportunity to work in cartoons in a dramatically different but highly profitable manner.

Summary Strategies for Mastering College

Diversify Your Learning Style to Get the Most From College

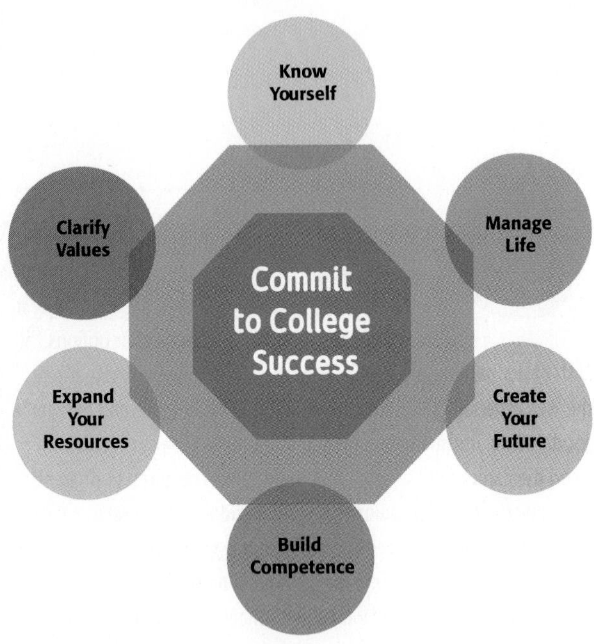

Focus on the Six Strategies for Success above as you read each chapter to learn how to apply these strategies to your own success.

1 How You Learn

- Identify your intellectual strengths and weaknesses.
- Understand how your sensory preferences shape your learning.
- Recognize what learning processes help you learn best.
- Understand what courses and majors are the best fit based on your intellectual profile, sensory preferences, and learning processes.
- Link your personality style to your classroom success.

2 Think Strategically about Your Learning

- Understand how effort relates to learning style.
- Recognize the difference between surface and deep learning.
- Commit to deep learning when time and resources permit.
- Develop adaptive strategies based on your learning style.
- Learn how the features of this book can impact your success in the course.

3 Build Positive Relationships with Instructors

- Select teachers whose style works well with your own in the beginning.
- Choose teachers who will build your resilience by developing your less-preferred styles as your learning matures.
- Understand the difference between a student-centered teacher and one who is content-centered.
- Make a good first impression to establish yourself with your instructors.
- Maintain strong connections through conscientious and ethical behavior.
- Solve problems through effective interpersonal skills.

4 Choose a Major That Fits Your Learning Style

- Consider majors with courses that match your learning style.
- Stretch your ability to use different learning styles to have more career options later.

Review Questions

1. List the nine types of intelligence that Gardner identified and circle the one that best represents you. How can you use this information to enhance your success in college?

    1. ______
    2. ______
    3. ______
    4. ______
    5. ______
    6. ______
    7. ______
    8. ______
    9. ______

2. List below the three types of sensory preferences for learning and circle the one that best represents you. How can you also use this to enhance your college success?

    1. ______
    2. ______
    3. ______

3. List below the four types of experiential learning preferences and circle the one that best represents you. Now consider the preferences you circled above. What does this imply about the types of courses in which you might be most successful?

    1. ______
    2. ______
    3. ______
    4. ______

4. In what ways can personality factors contribute positively and negatively to success in the classroom?

    ______

    ______

5. What are some important things to do to get off on the right foot in class? List at least three strategies you can use now to make the best possible impression on your teachers.

    1. ______
    2. ______
    3. ______

Know Yourself

SELF-ASSESSMENT 1

Your Intelligence Profile

Beginning courses in college will give you an opportunity to experiment with and improve different kinds of intelligence. See how different college courses promote specific kinds of intelligence. Then indicate your strengths by identifying all the characteristics that apply to you.

Mark the space using the following codes: 2, very much like me; 1, somewhat like me; 0, not like me.

Verbal-Linguistic (Great Books, Composition, History)

____ I like to read.
____ I enjoy finding out the meanings of new words.
____ I appreciate humor involving wordplay.
____ I enjoy telling or writing poems or stories.
____ I recall written or verbal material well.

Logical-Mathematical (Algebra, Philosophy, Chemistry)

____ I like working with symbols.
____ Math comes fairly easy to me.
____ I like to analyze and solve problems.
____ I like to discover logical weaknesses in an argument.
____ I enjoy listening to a good debate.

Musical (Music Appreciation, Orchestra)

____ I enjoy singing or making rhythmic sounds.
____ I like to listen to favorite tapes and records.
____ I sometimes make up my own tunes.
____ I would enjoy learning to play a new musical instrument.
____ I enjoy music deeply even when it has no lyrics.

Bodily-Kinesthetic (Recreation Studies, Engineering)

____ I enjoy working with my hands.
____ It's hard for me to sit still for long periods of time.
____ I am good in at least one sport.
____ I enjoy a well-executed physical movement.
____ I'm physically comfortable with my body.

Spatial (Geometry, Art, Computer Science)

____ I can easily visualize objects.
____ I tend to find beauty in things that others don't.
____ I can usually get around without going the wrong way.
____ I enjoy working on arts, crafts, or drawing.
____ People often comment on my "good taste."

Interpersonal (Psychology, Sociology, Nursing)

____ I like to be around people, and I make friends easily.
____ I have a knack for remembering names and faces.
____ I have demonstrated natural leadership tendencies.
____ I notice subtle differences among people.
____ I understand people better than many other people do.

Intrapersonal (Religious Studies, Film Studies)

____ I prefer solitary activities to group work.
____ I enjoy quiet time.
____ I am very sensitive to emotional experiences.
____ I know myself very well.
____ I prefer to have a few deep friendships rather than lots of friends.

Naturalist (Biology, Evolution, Forensic Science)

____ I have a strong curiosity about how nature works.
____ I enjoy looking for patterns in things.
____ I can learn more easily outdoors than indoors.
____ Science classes tend to be easy for me.
____ I have at least one collection that I keep in careful order.

Spiritual/Existential (Humanities, Philosophy, Religious Studies)

____ I like learning about religious practices in other cultures.
____ I wonder about life's absurdities and coincidences.
____ I have lots of questions about the nature of the universe.
____ I am not easily frustrated when big questions don't have easy answers.
____ College students spend too little time thinking about issues with cosmic significance.

Add up your scores in each category. This inventory can reveal which multiple intelligence area is a relative strength and which is a relative weakness. In which dimensions did you score the highest? In which did you score the lowest?

SELF-ASSESSMENT 2

Sensory Preference Inventory

Using the scale below enter the appropriate rating to each self-description in the open box.

Often = 5 points
Sometimes = 3 points
Seldom = 1 point

Then add up the numbers in each column to find out your dominant sensory preference.

		VISUAL	AUDITORY	TACTILE
1.	I can remember best about a subject by listening to a lecture that includes information, explanations, and discussion.			
2.	I prefer to see information written on a chalkboard and supplemented by visual aids and assigned readings.			
3.	I like to write things down or take notes for visual review.			
4.	I prefer to use posters, models, or actual practice and do other activities in class.			
5.	I require explanations of diagrams, graphs, or visual directions.			
6.	I enjoy working with my hands or making things.			
7.	I am skillful with, and enjoy developing and making, graphs and charts.			
8.	I can tell if sounds match when presented with pairs of sounds.			
9.	I remember best by writing things down several times.			
10.	I can easily understand and follow directions on maps.			
11.	I do best in academic subjects by listening to lectures and tapes.			
12.	I play with coins or keys in my pockets.			
13.	I learn to spell better by repeating words out loud than by writing the words on paper.			
14.	I can understand a news article better by reading about it in the newspaper than by listening to a report about it on the radio.			
15.	I chew gum, smoke, or snack while studying.			
16.	I think the best way to remember something is to picture it in your head.			
17.	I learn the spelling of words by "finger spelling" them.			
18.	I would rather listen to a good lecture or speech than read about the same material in a textbook.			
19.	I am good at working and solving jigsaw puzzles and mazes.			
20.	I grip objects in my hands during learning periods.			
21.	I prefer listening to the news on the radio rather than reading about it in the newspaper.			
22.	I prefer obtaining information about an interesting subject by reading about it.			
23.	I feel very comfortable touching others, hugging, handshaking, etc.			
24.	I follow oral directions better than written ones.			
Total each column of numbers to find your stronger sensory preference.		Visual Total	Auditory Total	Tactile Total

SELF-ASSESSMENT 3

Experimental Learning Preferences

Each choice here captures an aspect of how people prefer to learn. Think about each choice in relation to yourself and circle the number in front of all of those items that apply to you.

When I have to learn how to operate a new piece of equipment, I
1. watch someone who knows how to operate the equipment
2. carefully study the owner's manual
3. fiddle with the dials until I produce a desired effect
4. ignore the instructions and make the equipment suit my purposes

What I like best about lectures is (are)
1. the chance to record the ideas of an expert
2. a well-constructed argument about a controversial issue
3. illustrations using real-life examples
4. inspiration to come up with my own vision

My class notes usually look like
1. faithful recordings of what the instructor said
2. notes embellished with my own questions and evaluations
3. outlines that capture key ideas
4. notes with drawings, doodles, and other loosely related ideas or images

I prefer assignments that involve
1. emotional expression
2. analysis and evaluation
3. solving practical problems
4. creative expression

In class discussion
1. I'm a watcher rather than a direct participant
2. I'm an active, sometimes argumentative, participant
3. I get involved, especially when we discuss real-life issues
4. I like to contribute ideas that no one else thinks about

I would rather work with
1. stories about individual lives
2. abstract ideas
3. practical problems
4. creative ideas

My learning motto is
1. "Tell me."
2. "Let me think this out for myself."
3. "Let me experiment."
4. "How can I do this uniquely?"

Interpretation: Look over your responses and add up the number of times you circled each number:
1. ___ *(learn by reflecting)*
2. ___ *(learn by critical thinking)*
3. ___ *(learn by doing)*
4. ___ *(learn by creative thinking)*

The alternative you circled the most is your preferred learning process. You may discover that you strongly favor a particular approach. Or you may find that your preferences are spread across several categories. Your experiences in college will help you develop your skills in all areas so you will become more flexible and more resourceful.

Your Journal

REFLECT

1. A Matter of Style

You have had the opportunity to complete self-assessments designed to capture your strengths and style.

- List your strengths and weaknesses across the inventories.

___

- What new insights do you have about your learning potential?

___

- Did you learn anything that was distressing to you?

___

- Considering your whole profile, what is one positive change you might make based on your knowledge that will enhance your success?

___

2. The Deep End of the Pool

You probably recognized when you read about deep and surface learning that how comfortable you are as a learner may depend on the context. For example, you may easily comprehend complex ideas in a subject that you find intrinsically interesting. When subjects don't intrigue you, your efforts may feel shallow.
Think about the courses you are registered for this semester.

- Rank the courses in terms of how deeply you plan to learn in the courses.
- See if you can identify the factors that will influence your decision in each course. For example,
  - Is the course intrinsically interesting?
  - Are you drawn to the teaching style of the instructor?
  - Is a good performance in the course essential for making progress in your major?
- If you get into a bind this term, can you withdraw from the course in which your learning is the most shallow?

DO

1. Connect with a Special Teacher

Make an appointment with the instructor who seems most approachable to you. Interview that instructor and see if you can find out the following information:

- How did your instructor's interest in the discipline begin?

___

- What does your instructor remember about being a first-year college student from personal experience?

___

- What advice would the instructor offer on how to get the most from college and how to avoid pitfalls?

___

- How would your instructor describe his own learning style, and how does that influence course planning?

___

- How good is the match between the instructor's intention and your learning style?

___

Your Journal

2. Review a Syllabus

Consult the syllabus from the course you expect to be the most difficult for you. Examine it carefully, then try to predict how the class will proceed. What clues does the syllabus offer about how well the class demands will fit with your learning style? Ask yourself questions like these:

- "How labor intensive will the course be?"
- "Where will the peak periods of effort occur?"
- "How should I pace my reading?"
- "Will there be an opportunity to develop my group work skills?"
- "How can I connect with the instructor if I run into a problem?"

THINK CRITICALLY

1. The Stylish Major

You have probably given some thought to the kind of major for which you would be best suited. Think about whether the major you've declared or to which you're most inclined is best suited to your learning style.

- What major are you considering?
- What intelligences fit best with this major?
- What sensory preferences might work best in this major?
- What learning process might be most emphasized in this major: reflection, active learning, critical thinking, or creative thinking?
- Does your personality style lend itself to the demands of the career?
- What is your conclusion about how well you might be suited to this major based on your learning style?

2. Career Cruising on the Web

Instead of starting with the careers that you have been considering, go at it from another direction. Conduct a web search to identify five career options that would fit well with your learning style. Be sure to include some unconventional career choices. Explain what you think the connection is between the career choice and your learning style.

CREATE

1. Everything I Need to Know I Plan to Learn in College

Robert Fulghum wrote a wonderful book entitled *Everything I Need to Know I Learned in Kindergarten* that emphasized simple truths about success that we learn in childhood. Write down ten simple truths that might serve as the draft for a college-level version of his book. Especially if your personality style leans toward greater structure, your ten simple truths may be useful to post somewhere near your preferred study area.

2. Your Learning Metaphor

Think about what it feels like for you to learn in the college classroom. Do you feel like a sponge, soaking up every detail you can? Do you feel like a juggler? A prisoner? A butterfly? Are there other metaphors that describe your student experience? Describe or draw your metaphor and explain its significance. Go one step further and think about what your metaphor communicates regarding your personality style.

5 Expand Your Thinking Skills

© Digital Vision/Getty Images

KNOW YOURSELF

ONE OF YOUR PRIMARY PURPOSES IN COLLEGE is to become a better thinker. In this chapter, you'll explore ways to move beyond memorization to refine your thinking skills, including improving critical thinking, developing strong arguments, solving problems, making sound decisions, and becoming more creative. To get a current picture of your thinking skills, place a check mark next to only those items that apply to you.

- I can describe how critical thinking styles differ.
- I know how to ask good questions.
- I argue well.
- I use systematic strategies to solve problems.
- I practice an open mindset to improve my quality of life.
- I regularly make sound decisions.
- I can avoid routine thinking problems that prevent good decisions.
- I strive to be creative.

College will demand new ways of thinking to help your survive current challenges and prepare for the future.

CHAPTER OUTLINE

Think Critically

Ask Questions
Offer Criticism
Critical Thinking and the Internet

Reason

Make the Right Inferences
Learn How to Handle Claims
Refine Your Reasoning

Solve Problems

Find the IDEAL Solution
Acquire Problem-Solver Characteristics
Practice Mindfulness

Make Good Decisions

Avoid Snap Decisions
Expand Narrow Thinking
Contain Sprawling Thinking
Clarify Fuzzy Thinking
Recognize Factors in Good Decision Making

Think Creatively

Break the Locks
Foster Creativity
Discover "Flow"

Images of College Success

Anne Swift

An ordinary person might have been daunted by the setback, but Anne Swift turned major disappointment into a thriving career even before she graduated from college (Karlin 2006). When she found that she had trouble balancing her computer on her lap while riding on a train, she solved the problem by designing a flexible keyboard. A first-year student at the University of Western Ontario, she then began the arduous process of filing for a patent. Unfortunately, she discovered that someone else filed the idea during the period it took her to learn how to protect her intellectual property.

Rather than curse her fate, Swift turned her ingenuity in solving problems to securing patents and founded Young Inventors International to help other inventors under age thirty-five avoid similar frustration and disappointment. The organization has more than five hundred members from all over the world who benefit from a variety of activities that foster entrepreneurial spirit. Workshops, newsletters, and social gatherings are the vehicles through which young inventors can smooth out the rocky process of getting their ideas to the marketplace. The organization also helps young inventors locate corporate sponsors or mentors to assist them.

Swift's entrepreneurial spirit was evident even before college. As a high school junior she created and ran businesses involving database management and tutoring. She graduated with highest distinction in economics and political science from the University of Toronto and currently is pursuing an advanced degree in decision science from Carnegie-Mellon University. She consults as a motivational speaker and spends several hours a week raising funds for her nonprofit organization. To maximize success, she suggests first-year students get informed and get connected (Swift 2006). The more you know through reading the newspaper, the web, and other sources, the better your opportunities to come up with innovative ideas. Swift always carries a notebook to capture any insights that could turn into viable patents.

Anne Swift Enterprises, Inc.

ANN SWIFT'S problem-solving skills launched a promising career even before graduation from college.

Learning to think well provides a solid foundation for succeeding in college assignments and in any current or future career. As you read, think about the Six Strategies for Success listed to the left and how this chapter can help you maximize success in these important areas, particularly in building competence.

Think Critically

College may not prepare you for a specific career but it will teach you how to think more effectively, which in turn will prepare you for a broad range of career choices. During college you will learn innumerable facts and concepts that you might believe you would never use in your career, but the powerful by-product of that process should be refinement of your thinking skills. The array of courses that you take will provide much practice in developing critical thinking, reasoning, and problem solving. Along the way you also will make significant decisions and experience your creative potential. Let's explore the ways that college will help you become a more effective and powerful thinker.

You've probably heard the term *critical thinking*. It refers to the use of purposeful, reasoned thinking to reach your goals (Halpern 1997). Among other benefits, when you think critically you improve your ability to learn and retain new information. Clearly, this will benefit you in college and beyond.

The complexities of life in the twenty-first century underscore the need for critical thinking skills. Conserving the environment, managing nuclear energy, and remaining a competitive economic force are just a few of the tasks that require our best collective thinking. Such concerns have prompted national discussions about the role of colleges in helping citizens develop better thinking skills. One aim of a liberal arts education is to help you develop broad critical-thinking skills by sampling the various ways of thinking required in different disciplines (Ratcliff, Johnson, and Gaff 2004).

Different disciplines tend to approach critical thinking in distinctive ways. For example, the natural sciences often emphasize critical thinking skills as they relate to problem solving. The humanities focus on the critical analysis of expressive works.

Exposure to various disciplines should help you develop a broad base of perspectives that will serve as the basis for expert critical thinking. Your own knack for critical thinking will depend on your learning style and the successes you've had in various thinking challenges. For example, your ability to be effective as a critical thinker will vary with the commitment you make to study a discipline in depth. In some situations, your intrinsic interest in the topic will make it easy for you to grapple with the main ideas. In other situations, the content may seem hard to penetrate, so it may be more manageable to engage at a more shallow level.

> ***Two percent of the people think; three percent of the people think they think; and ninety-five percent of the people would rather die than think.***
>
> George Bernard Shaw
> *Nineteenth-century Irish playwright and literary critic*

© Carol Cable. Used with permission of the cartoonist.

Potter (2005) characterized three critical thinking styles that differ in their strategic success. "Information avoiders" engage in very little critical thinking; "they keep their minds on autopilot almost all of the time." Such individuals tend to go along with other people's opinions. They look for information that confirms what they already know and often feel overwhelmed by incoming data. "Consumers" are good at gathering information but don't tend to fare as well when the thinking challenge goes beyond memorization. They prefer their knowledge already processed. In contrast, "strategists" like to engage with information. They like to dig deep, play with ideas, and develop fresh insights. Figure 5.1, "Three Types of Thinkers," details how these knowledge styles differ. In addition, Self-Assessment 1, "The Critical Difference," on page 142 gives you an opportunity to evaluate how well your characteristics match those of good strategic thinkers.

Ask Questions

One sign of a good critical thinker is the ability to ask on-target questions. When you were little, you were probably constantly asking questions. But as you got older, you may have acquired more passive learning habits. Unfortunately, if you haven't been asking questions often, these skills may be dormant.

The problem may be fear of embarrassment. You may think of good questions to ask but worry about what others will think of you. Perhaps the instructor will think your question comes from left field. Or maybe other students will think you are showing off what you know. The problem with worrying so much about what others think is that you sacrifice chances to improve your own thinking and speaking skills. It's *your* education. If you don't take risks, you won't get to develop your mind as much as you deserve. The Journal activity "A Question a Day" on page 146 provides the opportunity to brush up on your question-asking skills.

> ***The start of finding great answers is asking good questions.***
> Anne Swift
> *Founder of Young Inventors International*

Another problem students have is not being sure what kind of questions to ask. Your question type will depend on what kind of information you are trying to learn. Your question can:

- *Read the lines.* These questions concentrate on identifying critical features or concepts. *What are the most important ideas being presented?*
- *React to the lines.* These questions facilitate an emotional response to the content. *How does the issue or concept make you feel?*
- *Read between the lines.* These questions emphasize your ability to analyze the content into component parts. *What factors explain how the key ideas developed?*
- *Read beyond the lines.* These questions prompt you to think about alternatives or future possibilities. *What difference will the ideas make in the long run* (Strong et al. 2002)?

Suppose you are studying the history of cartooning in an arts appreciation course. What kinds of questions illustrate these distinctions?

- *Read the lines.* What role does cartooning play in modern culture?
- *React to the lines.* What range of emotions do cartoons stir?
- *Read between the lines.* What political agenda regarding conflict in the Middle East might be expressed by a particular editorial cartoon?
- *Read beyond the lines.* Would you anticipate that cartoons will become more or less powerful as agents of social change over the next decade?

FIGURE 5.1 Three Types of Thinkers

Information Avoiders . . .	Consumers	Strategists
• often miss the point • don't like to try new things • rely on short-term memory strategies rather than more meaningful long-term learning • don't check their intuitions against the facts • avoid developing new ways to categorize information • feel overwhelmed by new information • reject uncertain or complex ideas • make rapid decisions to escape cognitive discomfort	• struggle with identifying the most critical elements of a message • memorize facts as "commodities" • rely heavily on expert opinion • prefer direction by others over self-direction • less adept at constructing new categories of information • adept at managing emotions while coping with information • concentrate on ways to reduce additional mental effort • favor efficiency over accuracy processing when the effort intensifies	• can distinguish central ideas from nuances • capable of memorizing and recalling detail for long periods of time • intrigued by the challenge of creative problem-solving • adept at creating new categories of information • transforms negative emotions into additional motivation to achieve goals • energized by complexity and chaos • favor accuracy over efficiency, rarely jumping to conclusions

From V. R. Ruggiero, Beyond Feelings: A Guide to Critical Thinking, *4th edition Copyright © 1995 by Mayfield Publishing Company.*

Get your curiosity out in the open. If you recapture your enthusiasm for asking questions, your college years will be more interesting and fun. A special kind of thrill occurs when your thinking generates good questions. Have you ever gotten chills when your question elicits a "Good question!" response from your instructor? "Expand Your Resources: "I Have a Question" gives some more tips on how to ask good questions.

Although instructors may reassure you that "there's no such thing as a stupid question," there are *unwelcome* questions. These include questions that detract from the momentum of the class, focus more on self-concerns than on the needs of the class, or demonstrate that the questioner has failed to pay attention. See "Build Competence: It's Not Therapy," for some strategies to help you discern if your questions stray off course.

© Royalty-Free/CORBIS

A student asking a question in class should look confident and at ease

Offer Criticism

Dr. Gray shuts off the videotape of the president's State of the Union address, then turns to the class and says, "What do you think?" Jeff dreads moments like this, because the question feels so open-ended. He's never sure what instructors want.

When a teacher offers you a chance to practice the higher-order skills of thinking critically and evaluating, it's easy to feel intimidated. However, some strategies can help you:

1. *Decide whether you like what you're being asked to judge.* Your general reaction can set the stage for detailed analysis later on. For example, were you smiling or frowning during the State of the Union address?
2. *Look for both positive and negative attributes.* Some people unnecessarily limit their thinking by focusing only on the attributes that support their emotional response. If you were thrilled by what the president said, try to find some weaknesses in the address. If you were dissatisfied, look also for positive features in what you heard.
3. *Use criteria to stimulate your thinking.* To what degree is the work you are evaluating

effective	*sufficient*
efficient	*adequate*
reasonable	*logical*
beautiful	*sensitive*
practical	*accurate*
thought-provoking	*stimulating*
justifiable	*comprehensive*
understandable	*relevant*

   Which of the criteria would apply to a presidential address? A work of art? A symphony? A public policy?
4. *Use examples to support your judgment.* Expect to explain your judgment. Which phrases or examples in the State of the Union stayed with you? What made the examples compelling? The Journal activity "The Great Debate" on page 147 gives you an opportunity to hone your critical-thinking skills.

EXPAND YOUR RESOURCES

I Have a Question

You can improve your analytic skills by learning to ask questions that will help you break open the ideas you're studying (Browne and Keeley 1990). Here are some questions that can help you strengthen these important skills

- What are the issues and the conclusion?
- What are the reasons?
- What words or phrases are ambiguous?
- Are there value conflicts?
- What assumptions are being made?
- What is the evidence?
- Are there other ways to explain the results?
- Are there flaws in the reasoning?
- Is any information missing?
- Do the conclusions fit the reasons?
- How do the results fit with my own values?

From Browne, M. Neil; Keeley, Stuart M., *Asking the Right Questions: A Guide to Critical Thinking,* 7th Edition. Copyright © 2004, p.13. Adampted by permission of Pearson Education, Inc., Upper Saddle River, NJ.

Critical Thinking and the Internet

The Internet has transformed nearly every aspect of our lives. Although it has dramatically expanded our access to information, surfing the net can produce a quagmire of data. An uncritical user can end up with too much, too little, or invalid information.

This problem poses a special threat for students who like the convenience of doing research on the Internet but may not have developed the critical-thinking skills necessary to separate the valid and valuable from the mass of material than can show up on the computer screen. Thinking critically about your search strategy will make your surfing profitable.

Locating What You Need Allow yourself a reasonable amount of time to play with different strategies to produce the best results. Identify and enter key concepts in a search engine. If you are operating in a particular discipline-based database, you may have the best luck by entering the basic concepts of the discipline to begin tracking down information. If you get an excess number of hits, refine your search by adding more parameters.

For example, you might limit your search to articles printed only in the last five years. Or you might conduct a Boolean search by combining two key terms. A Boolean search that specifies one term, then "OR," then another term will hit any article in which either term is present. "First ladies" or "foreign policy" will produce a broad search, identifying any online resource that addresses either term. By contrast, using "AND" instead of "OR" will narrow your hits to any resources that deal both with first ladies *and* foreign policy. You should be able to narrow down efficiently which first ladies had an influence on foreign policy.

What happens if there are too few hits to be helpful? Go back to the conceptual drawing board and expand your search. Think about an overarching term in which the key concept you have already tried could be embedded. Suppose you need to find information about an obscure tree disease for a botany class. If you come up empty-handed by entering the name of the disease, enlarge your search to "tree disease." Usually, however, the problem is too much rather than too little information.

> ***Curiosity is the very basis of education and if you tell me that curiosity killed the cat, I say only the cat died nobly.***
>
> Arnold Edinborough
> *Twentieth-century English publisher*

Finding the Best Data Determining what is sufficiently high quality is another challenge. What are some pointers to ensure your resources will be credible?

- Avoid opinion pieces that can't be substantiated. The Internet does not police itself.
- The Internet is the perfect vehicle for anyone with a point of view and a computer to try to capture and persuade an audience. Be vigilant about entries that appear to offer facts that can't be corroborated.
- Identify the author and verify the author's expertise. The most valuable websites will be those that present information by experts in the specific discipline in which you are conducting your search. Individuals with scholarly degrees, affiliations with well-known institutions, or well-established reputations will be easier for you to claim as credible sources. If the author's name is present, you can do an additional search to identify the author's credentials if those are not available on the website. Web pages that do not credit an author are suspect. Similarly, blogs contain a distinctly personal perspective that probably won't earn a place in your harvest of sound data.
- Check the date. Information on older websites may be sufficiently outdated that your including them will demonstrate that your search wasn't thorough.
- Trace information to its original source to strengthen your confidence. One of the best features of the Internet is that it can direct you toward original citations in published journals. Many of those may be online.
- Don't be taken in by aesthetically pleasing websites. Websites can be highly attractive and seductive, even when the information they contain isn't sound. Look for indicators that the scholarship is solid, such as well-defined concepts, charts and tables, sponsorship by reputable organizations, and so forth. Although the Internet contains a bounty of useful information, it also is a playground for con artists and hoax perpetrators who may try to entice you through compelling graphics and offers that are truly too good to be true. Evaluate the potential gems you discover by going beyond the introductory website. Consider visiting http://www.urbanlegends.com where you can find some examples of unfounded claims that have been debunked.

BUILD COMPETENCE

It's Not Therapy

Greg really looked forward to his college success class. He saw it as a wonderful opportunity to sort out events that had happened in his academic life to make him the successful student he had become.

Nearly every topic the instructor introduced had personal relevance to him, and he felt compelled to ask many questions and share his personal experiences with the class. Yet he noticed Dr. Turner's attitude toward him had begun to shift. In the beginning, she smiled and seemed genuinely excited about the examples he provided. More recently, she quickly shifted attention away by asking, "Does anyone *else* have an example?" He wasn't sure what to make of it.

Instructors provide cues about how solid your questions and contributions are in relation to their goals. Limited eye contact, diverting attention to others, and deferring your question until everyone else has spoken are signs from your instructor that your questioning skills may be overactive. When you see these signs, turn your critical-thinking skills to careful analysis of the questions that the other students are asking, to provide balance to the class.

- Don't settle for the first data you find. Although it may be easy to harvest information from Wikipedia, the open-source encyclopedia that consumers help to build and sustain, many professors will not accept citations from this source because they believe it is prone to distortion and error, whether your actual citation has that problem or not.

Reason

Sometimes you may find that you don't have all the information you need to understand a phenomenon, make a prediction, or solve a problem. Through reasoning, you can derive the missing elements. Reasoning represents a special kind of critical thinking that you will often have to use as your course demands get more sophisticated.

Good reasoners effectively make inferences, use logic, and create and defend arguments (Beyer 1998). Good reasoning isn't always easy, but you can learn it and get better at it.

Make the Right Inferences

As you head for class early in the morning during finals week, suppose you come across a student whom you don't know who is out cold, sprawled across the sidewalk, his books scattered on the ground (Halonen and Gray 2001). What do you think? There are many inferences you might draw based on what you observed. *Inferences* are interpretations that you derive from processing cues in a situation. For example, you could infer that your fallen campus colleague might be:

Man is the Reasoning Animal. Such is the claim. I think it is open to dispute.
Mark Twain
Nineteenth-century American humorist

1. exhausted from studying for finals
2. suffering from a serious health problem
3. passed out from drinking until the wee hours
4. a psychology major doing an experiment

All these inferences are plausible, meaning that they are logical, potentially accurate ways to explain what you saw. However, it's likely that one explanation is better than the others. You constantly make inferences, such as:

- Your roommate is scowling, so you infer she failed a test.
- You find the dishes piled up, so you infer that you'll have to do them.
- You get an unsigned note asking you to go out for coffee, and you infer who was most likely to have invited you.

Your interpretations of the events around you are based on your collected experiences.

Therefore, your inferences will reflect that experience and sometimes produce biases in interpretation. Go back to the example of the fallen colleague. If you inferred that the individual might be recovering from a hangover, your past experiences may have created a predisposition or bias in how you make sense of what you see in this situation. You may have heard about a huge frat party the night before, where everyone got totally wasted. But aren't you forgetting the books on the ground? Why would someone who is passed out from drinking too much be carrying books? To test this proposition further, imagine that the fallen colleague is female, not male. How does changing the gender of the person change your interpretive bias? Would you assume a woman is as likely to pass out from drinking too much? You can see how bias and previous knowledge can shape and possibly distort the reality that you experience.

Your ability to make accurate inferences is probably very good in most situations. However, inferences can be tricky. Notice in the examples given how easy it is to be wrong. In fact, think about a recent situation in which you jumped to the wrong conclusion.

A faulty inference was probably to blame. Sometimes inferences become *assumptions*, inferences that we accept as the truth. An assumption is not based on fact or reason and may be false. You may not recognize that you're operating from a faulty assumption until you learn otherwise.

© John Coletti Photography

What happened here? Your conclusions come from inferences you make from the clues in the scene.

Learn How to Handle Claims

Instructors may challenge you to sort fact from fiction. They may ask you to judge the *validity* (truthfulness) of a *claim* (a statement that can be either true or false but not both) (Epstein 2000). Claims are different from *facts*, which are truths that can't be disputed.

> *Fact:* The moon is full at least once a month.
> *Claim:* The full moon makes people a little crazy.

Notice how the claim is debatable and requires evidence before we can determine its validity; the fact cannot be challenged. When you evaluate a claim, you have three choices:

1. Accept the claim.
2. Reject the claim.
3. Suspend judgment until you have more information.

How will you rise to this challenge?

When to Accept a Claim There are three circumstances in which it's reasonable to accept a claim:

1. *Personal experience.* Trust your personal experience when your confidence level is high and there isn't a good contradictory explanation. For example, you may have been warned about the "freshman fifteen," the tendency for students to put on weight during the first year of college. Despite the warning, you notice the scale is starting to creep upward, which you attribute to increased snacking during study sessions. Although there may be some exceptions, you may notice that many of your peers are struggling with extra weight gain as well. Your personal experience suggests that the claim that the first year can layer on pounds seems true.
2. *Trustworthy expert.* If a claim is made by someone with a trustworthy track record or other similar credentials such as expertise, it's reasonable to accept the claim as true. This includes claims made in reputable journals and references. For example, claims about damage from smoking that are reported in the *New England Journal of Medicine* are usually trustworthy. Claims by your next-door neighbor about the value of vitamin B may not be as valid.

3. *Reliable media sources.* Unless the media source is going to profit from the claim presented, it's reasonable to accept the claim. For example, local weather forecasters regularly make claims about future weather patterns that generally are accurate. Some newscasters demonstrate their reliability with the accuracy of their predictions. However, just because someone is on the news doesn't make that person a reliable source.

When to Question a Claim Question claims that:

- *come from "unnamed sources."* If you can't verify the source, you shouldn't readily accept the claim.
- *confer an advantage.* Experts sometimes make large profits by supporting certain claims. Be suspicious of claims that can be linked to payoff. Jennifer Love Hewitt may be a beauty, but her endorsement of a health product is likely to be more of an advantage to her than to you.
- *are used to sell a product.* Advertisements and commercials are always making claims, which are often reputed to be based on solid research. However, the research may be biased, or there may be contradictory findings that are not reported. For example, influenced by claims in advertising, millions of Americans take herbal supplements to enhance their memory. Only recently has conflicting evidence suggested that the supplements are a waste of time and money.
- *offer personal experience as "proof."* Human memory can sometimes introduce distortions that can lead you to endorse a claim that simply isn't true. For example, the psychologist Elizabeth Loftus (1993) demonstrated that people can be tricked into recalling events in their childhood that never happened. The people in her study confidently recalled getting lost in a mall based on hearing others report the experience. Loftus suggested that we "reconstruct" memories that represent a blend of the truth, perceptual distortions, and wishes.
- *appeal to common beliefs and practice.* Just because "everybody does it" doesn't make it right or truthful.
- *use language in misleading ways.* Politicians are often accused of putting a "spin" on their claims. For example, they might report that the "vast majority" of Americans believe in vouchers for private school, when the actual statistic in favor might be 51 percent at the time. Beware of overblown language that can disguise the truth.

To swallow and follow, whether old doctrine or new propaganda, is a weakness still dominating the human mind.

Charlotte Gilman Perkins
Twentieth-century American social critic

Form Strong Arguments In formal reasoning, an *argument* is a set of claims. The argument begins with *premises*, initial claims that lead to a final claim called the *conclusion* of the argument (Epstein 2000). A good argument is one in which the premises (1) are true and (2) lead logically to the truth of the conclusion. Good arguments are also called *strong* or *valid* arguments.

Here's an example of a good argument:

Premise: All healthy dogs have fur.
Premise: Spot is a healthy dog.
Conclusion: Therefore, Spot has fur.

Some good arguments are reasonable because the premises and conclusion are sound, even though the conclusion may not be as absolute as the one in the example.

In most cases, these plausible arguments deal with probable outcomes instead of definitive ones.

Premise: Most dogs who live outside have fleas.
Premise: Spot lives outside in a doghouse.
Conclusion: Therefore, Spot probably has fleas.

Spot could be the rare exception, but the conclusion is logical if the first two premises are true. Here are some simple suggestions that will help you develop the most persuasive arguments:

1. Be sure that the conclusion follows logically from the premises.
2. Leave out faulty or dubious premises.
3. Use precise language to pinpoint your claim. (Vague or ambiguous language makes your position easier to challenge.)
4. Avoid making claims you can't prove.

The Journal Activity "Claims Detector" on page 146 allows you to practice evaluating claims made by commercials and to look for premises and conclusions.

BUILD COMPETENCE

Offensive Defense

What began as a simple exchange about an application of supply-and-demand principles in their marketing class had suddenly escalated. Tony was feeling pretty frustrated that Taneesha not only didn't understand what he was saying but kept asking for examples that would provide convincing evidence for his point of view. No matter what example he generated, Taneesha rejected the example, shaking her head. In the heat of the moment, Tony lost his cool: "Well, who's doing better in this course, then? I got an A on the last exam. What did you get?" When he calmed down, he recognized that he had violated a fundamental principle of making good arguments. You attack the argument, not the arguer.

Form Counterarguments In many classes you may be asked to find flaws in an argument. A counterargument challenges an argument by showing:

1. a premise is false
2. the conclusion is false
3. the reasoning is weak or faulty

In Figure 5.2, "Arguments: The Good, the Bad, and the Goofy," see whether you can determine exactly what weakens each argument.

Some counterargument strategies are ineffective. For example, ridicule is not a good way to counterargue. Ridicule or criticism of the person making the argument disrupts communication without improving anyone's understanding. Refer to "Build Competence: Offensive Defense" for an illustration.

Another ineffective strategy is restating the original argument in a distorted way and then disproving the distortion. Suppose you are debating with a classmate the need for welfare reform to improve employment opportunities. Your classmate introduces a recent study that suggests children on welfare perform poorly in school. He concludes that past welfare reform has been harmful to academic achievement and concludes that there is no basis to believe additional reform will enhance children's achievement. Note the drift and distortion in the argument. To be effective, your counterargument must accurately represent the original argument and defend against only that argument.

Refine Your Reasoning

You can improve your reasoning skills in the following ways:

Be Willing to Argue You may have to present a position in a term paper, in a speech, or in answer to a complex question in class. Students study reasoning as a formal science in logic classes, but you'll certainly have opportunities to create and defend arguments in many other formal and informal situations. Don't shrink from those opportunities, even if you have negative feelings about the word *argument* based on the tension that you've felt when in conflict with a friend or loved one. Intellectual arguments can generate passion, too, but they need not have the same emotional intensity or feelings of personal risk as differences you have with loved ones.

Use Inductive and Deductive Reasoning There are two types of argument: induction and deduction (Porter 2002). *Induction* involves generalizing from specific

FIGURE 5.2 Arguments: The Good, the Bad, and the Goofy

See if you can spot ways to challenge the following arguments.

© Sidney Harris. Reproduced by permission of ScienceCartoonsPlus.com.

Example 1
Premise: All cats have four legs.
Premise: I have four legs.
Conclusion: Therefore, I am a cat.
Both premises are true, but together they do not produce a logical conclusion, because the first premise does not state that *only* cats have four legs. The conclusion must follow logically from the premises.

Example 2
Premise: All birds have fur.
Premise: Tweetie is a bird.
Conclusion: Tweetie has fur.
The first premise is false, so the conclusion is implausible.

Example 3
Premise: Good dogs sit on command.
Premise: Spot sits on command.
Conclusion: Spot is a good dog.
Although the premises may both be true, the conclusion isnt su pported. Spot may engage in other behavior that makes him a bad dog.

Example 4
Premise: The dog show winner is the best dog in the country.
Premise: Spot won first place in the dog show.
Conclusion: Spot is the best dog in the country.
The conclusion follows logically, but what exactly is meant by "best"? And is the first claim likely to be true? There are many dog shows every year. Was the show that Spot won really the Super Bowl of dog shows? In other words, the first premise is suspect, so the conclusion is as well.

instances to broad principles. For example, perhaps you really enjoyed your first college foreign language class. Based on that experience, you might reason inductively that *all* language classes in college are great. Notice that your conclusion or rule—your *induction*—might be incorrect, because your next course may turn out to be disappointing. Inductive arguments are never 100 percent certain. They can be weak or strong.

In contrast, *deduction* moves from general situations or rules to specific predictions or applications. Deductive reasoning parallels the hypothesis testing procedures used in the sciences. For example, your chemistry professor may ask you to identify an unknown substance. By applying specific strategies of analysis, you narrow the possibilities until you know what the substance is. A deductive argument is 100 percent true if the premises are true and the reasoning is sound. When the premises are untrue or the logical connection between the premises and the conclusion is shaky, a deductive argument may be false. Look at the deductive examples in Figure 5.3, "Using

FIGURE 5.3 Using Induction and Deduction

From specific observations →	to general principles	=	INDUCTIVE REASONING
1. Maria has red hair and a bad temper. →	Most redheads probably have bad tempers.		
2. Waking up on the past three Mondays was a hard thing to do. →	Waking up on Mondays will probably always be a hard thing to do.		
3. T. S. Eliot's *The Wasteland* is a masterpiece. →	The rest of Eliot's poetry should be impressive.		
From broad generalizations, observations →	**to specific conclusions**	=	**DEDUCTIVE REASONING**
1. Butlers tend to have evil minds. →	The butler may have been the murderer!		
2. All cats have scratchy tongues. →	This is a cat. It must have a scratchy tongue.		
3. My roommate Ted seems really cranky after math class. →	He may have flunked his math test.		

Induction and Deduction." Is any one of these arguments completely convincing? Why or why not?

Check Your Assumptions It's easy to reach wrong conclusions from wrong assumptions. For example, the satirist Jonathan Swift caused a stir in the eighteenth century when he proposed one solution for two serious problems facing British society: too many orphaned children and not enough food. Swift proposed that both problems could be solved if the orphans were eaten! Those who *assumed* Swift was putting forward a serious position were outraged. Those who carefully examined Swift's real purpose, and discovered that he meant to bring serious attention to these social problems, were amused by his wit and sensitized to the problem. Identify your assumptions and then do your best to verify them.

Know Your Own Bias We all have strong preferences and prejudices that may prevent us from evaluating an argument fairly. By acknowledging your own preferences and prejudices, you can increase the likelihood of coming up with more effective arguments. For example, if you know that you feel strong sympathies for single parents, you can take this bias into account when you evaluate government policies that affect their lives. Good reasoners guard against their own "soft spots" to increase their objectivity. For example, if you know your political leanings are conservative, you may be less likely to scrutinize arguments and claims that come from well-known conservatives. You can guard against your political soft spot by paying even closer attention to the claims made by those with whom you fundamentally disagree.

Know the Lingo Missimer (2005) suggests some phrases to help you launch the analysis of an argument:

- I agree with the argument because. . .
- The argument could have been stronger. . .

- The reason supporting the argument is weak. . .
- The definition could be more precise. . .
- The author has not made assumptions explicit. . .

Take Time before Concluding Sometimes we short-circuit our reasoning. It's easy to get excited about a bright idea and stop the hard analytic work involved in thinking the problem through to the end. A premature judgment may work out, but it tends to make us even less exacting the next time we analyze a problem. Careful reasoners resist impulsive judgments. They thoroughly review an argument to make sure they have addressed all questions.

Solve Problems

The humorist Russell Baker once quipped, "I've had an unhappy life, thank God." His observation underscores the importance that problems play in building our character and resilience. You might think that living a problem-free existence would feel terrific.

Maybe it would . . . briefly. Problems add vigor and vibrancy to our lives; solid solutions bring a sense of accomplishment that makes the ordeal worthwhile. Wobbly or ineffective solutions provide an opportunity to learn new and better ways for the future.

Being in college will offer an array of problem-solving circumstances. Where do I get the cheapest textbooks? What field should be my major? How will I make friends who will support my academic goals and future dreams? How will I ever complete three term papers at the same time? Where can I park without getting a ticket? And the "Grand Problem" you will eventually have to solve: What will I do *after* college? Your experience in solving problems in college will be critical to your future success in professional life. See "Create Your Future: Career Connections" for how your reaction to solving problems can point you to a logical career choice.

Find the IDEAL Solution

Once a problem gets on your radar screen, it's tempting to hope that you can solve it without much thought. The fact is that good problem solving requires a great deal of thought, and a step-by-step approach often facilitates that thought process. Many people find it helpful to use a specific problem-solving system, such as the five-step IDEAL method (Bransford and Stein 1984). Let's see how that might apply to a common problem related to course scheduling.

> ***The shrewd guess, the fertile hypothesis, the courageous leap to a tentative conclusion—these are the most valuable coins of the thinker at work.***
>
> Jerome Bruner
> *Contemporary American Psychologist*

Look at a typical case. Then go to Journal activity "Your IDEAL" on page 147 for more practice applying this strategy to an issue in your life.

1. *Identify the problem.* Bernita discovered when she arrived at her first art appreciation class that her instructor had already started. The instructor looked distinctly displeased as Bernita took a seat in the back of the class. When she looked at her watch, Bernita discovered that she was two minutes late. Obviously, she didn't want to annoy her instructor by arriving late to class each day. How could she avoid being late?
2. *Define the problem.* Be as specific and comprehensive as you can in defining a problem. Outline the contributing factors. There are two parts to this problem. First is the fact that the professor is clearly a stickler about being on time to his class. The second is Bernita's lateness. Why does the professor start right on time? Does he always? What made Bernita late to class? Was her watch broken?

Was she carrying 60 pounds of books? Did she walk too slowly? Probably the main factor was the distance between the art class and the English class that Bernita had on the other side of the campus in the previous period. Even if she walked at top speed, she couldn't get to the art class on time.

Coming Up with Alternatives

These approaches may help you generate new ideas for resolving problems:

- Examine how you feel about the situation.
- Collect opinions about possible approaches.
- Research what the experts would do.
- Break the problem into smaller pieces.
- Think through the consequences of leaving the problem alone.
- Work backward from the preferred outcome.

3. *Explore alternative approaches.* Systematically gather and explore alternative solutions to isolate the best approach. Assuming that arriving late to class makes her uncomfortable enough to take action, what are some reasonable alternatives that Bernita could pursue? She can drop either class, or transfer into another section that prevents the conflict. She can talk to the instructor in her art class. Maybe there was something unusual about this day and he is usually more relaxed. He may be understanding about her arriving a couple of minutes late if he sees that there is a legitimate reason. Or she can ask the instructor to wait until she gets there (maybe not). Or perhaps she can talk to the English professor about leaving a couple of minutes early (maybe not). Manage Life, "Coming Up with Alternatives," suggests ways to generate solutions.
4. *Act on the best strategy.* Take specific action to resolve the problem. Include more than one strategy. Bernita decided to explain to her art instructor why she would be a few minutes late to class, added that she would do her best to get there on time, and asked for her instructor's support. The instructor verified that Bernita would be late only by two minutes and asked that she sit near the door to minimize disruptions. He also thanked Bernita for her courtesy.
5. *Look back to evaluate the effects.* The final step is to evaluate whether or not your solution works. You might be thrilled with how well it works and feel free to move on to your next challenge. Or you might discover that the solution didn't work. In this instance, Bernita's problem solving was successful. Her solution not only saved her from the trouble and expense of dropping the class but also gave her a better personal connection with her instructor. Complete Self-Assessment 2, "How Systematically Do I Solve Problems?" on page 144 to assess your own problem-solving strengths and weaknesses.

Acquire Problem-Solver Characteristics

Problem solvers tend to approach complex situations with a questioning attitude that can clarify the situation. For example, entrepreneur Anne Swift (2006) relies on "The Five Questions" to help her identify problems and get them resolved.

- **Who** . . . is affected? . . . should I talk to?
- **What** . . . are the issues? . . . are the resources?
- **Where** . . . is the problem? . . . can I find additional information?
- **When** . . . can I expect a solution? . . . can I move ahead?
- **Why** . . . is this an important challenge?

What are some other ways you can maximize your problem-solving skills (Whimbey and Lochhead 1991)?

- *Observe carefully.* Try to identify all the relevant factors in a problem from the outset. Superficial observation misses factors that hold keys to ultimate solutions. Careful observation involves analysis—identifying the relationships among the elements of the problem.

- *Stay positive and persistent.* Don't be beaten by frustration. Search for ways to make the struggle invigorating rather than frustrating.
- *Show concern for accuracy.* Pay attention to detail. It's easy to let small errors occur in moments of inattention. Take care not to leave out crucial information. Proofread statements and recheck calculations before submitting your work for review.

Practice Mindfulness

Developing the right frame of mind about possibilities is an essential ingredient in improving your ability to solve problems. There are many ways to practice mindfulness to improve your problem-solving skills (Dweck 2006, Langer 1997). Here are several that are particularly helpful in a college setting:

- *Create new categories.* We often dismiss things by categorizing them in a global way. For example, you might dismiss a "bad" instructor as not worthy of attention. However, if you look more closely at the various aspects of teaching, your perceptions will be richer. For example, perhaps the instructor's delivery is plodding but his choice of words is rich. Or his ideas are delivered without enthusiasm but his precise examples always make things easier to understand. A closer look can make us less judgmental and more tolerant.
- *Take control over context.* When you feel like your own options have been constrained, reexamine your circumstances to see whether you have overlooked some aspect of the situation that could make it more palatable or more rewarding. Anne Swift's refusal to adjust to given working conditions fueled her inventiveness to develop a flexible keyboard, giving her greater control over her working conditions.
- *Welcome new information.* We tend to disregard information that does not fit with what we already know. This is an especially important tendency to overcome when you conduct research. Staying open to new information maximizes your pool of ideas. You may begin with one idea of what you want to prove but find that another possibility is actually more exciting.
- *Use technology.* The world is at your mouse's command through the Internet. The World Wide Web offers unlimited examples of good and bad problem solving. The Journal activity "Creative Surfing" on page 149 explores what the Internet can tell you about human problem solving.
- *Maintain a growth mindset.* Be vigilant about the ways in which opportunities can lead to new learning. Even failure can provide powerful new insights that can help you more effectively in the long run. See "Clarify Values: Wounds that Reward" for an illustration.
- *Enjoy the process.* It's easy to become so single-minded about solving a problem that you forget to pay attention to the process of achieving it. Remember that the process is just as important as the outcome. At times the task before you may seem too large to finish. By taking a large project and breaking it into smaller, achievable deadlines and goals, you'll also stay mindful of the learning that occurs along the way. The Journal activity "Minding the Store" on page 146 will help you evaluate your mindfulness.

You see, but you do not observe.
Sherlock Holmes
Arthur Conan Doyle's nineteenth-century fictional detective

CLARIFY VALUES

Wounds that Reward

No one looks forward to failing, but sometimes the impact of "blowing it" can have a profound effect on your learning and, consequently, your attitude about failure. Take Celia's case. She went to a special evening lecture by one of her favorite professors. She had listened very casually, laughing at the jokes but not really taking anything in. When she approached the professor at the end to provide a gracious but empty compliment, the professor asked what she specifically liked about the lecture. Celia was sunk! It was embarrassing to be caught short. However, Celia used the opportunity to clarify her values of being honest and genuine. In the future she would commit to offering genuine feedback and to doing the hard listening and thinking that would justify good feedback. She was grateful to have failed the test with her professor for the long-term impact the experience provided.

Make Good Decisions

Solving problems often requires making good decisions. Some decisions have far-reaching consequences. For example, you decided where to go to college. To make that decision, you may have used some systematic criteria. Perhaps you wanted a college close to home with low tuition costs and specific majors. Or you may have decided to go to the campus you liked best when you visited. How satisfied you are now with your college experience may reflect how carefully you made that decision.

Four common problems interfere with good decision making (Swartz 2001). The following explores how these approaches might influence your own future career decisions.

Avoid Snap Decisions

We are inclined to make decisions too quickly, before we have had time to consider all of the options. Hasty decisions are much more likely when we are trying to solve short-term problems, leaving us vulnerable for long-term problems. You might take the first job offer you get. Although the offer might be a good match for your skills, such a quick decision precludes another alternative that might be even better.

Expand Narrow Thinking

We may simplify choices in a way that overlooks a broader array of options. Our rush to choose from column A or B may keep us from turning the page to see many other options in columns C–F. Many students feel pressured to establish their careers. You might decide advertising is the way to proceed and not consider any other options that might be more satisfying.

> ***One clear idea is too precious a treasure to lose.***
> Caroline Gilman
> *Nineteenth-century American writer*

Contain Sprawling Thinking

We may entertain too many options. By attending to too many possibilities, we may neglect the in-depth consideration that might make the best option stand out. If you find yourself making job interview appointments with more recruiters than you reasonably can prepare for, you may be suffering from thinking sprawl.

Clarify Fuzzy Thinking

We may not think through a problem carefully to isolate the key factors that will lead to a solution. Sadly, many students complete their majors using fuzzy thinking. They may graduate without any distinct ideas about what they can legitimately pursue as employment options.

But let's look at an example that might feel closer to home. If you find yourself struggling at midterm with diffuse feelings of failure, fuzzy thinking can be a problem. You can wallow in the mire or you can systematically think through what factors might be contributing to your problem. Perhaps you are taking too many credits to be successful? Maybe there is an instructor whose methods set your teeth on edge? You might be struggling from sleep deprivation linked to your roommates' snoring. Perhaps a broken heart might be distracting your concentration. The more specifically you can differentiate relevant factors, the more easily you can come up with a game plan that might address the issue.

"You take all the time you need, Larry."

Recognize Factors in Good Decision Making

In contrast, good decision makers know why they need to make a decision and examine as many options as appropriate. They consider both short- and long-term consequences of their decisions.

Good decision makers articulate the pros and cons of each option and weigh the advantages and disadvantages according to their values.

They choose an option that makes the most sense given the significance of the decision.

Making decisions involves not only using higher-order thinking skills but also integrating those skills with your own values and knowledge about yourself. Good decisions solve problems and make your life better. Bad ones often make a mess. See "Manage Life: The Pull Toward Bad Decisions" for some additional tips on avoiding bad decisions. Then complete the Journal activity "No Regrets" on page 146 to explore how those principles apply to your own life.

Think Creatively

College abounds with opportunities for you to build self-esteem by expanding your creative abilities. Start to become more creative by motivating yourself to exercise your creativity whenever you can. Seizing opportunities to develop your creative flair will go a long way toward building your self-confidence and self-esteem.

Creative people tend to have some common characteristics (Perkins 1984):

- They actively pursue experiences that are aesthetically pleasing. For example, they enjoy experiencing beauty in art or elegance in a scientific theory.
- They enjoy taking a unique approach to research, choosing new and exciting topics rather than going over more familiar territory that other students might address.
- They love the process of creating. For example, creative students may feel as good when they turn their work in as when they get back a successful grade.
- They are flexible and like to play with problems. Although creativity is hard work, the work goes more smoothly when taken lightly; humor greases the wheels (Goleman, Kaufmann, and Ray 1992). Playing helps them stay open to more possibilities and disarms the inner censor that often condemns ideas as off base.

Despite the stereotype that creative people are eccentric, most strive to evaluate their work fairly. Whether they use an established set of criteria or generate their own, they themselves ultimately judge the value of what they have created. Creative students thrive when they think of guidelines for assignments as a launching point for their imaginations. To evaluate your own creative style, complete Self-Assessment 3, "My Creative Profile" on page 145.

Break the Locks

Many people believe that they can't lead creative lives. You may be one of them. Despite childhoods filled with imaginative play, many of us surrender our sense of curiosity over time, harming our capacity for creativity. A variety of "mental locks" can prevent us from pursuing creative responses. Some of these locks and the "keys" for opening your mind include:

• I have to have the right answer.	Sometimes the "right" answer isn't as much fun or as satisfying as an alternative.
• I must be logical.	But I need to get in touch with my emotional side.
• I must follow the rules.	But breaking the rules can be really liberating!
• I have to be practical.	But not in every situation.
• Play is frivolous and wastes time.	And I miss it! I want those feelings back!
• That's not my area.	But it could be!
• I must avoid ambiguity.	But ambiguity can open new doors.
• I can't appear to be foolish.	But foolishness can be fun.
• To err is wrong.	I'm designed to derail from time to time.
• I'm not creative.	But I could be!

A flexible attitude sets the stage for creativity in school and throughout your life.

Creativity is allowing yourself to make mistakes. Art is knowing which ones to keep.

Scott Adams
Contemporary American cartoonist

Adventure is worthwhile in itself.

Amelia Earhart
Twentieth-century American aviator

Foster Creativity

Psychologists affirm that all people can be creative if they adopt the right attitudes and behaviors (Sternberg and Lubart 1995). The following basic steps can contribute to more creative and fulfilling lives:

1. *Don't accept other people's blueprints.* Question assumptions. Constantly look through and around problems to find a new approach. By moving away from how most people approach things, you may find yourself in the lead. For example, if everyone executes a PowerPoint presentation for a speaking assignment in a class, you will stand out by using the blackboard or newsprint to support your key ideas. Think about how others will execute an assignment and, within reason, choose a course that makes your work stand out positively.
2. *Be vigilant about what others can't see.* Look for new and intriguing ways to redefine the environment. Use your unique past experiences to help you pick up on things that other people will miss.
3. *Differentiate the good from the bad.* Creative people will generate many possibilities but not all of them will be appropriate. Don't linger on the ideas that don't have strong potential.
4. *Take the plunge* before *you are an expert.* You don't really need to know absolutely everything about something before coming up with some new connections. In fact, sometimes too much knowledge can produce stereotyped ways of looking at the relevant facts and can lead to more mundane solutions.

CREATE YOUR FUTURE

Career Connections

As soon as she was old enough to work, Rachel pursued a string of jobs to give her some spending money. Whether she was a receptionist in a hair salon, a shoe clerk, or a waitress, she seemed to take special joy in identifying, figuring out, and solving problems. Her employers commented on her initiative and regularly benefited from the creative suggestions she came up with to improve customer service. It was no surprise to those who knew her that computer studies would be a perfect match for her talents in problem solving. Her employment history and her liberal arts training gave her just the right background to thrive in her major and set her sights appropriately on a career in software engineering. That job provided an endless string of fascinating problems for her to solve.

Andy was just like most students who cringed in horror when they learned they had to give their first speech in college. Much to his surprise, he actually enjoyed making his first class presentation. He liked the challenge of coming up with an original idea, building an argument, and defending his position when challenged by classmates. He recognized that his careful research made him a real expert for the first time and he liked the feeling. By the time his college career came to an end, he decided the career that was best suited for his needs was becoming a college professor, a career that would allow him to recapture regularly the great feeling of expertise that he was introduced to in that first college assignment.

The Pull Toward Bad Decisions

All of us make bad decisions from time to time. We are likely to commit common judgment errors that could be avoided when you know the traps (Halpern 1997). These tips are especially helpful from the standpoint of managing life more functionally and smoothly.

- **Overconfidence.** Because we tend to be overconfident about the correctness of our past decisions, we usually neglect to notice that a path not taken might have been better than the one we chose. For example, you may be convinced that you chose exactly the right place to start your college education. However, you can't be completely positive, because you won't have any way to compare how you might have felt starting on other campuses.

Solution: Be a little skeptical when you evaluate how wise your past decisions have been.

- **Confirmation Bias.** We are inclined to look for evidence to support the outcome that we want rather than evaluating what is in our best interest. We also tend to ignore information that might change our minds. For example, you may be eager to avoid a particular course because you have heard lousy things about the instructor. You pay close attention to every report that supports the conclusion you have already drawn,

Solution: Look actively for evidence that could prove you wrong so that your final conclusion will be well-informed.

- **Overinvestment.** Once you've embarked on a course of action, especially if you've had to invest time or money, it may be hard to recognize a bad decision and choose a different course because you will lose what you have already invested. For example, if you've worked your hardest and just can't seem to do well in a particular class, don't stay there just because of the time you have already invested unless you have a good strategy that could make things change positively.

Solution: Be prepared to walk away when an investment sufficiently sours.

- **Hindsight bias.** It's easy to claim that we could have predicted something *after* it has already happened. Good decision makers don't waste time claiming they predicted what has become obvious. Also known as "armchair quarterbacking," coming up with explanations for the obvious can make you look foolish.

Solution: Recognize that what you "knew all along" may just be a function of what you know right now.

Adapted from Diane Halpern, Critical Thinking across the Curriculum *Copyright © 1997 by Lawrence Erlbaum Associates, Inc. Reprinted by permission of the publisher.*

5. *Concentrate on the big picture.* Attending to details will help you get your creative idea across the finish line, but adopting a more holistic, global approach will help you pursue a creative lifestyle.
6. *Take sensible risks.* All creative people will face obstacles. Successful creative people will overcome them. Having courage and staying open to new experiences will contribute to selecting reasonable risks. Creative people take risks and learn from their mistakes. Picasso created more than twenty thousand paintings; not all of them are masterpieces. Your learning will be limited if you don't stick out your neck once in a while. If you're considering a particularly creative approach to an assignment, however, share your plan with your professor ahead of time.
7. *Motivate yourself intrinsically.* If you concentrate on the joy of the process rather than the prospect of rewards, your creative approaches are likely to feel much more rewarding and easier to sustain over time.
8. *Shape environments that will support your creativity.* Find friends who will recognize your distinctiveness. Choose a major in which your individuality can shine. Avoid work environments that feel oppressive, mechanical, or uninspired.
9. *Actively pursue the creative life.* If you accept the proposition that you are not creative, then you won't be. If you open yourself to maximizing your creative potential, you begin the journey. See "Create Your Future: Take Charge of Your Imagination" to help you make the commitment.

Discover "Flow"

Creative people regularly experience a heightened state of pleasure from being completely absorbed in mental and physical challenges. Mihaly Csikszentmihalyi (pronounced ME-high CHICK-sent-me-high-ee) (1995, 1997) interviewed ninety prominent people in art, business, government, education, and science in a study on this subject and coined the term *flow* to describe this special state. He believes that everyone is capable of achieving flow. Some practices that can facilitate this state include:

- *Seek a surprise every day.* Maybe the surprise will be something you see, hear, or read about. Become absorbed in a lecture or a book. Be open to what the world is telling you. Life is a stream of experiences. If you swim widely and deeply, your life will be enriched.
- *Surprise at least one person every day.* In many tasks and roles you have to be predictable and patterned. Do something different for a change. Ask a question you normally would not ask. Invite someone to go to a show or a museum you've never visited. Buy a bagel for someone who shares your commute.
- *Write down each day what surprised you and how you surprised others.* Most creative people keep a diary, notes, or lab records to ensure that their experiences are not fleeting or forgotten. Start with a specific task. Each evening record the most surprising

event that occurred that day and your most surprising action. After a few days, reread your notes and reflect on the past experiences. After a few weeks, you might see a pattern of interest emerging in your notes, one that may suggest an area to explore in greater depth.

- *When something sparks your interest, follow it.* Usually when something captures our attention, it's short-lived—an idea, a song, a flower. Often we're too busy to explore it further or we think we can't because we're not experts. It's none of our business. But the world *is* our business. We can't know which part of it is best suited to our interests until we make a serious effort to learn as much about as many aspects of it as possible.
- *Wake up in the morning with a specific goal.* Creative people wake up eager to start the day. Why? It's not necessarily that they are cheerful, enthusiastic types but because they know that there is something meaningful to accomplish each day and can't wait to get started.
- *Take charge of your schedule.* Figure out which time of the day is your most creative time. Some of us are most creative late at night, others early in the morning. Carve out some time for yourself when your creative energy is greatest.

Try it out. Explore the Journal activity "I Wonder . . . " on page 147 to enhance your flow.

Take Charge of Your Imagination

If you accept the proposition that everyone has the potential to be creative, this means you, too! But you may need to rethink your environment to promote a more creative style. Here are some simple ideas to experience greater creativity on a day-to-day basis.

- *Decorate your door or bathroom mirror.* Find images, cartoons, headlines, and pictures that express who you are and put them up. The images will express to others your personality and values. You may generate some conversation with new acquaintances based on what images you post. The images can also remind you of your commitment to live a more creative life.
- *Use a thesaurus.* In writing projects, come up with new words that may have a stronger impact on your readers.
- *Use titles with pizzazz.* Don't settle for a mundane introduction to work that you have written. Imagine what ideas might be most captivating. Devote some time to helping your work stand out.
- *Sit in a different place.* Unless you are restricted by a seating chart, move around in classes or in the lunch room. Humans are creatures of habit. Break your habit. It may produce new perspective and new friends.
- *Think "connections."* Explore how what you are learning in one class might inform what you are learning in another. These connections may provide you with some novel insights that you can share during class discussion.
- *Go with your second impulse.* Your first impulse is likely to represent an easier path, perhaps arising from routine ways that you approach problems. Go with an approach that is less characteristic of your style.

Summary Strategies for Mastering College

Motivate Yourself to Expand and Deepen Your Thinking Skills by Taking Advantage of All the Opportunities You'll Have In and Out of the Classroom

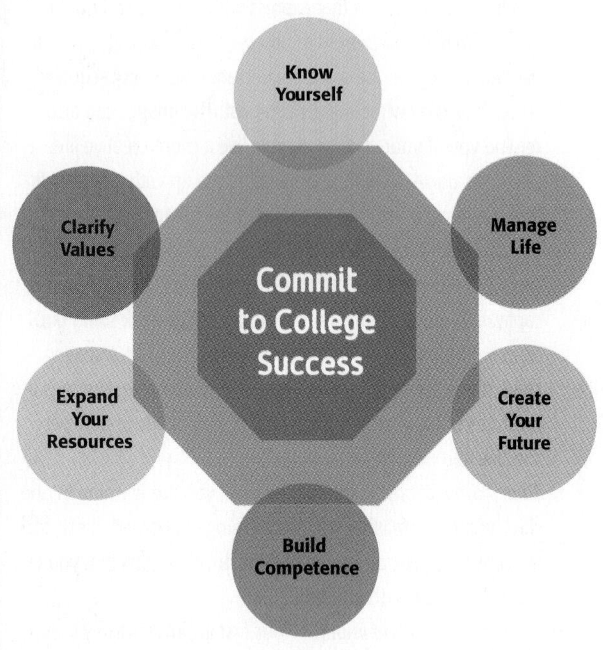

Focus on the Six Strategies for Success above as you read each chapter to learn how to apply these strategies to your own success.

1 Think Critically

- Recognize the role that college plays in promoting better thinking.
- Understand what critical thinking is and how it can benefit you now and in the future.
- Recognize the common features of good critical thinkers.
- Understand the different kinds of effective questions you can ask.
- Be wary about information gathered from the Internet.
- Know how offering criticism can enhance critical thinking.

2 Reason

- Make accurate inferences by attending to the proper cues.
- Reject claims that mislead, give an advantage, or have no valid source.
- Accept claims based on personal experience, expert opinion, or reliable media sources.
- Evaluate arguments by looking at the logic of the premises and conclusion.
- Refine your reasoning by being open to argument, using inductive and deductive thinking, checking your assumptions, understanding your biases, and taking time before reaching conclusions.

3 Solve Problems

- Use a systematic approach to problem solving, including evaluating the consequences.
- Demonstrate good observational skills, strategic approaches, persistence, and attention to detail.
- Use good questioning skills to prepare good solutions to problems.
- Practice mindfulness to improve your problem-solving skills.

4 Make Good Decisions

- Practice decision-making skills that integrate your knowledge, values, and thinking skills.
- Work systematically to make the most effective decisions.
- Avoid making snap decisions or applying narrow, sprawling, or fuzzy thinking.
- Overcome personal biases.

5 Think Creatively

- Understand and imitate people with creative characteristics.
- Adopt the attitude that creativity is possible.
- Live creatively to produce a state of "flow."

Review Questions

1. List three things that distinguish good critical thinkers from bad ones. Do these characteristics apply to you? If not, how can you improve your critical thinking skills?

   1. ______________________________
   2. ______________________________
   3. ______________________________

2. Write down a question you have about something you are currently studying. Is it a "good" question based on what you have read in this chapter? Analyze why or why not.

Your question: ______________________________

Your analysis: ______________________________

3. What steps can you take to construct a good argument?

____

____

____

4. Describe the IDEAL problem-solving strategy below.
   What are some other strategies for successful problem solving?

I: ______________________________

D: ______________________________

E: ______________________________

A: ______________________________

L: ______________________________

Additional Strategies: ______________________________

5. List some steps you can take now to improve your creativity.
   How can this help you achieve "flow"?

____

____

____

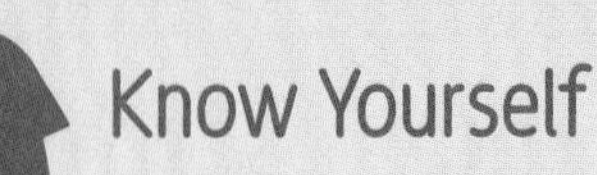

SELF-ASSESSMENT 1

The Critical Difference

For each of the 30 items below, choose the number that most closely corresponds with your profile.

0 = Not at all like me 1 = A bit like me 2 = Like me 3 = Very much like me

_______ 1. When I encounter a new idea in a course, I like to analyze it in depth.

_______ 2. The most important element in any course is a well-prepared teacher who can present the information clearly.

_______ 3. I don't like memorizing lots of material.

_______ 4. I like courses where we deal with a few topics but really analyze them in depth rather than courses where we cover many different topics but don't go into much depth on any one.

_______ 5. I dislike tests where you're supposed to guess what the teacher wants.

_______ 6. In many courses, I just can't get started.

_______ 7. While the teachers are lecturing, I often find myself thinking beyond the points they are trying to make.

_______ 8. It is important for teachers to hand out study guides before the test so I can know what I should study.

_______ 9. When I have a difficult problem, I like to "cut to the chase" and make a quick decision rather than doing a lot of work that might not amount to anything.

_______ 10. Not all ideas in a course are equally important; I like to decide for myself what is important more than I want my teacher to make that decision for me.

_______ 11. During class, I try to write down everything the teacher says.

_______ 12. My teachers usually lecture in a way that is hard to follow.

_______ 13. I get excited by challenges; the harder the challenge, the more excited I get.

_______ 14. I do not like the teacher to waste class time by getting off the track by telling irrelevant stories that won't be on the tests.

_______ 15. If I do not understand the course material, I try not to worry about it.

_______ 16. When I run into something that does not immediately make sense, I keep working with it and analyzing it until I really understand it.

_______ 17. I think test questions should be taken directly from the class notes. It's not fair when the teacher surprises me with a test question about material we did not cover in class.

_______ 18. I prefer that the teacher never call on me during class.

_______ 19. The learning challenge I like the most is the task of trying to make order out of chaos.

_______ 20. My confidence level in a course is highest when the course has a lot of well-organized facts that I can memorize easily.

SELF-ASSESSMENT 1

The Critical Difference

_______ 21. It is the teacher's job to motivate me to do my best work.

_______ 22. I'm the kind of person who likes to set my own goals for learning, even if they are very different from the teacher's goals in the course.

_______ 23. When I am exposed to new information, I want my teacher to tell me what is most important.

_______ 24. No matter how hard I work, I never seem to do as well as I would like.

_______ 25. When my teachers give reading assignments, I like it when they don't tell me what to look for in the reading; I like to determine what is important for myself.

_______ 26. I hate courses where the instructor gives you lots of readings and you have to figure out what is important in those readings.

_______ 27. If I don't learn much in a course, it is usually because the material was too hard.

_______ 28. I am often frustrated in courses when we don't examine something in enough depth to find out what is really going on.

_______ 29. During the first class meeting, I want to get an accurate idea of how hard the course will be.

_______ 30. When I get a low grade on a test or an assignment, I feel frustrated and it is hard to shake that feeling.

Score sheet:

1. ____	2. ____	3. ____
4. ____	5. ____	6. ____
7. ____	8. ____	9. ____
10. ____	11. ____	12. ____
13. ____	14. ____	15. ____
16. ____	17. ____	18. ____
19. ____	20. ____	21. ____
22. ____	23. ____	24. ____
25. ____	26. ____	27. ____
28. ____	29. ____	30. ____
Total ____	Total ____	Total ____

Circle the largest number of the three totals. If that circled number is more than twenty-five and the other two totals are below fifteen each, then the circled number indicates your dominant critical thinking style. If no total is more than twenty, and especially if all three totals are similar (within about seven points of each other), then you have a mix of styles. The right column represents the information avoider style. The middle column represents the consumer style. The strategist style is represented in the left column.

Know Yourself

SELF-ASSESSMENT 2

How Systematically Do I Solve Problems?

Think about the problems you've faced in your academic and personal life in the last month. Review how regularly you went through each of the stages of the IDEAL model.

	Usually	**Not Usually**	**Explain**
Identification: I accurately identify when something needs attention.			
Definition: I describe problems comprehensively, including all factors that might influence the problem.			
Evaluation: I figure out different approaches to take and decide on the best alternative.			
Action: I put my plans into action.			
Looking back: I purposefully examine how effective my chosen solutions are.			

As you examine the results of your review, which aspects of problem solving are your strengths? What elements do you need to practice to become more systematic in your problem solving? What ideas do you have for incorporating these skills into your problem-solving style?

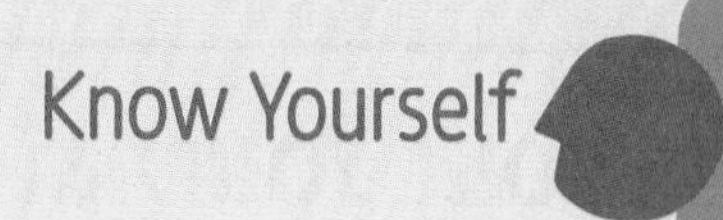

SELF-ASSESSMENT 3

My Creative Profile

To get some measure of your creative potential, answer the following:

1. If you were managing a rock group, what original name would you give it?
2. You've been asked to plan a birthday party for your five-year-old nephew. How would you make it different from other parties his friends have attended?
3. How many uses can you think of for a pencil?
4. What kind of musical instrument could you make out of the contents of the junk drawer in your family's kitchen?
5. You've just been invited to a costume party. What will you wear?
6. What theme would you propose for a sales campaign for your favorite shoe?
7. What business could you establish that would make the lives of your classmates easier? What would you call the business? How would you promote and develop it?
8. What is one strategy you could develop that would make people less afraid of failure?
9. You have to negotiate a late deadline for a paper with your professor. How might you do that creatively?
10. How many creative uses can you think of for a remote control unit?

This assessment highlights flexible thinking. If you found yourself stumped by most of the items, then you may not have developed the flexible mindset that helps creative people. If you answered a few of the questions, then you can probably point to a few creative areas in your life. If you felt exhilarated by the questions, chances are good that you're often creative.

Your Journal

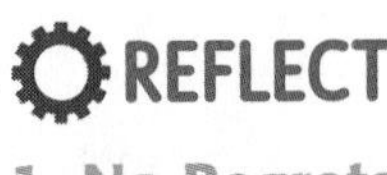

REFLECT

1. No Regrets

Do a postmortem about an important decision you made that was very satisfying to you. For example, did you select the right college to begin your academic career? What about the process helped to ensure that your decision would be right? What aspects of this process can you practice regularly in making sound decisions in the future?

___

___

2. Minding the Store

How often do you find yourself slipping up by not paying full attention to what you are doing? On a scale of 1 to 10, rate how mindful you are on a day-to-day basis. Next, think about the circumstances that tend to trigger greater mindfulness. When are you in top form, functioning in a mindful manner? What situations encourage you to be mindless? Speculate about some of the losses you may have incurred from mindless behavior. What would you have to do to make mindfulness your standard way of operating?

___

___

DO

1. A Question a Day

Sometimes it's hard to overcome the impression that if you ask questions, other people will think you don't know what's going on. Good questions show just the opposite—that you're alert, thoughtful, and invested. For at least one week, make a point to ask a good question in each of your classes. Bring it up in class, ask your instructor after class, or e-mail your question to the instructor. How did this improve your ability to ask questions? How did you feel about becoming more actively involved in your learning?

___

___

2. Claims Detector

Record the claims you hear in the media for one day. Commercials are especially good targets for this activity. Pick the claim that is most interesting to you and see if you can convert the commercial claims into premises and conclusions. Should you accept the claim, reject the claim, or suspend judgment based on the evidence offered?

CLAIM: ___

PREMISES: ___

___

___

CONCLUSION: ___

ACCEPT, REJECT, OR SUSPEND JUDGMENT: ___

Your Journal

THINK CRITICALLY

1. The Great Debate

Think about an issue or controversy that stirred your feelings in one of your classes and record it below. Perhaps it was a political concern or a strong reaction you had to a poem or painting. Briefly map your position on this issue by providing the key ideas that support it. Now assume you've been assigned to argue the opposite side in a debate. Map this position as well. Did careful mapping of the opposing side do anything to weaken your commitment to the original position?

Your Issue: ______________________________

Your Position: ______________________________

Key Ideas: ______________________________

____

____

Opposing Position: ______________________________

Key Ideas: ______________________________

____

____

2. Your IDEAL

Consider an important issue in your life right now and apply the IDEAL problem-solving strategy listed below. Did this help you come up with some ideas for resolving this issue? Why or why not?

Identify the problem: ______________________________

Define the problem: ______________________________

Explore alternative approaches: ______________________________

Act on the best strategy: ______________________________

Look back to evaluate the effects: ______________________________

CREATE

1. "I Wonder . . ."

Here is a simple exercise to increase your creative thinking. Each day for a week, take a few minutes to ask yourself a question that begins with "I wonder . . ." Ask this question about a particular aspect of your life. It's important not to censor yourself, no matter how impractical or outlandish the question sounds. After you practice doing this, pose your questions to your friends. Focus on something that you're sincerely curious about and that matters to others. Listen carefully to your friends' responses. You'll probably discover that your questions have some assumptions that deserve to be challenged or fine-tuned (Goleman, Kaufman, and Ray 1993).

2. Creative Surfing

Find out what the Internet has to offer concerning problem solving. Enter "problem solving" into a search engine and visit at least three sites that address the issue. List the sites and their main premises below. What did you learn about problem solving? Why has the Internet become such a boon to problem solving?

Site #1: ______________________________

Site #2: ______________________________

Site #3: ______________________________

6 Take It In: Notes and Reading

© Gary Connor/PhotoEdit

KNOW YOURSELF

TO SUCCEED IN COLLEGE, you need to take charge of new ideas and make good judgments about their importance to your learning. In other words, learn strategies for being *selective* about the information you take in. To see where you are right now, place a check mark next to only those items that apply to you.

- I'm very organized about the way I absorb information from lectures, group work, and textbooks.
- I use many different strategies to figure out what's most important to learn.
- I read assignments *before* going to the class.
- I know how to keep myself focused during difficult lectures.
- I'm familiar with different note-taking methods.
- I know the difference between primary and secondary research sources and the value of each.
- I pace my reading according to the depth of understanding I am striving for.
- I use various strategies to read more effectively and efficiently.
- I use my notes to improve my learning as well as my test performance.

As you read the following profile of Condoleezza Rice, consider how you could benefit from the successful strategies she used to gather information and use it in original ways.

CHAPTER OUTLINE

Commit, Concentrate, Capture, Connect

Take Charge of Lectures

Commit to Class
Concentrate
Capture Key Ideas
Connect Ideas

Take Great Lecture Notes

Develop Your Style
Choose the Best Method
Master Note-Taking Strategies

Take Charge of Your Reading

Commit to Reading Goals
Plan Time and Space to Concentrate
Capture and Connect
Identify Levels of Reading Effort
Pick Up the Pace
Know How to Read Primary and Secondary Sources

Master Reading in Different Disciplines

Take Great Reading Notes

Choose the Best Method
Follow Other Note-Taking Tips
Take What You Need from the Internet

Process Information Professionally

Images of College Success

Condoleezza Rice

Named the "most powerful woman in the world" by *Forbes* magazine in 2005, Condoleezza Rice has broken records and blazed new paths over the course of her life. Rice was born in Alabama and experienced profound personal loss at age eight when her friend Denise McNair died at the hands of white supremacists who bombed the Baptist church her friend was attending. Rice reflected that her early experiences with racial discrimination fueled her determination about what it took to succeed when times got tough. She concluded that to be successful she would simply have to be "twice as good" as nonminority members, and her record of success indicates she has succeeded in that goal. Early evidence of her motivation to succeed was apparent in her success in competitive figure skating. Gifted in musical talent as well, she initially planned to prepare for a career as a concert pianist. Her name, Condoleezza, derives from an Italian musical term meaning "with sweetness."

At age fifteen Rice attended the University of Denver, where she took a life-changing course taught by an international politics professor; that course redirected her to pursue graduate work as well as a career in public service. Graduating with a major in political science at nineteen, she went on to achieve her masters from the University of Notre Dame and her doctoral degree from the University of Denver. Along the way, she developed facility in Russian, German, Spanish, and French. Prior to her appointment as secretary of state, Condoleezza served as the youngest provost at Stanford. She became national security advisor to Bush based on her expertise in political systems across the globe. Her considerable ability to process and stay on top of a staggering array of information has made it possible for Condoleezza to serve in a variety of simultaneous roles, including acting on boards of directors of businesses, academic institutions, and charitable operations.

CONDOLEEZZA RICE demonstrates exceptional abilities in skillfully using information.

Motivate yourself by adopting helpful strategies to select, think about, and learn new ideas that college has to offer. As you read, think about the Six Strategies for Success listed to the left and how this chapter can help you maximize success in these important areas, particularly in building competence.

Commit, Concentrate, Capture, Connect

College requires you to sift through and master an extraordinary amount of information. Extracting what you need from lectures and textbooks is no small feat, especially given differences in learning styles that make some tasks more challenging for you than others. This chapter describes a simple, easy-to-remember approach for sorting through information and making good decisions about what you need to learn and how to best learn it—the "four Cs".

- *Commit* yourself to do your best work.
- *Concentrate* to eliminate distractions and focus on the material.
- *Capture* critical information.
- *Connect* new ideas to what you already know.

You can apply this approach to your classes and reading assignments to help you learn more effectively.

Take Charge of Lectures

First let's apply the four Cs to getting the most from classes.

Commit to Class

Some classes will be exciting from start to finish. You'll look forward to these lectures and linger after each. It's easy to follow through on your commitment to learning when courses match your learning style or personal interest. When the content of the class or the style of the lecturer is not a good match, making a strong commitment to attend class is even more important. This commitment involves more than just showing up, however. You commit to the work involved as well. Before each class, get ready to learn.

> ***The quality of a person's life is in direct proportion to their commitment to excellence, regardless of their chosen field of endeavor.***
>
> Vincent T. Lombardi
> *Green Bay Packers coach*

Anticipate Review your notes from the last class as well as your reading assignment. Identify any areas that are difficult to understand and think about questions that could clarify them. Or search the web to find other sources that might clarify these areas. Read your syllabus to determine the topics for discussion in class, and make sure you have done any reading associated with these lecture topics.

Think about the format for the class, and prepare appropriately. Will it be a lecture, lab, or seminar? A seminar requires a different type of attention than a lecture. These strategies will help you anticipate how the class will flow and what ideas will be most important.

Be on Time Even better, arrive a few minutes early. This gives you a chance to review your notes before class and to be ready to go as soon as the instructor begins. Well-organized instructors often use the first few minutes of class to review the previous class. This allows you to rehearse what you've been learning. Like reviewing your notes, it also sets the stage for how the upcoming class will unfold, which will help you get organized and figure out what's most important.

Don't Miss Classes The best way to be prepared is to attend all your classes. Even if you haven't done the assigned reading, the class will still be worthwhile. The lecture may be so fascinating that it makes it easier to sit down and do a double dose of reading in preparation for the next class. If you can't attend class, use good judgment about how to compensate. See "Manage Life: Any Old Notes Won't Do" for some good advice.

Do the Assignments Assignments aren't usually optional. Instructors design assignments to help students develop expertise in the content and skills that the course has to offer. If you decide not to submit an assignment, you don't just lose points. You lose ground. From the outset of the class, plan how to complete all your assignments to get the most from your courses.

Some students assume that reading assignments aren't all that important because the instructor will cover the material in class. This is not a wise assumption. Many instructors assign reading as a related but independent resource; they do not review the reading in class. Successful students complete assigned readings before class to better understand the lecture. Connections and overlaps between the lecture and reading reinforce their learning. Another reason to complete reading assignments is that you may be called on to report your impressions. It's embarrassing when you haven't got a clue of what to say.

Concentrate

Many things influence concentration. For example, if you're an auditory learner or have a natural interest in the topic, extracting what you need from a lecture may not be hard. Other circumstances, though, will require you to take a more strategic approach to concentration.

Minimize Distractions You can do many things to minimize distractions:

1. *Sit near the front.* If you can't see or hear clearly, find a spot where you can.
2. *Reduce noise.* The instructor may not realize how noisy the room is for you, so do what you need to ensure your best hearing. Close doors and windows to reduce unwanted noise. Move away from chatty neighbors.
3. *Reduce off-task pressures.* Get the sleep you need, and eat before class to quiet a growling stomach. If a specific worry keeps bothering you, write it down separately from your notes. Promise yourself that you'll worry about it later, so you can let it go for now.

© Colin Young-Wolff/Photo Edit

If you have to read in distracting environments, minimize the distraction. For example, on a crowded bus you might want to read while listening to music played at a low level on headphones.

4. *Stay tuned in.* If something in the lecture distresses you—either content or delivery style—concentrate on identifying more precisely what bothers you and how you can best resolve the problem. Focus on hearing what you most likely will be tested on. Breathe deeply and use other stress-management techniques to stay in tune. If you tend to get off track from too much daydreaming, see the Journal activity "Daydream Believer" on page 183 to help you conquer your drift.
5. *Track your progress.* Keep records of how much time you spend paying attention. At the end of each class, estimate what percentage of time you were on track and write it in the upper-right corner of your notes. Try to make regular improvements in your rate.

> ***You cannot truly listen to anyone and do anything else at the same time.***
>
> M. Scott Peck
> *Twentieth-century American psychiatrist and author*

Instructors differ in their abilities to lecture. Some make learning easy; others make it tough. Sometimes students react differently to the same lecturer. For example, some lecturers enchant students by sharing personal anecdotes, but some students find these examples annoying and time wasting. Develop your skills at listening so that you can compensate for any skills in speaking that the instructor may lack. See "Build Competence: Tame That Tough Lecture" for some pointers.

Listen Actively To succeed you need to concentrate. One way to do this is to listen actively. On average, speakers say about 150 words per minute, and listeners can process about 500 words per minute, more than three times the speed of speech (Nichols 1961). This means that even when instructors talk very fast, you should have plenty of time to understand them. Put that extra time to its best use through *active listening.*

Active listeners sort through the information they hear and figure out what's most important. They connect what

MANAGE LIFE

Any Old Notes Won't Do

Hallie was feverish and decided to stay in bed rather than struggle through government class and possibly spread whatever was troubling her to her classmates. She phoned her best friend Terry to let her know she wouldn't be there, and, so she wouldn't miss anything, she asked Terry to make a copy of her notes. When Terry passed Hallie the "notes" a few days later, Hallie was startled to see just three lines on the page. The notes said, "There was a guest speaker, Mr. Johnson, or something like that. He was really boring. You were right to stay home in bed." Unfortunately for Hallie, Mr. Johnson was a local city council member whose presentation served as the heart of the next exam.

When you miss a class, don't assume that any old notes will do. When life throws emergency conditions your way, be sure to borrow notes only from students who have demonstrated a good grasp of the course. Your best friend might not be the best person to ask.

> ***The first duty of a lecturer—to hand you after an hour's discourse a nugget of pure truth to wrap up between the pages of your notebooks and keep on your mantelpiece forever.***
>
> Virginia Woolf
> *Twentieth-century British novelist and literary critic*

they hear with things they already know. Although it's hard mental work, active listening is an efficient way to get the most from a lecture. The next sections provide some specific strategies to build your active listening skills.

In contrast, passive listeners merely write down the instructor's words without necessarily understanding the ideas or making judgments about their importance. This approach shifts actual learning to a later time, when the ideas have already faded. Don't delay the job of understanding. Putting it off not only makes ideas harder to learn, it also takes time from preparations for the next assignment.

Capture Key Ideas

Some instructors will help you spot their main ideas by starting with a preview, outline, or map of the material that a lecture will cover. Others won't, but they will still expect you to grasp their organization (even when it's obscure) and recognize key ideas. Successful note taking depends on your flexible use of structures and a format that will best serve your learning. You may need to experiment in each class until you find just the right note-taking groove. What are some strategies you can use to recognize key points?

Tame That Tough Lecture

THE FAST-TALKING LECTURER

Enthusiastic instructors may talk too fast for you to catch what they're saying. When you're confronted with a fast talker:

- **Say "Please slow down."** Most fast-talking instructors know they talk too fast. Many appreciate getting feedback so they can adjust their pace.
- **Encourage the instructor to write down the key terms.** Seeing them written down will help you understand them. Also, when the instructor writes on the board, you may be able to catch up.
- **Focus on the major thrust, not the detail.** Fast talkers are hardest for students who attempt to take notes word for word. Concentrate on the major ideas instead.

THE BEWILDERING LECTURER

Some instructors simply use more sophisticated language than you may be used to hearing. When your instructor is hard to understand:

- **Prepare for class carefully.** If you do the assigned readings before class, you'll already be familiar with many key terms.
- **Ask for restatements.** If you persist in asking for interpretations when an instructor's language is too complex, many instructors will simplify their language to avoid losing the time it takes to re-explain.
- **Change your attitude.** Think about this kind of instructor as eloquent rather than obtuse. He gives you extra education for your tuition dollar. You may emerge from the class with an enriched vocabulary.

Continued on next page

Identify Key Words, Themes, and Main Points Often these are ideas that the instructor repeats, highlights, illustrates with examples, supports with related facts, or displays on a blackboard or screen. Many instructors organize courses around a central set of terms. Any unfamiliar term or phrase is a new idea you need to learn. Such terms often represent the specialized language of the discipline you're studying. Recognizing broader themes may be more challenging. Sometimes your instructor will give you an overarching theme to help you organize what you're about to hear. If the instructor does not, make a point to think about what theme the details of the lecture suggest and how they relate to themes from previous lectures. Try to keep the big picture in mind so you don't feel overwhelmed by the details.

How can you tell the difference between a central idea and the details used to support the idea? Facts, stories, predictions, analogies, statistics, opinions, comparisons, and explanations provide the details to drive the main point home.

Recognize Organization Patterns in the Lecture Academic information comes in predictable patterns (Strong and others 2002). Listen for some key words that will signal these patterns of how main points and supporting details relate. This anticipation will help you to grasp the logic and flow of the lecture and minimize the tendency to get lost in details and digressions. Some examples of such patterns include:

- *Listing Patterns:* All the relevant facts, concepts, and events are presented in simple lists that reflect order of importance. Signal words include *first, second, also, in addition, another, moreover, next, furthermore.*
- *Comparison Patterns:* These patterns focus on similarities and differences. Signal words include *on one hand, similarly, in contrast, but, then, either, or, compared to, opposite of, like.*

- *Sequence Patterns:* Many times instructors will incorporate timelines, chronologies, or procedural steps or stages to show how things are fixed in a certain order. Signal words include *first, second, finally, while, now, then, next.*
- *Cycle Patterns:* Cycle patterns of organization show how trends end up where they started. Signal words include *first, second, finally, while, now, then, same, circular.*
- *Problem-Solving Patterns:* In these types of organization, the instructor identifies a problem, establishes conditions for solving the problem, explains the solution, and predicts the aftereffects. Signal words include *since, resulting, hypothesis, leading to, because, so, if . . . then, solution.*
- *Cause-and-Effect Patterns:* These patterns involve showing causal connections between two events. Signal words include *prediction, effect, causation, control.*
- *Example Patterns:* These patterns involve defining a concept and then offering examples or illustrations to clarify or explain the term. Signal words include *for example, for instance, other examples include, such as.*

Relate Details to the Main Point Instructors use stories, examples, or analogies to reinforce your learning of main points. They usually intend their stories to do more than entertain. Check to make sure you understand why the instructor chose a particular story or example. Pay attention to how much the instructor relies on important details at test time. Some instructors may expect you to be accountable for all the details. Others will pay less attention to your rote recall of minor details but will instead emphasize your ability to communicate your understanding of the main ideas with the most important details.

Listen for Clues Pay special attention to words that signal a change of direction or special emphasis. For example, note when a concept or topic comes up more than once. Such a topic is likely to show up on an exam. Transition speech, such as "in contrast to" or "let's move on to" or even "this will be on the next exam," signals the change of topics or emergence of new key points. Lists usually signify important material that is also easy to test. Instructors are most likely to test for ideas that they consider exciting, so listen for any special enthusiasm.

Work on Your "Sixth Sense" Some students just know when an instructor is covering key ideas, especially material that's likely to be on the test. They sit, pencils poised, and wait for the instructor to get to the good stuff. Actively categorize what your instructor is saying by asking yourself questions such as:

- "Is this statement central to my understanding of today's topic?"

THE DISORGANIZED LECTURER

Some lecturers organize poorly. They go off on tangents or don't teach from an organized plan. If you have a chaotic instructor:

- **Look at the big picture.** Concentrate on the larger themes so that you won't feel overwhelmed by disconnected details.
- **Rely on the textbook.** Be sure you use this important resource to fill in the blanks that a chaotic lecturer produces. The text publisher may offer other support features, such as a study guide or website, which can contribute to your understanding.
- **Form a study group.** Pool your resources to make sense of the teaching.
- **Impose organization.** Use note-taking strategies that will help you see the connections between the ideas. Try to organize the lecture materials to give them some structure; for example, create an outline.

THE TEDIOUS LECTURER

Instructors give boring lectures because they have lost interest in their work or don't understand classroom dynamics well. Some instructors even suffer from stage fright. If you have a boring instructor:

- **Make connections.** Breathe more life into the lecture by applying what you hear to what you already know.
- **Ask questions that encourage examples.** Stories have a natural appeal. They can arouse and sustain attention. By requesting an illustration of a key point, you may help the instructor add life to the lecture. Although this may be easiest to accomplish in small classes, you can also ask for examples in visits during office hours.
- **Show active interest in the lecture.** Sit in the front row, maintain good eye contact, nod your head, and smile occasionally to motivate teachers to give you their best work.

Reprinted by permission of Vivian Scott Hixon.

- "Does this example help clarify the main ideas?"
- "Is this a tangent (an aside) that may not help me learn the central ideas?"

To get some practice refining your ability to predict test questions, see the Journal activity "Analyze the Sixth Sense" on page 184.

Save Your Energy Don't write down what you already know. Besides covering new material, lectures usually overlap some with material in required textbooks. If you have read your assignment, you should be able to recognize when the lecture overlaps the text. Open your text and follow along, making notes in the margins where the instructor stays close to the text. Pay closer attention when what you hear sounds unfamiliar.

Connect Ideas

The best listeners don't just check in with the speaker from time to time. They work at listening by using strategies to create more enduring impressions of the lecture and to escape daydreaming.

Paraphrase What You Hear If you can't translate the ideas from a lecture into your own words, you may need to do more reading or ask more questions until you are able to do so.

Relate Key Ideas to What You Already Know When you can see how the course ideas connect to other aspects of your life, including your experiences in other courses or contemporary events, the ideas will be easier to remember. For example, if you're studying in sociology how societies organize into different economic classes, think about how those ideas apply to the neighborhood where you grew up or about ideas from your business or economics class.

Make a Note of Unknown Words Sometimes unknown words are a signal that you've missed something in a previous lecture. If you take notes on a laptop, you may be able to look up meanings in an electronic dictionary as you go. Consider making a file in your word processing program to store these terms for easy review. If not, write the word at the top of your notes and look it up right after class. Keep a running list of the words that gave you trouble. Your list becomes a natural tool for review before exams.

Own Your Confusion It's inevitable. Sometimes you will be confused. The instructor may use terms you don't understand or present relationships that may be too subtle to grasp the first time you hear them. If English is your second language, there may be other reasons why you lose your way. The instructor may speak too fast for you to process the information. Clearly mark your notes with a question mark or other code that identifies this is an area you need to revisit. Make a point to confer with classmates, check on the Internet, explore your text for backup support, or even talk with the instructor after class until you get back on the right path.

Get Involved When you determine the direction the class will take, you can come up with examples that make ideas more compelling. Suggest those examples to the instructor. Say, "Would this be an example of what you are talking about?" Ask questions. Answer questions when the instructor asks them. Participate in discussions that are prompted by the lecture. No matter what form your involvement takes, it will help you stay engaged with the ideas in the lecture.

Take Great Lecture Notes

Taking great notes is your opportunity to think and learn actively during your time in class. With proper planning and monitoring, great notes will cut your review time and help consolidate your learning.

Develop Your Style

Successful students take good notes. The quality of their work is based on the quality of their drive. By connecting your work during lectures with your future prospects, you can find the energy to excel.

A successful note-taking style reflects not just the complexity of the course content and the lecturer's style but your own learning preferences as well. If you're a visual learner, use images, arrows, or other graphic organizers to help you remember the important material and relationships more easily. Color-code parts of your notes or draw sketches. Use any strategy that will help the key ideas stand out. If you're an auditory learner, you may thrive in lectures; however, you may be tempted to take down every word. See "Build Competence: It's Not Transcription," for some good advice.

Sometimes students use note taking to dodge the hard work of paying careful attention in class. Writing notes occupies their attention, although their learning might be better served by devoting 100 percent attention to the lecture. Experiment with your ability to concentrate in class. Make a prior arrangement with a classmate who takes notes successfully to show you what she records. Rather than taking notes yourself, attend completely to the lecture. Then examine your friend's notes afterward to see how effectively you have learned. Taking responsibility to learn—rather than record—may make some permanent changes in how you approach note taking.

Technology can also enhance your note-taking prowess. Many students like to bring laptops to class to capture information. Unless you have developed facility with a graphics program, you are more likely to rely on the word processing program to help you with the verbal details of the class. However, many newer model laptops convert written notes into typewritten text and graphics. Recognize that instructors may monitor your use of the laptop to ensure that you are paying attention rather than cruising the Internet in an off-task activity, so don't let the attractions of the Internet lure you away from your primary job of taking effective notes.

There is no short cut to achievement. Life requires thorough preparation—veneer isn't worth anything.

George Washington Carver
Nineteenth-century American horticulturalist and chemist

Choose the Best Method

Once you get beyond the idea of taking notes verbatim, you have numerous good options. Choose one that suits your learning needs and preferences. Here are several popular note-taking methods:

Summary Method In this approach, you'll monitor the lecture for critical ideas and pause at intervals to summarize what you think is most important. Summarizing appeals most to students with auditory learning preferences. They are comfortable in the world of words and have learned to trust that they can extract the key ideas after the fact. Translating the material into their own words provides great writing practice.

Writing summaries may be somewhat time-consuming, but it helps you take responsibility for judging what is crucial and relating that to other aspects of the course. It's also an effective way to handle a disorganized lecturer. However, with the summary method you run the risk that you might overlook some key ideas.

Outlining An outline summarizes key points and subpoints, as demonstrated in Figure 6.1. The summary of headings at the beginning of each chapter of this book is another example of an outline. When you use an outline form, your results are neat and well organized. Naturally, outlines are easiest to create when the lecture itself is well organized. Some outliners don't use numbers and letters because the task is too distracting. They simply use indentations to signify subpoints. What kind of learner likes to outline? The distinctiveness of an outline appeals to students who are especially good at analysis and critical thinking.

Students who like to analyze tend to enjoy constructing a representation of the lecture that clearly highlights the main points, with supportive details tucked neatly under subheadings. The outline shows the relationship among ideas and reduces distracting verbiage to its key points, showcased by a systematic visual display that can be easier for visual than auditory learners.

However, it may not always be easy to impose a crisp outline on a messy presentation. That challenge can sometimes divert the outliner's attention from listening to the content of the lecture to the process of creating an acceptable outline. However, outlining will sharpen critical thinking skills because, when done properly, it provides practice in analyzing the course content.

The Cornell Method Draw a vertical line down your loose-leaf or notebook page, about 2½ inches from the left edge of the page as shown in Figure 6.2. Draw a horizontal line across the page, about 2 inches from the bottom. Use the largest area on the right side of the page to take your notes during class. After class is over, use the blank left side of the page to write short headings or questions for each part of your notes. Use the bottom of the page for a summary or other comments and questions.

The Cornell Method creates a great tool for reviewing. Cover up the right portion of the page and use the phrases or questions on the left side as prompts. As you read each prompt, practice recalling the details on the right. Choose the Cornell Method if

FIGURE 6.1 Take It In

This format organizes lecture coverage by main headings and subheadings.

Chapter 6
Target Information
I. Commit, Concentrate, Capture, Connect
  A. Identifying what you need is hard work
    1. From lecture
    2. From text
  B. 4-part approach can help make good decisions
II. Take Charge of Lectures
  A. Commit to the course
    1. Not hard to commit when interest is high
    2. When not a good match . . .
      a. Be present
      b. Be ready
      c. Be punctual
  B. Concentrate
    I. Overcome distractions
      a. Sit near front
      b. Reduce noise
      c. Reduce off-task pressures
      d. Stay tuned in
      e. Track your progress
    2. Adapt to Teaching Styles
      a. To cope with fast talkers
        (1) Tell them ìSlow down"
        (2) Ask them to write down key words
        (3) Focus on key ideas
      b. To cope with bewildering lecturers . . .

FIGURE 6.2 The Cornell Method

The Cornell method separates running notes taken during class from summary phrases and an overall summary or comments added after class. To review, cover the material on the right and practice recalling it from the cues on the left.

	Dr. Kong--Psychology 21 Tues. 9-14-02
	<u>Topic: Optimism & Pessimism--Seligman's theory</u>
Success: 2 keys or 3?	Talent and desire, 2 keys to success. Is there a 3rd key-- "optimism"? (=<u>expecting</u> to succeed)? The real test=how you react when something bad happens. Give up or fight on?
Lab studies on learning/unlearning helplessness	Psych lab experiments can teach dogs to be helpless. If dog is trained to think it has no control over when it will get shocked, it starts acting helpless even when it could jump away & not get shocked. Same type thing happens to people in childhood. If they don't think they can change things, they act helpless: <u>pessimistic</u>. But you can also train a dog <u>out of</u> being helpless. All depends on <u>expecting</u> to be or not be in control.
	How optimists vs. pessimists explain bad events.
	Pessimist:
	1. <u>Personal</u>--"Bad things are my fault."
"P P P"	2. <u>Permanent</u>--"Can't get better."
	3. <u>Pervasive</u>--"Affects everything I do."
	Optimist:
	1. Impersonal--"Bad things not my fault."
	2. Momentary--"Can change tomorrow."
	3. Particular--"Doesn't affect the rest of me."
Pessimism → depression	Everyone can get depressed, but pessimists <u>stay</u> depressed longer. Why? Because of how they <u>explain</u> things.
Therapy = Change explanations	<u>Cognitive therapy</u>: Change the way pessimist explains things to cure their depression. How? First get them to hear what they tell themselves when things go bad. Then get them to change what they say.

Seligman found that desire and talent don't always win. Optimism also important. Pessimists can become "helpless" in hard times. Optimists recover faster. Training pessimists to think more optimistically might reduce depression.

Q: But how does it work? Find out Thursday!

BUILD COMPETENCE

It's Not Transcription

The worst strategy students can adopt when taking lecture notes is trying to get down every word the instructor says. They become *transcribers*, trying to reproduce the lecture word for word. This approach to note taking pays off for medical records transcribers but not for students.

Recall the time advantage that the listener has in processing information. You usually can think and listen more than three times faster than a speaker can talk. Professional transcribers, who are adept at using shorthand, do well if they can get down eighty to ninety words a minute using shorthand. By contrast, students who transcribe an instructor's words without using shorthand may write at fewer than twenty words per minute (Kierwa 1987). By concentrating on capturing individual words, they get only a portion of the message and certainly miss the big picture.

you demonstrate a preference for auditory learning and are conscientious about review. The format commits you to working actively with verbal representation of the notes, capturing themes, analyzing trends, and generating questions. You can also combine the Cornell Method with summarizing or outlining to take advantage of the strengths of those approaches.

The Question Technique An adaptation of the Cornell System may be especially helpful in getting you ready to take exams (Pauk 2000). Rather than highlighting key phrases or words in the left column, formulate specific questions that are answered by the material you have written on the right. For example, suppose you are learning about photosynthesis in botany class. Your class notes might begin with defining photosynthesis. Your question cue on the left might be, "How do you define photosynthesis?" The questions provide a good review of material the way it might be framed on an exam.

Concept Maps A concept map provides visual cues about how ideas are related, as shown in Figure 6.3. Some students construct concept maps from lecture notes during class. Others may draw concept maps after class as a way to review the material.

Concept maps appeal to visual learners with a creative flair. They are more engaging to create and facilitate recall better than other formats for visual learners. A risk with this method, however, is that the concept mapper can be more drawn to the creative process and committed to making an aesthetically pleasing map than he is to listening to the content of the lecture and correctly identifying the relationships being represented.

Master Note-Taking Strategies

You'll learn a great deal by taking careful notes. Whichever format you choose, combine it with the following strategies:

Clearly Identify the Class Be sure to include the topic or title of the lecture, if any, along with its date. This notation will make it easier to track down specific information in sequential order when it's time to review. Include your name and e-mail address or phone number, in case you lend your notes to a classmate or they become lost.

Reduce to Key Ideas Simplify what you record from lectures to the fewest words possible to capture the key ideas. Shorter notes will facilitate easier review and allow you to concentrate on the most critical details.

Take Notes from All Relevant Input Some students believe that only the instructor's input is worth recording. However, the instructor may treat any class material as fair game for testing, even when other students introduce the ideas. Also remember to summarize the relevant details from videos or films that are shown in class.

Don't Erase Mistakes Erasing takes more time than crossing out an error. Drawing a line also lets you restore the information later if you need it.

Abbreviate Use standard abbreviations to record information quickly. Figure 6.4, "Common Abbreviations for Notes," suggests some simple substitutions. Develop

FIGURE 6.3 The Concept Map

A concept map is a helpful tool for visual learners. It displays the key ideas in a lecture or resource and shows how the ideas relate to each other.

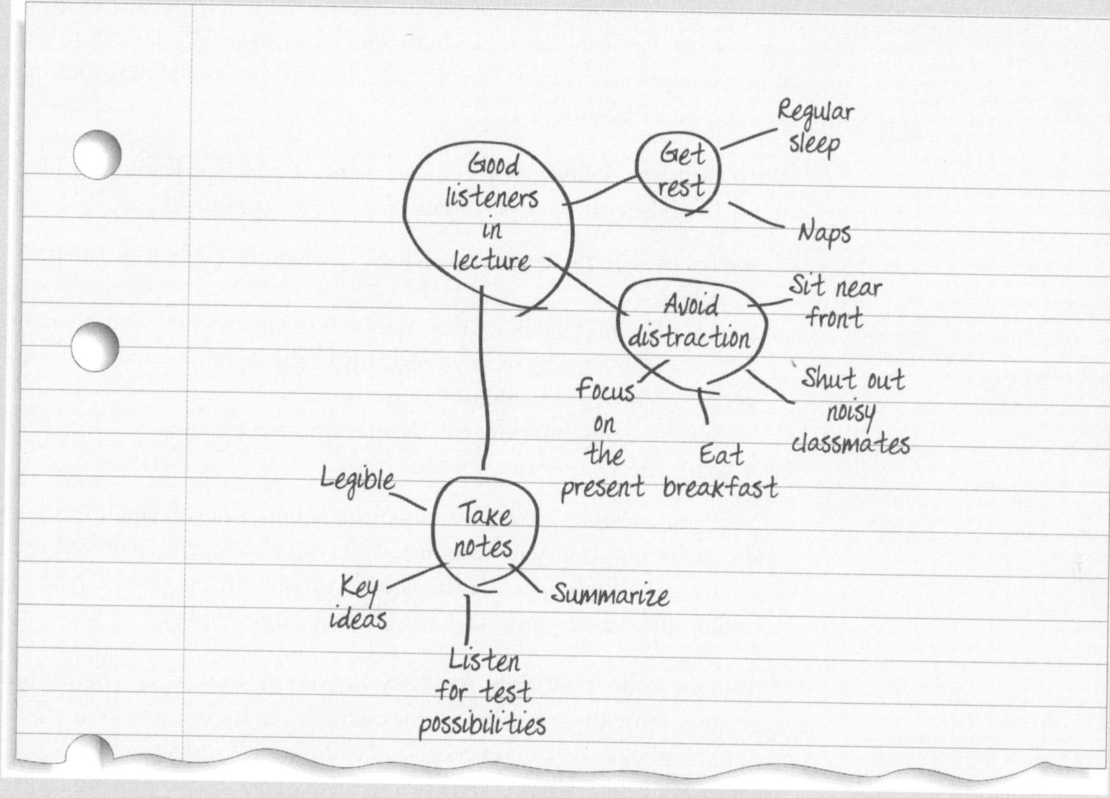

FIGURE 6.4 Common Abbreviations for Notes

Using your own abbreviations or the standard abbreviations in this list will save you time when you take notes.

i.e. = that is (to clarify by restating a point)	< = less than
e.g. = for example (to clarify by adding a typical case)	> = more than
vs. = versus (to identify a contrasting point)	k = $1,000 (as in 10 k for 10 thousand; k = kilo)
∴ = therefore (to come to a conclusion)	~ = approximately
∵ = because	?? = I'm confused
w/ = with	* = important, testable
w/o = without	@ = at
→ = leads to	

your own abbreviations for words that you need to write often. For example, you can abbreviate academic disciplines, such as *PSY, BIO, ENG,* and *LIT.* When instructors use terms regularly throughout the course, develop abbreviations for them as well. For example, *EV* might stand for *evolution* or *A/R* for *accounts receivable.* When you use personalized abbreviations, write their meanings inside the cover of your notebook as a handy reference.

Review Your Notes Often Review your notes right after class whenever possible. Some students like to rewrite or keyboard their notes after class as a way of consolidating information. If you don't rewrite, at least reread your notes to add whatever might be missing. Highlight certain phrases, identify the key points, or revise notes that are unclear. Review your notes between classes to consolidate your learning. Some students review notes from the previous class just before the next meeting as a way to get back into the subject.

Tape Lectures Selectively Some students like to tape lectures as a backup for the notes, but it isn't always a good idea. Tape the lecture only if you:

- need the complete text of a lecture, as when the content is extremely difficult or tricky
- have a learning disability that hinders listening carefully or accurately
- have a plan for how to listen regularly to the tapes
- take advantage of commuting time to listen
- must be absent but can get a classmate to tape for you
- secure the lecturer's permission

Without a plan or special need to justify taping, you will end up with a stockpile of audio recordings that you never listen to. You also may be tempted not to listen as carefully as you might while the class is actually in progress. If you don't use the recording afterwards, you'll have lost a learning opportunity.

Organize Your Materials for Easy Retrieval Keeping a separate notebook or a separate compartment in a binder for each subject can improve your efficiency. Three-ring binders allow you to rearrange and add pages. Write on only one side of the page to make your notes easy to arrange and review later. Some students, especially tactile learners, use index cards because they're easy to carry, organize, and review.

If you use electronic note taking, experiment with the best way to manage your records. At minimum, maintain a separate folder for each course on your hard drive or desktop to help you separate and sort your classes. A file for each class experience housed in the appropriate folder will help you keep the activities appropriately sequenced and make it easier to review. With a little discipline, you may also be able to set up an ongoing glossary of terms, which will facilitate easier review when it's time to commit the material to memory.

"As I get older, I find I rely more and more on these sticky notes to remind me."

Request Feedback about Your Notes Especially in classes where you struggle with note taking, see your instructor during office hours and ask for help. Ask whether you are capturing the main ideas in your notes; if not, discuss ways to improve your note taking. Complete the Journal activity "Show and Tell," on page 183 to prepare you to get that extra support.

Evaluate Your Note-Taking Strategy When you get a test back, examine the structure of your notes to see what accounted for your success. Continue to practice the strategies that served you well. Modify practices that may have made it hard for you to learn or test well. Evaluate your own style of listening by completing Self-Assessment 1, "Auditing Your Note-Taking Style for Lectures" on page 180. The results will show where you can improve.

Take Charge of Your Reading

The four Cs—Commit, Concentrate, Capture, and Connect—work as well for reading as for note taking. A systematic approach to reading will allow you to achieve your reading goals and make your learning more efficient.

Commit to Reading Goals

In college, attending class and doing the reading assignments is your job. Although these tasks should be your first priority if you hope to be successful in college, circumstances often conspire to divert your attention and undermine your intentions. See "Clarify Values: The Importance of Reading" to reinforce your good intentions.

The Importance of Reading

Here's a surprising fact: Most college students don't do their assigned reading at the time that would be most useful to build their learning, if at all (Nilson 2006). There are several possible explanations. Many students sandwich their reading assignments between intense work and social obligations. Most college students are sleep deprived and find it easier to drift off than follow through. Some students don't bother to buy course texts, assuming—sometimes disastrously—that all the important "stuff" will be covered in lectures. They plan to get by with merely course credit, rather than investing fully to maximize the impact of their tuition dollars.

Think about how you will stand out among your peers and establish yourself as a genuine scholar if you do the reading—and do it well.

Use Self-Assessment 2, "What's Your Reader Profile?" on page 181 to see how your reading skills stack up. Then consider these additional strategies for improving your skills:

- *Stay positive.* Keep a positive attitude. Others have succeeded before you. If they could manage, so can you. If you approach your reading with a feeling of defeat, you may give up instead of pulling through.
- *Make the author your companion.* Most authors envision themselves talking to their readers as they write. As you read, imagine talking to the author as a way of making your reading more lively. When you approach reading as one end of a conversation, it may be easier to make comments, to see relationships, and to be critical.
- *Pace yourself according to the difficulty level.* When you're naturally drawn to a reading or it fits in well with your abilities or interests, you may not have to struggle to get the key ideas. However, you may need to read some difficult writing three or four times before it begins to make sense. When you have two or more kinds of reading to complete, read the harder or duller one first, while your concentration is strongest. We all struggle with hard material—that's normal.
- *Monitor your zoning out.* Your brain operates at a speed that is not always compatible with the reading. It is normal to find yourself off task, especially when the material doesn't grab you. If your rate of zoning out produces real interference with your learning, consider getting a consult from the learning center to see whether some specific strategies will help keep you on task.
- *Take breaks.* Plan to take breaks at regular intervals throughout a reading session. How long you can read between breaks depends on how hard you have to work to grasp the ideas. Examine the material to see whether there are natural breaks, such as the ends of sections, that correspond to your attention span. Reward yourself when you've completed each reading goal. Go for a walk, visit briefly with someone, or do some pleasure reading.
- *Shift gears when you do not make progress.* A fresh start may be required if you find yourself reading and rereading the same passage. Try writing a note on the reading. Take a break. Get something to drink. Call a classmate to confer about your struggle. Return to the passage with an intention to read more slowly until the clouds part.
- *Find other sources if the reading is confusing.* Sometimes an author's style is hard to comprehend. For nonfiction, find a clearer book on the same topic at the library or bookstore. Make sure that it covers things similar to your assigned test. Browsing the

Internet may be helpful as well. Some bookstores sell guides to certain disciplines that may help to clarify basic ideas. Your course textbook may provide either a published or an electronic study guide to help you practice the key ideas. Keep your introductory textbooks as references for when you are challenged in later, tougher courses. Get help from an instructor or tutor in finding other sources.

- *Build your vocabulary.* College is a great place to expand your vocabulary. In the process of learning the specialized languages in a discipline, you'll also expand your general vocabulary. Get a dictionary or use the electronic version on your computer to look up words you don't know. Once you look up a word, practice using the word to help you remember it. Visualize some situation related to the word. Keep a list of new words and their meanings on an index card to use as a bookmark or in an electronic file on your computer.

FIGURE 6.5 Word Attack Skills

Prefixes (word beginnings) and suffixes (word endings) provide clues about word meanings. Here are some common examples from Latin and Greek.

Prefixes	Meaning	Example
a, ab	without or not	*a*theist: nonbeliever in God
ad	to	*ad*vocate: to speak for
ambi	both	*ambi*valent: uncommitted
con	together	*con*vention: formal gathering
de	from or down	*de*spicable: abhorrent
dis	not	*dis*interest: boredom
ex	over	*ex*aggerate: to magnify
hyper	above	*hyper*active: overactive
hypo	under	*hypo*dermic: under skin
mono	single	*mono*lingual: speaking one language
non	not	*non*responsive: not reacting
pro	forward	*pro*duction: process of making
re	back, again	*re*vert: return to former state
sub, sup	under	*sub*ordinate: in a lower position
trans	across	*trans*pose: to change places

Suffixes	Meaning	Example
-able, -ible (adjective)	capable of	respons*ible:* in charge
-ac, -al, -il (adjective)	pertaining to	natur*al:* related to nature
-ance, -ence (noun)	state or status	dalli*ance:* playful activity
-ant, -ent (noun)	one who does	serv*ant:* person who waits on others
-er, -or (noun)	one who does	contract*or:* one who builds
-ive (adjective)	state or status	fest*ive:* partylike
-ish (adjective)	quality of	fool*ish:* like a fool
-less (adjective)	without	heart*less:* harsh, unfeeling
-ly (adjective/adverb)	like	miser*ly:* like a miser
-ness (noun)	state of	peaceful*ness:* state of peace

If you don't have a dictionary nearby when you need it, you may be able to use "word attack" skills to understand a word. That is, you can often divide a word into parts that give you hints about the meaning. Knowing common prefixes and suffixes (word beginnings and endings) can help. See Figure 6.5, "Word Attack Skills," for some common examples. Sometimes you can also determine the meaning of a word from the context of the sentence.

- *Work on reading faster.* Fast readers tend to be more effective learners than slow readers, not only because they remember more of what they read but also because they save valuable time (Armstrong and Lampe 1990). Evaluate your reading speed by completing Self-Assessment 3, "How Fast Do You Read?" on page 182. Improve your reading speed by concentrating on processing more words with each sweep of your eye across a line of text. For example, if you normally scan three words at a time, practice taking in four words with each scan or scan to read whole phrases instead of individual words. You can also ask to have your reading abilities tested formally by reading specialists at the college. They can help you identify specific problems and solutions. See "Build Competence: Reading Habits: Bad and Good," for some other pointers about reading speed.
- *Set goals.* Make commitments that will help you feel more responsible for what you've read. Join a study group or promise to tutor another student who needs help. Shy students can approach their instructors with a plan about how they want to contribute to class on a given day to help them develop confidence about class participation. For example, you might share with the instructor that you have a personal goal to improve your class participation and enlist the instructor's help by calling on you in relation to material you have especially well prepared. Instructors will be drawn to help students who take this unusual but constructive approach because it demonstrates your motivation while sensitizing the instructor to the fact that participation is hard for you.

Always read stuff that will make you look good if you die in the middle of it.

P. J. O'Rourke
Contemporary American political humorist

Plan Time and Space to Concentrate

College reading takes concentration. Schedule blocks of time for reading in a place where you won't be interrupted. On your main schedule, set aside times for study. Clear other concerns from your mind so you can concentrate.

Students differ about where they prefer to read. Many like the library. Others find it *too* quiet or too full of distracting people. Try out a few settings to find out which ones work best for you.

If you can spend only a little time on campus, you may face particular challenges in securing quiet space and uninterrupted time. Some commuters on public transportation can read and review while they travel. If you're stuck with reading an assignment in a noisy environment, you may want to wear headphones with familiar instrumental music just loud enough to block distractions. If you have a long drive to school, you can listen to taped classes in the car.

If you have to combine reading with child care:

- Plan to read during children's nap times, after they have gone to bed, or before they get up.
- Set a timer for fifteen minutes and provide activities that your children can do at the table with you. Let them know that at the end of fifteen minutes—when the timer goes off—everyone will take a play break.

Reading Habits: Bad and Good

One bad habit that many students fall into is *subvocalizing*, or concentrating on sounding out words as they read. Some students actually mouth words as they read, which is quite inefficient. However, others subvocalize with their mouths closed. Subvocalizing dramatically slows down your reading because it limits your reading speed to how fast you talk. Some students also trace the words in the text with their fingers to pace their reading. Unless you specifically need the additional tactile feedback to support your learning, this physical constraint will only slow you down.

One good habit is concentrating on sweeping the line of text with your eyes, fixating between meaningful phrases. For example, you might try to read the last line as "One good habit • is concentrating on • sweeping the line of text • with your eyes • fixating between meaningful phrases." As you work to take in larger units of meaningful text, both your speed and comprehension should increase.

- Find other students with similar child-care needs. Pool your resources to hire a regular babysitter or trade babysitting services to free up more time for reading.

Capture and Connect

Think about the challenge facing Condoleezza Rice in the information processing required to execute her responsibilities. The scope and complexity of information bombarding her requires that she put in place sophisticated strategies for how to approach information. Some information must be studied for complete mastery to avoid embarrassing lapses in public contexts; other information requires merely a "drive by." Rice's political success depends on enacting the right information-processing strategies.

You have similar choices to make. How well you read will depend on your interest level, the complexity of the material, the time you have to do the reading, and your reading skill. If you're very interested in a topic and already know something about it, you may not need specific strategies to comprehend the reading. Just dive in and take appropriate notes. But what if the reading is unfamiliar and difficult? Read both selectively and systematically. Your system will probably include some of the following types of reading: preview, skimming, active reading, analytic reading, and reviewing. Figure 6.6 demonstrates how these different strategies are related.

Before You Read It is always a good idea to preview the material before you sit down to read. This helps you estimate how intense your reading effort will need to be and how much time it will take to complete the assignment. It also gives you a broad overview of the material, which can make it easier to understand and remember the details.

Preview Dave, an education major, always previews his reading assignment no matter what the subject. During the preview, Dave looks at:

- *The context for the assignment.* To see how the assignment fits into the course, Dave thinks about the class activities that have led up to the assignment.
- *The length of the reading.* By applying his reading speed to the number of pages in the assignment, Dave can estimate how long he will need to devote to the job.
- *The structure and features of the reading.* A good time to take a reading break is at the end of a section. Knowing a text's structure can help Dave plan ahead. Textbook features such as summaries can help him rehearse his learning.
- *The difficulty of the reading.* Higher-level material may require more than one reading.

Identify Levels of Reading Effort

There are several different levels at which you can read, depending on the difficulty and importance of the material and the time you have to devote to the task.

Skimming Whereas previewing helps you size up the reading, skimming covers the content at a general level. When you skim, you read at about twice your average rate.

Focus on introductory statements, topic sentences (usually the first sentence in the paragraph), and boldface terms. Slow down to examine summaries carefully. Make sure you understand the points that the author intends. Karen, a management major, likes to skim a text before she settles down to read more intensely. Skimming gives her a sense of the kind of information her assignment contains. She recognizes that the concepts in many of her courses overlap. By skimming the material, she can see where the assignment contains new ideas that she'll have to read more carefully.

FIGURE 6.6 Elements of Your Reading Plan

Approaching your reading assignments strategically means adopting different reading strategies. The type of reading you choose depends on your available time, the complexity of the material, and your motivation to master the ideas. As you go from the top to the bottom of the pyramid, the intensity of your effort increases: You become more involved with the material, and the reading task becomes more demanding. The consequences of your review may return you to the reading to skim, read actively, or read analytically.

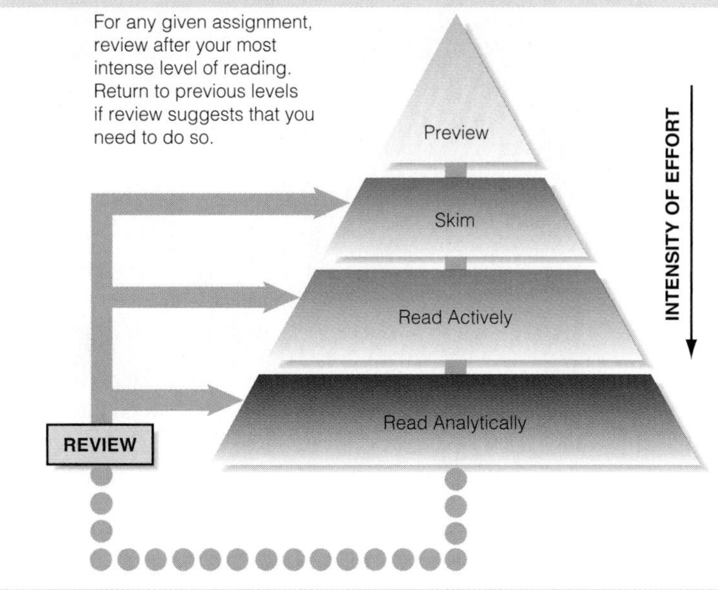

Markie, a full-time communications major with a half-time job, doesn't always have the time to read her assignments as thoroughly as she should. Rather than abandoning her reading, she skims some assignments. She usually reserves the strategy for easier courses so she can concentrate more intensely on her tougher ones.

You don't always need to read every word of every assignment (Frank 1996). Your ability to read selectively improves as you grow accustomed to how readings relate to a course and how your instructor chooses test material. Skimming provides you with the surface structure of the ideas in the text when that is all you have time for. Successful skimmers can usually participate in class discussions with some confidence if they rehearse the main ideas and have read some key passages.

> ***He has only half learned the art of reading who has not added to it the more refined art of skipping and skimming.***
>
> Arthur James Balfour
> *Nineteenth-century British statesman*

Active Reading Takima, a music major, was distressed to reach the bottom of a page of her science book only to discover that she had absorbed no information from her reading. You've probably experienced something similar. It's easy to engage in empty reading. Your eyes track across the lines of text but your brain fails to register anything meaningful.

Read texts *actively* to prevent the wasted time of empty reading or to avoid having to read the same material again. Immerse yourself in what the author is trying to say. Identify the main ideas and understand how the supporting points reinforce those ideas. Also construct the meaning in what you read by linking the information to your own personal knowledge or experience. Use these questions as guidelines for active reading:

- Have I ever experienced anything similar to what is described in the reading?
- How does this relate to things I already know?
- How might this be useful for me to know?

Sifting through the vast array of information on the Internet to get what you need takes time, energy, and careful attention.

- Do I like or agree with these ideas?
- How does the reading relate to current events?

Active readers form as many links as possible between their personal experience and knowledge and what they're reading.

Analytic Reading Joshua, majoring in premed, likes to read his assignments intensely. Like other analytic readers, he likes to break ideas open or dig underneath their surfaces. He tries to spot flaws in the writer's logic and identifies which elements are clear and which are confusing. He compares the quality of the work to that of other works he has read. He examines whether the materials are persuasive enough to change his own viewpoint. Good analytic readers question both the author and themselves as they dig their way through a reading. The following questions may help you become an analytic reader:

- What are the author's values and background? Do these influence the writing? How?
- Does the author's bias taint the truthfulness of what I'm reading?
- What implicit (unstated) assumptions does the author make?
- Do I believe the evidence?
- Is the author's position valid?
- Are the arguments logically developed?
- What predictions follow from the argument?
- What are the strengths and weaknesses of the argument?
- Is anything missing from the position?
- What questions would I want to ask the author?
- Is there a different way to look at the facts or ideas?
- Would these ideas apply to all people in all cultures or in all situations?

After You Read The final step in a successful reading plan is to review the material after it has been read. There are several different strategies for reviewing.

Review An anthropology major, Sanjay likes to review his reading assignments to help consolidate his learning. He reviews his notes immediately after class and before he begins his next reading assignment. Reviewing the assignment makes the main points stand out and makes them easier to remember.

Think of reviewing as an opportunity to test yourself on your own comprehension. Question yourself on details or write out summaries of what you've read. The quality of your notes can make all the difference when it's time to study for a test. With well-constructed notes that you have reviewed systematically after your classes, your final review should be a breeze. Figure 6.7 recommends some combinations for different reading tasks. To understand your own reading patterns, complete the Journal activity "How Do You Read?" on page 183.

"We think you may be suffering from information underload."

Pick Up the Pace

Another strategy to address level of effort is thinking about the overall pace of reading required for the purpose (Schaffzin 1998). In general, textbook reading requires a slow pace because your goal is mastery of the material. You most likely will have to study and memorize the details to survive a test. It pays to go slowly. In contrast, some reading, such as the kind you would find in newspapers, magazines, and memos, can be grasped using a medium reading speed. You are not likely to be tested on this material, but your reading should strive to produce an overall grasp of the main themes and ideas with less attention to the details. Finally, some writing lends itself to a fast pace, such as fiction and other narrative forms.

Know How to Read Primary and Secondary Sources

There are two general types of readings for courses: primary sources and secondary sources. A primary source is material written in some original form, such as autobiographies, speeches, research reports, scholarly articles, government documents, and historical journal articles. For example, you may read the U.S. Constitution as a primary source in your political science class.

Secondary sources summarize or interpret these primary sources. A magazine article that discusses politicians' interpretations of the Constitution generally would be considered a secondary source. Textbooks are secondary sources that try to give a comprehensive view of information from numerous primary works.

You have many more opportunities to read primary sources in college than you did in high school. Most people find reading original works exhilarating. For example,

Reading a book is like re-writing it for yourself. You bring to a novel, anything you read, all your experience of the world. You bring your history and you read it in your own terms.

Angela Carter
Twentieth-century British writer and educator

FIGURE 6.7 Reading Strategies for Different Situations

When you want to develop understanding of the ideas:
Preview → Active reading → Review
When you want to practice critical thinking about your reading:
Preview → Analytic reading → Review
When you have trouble retaining what you read:
Preview → Skim → Active reading → Review → Review
When you don't have time to read for mastery:
Skim → Review
(pay close attention to summaries and boldface terms)

My friend invented Cliff's Notes. When I asked him how he got such a great idea, he said, "Well, first I . . . I just . . . well, to make a long story short. . . ."

Stephen Wright
Contemporary American actor and writer

reading a speech by Frederick Douglass about the abolition of slavery will likely stimulate you more than reading interpretations of his speeches. However, primary sources may be more difficult to read than secondary sources. Primary source vocabulary may be more obscure, encouraging you to sit with a dictionary close by to help you decode the meaning. Secondary sources often summarize and interpret the meaning of the primary source. While original works must be chewed and digested, the secondary source does some of the chewing and digesting for you.

Interpreting original ideas is also more challenging than accepting others' interpretations. When reading primary sources, learn as much as you can about the intentions of the authors and the historical context in which they were writing. Understanding a historical period will help you interpret texts written at that time. Check out the Journal activity "Primary versus Secondary Accounts" on page 183 to clarify how these differ.

Master Reading in Different Disciplines

As you've already discovered, some readings are more challenging than others. That's normal. Obviously, you'll learn material more easily if it matches an area in which you have special interests and intellectual strengths. However, liberal arts programs almost always require reading about topics that don't come naturally. In some readings, technical terms may slow you down. Other readings may require more imagination. Let's explore some tips that will help you read more efficiently in a variety of disciplines, some of which will be more challenging for you than others.

MANAGE LIFE

Fiction in the Crunch

Despite your best intentions, you may find yourself with an assigned novel and no time to chew and digest the work on your own. What are some recommendations to help with the time crunch if you can't complete the work (cf. Schaffzin 1998)?

1. Read the first and last chapter completely. You should have enough detail to help you with the basics.
2. Scan the book to see if you can trace the plot. Skip any details, such as dialogue, that don't shed more light on plot.
3. Identify repeated imagery. Symbols and themes will be repeated in the work, and being able to describe such special features can impress a professor.
4. Cruise shortened versions. Checking out *Cliff's Notes* is better than nothing, but don't expect to get the rich impact from these interpretations that you would from the original assignment.
5. Should you watch the movie version? If you have two hours, you would probably be better off digesting the book directly. Films can sometimes take the book in a different direction than the author originally intended. Relying on the film can expose the fact that you haven't really done the reading assignment.

Literature In literature courses, you study poetry, novels, plays, and short stories. Appreciation of these forms comes most easily to people who enjoy reflective learning and who like to think critically. For them, many great works provide delight. But what strategies can help you when reading literature is challenging?

- *Use your imagination.* Visualize the action. Participate at the level the author intended: Use as many senses as the author used—taste, smell, sound—as you recreate the author's world in your imagination.
- *Look for connections.* Are any of the experiences like your own? Do the characters remind you of anyone you know?
- *Monitor theme development.* Most powerful literature concentrates on specific themes. Look for emerging themes and keep track of the manner in which the author pursues the theme. This practice will help the work hang together more effectively as you read and later try to remember the elements for testing purposes.
- *Make the author real.* Search the Internet for a good biography or personal details about the author that might help you understand the author's motivation to create the work.
- *Make a chart.* If the reading is complex, make a list of key figures as they are introduced so you can easily review as the story progresses.
- *Predict what will happen.* Once you understand the direction the work is taking, see whether you can anticipate what happens next.

- *Read aloud.* Some great works are savored best when read aloud. Find a study partner and share the task. Remember to allow more time for this strategy, but the investment will be worthwhile because you will generate more-vivid memory cues using this approach.
- *Budget sufficient time.* Complex reading takes time. Be sure to set aside sufficient time not just for reading but for thinking, too. When your life conditions prevent you from following through on your plan, refer to "Manage Life: Fiction in the Crunch."

"Read the book!" "See the movie!"

History Some students love history because they believe that we are all the walking expression of history. Others enjoy history because historical insights illuminate the present and set our direction for the future. Either way, history texts provide a great opportunity to use your imagination which will come alive if you let it. Good readers in history put conscientious effort into seeing how events, places, and people interconnect. There are a number of approaches for accomplishing this:

- *Put yourself in the picture.* As you read about events, think about how you might have reacted to them at the time.
- *Change history.* Predict an alternative course of history by changing a critical event or two. How might the ripple effect have changed some element of your life?
- *Distinguish central ideas from supporting ideas.* You won't be tested on every detail you read. Practice identifying the most critical aspects of what you read that seem more "testworthy."
- *Imagine or draw the timeline.* See whether you can determine how one event leads to another. Impose pictures on the timeline that capture the flavor of the era or the action.
- *Make it into a movie.* Imagine a cast of film stars in the roles of the historical figures you're reading about. It may help you visualize the action better.
- *Reinforce what you know by watching relevant films critically.* If you have the chance to see a movie that depicts the era in history that you are studying, watch the film carefully to spot mistakes that expose what the filmmaker didn't understand about the era.
- *Don't forget the big picture.* Keep in mind how each new event or person you encounter in your learning adds to your understanding of the grander historic scale.

Natural and Social Science The sciences can be especially challenging because of the level of abstraction in some scientific writing. The terminology presented in the sciences represents a kind of shorthand that allows scientists to communicate with each other. Learning these terms can be a challenge without some helpful strategies such as:

- *Keep a running glossary of terms.* Treat the sciences like a foreign language. Each new term stands for a concept. Study the meaning of each and develop a reliable repository for the ideas. Some students like to write terms inside the cover of the text or a notebook, or you can create a terms bookmark that can help you keep track of your progress in the text.
- *Accept the role of numbers.* If you aren't comfortable with numbers, you may be turned off by the practice of measurement and statistics that pervades most sciences. Don't be. When numbers accompany text, spend extra time understanding their significance.

- *Think practically.* See whether you can come up with a practical application of the scientific relationships you're reading about. For instance, imagine yourself as the head of a lab charged with exploiting the new scientific finding for public benefit. Or perhaps you could make some predictions about the potential risks of implementing the findings. You can even turn science into science fiction! How could these principles develop a great science fiction plot?
- *Look for links in the news.* The sciences regularly issue progress reports that may enhance your understanding or clarify concepts. Many publications and news magazines also feature regular science columns that discuss applications of science and technology to daily life, health, the environment, and so on. Even if you've never read them before, get in the habit of looking for them and finding topics that relate to your class.
- *Cruise the Internet.* Chances are good that the Internet will provide ideas that will help you with the vocabulary of science. Find information about the scientists themselves that will help make the enterprise feel more real to you.
- *Look for overlaps.* Where does your life intersect with the scientific ideas you're trying to learn? If the material doesn't have any relevance for you now, would it be relevant for your relatives or for you at a later time in your life?

Take Great Reading Notes

The expertise you develop in taking good notes during lectures can also help you take effective notes from reading assignments. The principles are the same:

- Capture the main ideas.
- Show how secondary information connects and supports main ideas.
- Choose a note-taking format that maximizes your retention and learning.

Choose the Best Method

There are three general strategies for taking reading notes: highlighting the text, personalizing it, and making external notes as you read.

Highlight Text Using a highlighter helps many students concentrate as they read and makes it easier for them to review for tests. Ideally, highlight topic sentences, key words, and conclusions, which usually make up much less than one-quarter of a text.

Although this strategy may keep you engaged with the reading, it presents several hazards. You may highlight too much material so that you are faced with rereading nearly the entire text when you review. It's easy to find yourself mindlessly highlighting text, giving yourself the illusion of reading when you haven't really absorbed the key ideas. Also, simply highlighting does not show why you thought that passage was important. And when it's time to review, you still need to carry the complete text with you. Finally, if you sell your text after the course is over, the highlighting may reduce its value. Other strategies that promote greater involvement are likely to be more helpful in the long run. See Figure 6.8, "Highlighted Notes," for a model of effective highlights.

Personalize the Text Some students find that they can absorb a text more easily by using the margins to simulate an interaction with the author. Think of the margin notes as your opportunity to engage in an imaginary conversation with the text's author. Contemplate what questions you would like to ask. Identify areas that might not make sense to you. Jot down a personal example that illustrates a key point. Fill the margins with your good connections. To make your learning more vivid, you can draw arrows or thumbs-down signs when you disagree, and circle key terms. Draw symbols. Write summary notes.

Take Notes as You Read Earlier in the chapter, you learned about four techniques for taking notes from lecture: summarizing, outlining, the Cornell Method, and Concept Mapping. These techniques also work for notes that you take from reading. What are some advantages of applying these methods to taking notes from texts?

Summarizing This technique helps you extract the key ideas from passages and put them in your own words. Plan to summarize after each major subdivision in your reading. If the text has no headings, try to summarize after you have read a small or sufficient number of pages. The author's summaries will highlight the important key ideas, but they may glance over details that could be critical to your success at exam time.

> ***I had the worst study habits and the lowest grades. Then I found out what I was doing wrong. I had been highlighting with a black magic marker.***
>
> Jeff Altman
> *Contemporary American comedian*

Outlining Outlining imposes a systematic organization with predictable headings (I, A, 1, a . . .) to represent faithfully the complexity of the materials you read. Outlines distinguish main points (headings I and A) from supporting points (1 and a) and facilitate quick review for exams. Outlining tends to be a preferred note-taking mode for people who enjoy making explicit the nature of the relationship among concepts in the reading. Outlining from texts works best when the assigned reading materials are logically organized. If they are not, less-rigid strategies will work better.

The Cornell Method When applied to notes from texts, the Cornell Method combines the best features of creating external notes with the personalization of making notes in the margin of your book. When you use this method, you subdivide the note page into a main portion summarizing what you read and smaller sections for your responses, answers, questions, and connections, as discussed earlier. Figure 6.9, "Cornell Notes on Reading," provides good examples of note taking.

Concept Mapping This strategy turns the content from the reading into a visual representation. Developing maps strongly appeals to visual learners. Concept maps can get messy if the text contains dense, interrelated content, but they also provide a great tool for review. Consider the Journal activity "Note Taking Now" on page 184 to practice some of these methods.

Follow Other Note-Taking Tips

Regardless of the method you choose, there are some general strategies that will maximize your effectiveness:

- *Write your notes in your own words.* Translating an author's words into your own increases the personal connections you make to the material and makes it easier to remember. It also helps you avoid plagiarism when you use the notes to write a paper. When you literally lift the words of an author from a text and later present these words as your own, you are stealing the thoughts and expressions of another. Instructors may view this as laziness or deceit and may penalize you.
- *Avoid writing down things you don't understand.* You simply won't understand some

"All very well and good—but now we come to chart B."

FIGURE 6.8 Highlighted Notes

Minorities and Stardom

Stark, R. (1994). *Sociology.* 5th Edition.

NBA = African-American?

The majority of players on every team in the National Basketball Association are African American. White boxing champions are rare. A far greater proportion of professional football players are African American than would be expected based on the size of the African-American population. Furthermore, African Americans began to excel in sports long before the Civil Rights Movement broke down barriers excluding them from many other occupations. This has led many people, both African American and white, to conclude that African Americans are born with a natural talent for athletics. How else could they have come to dominate the ranks of superstars?

main question

The trouble with this biological explanation of African Americans in sports is that it ignores an obvious historical fact: It is typical for minorities in North America to make their first substantial progress in sports (and, for similar reasons, in entertainment). Who today would suggest that Jews have a biological advantage in athletics? Yet at the turn of the century, the number of Jews who excelled in sports far exceeded their proportion in the population. And late in the 19th century, the Irish dominated sports to almost the same extent as African Americans have done in recent decades.

example: Jews showed same pattern 19th cent.

By examining an encyclopedia of boxing, for example, we can draw accurate conclusions about patterns of immigration and periods at which ethnic groups were on the bottom of the stratification system. The Irish domination of boxing in the latter half of the 19th century is obvious from the names of heavyweight champions, beginning with bareknuckle champ Ned O'Baldwin in 1867 and including Mike McCoole in 1869, Paddy Ryan in 1880, John L. Sullivan in 1889, and Jim Corbett in 1892. The list of champions in lower-weight divisions during the same era is dominated by fighters named Ryan, Murphy, Delaney, Lynch, O'Brien, and McCoy.

Early in the 20th century, Irish names became much less common among boxing champions, even though many fighters who were not Irish took Irish ring names. Suddenly, champions had names like Battling Levinsky, Maxie Rosenbloom, Benny Leonard, Abe Goldstein, Kid Kaplan, and Izzy Schwartz. This was the Jewish era in boxing.

Then Jewish names dropped out of the lists, and Italian and eastern European names came to the fore: Canzoneri, Battalino, LaMotta, Graziano, and Basilio; Yarosz, Lesnevich, Zale, Risko, Hostak, and Servo. By the 1940s, fighters were disproportionately African American. Today, African-American domination of boxing has already peaked, and Hispanic names have begun to prevail.

history of boxing:

Irish

Jews

Italians

Af. Am.

The current overrepresentation of African Americans in sports reflects two things: first, a *lack of other avenues to wealth and fame*, and, second, the fact that minority groups can overcome discrimination most easily in occupations in which *the quality of individual performance is most easily and accurately assessed* (Blalock, 1967). These same factors led to the overrepresentation of other ethnic groups in sports earlier in history.

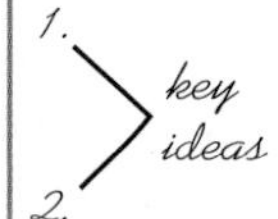

1. 2. key ideas

It often is difficult to know which applicants to a law school or a pilot training school are the most capable. But we can see who can box or hit a baseball. The demonstration of talent, especially in sports and entertainment, tends to break down barriers of discrimination. As these fall, opportunities in these areas for wealth and fame open up, while other opportunities remain closed. Thus, minority groups will aspire to those areas in which the opportunities are open and will tend to overachieve in these areas.

this is why

ideas on a first reading. You may feel tempted to write down unclear ideas with the intention of returning to them later. Don't. Instead, mark the passage with a question mark and do what you can to clarify it before you record it and move on.

FIGURE 6.9 Cornell Notes on Reading

	Stark, R. (1994), Sociology. Belmont, CA: Wadsworth. p.333
	Minorities and sports
"Natural talent" of A-A's in sports?	Popular biological view: African-Americans born with natural athletic talent because so many pro athletes are A-A, compared with their percentage in U.S. pop.
But similar pattern for other minorities	But other minorities also made their first big progress in sports (& entertainment). See lists of boxing champions: * Irish dominate last half 19th century * Jews around 1900 * Italians dominate after Jews * A-A dominate after Italians * Hispanic champions now (& future)?
	Proposed sociological reason for numbers of A-A in pro sports?
Real reasons for current number of A-A's in sports?	1. "Lack of other avenues to wealth and fame" 2. "Quality of individual performance easily and accurately assessed" in sports.
	Importance of talent in sports & entertainment tends to break down discrimination barriers in these areas before other areas of life.

People say A-A's excel in pro sports now due just to "biology." But other minorities have gone though the same pattern of excellence in sports until they were accepted in other fields. In sports individual talents can be seen, so discrimination barriers not as bad as in other fields.

Q: What about other sports beside boxing? What about music? Same pattern? How much are opportunities changing for A-A's outside sports?

- *Think and record in pictures.* Try to turn information from the text into some other form, such as a list, table, graph, or picture, to make it easier for you to recall. Diagrams and tables also can be tools for summarizing.
- *Explain yourself.* College reading is often complex and abstract. It's easy to read a mass of material and think you understand what you've read when in fact you missed a key idea. Imagine that you have a study companion who doesn't read as well as you do and struggles to understand the central ideas in assignments. Regularly explain the key ideas in the reading to your "friend," particularly when the material is harder or less interesting for you than usual. When you can't explain the passage easily, you need to review it. Of course, if you use this strategy, please tell your roommates about it so they won't think you're cracking up!
- *Periodically evaluate the quality of your notes.* Especially after an exam, review your notes to see how well they worked. To make some comparisons of note-taking strategies across different course contexts, complete the Journal activity "A Shared Path to Success" on page 184.

Getting information off the Internet is like taking a drink from a fire hydrant.
Mitchell Kapor
Contemporary American computer expert

Take What You Need from the Internet

The Internet is one of your best learning resources, but you have to use it properly at the college level to maximize your benefits.

Check before you search You may plan to conduct your research process completely online for your convenience. Although there is a lot of valuable information on the Internet, many instructors have strict requirements about what may or may not be used in their assignments. Many exclude Internet sources because of uncertainty about quality.

Navigate to the right spot If you are starting a cold search on the Internet, you may have to spend some time playing with the key terms to help you find the most valuable resources. An ambiguous or poorly defined search can produce too many hits for you to review, especially if you are in a time crunch. Cut back on your harvest of information by adding some terms to the search or more sharply define the key terms you are using.

Monitor quality of the resource Not everything on the Internet is credible. Some sites are simply not appropriate for work you need to submit at the college level. Your best bet will be using information developed by recognized experts in the field. If you have questions about the suitability of a resource, ask your instructor.

Beware of cut-and-paste strategies The information on the Internet is so easy to transport from one context to another that it may be tempting just to capture the information by executing a cut-and-paste command from the Internet to your computer. Although it may give you the data you need, this approach can promote plagiarism. When you intend to use the information in your own paper, be careful to paraphrase what you have captured. Many instructors use special programs to detect materials that have been downloaded from the Internet into student papers, and the penalty for evidence of plagiarism can be severe.

Make durable and protective records Create an electronic document for every research citation you produce (Rosen 2006). The best strategy is to cut and paste the passage that you want to capture as the foundation of the note you wish to make—but don't stop there. Be sure to include the URL (internet address of the web page), and date the record to indicate when you retrieved the information. If available, write down the author and the date the author originally submitted the information. Finally, write down in your own words what you intend to do with the passage. This final step can help you avoid inadvertently cutting and pasting another person's work into your writing.

Bookmark important resources Sometimes you get lucky. You may find a superb website that will continue to provide helpful information to you for the duration of a course. Enter the site into your list of favorites so you can easily refer to it again.

Putting Study Skills to Work

Marty loved to read. He saw research assignments as a great opportunity to test his detective skills and especially enjoyed projects that allowed him to find obscure information. He honed his research skills so well that he embarked on an unusual career path that regularly gave him the opportunity to read and conduct research as a lifestyle. He became a fact-checker for novelists. One of his clients liked to write complex techno-thrillers that required a lot of technological background. Marty routinely might figure out how to incorporate the latest developments in bioterrorism or nuclear weaponry to help his clients produce best-selling but factually accurate works.

Kirsten liked the intellectual challenge of taking good lecture notes. Early in her college career she prided herself on her ability to deal with the most complex lectures. She worked out an extensive personal coding system to maximize her efficiency in recording key ideas and distinguishing her interpretations from the facts of the matter. Because she was so curious about human nature, she pursued a job in journalism, where her exceptional ability to identify and report key themes were essential to her success.

Process Information Professionally

When you think about how much time you will spend over the course of your college career learning from text and lectures, you may feel a bit resentful. Sometimes such systematic study can feel like busy work, especially if the process you go through doesn't quite translate into the grades that you want. However, think again. Such work can be quite useful, as seen in "Create Your Future: Putting Study Skills to Work."

Any profession that you pursue will test you regularly on how well you can read and listen. The good habits that you develop in college should carry over into successful work contexts. Remember that creating your future is one of your six key strategies for success—it is never too soon to start preparing for the future. Among other responsibilities, you may need to:

- record and implement a medical program for a client
- absorb the key points from a proposal to increase sales, based on what you hear at a marketing meeting
- extract principles from a legal precedent to prepare a legal brief
- identify, communicate accurately, and take action on the primary complaints of a dissatisfied customer
- search the Internet to find news relevant to a current dilemma that influences social policy

Note how each of these situations will benefit from conscientious practice at being a good listener, note taker, and reader. See the Journal activity "Taking Advantage" on page 184 to size up how your future plans might benefit from refining your skills in information processing.

Summary Strategies for Mastering College

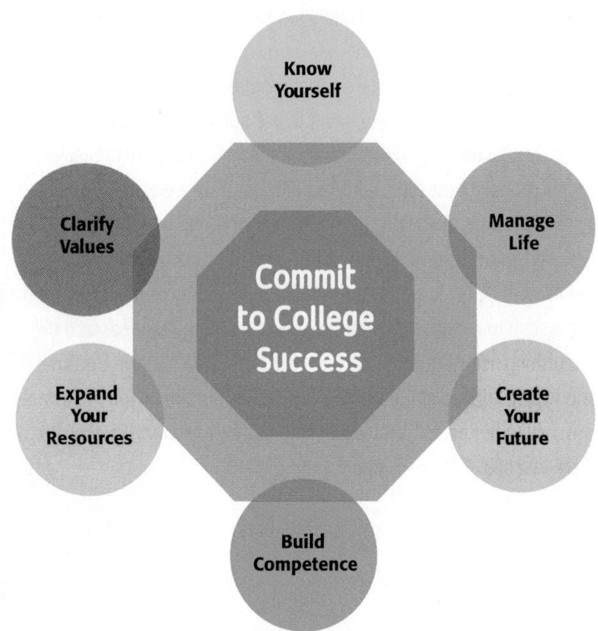

Focus on the Six Strategies for Success above as you read each chapter to learn how to apply these strategies to your own success.

1 Commit, Concentrate, Capture, Connect

- Summarize information in ways that fit your learning style.
- To make your strategies successful, you need to make a commitment, concentrate, capture key ideas, and make connections.

2 Take Charge of Lectures

- Commit to attending class to get the most out of lectures.
- Overcome distractions to improve your concentration.
- Adapt your listening skills to the demands of the course and the style of the teacher.

3 Take Great Lecture Notes

- Find a note-taking format that works well with your learning style.
- Use your notes strategically to improve your ability to recall information.

4 Take Charge of Your Reading

- Find the right time and space to make your reading effective and efficient.
- Tailor your reading intensity and speed to the course requirements.
- Approach disciplines with different strategies depending on your interest level and complexity of the material.

5 Take Great Reading Notes

- Experiment with note-taking strategies that will help you identify and retain the most important ideas.
- Use your own words to record ideas from texts in order to learn the material well and avoid plagiarism.
- Harvest what you need from the Internet by using strategic search methods.

6 Process Information Professionally

- Show patience with how much effort will be required in information processing in your classes.
- Imagine how refined note taking and reading skills will benefit you in the future.

Review Questions

1. Write down the four Cs of learning new information. Also include a few ways each can be applied to learning from lectures and reading assignments.

   1. C: ______

   2. C: ______

   3. C: ______

   4. C: ______

2. What are three tips for listening most effectively to challenging lectures? How can these tips also be applied to absorbing information from difficult readings?

   1. ______

   2. ______

   3. ______

3. What style of note taking makes the most sense for each of the classes you're currently taking? List your classes below, followed by the best method.

   1. ______

   2. ______

   3. ______

   4. ______

   5. ______

4. List the three ways to process information as you read. How can each style help you succeed in your various college courses? What type do you currently use most often and why?

   1. ______

   2. ______

   3. ______

5. What are some good strategies for taking notes on your readings? List a few pros and cons of each.

SELF-ASSESSMENT 1

Auditing Your Note-Taking Style for Lectures

	Always	Sometimes	Never
I approach listening actively.			
I select note-taking formats to suit the various courses I take.			
I organize my notes in one place.			
I label the lecture with title and date.			
I take notes from all participants in class.			
I concentrate during class.			
I work to build my vocabulary.			
I cross out errors instead of erasing them.			
I try not to write dense notes. I leave space for adding more later.			
I listen for directional cues or emphasis.			
I avoid shutting down when I have a negative reaction to what I hear.			
I highlight key ideas or themes.			
I use abbreviations to save time.			
I personalize my notes.			
I review my notes after class.			
I pay attention to the quality of my note-taking process as I go.			
I would consider asking the instructor for help in constructing better notes.			

Results: Look at the pattern of the responses that you made on this assessment. Your best note-taking strategies are reflected in checks in the Always column on the left. If the majority of your checks fall in the Always column, you are establishing a good foundation for study with your note-taking practices. Now look at the items marked Never. What would it take for you to add each of these items to your note-taking toolbox?

SELF-ASSESSMENT 2

What's Your Reader Profile?

Circle the alternative that best describes you as a reader.

1. When I have an assignment to read,
  a. I'm usually enthusiastic about what I'll learn.
  b. I like to wait to see whether what I have read will be valuable.
  c. I'm generally apprehensive about reading assignments because I'm afraid I won't understand them.

2. What is my attitude toward the authors of my college books?
  a. I think of them as human beings with an interesting story to tell.
  b. I haven't really given the writers much thought.
  c. I think of them as people who will probably talk over my head.

3. When I plan my reading,
  a. I think about how the assignment fits in with the objectives of the course.
  b. I review the prior assignment to set the stage for current work.
  c. I plunge in so I can get it done.

4. I take breaks
  a. to consolidate the information I read.
  b. to help me study longer and more productively.
  c. whenever I lose interest in my reading.

5. When I don't know a word,
  a. I look it up, write it down, and practice it.
  b. I try to figure it out from the context of the sentence.
  c. I usually skip over it and hope it won't make too much difference in the meaning of the passage.

6. When I can't understand a sentence,
  a. I reread the sentence more carefully.
  b. I try to figure out the sentence from the context of the paragraph.
  c. I skip the sentence, hoping it will make sense later.

7. When the whole assignment confuses me,
  a. I try to find more materials that will shed some light on my confusion.
  b. I ask the instructor or someone else for ideas about how to cope with the assignment.
  c. I tend to give up on it.

8. When I read,
  a. I try to read as fast as I can while still understanding the meaning.
  b. I try to sweep as many words as I can at a glance.
  c. I take it one word at a time—speed doesn't matter to me.

Results: Alternatives a and b of each question indicate successful reading habits. Revisit any c alternatives that you marked. Think about possible causes of these less-successful patterns. You may benefit from a visit with a reading specialist on campus.

SELF-ASSESSMENT 3

How Fast Do You Read?

Select a text from one of your courses. Set a timer for five minutes and start reading. When the timer goes off, stop reading. Count the number of lines you read in the five-minute period. Pick several lines at random in the text and count the number of words in the lines. Multiply the number of lines you read by the average number of words per line. This will give you an approximation of the total words you read in the five-minute period. Finally, divide by five to produce your reading speed in words per minute.

Content area: ______________________________

Date of assessment: ______________________________

Number of lines read: ______________________________

× Number of words per line: ______________________________

= Approximate total words: ______________________________

Divided by 5 (minutes): ______________________________

Approximate words per minute: ______________________________

How does your reading speed compare with these average speeds for different kinds of reading (Skinner 1997)?

Skimming	eight hundred words per minute
Active reading	one hundred to two hundred words per minute
Analytic reading	under one hundred words per minute

Results: Use this estimate as a baseline for your reading speed. If the material was well suited to your interest areas, you were probably able to read within the range for effective active reading. If the material was very familiar, your rate was probably higher, approaching the rates found in skimming. If your reading rate was below one hundred words per minute, this may be a cause for concern. Although that reading rate is acceptable for complex materials, a slower reading rate on routine materials predicts that you may have difficulty keeping up with your reading assignments.

Consider going for a more thorough evaluation of your reading strengths and weaknesses at the campus study skill center. Professional assistance can pinpoint the problem and make your future reading strategies much more successful.

Your Journal

REFLECT

1. Show and Tell

Carefully look over the notes that you have taken in a course where your learning isn't coming easily. Think about what clues to your struggle may be present in how you take notes. For example,

- Are you staying tuned in throughout the class?

___

- Are you writing down words that you don't understand?

___

- Do the lecture notes fit with the big picture?

___

Then follow up on your reflection by visiting your instructor during posted office hours. Take your notes and your observations with you. Ask the instructor to review your approach to see if other suggestions might improve your gains from note taking.

2. Daydream Believer

One of the biggest obstacles to successful listening in class is the tendency to daydream. Monitor your listening in your current courses for one week. In which class did you daydream the most? Why do you think this is happening? Perhaps the room is too hot or the lecture falls right after lunch. List some possible reasons below. Now list some strategies for conquering your daydreams and implement these strategies next week.

Daydreaming in class: ___

Possible reasons: ___

Strategies: ___

DO

1. Primary versus Secondary Accounts

Read a newspaper account (a secondary source) of a recent scientific achievement or issue and list it below. Then ask a librarian to help you track down the original work (the primary source) in a scientific journal at the library or online. Compare the length of the reports, the language level difficulty, the order of importance of ideas, and any other contrasting features. Based on your observations, how would you say that primary and secondary sources differ?

Scientific achievement or issue: ___

Focus of secondary source: ___

Focus of primary source: ___

How do they differ? ___

2. How Do You Read?

Monitor how you read your assignments for one week. Then rate how regularly you engage in different kinds of reading:

	Regularly	Sometimes	Rarely
Previewing:	___	___	___
Skimming:	___	___	___
Active reading:	___	___	___
Analytic reading:	___	___	___
Reviewing:	___	___	___

In what area are you the strongest, and how might this impact your academic performance? In what area do you need the most practice?

___

Your Journal

THINK CRITICALLY

1. A Shared Path to Success

Form a small group in your college success class to compare your strategies for taking notes in this course. If you have another course in common, compare your approaches to that content area as well. See whether as a group you can determine which approaches are most effective in capturing the critical ideas in these contexts. How does the type of course influence note-taking strategies?

2. Analyze the Sixth Sense

Some students seem to have an uncanny ability to figure out what information given in class will show up on the tests. Think about what kinds of cues they're picking up on in class and apply them to one of your courses.

- How do the instructor's vocal cues tell you what's important?
- What kinds of words show an instructor's intent?
- What behaviors show an instructor's excitement about concepts?
- How does your instructor tend to stress important concepts?

CREATE

1. Taking Advantage

Effective organizational strategies will serve you well not only in college but also throughout life. Think about your future. How will the ability to process information effectively and efficiently influence the quality of your work? Think about the advantages you can gain by developing good information-processing skills now.

2. Note Taking Now

Spend the next ten minutes skimming the next chapter in this text and creating an outline of its content. After you are done, compare your outline with the one the authors provide on the first page of the chapter. How was your outline similar or different? Did you miss any main ideas or capture any additional points? Think about how your presentation of content might differ if you had made a concept map or summary. What strategy do you think works best for you?

7 Enhance Your Study Skills and Memory

© John Henley/CORBIS

KNOW YOURSELF

Studying works best when you know how to make good use of your study time. This chapter explores ways to bring your study habits under your control, improve your memory, and get the most from your study of various disciplines. To evaluate where you stand right now, place a check next to only those items that apply to you.

- I choose appropriate places and times to study.
- I set reasonable goals for study sessions.
- I review regularly to learn course information better.
- I organize materials and use strategies to make ideas easier to learn and remember.
- I pursue deep learning strategies when I can.
- I adapt my study strategies to suit different disciplines.
- I take my learning style into account when I study.
- I form study groups to expand my learning resources.

Think about how Janeane Garofalo's life illustrates some important features about memorizing and studying.

CHAPTER OUTLINE

Plan Your Attack

Where to Study
When to Study
What to Study

Master the Disciplines

The Humanities
Natural Science and Math
Social Science
Foreign Languages

Join a Study Group

Making Study Groups Work
Overcoming Group-Work Obstacles

Overcome Learning Disabilities

Evaluate Your Issues
Know Your Rights
Compensate

Improve Your Memory

How Memory Works
How to Memorize
Additional Memory Strategies
Evaluate Your Progress

Images of College Success

Janeane Garofalo

At 5 foot 1, Janeane Garofalo is a surprising comedy giant (Kappes 2001).

Her alternative stand-up, a refreshing mix of jokes and self-deprecation that Janeane describes as "hit-and-run confession," has won fans across generations. Janeane's most popular film, *The Truth about Cats and Dogs*, cast her as a veterinarian who hosts a successful talk show about managing pet problems, but she has dubious success managing her own love life. This breakout role established her on- and off-screen persona as hip, sarcastic, and smart.

Janeane began to study popular comedy styles in high school, memorizing the routines she liked best. During her senior year at Providence College, she participated in an open-mike night at a comedy club. Janeane works hard to keep her stand-up fresh. She carries a notebook to record elements that will become the heart of her future monologues. To make sure that the delivery of her carefully memorized observations will appeal to the audience, she continuously reorganizes the materials, changing the order of what she has stored in memory and making new connections among the ideas. She also reads extensively. She claims that waiting around for filming to start is a great way to stay on top of the stack of books she wants to read. Her favorite book, Viktor Frankl's *Man's Search for Meaning*, is a classic that is often assigned during first-year humanities courses.

© Pace Gregory/CORBIS SYGMA

JANEANE GAROFALO has a successful stand-up routine that is based on a disciplined approach to memorizing skills.

As you read, think about the Six Strategies for Success listed to the left and how this chapter can help you maximize success in these important areas. For example, effective study flows from solid planning based on your goals. Use these goals to motivate yourself to maximize your study skills and resources.

Plan Your Attack

To do well in college, most of us need concentrated study time with notes we've made from readings and classes. A systematic study strategy will make your investment of time and effort pay off. Studying accomplishes many objectives. It makes recalling the core material of the course easier. It helps you develop richer insights. It also promotes good work habits that will carry over into your career.

The amount of time students report doing assignments or studying is related to many aspects of college success (Astin 1993). Students who study more hours say they are more satisfied with college than are students who study less. Also, those who invest more time studying report that college improves their cognitive skills and emotional life. But studying *more* is only one way to improve. Studying *more effectively* also can help. Among other benefits, sensible study methods save you time so you have more of it for social life and other interests.

> ***Those who do not study are only cattle dressed up in men's clothes.***
> Chinese proverb

Imagine the motivation that it took for Janeane Garofalo to learn the comedy routines she memorized. Garofalo was motivated because she loved performing the routines and imagined that it would make her feel good to get up in front of an audience and make people laugh. She created her future by understanding herself and purposefully developing skill sets that helped her achieve her goals.

Visualizing success also makes your goal easier to accomplish. Imagine yourself, after a good study session, coming to class and participating actively in a discussion. Imagine raising your hand to answer one question after another and contributing to the class discussion so effectively that the entire class is responding to your comments. Would that make you feel good? How about getting back a test with a big fat "A—Good Job" on the top? If you can't get motivated to study, just imagine the positive outcomes that can make you feel at the top of your game. They'll help you manage the hard work in between.

Where to Study

The phone rings. Your downstairs neighbor is throwing a noisy party. Your roommate insists on watching *American Idol* full blast. And your relentless appetite demands a

© Kelly-Mooney Photography/CORBIS

Some students can study effectively in uncomfortable postures and distracting environments, but many students prefer to study at a desk or a table. Have you figured out where you study best?

hot fudge sundae. At times the world is so full of distractions that it seems impossible to find the right time and place to study. But your success as a student depends on your conquering these distractions and sticking to a good study routine.

The Best Available Space Find the best place you can to work, and study there consistently. The best place is usually private, quiet, well lit, and a comfortable temperature. For many students, the best place will also offer access to a computer and an online connection. That way you can have Internet resources available to support your work and still maintain a quick fix for the social deprivation that can happen during long periods of study.

Narrow your study sites to one of a few places that provide you with the working space, storage space, and electronic access that will make your work efficient. Finding a study space at home is easiest, but you have other options as well. Colleges usually try to maintain other quiet spaces on campus, which include access to general-use computer labs, wireless hubs, or laptop hookups to facilitate both studying and maintaining your personal network. You may find just the setup you need in the library, a dedicated lab, or even quiet but wired spaces of some campuses. Residence halls often set aside study spaces away from noisy roommates. Ask other seasoned students about good study places on campus to find the most promising and productive sites.

Commuters can use driving time to review audiotapes of complicated lectures. Some instructors are making podcasts of their lectures more commonly available to facilitate review. Carpooling with someone in class also provides review time. Riding on a bus or train, especially if the commute is long, provides blocks of study time, if you can study well in this type of environment. You might even be able to use your laptop effectively if you take precautions regarding computer safety and power needs.

The Right Conditions Although some students can concentrate in strange places and odd postures, most find that sitting at a desk improves concentration. Desks provide storage for study materials and help you stay organized. If you don't have a desk, use boxes or crates to contain and organize your supplies and books. Set up a simple filing system if you can. See "Manage Life: Home Schooling," to see how to adapt to challenging conditions at home.

> ***Patience and tenacity of purpose are worth more than twice their weight in cleverness.***
>
> Thomas Henry Huxley
> *Nineteenth-century English biologist*

Wherever you study, minimize noise. Many people study best when the CD player, radio, and television are off. Some people like music in the background to mask other sounds and give a sense of control over the environment. If you can't control the noise around you, use headphones and soft instrumental music to minimize distraction. How can you pull together these ideas to develop the most supportive study environment? See the Journal activity "Creative Space Management" on page 212 for help.

When to Study

Although some study strategies can make you a better learner, there is no denying the need to study long hours for academic success. How can you best use those hours wisely? How can you motivate yourself to orchestrate your time to maximize available hours for study? See "Clarify Values: Hour by Hour" to evaluate your general commitment to study.

When to Review Review your notes immediately after class. This practice allows you to rehearse new ideas and identify unclear ones while they are fresh, so you can then clarify them with your instructor or in your reading. See "Build Competence: After Class Is Over" for tips on how to review. Reviewing your class notes and notes on reading assignments before the class meets again adds another rehearsal session that prepares you to participate in the next class more effectively. It also reinforces your memory on those concepts. Successful students often get to class about ten minutes early to review their notes. Taking this preparation time to anticipate class events can save you time in the long run.

Schedule regular cumulative review sessions. Devote some time to seeing the big picture in each of your courses. Look at how each lecture fits the broader course objective.

If you regularly review your notes during the term, you'll need less review time right before exams.

MANAGE LIFE

Home Schooling

What if you have to share study space at home with others, even children? Family squabbles over space can subtract dramatically from your study time.

Together, figure out how best to share the space. Some suggestions are:

- Assign desk drawers to everyone who will be sharing the space.
- Hang a bulletin board near the workspace to display everyone's best work and to provide good motivation.
- Tidy up after each study session, especially if you are using the kitchen table, unless you make other arrangements with your family.
- Develop a schedule for access to the family computer. Practice saving your work and respect the privacy of others who share your equipment.

Listen to Your Body Pay attention to your natural rhythms. Research suggests that many young adults undergo developmental changes that predispose them to being night people (Carskadon 1999). They require more rest to cope with those changes and may not get in sync until later in the day. Sometimes that preference lingers so that even older students may feel more functional later in the day than early in the morning.

If you're a night person, review sessions may be most effective after supper and late into the evening. If you're a morning person, you need to study earlier in the day to maximize your attention and concentration. Complete Self-Assessment 1, "Early Bird or Night Owl?" on page 208 to evaluate your high- and low-energy periods.

If you aren't getting the proper amount of rest, studying will be very difficult. You should be able to stay awake and alert if you have had sufficient sleep. Sleep experts (Maas 1999) suggest that traditional-age college students need ten hours of sleep per night because of the significant physiological changes that are unfolding. However, college students report an average of only six hours of sleep—a four-hour deficit each night–that can take a toll on memory, mood, concentration, and other crucial ingredients of college success.

CLARIFY VALUES

Hour by Hour

Most professors advocate studying at least two hours *outside* class for every hour you spend *in* class. Which of the following represents your general orientation toward study?

- I study every minute I'm not committed to some other activity.
- I try to schedule systematically two or more hours for each hour in class.
- I average about one hour outside of class for each hour in class.
- I'm lucky if I can squeeze in any study outside of class.

Constant study is likely to lead to problems of burnout or other problems related to leading an imbalanced life. Sandwiching studying in between other commitments is unlikely to lead to academic success. The middle two strategies are your best bet for academic success.

But what if the demands of your schedule prevent you from getting all the sleep that you want or need? Avoid getting too comfortable; it is just an invitation to doze. See "Manage Life: Stave off the Sleep Invasion" for other ways to beat the urge to sleep while studying.

What to Study

Use the daily and weekly calendar you established in Chapter 3 to decide when your activities must intensify or when you can take a much-needed recreation break. Keep

BUILD COMPETENCE

After Class Is Over

1. **Rewrite and reorganize your notes.** This not only allows you to create a neater, clearer set of ideas for study but also provides an immediate review to help you take in and organize information.
2. **Highlight the most important ideas.** Underline or color-code the ideas you think may appear on a test. Write notes in the margins that will make the material more meaningful to you.
3. **Write a summary paragraph of the main ideas.** What were the main points covered in class? How did this class fit into the overall course?
4. **Identify any ideas that are still confusing.** Make notes about what remains unclear so you can look up the answer in your reading. You also can ask other students or the instructor.

your long-term goals posted in your study area or use them as your screen saver so you can have easy access to reminders about what your commitments will require.

Set subgoals for each study session. Plan how long your study session will be as well as what specific tasks you want to accomplish and in what order. Build in some break time to help your concentration stay fresh. Monitor how well you're achieving these subgoals and adapt your planning and resources accordingly.

The Original Bloom's Taxonomy College instructors sometimes rely on a classic framework, Bloom's Taxonomy, which clarifies different kinds of learning and organizes them according to complexity. Some may explicitly identify their use of Bloom's Taxonomy in their syllabi. In other cases, instructors use the basic idea—the scaffolding of cognitive skills—implicitly in the design of their courses.

Benjamin Bloom and his colleagues (1956) developed their hierarchy of cognitive skills to describe the kind of work that college courses require. Bloom and his colleagues originally distinguished *lower-order thinking skills*, such as knowledge and comprehension, from *higher-order thinking skills*, such as application, analysis, synthesis, and evaluation. Some instructors introduce Bloom's Taxonomy as a framework to help you understand how to delve more deeply into your studies.

Beginning courses tend to emphasize the *lower-order* cognitive skill of remembering, which is usually assessed using multiple-choice tests. To study for tests that involve lower-order learning, rely on effective memory strategies discussed later in this chapter.

Advanced courses tend to emphasize *higher-order* cognitive skills, including applying, analyzing, evaluating, and creating. Application skills help you transfer your knowledge to novel examples. Practice in analysis contributes to your effectiveness in reasoning and asking questions. Evaluating requires making decisions or judgments. Creating involves the integration of ideas into a new creation or perspective. Higher-order tasks require you to show greater independence and creativity in your thinking.

The New Bloom's Taxonomy Recently, Bloom's colleagues (Anderson and Krathwohl 2001) modernized the original taxonomy with the following, arranged from lower-order to higher-order cognitive skills:

- **Remember.** Retrieve pertinent acts from long-term memory *(recognize, recall).*
- **Understand.** Construct new meaning by mixing new material with existing ideas *(interpret, exemplify, classify, summarize, infer, compare, explain).*
- **Apply.** Use procedures to solve problems or complete tasks *(execute, implement).*
- **Analyze.** Subdivide content into meaningful parts and relate the parts *(differentiating, organizing, attributing).*
- **Evaluate.** Come to a conclusion about something based on standards/criteria *(checking, critiquing, judging).*
- **Create.** Reorganize elements into a new pattern, structure, or purpose *(generate, plan, produce).*

You can follow the spirit of Bloom's Taxonomy in your own approach to studying. Challenge yourself to go one level above what the course requires. For example, if your instructor emphasizes the learning of facts and figures in assignments, practice applying course materials to new situations. This emphasis will promote learning that endures. Try the Journal activity "Deep Study" on page 211 to see how Bloom's Taxonomy can help you study more effectively for exams.

Master the Disciplines

If you're majoring in an area that will train you for a specific profession such as business or medicine, you may wonder why you also need to take liberal arts courses. Each discipline represents a specialized way of thinking about human experience that should help you develop a richer perspective on life and more ways to view and handle problems.

According to Gardner (1999a), students must get beyond memorizing facts and concepts to understand how disciplines uniquely flavor the interpretation of fact.

Gardner suggested that proper education provides a "shopping mall of the disciplines," which ultimately can help students choose which ones they will master.

Courses differ in how much they make you think. You may have already noticed that you have to adjust your study strategies to different disciplines, especially when a class isn't a great match for your learning style. Here is a four-part framework that we will apply to the major disciplines to help you adjust to these differences and maximize your results:

- *The Rules.* Although each discipline requires memorizing new content, each also has sophisticated frameworks and theories that require deeper levels of thinking and understanding.
- *The Risks.* Each discipline tends to have special challenges associated with developing mastery.
- *The Resources.* Your learning style will make some disciplines more successful than others for you. Which elements of your learning style facilitate that success?
- *The Remedy.* If you're studying a discipline that doesn't match your learning style, there are things you can do to improve your efficiency and effectiveness.

Stave off the Sleep Invasion

1. **Use your desk *only* for studying.** When you drift asleep at your desk, you learn to associate your desk with napping, a cue you may not be able to afford.
2. **Set an alarm.** Buy a wristwatch that can signal you at reasonable intervals to keep you focused.
3. **Make a commitment to others.** Study with others and use the social contact to keep you from dozing off.
4. **Take a five-minute fresh-air break.** A brisk walk can clear your mind so you can focus better when you return to your studies.
5. **Stay involved in your reading.** The more invested you are, the less tempting it is to give in to sleepy feelings.
6. **Get enough sleep to begin with.** You can manage a late night every once in a while, but a steady diet of all-nighters guarantees that you'll be fighting off the sandman.

The Humanities

Humanities courses develop your understanding of human experience. Most emphasize exploring your subjective experience as you read literature, examine specific periods in history, or evaluate the ideas of philosophers.

The Rules Typically each humanities course is built around a particular *framework*, or set of concepts or theories, that will help you develop a new perspective or richer appreciation for the human condition. For example, learning about literature will expose you to various frameworks of literary criticism, such as psychoanalytic or feminist criticism. Each framework in turn is built on a distinct set of values and assumptions.

Applying the frameworks to literature will probably lead you to different kinds of conclusions. A psychoanalytic framework prompts you to look at unconscious motivations; a feminist framework sensitizes you to social forces that create different options for women and men. You can apply these frameworks to expand your personal

Deep Study Strategies for the Humanities

Suppose you've enrolled in a film appreciation class. You've just read a chapter about the works of Steven Spielberg. Asking the following (or similar) questions during your review session will help you probe the material most deeply:

Remember. What are the names of Spielberg's past films? When did his first film debut?

Understand. Name the ways his films could be regarded as successful. What themes does he regularly present in his films?

Apply. What other filmmakers tend to borrow from Spielberg's methods? Think about how a different director might have directed the film *Artificial Intelligence: AI.*

Analyze. Why are his films so financially successful? What role has technology played in his productions?

Evaluate. In what ways do you think his work is unique? Rank Spielberg's films from best to worst.

Create. Propose a story line that would be intriguing to Spielberg. How might his films have been different if he'd been born twenty years earlier?

insight. Humanities instructors look to your insights as evidence that you understand the frameworks.

The Risks You may fear that your personal interpretations will get you in trouble in humanities courses. You may assume that there is only one right answer and may be afraid that you'll look foolish if what you say is "wrong." However, the objective of most humanities courses is to encourage breadth of thinking. Take the risk of sharing your insights. You may end up offering ideas that your class members have never heard. "Expand Your Resources: Deep Study Strategies for the Humanities" illustrates one helpful approach based on Bloom's Taxonomy.

Notice that by using your imagination to think about your assignments, you also make new connections to the assigned material. The more connections you make, the easier it will be for you to recall information. This strategy also helps you anticipate and practice for essay tests.

The Resources Because of their learning styles, some students have a natural advantage in humanities courses. Those who will be drawn to humanities as a major tend to have the following characteristics:

- If you have verbal-linguistic intelligence, you bring a love of words and their meanings to complex humanities assignments.
- If you're skilled in auditory processing, you can track difficult lectures with ease.
- If you enjoy assignments that emphasize reflection and creative learning styles as well, humanities assignments offer you wide latitude for personal interpretation.
- If you like to think critically and creatively, you'll have many opportunities to create and defend your perspective.

The answers you get from literature depend on the questions you pose.

Margaret Atwood
Contemporary Canadian novelist

The Remedy Not everyone has a learning style that makes learning in the humanities easy. What are some strategies you can use to enhance your success in humanities classes?

- *Keep a dictionary nearby.* You're bound to run into new terms that will slow down your reading.
- *Compare ideas.* Exploit any opportunity to discuss central ideas or identify challenging concepts.
- *Practice making conclusions.* Rehearse aloud or on paper the key ideas and principles you draw from the assignment.
- *Read to make connections.* The more you read about a topic, the more you'll have to reflect on.

Natural Science and Math

Natural science courses such as chemistry and physics explain the natural phenomena of the world, including everything from how fast an apple falls from a tree to the mysteries of the cell. Mathematics provides the tools to measure observations and assess change.

The Rules Natural science and math are loaded with theorems, laws, and formulas that you'll probably need to memorize, but comprehension should be your primary objective. Most of the activities that you undertake in science and math provide practice in application; you apply the rules to produce a specific outcome or solution. Obviously, the more you practice applying the principles or formulas, the more enduring your learning will be.

The Risks Natural science and math often have an unappealing reputation. The stereotype is that only science and math "geeks" do well in these courses. It will help if you deflate your images about science slightly. For example, you regularly act like a scientist does when you figure out how things work, although you may not be as systematic or careful in your observations as scientists are. With some practice, you, too, can do real science.

The Resources The natural sciences and mathematics attract students who have particular strengths in the logical-mathematical and naturalist dimensions of intelligence. Although the stereotype suggests that scientists do their work alone, progress in science depends on collaboration. Therefore, interpersonal intelligence also facilitates discovering and sharing new scientific knowledge.

Visual learners manage the challenges of mathematical formulas and also bring strong observational skills to science problems. Kinesthetic learners function well in laboratory exercises or field applications. Solving problems in natural science and mathematics also offers opportunities to exercise critical and creative thinking, thoughtful reflection, and active learning.

The Remedy If you don't have natural abilities to support your learning in the natural sciences and mathematics, see "Expand Your Resources: Improve in Science and Math" for some ideas that can help.

Social Science

Because the social sciences use scientific methods to understand human experience, they often draw on both the sciences and the humanities.

The Rules The social sciences produce laws and theories to explain the behavior of individuals and groups. Concepts in the social sciences often serve as shorthand for complex patterns of behavior. For example, *social stratification*, a sociological concept, refers to how people in a society can be classified into groups according to how much money they make, what types of jobs they have, how much power they wield, and so forth. Much of what students need to memorize in social science courses comprises new terms—such as *stratification*—that explain human behavior.

The Risks Learning in the social sciences can be challenging because what you are expected to learn may conflict with what you previously believed. Say, for example, that you heard on television and from your Uncle Ernie that it's dangerous to wake up a sleepwalker. It made sense to you, so you believed it. In your psychology class, however, you discover that this

Improve in Science and Math

- **Talk about what you already believe.** Sometimes pre-existing notions can interfere with learning new ideas in science. If you state what you really know or think about a scientific event, it may be easier for you to see where your explanation may not be adequate. Scientific explanations may then offer a clear improvement.
- **Make a total commitment.** Go to every class. Read every page of the text. Work every sample problem. Find other similar problems to solve. You may need to invest even more than the standard 2-to-1 ratio to get the basics.
- **Practice every day.** Committing to a little time each day will help you master the scientific terminology and formulas that facilitate scientific and mathematical competence.
- **Collaborate with others.** Most scientists do not work in isolation. Collaboration is a good model for beginners as well. By talking through problems with other students, you can improve your scientific problem solving.
- **Generate applied examples.** Identifying personal connections to the material will make abstract ideas more concrete.
- **Change representational strategies.** Some students find science and math too abstract. By changing the format of the problem, you may discover a clue about how to work with the ideas involved. For example, if a problem is presented in pictures or symbols, translate those to words. If you have a difficult word problem, try using pictures or symbols.
- **Know why you're studying.** Keep the big picture in mind. What will you accomplish by learning the skills involved in any given assignment? The long-range goal may help you stay motivated through the hard parts.
- **Be persistent and check your work.** Some problems don't yield a fast answer. Keep working, seeking, and persisting until you gain the insight you need to crack the problem. Be sure to check your answers so you don't lose credit because of carelessness. Scientists value precision and accuracy.
- **If you get confused, find another class section and sit in.** Sometimes it helps to sit through a class twice, which may be possible if your instructor teaches multiple sections.
- **Don't let anxiety overwhelm you.** Practice the skills and try to relax. If that doesn't work, seek counseling or tutoring.

knowledge is inaccurate, and that it is more dangerous to allow a sleepwalker freedom to walk into trouble. You have to reject some things you thought were true—such as opinions from Uncle Ernie—to make room for new ideas derived from social science research.

Social scientists draw on multiple theories to explain the same thing. Social science is considered to be a "soft" science, because it has to explain many deeply complex problems that depend on numerous circumstances.

The Resources Both interpersonal and intrapersonal intelligence can help you understand the social part of social science. Logical-mathematical and naturalist intelligence support the science part of social science. Auditory and visual sensory styles help social scientists do what they do. The strong analytic requirements of social science tend to reward critical thinking, although other kinds of processing can also help.

The Remedy

- *Expect complexity.* You're less likely to be disappointed by the limits of social science if you understand that not all your questions will have clean answers. The most interesting topics are complex and do not present simple answers.
- *Use your own experience.* Most of the topics you'll study correspond to things you've already experienced. When you connect concepts to your experiences, you can bring additional associations that will make them easier to learn. However, don't restrict yourself to understanding only what you've personally experienced.
- *Stay open to alternative explanations.* Recognize that your experience may not be typical of the systematic observations in science. You'll need to practice staying objective as you evaluate evidence, which may include re-evaluating the firm conclusions you have drawn from your personal experience.

Foreign Languages

Many colleges require students to study a foreign language to help them step outside their own culture and develop a broader perspective.

The Rules The study of a foreign language is loaded with rules. Proper grammar, verb tenses, and noun forms such as feminine and masculine all represent rules that you must learn to acquire a new language. You may also learn the norms and practices of the culture in which the language is practiced.

The Risks Many foreign languages have new sounds that may not be natural to you. You may fear revealing any shortcomings in your "ear" for language. The amount of time you have to spend drilling can also be daunting. Overcoming the risks and succeeding in foreign language classes involve understanding and memorizing as much as you can.

The Resources If you're blessed with a good ear for language, chances are that you have a strong auditory sensory preference. Your fascination with words and meanings in another language point to verbal-linguistic intelligence. Because learning a new language requires a lot of memorization, the learning process of reflection may be the best tool available to help you learn a new language.

The Remedy

- *Use color-coded materials.* Color-coded flash cards may give you additional cues about the kinds of words you're trying to learn. For example, use blue cards for verbs, yellow for nouns, and so on.
- *Construct outrageous images.* Construct an image from the sounds of the language that will help you recall the vocabulary. For example, suppose you are trying to memorize the French word for *five*. The word is *cinque* (pronounced *sank*).

Picture the numeral five sinking below a water line to make it easier to recall.

- *Talk out loud.* Label objects that you know. Rehearse routine conversations and stage practices with classmates when you can. Read your assignments aloud to improve your ear for the language.
- *Don't get behind.* Keep up, because this type of class work will pile up fast.
- *Distribute your practice sessions.* Although using shorter but frequent study sessions to memorize college material is good in general, it's *essential* when you're learning a foreign language. Regular practice sessions make your learning last longer.
- *Immerse yourself.* Try to find some natural exposure to the language you're studying.
- *Find a pen pal.* Watch movies or television programs that feature the language you're studying.

Now that you have had the opportunity to explore how to develop effective study strategies across the disciplines, complete the Journal activity "Reduce Your Disciplinary Risks" on page 211 to facilitate your best study habits in disciplines that you find challenging.

"I'm a social scientist, Michael. That means I can't explain electricity or anything like that, but if you ever want to know about people, I'm your man."

Join a Study Group

Working in a study group adds a vital element to your education and expands your resources. Besides learning the course content better, you can improve your ability to communicate, develop your project skills, and deal better with conflict. How can you make group work most efficient and effective?

Don't wait for an instructor to convene a study group. Find interested, competent classmates to meet regularly and talk about a challenging course. Once you have made the commitment, stay the course. Some additional strategies include:

- Identify the hardest concepts or ideas you've encountered.
- Talk about the problems or ideas you especially like or dislike.
- Discuss which parts of the readings interest you the most.
- Help one another share and clarify everyone's understanding of the material.
- Discuss strategies for remembering course material.
- Generate questions to prepare for tests.
- Keep your commitments.

> ***A special kind of beauty exists which is born in language, of language, and for language.***
> Gaston Bachelard
> *Twentieth-century French scientist*

Making Study Groups Work

Whether the group is working on a ten-minute discussion project in class or a challenge that spans several weeks, effective groups usually work in stages such as the following:

1. *Plan the task.* As the group convenes, lay the groundwork for working together efficiently by doing four things:
   - Introduce group members ("Who are we?").
   - Identify the purpose of meeting by agreeing on goals and objectives ("What tasks do we need to do?").

- Create a plan for working together ("How can we work together efficiently?").
- Set criteria for success ("How will we know we've succeeded in our task?").

2. *Come to a consensus.* Once the ground rules have been established, your group can address the specific task at hand. You don't have to choose a formal leader, although that might be helpful. Group members who ask questions and move the group along help through informal guidance.
3. *Evaluate the results.* In the final stage of the discussion, summarize what has been accomplished and evaluate how well the group has performed so you can improve its efficiency. Then, plan your next meeting. To determine how useful study group strategies might be for you personally, complete the Journal activity "Study-Group Savvy" on page 211.

My grandfather once told me that there are two kinds of people: those who work and those who take the credit. He told me to try to be in the first group; there was less competition there.

Indira Gandhi
Twentieth-century Indian politician

Overcoming Group-Work Obstacles

Group work can provide some of your most exciting—and most frustrating—learning. When you join others to solve a problem or explore the meaning of a work of art, your pooled brainpower can result in insights you might never have had on your own. Effective groups tend to bring out the best in their members.

However, people regularly have problems working in groups. Figure 7.1, "Common Problems and Sensible Solutions for Study Groups," describes some common group-work problems and what to do about them. In addition, the Journal activity "Call Waiting" on page 196 provides a common example of problems that arise in study groups to help you polish your social problem-solving skills and build your self-confidence.

Overcome Learning Disabilities

People with learning disabilities have been found in all nations of the world (Lerner 2006). Nearly one in ten people in the United States experience complications in learning caused by learning disabilities that interfere with incoming information by scrambling printed words, garbling spoken words, or causing confusion regarding numbers. As a result of confused input, people with disabilities can show problems in expression, including impaired short-term memory, problematic spelling, confusion about terminology, substandard grammar, and poor math skills.

Clearly, students with learning disabilities face daunting problems, including some unfounded prejudices of professors and students who equate learning disability with low intelligence. This challenge is sufficiently problematic that some researchers (Levine 2003) advocate for the use of the term *learning difference* rather than learning disability to reduce the stigma associated with being "LD."

However, many individuals with learning disabilities find great success in school and afterward in their careers. In fact, West (2003) cites a disproportionate number of successful CEOs of companies with dyslexia, one of the most common learning disabilities that involves interference with a person's ability to read. People with dyslexia report that words and sentences are hard to decode. Because they worry about performance and their slower rate of reading, students with dyslexia often feel singled out in classes for "not trying" or for "failing to live up to their potential," despite the fact that they try hard to keep up. West argued that such experiences appear to produce even greater motivation for individuals with learning disabilities to succeed and they work hard to develop successful compensating strategies.

Mercer and Mercer (2005) distinguished characteristics of those with learning disabilities who manage to thrive versus those who fail to accomplish much. Successful

LD students seek support systems to help them cope, stay positive, show strong verbal abilities, and find careers that play to their strengths as well as minimize their deficits. They persevere. In contrast, unsuccessful LD students fail to come to grips with the challenge. They don't take control of the situation and do not put in place emotional or academic support to help them weather the challenges. They often put themselves in situations that expose their weaknesses and may show higher rates of unemployment.

> ***Perseverance is the hard work you do after you get tired of doing the hard work you already did.***
>
> Newt Gingrich
> *Former speaker of the House of Representatives*

Evaluate Your Issues

Given the crucial importance of getting support systems in place, students who suspect they might be learning disabled should seek a formal evaluation of their status. However, many students think they might have learning disabilities when they really don't. Sometimes they simply don't put in enough study time or their anxiety sabotages them on tests. When you confer with your adviser about your academic struggles, prepare an honest evaluation of how much work you're putting in on your studies. Your problems may lie in ineffective study strategies rather than a learning disability.

If you've experienced criticisms about your performance even though you're trying hard, you may find it helpful to complete Self-Assessment 2 "Could I Have a Learning Disability?" on page 209, which identifies many characteristics of learning

FIGURE 7.1 Common Problems and Sensible Solutions for Study Groups

PROBLEM →	SOLUTION
Failure to do groundwork → Group members may be so eager to get on with the task that they jump into a chaotic and unsatisfying discussion.	**Establish goals** Your group will collaborate more efficiently if you have a clear picture of what the group wants to achieve and how you hope to achieve it.
Conflict avoidance → Some groups become disorganized as disagreements emerge. Conflict is valuable because differences of opinion can lead to a better discussion or well-considered solution.	**Legitimize difference of opinion** When conflict emerges, ask group members to support their opinions with evidence. Let the quality of evidence persuade the group.
Unequal participation → When groups are large and some members take charge, shy or unprepared members may be less likely to participate.	**Specify useful roles** Ask quiet members to serve the group by taking notes or summarizing the key ideas. Ask them directly about their opinions.
Domination by one member → Sometimes leaders push too hard and end up alienating other group members. They may not recognize the value of involving all members to improve the quality of the groupís conclusion.	**Ask for space and cooperation** When leaders get too pushy, suggest that other members need more time and space to express their ideas. If this gentle confrontation does not work, be more forceful. Point out what the group may lose when some don't participate.
Off-task behavior → Less committed members may engage in behaviors (such as popping gum) that distract the group.	**Ask for concentrated effort** Suggest that the offending person change the behavior to help promote a more favorable, quiet working environment.
Members who coast → Some group members may not contribute once they sense that the group will succeed by the work of the more energetic or motivated members.	**Clarify expectations** Express your disappointment and anger about the unfair distribution of work. Propose some consequences for those who aren't doing their fair share.

disabilities. This inventory will not tell you whether you have a learning disability; it merely provides a rough outline of concerns that you can raise with your academic adviser to sort out whether more diagnostic testing is in order.

Know Your Rights

If you have a learning disability, your academic outlook can still be good. Students whose learning difference can be verified by a qualified examiner may apply for special education support through the Education for All Handicapped Children Act of 1975. In addition, the Americans with Disability Act encourages campuses to support the special needs of students with disabilities. Many instructors have developed their own strategies to assist students. For example, they may offer longer test periods for students with language-processing problems.

"Manage Life: Learning Disability Accommodation Requests" offers some questions you might pursue with your instructor to help you stay competitive. Then complete the Journal activity "Thrive Even with Learning Differences" on page 211 to round out your strategy.

© Daniel Acker/Bloomburg News/Landov

© Frank Trapper/CORBIS

© Ethan Miller/Reuters/Landov

© Fred Prouser/Reuters/Landov

Learning disabilities do not prevent professional success. Businessman Charles Schwab and entertainers Patrick Dempsey, Jay Leno, and Whoopi Goldberg have all revealed their struggles with learning disabilities.

Compensate

If you do have a learning disability, you'll need to develop a set of strategies to compensate for the challenges your learning style presents. Among other things, you can:

- Set up a study group to discuss course material with others.
- Compare your notes with a friend's after each class to see if you've missed any important details.
- Use audio versions of textbooks when available.
- Use a spell-checker.
- Get support from the campus study skills center.
- Ask friends to proofread your written work.
- Alert your instructors to your special needs.
- Restrict yourself to using just one calendar to minimize confusion.

The compensating strategies you develop in college will continue to serve you throughout life.

Improve Your Memory

No matter what your learning profile, you will spend a substantial amount of time in college committing important facts, idea, and theories to memory. Memorizing is a fundamental skill that expands your knowledge base and lays a foundation for more sophisticated thinking skills as you learn about different disciplines. Especially in your early courses, your tests may depend entirely on memorization; for example, naming the levels of the phylogenetic scale in zoology or recognizing the musical instruments in a symphony requires memorization. Let's explore how memory works before we look at methods for improving your memory.

How Memory Works

Two important memory systems are involved in academic learning: *short-term memory* and *long-term memory.*

Short-Term Memory Short-term memory ("working memory") enables us to get some work done without cluttering up our minds. For example, when you look up a new phone number, it doesn't automatically go into your long-term memory for important numbers. Short-term memory lets you retain it briefly, for thirty seconds or so, just long enough to get the number dialed. Then it vanishes. Besides being brief, short-term memory has other features:

- *It's fragile.* Unless you rehearse the information in short-term memory, it will disappear. If you're interrupted while rehearsing the information—suppose someone asks you a question after you have looked up a phone number—your short-term memory will be disrupted and you'll probably lose the information.
- *It has limited capacity.* Short-term memory can hold approximately seven "chunks" of information before the system becomes overtaxed and information is dumped

Learning Disability Accommodation Requests

If you do have a learning disability, exercise your right to level the playing field by asking for appropriate accommodations from your instructors. Here are some questions you can ask your instructor to help you stay competitive and show your intention to do your best in spite of your limitations:

- Do you mind if I audiotape your lecture?
- Have you worked with learning disabled students before?
- Do you have any special advice to help me stay current in the course?
- May I use a spelling device to help me during testing?
- May I arrange for extended time to finish exams? Can we arrange for someone to monitor me?
- Is it possible to get assignments in advance?
- Can you recommend a tutor in case I run into difficulties in your course?
- When would be a good time for me to talk with you to clarify concepts I've learned in class?
- Would you like to have more information about my learning disability?

out of awareness (Miller 1956). Have you ever wondered why telephone numbers have seven digits?

- *It can be tricked.* You may be able to trick short-term memory into holding more detail through a process called "chunking": making each memory "chunk" represent more than one piece of information. This is the basis for the *mnemonics*, or memory aids, discussed later.

Long-Term Memory You've already stored a mountain of facts and impressions in your long-term memory from your education and life experience. Cognitive scientists describe long-term memory as partitioned into two special functions:

- *Procedural memory:* consists of the "how" of memory, the repository of directions for various activities that you have internalized. When you enact a protocol for finding something on the Internet, climb onto a bicycle seat and begin pedaling, or put in a contact lens, you are exercising procedural memory.
- *Declarative memory:* consists of the "what" of memory, the great store of facts and ideas that constitute your personal encyclopedia. Declarative memory is further subdivided into two more functions (Tulving 1972):
  - *Semantic memory:* represents your recall of basic facts and ideas. What is the meaning of *prerequisite*? When did the Great Depression begin? What was Edgar Allan Poe's most famous poem? The content of semantic memory is routinely the target of game shows such as *Jeopardy* and *Who Wants to be a Millionaire?*
  - *Episodic memory:* consists of your recall of personal details in your life. What was the best movie you ever saw? Where did you go on your last group date? When did you last see your car keys?

Each memory exists in your long-term memory. Ideally, you can retrieve it as needed.

What are some other features of long-term memory (LTM)?

- *LTM appears to have no limits.* Many long-term memories endure. For example, you may be able to recall the name of your first-grade teacher even though you

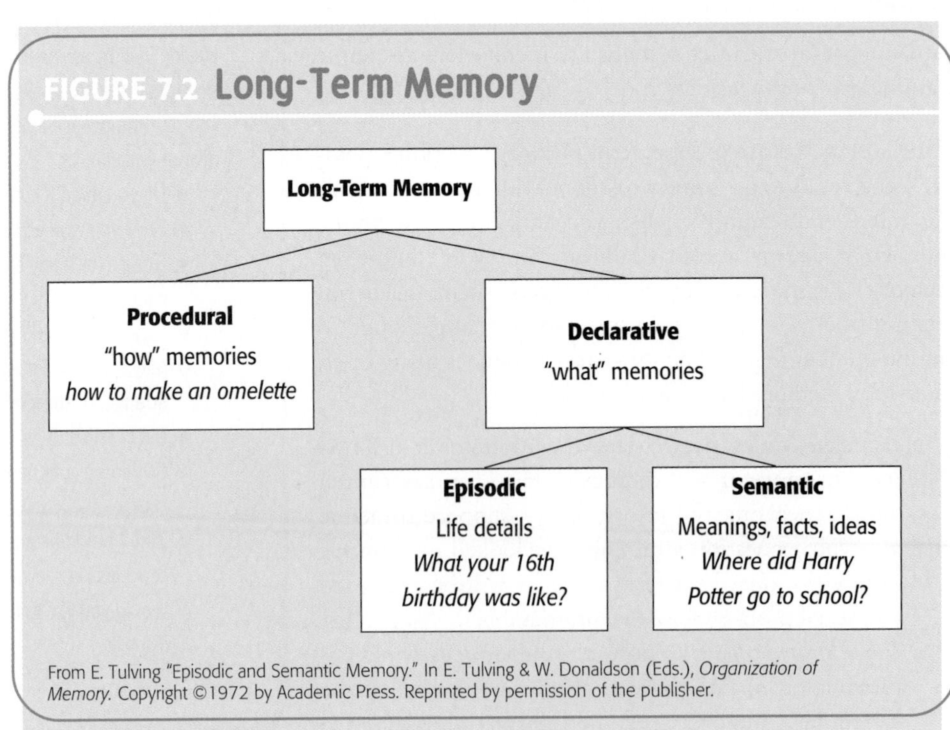

From E. Tulving "Episodic and Semantic Memory." In E. Tulving & W. Donaldson (Eds.), *Organization of Memory.* Copyright ©1972 by Academic Press. Reprinted by permission of the publisher.

haven't thought of her in a long time. We can also remember vivid information without much practice.

- *LTM is built through association.* The more you know about a topic, the easier it is to learn more, because you have more ways to make associations between new ideas and what you already know. For example, if you're a fan of old movies, you may devote a great deal of memory storage to retaining odd facts about directors, movie locations, and favorite actors. If you're *not* a sports fan, then you'll feel bewildered when your sports-focused friends discuss obscure statistics related to the Super Bowl. People easily store vast quantities of information in long-term memory on the topics that interest them most. If you don't know much about a subject, then your task is harder. You'll be building your concept base from the ground up. This is why some course materials are harder to learn than others. You have to work harder to make associations.
- *LTM can be tricked.* Memory research suggests that long-term memory can be remarkably creative . . . and deceptive. In a series of clever experiments, Elizabeth Loftus (1980, 2003) demonstrated that people could report vividly recalling events that had never really happened to them. Once we are convinced that we know something, we may fill in the gaps without realizing how much we've invented.
- *LTM can fail.* Unfortunately, no matter how hard you study, you're bound to forget some things you learn. There are two main reasons why we forget: interference and decay.

Interference can crowd out memories, making them difficult to retrieve. For example, when you take a full academic load, the sheer volume of the material may cause interference among the subjects, especially when courses use similar terms for different purposes.

Memory decay is the disintegration of memory that occurs when the ideas are not kept active through use. If you fail to review regularly or do not practice retrieving information, you may find it impossible to recall it when you want it, such as during a test. This is why it is important to regularly review what you have learned.

Ideally, you'll gear your learning strategies toward building your long-term memory with important and meaningful information. Learn course information so you can recall it not just for tests but well beyond the end of the course.

How to Memorize

Four general principles that provide a foundation for effective long-term memory (Higbee, 2001) are:

- ***Pay attention:*** Don't allow yourself to be distracted when you're processing information about things you must do or remember. Some absentmindedness is caused by failing to absorb the information in the first place.
- ***Pursue meaning:*** Memorizing through rote rehearsal is one route to long-term memory, but it tends to lead to superficial learning. Digging deep to comprehend information will produce more enduring learning than investing time committing meaningless information to memory.
- ***Impose organization:*** Organize concepts in a tree diagram or concept map, as shown in Figure 7.3, to provide additional cues for remembering ideas. For example, suppose you're studying important events in U.S. history in the 1950s. Construct a map that captures the important, related details of the period to make them easier to remember. You don't have to be artistic to draw pictures, make arrows, or create stars in the margins of books or notes. Adding images can make recalling details easier. Draw pictures of the comparisons that your instructor uses to clarify concepts. For example, if your psychology instructor describes

Freud's view of the unconscious as similar to an iceberg, draw a large iceberg in the background of your notes. Drawings are especially helpful for visual learners.

- ***Expand association:*** Personal connections will make learning and recalling unfamiliar or abstract ideas easier (Matlin 1998), especially if you're a visual learner. For example, in history you may have to learn about periods that seem quite remote to you. Think about how these periods might have involved your own ancestors. For example, would your great-grandmother have been a flapper during the Roaring Twenties, or would she have led a different kind of life? Make her the focal point of your learning about this era. If you don't know anything about her, imagine her.

Ask yourself questions about what you've read or what you've recorded about class activities. Expand the number of associations you make with the information. This makes the ideas easier to recall. Add this activity to your rehearsal time. The following questions, and others like them, can help you create additional links to course concepts:

- Have I ever seen this concept before?
- Do I like or dislike the ideas?
- What are some practical examples of the concept?
- Are there other ways to explain the concept?

This practice will improve not only your memory for course concepts but also your ability to think critically about them.

Memory is a complicated thing, a relative to truth, but not its twin.
Barbara Kingsolver
Contemporary American novelist

Additional Memory Strategies

These strategies provide additional help for memorizing different types of information.

Adopt the Right Attitude Memorizing new material is a challenge, but a positive attitude helps. Make a serious effort to develop interest in the subject you must study. Study to meet specific learning objectives. Think about the potential professional value the course may provide, even if you have to use your imagination a bit.

Stay Focused Concentrate on one thing at a time. You may have to study multiple subjects in one session. If so, try to focus your attention on the subject at hand. Study the most difficult subjects first because you need more energy for harder material. Reward yourself at the end by saving the subject you enjoy most for last.

Minimize Interference If you're taking two similar subjects, they may offer overlapping or conflicting ideas. To keep the ideas separate in your mind and reduce the amount of interference between them, space these subjects apart when you study. If you must study for multiple tests in a short time frame, schedule your final study session in a particular subject as the last thing you do before the test.

Use Mnemonics Mnemonics (*ne-MON-ix*) are strategies that expand visual or auditory associations and help you learn. They involve linking something you want to remember to images, letters, or words that you already know or that are easy to recall because of how you've constructed the mnemonic. They can be visual or text based, logical or goofy, complex or simple. See Figure 7.4 for some examples of mnemonics from a variety of disciplines.

The following strategies provide additional help for memorizing different types of information:

Rhymes If you were raised in the United States, you most likely learned when Columbus came to America through rhyme: "Columbus sailed the ocean blue/In fourteen hundred ninety-two." The rhyme leaves an indelible impression. Eventually you don't have to repeat the rhyme to remember the date. Here's another example from first aid: "When the face is red, raise the head. When the face is pale, raise the tail." Remembering the rhyme allows you to make a swift decision about appropriate treatment.

Songs Melodies also can produce enduring memories. A generation of U.S. children learned how to spell *encyclopedia* by singing its spelling along with Jiminy Cricket on *The Mickey Mouse Club* in the early days of television. Many children learn their phone numbers or addresses when parents sing the information to them using a familiar melody.

Acronyms Acronyms are special words (or sentences) that you construct using the first letter from each word in the list you wish to memorize. (See Figure 7.4 for some examples.) The acronym cues you not only to the items on the list but also to their proper order.

Method of Loci (LOW-sigh) In another mnemonic, you associate the parts of a list with a physical sequence of activities or a specific location that you know well. For example, you can remember a long and difficult speech by thinking about walking through your home and associating a piece of the speech with each of the rooms. Another example of the method of loci can be found in a creative pharmacy major's attempt to remember the path of a red blood cell by imagining an imaginary oversized body lying on a floor in a familiar room and walking his way through the heart, arteries, and veins.

> ***God gave us memory so that we might have roses in December.***
> Sir James M. Barrie
> *Author of* Peter Pan

Visualization Using your imagination to come up with provocative images can provide memory cues. Making visualizations ridiculous is the best way to make them memorable (Lorayne and Lucas 1996). Substitute or combine objects, exaggerate their features, make them disproportionate, or involve action in an image to make it distinctive.

Use Props Create a set of flash cards and carry them with you. Rehearse while you wait in grocery store lines, at the laundromat, and at doctors' offices. Consider creating audiotapes of the ideas you want to memorize, and review those while driving or doing chores.

Construct a "Cram Card" Whenever you can't commit important information to long-term memory through regular study and rehearsal, write down the essential points on a small card (Frank 1996). Don't overload it with detail. Study the card before your test, up to the point when your instructor says to put materials away. Then rehearse the information until you can write it down in the margins of your test booklet. In this way, your short-term memory can help you when your long-term memory cannot. Be sure to put the card away before the test begins. It could easily be mistaken for a cheat sheet.

Strive to Overlearn When you think that you really know your stuff, study just a bit longer to "overlearn" the material. Overlearning improves the integration and the endurance of your learning and helps you avoid partial memories.

Partial memory occurs when you remember something about a concept but not enough to help you. For example, you may recall

FIGURE 7.3 Tree Diagrams

Tree diagrams or concept maps branch out to organize important information.

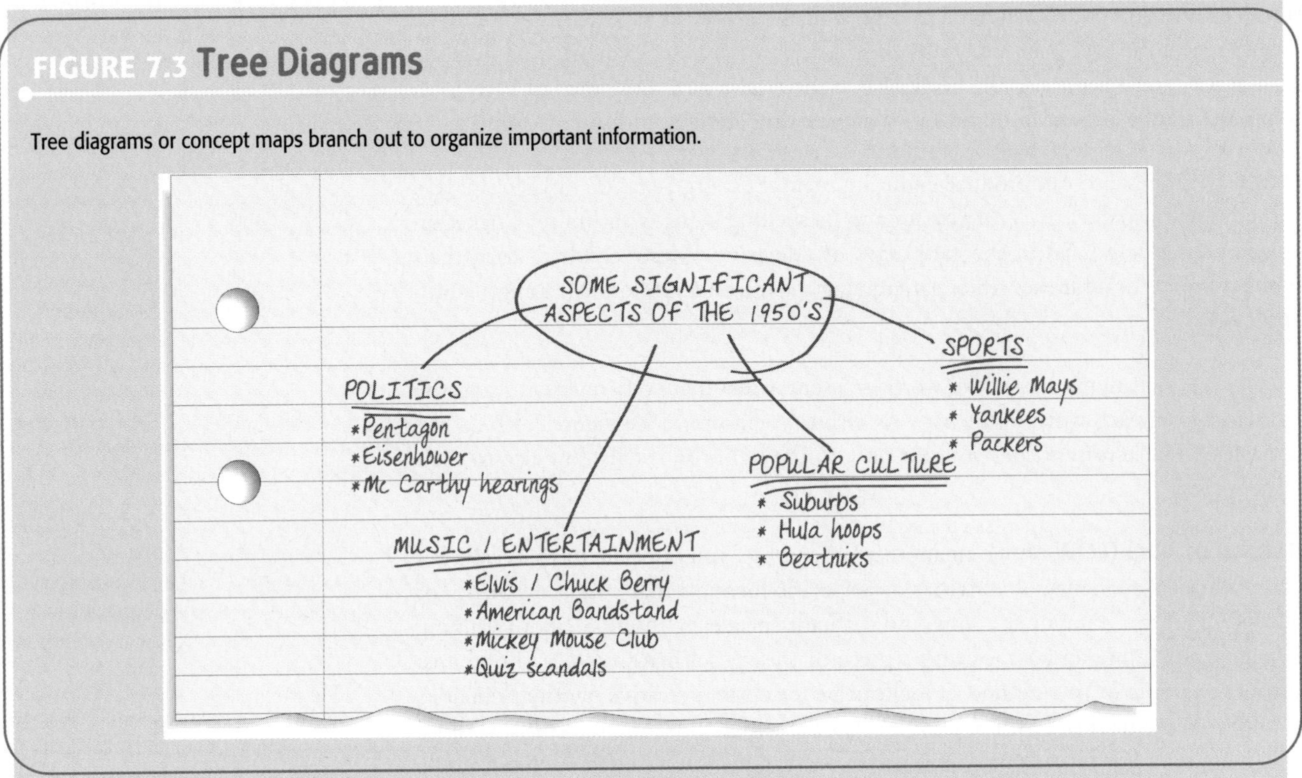

FIGURE 7.4 Examples of Mnemonics from Various Disciplines

Discipline	Mnemonic	Meaning
Business	SWOT	Strengths, weaknesses, opportunities, threats (a technique for analyzing problems)
Physics	ROY G. BIV	Red, orange, yellow, green, blue, violet (the visible colors in the light spectrum)
Geography	HOMES	Huron, Ontario, Michigan, Erie, Superior (the Great Lakes)
Music	Every	E
	good	G
	boy	B
	does	D
	fine	F (the lines of the treble clef)
Astronomy	My	Mercury
	very	Venus
	elegant	Earth
	mother	Mars
	just	Jupiter
	served	Saturn
	us	Uranus
	nine	Neptune
	pickles	Pluto (nine planets in order from the sun)

where a concept appeared on the textbook page but fail to remember its meaning. Or you may be able to remember that a concept starts with *p*, but the rest of the word eludes you. Instances of partial memory suggest that your study strategies need more work.

When you partially recall important information, you may be able to retrieve the whole of what you stored in memory if you temporarily change the direction of your thinking. Focusing away from the problem gives your mental circuits more time to "warm up," sometimes causing a term or name to surface.

Exploit Situational Cues If you can, when you take an exam, sit in the seat you normally sit in for class. Being in the same place may help you dredge up memories that might be hard to remember without context cues. The Journal activity "What's in a Name?" on page 212 also will give you an advantage in dealing with the enormous amount of memorizing that lies ahead.

CREATE YOUR FUTURE

Career Connections

Alan was almost supernaturally good in recalling obscure sports facts. Early on in his life he amazed people with the quantity and quality of the facts he was able to retrieve from his memory. He recognized that the more he knew about a team, the easier it was to attach additional, interesting, related details to his fact warehouse. He was happiest when he could engage in discussion with other sports enthusiasts, comparing the details of what they could recall. Alan was surprised and disappointed to discover that memorizing facts in his college courses was not as easy. However, he recognized that he could pursue a career in sports broadcasting that would make the most of his skills and interests.

He opted for a major in communication arts with an emphasis in broadcasting. His senior internship allowed him to live the life of a broadcaster for ten hours a week. His knowledge and enthusiasm were so impressive that Alan received a job offer shortly after graduation. Within a few years, he was a sports reporter at a small radio station, living the life he had dreamed of.

Julia had always wanted to be a teacher. She thought it would be very gratifying to teach children about music and watch the impact of their new appreciation of cultural activities on their lives. She was profoundly disappointed when she took her music appreciation course in college because the professor required that her students memorize long passages of music so they could recognize them at test time in as few bars as possible. Although she understood recognizing music from memory could enhance musical appreciation, she doubted that it would produce the kind of transforming effect on children that she wanted to produce.

In her field placement, she began experimenting with ways to allow children to create music and to criticize what they heard. She began to see the kinds of excitement that she thought could sustain her in her teaching career. To no one's surprise, Julia easily captured her dream job after graduation and also went on to earn teaching awards that recognized her creativity.

Evaluate Your Progress

How skilled are you in using memory-enhancing strategies to achieve your goals? Complete Self-Assessment 3, "Am I Ready to Learn and Remember?" on page 210 to identify strategies that you use now and ones that show promise for helping you study more effectively in the future. Another way to evaluate your progress involves examining your test results to determine whether your strategies worked. You may need to study for longer periods or to seek new, more efficient methods for learning new ideas.

If you prefer memorizing information to other kinds of academic work, you're in good company. Most beginning students prefer well-structured, simple learning tasks (Baxter Magolda 1992). Memorizing basic facts feels like a manageable challenge in most courses. However, college courses will routinely challenge you to go beyond rote memory and learn more deeply. One reason to accept these challenges now is that they can build your confidence for upper-level courses that you'll take later on. Overall, you'll emerge from college with greater pride in what you've accomplished. Now complete the Journal activity "How to Remember" on page 212 to further practice some strategies for improving your memory.

Summary Strategies for Mastering College

Enhance Your Study Skills by Using Strategies That Match Your Resources to the Demands of the Work

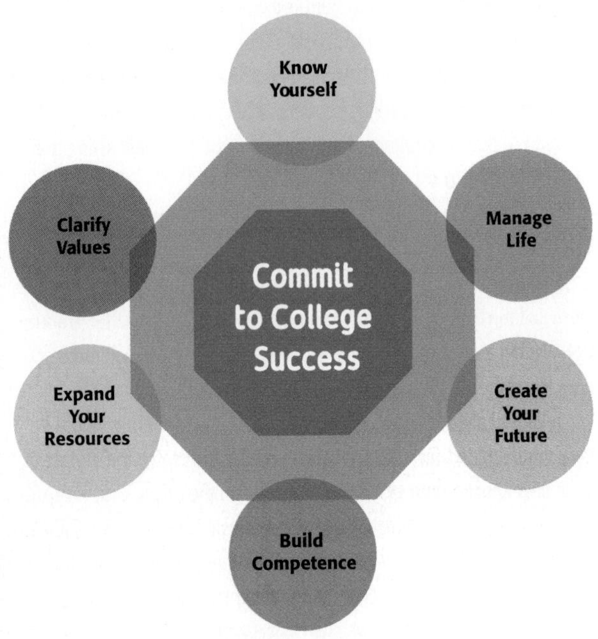

Focus on the Six Strategies for Success above as you read each chapter to learn how to apply these strategies to your own success.

1 Plan Your Attack

- Find a quiet place and use it consistently.
- Schedule study times that work with your energy level and course demands.
- Set goals for what you want to accomplish in a study session.
- Recognize how surface and deep learning differ.
- Push yourself to work at deep levels to help learning endure.
- Consider Bloom's Taxonomy to maximize study gains.

2 Master the Disciplines

- Prepare to think more abstractly as course work deepens.
- Understand the rules, risks, resources, and remedy for each discipline.
- Know how your learning style fits with a given discipline.
- Share your personal insights in humanities courses.
- Strengthen your logic and math skills to succeed in science and math.
- Expect complexity in social science.
- Memorize rules and terminology to optimize language learning.

3 Join a Study Group

- Form study groups to learn course concepts.
- Assign roles, plan tasks, set criteria for success, and evaluate your progress to ensure an effective study group.
- Solve routine problems that compromise group progress.

4 Overcome Learning Disabilities

- Recognize how confused input affects student performance.
- Undergo special testing if your results don't match your effort.
- Rely on the Americans with Disabilities Act to secure the help you need.
- Develop compensating strategies to minimize the effects of a learning difference.

5 Improve Your Memory

- Know the differences between short- and long-term memory.
- Approach memorizing with the right attitude.
- Attend, concentrate, and minimize interference among subjects.
- Use mnemonics to build personal connections to your course work.

Review Questions

1. List a few important issues to consider when deciding where to study, when to study, and what to study.

2. What is the difference between lower-order and higher-order cognitive skills? Provide a few examples of each.

3. How do the different disciplines encourage different kinds of study? List some specific strategies for success in the discipline area you are considering for your major.

4. List three pros and three cons of working in study groups. Now write down a strategy for addressing each con.

   Pro: ________

   Pro: ________

   Pro: ________

   Con: ________ Strategy: ________

   Con: ________ Strategy: ________

   Con: ________ Strategy: ________

5. How can learning disabilities influence study success? What can be done to address such disabilities?

6. Describe the difference between short-term memory and long-term memory. How can you use this information to improve your study strategies in the future?

SELF-ASSESSMENT 1

Early Bird or Night Owl?

To determine your typical energy level, check all the characteristics that apply to you. Then consider the strategies listed below for each type.

How's Your Energy?	Respect Your Natural Energy
____ I roll out of bed eager to face the day. ____ I manage to get up without an alarm. ____ My friends complain that I'm too chipper early in the morning. ____ I tend to run out of steam in the middle of the afternoon. ____ I prefer intense activity before noon. ____ I can't function without a minimum amount of sleep. ____ I leave parties early.	• Schedule classes as early as you can. • Avoid commitments when your energy dips in the afternoon. • Consider an afternoon catnap. • Study your hardest coursework before your energy lapses. • Don't plan to study late at night unless you absolutely must.
____ I drag myself out of bed, sorry the day has started. ____ I regularly use the snooze button on my alarm clock. ____ My friends complain that I'm too crabby in the morning. ____ I tend to start hitting my stride in the middle of the afternoon. ____ I prefer intense activity after noon. ____ I can function on little or no sleep. ____ I leave parties late.	• Schedule your classes in the late morning and early afternoon. • Try night classes. They may be a perfect match for your energy. • Buy a good alarm clock (maybe even a backup alarm). • Don't study when you're groggy. • Study late and fall asleep. It may help you retain information.

Are you an early bird or a night owl? The category with the most check marks reveals your energy profile, which suggests when study strategies and class scheduling will produce the greatest payoff. Early birds should make their most serious efforts before late afternoon. Night owls should avoid making commitments before late morning.

SELF-ASSESSMENT 2

Could I Have a Learning Disability?

You may have a learning disability if you have the following difficulties. Check any that apply to you.

Misunderstand simple printed materials _____

Have a great deal of trouble working with basic math problems _____

Have difficulty writing and speaking _____

Approach studying in a haphazard manner _____

Get easily distracted _____

Confuse *left* and *right* or other spatial words _____

Arrive late often (such as frequent late arrival to class) _____

Struggle with categories and comparisons _____

Have trouble with fine motor skills or finger control _____

Feel awkward in gross motor (body) movements _____

Misinterpret subtle nonverbal cues _____

Have difficulty following instructions _____

Reverse letters in words or words in sentences _____

Hear teachers complain that you "are not living up to your potential" _____

If you feel frustrated in any of these areas, you may want to see if you have a learning disability. First, talk with your adviser about the nature of your difficulties. She can recommend changes in your study strategy or refer you to a specialist on campus who can help you with diagnostic testing. On some campuses this evaluation is expensive, but you're likely to get advice that makes the investment worthwhile.

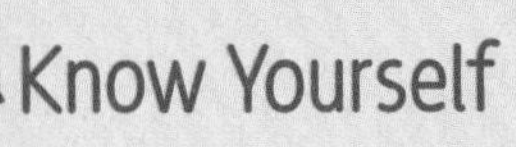

SELF-ASSESSMENT 3

Am I Ready to Learn and Remember?

Review the elements of effective study strategies below and decide whether each statement is something you already do well or something you need to improve.

	I Do This Well	I Could Improve This
To take advantage of my best energy levels, I purposefully schedule when I will study certain subjects.	________	________
I select study environments that have few distractions.	________	________
I review course materials regularly to spread my learning out over time.	________	________
I try to find some angle in my assignments that will increase my interest.	________	________
To ensure my understanding and increase my personal involvement, I question what I read.	________	________
I look for ways to add meaning to course ideas during review sessions.	________	________
I rehearse key ideas to the point of overlearning.	________	________
I use mnemonic strategies for memorization. (List several specific strategies you use):	________	________

____

____

When I feel frustrated by partial recall, I divert my attention to recover more details.	________	________
I schedule an intensive review session before a test.	________	________
I avoid cramming whenever I can.	________	________
I use review tests to see whether I need to change my study strategies.	________	________

Look over your answers. Could the areas you need to improve mean the difference between a mediocre performance and honor-quality work? What would you need to do to improve? How could you reward yourself for adopting better strategies?

Your Journal

REFLECT

1. Study-Group Savvy

In which courses would you benefit from forming a study group?

____

____

What special talents would you bring that would help the group succeed? Do you have any personality quirks or negative work habits that could adversely affect the group's outcomes? What can you do to address those problems in the study group?

Positive talents: ____________________

Negative traits: ____________________

2. Reduce Your Disciplinary Risks

Many people have fears related to disciplines they are required to study to complete their education. In what discipline are you least comfortable? Describe the source of your concern. What might you do to get more comfortable with this discipline? Can you identify any role models who can help you develop a more positive attitude?

Discipline: ____________________

Issues of concern: ____________________

Strategies for greater comfort: ____________________

Potential role models: ____________________

DO

1. Thrive Even with Learning Differences

Who is the learning disabilities specialist on campus? Find out and write down the contact information below. If you suspect you might have a problem, make an appointment with this individual to find out about further testing. If you don't think you have a learning disability, talk with a classmate who does. Find out what kinds of compensations seem to be most effective for him. Do some of the compensations seem like they might also be useful to you? Which ones?

Learning disabilities specialist: ____________________

Phone number and e-mail address: ____________________

Information on testing: ____________________

Helpful compensation strategies: ____________________

2. Deep Study

Pick a topic area from a subject you're currently studying. Develop a question based on each order level of Bloom's Taxonomy. Now come up with a tentative answer for each question. How much harder do you have to work to come up with a good answer to a higher-order question than a lower-order one? Think about the balance of lower-order and higher-order questions across the courses you are taking. What should this balance suggest about how you study in your courses?

Remember: ____________________

Understand: ____________________

Apply: ____________________

Analyze: ____________________

Evaluate: ____________________

Create: ____________________

Your Journal

THINK CRITICALLY

1. Call Waiting

You're assigned to a discussion group that will meet throughout the semester, but one of the group members brings her cell phone. The phone usually rings five minutes into the meeting. She excuses herself to take the call and usually misses more than half of each meeting. What strategies could you and your group use to address this challenge?

____

____

2. How to Remember

What is something that you frequently forget? It could be an important concept from one of your classes, a particular type of appointment, or where you last left your keys. List a few strategies that might help you address this memory lapse. Try each one. Which strategy worked best and why?

Strategy 1: ______________________________

Strategy 2: ______________________________

Strategy 3: ______________________________

CREATE

1. What's in a Name?

Select one list of information from any chapter in this book. Develop a mnemonic device for remembering the items in that list. Write it here. Revisit this mnemonic tomorrow and see how well you can remember the items it represents. Did the mnemonic help? Try applying this strategy to other aspects of this course.

Your mnemonic: ______________________________

2. Creative Space Management

Identify a place where you have a hard time studying, such as a bus, a noisy dorm room, or a crowded kitchen table. List three strategies that would help you make this place better for studying.

1. ______________________________

2. ______________________________

3. ______________________________

Now try each one. Did they work? Why or why not? What did this teach you about your ideal study location?

____

____

____

8 Succeed on Tests

© Royalty-Free/CORBIS

KNOW YOURSELF

BY THIS POINT IN THE TERM, you've probably already faced one ongoing challenge that all college students encounter—tests! Happily, some tests match how well you've studied and what you've learned. Other exams, however, may have led you to think that you and the instructor weren't on the same planet, let alone in the same classroom. To evaluate where you stand right now with regard to test taking, place a check next to only those items that apply to you.

- I pace myself effectively to get ready for a test.
- I figure out ahead of time what will be on the test and try to predict the test questions.
- I control my nervousness about test performance.
- I size up the test to know what I need to do and read all directions carefully before I start.
- I know effective strategies for scoring well on multiple-choice tests.
- I know how to do well on essay questions.
- I regularly complete tests in the allotted time.
- I know how to analyze test results to improve my learning and future test performances.
- I know the consequences of academic dishonesty at my college.

The physicist Albert Einstein was a notoriously poor student and test taker until the right learning climate helped him to thrive as a learner. Think about how this problem might apply to you as you read his profile on the next page.

CHAPTER OUTLINE

Get on with It!

Get in Gear

Plan for the Long Term
Plan for the Short Term
If You Must, Cram Strategically
Set the Stage for Test-Taking Success
Control Your Test Anxiety
Handle Emergencies Honestly

Meet the Challenge

Use General Test-Taking Strategies
Master Multiple-Choice Strategies
Master True/False Strategies
Master Fill-in-the-Blank Strategies
Master Short-Answer Strategies
Master Essay-Question Strategies

Make the Grade

Recover Your Balance
Review Your Work
Know When to Challenge
Understand Grading Systems

Build Your Character

Understand Cheating
Show Integrity and Resist the Impulse

Images of College Success

Albert Einstein

When he was a small child, no one could have predicted the extraordinary future of Albert Einstein. He was slow in learning to talk and painfully shy. Although he loved science and mathematics, he struggled with the style of his formal education. His teachers at the Luitpold Gymnasium in Munich, Germany, taught by constant drilling, which Einstein found boring. He often skipped classes or was ill prepared, resulting in punishment for his disobedience and scorn from his classmates.

Although his teachers thought he was dull, Einstein simply hated the persistent drilling he faced in school. When his father's business failed and the family moved to Italy, Einstein purposefully failed so many tests that he was asked to leave his school. One teacher told Einstein that he was glad to see him go because the teachers thought he encouraged other students to be disrespectful.

When his family later suggested that he needed to prepare for a career, Einstein applied to a technical school in Switzerland. To be admitted, he had to pass rigorous entrance examinations. Although his scores on his math and science exams clearly showed promise, he was a dismal failure in zoology, botany, and language. A remedial year at a relatively creative school, where his questioning was encouraged rather than discouraged, allowed him to catch up. He passed his entrance exams on his second attempt and went on to revolutionize the field of physics. Ironically, the Luitpold Gymnasium, an institution once offended by Albert Einstein's uncooperative and dull academic performance, was renamed in honor of him before he died (Levinger 1949).

Einstein himself would have been quite amused at the extent to which his own ideas would become the basis for testing millions of physics students who struggle to understand his creative conceptualization of energy and matter. When asked to explain the theory of relativity, Einstein once joked, "Put your hand on a hot stove for a minute and it seems like an hour. Sit with a pretty girl for an hour and it seems like a minute. That's relativity!"

What can we learn from **ALBERT EINSTEIN'S** experiences in testing?

As you read, think about the Six Strategies for Success listed to the left and how this chapter can help you maximize success in these important areas. Effective test-taking strategies can build your competence, but in this chapter we also pay special attention to clarifying the values that will lead to making decisions with integrity.

Get on with It!

No matter what course of study you pursue, your efforts are going to be evaluated. Believe it or not, tests can benefit you. They can help:

- *Pace your reading.* College reading assignments can feel overwhelming, so it's easy to get behind. Tests throughout the term push you to do the work on time.
- *Consolidate your learning.* Tests encourage you to study the course material more intensively and retain the ideas longer. Your effort in preparing for tests can produce insights you might not have made without the pressure of the exam.
- *Improve your thinking.* Tests sharpen your critical-thinking skills. Whether you're figuring out which multiple-choice alternative to eliminate or determining how to structure an essay, tests give you practice in careful observation, analysis, and judgment.
- *Get feedback.* Test results tell you whether your study strategies have worked. Good results confirm that you're on the right track. A string of poor scores suggests that you need to improve your motivation or study skills.
- *Achieve special status.* As demonstrated in the introductory story about Albert Einstein, test results can confer special status. For example, good results might qualify you for a scholarship or allow you to skip preliminary courses and move on to more advanced ones.

> ***Difficulties, opposition . . . there is a special joy in facing them and in coming out on top.***
>
> Vijaya Lakshmi Pandit
> *Twentieth-century Indian diplomat*

Get in Gear

You know that instructors are going to test you. What can you do to show them you've got the right attitude to succeed? First, recognize that there are important differences between tests in high school and those in college. Most students regularly take more tests and quizzes in high school but experience tests in college as harder. See Figure 8.1, "How Grades Can Change," to see how grades tend to drift downward as testing difficulties intensify.

"You're kidding! You count S.A.T.s?"

Learn How *Not* to Cram

- **Concentrate on the big picture.** Keep a master calendar for the term. Put all your scheduled tests on it. Post the calendar in your study area.
- **Design your test preparation across courses.** Plan how you'll read, study, and review assigned materials and class notes according to the test demands in all your courses. Wherever possible, distribute your study sessions over time to minimize interference among courses.
- **Keep up with your reading.** If you keep up with your reading, class experiences will reinforce your learning. Avoid massive catch-up reading the night before the test–there will probably be too much ground to cover, understand, and remember.
- **Reward yourself for staying on target.** A shiny A would be a powerful reward for strong test-preparation habits. However, that reward may come too far in the future to help you sustain better test preparation. Instead, reward yourself on a regular basis for sticking to your study plan. For example, after you've studied hard each evening, watch a tape of a favorite TV show, listen to some music that you really like, or talk with someone you enjoy.
- **Schedule a concentrated review session.** If you've kept up, a solid review session the night before your test should be adequate.
- **Don't skip a class to cram.** This strategy is a real problem in the weeks that lead up to final examinations, because all your instructors may use that time to give exam pointers or review essential material that may be critical to your success.

The Journal activity "Then and Now," on page 239 examines how your high school patterns might predict success. Then, use the following systematic approach to do your best on future tests.

Plan for the Long Term

Successful test taking requires good long-term and short-term planning. Good long-term suggestions include the following:

Pace Yourself Don't count on cramming! Eleventh-hour learning is fragile. It may crumble under pressure. The strategies offered in "Build Competence: Learn How *Not* to Cram," will help you pace yourself so you won't have to go through a last-minute rush to learn.

Meet Your Social Need If you have an extraverted style, studying with others will motivate you to do your reading and help to identify trouble spots. Ask other students who seem to understand the course—at least as well as you do, if not better—to join a study group. Screening helps to ensure that the group will be productive and not slowed down by students who don't reliably do their work. To improve testing success, study-group members can compare notes to create the most comprehensive understanding, share hunches about likely test material, develop practice questions, and challenge fuzzy explanations.

On the other hand, if the stimulation of a study group is not compatible with your introverted style, find less socially intense support strategies. For example, identify another strong student with a similar style and make a commitment to connect via e-mail to clarify questions or try out test-taking strategies.

Protect Your Health If you stay healthy throughout the term, you'll have fewer problems in managing your study schedule and fewer distractions at test time. You can't do your best if you're fighting off the urge to nap, feeling bad from a hangover, or coming down with a cold.

Adopt the Right Attitude Examinations can be emotional events. Nearly everyone feels some test anxiety, but some are overwhelmed by it. Others view testing as doing battle. They cast the instructor as a villain out to trick them and bring them down. These students get distracted into trying to "outfox" the instructor rather than learning the material. To go boldly into a test on hope rather than solid preparation will rarely achieve the outcome you want. Instead, facing the test with the confidence that comes from conscientious planning and systematic study is the best way to overcome unproductive attitudes and emotions.

Plan for the Short Term

Following are some suggestions to improve your short-term planning for taking tests.

FIGURE 8.1 How Grades Can Change

As you can see in the graph, grades drifted downward from high school to college. This means that you have to study harder to maintain the same grade point average in college.

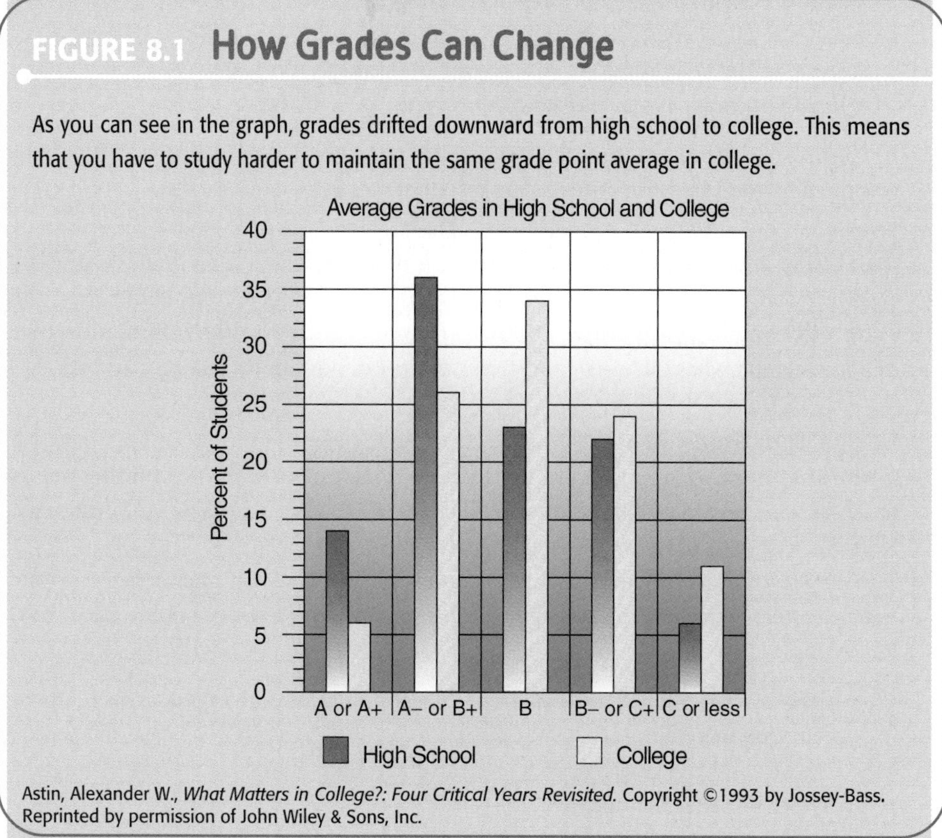

Astin, Alexander W., *What Matters in College?: Four Critical Years Revisited.* Copyright ©1993 by Jossey-Bass. Reprinted by permission of John Wiley & Sons, Inc.

Know What to Expect Test conditions vary. In large lecture classes, security issues may be intense. For example, your instructor may require you to sit in alternate seats to reduce cheating. Proctors may roam the aisles and retrieve all materials after the test. Your instructor may not even be present, so you might want to get all your questions answered before the day of the test. In smaller classes with the instructor present, you may be able to clarify issues as they arise. Either during the class or in the syllabus, most instructors describe the kinds of tests they are planning.

Some instructors even make sample tests from prior semesters available for study purposes. Many welcome questions about how to prepare. "Build Competence: Will This Be on the Test?" suggests questions you can ask your instructor to clarify the nature of the exam. You may know some students who have completed the course before you. Find out what they did to succeed or what strategies didn't work. Don't be afraid to research your instructor's test-construction practices.

"Psych out" the Teacher Some students seem psychic when guessing what will be on a test. How do they do it? They size up the instructor by identifying what concepts have been stressed enthusiastically during class lectures and discussions. Instructors often use specific cues to identify important and *testable* material (Appleby 1997). They may be signaling test material when they:

- repeat or emphasize certain concepts
- illustrate key ideas with examples
- stop pacing back and forth behind the lectern
- intensify eye contact
- use gestures in more dramatic ways
- change their tone of voice

- say "in conclusion . . . " or "to summarize . . . "
- pause to allow you time to write your notes
- write on the board or point to ideas on an overhead transparency
- highlight ideas in their introductory remarks or conclusion

Complete the Journal activity "Construct Your Own Exam" on page 239 to help you develop good skills for anticipating test design.

> ***Before everything else, getting ready is the secret of success.***
> Henry Ford
> *American inventor*

Don't Skip the Prior Class Most instructors devote at least a few minutes of the last class to narrow down the most critical material or even to give hints about what the exam will contain (McWhorter 2000). Pay close attention to the information that might telegraph what the instructor thinks is most important for testing purposes.

Design Your Study Strategy Your success depends on adapting your learning style to the kind of thinking measured by the test. Take responsibility for finding out as much as you can about what the test will cover. Then plan a suitable study strategy. Keep track of your progress as you prepare for the test.

Many tests, especially in introductory-level courses, focus on memorization. Your most effective memorization strategy will use your preferred sensory mode effectively. For example:

- *Visual learners* should use visualization techniques or drawings and diagrams to memorize material.
- *Auditory learners* may prefer to rehearse key ideas aloud or make up songs or rhymes to fix facts in memory.
- *Tactile learners* may try role play or other hands-on strategies to add cues that help them recall information.

Other types of tests may focus on more sophisticated kinds of thinking. Find out what the format of the test will be ahead of time. Know how points will be distributed across the test. This knowledge may help you decide where to spend your time if it's clear you won't be able to finish. For example, the multiple-choice section may be worth twenty points, and the essay section fifty points. Even though the multiple-choice questions come first, you may want to start with the essay, which counts for more. Find out whether there are penalties for guessing.

BUILD COMPETENCE

Will This Be on the Test?

Some instructors don't offer many clues about the tests they give. If you have one of these instructors, you might ask these questions:

- How long will the test be?
- What types of questions will be on it?
- Are there any particular aspects of the work we've been doing that you'll emphasize?
- What topics *won't* be on the test?
- Are there penalties for wrong guesses?
- Will this material also be covered on a cumulative exam at the end of the term?

Objective Tests Memorizing facts is usually a good strategy for answering simple, objective, test questions. These include tests with multiple-choice, matching, true/false, and fill-in-the-blank items. Successful memorizing strategies include using flash cards, making a concept vocabulary list, reviewing a text's study guide, and reorganizing your notes. Find the memorizing strategy that works best for your learning style.

At the college level, most instructors ask objective questions that require more than just rote memory. When you have to do more than recall facts, your study strategy will also be more complex. Draw organizational charts or diagrams to identify relationships. Design some practice questions that exercise your ability to reason.

Essay Tests Digesting a whole term's worth of material for an essay can be a challenge. If you know the specific topics ahead of time, scan the notes you've made and highlight all related ideas in a specific color. This will let you concentrate on those ideas as you think about questions or practice answers. If you don't know the essay topics ahead of time, go back over your course and reading notes and write a paragraph for each text chapter or course lecture. These paragraphs should summarize the key ideas in the passage.

© David Young-Wolff/PhotoEdit

To succeed on tests, you need to review your notes to think about how the ideas can be incorporated in designated test formats.

Procedural Tests Some types of tests ask you to demonstrate specific procedures, such as applying a formula to solve a math problem, conducting an interview in nursing, or solving for an unknown in chemistry. To prepare for procedural tests, perform the target skill until you're comfortable with it. If test time will be limited, build time limits into your practice.

Protect Your Study Time Classmates may request your help at the last minute, especially if you live with them. You may happily accept. Helping others can build your self-esteem and can also help you rehearse material. Or you may need to use the time alone to master the material yourself. If giving help does not work with your study schedule, explain that you've planned out your study strategy and need every minute to concentrate to do your best.

What if a loved one makes demands on your time that interfere with your study schedule? Explain to partners or family members, including children, that you need extra help from them before a test to make it as easy as possible to study. Promise them that you will spend time with them after the test. Then keep your promise. The Journal activity "Find Your Quiet Place" on page 240 provides some additional pointers on ways to envision and manage your study environment to produce the best test-preparation conditions.

If you practice good long-term and short-term strategies, your work is much easier as the test gets closer. Figure 8.2, "A Timetable for Sensible Study Strategies," summarizes strategies for pacing yourself for the least stressful test preparation.

If You Must, Cram Strategically

There is no substitute for hard work.

Florence Griffith Joyner
American Olympian

It's a bad idea to depend on cramming, but sometimes it can't be helped. You may have too many courses to manage any other way. What are some of the best ideas for last-minute, concentrated study?

- *Clear the decks.* Dedicate your last study session before the test to only that exam. Studying anything else can interfere with the test at hand.
- *Use textbook study aids.* The chapter headings and chapter end matter can help you organize your last-minute study strategies by identifying key ideas before you begin reading. First, go through and look at the headings—in a good textbook, these will provide you with an outline of the key ideas in the chapter. This practice is especially appropriate in an introductory book. Then read the summary, and look at the key terms and review questions. You will get a pretty good idea of the most important material in the chapter.
- *Skim for main ideas.* Once you know what to look for, skim the chapter with the key ideas in mind. You may even want to skim just to answer the review questions. Scan each paragraph in relevant readings for the key ideas. Topic sentences that capture the central idea of each paragraph are usually the first or the last sentences in the paragraph. Skim the entire assignment to improve your chances of remembering the material.
- *Divide and conquer.* Once you've skimmed the entire body of study materials, size up how much you have to learn in relation to your remaining time. Divide the

FIGURE 8.2 A Timetable for Sensible Study Strategies

After each assignment	Write a summary paragraph of what you learned and how it relates to the course objectives.
After each class	Review your notes to consolidate your learning.
During the last class before the test	Find out about the test: What will be and wonít be on the test The format of the test The contribution of the test to your grade Clarify any confused ideas from past classes.
After the last class before the test	Plan your final review session.
The night before the test	Organize your notes for systematic review. Study the test material exclusively—or last—to reduce interference. Practice the kind of thinking the test will require: Rehearsal and recital for objective tests Critical analysis for subjective tests Identify any fuzzy areas and confer with classmates to straighten out your confusion. Get a good night's sleep.
The day of the test	Organize your supplies. Eat a good breakfast/lunch/dinner. Review your notes, chapter summaries, and/or course glossary.
The hour before the test	Review your notes. Go to the classroom early and get settled. Practice relaxing and positive thinking.

information into reasonable sections and make your best guess about which will have the largest payoff. Master each section based on whatever time you have left. Even if you don't get to the lower-priority material, your test performance may not suffer much.

- *Stay focused and alert.* Study in good light away from the lure of your bed. Take regular breaks and exercise mildly to stay alert through your session. Caffeine in moderation and regular snacks also may help.
- *Be cautious about professional summaries.* Use professional summaries of great works if you can't complete a full reading. If you rent a film version of a great work of literature, be aware that films and even professional summaries often depart from the original in ways that may reveal your shortcut.
- *Learn from your mistakes.* When you enter a test feeling underprepared, you've undermined your ability to succeed. Even if you luck out and do well, this strategy shortchanges what you think and learn over the long term. Consider the factors that left you in such desperate study circumstances. Commit yourself to doing all you can to avoid getting stuck in a situation where you have to cram.

Set the Stage for Test-Taking Success

It's almost here. Whether you're filled with dread or eager to show what you know, the following last-minute strategies give you the best chance of doing well.

- *Get a good night's sleep.* Research shows that you need **at least** eight hours of sleep to stay alert and do your best thinking, problem solving, and communicating. If you deprive yourself of that dose of sleep, you are already at a disadvantage before you even begin.
- *Bring supplies for your comfort.* A bottle of water or cup of coffee may keep up your spirits (and your caffeine level). Instructors usually specify what comforts you can bring to class. Avoid causing distractions, such as unwrapping noisy candy wrappers; other students are likely to be as nervous and distractible as you are. If you get stress headaches, don't forget to pack your pain reliever.
- *Bring required academic supplies—and spares.* You may need to bring a blue book (a standard lined essay book for handwritten responses). Bring a sharpened pencil or pen and a backup, a calculator, scratch paper, or whatever other supplies the instructor allows. Make sure you have a watch or can see a classroom clock so you can pace your work.
- *Organize your resources.* In some cases, instructors may let you bring a summary of notes to jog your memory during the test. They even may let you have open access to your books and notes (a sure sign that the test will be hard). Write your summaries clearly so that you don't lose time trying to decode your own writing. Attach some tabs, use marked index cards, or highlight your resources in other ways that will make them easy to navigate under pressure.
- *Bring permitted reference aids.* If you struggle with writing and spelling, bring a dictionary or a spell-checker if it is permitted. Many instructors will let you use such an aid because it shows your desire to do good work. Some instructors will refuse because of concerns about security and fairness.

Sixty minutes of thinking of any kind is bound to lead to confusion and unhappiness.
James Thurber
Twentieth-century American humorist

Control Your Test Anxiety

Just moments before your instructor hands out an exam, you may feel as if you're in the first car of a roller coaster about to hurtle down the first drop. Your heart pounds. You're sweating. The butterflies just won't go away.

A few butterflies are okay. A little anxiety even can be a good sign. It encourages you to prepare for the test and can motivate you to do your very best. Too many butterflies, though, can cripple your test performance. Nervousness and worry activate the emergency systems in your body. Your pulse increases. Your heart beats faster. Your hands perspire. These responses prepare you to flee or to fight. In stressful circumstances, they help you survive. But in the quiet of the classroom, they interfere with your ability to focus on the test. Self- Assessment 1, "How Serious Is My Test Anxiety?" on page 236 will help you determine if your test anxiety is interfering with your performance.

Sabotaging Success Test-anxious students sabotage their own efforts because they focus on themselves in negative ways (Kaplan and Saccuzzo 1993). Preoccupied with the certainty of their own failure, they can't free up the energy to perform well. This reaction increases their chances of failure. Text-anxious students interpret even neutral events as further proof of their own inadequacy. For example, if a test proctor looks troubled, test-anxious students may assume that their own behaviors somehow caused the troubled look. They are more likely to experience stress-related physical symptoms, such as upset stomachs or stiff necks, which further hinder performance.

If you have anxiety about tests, you need to do two things (Zeidner 1995):

- Cope with your anxiety.
- Improve your study skills to build your competence and confidence.

"Hello, you've reached the office of Professor Arte. If your excuse for not turning your paper in on time is that your computer broke down, press '1.' If your excuse is that you had psychological problems, press '2.' If your excuse is that your grandmother died, press '3.' If your excuse is . . ."

BUILD COMPETENCE

Get a Grip

When people are under stress or feel anxious, they may be inclined to overbreathe or hyperventilate (Zuercher-White 1997). The signs of hyperventilation include shallow, heavy breathing, mouth breathing, gasping for air, yawning, and frequent clearing of the throat. Although it won't hurt you, hyperventilation can make you feel like you are suffocating.

Ironically, your sense of smothering is caused by taking in too much air. What can you do to get a grip and breathe more normally during exams?

- **Hold your breath.** If you can devote a minute or two to holding your breath in several ten-to-fifteen–second spurts, carbon dioxide will build up and counter hyperventilation and feelings of panic.
- **Breathe into a paper bag.** You may look a little funny, but this trick works. Exhale carbon dioxide into a paper bag that covers your mouth and nose. Then rebreathe the carbon dioxide until you feel calmer.
- **Breathe from your diaphragm.** You may have to practice this technique ahead of time to deploy it in the classroom. To learn diaphragm breathing:
  1. Find a comfortable place to recline and place a pillow on your stomach. Breathe in slowly through your nose and watch the pillow rise. Breathe out slowly and watch the pillow lower.
  2. Once you get the hang of it, remove the pillow but place your hand on your stomach. You will be replacing visual cues with kinesthetic cues that will be helpful when you try breathing in different postures. Concentrate on your stomach as it moves up and down with your measured breathing.
  3. Practice diaphragm breathing in different postures, without your hand on your stomach. Emphasize rehearsal of the skill while sitting, for greatest help during the exam.
  4. Slow down your breathing. Pause before inhaling. This practice will give you the greatest sense of control over your feelings of panic.
  5. Once you have achieved success, practice twice a day. Maximum success will occur when you can move easily into controlled breathing at the first hint of panic. Practice will facilitate your command.
- **Find support.** Most campuses offer support groups for test anxiety. These groups emphasize study strategies, anxiety management techniques, and moral support.

If you learn to cope with anxiety but don't improve your study skills, you'll feel calmer and more in control but won't improve your performance. By contrast, if you improve your study skills but don't master your anxious feelings, your performance may still erode. It will take some effort to do both things, but consider the long-term rewards.

Mastering Anxiety What are some specific things you can do to master test anxiety?

- *Invest your time properly.* Think about it. If you haven't spent as much time preparing for a test as you should, it makes sense to be frightened about performing poorly. Test jitters may only mean that you need to invest more time. If the format your professor will be using doesn't play to your strengths as a test taker, allocate more time to compensate for this challenge. See the Journal activity "Format Fever" on page 239 to help you think about testing formats that will demand more from you.
- *Neutralize anxiety.* One simple strategy is to neutralize your anxious feelings by learning to breathe in a relaxed manner under stress. See "Build Competence: Get a Grip," for some pointers on how to achieve greater control.
- *Talk positively to yourself.* Test-anxious students often make their anxieties worse by predicting their own failure. Instead of tormenting yourself with criticism and dire predictions, substitute positive statements, such as "I will overcome this challenge" or "I feel confident I will do well." Practice an optimistic outlook and more positive self-esteem will follow.
- *Exercise regularly.* Many students find relief from their anxieties by building a regular exercise program into their busy schedules. Exercise is a great stress reliever. It also promotes deeper, more restful sleep.
- *Avoid drugs.* Monitor your caffeine intake. Too much can compound agitated feelings. But this is minor compared with problems that result from using harder drugs to ward off anxiety or to stay alert. See "Manage Life: Just say 'Whoa'," to learn more about the cost of drug abuse.

Handle Emergencies Honestly

What happens if you can't make it to the test? Most instructors have strict regulations about taking scheduled tests on time to ensure fair treatment for all students. However, sick children, car accidents, and deaths in the family can interfere both physically and emotionally at test time.

If you can't report at the scheduled time, call your instructor *before* the test. Explain your situation. Ask whether you can take a makeup exam. Being courteous encourages your instructor's cooperation. Instructors may ask you to document your absence (for example, with a doctor's excuse) before they'll let you make up a test. Do all you can to take tests on schedule to avoid this kind of complication. See "Clarify Values: The World's Toughest

Test," to see what can happen when you fail to exercise personal responsibility about testing demands.

> ***Anxiety is the interest paid on trouble before it's due.***
> William R. Inge
> *Twentieth-century American playwright*

Meet the Challenge

The test is just moments away. You take your seat. The class quiets down as the instructor hands out the questions. How can you maximize your performance?

Use General Test-Taking Strategies

The following general strategies will help make the most of your studying to succeed on tests:

- *Relax.* Take a deep breath. The calmer you stay during a test, the better you'll do. Take relaxing breaths at the start and continue breathing calmly throughout the test. Concentrate on breathing slowly from your diaphragm. When you do this right, your stomach will move out as you breathe in, and in as you breathe out. "Chest breathing" can make you feel more agitated.
- *Look at the entire test.* Examine the structure. Count the pages. Think about how to divide your time, given your strengths and weaknesses. If the test includes different types of questions (such as multiple-choice and short essay), begin with the type you do best on to build your confidence. As you plan how to allot your time, leave more time for parts that require more effort or that make up more of your total score. Plan some time at the end to review your work.
- *Read the instructions . . . twice!* You'll be very upset if you discover near the end of the exam time that you were supposed to answer only certain questions rather than all the questions on the test. Read the instructions carefully to make optimum use of your available time.
- *When you get stuck, identify the problem and move on.* You'll be taking most exams under time pressure, so you can't afford to spend too much time probing the depths of your memory. If time is left over after you've finished the parts of the exam that you could answer with confidence, return to the parts you skipped.
- *Concentration despite distractions.* If you start daydreaming, circle the item that got you off task and come back to it later. Avoid getting caught up in competition with any students who complete the test early. Do the test at your pace—don't worry about who gets done first.
- *Ask for clarification.* When you're confused, ask your instructor or proctor for help. Most instructors try to clarify a question if they can without giving away the answer. An instructor may even decide that the question doesn't work and will throw it out.
- *Learn from the test.* The test itself may jog your memory. One area of the test may hold clues that can help you with other areas.

MANAGE LIFE

Just Say "Whoa"

Gary stared at his test paper and realized that what he had written didn't make sense. But he couldn't stay focused long enough to fix it. His hands were starting to shake. He looked at the clock and prayed for the hour to be over. He hadn't planned to run out of time in getting his reading done. When his roommate offered him a hit of speed to help him stay up to finish the material the night before the exam, he thought, "This could give me just the edge I need to get this done" and took it. However, as he struggled to get control of his work, Gary recognized that experimenting with drugs, especially the night before an exam, had just undermined, rather than helped, his performance.

Under the pressure of trying to meet the demands of multiple courses, some students turn to drugs to sustain a higher level of energy and attention. Stimulants can stave off sleep, but at a cost. You may feel out of control when the drug kicks in. You may "crash" after using stimulants. This will just put you further behind and maintain the incentive to keep using the drugs. It's a losing proposition. Don't even start.

CLARIFY VALUES

The World's Toughest Test

Whatever your complication in taking the test on time, it pays to be honest when trying to negotiate alternate arrangements, as the unusual saga of one college instructor illustrates.

Two of the instructor's first-year students became overconfident about their course performances so they partied heavily at another campus instead of preparing for the final. They returned to campus late with major hangovers. When they contacted their instructor the next day, they "explained" that they had been away for the weekend, got a flat tire on the way home, and couldn't get help. They begged for mercy and asked if they could reschedule the final. The instructor thought about it and then agreed. At test time, he sent the students to separate rooms. The problem on the first page was worth five points and dealt with a simple application about molarity and solution.

When they turned the page, they were surprised by the second and final question: (ninety-five points) Which tire?

- *Proofread your work.* Whether it's a series of math problems or an extended discussion on Japanese haiku, review your work. Under pressure, it's easy to misspell, miscalculate, and make other errors, even on things you know well. Using clear editing marks on your test paper demonstrates that you were being as careful as possible about your work.

Master Multiple-Choice Strategies

You'll probably face many tests that are mainly multiple choice: "question stems" or incomplete statements, followed by possible answers from which to choose. Figure 8.3, "Multiple-Choice Format," provides an example. The following strategies will help improve your scoring on multiple-choice questions:

- *Read the test items carefully and completely.* Cover up the alternatives and read just the stem. See whether you can answer the question in your head before you look at the alternatives. Then read *all* the alternatives before you identify the best one. This is especially important when your instructor includes "All of the above" or "A and C only" types of choices.
- *Strike out wrong answers.* When you can't easily identify the correct answer, eliminate the wrong choices so you can concentrate only on real contenders. Sometimes instructors include humorous distractors that can easily be dismissed. Don't dwell on their motives or allow yourself to get distracted. Strike those answers and move on.
- *Mark answers clearly and consistently.* Use the same method of marking your choices throughout the test. This may be important if questions arise later about an unclear mark. If your test is machine scored, avoid having extra marks on the answer sheet. They can be costly.
- *Change your answers cautiously.* Make sure you have a good reason before you change an answer. For example, change your answer if you mismarked your exam, initially misread the question, or clearly know you're moving to the correct alternative. If you aren't certain, it's best not to change. Your first impulse may be best.
- *Guess.* Some instructors subtract points for incorrect answers. In such a case, answer only the questions that you know for certain. However, most multiple-choice tests give credit for correct answers without extra penalty for wrong answers. In this situation, guess. If the question has four alternatives, you have a 25 percent chance of being correct.
- *Look for structural clues.* When the item involves completing a sentence, look for answers that read well with the sentence stem. (See Figure 8.4 for examples.) Sometimes instructors don't pay close attention to how the wrong alternatives read. If a choice does not work grammatically with the stem, it's probably not the right choice. In complex questions, the longest alternative may be the best one. The instructor may simply require more words to express a complex answer.

FIGURE 8.3 Multiple-Choice Format

The best way to succeed on multiple-choice tests is	*[question stem]*
A. Read the question carefully	*[contender]*
B. Check on the weather	*[distracter]*
C. Look for language cues to throw out choices	*[contendor]*
D. Cry like a baby	*[distractor]*
E. A & C	*[correct answer]*

FIGURE 8.4 Using Grammar Tools to Find Multiple-Choice Answers

In this example, spot the grammar clue that can help you determine the correct answer.

Don't change your multiple-choice answers unless you can find an

A. Error in how you marked your test booklet

B. Typo in the sentence stem

C. Justification from peeking at your lecture notes

D. Clues from cloud formation out the classroom window

Master True/False Strategies

True/false questions ask you to make judgments about whether propositions about the course content are valid or truthful. For example, consider this item: "True or False: It is always a bad idea to change your answer." This would be a good true/false question to assess your understanding of the last section on multiple-choice questions. (The answer is "False.") To maximize your performance on true/false items:

- *Go with your hunch.* When you don't know the answer on a true/false question, you have a 50 percent chance of being right when you guess. Choose the alternative with the intuitive edge.
- *Don't look for answer patterns.* Instructors generally strive to make the order of true/false answers random. This means there is no particular pattern to the answers. Selecting "False" on question thirty-five should have no bearing on how you answer question thirty-four or thirty-six. Focus your energy on the questions themselves rather than on trying to detect nonexistent patterns.
- *Honor exceptions to the rule.* If you can think of exceptions to the statement, even one exception, then the statement is probably false. In the earlier example, if you can think of even one circumstance in which changing your answer is a good idea, then the statement should be marked "False."
- *Analyze qualifying terms.* Pauk (2000 90) describes qualifying terms that suggest a question is true without exception as "100 percent words." Those terms suggest an unlikely or unwarranted generalization. Notice in our example, "It is *always* a bad idea to change your answer," the word *always* makes the statement invalid, because there are some times when changing your answer makes sense. Other 100 percent words include *never, none, every, all, entirely, only, invariably, best,* and *worst.*

Master Fill-in-the-Blank Strategies

Like multiple-choice questions, fill-in-the-blank questions test how well you recall information. An example of a fill-in-the-blank format is "Instructors try hard to make a _______ pattern of answers on true/false tests." (The answer is "random.") You either know or don't know the answers to these kinds of questions, but you may recover some answers that you don't know initially by skipping them and returning to them after you complete the rest of the test. This process may cue you to come up with just the right fill-in answer.

Master Short-Answer Strategies

Short-answer questions demonstrate how well you can explain concepts briefly. For example, a short-essay question might be "Describe some strategies for doing well on true/false questions." To maximize your score on short-answer questions, write clear, logical, and brief answers. Writing a great deal more than asked, or including information not asked for, suggests that you do not understand the concepts. When you skip a short-essay question because it stumps you, look for cues in the rest of the test that may help you go back and answer it later.

Master Essay-Question Strategies

Essay questions evaluate the scope of your knowledge and your ability to think and write. They tend to be much more demanding than objective test questions. What are some steps you can take to do your best on essays?

- *Anticipate possible questions.* If you were in your teacher's shoes, what questions would you ask? If you practice predicting and answering questions, your performance is likely to improve even if your predictions aren't on target. For example, an essay question that you could predict about the material in this section could be "Compare and contrast multiple-choice and essay-question strategies as a way of measuring your learning."
- *Read the question carefully.* A well-developed answer won't help you capture points if you don't answer the right question.
- *Highlight the requested action.* For example, in our earlier sample question you could underline *compare* and *contrast* to keep you focused on the most successful approach. See Figure 8.5, "Decode Essay Questions," for help. Then turn to the Journal activity "Decode Essay Instructions" on page 240 for practice.
- *Outline the key ideas.* A systematic blueprint can help you capture the most important ideas in your answer (as shown in the following example):

  I. How are multiple-choice and essay questions alike?
     A. They're constructed from the same material.
     B. You start with remembering concepts.
     C. You demonstrate your mastery of material.
  II. How are multiple-choice and essay questions different?
     A. Multiple-choice questions usually rely more on rote memory—recognition or recall of terms. Essays usually involve higher-order thinking skills.
     B. Multiple-choice questions can be answered more quickly.
     C. Multiple-choice questions usually have precise right answers.
     D. Essay questions are usually harder to answer.
     E. Essay questions are probably harder to grade.
     F. Well-written essays require planning and outlining.

- *Represent the question in your opening sentence.* Don't waste time rewriting the question. Set the stage for the information that will follow such as: "Instructors use multiple-choice and essay questions to evaluate how much you have learned from a course. These strategies share some similarities, but each offers some strategic advantages over the other."
- *Develop the main body of the essay.* Each paragraph should address an element required in the question: "The common characteristics of multiple-choice and essay questions include .

FIGURE 8.5 Decode Essay Questions

Look carefully at the verbs your instructor uses in essay questions. This chart offers some hints about how your instructor wants you to construct your answer.

When your instructor wants you to . . .	Your answer should . . .
ANALYZE	break into smaller parts and interpret importance
APPLY	extend a concept or principle to a new situation
COMPARE	identify similarities between two concepts
CONTRAST	distinguish important differences between two concepts
CRITICIZE	judge the positive and negative features of a concept
DEFINE	offer the essential idea behind a concept
DESCRIBE	provide sufficient details to establish key ideas in a concept
DESIGN	develop a new strategy to accomplish a goal
EXPLAIN	clarify the meaning of a concept through detail or example
EVALUATE	make a well-reasoned judgment about value or worth
GENERALIZE	apply a principle to make predictions about a new problem
HYPOTHESIZE	develop a specific prediction about a complex situation
IDENTIFY	designate the key elements involved
ILLUSTRATE	provide examples or details to clarify
INTERPRET	offer your distinctive point of view about a concept's meaning
LIST	identify factors in a systematic or comprehensive manner
PREDICT	offer your best guess about an outcome
PROVE	create your best argument using examples or reasoning
RECOMMEND	put forward a preferred course of action with a rationale
RELATE	draw connections among ideas
REVIEW	discuss the most important aspects of the concept
SUMMARIZE	briefly identify the most critical ideas

. . . Multiple-choice and essay questions also differ in what information they impart about a student's learning . . . ."

- *Summarize only if you have time.* Write like a reporter; present key ideas first and follow with details. This practice increases the likelihood that you'll cover the most important and point-scoring information before you run out of time.
- *Write legibly.* If your handwriting gets worse under stress—slow down. Instructors can't give credit for what they can't decipher. For some other pointers about good essay format, see "Build Competence: Get Your Essay Points."
- *Proofread your work.* Under time pressure, your written language can easily escape your control. Go back over your work and make any corrections the instructor will need in order to understand you clearly. Don't worry about the mess. Your own editing marks show that you care about the quality of your thinking.

- *Don't bluff.* The longer you write and the more you ramble, the more you expose what you really don't know.
- *Use humor carefully.* Unless you have clear cues from your instructors that they would appreciate a light-hearted response, don't substitute humor for an effective answer.

Self-Assessment 2 "How Well Do I Test?" on page 237 reviews many points that we've just covered. Use it to evaluate your current test-taking methods and to identify areas that need improvement.

Make the Grade

Grades don't change what you learned for the test, but grades can affect your self-esteem and motivation to study in the future, two important strategies for success. For example, good grades make you feel proud. They encourage you to stick with the study strategies that worked. Bad grades prompt you to make changes in order to succeed. But bad grades also can harm your self-esteem.

My imperfections and failures are as much a blessing from God as my successes and my talents.

Mahatma Ghandi
Nineteenth-century Indian philosopher

Recover Your Balance

At some point in your college career, you may not perform as well on a test as you hoped you would. Sometimes instructors don't design tests effectively. At other times, you simply may be pushed in too many directions to concentrate and do your best. Or the course may be a bad match for your natural skills and interests.

Don't let yourself become undone by one failure. Frame this disappointment as an opportunity to do some good critical thinking to figure out the causes of poor performance and to craft some new strategies to improve your situation. This approach can start by a careful review of your test results.

Review Your Work

Some reviewing of your test results will help you do better on the next test. Review to:

- **consolidate** your learning
- **analyze** what worked and what didn't work in your study strategy
- **ensure** that the grade was accurate

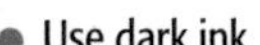

Get Your Essay Points

- Use dark ink.
- Carefully cross out parts that you no longer want evaluated.
- Avoid drawing numerous arrows to redirect your instructor's attention.
- Write on just one side of the paper.
- Use organizing notations, headings, or subpoints to clarify the order of your thoughts.
- Leave space between answers so your instructor can give you feedback or you can add ideas that you think up later.

Review all items, not just ones on which you made mistakes. Review and rehearse one more time the material that your instructor thinks you need to learn in the course. This can help you in the long run, especially if you have a cumulative exam at the end of the term.

Your test review should tell you whether your study strategy worked. Did you spend enough time studying for the test? Did you practice the right kinds of thinking to match the particular demands of this teacher? How can you use your study time more efficiently for the next test? Talk with the instructor about better ways to prepare.

What if your instructor doesn't allow extensive time for review of your exam during class—or worse, doesn't return the exams at all but only posts the grades? Visit your instructor during office hours and ask for the chance to review your test results. This visit also allows you to clarify any questions you have about your instructor's testing or grading practices, and shows that you are taking personal responsibility for your learning.

Know When to Challenge

Check the grading. Instructors can easily make errors when applying test keys or counting up point totals. Also identify questions that were not clearly written. Even if your critique of a question does not persuade an instructor to change your grade, your review may give you insight into how the instructor constructs tests, which can help you on the next one. Instructors are unlikely to change a grade without good reason. Most construct tests carefully and grade them as fairly as possible. However, if you believe the instructor misunderstood you or made an actual error in calculating your score that affects your grade, by all means ask for a grade change. Remember, though, that instructors can't give you extra points if it gives you an unfair advantage over others in the class.

If you view grades as a key to the future, you may want to fight for the grade you deserve. Some strategies for getting maximum consideration from your instructor are shown in "Build Competence: Negotiate a Grade Change."

> ***Do not on any account attempt to write on both sides of the paper at once.***
> W. C. Sellar
> *Twentieth-century British writer*

Understand Grading Systems

What systems of grading do most colleges use?

Traditional Grades Most schools use the traditional A–F grading system. Many also include plus (+) and minus (–) to make even finer distinctions in quality of work. Schools that use the traditional system convert grades into a grade point average, or GPA. In this system, A = four points, B = three points, C = two points, and D = one point. The point values of grades in all your courses are added up, then averaged to create your GPA. For example,

American History	C	2 points
College Algebra	A	4 points
Intro to Business	A	4 points
Sociology	B	3 points

GPA = 13 points divided by 4 courses = 3.25

A higher GPA improves your chances of getting a good job after college or of being accepted into graduate school. A GPA also has special meaning at some colleges. For example, GPAs of more than 3.5 may qualify you for the dean's list, the roster of students recognized for academic excellence. Some academic honor societies, such as Phi Beta Kappa and Phi Kappa Phi, invite students to join on the basis of GPA.

If your GPA falls below 2.0, you may be placed on academic restrictions or probation. On some campuses, probation limits the number of courses you can take in the next term and slows down your progress in your major. Because GPA is averaged across terms, a bad term's GPA will exert a heavy weight on your overall record, even if your performance improves in later terms. If your GPA remains low, you can flunk out.

Instructors sometimes assign test or course grades by using a curve. The overall results of the test for the class

BUILD COMPETENCE

Negotiate a Grade Change

At some point in your college career, you may disagree with an instructor's evaluation of how well you have performed. If getting your points restored is critical to your grade, by all means, get the points you deserve by conferring with your instructor. You will enhance your success by using the following strategies:

- **Ask for time after class to present your case.** Most instructors will not spend class time on the challenges of one student.
- **Develop your argument.** Point to evidence, such as an interpretation in the book that conflicts with something said in lecture, to support your request.
- **Explain your interpretation.** If you misinterpreted a question, describe your interpretation. Instructors will sometimes grant partial credit for a well-argued but off-base interpretation.
- **Avoid labeling a question as "bad."** Placing blame on the instructor will probably not encourage a helpful response.
- **Be gracious, whether you win or lose.** Most instructors remember and admire students who effectively advocate for themselves.

are tied to the strongest performance in the class. Other students' scores are judged in relation to that strongest score. For example, suppose that on a test with 100 points the highest score was 85. An instructor who is grading on a curve might give As to scores of 76–85, Bs to scores 66–75, and so on. Instructors may do this when a test turns out to be much harder than originally intended. However, even when most of the class performs poorly, some instructors don't curve the grades.

Building a satisfying grade point average will help you achieve your goals. See "Create Your Future: Targeting Your GPA," to explore some strategies for achieving the outcomes that will maximize your future options.

Pass-Fail Systems Some schools determine progress on a pass/fail basis, giving only pass (P) and fail (F) grades. When this is the only grading system a college uses, students may get extensive feedback about how well they have met their learning objectives. Instead of a grade point average, students graduate with other indicators of the quality of their work, such as a *narrative transcript.* In this document, their instructors describe their academic work and how well they achieved their goals.

Some colleges use both A–F and pass-fail grading. For example, students might get A–F grades in most of their courses but be allowed to take a certain number of credits outside their majors on a pass-fail basis. This dual system allows students to take some courses that they otherwise might avoid because of a potential mediocre grade.

The presence of grades appeals to externally motivated students who find they can more easily settle down and do the work when they know feedback will help them stay the course. Other students with stronger intrinsic motivation think grades and the pressures that go with them are distracting. Which do you prefer? See the Journal activity "Grades: Carrots or Sticks?" on page 240 to clarify your thinking.

Build Your Character

Each test that you take actually tests you twice, once on the course content and once on your character. Every test gives you an opportunity to demonstrate your personal integrity, and integrity matters. In *The Cheating Culture,* David Callahan (2004) argues that moral values are in dramatic decline and suggests that widespread cheating in college is a reflection of the significantly larger cultural problem. In addition, new technologies offer students inventive ways to procure high grades by circumventing all of the hard work in the course (Glater 2006). Students with integrity problems use cell phones, iPods, and Internet cruising to engineer favorable exam results just as they shop for term papers online rather than write them.

Unfortunately, cheating is widespread in college. The first multicampus survey on cheating (McCabe, Trevino, and Butterfield 1993) examined more than six thousand American undergraduates on more than thirty campuses and revealed that 78 percent of college students cheat at least once; over half of the respondents claimed that they cheated on tests. A more recent analysis (Athanasou and Olasehinde 2002) compared results across many years of surveys on cheating and estimated that approximately 60 percent of both males and females cheated in college.

What behaviors constitute cheating? Three distinctive categories of behavior reflect compromises in academic integrity (based on Cizek 1999):

- taking, giving, or receiving information illicitly from others (includes copying from others' work with or without their permission, submitting purchased essays, or recycling papers from prior courses without permission)
- using inappropriate information or material (includes improper paraphrasing and copying material without appropriate acknowledgment, fabricating data or references, or collaborating inappropriately when required to work individually)
- evading standard assessment conditions (includes substituting someone else's performance, giving untruthful excuses or engaging in other behavior such as offering sexual favors or threats to secure special treatment, destroying resource materials to handicap other students' performance, securing advance information about examination, or smuggling restricted information into testing contexts)

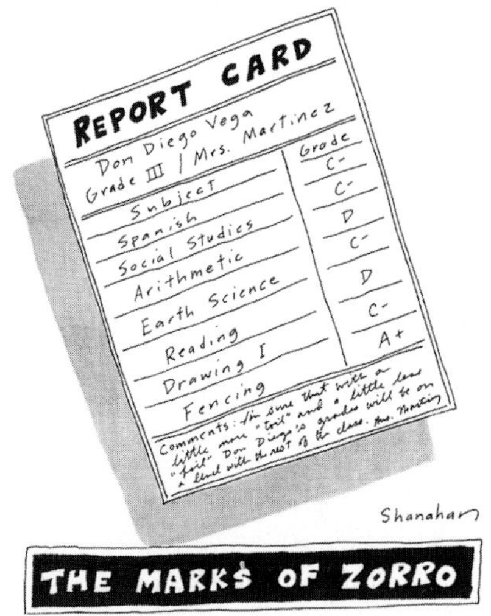

Most students won't report other students' cheating. In one survey, three-fourths of the students witnessed cheating by others but only one in a hundred informed the instructors (Jendrick 1992). Many of the students ignored the situation even though it made them angry or upset. One third of the students said cheating didn't bother them. Some researchers (McCabe, Trevino, and Butterfield 2002) concluded peer attitudes toward cheating have a stronger influence on individual student decisions to cheat than any other factors the researchers studied.

Understand Cheating

Cheating in college has many causes (Whitley and Keith-Spiegel 2002). Often students who cheat feel pressure to succeed. They feel overwhelmed by the demands of so many deadlines and can't see any other way to get by. Successful cheating gives students better grades with less effort.

Many students and instructors simply expect people to cheat if they have the opportunity. Some students reason that because other students cheat, it's okay for them to cheat, too. Instructors sometimes make it easy to cheat by not monitoring tests closely.

Often students who cheat do not get caught or aren't punished when they are caught. Although most students recognize that cheating involves some risk, they report that they have seen students cheat and get away with it. Many instructors don't feel confident in challenging students who cheat, so they overlook suspicious acts. Inaction by the instructor encourages others to cheat.

Some students who cheat may not recognize when they are cheating (Keith-Spiegel 1992). Some students "work together" and share answers either before or during a test.

They believe that there is nothing objectionable about sharing answers as long as both parties agree to collaborate. These students don't recognize that how they arrive at answers is just as important as the answers themselves.

How else do students justify cheating? Figure 8.6, "Excuses for Academic Dishonesty" (Whitley and Keith-Spiegel 2002), summarizes explanations that students offer for their behavior. Complete Journal activity "What's the Risk?" on page 239 to explore motivations for maintaining integrity on your own campus.

CREATE YOUR FUTURE

Targeting Your GPA

Imagine yourself at the end of your college career. How important will your GPA be toward securing the future you have in mind? Not all opportunities following college require a 4.0.

However, if you decide to continue your studies in graduate school, you need to start right now building a GPA that gives you the widest options. Write down the GPA range that you think would be most desirable at the conclusion of your career. Be realistic. Keep in mind how willing you are to make the sacrifices that will be required to excel.

Now think about whether you have laid the proper foundation to achieve that outcome. If you have, congratulations! If you haven't, list three things you could do to get on track.

Show Integrity and Resist the Impulse

Would you want to be cared for by a physician who cheated her way to a medical license? When the outcome of education involves life-and-death decisions, we clearly want to be cared for by someone with sound knowledge and skills.

Even if you don't plan to become a physician, you'll benefit from direct and accurate measurements of what you know. For example, your survival in more difficult, advanced courses may depend on your learning from an earlier course. By cheating, you increase the likelihood of serious academic problems in the future. Explore your own reasons for choosing responsibly in the Journal activity "Reflect on Cheating" on page 239.

In their mission statements, most colleges pledge to foster moral and ethical behavior.

Some colleges have a stringent honor code. The principles of the code, usually described in the student handbook, recognize that students will have plenty of opportunities to cheat. When you exercise integrity, however, you demonstrate not just to your instructor but also to your classmates that you're a trustworthy, moral person.

> ***Character is destiny.***
>
> Heraclites
> *Greek philosopher, 500 BCE*

Cheating can have ugly consequences. Even if they get away with cheating, some students struggle with a nagging conscience. The relief they initially feel in escaping a bad grade can be replaced by self-doubt, dissatisfaction, and guilt. These students suffer because they have fallen short of their own ideals, creating long-term harm for their self-esteem and self-confidence. Furthermore, once they cheat and get away with it, they may be tempted to do it again the next time they aren't as prepared as they should be.

When cheaters do get caught, they face multiple risks. Being accused of cheating in front of others is humiliating. Being found guilty of cheating means that the accused may have to explain this judgment to their friends or parents. Worse, some instructors will turn those accused over to a student court for punishment, spreading their humiliation even further. Penalties for cheating differ. An instructor may give cheaters a 0 on the exam or an automatic F in the course. On campuses that practice a strict honor code, one episode of cheating leads to expulsion. On some occasions, cheating students have experienced surprising consequences. See "Clarify Values: Protecting Your Options," for one example of the long-term consequence of giving in to the temptation to cheat.

What will you do when faced with an opportunity to cheat? If honesty is an important value for you, then you may have already committed yourself to making sure that you take no shortcuts to success. But what if you're not persuaded? Perhaps you've seen dishonest people get away with too much. After all, if 78 percent of students report that they have cheated, how wrong can it be? See "Create Your Future: Test Your Way to Your Career" for examples of how your attitudes towards tests, grades, and cheating can carry into your career.

Cheating is not a victimless crime. Students who cheat potentially rob themselves of learning that may be useful to them in the future. If you aspire to true excellence, you can't really do so by being a fraud. If you can't be a trustworthy student, how can you be a trustworthy partner or friend? To explore your

CREATE YOUR FUTURE

Test Your Way to Your Career

From the beginning of her college career, Sue was quite taken with the whole process of test taking. She was intrigued to see how a professor's personality shaped the manner in which she would end up being tested. She began to notice that some professors crafted tests with great care whereas others threw their tests together haphazardly. The latter situation made it much easier for Sue to argue adjustments to her score based on her ability to identify flaws in test construction. After four years of test-taking experience, Sue decided to go into a graduate program in educational psychology to learn more about test design and administration. Later, degree in hand, she applied to a large firm that developed national achievement tests, where she could continue to analyze test quality for fun and profit.

Mischa was distressed to find that cheating was rampant in his college classes. He believed that cheating was simply wrong and felt compelled to promote a different standard of character. He pursued and won a position on the committee that reviewed complaints about student integrity. This committee, comprised of students and faculty, had to make judgments about whether students had violated the integrity code and decide on the appropriate consequence. Mischa was surprised at how satisfying this work turned out to be. He decided a future in law would allow him to have a career in which he could put his high standards and analytic skills to work for the common good.

FIGURE 8.6 Excuses for Academic Dishonesty

Denial of Injury:	*Cheating hurts no one.* *Cheating is only wrong in courses in your major.*
Denial of Personal Responsibility:	*I got the flu and couldn't read all the chapters.* *The course is too hard.*
Denial of Personal Risk:	*Professors won't do anything to you.* *No one ever gets caught.*
Selective Morality:	*Friends come first and my friend needed my help.* *I only did what was necessary at the time.*
Minimizing Seriousness:	*It's only busy work.* *Cheating is meaningless when it has little weight on my grade.*
A Necessary Act:	*If I don't do well, my parents will kill me.* *I'll lose my scholarship if I don't get all B's.*
Dishonesty as a Norm:	*Society's leaders do it, so why not me?* *Everyone does it.*

Adapted from Academic Dishonesty by Bernard E. Whitley Jr. and Patricia Keith-Spiegel. Copyright © 2002 by Lawrence Erlbaum Associates, Inc. Reprinted by permission of the publisher.

own perspective about cheating, complete Self-Assessment 3, "Your Personal Honor Code," on page 241. Also see the Journal activity, "Promote Better Test Preparation," on page 240 for a creative way to summarize what you have learned about test preparation.

CLARIFY VALUES

Protecting Your Options

Randy had a weak moment in his sophomore year. He had not set aside enough time to complete the take-home test assigned in his French class. However, he remembered that his roommate had taken the course the semester before and had done very well. He scanned the hard drive of the computer they shared and found his roommate's exam. "Just this once," he thought as he downloaded the exam, modified parts of the essay, and submitted it as his own work.

His instructor recognized the essay because the work had stood out the first time. Busted, Randy had to take a zero in the course. He lost "face," the tuition, the time, and the course credit. What he didn't expect was that because of his lack of integrity, his adviser refused to write him letters of recommendation for graduate school. Randy was surprised to learn that one impulsive act had such serious long-term impact on his future.

Summary Strategies for Mastering College

Tests Can Help You Refine Your Skills in Planning and Achieving Goals as You Build Your Knowledge Base and Your Personal Integrity

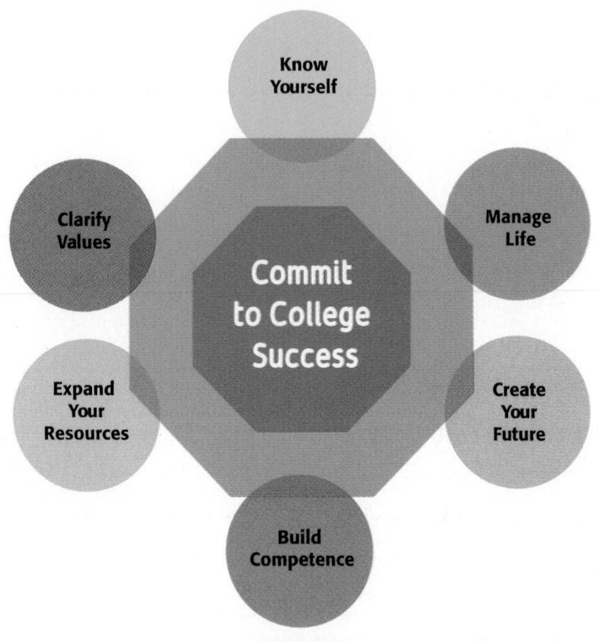

Focus on the Six Strategies for Success above as you read each chapter to learn how to apply these strategies to your own success.

1 Get on with It!

- Accept that tests are a fact of life in college. They offer feedback for how well you're learning and give you a sense of accomplishment when you succeed.
- Tests also help you pace your reading, consolidate your learning, improve your thinking, and achieve special status.

2 Get in Gear

- Use long-term strategies: pacing yourself, protecting your health, and getting in the right frame of mind.
- Use short-term strategies: knowing what to expect, sizing up the teacher, and designing study strategies that suit your learning style.
- Cramming happens. Concentrate your efforts in the home stretch if you haven't had time to prepare.
- Reduce your test anxiety through positive self-talk, appropriate preparation, and relaxation strategies.
- Handle emergencies immediately and honestly.

3 Meet the Challenge

- Plan how to use your time in each testing challenge.
- Use a variety of general test-taking strategies to improve your performance.
- Look for cues in objective tests to help you determine the best answer.
- Produce precise responses to do your best on short-answer questions.
- Do your best on essay questions by planning, expressing yourself precisely, and writing legibly.

4 Make the Grade

- Review your results to consolidate your learning and to plan better study strategies.
- Use good judgment when you challenge your instructor's judgment about the fairness of a grade.
- Don't waste a semester. A bad semester will have a whopping impact on your cumulative GPA.

5 Build Your Character

- Demonstrate your academic integrity by resisting cheating.
- Recognize the motives that drive students to cheat.
- Set a high personal standard to build your character.
- Avoid the ugly personal outcomes of cheating, including possible expulsion from school if you are caught.

Review Questions

1. How does a positive attitude influence your success on tests? List three other strategies you can implement to improve your test performance in the future.

   1. ____________________
   2. ____________________
   3. ____________________

2. How should your study strategies vary according to the kind of test you'll be facing? List a few specific types of tests, followed by a description of an appropriate study strategy.

   Test: __________ Study Strategy: __________

   Test: __________ Study Strategy: __________

   Test: __________ Study Strategy: __________

3. Describe a few specific ways to overcome test anxiety.

4. Why should you review your test results carefully when the instructor returns your work? What else should you do after a test to maximize your overall grade in the course?

5. What advantages follow when you avoid the temptation to cheat on tests? List three disadvantages that can result from cheating.

   1. ____________________
   2. ____________________
   3. ____________________

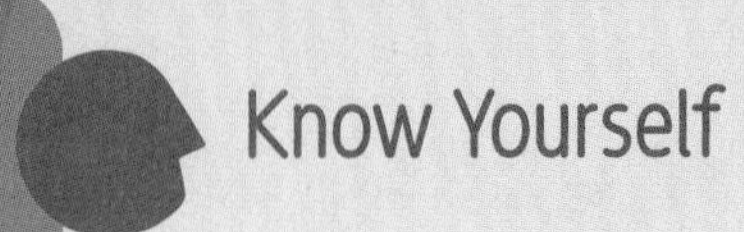

SELF-ASSESSMENT 1

How Serious Is My Test Anxiety?

Check the category that best describes the way you feel when you take tests:

	Never	Occasionally	Regularly
I feel physically ill just before a test.			
I fail to complete tests, because I fret about what will happen when I fail.			
I can't seem to organize my time to prepare well for exams.			
I know I could do better if I could ignore how nervous I feel during tests.			
I struggle with stomach pain and bathroom urges just before a test.			
My mind has gone completely blank during the middle of an exam.			
I fear that I'll end up turning in the worst performance on the test in the entire class.			
I have difficulty getting a good night's sleep before a test.			
I'm very concerned about what my instructor will think of me if I don't do well on a test.			
I get more distracted during the test than other students seem to.			
I start to panic when other students finish their exams while I'm still working.			
I know the material better than my exam score indicates.			
I know I won't be able to have the kind of future I want unless I can get a better grip on my testing fears.			

These items give you a general idea about how seriously test anxiety may be interfering with your test performance. If you marked any items "regularly" or marked several "occasionally," you might benefit from a more in-depth assessment of your test anxiety. Contact the study skills center on your campus.

After evaluating the nature of your difficulty, the study skills specialists can make specific recommendations to help you master your anxiety. If you're seriously troubled by test anxiety, seek counseling.

SELF-ASSESSMENT 2

How Well Do I Test?

Rate how often you use these skills.

	Always	Usually	Sometimes	Never
As part of my general test-taking strategy	____	____	____	____
I stay relaxed during the exam.	____	____	____	____
I look at the entire test before I start.	____	____	____	____
I read the instructions carefully.	____	____	____	____
I concentrate even when distracted.	____	____	____	____
I ask the instructor for help when I'm confused.	____	____	____	____
I move on when I get stuck.	____	____	____	____
I look for cues in other parts of the test.	____	____	____	____
I proofread my work.	____	____	____	____
In multiple-choice questions				
I read the test items carefully and completely.	____	____	____	____
When I'm uncertain which answer is right, I take steps to rule out the alternatives that are wrong.	____	____	____	____
I mark the correct answer clearly and consistently.	____	____	____	____
I change my answers only when I'm certain I should do so.	____	____	____	____
When I don't know an answer, I guess.	____	____	____	____
When stumped, I look for cues in the question's structure.	____	____	____	____
On true/false items				
I go with my hunches.				
I avoid looking for patterns on the answer sheet.				
I analyze qualifying terms (such as *always, never*).	____	____	____	____
I try to find exceptions to the rule.	____	____	____	____
On fill-in-the-blank questions				
I don't loiter when stumped.	____	____	____	____
In short-answer questions				
I write brief, logical answers.	____	____	____	____
In essay questions				
I underline the verbs in the question to help figure out what kind of thinking I need to do.	____	____	____	____
I think and outline before I write.	____	____	____	____
I reflect the question in my opening sentence.	____	____	____	____
I write main ideas first and fill in details and examples later.	____	____	____	____
I don't bluff when I don't know.	____	____	____	____
I write for readability.	____	____	____	____
I'm careful about using humor.	____	____	____	____

Now go back over the list and circle the test-management skills that you marked "rarely" or "never." Check your calendar for the date of your next exam. Use your goal-setting skills to make improvements for that exam.

SELF-ASSESSMENT 3

Your Personal Honor Code

Check the items with which you agree.

Under what circumstances do you think most students might be inclined to cheat?

when it's unlikely that they would be caught ________

when they feel desperate to get a better grade ________

when a great deal is riding on a particular grade ________

if they haven't managed their time well enough to study effectively ________

when they might be teased by their peers if they refused to cheat ________

Other: ____

If someone is caught cheating, which consequence do you think is the most appropriate?

expulsion from school ________

failure in the course where the cheating occurred ________

failure of the assignment on which the cheating occurred ________

review by the school's honor board ________

public censure ________

repeating the assignment without cheating ________

depends on the cheater's history ________

Other: ____

Rank the things that discourage you from cheating:

I would lose my self-respect. ________

I would be frightened of getting caught. ________

I want my test results to reflect my learning accurately. ________

I consider it my honor to uphold academic integrity. ________

I don't want to give in to group pressure to do things that I don't believe in. ________

Other: ____

Will you be able to withstand the temptation to take the easy (but risky) way out of making the grade?

Your Journal

REFLECT

1. Then and Now

Think about the grades you made in high school. How much time did you put into studies then compared with now?

- Are you managing the same levels of achievement?
- Have you had to increase your effort just to hold your ground?
- Are you now studying harder than you ever have?
- Is that effort resulting in the achievement you're aiming for? If not, what steps should you take to feel more satisfied?

2. Format Fever

Students differ in the preferences they have for the formats in which they are tested. Some students love the challenge of crafting a solid essay response to a well-framed question. They may dislike the precision required in multiple-choice questions. Other students live in stark fear of having to write what they know. Instead they thrive on the opportunity to hammer a set of multiple-choice questions. Rank the following test formats in the order of your preference:

___fill-in-the-blank
___multiple-choice
___true-false
___essay

In your journal, speculate about why you ordered the formats as you did. How does your achievement history influence your choice? Does your learning style dictate which formats are more appealing?

3. Reflect on Cheating

You've probably experienced a situation in which you could easily have cheated but you resisted the opportunity.

- Describe what would have made the cheating easy.
- Identify the feelings and values that were involved in resolving this problem.
- Were you satisfied with the resolution?
- What actions, if any, did you take to feel comfortable with the outcome?

DO

1. Construct Your Own Exam

Construct a sample test for the next real test you'll face. If you were the teacher, what would be the most important concepts to test for? How would you go about assessing them? If you think it would be helpful, make an appointment with your instructor to compare your own strategy with the one you have created. What insights can you gain from the conversation that will make you even more effective at predicting test design?

___

___

2. What's the Risk?

Locate a copy of your school's honor code or procedures that govern academic integrity. Review it to determine the risks involved in cheating. In most cases, the outcomes of being caught and punished for cheating are fairly severe. How can you reconcile this outcome with the fact that 75 percent of college students report cheating at some point in high school or college or both? Consider how learning styles and personality factors might influence the decision to cheat.

___

___

Your Journal

THINK CRITICALLY

1. Decode Essay Instructions

Find some examples of essay questions, preferably ones from tests you took this term. Circle the verbs that represent the kind of thinking the instructor has asked you to do in completing the essay. Think about what kind of question is being asked. How will this decoding exercise influence your study strategy for the exams you will face in the future?

___

___

2. Grades: Carrots or Sticks?

Many students thrive in graded systems. They like the clear-cut messages they get when their efforts are rewarded by good grades. However, other students find grades less rewarding. They think competition for grades undercuts meaningful learning and feel stressed out by the process. With a group of students, discuss the advantages and disadvantages of using grades to evaluate learning. Which system would most effectively motivate your learning?

___

___

CREATE

1. Promote Better Test Preparation

Create a website for one of your courses in which you explore the hazards of cramming or offer six bits of good advice about how to succeed on tests in that class. Make an appointment with the instructor for feedback. If the feedback is positive, perhaps your website can be incorporated in the planning the next time the course is taught.

2. Find Your Quiet Place

Imagine your favorite peaceful place. Where would it be? What would you be doing there? Think of this calming refuge to help you ward off anxiety while studying or test taking.

What would you need to do to make this image one you can rely on during stress to restore your peace? Try the exercise "Learn to Relax" on the CD-ROM that came with this book.

___

___

9 EXPRESS YOURSELF

- I pursue opportunities to practice effective communication skills.
- I can design and execute projects involving research.
- I polish writing projects to showcase my ideas properly.
- I know how to avoid problems with plagiarism.
- I seek criticism from other people to improve the quality of my work.
- I use strategies to engage the audience during speeches.
- I know how to control jitters when communicating.

© DesignPics, Inc./IndexOpen

College offers unique opportunities to refine your speaking and writing skills.

CHAPTER OUTLINE

Express Yourself!

Prepare Before You Write

Clarify Your Goal
Define Your Purpose
Select a Topic
Narrow Your Topic
Develop a Working Thesis

Do Your Research

Gather Sources
Master the Library
Use the Internet

Get Organized

Establish Your Writing Routine
Develop Your Writing Plan
Prepare Outlines

Write with Impact

Prepare Your First Draft
Revise and Revise Again
Edit
Finish in Style

Solve Writing Problems

Learn from Feedback
Find Your Unique Voice
Stop Procrastinating
Unlock Writer's Block
Build Your Integrity

Speak!

Pursue the Spotlight
Write a Good Speech
Deliver a Good Speech
Improve Your Speaking Skills

Images of College Success

J. K. Rowling

She was the first person to write her way into the billionaire's club. J. K. (Joanne Kathleen) Rowling was stalled in a train between Manchester and London when her world-famous hero, Harry Potter, just "strolled into my head." She began work on the manuscript the moment she got home. Currently, Rowling is working on Harry's seventh adventure, but her track record is awe-inspiring. Her *Harry Potter* books have been published in fifty-five languages, and she has won numerous awards and recognitions for this imaginative work that integrates critical thinking, problem solving, and creativity.

Rowling was born in England near a town called Dursley, familiar to her fans as the last name of Harry Potter's foul adoptive family. She always wanted to be a writer, penning her first work at age six about a rabbit with measles. She majored in French and classic literature at the University of Exeter. A fan of writers Jane Austen and C. S. Lewis, Rowling worked for a while as an English teacher. She became a secretary for Amnesty International and later for a publishing house, where one of her duties was sending out rejection letters to hopeful authors. Ironically, she received nine rejections of her first Potter manuscript before someone wisely saw her promise and offered her a breath-taking hundred-thousand-dollar advance.

Despite the enormous wealth and worldwide fans her imaginative work has generated, Rowling's life hasn't always been easy. She constantly must contend with rumors that she was so impoverished when she wrote the original Harry Potter novel that she scribbled it on napkins in cafes, to avoid the discomfort of her unheated flat. She responded to that romantic and erroneous imagery this way: "I'm not stupid enough to rent an unheated flat in Edinburgh in mid-winter." That is no surprise to fans of the Harry Potter series, since Rowling admits that she based the all-knowing character Hermione loosely on herself, although, Rowling adds, "I was neither as clever or annoying (I hope!)." (Imbornoni, 2006).

J. K. ROWLING'S massive success in writing has evolved into many opportunities to speak in public as well.

When employers are asked what they seek most in college graduates, the consistent answer is "communication skills." Thus, mastering communication skills will benefit you not only in college but in future careers and many other aspects of your life. As you read, think about the Six Strategies for Success listed to the left and how this chapter can help you maximize success in these important areas.

Express Yourself!

If you are not interested in becoming an author like J. K. Rowling, you may wonder why you need to learn how to write. You may want to go into business or law or medicine. However, in most professional worlds, skilled writing and public speaking can be critical to your success. If you choose your college opportunities carefully, you'll learn to express yourself in writing and speaking with precision, poise, and polish. Even if you think that you're not a good writer, you can learn. Writing is not an innate skill.

Writing essays, lab reports, and papers in college prepare you to write effective memos, proposals, and reports in the work world. Practice in editing and proofreading will improve your attention to detail. Writing projects also encourage the kind of creativity that would be highly valued in fields like advertising, publishing, and marketing.

Classroom speaking provides practice for interviewing, supervising, persuading, negotiating, selling, and other aspects of working with the public. Enhance your future career prospects by honing your writing and speaking skills now.

If you connect well with others and can usually think of the right thing to say at the right time, you may be a natural communicator. Most of us need practice and hard work. Bringing personal expression under your control through a variety of projects in college will give you great flexibility for the challenges you'll face after graduation.

Beginning communication assignments concentrate on writing and speaking about personal experiences. As you progress further into your major, communication performances will become more challenging, tailored to your chosen discipline. With some practice, you can significantly improve your skills by graduation. How much better you become will depend on your making the most of your opportunities. Build your self-confidence as a communicator by exploring "Manage Life: Conquer Your Communication Qualms."

Prepare Before You Write

Whether your project involves writing or speaking, the following strategies can help you produce your best effort.

> ***Good communication is as stimulating as black coffee, and just as hard to sleep after.***
> Anne Morrow Lindbergh
> *Twentieth-century American poet*

Clarify Your Goal

Make sure you understand the goal of the assignment from the instructor's point of view. Look at the syllabus and try to link the specific assignment to the overall goals of the course. Ask questions to clarify anything that is unclear. Compare your ideas with your classmates' perceptions. Actively evaluate how the goal of the assignment can help you achieve your writing goals. For example, if your assignment is to write a three- to five-page essay, you might opt for the shorter three-page goal to help you work on developing short, coherent arguments. By contrast, if you receive feedback that you need to develop your ideas in greater depth, go for the five-page limit. You also might want to tailor assignments to your career goals. For example, if you are interested in advertising, you might choose to write a persuasive essay.

Define Your Purpose

If you're lucky, you'll have an opportunity to write in a variety of formats that will prepare you for the diverse writing demands in professional life. Strong writing skills are a great asset in virtually every professional career. Before you begin writing, review the directions and make sure you understand the purpose of the assignment. There are five basic reasons for writing:

- *To explain an idea or provide information (expository).* Research papers and essays often have this purpose. Instructors often assign research papers to develop your research skills as well as your writing skills. Essays develop your writing and reasoning skills, and demonstrate your ability to think analytically about the subject you're learning.
- *To persuade or argue a point.* This type of assignment often combines writing and problem-solving skills and can benefit from the following organizational strategy:
  - Define the problem and its impact clearly.
  - Describe the origin of the problem.
  - Identify any other relevant factors.
  - Propose a solution.
  - Predict the impact of the solution, including negative outcomes.
  - Develop a follow-up strategy.

© Jeff Greenberg/PhotoEdit

Compare your ideas with those of a classmate to clarify your understanding of confusing ideas or concepts.

- *To describe an experiment or process or to report on lab results.* In science classes, you may work independently or collaborate on a lab report that describes a specific scientific procedure.
- Lab reports are usually highly structured, based on a set of conventional headings. For example, a botany instructor might ask you to experiment with how different nutrient levels affect plant growth. The lab report will contain the following sections:
  - *Introduction:* the nature of the problem, including relevant research
  - *Methods:* the procedure used to investigate the problem
  - *Results:* the findings
  - *Discussion:* the significance of the results; improvements to the procedure
- *To reflect on your own experience.* Journal writing lets you explore the personal significance of what you are studying. Instructors usually don't grade journals in a traditional way. They will give you feedback about your insights or the seriousness of your effort. Although research may not be required in such projects, it's a good idea to connect with course concepts to show what you have learned.
- *To create an original piece of writing.* Literature instructors may assign creative writing projects, such as poetry and short stories, to foster an appreciation of these genres. Don't rule out doing research in reflective assignments. Locate authors whose style you admire. Do some background reading on a topic that might focus your work.

Conquer Your Communication Qualms

It's normal to fret a bit about whether you will fare well in the writing and speaking assignments that lie ahead. What kinds of strategies can you use to gain confidence in your ability to get your message across?

- **Seek opportunities.** When something is unsettling, it is human to try to avoid similar situations. However, the only way you can improve in this vital skill of communication is through practice, practice, practice. Whenever you are given an opportunity to write or speak in a class, grab it!
- **Build from strength.** Audit what you do well in communication assignments and concentrate on adding one more area of strength with each new assignment. For example, suppose you can write a good sentence but have trouble stringing sentences together in paragraphs that have impact. Concentrate on coherent paragraph development as the next area to master.
- **Develop an overarching plan.** Feedback on your communication skills is generally helpful, regardless of the class in which it originates. For example, one of your instructors may point out that you need to develop your ideas more. Consolidate such feedback from multiple sources. Then set some overall goals for improving those skills in all of your assignments. See the Journal activity "What Are Your Writing Trends?" on page 276 to help you develop a master strategy.
- **Pursue balanced feedback vigorously.** Your skills will grow best when your critics reinforce your strengths as well as point out your deficits. Make certain that you get confirmation on what you did well, to build your confidence. Find additional reviewers if you can't get positive feedback from your instructor.
- **Don't crumble if you misfire.** The most talented communicators foul up from time to time. A shaky speech or a less-than-ideal paper should encourage you to better prepare or rehearse so you improve next time.

Select a Topic

Many instructors will select your topic, at least in a general way. However, you still may have to narrow it down. Choosing well can help you take responsibility and embrace the work that lies ahead. What strategies can help?

1. Look through your notes. What concepts stand out as the most interesting to you?
2. Examine your textbook and course readings, explore the encyclopedia, or cruise the Internet to spark your imagination.
3. Explore your personal experience. Think about aspects of the assignment that naturally connect to your own life. For example, J. K. Rowling modeled Harry Potter's friends after people she grew up with. Refer to the Journal activity "Exploiting Your Life" on page 271 to develop a reservoir of good ideas for future projects.
4. Consider what topic would be the most fun or would have the most future value for you. Are there topics that will connect in a meaningful way to your future career plans? Give those ideas top consideration.
5. Carry a small notebook or maintain a separate file in which you can capture ideas that come to you. Think often about your topic to sensitize yourself to ideas that might strengthen the development of your argument. Although popular media resources such as magazines and television programs may not be acceptable resources for a formal research paper, they can suggest interesting directions for more formal research.

6. Consider developing a "research stream." Good students see the value of an ongoing focus for their college papers (Hansen and Hansen, 1997). They develop a research stream that begins with the first paper they write and builds with each new project. This way they don't have to start from scratch with each assignment, and they can manage greater depth each time.

For example, Paulo enjoys thinking about environmental issues. He looks for opportunities in his writing assignments to read what he enjoys. He writes about literature with ecological themes, evaluates ecology-related legislation in social science classes, and explores environmental crises in natural science term papers. As a result, Paulo knows his material very well and expands what he knows with each project. His focused writing may serve his job-hunting future better than a hodgepodge of unrelated essays. When you choose topics for papers and other projects, keep your long-term career goals in mind.

> ***One of the advantages of being disorderly is that one is constantly making exciting discoveries.***
>
> A. A. Milne
> *Author of* Winnie the Pooh

Narrow Your Topic

As you explore possible topics, avoid ones that are too large, too obscure, too emotional, or too complicated for you to work with in the allotted time. Do not write or speak about areas where you have little knowledge because it's easier to stay engaged with a project where you have personal interest. Conduct research until you have the knowledge you need to succeed. You may need to redefine the project several times before settling on a topic that speaks to you. Although there are a number of techniques for narrowing your topic, once you have a general idea of what you want to write about, "mess around" with the ideas to begin to make them your own.

Free Write Free writing involves writing without stopping for a set period of time, usually five to ten minutes, to help get your thoughts on paper. After free writing, review your work to see if any key ideas stand out. When you have identified key concepts in your writing, do another free write on these topics until you have a more specific concept for your paper. Spontaneous writing may help you uncover new ideas, questions, and connections. Simply write whatever you think about the topic and save the parts that have potential.

Pausing during group process to freewrite may produce a wealth of new insights.

Brainstorm Concentrate on the assignment and write down all of the concepts or ideas that occur to you. Don't worry about the order, clarity, or meaning of the ideas. Just write down everything that comes to mind. Following your brainstorming session, impose some order on what you have produced. Draw connecting lines. Strike out distractors. Make new concept maps that display the most meaningful connections as the basis for your writing.

Talk It Out You may find it easier to narrow your topic by pretending that you're talking to a friend. Once you have some ideas to work with, jot down the parts of the conversation you liked and proceed to the formal aspects of writing. Or talk to real friends and colleagues. Use the most interesting parts of that conversation to launch your own perspective.

Ask Questions Journalists follow a specific protocol that can be helpful to generate good writing. Go after your task with *who?, what?, when?, where?*, and *why?* Answers to those questions can provide new direction to your work.

Begin Reading on the Topic If the assignment is relatively focused to begin with, you may just be able to start reading, and that will spark ideas and interest.

Develop a Working Thesis

After you have narrowed your topic to an area of specific interest to you, refine it even further by developing a **thesis.** Your *thesis statement* conveys your general position on the topic and guides the direction of your writing, which supports your thesis. The thesis is essential because it focuses your topic and provides a clear direction for your thinking, research, and writing.

A good working thesis:

1. reduces the topic to a single controlling idea, unifying opinion, or key message
2. presents your position clearly and concisely, in one sentence
3. makes a statement that can be supported by statistics, examples, quotes, and references to other sources within the time and space constraints of the assignment
4. creates interest in the topic
5. establishes the purpose of the paper
6. establishes the approach or pattern of organization

Each paragraph should develop a separate but connected point that supports your thesis. For example, your art history instructor might ask you to contrast the work of two Impressionist painters. Your thesis statement might read as follows: "Both Manet and Monet are important Impressionist artists, but Monet's work has achieved wider popularity." Subsequent paragraphs could address the following elements of the thesis statement:

- What is Impressionism?
- Why are the artists considered important?
- What distinguishes the work of each?
- What evidence suggests that one artist is more highly regarded than the other?

To answer each of these questions, include expert opinions found in your research. Don't be afraid to modify your thesis. If your research is not supporting it, restate your thesis to reflect the supporting evidence. Sometimes you will need to do some preliminary research before you can even write your thesis statement.

Do Your Research

Many writing and speaking assignments require research to flesh out facts, figures, and background information about your topic. Good research involves gathering reliable sources of information from a variety of resources such as books, journals, and Internet sites.

Gather Sources

> ***Research is to see what everybody has seen, and to think what nobody else has thought.***
> Albert Szent-Györgyi
> *Twentieth-century Hungarian biochemist*

How many research sources should you include in your paper? Sometimes instructors will specify a minimum number; sometimes they won't. You may not have a clear idea about what will work best until you have done some research. Think responsibly about how many sources you will actually need to develop the most effective argument, but plan to look at more materials than you ultimately will refer to in your work. Not every resource you read will be relevant in the end. Choose those that help you develop a sound argument. Quality of evidence, not quantity, will impress your instructor.

Good researchers find, and carefully show, appropriate, persuasive evidence. For example, you can include statistics in a political science essay because numerical evidence communicates information about voting trends. However, citing statistical evidence in an expressive essay or a piece of literary criticism assigned in a humanities class probably won't work. The point of any formal expressive assignment is to demonstrate your knowledge of course-related ideas.

As you do your research, also find sources that argue *against* your assertions. This practice may surprise you. Anticipating criticisms that the reader might have and defending against them in your writing strengthens your overall argument.

Write down the complete reference for each source *as you go*. It's frustrating to assemble a reference list at the end of your work only to discover that you forgot to write down the year a book was published, an important page number, or an Internet address.

Master the Library

Get to know your library's resources so you can locate information quickly. Take a tour if you haven't already done so. If you have trouble locating what you need, ask! Most librarians enjoy helping students. Approach the librarians who appear friendliest or pursue those with the most specialized knowledge on your topic.

© JP Lafont/Sygma/CORBIS

Knowing the significance and location of different kinds of resources can save you valuable time in the library.

Library searches often start in the reference room, which usually houses both paper and electronic databases. From there you may be routed to other areas of the library where you can locate original or *primary* sources (for example, books and journal articles), *secondary* sources (for example, textbooks and other sources that review primary works), or popular press items. References to research or expert opinions that you use in your research are called *citations*.

Your research assignment may specify which types of sources you can use. Most instructors prefer original (primary) sources. They also are more impressed by journal articles that are "peer reviewed." This means that the article was critically analyzed and then approved by other experts in the field. Check with your instructor whether some sources are off-limits, such as popular magazines.

Once you've collected several sources, discard the unhelpful ones. Read those with potential carefully, taking notes that will help you represent the author's ideas. It can be helpful to collect pertinent information on three-by-five–inch notecards that you can easily reorganize during the writing process.

Use the Internet

Whether you use the library or the Internet or both, your search will begin with a key word or two that you'll enter into an appropriate database. Do key word searches on several search engines to see what the nature of the discussion might be on the topic you have in mind. For example, if your environmental science class requires a paper on effective recycling strategies, start with the word *recycling.* Using that key word may produce so many "hits" that you could be overwhelmed. Narrow your search to something more specific such as *newspaper recycling* to find more targeted information. If your search produces too few hits, broaden the concept until you find some resources that will help you.

Relying on the Internet, however, can be risky. Most instructors still favor library research that will help you locate printed publications and peer-reviewed sources. The information on the Internet isn't always reliable. Anyone can post anything, making it hard to sift out the gold. Don't assume that an Internet source will be acceptable.

However, instructors may be willing to accept Internet citations that are:

1. written by a recognized authority in the field
2. supported by a reputable host group
3. peer reviewed
4. credible and unbiased

Good research is important for many types of writing and speaking assignments, providing the basic information you then craft into your final presentation. Following are some additional strategies for organizing your work to maximize success.

Get Organized

For some people, coming up with ideas isn't the hard part of good writing. Developing the organization and having the discipline to bring good ideas under control can be difficult aspects of successful writing.

Establish Your Writing Routine

A writing routine can help you get down to business and avoid wasting both time and energy.

Stock Your Reference Shelf Good writers rely on expert help. Invest in references that will help you develop and express your ideas. For example:

- A *dictionary* can help you with definitions, pronunciation, and spelling.
- A *thesaurus* provides synonyms and can help expand your vocabulary.
- An *atlas* provides geographic facts and figures.

- A style manual can help you with grammar and writing conventions, such as the *American Psychological Association* and *Modern Language Association* procedures.
- A book of quotations provides proverbs and memorable quotations organized by topic, author, or key phrases.

Find a Place to Write Most writers say that they need uninterrupted time to think about their writing. Find a quiet place where you won't be interrupted. Hang a "Do Not Disturb" sign on your door to reduce distraction. Don't answer the phone or e-mail messages.

A #2 pencil and a dream can take you anywhere.

Joyce A. Myers
Contemporary American businesswoman

Develop Your Writing Plan

Many students overconfidently sit down the night before a paper is due and dash off a first draft to submit the next day. In most cases, that plan will guarantee unhappy feedback. Good writing requires time and a plan for how to use that time most effectively.

Examine the due date for the assignment and work backward to allow the right amount of time to get the job done. Make sure that you factor in how assignments in other classes must be addressed in your overall timetable. Chapter 3 offers some helpful hints about time management for writing projects. In addition, Figure 9.1, "A Sample Timetable for a Writing Deadline," offers guidance.

Prepare Outlines

Generate outlines before you write that allow you to represent the scope of your thoughts, incorporate your research, and make your best argument.

The Informal Outline An informal outline lists the points to be covered in your paper. Putting them down allows you to begin to organize and group them into related clusters. As you find connections and consolidate points, you should revisit your thesis. Does the evidence still support it? Do you need to restate it? If you haven't already written a working thesis, this consolidation of ideas should lead to one. Outlining often reveals areas that require further research.

The Formal Outline A formal outline provides a more structured order to your points, identifying which are the key ideas and which are subordinate. The key ideas become paragraphs, with the subordinate ideas providing supportive evidence.

Write with Impact

Over time, writing projects improve your writing skills, develop your confidence as a writer, and build your self-esteem, one of the important steps to success listed at the beginning of this chapter.

Prepare Your First Draft

The draft stage is an important first step in the process of actually writing your paper or speech. However, don't confuse a first draft with a final presentation. Following are some important things to keep in mind when first drafting your assignment.

Know Your Audience Knowing your audience can help you make the right decisions. For example, some tasks require objective and precise presentation of the facts.

FIGURE 9.1 A Sample Timetable for a Writing Deadline

One to two months before the deadline	Select your topic. Map your ideas. Develop your writing plan. Begin to develop a thesis statement. Start your research.
Two weeks before the deadline	Develop individual sections of your paper. Revise with vigor. Complete your research. Finalize your thesis statement.
The week before the deadline	Polish the individual sections of the paper. Create an interesting title. Check your references for accuracy. Obtain some feedback from a friend.
The night before the deadline	Combine the parts of the paper. Print the final draft. Proofread your paper. Assemble the paper.
The morning of the deadline	Proofread your paper one more time.

In other projects you must be exploratory and imaginative. Some projects work best with a casual tone; others may require a polished, professional presentation.

Keep It Casual, and Keep It Moving In your first draft, don't get bogged down. Write quickly. If you've done your research, and have given yourself enough time to think about the project, you'll be surprised at how much you know without referring to your note cards.

You don't have to write in a particular order. Develop the points first that you know best and end with those that require more thinking or references to research. Consider writing your introduction last, and your conclusion first. This way you will know where you're going and all paragraphs must lead to that ending. Set subgoals for how much writing you want to accomplish in any given sitting. For example, it may help to draft the conclusion one day and key paragraphs on other days.

Organize Your Argument Formal papers usually have three parts: an introduction, a body, and a conclusion:

- *Introduction.* The introduction, which contains the thesis statement, lays a foundation for the rest of the piece. Good writers establish the *context* or the purpose for writing, even when the instructor is the audience. They state their intentions early and anticipate the kinds of information readers might want to know to help them understand the motive in writing. Throughout the paper, keep in mind what your audience already knows and what they need to know.
- *The body.* The body of the paper should include your opinions and the evidence that supports your argument. Each paragraph in the body should introduce a

separate idea and support it with details such as quotes, examples, statistics, and references to other sources. Each paragraph should follow logically from the one before, and all paragraphs must relate to the thesis of the paper. The body should use a clear pattern of organization such as listing patterns, comparison patterns, sequencing patterns, cycle patterns, problem-solving patterns, cause/effect patterns, definition/example patterns, and topical/categorical patterns, as discussed earlier in the text.

- *The conclusion.* In a long paper, your conclusion should summarize your argument or review your main points. Make sure that your conclusions fit with the thesis statement you established at the beginning. See "Build Competence: Finishing Touches" for more suggestions.

Revise and Revise Again

Always leave plenty of time for revision. It is the single most important part of the writing process. In fact, you should plan to spend at least 50 percent of your time on this part of the writing process. You may have several working drafts before you reach the final draft.

Assess It After you have finished the first draft, put it aside for a couple of days. Each draft should be separated by at least a day of time away from the paper. This "away time" gives your brain a chance to process the material at a subconscious level, and allows you to come back to it with a fresh perspective.

Reread It Before you begin your revision, read it aloud to yourself or someone else. How does it sound? Does it flow? Does it make sense? Is it too long or too short? You may find you need to do more research to expand on certain points that don't seem adequately supported. You should go through and put a check next to the passages that are fine and a question mark next to any that require work. Check out the Journal activity "One More Go-Around" on page 271 to help you practice your revision skills.

Give It to Others to Read Writers can lead solitary lives, but that stereotype isn't necessarily accurate. Most writers benefit from reviews by others. When your draft is almost finished, get feedback from others who write well. Ask them to point out places where you're not clear or to identify points that need further development. Avoid getting feedback from friends who may be struggling with their own writing or you could pick up their bad habits. Your campus may have a writing center where experts can help you improve your writing or can recommend a writing tutor. Your instructor also may be willing to read an early draft of a paper.

Write the Appropriate Length Beginning writers sometimes struggle with knowing how much to write. Typically, they write too little rather than too much. Check your writing to see that you explained your intentions to the reader. Provide good examples. Make sure that the parts connect to each other with good transition sentences. All writing elements should follow logically from your original thesis statement.

Some writers have the opposite problem. Their long-winded sentences contain nonessential elements. For example, phrases such as "It is well known that" or "There are many things that"

BUILD COMPETENCE

Finishing Touches

You've spent a great deal of time developing just the right approach in your essay, but some closing strategies can weaken the impact of your work (based on Raimes 2002). Monitor how you conclude your work to maximize your writing success:

- **Don't apologize.** If you find yourself apologizing either for the inadequacy of your argument or the substandard quality of your writing, you simply need to keep refining your work.
- **Don't bore your reader.** Although you may be communicating many of the same ideas that you did in the introduction, be sure to vary how you express the ideas. Repetitive writing feels flat and may alienate interest in your work.
- **Don't introduce new ideas.** If you open up new questions, you owe the reader a longer paper and a later conclusion.
- **Don't contradict yourself.** Your point of view throughout the paper should be consistent or your reader will be confused about your purpose.

are usually unnecessary; they flatten good writing. Using too many adjectives and adverbs also slows down the reader and reduces your writing's impact. In good writing, "less is more." What if the instructor doesn't specify how long a paper should be? See "Manage Life: As Long as It Takes" to help decipher what your instructor may want.

> ***Blot out, correct, insert, refine,***
> ***Enlarge, diminish, underline,***
> ***Be mindful, when invention fails,***
> ***To scratch your head, and bite your nails.***
>
> Jonathan Swift
> *Eigteenth-century English satirist*

Edit

Editing involves stylistic changes, as well as modifying sentence structure and correcting spelling, punctuation, and grammatical errors.

Refine Your Style Your communication should provide a showcase for your distinctive point of view. When it captures exactly what you think and feel, the thrill can be comparable to shooting a hole-in-one or taking a first prize. What are some strategies to achieve a memorable style in your writing and speaking? McKowen (1996) offers the following suggestions:

- Add more words only when it will enhance your impact.
- Remove words, brutally if necessary, to clarify your meaning.
- Replace words when you know there's something not quite right about your choice.
- Shorten sentences to make your writing crisper.
- Rearrange sentences until you find what works best.

Write with an active voice, using action verbs. Be specific, using descriptive language that: draws on the senses; uses specific, concrete nouns; and avoids too many adverbs and adjectives.

Resist the urge to use overblown language just because you are in college. Journalist Edwin Newman (1976), in *A Civil Tongue*, suggested that we embellish language to appear smarter than we really are. He cites as examples these gems from his personal experience:

- "After ingesting alcohol, exclude vehicle use." (Don't drink and drive.)
- "In order to improve security, it is requested that, effective immediately, no employees use the above subject doors for ingress or egress to the building." (Don't use these doors.)
- "I don't wish to defray, but I'll particularize that with more specificity at a later date." (I'll give you more details later.)

You don't want your readers to scratch their heads in wonder because they can't decode your message. Strive to use precise, clear language to the best effect. Limit your use of extreme adjectives and superlatives. Think of how often we hear "amazing," "fantastic," "incredible," "awesome," and so on. Overuse of such words can have adverse long-term effects on how people interpret your experience. For example, if you are "desolate" at missing a dinner date, how would you describe your feelings when someone close to you dies? If your new computer game is "awesome," how would you describe the Grand Canyon? Which actually fills you with awe? Invest some time in selecting just the right word to get your point across. The English language is rich with options.

MANAGE LIFE

As Long as It Takes

You've probably heard this unhappy exchange at least some time in your academic career. Student: "How long should this paper be?" Teacher: "As long as it takes." The student feels exasperated by the teacher's answer, and the teacher feels discouraged by the student's question.

The student wants a straightforward answer, such as "five pages," so that she can plan how to go after the right number of resources to fit the assignment length. In effect, the desired length of the assignment will dictate the intensity of the effort that will go into her final product.

The teacher's response comes from another perspective. The teacher developed the assignment to encourage the student to explore an interesting idea. The teacher would much rather give free reign to the student's exploration than constrain the process with an artificial boundary.

What strategy would work better to get the help that you need? Communicate your interest in the topic you have chosen and express the concern that you may be tempted to write too much. Ask if there are upper limits that will stress the patience of the teacher. You may be able to ask to see some successful past models on similar assignments if you establish your intention to invest yourself in the assignment's central ideas rather than unintentionally communicating that you will be striving to meet the teacher's minimum expectations.

Will the time you spend on refining your style pay off? This principle is illustrated nicely by a sign posted on the office door of a writing teacher:

First draft:

"I think about you all the time and admire you for all your many qualities.
I probably even love you.
I could go on and on. . . . "

Final draft:

"How do I love thee? Let me count the ways."

—Elizabeth Barrett Browning, *Nineteenth-century poet*

Follow the Rules Effective writers are careful about following the rules or *conventions* (for example, grammar and spelling) of good writing. As you get closer to your final draft, you should make sure your writing has followed these rules. Specific *style manuals* will also help you adjust to different disciplinary conventions.

The American Psychological Association (APA) offers the standard for writing in the natural and social science disciplines; online tips for using APA style can be found at http://www.apastyle.org. The Modern Language Association (MLA) publishes another common set of guidelines, and helpful pointers for this approach are posted online at http://webster.commnet.edu/mla/index.shtml. Ask your instructor which style manual is best for your purpose.

Instructors vary in how much they care about such conventions. Some simply reject papers that include substantial problems with spelling, grammar, and sentence structure. Others overlook these matters if the ideas expressed in the paper are good. Some instructors are sticklers about learning and implementing APA or MLA format. They may provide a *style sheet* that states how the paper must be written. Others may not specify guidelines but expect you to observe general principles of good writing that you've learned in composition class.

Grammar Even seasoned writers have questions about grammar in their writing. Have a reference manual handy during polishing and proofreading. Consult "Build Competence: Top Ten Grammar Violations in College" to help your papers get the most enthusiastic reception.

Punctuation Punctuation marks pace how the audience reads your writing. Here are some general rules for the most challenging punctuation uses:

- Semicolons: Use to connect thoughts that are closely related; use these sparingly. Semicolons go well before *however, therefore, for instance,* and so on. They also should be used to separate items in a series that contain commas.
- Dashes and exclamation marks: These marks—favorites of the tabloid press—add drama. Use them in informal projects or in limited ways in formal work.
- Quotation marks: Quotes longer than three lines require special indentation and marking. In shorter uses, punctuation marks belong *inside* quotation marks.
- Apostrophes: Use for contractions (for example, *can't, don't, wouldn't*) and possessive indicators (*Ted's, the child's, the women's*). Good writers generally avoid using contractions in formal work. Take note that *its* and *it's* are not the same. *Its* is the possessive form of the pronoun *it. It's* is a contraction of *it is* and does not indicate possession. (Example: *It's* a good thing that working hard is *its* own reward.)

"This has merit, but could you go back through and add more 'like's and 'you know's?"

www.cartoonbank.com, ID: 39720 published in *The New Yorker*, June 22, 1998.

Spelling Some lucky people are naturally good spellers. They imagine how each word looks, sound words out, and memorize spelling conventions (for example, "*i* before *e* except after *c*"). However, even good spellers use the dictionary or the computer's spell-checker to help polish their papers.

A spell-checker won't catch all errors. Be vigilant about the challenges of *homonyms*, words that sound alike but mean something different. They can easily slip into writing and elude even careful proofreaders. For example:

- *two* versus *too* or *to*
- *their* versus *there*
- *hear* versus *here*

Finish in Style

Before you submit your final paper, there are still a few more steps you can take that will help it stand out in the pile your instructor will be evaluating.

Pick a Compelling Title Many assignments require a title. Some writers wait until the project is almost completed before creating a title that captures the appeal of the work. Strive to create one that compels the reader to read further. Which paper would you rather read?

An Analysis of the Poetry of the Beat Generation

OR

The Poet's Place in the Beat Generation

OR

Where Has All the Rhyming Gone? Poetry from the Beat Generation

Both the second and third options are likely to engage the reader more successfully than the flat approach in the first title. Refer to the Journal activity "Entitlement" on page 272 to further explore how creative titles can enhance reader interest.

Produce a Professional Product Your writing is an extension of yourself. Your final product not only reveals your ability to construct an argument but also communicates your pride about your own work. Smudge-free, easy-to-read writing says a great deal about your high standards and professionalism. Most instructors expect you to use a computer with word processing software to produce your paper. That way you can revise easily.

Although word processors can save time, they can also frustrate you if you overlook some simple precautions. Nothing is more frustrating than having the power go down after you've been working on your computer for hours. In this situation you'll lose everything that has not been saved. Develop a habit of frequently saving as you write. For example, save your work every time you complete a section or a page of writing. Or, turn on the automatic save function so you won't have to think about doing it manually. Make a backup copy—just in case. Label your disks so you don't have to waste time searching multiple disks to find your paper.

Have a backup plan**.** Even the most reliable computer can fail when you need it most. If you've duplicated your work on a portable medium, make sure you know where you can find a compatible system to use in a pinch. Your campus computer center will provide some backup machines.

Include a cover page with the title of the paper, your name, your instructor's name, the course, and the date, unless your instructor requires a different format. Be sure to number the pages. Ask your instructors for other format preferences, including whether they like fancy covers. Many instructors disdain plastic folders or binders as a waste of money and resource. By contrast, some think a cover gives a more professional look.

Top Ten Grammar Violations in College

What are some of the most frequent grammar violations that trigger a negative mindset in your instructors when they grade your writing? Teachers tend to recoil when they see grammar errors like these:

- "Me and Todd went to the store."
  → "Todd and *I* went to the store." (proper pronoun use)
- "A person should follow their own dream."
  → "*People* should follow *their* own *dreams.*" (noun–pronoun agreement)
- "The football was thrown by the quarterback."
  → "The quarterback *threw* the football." (active voice)
- "Do you know where you're going to?"
  → "Do you know where you are *going*?" (excess prepositions; avoid using *where at* and *where to*)
- "I really like the TV show *24.*" (You don't need *a lot*, or worse *a lot.*)
- "I like the show 24 a lot."
- "I *except* your apology."
  → "I *accept* your apology." (if I want to make up)
  → "I take *exception* to your apology." (if I'm still angry) (This is the proper use of *accept*, meaning to go along with, and *except*, meaning to set aside.)
- "My homework effects my mood."
  → "My homework *affects* my mood." (As a verb, *affect* means to influence; *effect* means to create, but is used more rarely.)
- "I plan to win irregardless of what you do."
  → "I plan to win *regardless* of what you do." (*Irregardless* is not a proper word.)
- "I could care less."
  → "I *couldn't* care less." (If you could care less, it means you are still bothered.)
- "I can't hardly finish my work."
  → "I *can* hardly finish my work." (*Can't hardly* is a double negative.)

Proofread the Final Draft Proofreading can be tricky. You may be so close to what you've created that you can't spot errors easily. A break can help. For example, Bret likes to get a good night's sleep before he proofreads and prints his final draft. By returning to the paper later, he feels more confident about catching the subtle errors that he might miss when he is tired. Proofreading your paper aloud may help you catch more errors.

Altering your usual method of reading may help you see weak sentence structure. When you think that you've caught all errors, proofread one more time. If the errors are minor, you won't need to print another copy. Making last-minute proof marks on your paper signals to your instructor that you made a final pass to ensure the work represents your best effort.

Evaluate Your Work Once a paper is finished, good writers assess the quality of their work. Complete Self-Assessment 1, "What Are My Writing Strengths and Weaknesses?" on page

268 to explore reviewing skills that will lead to better papers. If you formally evaluate the quality of your work early enough, you still may have time to revise it and earn a better grade.

Meet Deadlines Turn projects in on time or negotiate an exception with an instructor *before* the deadline. Even if you've written the best paper in the history of the class, many instructors penalize late submissions. Some even refuse to accept them.

Solve Writing Problems

Even the best writers sometimes run into problems that can keep them from achieving their goals. The first problem may be that they only look at the grade that comes back on a paper, never taking the time to read and carefully consider the instructor's comments. Other common problems include difficulty developing a distinctive voice, procrastination, and writer's block.

Learn from Feedback

Instructors vary in the methods they use to evaluate papers. Some simply assign a grade that captures the overall quality of your work. This approach is sometimes referred to as *holistic grading.* Others provide detailed feedback, often relying on a *rubric*, or formal set of criteria, to detail your strengths and weaknesses. When you get detailed feedback, read it carefully so you can learn something that will help in future assignments.

A river of red ink can be hard to take. Read extensive criticisms quickly, then take some time to recover before you try to learn from the feedback. Let yourself be disappointed. Maybe even mope a little. Then return with the intention of learning what to do to improve your writing. Remember, we all often learn more from mistakes than from successes.

Ask for feedback if you don't understand your grade. Many instructors believe students are willing to settle for a summary judgment—a grade—with little or no justification. However, when you don't understand how your instructor derived your grade, ask. Specific feedback on your strengths and weaknesses is essential to becoming a good writer.

Watch your growth as a writer by keeping track of how your papers are improving. Review your collection of papers now and then, especially when you're disappointed by an evaluation. In some college programs, you may be asked to construct a portfolio of your work to track your progress. Establishing a portfolio (a folder or binder of past papers, organized chronologically) will also help you establish a research stream, as discussed earlier in this chapter. Also complete the Journal activity "What Are Your Writing Trends?" on page 272 for some ideas on using past writing assignments to improve your future performance.

© Richard Hutchings/CORBIS

Seeking additional feedback from your instructor will make you a stronger writer.

Find Your Unique Voice

Some college students struggle with self-esteem issues, and expressive projects expose personal uncertainty. From past experience, some worry that their ideas will be poorly received. Communication projects provide a way to discover, express, and polish your thoughts. Your instructors don't expect perfection. In fact, projects that are too well crafted can generate concern and suspicion.

Most instructors enjoy working with you to find your voice. Your self-esteem as a communicator will grow with your serious effort.

Although most instructors favor logical and uncluttered writing, many respond enthusiastically to work that has a creative flair. Consider what it must be like for the instructor to grade one essay after another that strives merely to meet a narrow set of criteria.

Like most other people, instructors generally appreciate variety, unusual insights, and even some humor in their students' assignments. You can build a distinctive approach in various ways. Find out what other students typically do, then do something different. Consider a unique slant for the project. Create an engaging title. Use a thesaurus to expand your word choice. Add interesting quotations. See the Journal activity "The Liberal Arts Flair" on page 272 for some practice.

> ***I love criticism just so long as it's unqualified praise.***
>
> Noel Coward
> *Twentieth-century English playwright*

Stop Procrastinating

Like many writers, you also may struggle with getting down to business. Sometimes other more pressing projects intrude or distract. Or the project may be one in which you have little interest. In any case, you may suddenly find yourself with a deadline looming before you and end up submitting an assignment that you dashed off at the last minute. Submitting a rough draft may make your instructor think that you weren't taking the task seriously. To combat procrastination, plan a reasonable schedule that breaks your research and writing into manageable parts, like the one outlined in Figure 9.1. Then stick to it. Reward yourself for completing each phase. For some other strategies to help reduce procrastination, see "Manage Life: Good Intentions."

Unlock Writer's Block

Sometimes you have nothing to say. Don't panic. All writers face times when inspiration fails and words don't come easily. Interestingly, one good response is to write about your writer's block. Write about how it feels to be empty. Describe the nature of your blocks. You may gain insight into your resistance and find ideas that will get you moving. Another good step is asking for a conference with your instructor.

By talking about the assignment, your instructor can offer tips or hints that can unleash your creativity. Ask whether your instructor has any model student papers. By observing how others tackled related problems, you may be able to spark some ideas of your own.

You also can try a creativity-generating computer program that provides a systematic approach to helping you explore your ideas. IdeaFisher and Inspiration are two popular programs. Explore some other options by visiting this Internet site: http://members. ozemail.com.au/~caveman/Creative/ Software/swindex.htm.

Build Your Integrity

Communication projects can be both exciting and challenging. Sometimes this challenge encourages students to cut corners, presenting others' work as their own. Make a communication project an opportunity to practice honest, appropriate behavior and build your integrity.

Understand Plagiarism *Plagiarism* means presenting someone else's words or ideas as your own. This is a serious academic offense. Most campuses specify harsh outcomes for those found guilty. Plagiarism can shortchange your learning, severely risk your academic health, and ruin your reputation. A recent high-profile plagiarism case underscores the danger. Harvard student Kaavya Viswanathan was publicly disgraced when it was revealed that her book, *How Opan Mehta Got Kissed, Got Wild, and Got a Life,* was derived from other authors' works. A promising literary career ended up stalled just as it began.

MANAGE LIFE

Good Intentions

Katie knows that she needs to get started on her term paper, due the next day, but she can't concentrate. She decides to do some laundry first. She notices that the laundry area needs straightening. "Looks like the washer could use a wipedown," she thinks. Before she knows it, two hours slip away. The laundry room is squeaky clean, but all she has to show for her term paper are good intentions. At least she will have a clean T-shirt when she has to explain to her instructor where her paper is.

Types of Plagiarism Experts suggest that students who plagiarize generally fall into one of two categories: those who inadvertently plagiarize and those who do it on purpose (Harris 2001). The penalties for inadvertent plagiarism can be just as severe as for intentionally misrepresenting your work, so make sure you understand the rules.

Accidental Plagiarism Inadvertent plagiarizers can fall into the trap by not knowing the rules that govern appropriate citation. For example, some students erroneously believe that they can lift words from a source if they simply cite it. Wrong! Importing an author's words directly into your own work requires quotation marks and proper citation. Some students believe if you change a word or two in a sentence, that's good enough. It's not. Both strategies can make you vulnerable to charges of plagiarism by alert instructors. See Figure 9.2, "From Original Source to Proper Citation," for some examples that will help you avoid plagiarism by accident. Then check out your understanding of the rules by taking Self-Assessment 2, "Are You at Risk for Plagiarism?" on page 269.

Purposeful Plagiarism Why would anyone plagiarize on purpose? Harris (2001) offers many reasons. Some students may have been trained in a different tradition. For example, some foreign students have learned to cite a source word for word to "honor the writer" (Harris 2001, 12). However, others may be looking for a shortcut to produce a project that they can submit for a grade. They may feel swamped by too many deadlines or insecure in their own writing skills. They may believe their instructors don't really read the papers so that justifies not going to the trouble of writing one. Unfortunately, some students also enjoy defying authority. They relish the opportunity to outsmart the professor by not getting caught when submitting the work of others as their own.

Think about examples you have seen of students who plagiarize to meet their course requirements. Consider the Journal activity "The Cost of Plagiarism" on page 272 to determine whether there are other explanations. How do they do it? They may borrow a paper from a friend, download a paper from the Internet, build a paper from multiple cut-and-pasted resources, "recycle" a paper from a prior class, or even buy a term paper on the Internet.

How do they get caught? According to Harris, not all faculty members pay careful attention, but the ones who do have well-developed strategies that can identify plagiarism. Among obvious factors, instructors look for:

- inconsistent "voice" throughout the paper
- vocabulary that doesn't fit with what the student should know
- sentence structure that is too complex for the student's level
- content that doesn't quite fit with the topic
- parts of the paper don't fit together well

FIGURE 9.2 From Original Source to Proper Citation

Suppose you are writing a paper for psychology class about the meaning of body piercing in contemporary culture.

From your literature review imagine that you have found a great resource in a recent article published in a peer-reviewed journal by Lydia Gray.

How do you incorporate Grays i deas to support your argument? You have two options:

Appropriate Citation with Quote:

Gray (2001, p. 55) stated, "Body piercing represents a teenager's attempt to shock her parents and distance herself from their values."

Your citation gives full credit to the person who originated the idea. The quote marks tell the reader that the author stated the argument in these words on a specific page in the original resource. Use quotations sparingly, but do so when the author has used especially vivid words or examples and their impact would be lost by paraphrasing.

Appropriate Citation with Paraphrase:

Gray (2001) speculated that adolescents may alienate their parents on purpose by certain behaviors, such as body piercing, that don't fit with their parents' value system.

Your citation gives credit to the original author, but you translate the original idea into your own words. This approach is the preferred way to cite evidence in most cases. It honors the author and the idea but relies on your ability to translate the idea into your own words.

When do you run the risk of being accused of plagiarism?

Overt Plagiarism: Direct Use of Author's Words, No Paraphrase, No Citation

Gray originally stated,

"Body piercing represents a teenager's attempt to shock her parents and distance herself from their values."

You write in your paper:

Body piercing represents a teenager's attempt to shock her parents.

Using this line, word-for-word, in your paper misrepresents the idea as your own. Merely leaving off the last half of the sentence does not protect you from the accusation of stealing the author's words.

Overt Plagiarism: Direct Use of Author's Ideas, Insufficient Paraphrase, No Citation

Gray originally stated,

"Body piercing represents a teenager's attempt to shock her parents and distance herself from their values."

You write in your paper:

Body piercing can be a girl's attempt to upset her parents and distance herself from their values.

Substituting a few words in the author's original sentence and not giving credit to the author for the original idea counts as plagiarism.

- missing important recent references
- inconsistent format throughout the paper

In addition, some students plagiarize sloppily. They leave clues for a careful reader that will lead to their downfall, such as the date when the paper was written for another class. Instructors can also test-drive portions of papers through electronic databases to identify whether a project is original.

Protect Yourself Being accused of plagiarism can be extremely stressful, both for you and your instructor. How can you avoid the complications of being involved with a plagiarism accusation? "Clarify Values: Prevent Plagiarism" offers a few good ideas.

If you end up getting drawn into a plagiarism inquiry, cooperate with your instructor. You have the right to due process. Be prepared to bring your resources, to share what you know about the information in the project, and describe how you completed your work. You may be able to resolve the problem with a sound explanation. If that approach is unsuccessful, familiarize yourself with your campus procedures and batten down the hatches. It's going to be a stormy sea ahead.

Speak!

Although both speaking and writing provide an opportunity to express yourself, speaking differs from writing in significant ways. When you write, you can refine your work until it says exactly what you want. However, when you speak, even though you can practice to a fine point, the reality of live performance adds a whole new communication challenge.

Pursue the Spotlight

College should offer several opportunities for you to improve your speaking skills in the contexts of working individually and collaborating with others. For instance, you may be asked to address the class formally by delivering a carefully researched position or to give an extemporaneous speech on a topic given just moments beforehand. Some courses promote expressive reading of dramatic works. These opportunities will refine your public-speaking skills, including pacing, voice quality, and connecting to the audience.

Group speaking projects include case presentations, panel discussions, and debates. These projects are most successful when group members can coordinate their individual pieces and practice together. However, having to work in a group can sometimes make these assignments even more challenging.

You also can learn about speaking by observing good speakers. College campuses often host dynamic speakers who can show you how it's done. In addition, you can get experience in the spotlight by asking questions at the end of the speech. If that option feels overwhelming at first, approach the speaker with your questions or comments when the speech is over. Most speakers want your feedback. By being an active audience member, you can learn a great deal about good speaking skills.

Videotape has captured a variety of brilliant speeches that showcase masterful communication. Some of these may also be available on DVD or over the Internet. Take advantage of lessons from speakers at the height of their persuasive skills to inspire you to do your best.

CLARIFY VALUES

Prevent Plagiarism

Commit to expressing only your own ideas, not solely to avoid the punishing consequences of plagiarism suspicion but to take advantage of showcasing your best ideas. Following are some strategies to help you avoid being accused of plagiarism during your college career.

- **Paraphrase when you do research.** As you take notes from various resources, translate the ideas of others into your own words. Compare what you have written with the original source to make sure that your paraphrase captures the spirit of the ideas written, not the actual words and phrases themselves.
- **Give proper credit.** When you directly quote or refer to the ideas of another writer, provide source information in the format required by your instructor.
- **Make your own observations stand out in your notes.** Put your own ideas in the margin or print them so that they look physically different from the ideas you received from others. Later you can use your own observations without fear of committing plagiarism.
- **Use quotations sparingly.** Rely on the words of experts only when their writing is so elegant that your paraphrase will not do it justice. Using many or long quotations is a sign that you're uncomfortable expressing your own ideas.
- **Don't help others plagiarize.** Lending someone else your paper when you suspect the borrower plans to submit something based closely on your work implicates you in plagiarism. If the borrower's submission is questioned, you may find yourself in the unpleasant situation of explaining why you lent your paper for an unethical purpose.
- **Guard against others plagiarizing your work.** If you use a community-based computer, do not store your work on the computer's hard drive. Others who use the computer can easily download your writing and submit it as their own without your knowledge or permission.

Write a Good Speech

All famous speeches were written before they were delivered and became memorable. Keep in mind that the skills involved in preparing good papers also apply to good speeches. For example, you will want to develop a thesis statement, research your topic, create an outline, and organize your points into an introduction, main body, and conclusion. What additional strategies can you apply?

Define Your Purpose Know your goal. Are you supposed to persuade? Inform? Entertain? Debate? Your purpose will determine how to use resources and structure

© Noel Henderson/Photographer's Choice/Getty Images

Rehearse using available technology to ensure a smooth and effective presentation.

your speech so you can achieve success. It also will help you avoid running too short or too long. To enhance your success, talk with your instructor about your intentions. Submit a thesis statement, outline, or concept map before your scheduled presentation time. Ask for comments to help you stay close to the goal of the assignment.

Engage Your Audience Most college audiences will be sympathetic. After all, your peers will be in your shoes before the term is over. A college audience usually provides a uniquely supportive learning environment in which to give a speech. If you assume that your audience is supportive, you may feel less apprehensive about giving the speech. Identify your purpose early in your speech. Keep in mind what your audience knows already and what it needs to know. However, never omit your purpose, even if the audience already knows it. It's best to be brief but clear.

Effective speakers address the audience on its level. For example, if your college recruits you to talk to high school students about college life, your vocabulary and examples might be different than those in the same kind of speech given to the students' parents. Good speakers also try to understand the values of their audience so they appeal to their listeners more effectively.

> ***The best impromptu speeches are the ones written well in advance.***
> Ruth Gordon
> *Twentieth-century American actress and writer*

Build Your Message An anonymous speech instructor once recommended the perfect structure for public presentations, "Tell 'em what you are going to tell 'em, tell 'em, then tell 'em what you told 'em." Although this approach might sound boring, repeating the key ideas of a speech really helps. As in good writing, the main point of the speech serves as the backbone, and each portion of the speech must support it.

Many speakers hand out a printed outline of a speech or rely on PowerPoint slides so the audience can follow the speech better. As you construct the body of your talk, pay attention to the kinds of support that appeal most to the audience. You don't have to overwhelm your audience with statistics and stories to make your point. Choose your evidence carefully to create both emotional and logical appeal. Class speeches should reflect what you've learned from the course. You can draw ideas from the textbook, class notes, or other readings that relate to what you're studying. However, if you give a speech that shows no evidence of what you've learned from the course, your grade will probably suffer as much as your audience.

> ***We don't know who we are until we see what we can do.***
> Martha Grimes
> *American mystery writer*

Deliver a Good Speech

If you have invested time wisely in getting your ideas together, a speech gives you the opportunity to shine. How can you get the most out of these opportunities?

Rehearse The time put into rehearsal often makes or breaks a speech. If you know your speech well enough, you should need your note cards only for cues about what you intend to say. Otherwise, you may be tempted to read what you've written, which disconnects you from the audience. Because effective speakers know their own intentions and order of ideas, they don't need to rely heavily on their notes or a memorized script. They give the impression of connecting with the audience by talking with them rather than reciting from memory or reading directly from a prepared text.

Look the Part How you look will influence your speaking success. Dress to meet the expectations of the audience. For example, some formal speeches may work better if you dress less casually. How you dress should not distract from your message. Your clothes should be comfortable without being distracting. Make sure your shoes match. Avoid playing with your hair and jewelry. You will want the audience to pay attention to your message, not your fashion sense.

Start your speech with a personal experience or a joke. Introduce an interesting news item, quotation, or event that the audience will remember. In all cases, conclude your opening with a statement of your objective and a description of where you intend to go.

> ***If you have an important point to make, don't try to be subtle or clever. Use a pile driver. Hit the point once. Then come back and hit it again. Then hit it a third time—a tremendous whack!***
>
> Winston Churchill
> *Twentieth-century British prime minister*

Polish Your Delivery Stand straight and breathe in a controlled manner. Speak clearly and confidently. Make gestures that are purposeful, directing attention to underscore what you are saying. Look your audience in the eye. And don't forget to smile or frown appropriately to express the emotion you feel about your topic. Even casual speeches benefit from the polish that comes from practice. Minimize the number of pauses, "ums" and "ahs," or other interruptions that invite your audience to stop listening.

Effective speakers also project their voices to reach people at the back of the room; these speakers put life in their voices to keep people's attention. A monotone delivery, bad grammar, or sloppy sentence structure can be lethal. When you practice giving your speech to a friend, ask for specific feedback on grammar and language.

Use Media Effectively Good speakers use a variety of means to make their ideas believable, including stories, video clips, quotations, statistics, charts, and graphs. Every element should play a meaningful role in the development of the speaker's position.

If you use an overhead projector, computer-generated images, or PowerPoint slides, practice with the equipment before the speech since its use can be tricky. Make the lettering large and easy to read. (To test the size of your lettering, put the transparency on the floor and stand over it or walk a few feet away from your computer screen. If you can read from this position, the font is probably large enough.) Prepare typed overheads; handwritten ones suggest a lack of pride in your work. If you use audiotapes or videotapes to support your presentation, be sure to wind the tape to the appropriate starting point ahead of time.

For other suggestions on delivering great presentations with PowerPoint, see "Build Competence: All Power, No Point." Also complete the Journal activity "PowerPointers" on page 271.

Finish Gracefully When you conclude your speech, return to your key themes. Summarize what you've covered, and identify any actions the audience should take as a result of your speech.

If you've given a long speech, repeat your objectives. Then smile and prepare to receive your applause. Many instructors include a question-and-answer period following a student's speech. Such activity encourages you to think on your feet and to learn how to manage unexpected events. See "Expand Your Resources: Winning in the Home Stretch" for how to manage the question-and-answer period.

BUILD COMPETENCE

All Power, No Point

The use of PowerPoint for presenting visual support in lectures and speeches has become rampant, but many presentations violate good communication standards, leading one pundit to suggest that a PowerPoint presentation was "all power, no point." What are some pointers for making PowerPoint work?

- Don't use PowerPoint if the light conditions will make it hard to see your visuals.
- Use bullets, not complete text.
- Limit content to four to five ideas per slide.
- Use colors that complement each other.
- Use sound effects sparingly, if at all.
- Don't turn your back on the audience to read your slides.
- Rehearse on the system that you will use to deliver your presentation.

Winning in the Home Stretch

When your classmates ask questions that stump you after you've given a speech, consider these strategies for coping with the strain:

- **Ask for a restatement of the question.** This can give you clues to help you answer the question or provide extra time to think through your response.
- **Say "I don't know."** Sometimes it's best to admit that the questioner poses a new topic for you, then move on. No one expects a speaker to have all the answers. You can also use logic to speculate about an answer, but identify your answer as speculative.
- **Ask the questioner for an opinion.** Many people who ask questions have their own ideas about what constitutes a satisfying answer. Your willingness to share the stage will be seen as gracious, and the gesture gives you more time to respond.

Improve Your Speaking Skills

Good speaking skills don't just develop overnight. By revisiting your performances after the fact you can improve for the future.

Evaluate Your Work Good speakers check the quality of their speaking as they rehearse, as well as during and after the actual performance. Complete Self-Assessment 3, "What Are My Speaking Strengths and Weaknesses?" on page 270 to examine your speaking skills in detail.

Solve Delivery Problems You will be experiencing a variety of speeches throughout your college career. Some will dazzle you. Others will be painful to watch. Many students choke, tear up, or show other obvious signs of nervousness when they speak to a group. See the Journal activity "The View from the Audience" on page 271 to explore some lessons offered by your classmates' problematic speeches. See "Clarify Values: With All Due Respect" to optimize your gains from the work of your classmates.

Delivery problems can undermine your effectiveness. However, there are several strategies that can put you at ease.

> ***It is no sin to attempt and fail. The only sin is not to make the attempt.***
>
> SuEllen Fried
> *Contemporary American social activist*

- *Diagnose your problem carefully.* If you routinely choke during oral presentations, identify when the problem occurs and whether there are any consistent causes. Contrast those situations with other performances that have been more satisfying. This analysis will help you find ways to improve your delivery.
- *Anticipate what your body needs.* Breathe deeply and stretch your muscles to give your body signals about your intention to control your nervousness. Take a bathroom break before your talk begins. Have a glass of water handy to relieve parched lips and give you time to regain your composure.
- *Organize yourself to maintain control.* Prevent losing your place by using well-organized, easy-to-read note cards. Number the cards so that you can restore their order quickly if you drop the stack. It happens!
- *Use technology strategically.* A tape or video recorder during rehearsal can provide clues about where your delivery suffers. If you use technology during your presentation, rehearse blending these elements with your talk. A graceful pause to review a slide can focus audience attention on your content and away from your own anxiety.
- *Note any mannerisms or gestures that may distract your audience.* Practice reducing these problems until you're satisfied that you can perform smoothly.
- *Enlist audience support.* If you announce that your hands are shaking or your knees are knocking, your audience will think about your hands or knees and not your ideas. If you lose your place, however, admit the problem to the audience, then stop and regain your control. If you lose your composure because you feel overwhelmed, tell the audience that this topic is hard for you. They'll appreciate your candor and support you.

CLARIFY VALUES

With All Due Respect

If you happen to take a class where all students must deliver speeches, you might think these are opportunities to kick back and take it easy while your classmates take their turns. Reframe these experiences as opportunities to practice the values and behaviors that demonstrate good collegiality. Listen carefully to each speech. Think about questions you could ask that would allow your classmates to demonstrate more fully what they know. Engage with the presentation as fully as you can. Close attention will bring intellectual gains from the content and interpersonal gains from your good classroom citizenship.

Seek a Second Chance All great speakers suffer an occasional bad performance. Recognize your potential to learn from experiences that don't go well. Commit yourself to better preparation, goal setting, and improved performances in the future. See if you can work out a second chance with your instructor. Sometimes your speech can be videotaped in the college media facilities so the instructor can review it at a convenient time. Whether this second chance improves your grade or not, your positive practice will help you turn in a performance in which you have greater pride.

"I could have been a big celebrity but for my fear of public speaking."

CREATE YOUR FUTURE

Career Connections

Myra loved to write. She had always received great feedback from her instructors throughout high school. She was tempted to major in English in college but was surprised to discover how much she liked her science classes. The lectures offered answers to the questions she had entertained about how the universe worked. She seemed especially drawn to mysteries about the functioning of the human body. Although she enjoyed the labs that usually accompanied her courses, what she most enjoyed was writing about science. Her biology instructor made a comment on one of her papers that became a turning point in her life decisions: "You write so well. You should consider writing about science as a career!" Before that comment, she had never really considered that there might be a career that would combine her two loves. With the help of a career counselor, she discovered a variety of interesting career opportunities, including science fiction writing, grant development, magazine writing, and science journalism.

Todd hated public speaking in high school. His knees used to knock and he would feel nauseous at the thought of having to share his ideas. When he took a required public speaking course, the practice involved in having to design and deliver four speeches in the course of a semester got him past the "willies." He began to relax and enjoy the challenge of presenting his ideas. He discovered that he enjoyed persuasive opportunities the most. By the time he graduated, he targeted a career in pharmaceutical sales, a choice that was effectively supported by a major in communications and a minor in chemistry.

Summary Strategies for Mastering College

Refine Your Expressive Skills by Seizing Every Opportunity to Practice Communicating, Prepare Properly, and Evaluate How Well You Met Your Goals

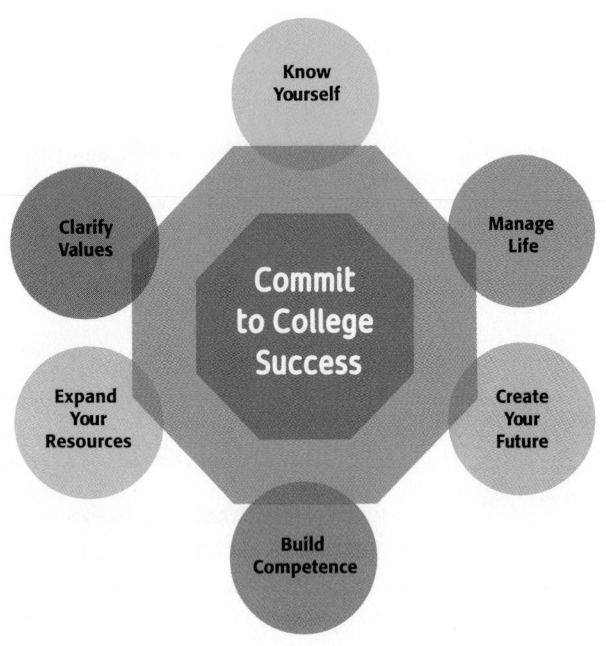

Focus on the Six Strategies for Success above as you read each chapter to learn how to apply these strategies to your own success.

1 Express Yourself!

- Recognize why future employers place great value on communication skills.
- Know your audience and write with a specific purpose in mind.
- Use credible resources to support your ideas.
- Develop your writing strategy and stick to the plan.
- Overcome common problems that block expression.

2 Speak!

- Practice speaking in different contexts to polish your skills.
- Learn to relax to overcome speech jitters.
- Follow instructions carefully to achieve the best outcomes.
- Rehearse until you aren't dependent on notes.
- Use technology wisely to support your ideas not distract from them.

Review Questions

1. List a few ways that good writing and speaking skills can improve your job performance.
   1. ______
   2. ______
   3. ______

What is a thesis statement?

______

Why is it important?

______

3. Why should students avoid plagiarism? List a few strategies for making sure you don't plagiarize.

______

4. What are some typical problems faced in giving formal speeches and how can these be overcome?

______

5. What are some ways to recover from disappointing performances in communication?

______

Know Yourself

SELF-ASSESSMENT 1

What Are My Writing Strengths and Weaknesses?

Once you've completed at least one formal college writing assignment, examine your work using the guidelines here (based on Alverno College 1995). The feedback or grade you received from your instructor may provide some clues about areas that you need to improve. Keep the writing criteria handy to help guide your future writing projects.

Writing Criteria	**Completely**	**Partially**	**Barely or Not At All**
I followed the instructions.			
	Effectively	**Partially**	**Barely or Not At All**
I established *appropriate context* and kept this focus throughout.			
I crafted the *style* of the paper and selected *words* carefully to suit the purpose.			
I showed conscientious use of appropriate *conventions*, including spelling and grammar.			
I *structured* the paper, including an introduction, main body, and conclusion.			
I included *evidence* to support my thesis.			
I added *content* that reflected learning specific to the course.			

Now review your responses to these criteria and answer the following:

- *What are your writing strengths?*
- *What do you need to improve?*
- *Is this pattern typical of your writing projects?*
- *What strategies will help you improve?*
- *Would it be useful to consult with the campus writing center?*

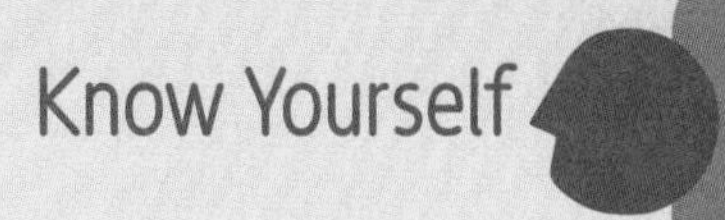

SELF-ASSESSMENT 2

Are You at Risk for Plagiarism?

Which of the following are acceptable ways to acknowledge the ideas of others in your own writing?

_____ reproducing the writer's original words—with quotation marks

_____ reproducing the writer's original words—without quotation marks

_____ leaving out a portion of the writer's original sentence

_____ rearranging the words in the writer's original sentence

_____ substituting a few words in the writer's original sentence

_____ identifying the writer, but putting the original sentence in your own words

_____ without identifying the writer, putting the original sentence in your own words

There are only a few appropriate strategies you can use to acknowledge the work of others. These include:

- *reproducing the writers original words—with quotation marks*
- *identifying the writer, but putting the original sentence in your own words*

Keep this in mind when preparing all of your writing assignments, regardless of the discipline.

SELF-ASSESSMENT 3

What Are My Speaking Strengths and Weaknesses?

Even if you haven't already had a speaking assignment in college, you've probably developed a sense of your strengths and weaknesses in giving presentations. Review the following, based on Alverno College's *Writing and Speaking Criteria* (1995), to determine how effective you are as a public speaker. Keep these speaking criteria available to help you in future speaking assignments.

Speaking Criteria	**Routinely**	**Often**	**Rarely**
I connect with the audience by talking directly to them rather than reading my notes or delivering a memorized script.			
I state my purpose and keep this focus throughout.			
I craft the style of the speech and select words carefully to suit the purpose.			
I effectively deliver the speech, using eye contact, supportive gestures, and effective voice control.			
I follow appropriate conventions, including grammar.			
I organize the speech well, including the introduction, main body, and conclusions.			
I include evidence that supports and develops my ideas.			
I use media effectively to help the audience grasp key ideas.			
I include content that reflects my learning from the course.			

Now review your accomplishments in speaking:

- *What are your strengths?*
- *What criteria show that you need to improve?*
- *Is this pattern typical of your speaking projects?*
- *What strategies should you pursue?*

Your Journal

REFLECT

1. The View from the Audience

Recall a time when you observed someone making a bad speech.

- At what point did you recognize the speech would be unsatisfying?

____

- Did the speaker make any attempts to correct the failing outcome during the speech?

____

- How did you feel as you watched the speech flop?

____

- What advice could you have offered the speaker to turn the speech around?

____

- How should these observations influence your preparation for future speaking challenges?

____

2. Exploiting Your Life

J. K. Rowling exploited many elements of her own personal life when she constructed her *Harry Potter* series. Make a list of important events in your own life that might become a resource for future expressive writing projects. Keep the list in your day planner or somewhere else that you can refer to easily throughout your college career.

DO

1. PowerPointers

You have probably already been exposed to many PowerPoint lectures that vary in their quality. Select a lecture and think about ways that the delivery of information could have been improved. Make some notes about what worked and what didn't work. How might your critique influence your own strategies when it is your turn?

2. One More Go-Around

Commit yourself ahead on the next writing assignment to leaving extra time at the end of the process. Finish your work one week ahead of the deadline. Try several different revision strategies:

- Sleep on it.
- Read it aloud to friends.
- Work your way backward through the paper paragraph by paragraph.
- Scrutinize word choice to see if you have chosen the right word for the right effect.
- Use computer functions to check spelling and grammar.
- Proofread two hours before the deadline to catch any final errors.

Which of these strategies seem to work best to help you produce your most effective writing?

____

Your Journal

THINK CRITICALLY

1. The Cost of Plagiarism

List some reasons why students you have known resorted to plagiarism to satisfy their course requirements. After each reason, list a potential justification for this act. Finally, list all of the consequences of plagiarism, whether the student is caught or not.

1. Reason: ______________________ Justification: ______________________

2. Reason: ______________________ Justification: ______________________

3. Reason: ______________________ Justification: ______________________

Consequences: ______________________

How does this exercise influence your own resilience in resisting taking the easy way out on writing assignments?

____

2. What Are Your Writing Trends?

Begin a collection of papers from your courses to establish your writing portfolio. Arrange them in chronological order in a file folder or binder. What trends are apparent in the feedback that you are receiving?

____

Is the positive feedback you are getting consistent with your own self-image as a writer?

____

Is the negative feedback you are getting a clue about where you should concentrate your efforts to improve?

____

Do you see a potential "research stream" that you can capitalize on in future writing projects?

____

CREATE

1. Entitlement

Think about a writing assignment you are working on now, or look over your course syllabi for one that is due later in the semester. List the course below, along with the topic you are or will be studying when the writing project is assigned.

Course: ______________________ Topic: ______________________

Now start brainstorming about potential titles, based on that topic area. Don't be afraid to be creative or silly—this is just an exercise. Revisit this list of ideas once you actually sit down and start working on the assignment. You are already ahead of the game.

2. The Liberal Arts Flair

Many expert communicators find that the well-placed quotation can be an effective way to craft elegant writing. Quotations can be used to open or close a speech or a paper with some drama. Examine your upcoming work assignments to identify some possibilities to cruise for quotes to elevate the stature of your writing. Use either print quotation sources or go online to exploit any of the great quotation sites that will help you find just the right embellishment. Locate at least five quotes that would produce your intended effect.

Alverno College. *Writing and Speaking Criteria* (Milwaukee, WI: Alverno Productions, 1995).

10 Take Charge of Your Physical and Mental Health

© Kathrine Wessel/CORBIS

KNOW YOURSELF

There is no getting around it—college has many stressful moments. Cherish your physical and mental health. Motivating yourself to be physically and mentally healthy will help you to balance life and help you stay on track as you pursue your academic goals. To evaluate how well you take care of your health, place a checkmark next to only those items that apply to you.

- I live a healthy lifestyle.
- I exercise regularly.
- I get enough sleep.
- I eat right.
- I don't smoke.
- I don't take harmful drugs.
- I make good sexual decisions.
- I cope effectively with stress.
- I am not depressed.
- I know where to seek help for mental health problems.

As you read about Brooke Ellison, think about the physical challenges she overcame in her college career. What can you learn from her story?

CHAPTER OUTLINE

Value Health and Adopt a Healthy Lifestyle

Value Your Health
Risks to College Students

Pursue and Maintain Physical Health

Develop Healthy Behaviors and Address Problems
Exercise Regularly
Get Enough Sleep
Eat Right
Don't Smoke
Avoid Drugs
Make the Right Sexual Decisions

Safeguard Your Mental Health

Cope with Stress
Tackle Depression
Understand Suicide
Seek Help for Mental Health Problems

Images of College Success

Brooke Ellison

Brooke Ellison's life took an unexpected turn as she passed the fire station walking to school on her first day in the seventh grade. A car struck her, paralyzing her from the neck down and rendering her unable to breathe. She credits the prompt response of emergency workers and police for saving her life. However, the accident left Ellison a quadriplegic.

A tragedy of this magnitude would prompt many people to throw in the towel, but Ellison claims that the accident inspired a deeper faith: "My situation has given me a different perspective on life. I see things with different eyes. I see the value in things that are sometimes overlooked by other people—having family and friends, being able to appreciate a beautiful, sunny day. These are things I came so close to losing" (Gewertz 2000).

When Ellison gained entry to Harvard, the challenges of college life for a student with such substantial physical limitations were daunting. Ellison's mother moved into her dorm at Harvard to help her with everything from her health care needs to turning pages of her college texts.

Ellison graduated from Harvard with a degree in cognitive neuroscience. She is drawn to research on regenerating spinal tissue, because she is optimistic about her prospects for recovery. Her own studies on resilience suggest that people can learn how to be hopeful in the face of extraordinary obstacles to success.

Since her graduation, Ellison has cowritten a book with her mother, *Miracles Happen*, and worked as a motivational speaker. She plans to attend graduate school at Harvard's Kennedy School for Government and hopes this experience will prepare her to help shape policies and issues that directly impact lives. In addition, the late Christopher Reeve, who also suffered quadriplegia, directed a TV movie based on her story.

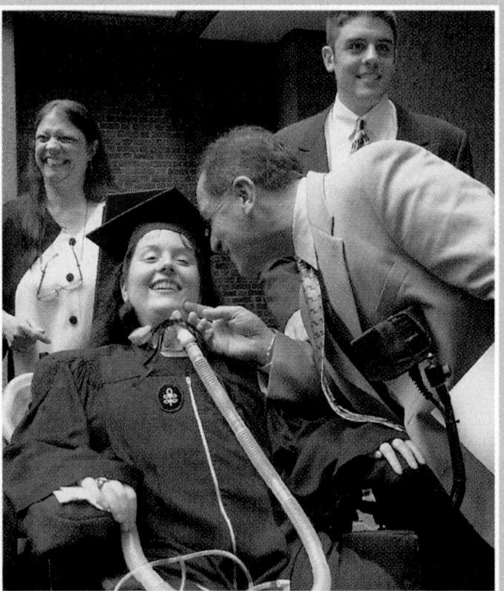

CONGRATULATED BY HER FATHER, Brooke Ellison graduates from Harvard with a degree in cognitive neuroscience. Her mother (left) helped her overcome tremendous physical obstacles in reaching her academic goals.

As you read, think about the Six Strategies for Success listed to the left and how this chapter can help you maximize success in these important areas. For example, maintaining good physical and mental health gets you in shape to reach your academic goals. Your self-esteem is also closely linked to your health.

Value Health and Adopt a Healthy Lifestyle

Your health is influenced by many factors—heredity, the environment, health education, the availability of health care, and lifestyle. Most of these factors are out of your personal control, but the one factor that is probably the most important, and entirely in your control, is lifestyle. Lifestyle is your way of living—your attitudes, habits, choices, and behavior. To evaluate your lifestyle now, complete Self-Assessment 1, "Is Your Lifestyle Good for Your Health?" on page 296.

What did you find out from this assessment? Are your lifestyle choices promoting good health, or are they placing you at risk for developing serious health problems?

Value Your Health

How much do you value your physical and mental health? Like other achievements, strong physical and mental health are supported by setting goals, planning how to achieve them, and monitoring progress. Like everything worthwhile, your vigor and health depend on your values and motivation. Self-esteem also follows from physical and mental health, and vice versa. If you have high self-esteem you're more likely to embark on a program of improvement than if you have low self-esteem. If you're fit, you'll tend to have higher self-esteem. As you can see, your health is closely linked with many of the strategies for success listed earlier.

Consider having a healthy body weight. Individuals who place a high value on this are more likely to be motivated to eat balanced, healthy meals and to exercise. If they begin to become overweight, they are likely to set goals, plan, and monitor their progress toward the goal of returning to a healthy weight. Further, setting and reaching weight goals, getting motivated, and valuing a healthy weight tend to increase self-esteem.

High self-esteem increases the likelihood that people will actually put forth the effort to reach a more healthy level of weight.

> ***Nothing can be changed until it is faced.***
>
> James Baldwin
> *Twentieth-century American novelist*

Good health requires good health habits. By making some lifestyle changes, you may be able to live a much longer, healthier, happier life. In fact, as many as seven of the ten leading causes of death (such as heart disease, stroke, and cancer) can be reduced by lifestyle changes, yet most of us tend to deny that the changes we think *other* people need to make also apply to us.

Risks to College Students

If you are like many college students, you're not nearly as healthy as you could be. In a national survey of first-year students, half said their health could be improved (Sax and others 2001). Male college students engage in riskier health habits than females do. For example, they are less likely to consult a physician or health care provider when they have unfamiliar physical symptoms, less likely to go to scheduled health checkups, and more likely to be substance abusers (Courtenay, McCreary, and Merighi 2002).

Young adults have some hidden health risks. Ironically, one risk stems from the fact that they often bounce back quickly from physical stress and abuse. This resilience can lead them to abuse their bodies and neglect their health. The negative effects of abusing one's body do not always show up immediately. However, at some point later one may pay a stiff price.

The following lifestyle patterns have been linked with poor health in college students: Skipping breakfast or regular meals, relying on snacks as a main food source, overeating, smoking, abusing alcohol and drugs, avoiding exercise, and not getting enough sleep. Do any of these habits apply to you?

Pursue and Maintain Physical Health

Are you as healthy as you can be? What did Self-Assessment 1 reveal about your current lifestyle choices?

Develop Healthy Behaviors and Address Problems

Let's look at specific aspects of your health. Are you putting your health knowledge to work by developing good health habits? If you had low scores on the self-assessment, ask yourself some frank questions. You're probably not doing all that you can to be healthy.

Seek medical attention without delay if you experience any of the following (Hahn, Payne, and Lucas, 2007; Teague, Mackenzie, and Rosenthal 2007):

- develop a lump in your breast
- have unexplained weight loss
- experience a fever for more than a week
- cough up blood
- encounter persistent or severe headaches
- have fainting spells
- develop unexplained shortness of breath

In some circumstances, these symptoms can signal a cancer or other serious problems. In many cases, though, a thorough medical exam will confirm that nothing serious is wrong. Either way, it is always best to be well-informed about your health.

Exercise Regularly

In recent research, exercise has been shown to:

- generate new brain cells
- improve the ability to process information
- increase cardiovascular fitness
- create lean body mass and reduce body fat
- increase strength and muscular endurance
- improve flexibility
- produce a greater life expectancy
- reduce stress symptoms
- improve mood and lessen depression
- raise self-esteem

Clearly, exercise alone is not going to ensure that you reach your academic goals. However, the fact that it can help you generate new brain cells is linked with thinking and learning. What are some other ways the benefits listed previously might help improve academic performance?

Exercise is certainly good for you and includes both aerobic or anaerobic activities (Wuest and Bucher 2006):

- *Aerobic exercise* is moderately intense, sustained exercise that stimulates your heart and lungs, while increasing your heart rate and the flow of oxygen through your body. Jogging, cycling, and swimming are examples of aerobic activities.
- *Anaerobic exercise* requires more oxygen than your body can take in, so it can only be done at short intervals. It often involves quick or intense movement such as doing pushups or running a hundred-yard dash. In contrast, running a long distance is mainly aerobic.

Motivate Yourself to Exercise

- **Visualize no change.** Ponder for a moment what the outcome will be of making no change in your health practices. Weight problems, physical inflexibility, and chronic health issues will drain away your quality of life.
- **Make time for exercise.** It's easy to sabotage your own commitment to exercise with excuses. If your excuse is, "I don't have time," find it. Ask yourself, "Am I too busy to take care of my health? What do I lose if I lose my health?"
- **Schedule exercise.** Make exercise a high priority in your regular commitments. Don't let unimportant things interfere with your exercise routine. Don't make excuses.
- **Find serious partners.** If you have a commitment to exercise with someone who is serious, it will be a lot harder to blow off your exercise in favor of a less healthful activity.
- **Chart your progress.** Record each of your exercise sessions in a systematic way. Use a notebook or a calendar, for example. This practice can help you to maintain the momentum you need to work out regularly.
- **Learn more about exercise.** The more you know about exercise, the more you're likely to continue it. Examine the resources on the website for this book to read more about exercise.

Aerobic exercise has significant cardiovascular benefits and burns fat (what you want for weight loss). Anaerobic exercise builds muscle tissue but does not help you lose weight as much. Many exercise activities are both aerobic and anaerobic, such as tennis, basketball, and circuit training (circulating among different exercise machines and stations).

If you don't exercise now, how can you motivate yourself to get going? "Manage Life: Motivate Yourself to Exercise" provides some good hints.

Get Enough Sleep

Most of us have occasional sleepless nights. Maybe we are stressed out and can't sleep soundly. In this case, we don't deliberately lose sleep. However, many college students deliberately pull all-nighters now and then to cram for a test. More common than all-nighters are successive nights with significantly reduced sleep because of parties, talking late with friends, and studying late. Just living with other students can produce irregular sleep patterns.

The residence hall might be noisy, or your roommate might not have a class until noon and stays up late while you have a class at 8 a.m. How might you deal with these situations? In many instances, college students don't get adequate sleep as a result of their own choices. Take the responsibility of saying no to staying late at parties, going out late when you have an early class, or staying up late when some friends just want to talk. You can set aside a time during the next day to talk with them if it is not an emergency. Many students think that sleeping late on the weekends makes up for lost sleep, but research recently has shown that this is not the case (Carskadon 2006). College students have twice as many sleep problems as the general population (Brown, Buboltz, and Soper 2001).

How Much Sleep Do You Need? The amount of sleep needed varies from person to person. Most students need at least eight hours of sleep to function competently the next day. Researchers have found that many college students do not get this much sleep and, therefore, do not function at optimal levels the following day (Dement and Vaughn 2000). Some experts argue that a more realistic total for traditional-age students who are at the end of substantial physical changes during adolescence is ten hours a night (Maas 2002). College students average only about six and a half hours of sleep per night. Many are unaware that their academic difficulties may be related to their sleep habits (Brown and Buboltz 2002). In addition to academic problems, sleep deprivation is associated with higher levels of stress, headaches, inability to concentrate, less effective memory, irritability, and possibly increased susceptibility to illness (Taylor 2006).

Why Might You Be Having Sleep Problems? As many as one in five students have *insomnia*, a sleep disorder that involves an inability to sleep. Alcohol, nicotine, and caffeine can interfere with your sleep and contribute to sleep problems. For example, drinking before you go to sleep keeps you from getting a full night of restful sleep, because it dehydrates you. Stress also can cause sleep problems.

For more information on good sleep, see "Manage Life: How to Sleep Better." The Journal activity "Evaluate Your Sleep" on page 300 also provides an opportunity to critically evaluate your current sleep habits.

MANAGE LIFE

How to Sleep Better

- **Get into a regular daily routine.** Go to sleep and wake up at approximately the same time each day.
- **Do something relaxing before you go to bed.** Soft music can help you unwind at the end of the day, but don't do homework right up to the moment before you want to drop off.
- **Avoid discussing stressful problems before you go to bed.** Don't bring up money or relationship problems if you expect to fall asleep quickly.
- **Make sure your sleeping area is good for sleeping.** Your bedroom should have minimum light, minimum sound, and a comfortable temperature.
- **Cut out naps.** It is okay to take a brief nap after lunch, but do not take naps that last more than an hour, and make sure to take them no later than 3 p.m. Napping during the day can interfere with night sleeping.
- **Engage in regular exercise.** However, don't exercise just before going to bed, because exercise increases your energy and alertness.
- **Manage your time effectively.** You should get at least seven to eight hours of sleep every night, maybe more, to be at your best.
- **Manage your stress.** Learn how to relax and cope with stress effectively.
- **Contact your college health center.** If the above strategies don't work, get some help from health professionals.

Eat Right

Many college students have poor eating habits. A study of eighteen hundred college students found that 60 percent eat too much artery-clogging saturated fat and 50 percent don't get enough fiber in their diets (Economos 2001). Almost 60 percent said that they know their diets have gone downhill since entering college.

Being Overweight Obesity has become a major health risk in the United States and in many countries around the world. Strong evidence of the environment's influence on weight is the doubling of the rate of obesity in the United States since 1900. More than 60 percent of U.S. adults are currently either overweight or obese (National Center for Health Statistics 2006). This dramatic increase is likely because of greater availability of food (especially food high in fat), the use of energy-saving devices, and declining physical activity. In 2000, U.S. women ate 335 calories more a day and men 168 more a day than they did in the early 1970s (National Center for Health Statistics 2004). Obesity is linked to increased risk of hypertension, diabetes, cardiovascular disease, and early death (Wardlaw and Hampl 2007).

The "freshman 15" refers to the approximately 15 pounds that many first-year students gain. The weight often shows up in the hips, thighs, and midsection. Why do first-year students gain this weight? During high school many students' eating habits are monitored by their parents, so they tend to eat more balanced meals. Once in college, students select their own diets, which often consist of chips, chips, and more chips, fast food, ice cream, late-night pizza, and beer. Once the extra 15 pounds arrive, what do first-year students do? They diet.

Dieting has become a way of life for many individuals, including college students. Be wary of diets that promise quick fixes or that sound too good to be true. Aim for a long-term plan that involves eating a variety of vegetables, fruits, and grains, and being physically active on a daily basis. This plan may produce slower results, but it works far better over the long term and is much healthier for you. To think more about your own diet, complete the Journal activity "Think About Your Diet," on page 299.

One of the best sources of nutritional advice, the *Dietary Guidelines for Americans*, is issued by the U.S. Department of Health and Human Services. These guidelines are revised every five years. The most recent ones support these six principles:

1. *Eat a variety of foods.* Use the four basic food groups to evaluate your diet:
   - the milk group (cheese, yogurt, milk)
   - the fruit and vegetable group
   - the grain group (cereals, bread, noodles)
   - the meat group (poultry, fish, red meat, and nuts)

   Healthy adults need to eat at least three servings of vegetables, two of fruit, and six of grain products every day. Megadose supplements of vitamins are no substitute for a healthful diet, and they can be harmful. Avoid them.
2. *Maintain a healthy weight.* Some college students are overweight, others underweight. Preoccupation with dieting can lead to dangerous loss/gain cycles that are hard on your body. Strive to maintain a reasonable, manageable weight.
3. *Follow a diet low in fat, saturated fat, and cholesterol.* Unfortunately, many of the best-tasting foods are the worst for you. Fat is found in large quantities in fried foods (fried chicken, doughnuts), rich foods (ice cream, pastries), greasy foods (spare ribs, bacon), and many spreads (butter, mayonnaise). In contrast, yogurt is low in saturated fat. Cholesterol, a key contributor to heart disease, is found only in animal products.

   Fitness expert Covert Bailey (1991) says that if you throw a pound of butter in a swimming pool, it will float just like a cork. The fat in your body will float in the same way, so the fatter you are, the more you'll float. Bailey says that he once had a friend who floated so well he could read a book while coasting along on top of the water in a swimming pool. If you have more than 25 percent body fat, you'll float easily. At 13 percent or lower, you'll sink quickly. Healthy body fat percentages vary for women and men. The highest healthy body fat content is 22 percent for women, 15 percent for men. Unfortunately, the average woman has 32 percent body fat, the average man 23 percent.
4. *Substitute plenty of vegetables, fruits, and grain products for unhealthful foods.* Replace fatty foods with more healthful sources of starch and fiber. This involves eating grain products, legumes (dried beans, peas), fruits, and vegetables not cooked in fat.
5. *Use sugar only in moderation.* In addition to table sugar, other common sugar products include brown sugar, syrups, honey, jams, jellies, ice cream, cookies, cakes, and most other desserts. If you eat dessert, try eating fresh fruit instead of foods with added sugar. Replace soft drinks with water.
6. *Use sodium in moderation.* Some people are sensitive to sodium and are at risk for hypertension (persistent high blood pressure). To reduce the sodium in your diet, eat less salt. Flavor your food with lemon, spices, herbs, or pepper.

Anorexia Nervosa and Bulimia Nineteen-year-old Andrea gradually eliminated foods from her diet to the point where she lived on Jell-o and yogurt. She spent hours observing her body. She wrapped her hands around her waist to see whether it was getting any thinner. She fantasized about becoming a fashion model. Even when her weight dropped to 80 pounds, Andrea still felt fat. She continued to lose weight and was hospitalized for *anorexia nervosa*, an eating disorder that involves the relentless pursuit of thinness through starvation. Anorexia nervosa can eventually lead to death.

Most anorexics are white female adolescents or young adults from well-educated middle- and upper-income families. They have a distorted body image, perceiving themselves as overweight even when they become skeletal. Numerous causes of anorexia nervosa have been proposed. One is the current fashion image of thinness, reflected in the saying, "You can't be too rich or too thin." Many anorexics grow up in families with high demands for academic achievement. Unable to meet these high expectations and control their grades, they turn to something they can control: their weight.

Bulimia is a disorder that involves binging and purging. Bulimics go on an eating binge then purge by vomiting or using a laxative. Sometimes the binges alternate with fasting. However, they can also alternate with normal eating. Anorexics can control their eating; bulimics cannot. Bulimia can produce gastric and chemical imbalances in the body, as well as long-term dental damage. Depression is common in bulimics. If you have anorexic or bulimic characteristics, go to your college health center for help. Be positive; see "Create Your Future: Turning Problems and Interests into Careers" for inspiration.

Don't Smoke

Some stark figures reveal why smoking is called suicide in slow motion:

- Smoking accounts for more than one-fifth of all deaths in the United States.
- It causes 32 percent of coronary heart disease cases in the United States.
- It causes 30 percent of all cancer deaths in the United States.
- It causes 82 percent of all lung cancer deaths in the United States.
- Passive smoke causes as many as eight thousand lung cancer deaths a year in the United States.

Most smokers want to quit. Can they? Unfortunately, the same survey offers some more bad news. About half of the smokers had seriously tried to quit smoking but had lost the battle. The immediate addictive, pleasurable effects of smoking are extremely difficult to overcome. There was some good news, though. About half of the people in the United States who ever smoked have quit.

I'm glad I don't have to explain to a man from Mars why each day I set fire to dozens of little pieces of paper, and then put them in my mouth.

Mignon McLaughlin
Contemporary American humorist and writer

If you're a smoker, how can you quit? Many different strategies have been tried to help people quit smoking. They include drug treatments, hypnosis, and behavior modification. Drug treatments include *nicotine gum*, a prescription drug that smokers chew when they get the urge for a cigarette. Another drug treatment is the *nicotine patch*, a nonprescription adhesive pad that delivers nicotine through the skin. The dosage is gradually reduced over eight to twelve weeks. Some smokers, usually light smokers, can quit cold turkey.

The resources on the website for this book include good information about ways to quit smoking.

Avoid Drugs

We are a drug-using society. Hardly a day goes by when most of us do not take a drug, although we don't always call it that. For example, many cola beverages contain the drug caffeine. With the popularity of Starbucks and other coffeehouses, we have become a coffee culture. Many students love sitting in coffeehouses for hours, sipping coffee, studying, and socializing. Unfortunately, imbibing highly caffeinated coffee and abusing many other drugs are not good for your health.

Many college students take drugs (including alcohol) more than they did in high school (Zucker and others 2006). Among the reasons for the increased use of drugs among first-year college students are:

- greater freedom from parental supervision
- high levels of stress and anxiety associated with academic and financial concerns
- peer use of drugs for recreational purposes

Depressants, Stimulants, and Hallucinogens The drugs that college students take can be classified in three main categories: depressants, stimulants, and hallucinogens.

1. *Depressants* are drugs that slow down the central nervous system, bodily functions, and behavior. Among the most widely used depressants are alcohol, barbiturates, and tranquilizers.
2. *Stimulants* are drugs that increase the activity of the central nervous system. The most widely used stimulants are caffeine, nicotine, amphetamines, and cocaine.
3. *Hallucinogens* are drugs that modify perceptual experiences and produce hallucinations. LSD, marijuana, and Ecstasy are hallucinogens.

Ecstasy, which has seen increased use in recent years by college students, also has stimulant properties and is popular at raves. Ecstasy users often become hyperactive and sleepless, and using Ecstasy can lead to dangerous increases in blood pressure, as well as a stroke or heart attack (Johnston and others 2006).

A summary of the medical uses, short-term effects, and health risks of depressants, stimulants, and hallucinogens is presented in Table 10.1, as is information on overdoses and the risk of physical/psychological dependence on these drugs.

Why Do People Take Drugs? Drugs help people adapt to or escape from an ever-changing, stressful environment. Smoking, drinking, and taking drugs can reduce tension and frustration, relieve boredom and fatigue, and help us to ignore the world's harsh realities. Drugs can give us brief tranquility, joy, relaxation, kaleidoscopic perceptions, and surges of exhilaration. They sometimes have practical uses; for example, amphetamines can keep you awake all night to study for an exam, although the quality of study in such conditions may not help you achieve your academic goals. We also take drugs for social reasons. We hope they will make us feel more at ease and happier at parties, on dates, and in other anxious social contexts.

However, the use of drugs for personal pleasure and temporary adaptation can be dangerous. The use can lead to

Turning Problems and Interests into Careers

Stacey had always been a few pounds overweight and had been teased by some of the kids in high school. Once she was finally away from home and on her own in college, she was determined to alter her image. She went on an extreme diet, cutting out all carbohydrates and subsisting mainly on peanut butter and yogurt. At first she looked great, but by Christmas she was too thin, yet still determined to lose even more weight.

When this continued into the spring, her hair began to fall out and she lost all energy, barely able to drag herself to class each day. Finally her roommate convinced her to visit the college health center, where she was diagnosed with anorexia. The nurse called in a nutritionist with whom Stacey met on a regular basis, working on a diet that would aid her recovery. At first it was difficult for Stacey to see herself regaining some of the weight, but the nutritionist taught her about the importance of different types of food for her health and the dangers of extreme dieting.

That experience convinced Stacey to change her major to dietetics and nutrition, and she began planning for a career as a dietitian. She now works as a consulting dietitian and nutritionist in a local school system, helping to promote sound eating habits in students through education and counseling. Her goal is to help prevent others from experiencing the negative health impact of extreme diets, anorexia, and bulimia.

David had always been an avid athlete and was crushed when he was cut from the baseball team his freshman year. He turned his free time toward partying, gaining ten pounds while his grades plummeted. His adviser discussed the importance of athletics in providing structure for his life as well as the importance of healthy exercise, and he steered David toward intracollegiate athletics. David quickly became a standout in the baseball program.

His interest in sports and the positive impact it had on his life led him to a career in coaching. He wanted to remain active after graduation and help other students gain the benefits from athletics that he had experienced. He got a job coaching junior varsity baseball at a high school in his hometown, substitute teaching on the side to help make ends meet. He liked working with the kids both in and out of the classroom and eventually decided to go back to school to get his teaching degree so that he could teach and coach full time.

drug dependence, personal distress, and in some cases fatal diseases. What initially was intended for pleasure and adaptation can turn into pain and maladaptation. For example, on a short-term basis, a few drinks help some people to relax and forget about their problems. However, drinking can become an addiction that destroys relationships, careers, minds, and bodies. Ruptured lives and families, permanent liver damage, and depression are common outcomes of alcoholism.

> ***Alcohol is a good preservative for everything but brains.***
> Mary Poole
> *Contemporary American writer*

Alcohol Alcohol abuse is a special concern. Alcohol is the most widely used drug in our society. More than 13 million people in the United States call themselves alcoholics. Alcoholism is the third leading killer in the United States. Each year about 25,000 people are killed, and 1.5 million injured, by drunk drivers. More than 60 percent of homicides involve the use of alcohol by either the offender or the victim. About two-thirds of aggressive sexual acts toward women involve the use of alcohol by the offender.

In a recent national survey, almost half of U.S. college students say they drink heavily (Wechsler and others 2002). In this survey, almost 75 percent of underage students living in fraternities and sororities were binge drinkers (defined as men who drank five or more drinks in a row and women who drank four or more drinks in a row at least once in the two weeks prior to the survey), and 70 percent of traditional-age college students who lived away from home were binge drinkers. The lowest rate of binge drinking—25 percent—occurred for students living at home with their parents. See "Clarify Values: Let's Get Wasted" to think further about binge drinking's negative effects.

Almost half the binge drinkers reported problems that included missed classes, injuries, troubles with police, and unprotected sex (see Figure 10.1). Binge-drinking college students were eleven times more likely to fall behind in school, ten times more likely to drive after drinking, and twice as likely to have unprotected sex than were college students who did not binge drink.

Date rape also is far more likely to occur when one or both individuals have been drinking heavily. Self Assessment 2, "Do I Abuse Drugs?" on page 297 can help you judge whether you are a substance abuser. If you have a substance abuse problem, what can you do about it?

- *Admit that you have a problem.* This is tough. Many students who have a substance abuse problem won't admit it. Admitting that you have a problem is the first major step in helping yourself.
- *Listen to what others are saying to you.* Chances are that your roommate, a friend, or someone you've dated has told you that you have a substance abuse problem. You probably denied it. They are trying to help you. Listen to them.
- *Seek help for your problem.* There are numerous resources for students who have a substance abuse problem. These include Alcoholics Anonymous, Cocaine Anonymous (CA), Al-Anon, and Rational Recovery Systems. Most towns have one or more of these organizations, which are confidential and are led by people who have successfully combated their substance abuse problems. They can help you a great deal. Also, the health center at your college can provide help.
- *Use the resources on this book's website.* Examine the resources for reducing drug use. They include phone numbers, information about organizations that can help you overcome your problem, and links to other relevant websites.

CLARIFY VALUES

"Let's Get Wasted"

Art tells his friend, "It's been a bummer of a week. I blew two tests. I'm depressed. Let's get wasted." And they do. They drink a fifth of gin and pass out. Sound common? Sound harmless?

It's common. It often is not harmless.

When students get wasted, they can get arrested and go to jail, have car wrecks, get monster hangovers, accidentally set dorm rooms on fire, flunk out of school, damage property, and make bad sexual decisions. Getting drunk as a chronic condition gives evidence that you place greater value on short-term pleasure seeking even at the sacrifice of important, long-term, life goals.

Limit your time with someone who likes to get wasted. Don't go to or linger at parties where getting wasted is the main objective. If you get tempted, keep in mind all the things that can go wrong when you lose control and consciousness. Also, keep thinking about how you'll feel the next day.

TABLE 10.1 Psychoactive Drugs: Depressants, Stimulants, and Hallucinogens

Drug Classification	Medical Uses	Short-Term Effects	Overdose	Health Risks	Risk of Physical/ Psychological Dependence
Depressants					
Alcohol	Pain relief	Relaxation, depressed brain activity, slowed behavior, reduced inhibitions	Disorientation, loss of consciousness, even death at high blood-alcohol levels	Accidents, brain damage, liver disease, heart disease, ulcers, birth defects	Physical: moderate; psychological: moderate
Barbiturates	Sleeping pill	Relaxation, sleep	Breathing difficulty, coma, possible death	Accidents, coma, possible death	Physical and psychological: moderate to high
Tranquilizers	Anxiety reduction	Relaxation, slowed behavior	Breathing difficulty, coma, possible death	Accidents, coma, possible death	Physical: low to moderate; psycho-logical: moderate to high
Opiates (narcotics)	Pain relief	Euphoric feelings, drowsiness, nausea	Convulsions, coma, possible death	Accidents, infectious diseases such as AIDS (when the drug is injected)	Physical: high; psychological: moderate to high
Stimulants					
Amphetamines	Weight control	Increased alertness, excitability; decreased fatigue, irritability	Extreme irritability, feelings of persecu-tion, convulsions	Insomnia, hyperten-sion, malnutrition, possible death	Physical: possible; psychological: mod-erate to high
Cocaine	Local anesthetic	Increased alertness, excitability, euphoric feelings; decreased fatigue, irritability	Extreme irritability, feelings of persecu-tion, convulsions, cardiac arrest, possible death	Insomnia, hyperten-sion, malnutrition, possible death	Physical: possible; psychological: mod-erate (oral) to very high (injected or smoked)
Hallucinogens					
LSD	None	Strong hallucina-tions, distorted time perception	Severe mental disturbance, loss of contact with reality	Accidents	Physical: none; psychological: low
Marijuana	Treatment of the eye disorder glaucoma	Euphoric feelings, relaxation, mild hallucinations, time distortion, attention and memory impairment	Fatigue, disoriented behavior	Accidents, respiratory disease	Physical: very low; psychological: moderate

FIGURE 10.1 The Hazardous Consequences of Binge Drinking in College

©Paula A. Scully

The Troubles Frequent Binge Drinkers Create for . . .

Themselves[1] (% of those surveyed who admitted having had the problem)		**and Others**[2] (% of those surveyed who had been affected)	
Missed a class	61	Had study or sleep interrupted	68
Forgot where they were or what they did	54	Had to care for drunken student	54
Engaged in unplanned sex	41	Were insulted or humiliated	34
Got hurt	23	Experienced unwanted sexual advances	26
Had unprotected sex	22	Had serious argument	20
Damaged property	22	Had property damaged	15
Got into trouble with campus or local police	11	Were pushed or assaulted	13
Had five or more alcohol-related problems in a school year	47	Had at least one of the above problems	87

[1]Frequent binge drinkers were defined as those who had had at least four or five drinks at one time on at least three occasions in the previous two weeks.

[2]These figures are from colleges where at least 50% of students are binge drinkers.

H. Wechsler, A. Davenport, G. Dowdall, B. Moeykens, and S. Castillo, "Heath and Behavioral Consequences of Binge Drinking in College" *from Journal of the American Medical Association, Vol. 272, No. 21, Dec 7, 1994.*

Make the Right Sexual Decisions

Making smart sexual decisions has never been more important than today. AIDS, other sexually transmitted diseases, and unwanted pregnancy pose life-altering challenges (Crooks and Bauer 2005). Individuals vary in the extent to which they believe it is acceptable to engage in various sexual behaviors (Caroll 2007). To evaluate your sexual attitudes, complete Self-Assessment 3 "My Sexual Attitudes" on page 298.

Avoid Sexually Transmitted Infections *Sexually transmitted infections (STIs)* are diseases contracted primarily through sex. This includes intercourse as well as oral–genital and anal–genital sex. STIs affect about one of every six adults.

Symptoms With certain STIs, you may be showing no immediate symptoms and yet still pass the infection on to someone else who will suffer. Following are some symptoms for which you should certainly see a doctor or visit a clinic as soon as you can.

Men:

- foul-smelling, cloudy discharge from the penis
- burning sensation when urinating
- painless sore on the penis
- painful red bumps in the genital region, usually on the penis, turning into tiny blisters containing clear fluid
- warts in the genital area, either pink/red and soft or hard and yellow/gray

Women:

- yellow-green discharge from the vagina
- painful sore on the inner vaginal wall or cervix
- burning sensation during urination
- painful red bumps on the labia, turning into tiny blisters containing clear fluid
- warts in the genital area, either pink/red and soft, or hard and yellow/gray

No single STI has had a greater impact on sexual behavior or created more fear in the last decade than HIV-AIDS. Experts say that AIDS can be transmitted by sexual contact, sharing hypodermic needles, blood transfusion, or other direct contact of cuts or mucous membranes with blood or sexual fluids (Hyde and DeLamater 2006). It's not who you are but what you do that puts you at risk for getting AIDS. *Anyone* who is sexually active or uses intravenous drugs is at risk. No one is immune.

Reduce Your Chances What can you do to reduce the likelihood of contracting an STI? First, recognize that the only completely effective strategy is abstinence. But if you do choose to have sex, here are some ways to reduce your chances of being infected (Crooks and Bauer 2005):

1. *Assess your and your partner's risk status.* If you've had previous sexual activity with others, you may have contracted an STI without knowing it. Have you been tested for STIs in general? Remember that many STIs don't produce detectable symptoms. If you care enough to be sexually intimate with a new partner, you should be willing to be open with him or her about your own physical sexual health.

   Spend time getting to know a prospective sexual partner before you have sex with him or her. Ideally, this time frame is at least two to three months. Use this time to convey your STI status and inquire about your partner's. Keep in mind that many people are not honest about their sexual history. It is dangerous to presume good will and good health from unfamiliar sexual partners, and the consequences of risk taking could be lethal.
2. *Obtain prior medical examinations.* Many experts on sexuality now recommend that couples who want to begin a sexual relationship abstain from sexual activity until

both undergo medical and laboratory testing to rule out the presence of STIs. If cost is an issue, contact your campus health service or a public health clinic in your area.

3. *Use condoms.* When correctly used, condoms help to prevent the transmission of many STIs. Condoms are most effective in preventing chlamydia, gonorrhea, syphilis, and AIDS. They are less effective against the spread of genital herpes and genital warts. Recommendations for the effective use of condoms include the following:
    - Put on a condom before any genital contact has occurred.
    - Make sure the condom is adequately lubricated.
    - Don't blow up the condom or fill it with water to test it for leaks (this stretching weakens the latex).
    - Don't unroll the condom first like a sock and then put it on, but instead unroll it directly onto the erect penis.
    - Twist the end of the condom as it is rolled onto the penis to leave space at the tip.
    - If the condom breaks, immediately replace it; never reuse a condom.
4. *Avoid having sex with multiple partners.* One of the strongest predictors of getting AIDS, chlamydia, genital herpes, and other STIs is having sex with multiple partners.

© Casey Cohen/PhotoEdit

If you have sex, be proactive rather than reactive. Use effective contraception and protect yourself against STIs. Promiscuity greatly increases your chances of contracting AIDS and other STIs. Think before you act. Too often enchanted evenings are followed by disenchanted mornings.

Protect Against Unwanted Pregnancy Most college students want to control whether and when they have children. That means either abstaining from sex or using effective contraception. Students who feel guilty and have negative attitudes about sexuality are less likely to use contraception than are students who have positive attitudes about sexuality.

Following are the main contraceptive choices (American Pregnancy Association 2006):

- *Abstinence.* This is the only strategy that is 100 percent effective in preventing unwanted pregnancy.
- *Oral contraceptive.* Advantages of birth control pills are a high rate of effectiveness and low interference with sexual activity. However, the pill can have adverse side effects for some women, such as blood clots, nausea, and moodiness.
- *Male condom.* A main advantage is protection against STIs. A small proportion of condoms break. Improve protection by using a spermicide with condoms. Failure rate for male condoms is about 14 percent.
- *Female condom.* A sheath, usually made of latex rubber, that is inserted into the vagina. Failure rate for the female condom is about 21 percent.
- *Emergency contraception.* Emergency contraception, also called the "morning-after pill," can prevent pregnancy when taken within seventy-two hours after unprotected intercourse.
- *Ortho Evra patch.* An alternative to the pill, the hormonal patch is placed on the body once a week for three weeks and then removed to allow for a menstrual

period. If used as directed, the patch has a very effective rate of preventing pregnancy.

- *Diaphragm.* This consists of a latex dome on a flexible spring rim that is inserted into the vagina with contraceptive cream or jelly. The diaphragm must be fitted by a skilled medical practitioner. The diaphragm has few negative side effects and a high effectiveness rate when used properly. Failure rate for the diaphragm is appxoximately 20 percent. A cervical cap is like a miniature diaphragm that fits over the cervix. It also has a 20 percent failure rate when used before having a child, but a 40 percent failure rate after having a child.
- *Spermicides.* These include foam, suppositories, creams, and jellies that contain a chemical that kills sperm. Advantages include a lack of serious side effects. Disadvantages include potential irritation of genital tissues and interruption of sexual activity. Most experts on sexuality say not to rely on spermicide alone for contraception.
- *Intrauterine device (IUD).* The IUD is a small plastic device that is inserted into the vagina. The IUD's advantages include uninterrupted sexual activity and simplicity of use. Possible disadvantages include pelvic inflammation and pregnancy complications.
- *Norplant.* Norplant consists of six thin capsules filled with a synthetic hormone that are implanted under the skin of a woman's upper arm. The implanted capsules gradually release the hormone into the bloodstream over a five-year period to prevent conception. Working like a mini-birth control pill, Norplant provides highly effective contraception. Its negatives include potential bleeding and hormone-related side effects.
- *Depo-Provera.* Depo-Provera is an injectable contraceptive that lasts three months. Users have to get a shot every twelve weeks. Depo-Provera is a very effective contraceptive method but can cause menstrual irregularities.
- *Tubal ligation.* This is the most common sterilization procedure done for women. It involves severing or tying the fallopian tubes.
- *Lunelle injection.* A hormonal injection given every month to prevent ovulation. It has a very low failure rate, similar to that of oral contraceptives.
- *Vasectomy.* This is a male sterilization procedure that involves cutting the sperm-carrying ducts.

Using no contraceptive method, trying to withdraw the penis just before ejaculation, and periodic abstinence are not wise strategies. If you're sexually active, compare the various contraceptive methods and choose the method that is the safest and most effective for you.

As you have learned in this section, maintaining good physical health is important for your success in college and beyond. For some additional strategies for improving your health, see "Manage Life: Your Physical Health." The Journal activity "Promoting Safe Sex" on page 300 also provides an opportunity for you to think more about ways to promote safe sex on your campus.

Safeguard Your Mental Health

As we said at the beginning of the chapter, an important factor in being mentally healthy is having high self-esteem. This section describes several strategies for improving mental health, all of which are linked with building self-esteem.

MANAGE LIFE

Your Physical Health

Throughout this book, we have emphasized how important it is for you to take responsibility for your behavior. Your physical health is no exception. Exercising regularly, getting enough sleep, eating right, not smoking, avoiding drugs, and making the right sexual decisions all require you to consistently take charge of your life and not let yourself slide into bad habits.

Five steps in developing a self-control program to improve your health are (Martin and Pear 2006):

1. Define the problem.
2. Commit to change.
3. Collect data about yourself.
4. Design a self-control program.
5. Make the program last–maintenance.

1. *Define the problem.* What would you like to change? Which aspect of your health would you like to more effectively control? For one person, this might be "lose thirty pounds," for another it might be "quit smoking," and for yet another person it might be "engage in aerobic exercise for thirty minutes, four days a week." What aspect of your health do you want to change?
2. *Commit to change.* When college students commit to change, they become better self managers of their smoking, eating, exercise, and other aspects of their lives. Some good strategies for committing to change are:
    - Tell others about your commitment to change–they will remind you of your commitment.
    - Rearrange your environment to provide frequent reminders of your goal, making sure the reminders are associated with positive benefits of reaching your goal.
    - Plan ahead for ways that you can deal with temptation, tailoring these plans to your program.
3. *Collect data about yourself.* This is especially important in decreasing excessive behaviors such as overeating and frequent smoking. Make up a chart and monitor what you do every day in regard to what you want to change.
4. *Design a self-control program.* A good self-control program usually includes both long-term and short-term goals and developing a plan for how to reach those goals.
5. *Make the program last.* Establish specific dates for postchecks. Establish a buddy system by finding a friend with a similar problem. The two of you can set maintenance goals and once a month check each other's progress.

Cope with Stress

There is no doubt that stress is a factor in your mental health. However, do you know how important it is? According to the American Academy of Family Physicians, two-thirds of all medical office visits are for stress-related symptoms. Stress is also a major contributor to heart disease, accidental injuries, and suicide. A number of life events have been identified as stressful enough to significantly affect one's physical health.

What are the most common stressors for college students? In one study (Murphy 1996), the academic circumstances creating the most stress for students were tests and finals, grades and competition, professors and class environment, too many demands, papers and essay exams, career and future success, and studying. Do any of these apply to you?

In this same study, the personal circumstances that created the most stress for students were intimate relationships, finances, parental conflicts and expectations, and roommate conflicts. Another study showed that the first year of college was by far the most stressful for students (Sher, Wood, and Gotham 1996).

Coping with stress is essential to making your life more productive and enjoyable (Blonna and Paterson 2007). Coping means managing difficult circumstances, solving personal problems, and reducing stress and conflict. Not everyone responds the same way to stress; some of us have better strategies than others. The Journal activity "Examine Your Coping Style" on page 299 provides an opportunity for you to analyze how well you cope.

The good news is that if you don't currently cope with stress effectively you can learn to do so (Taylor 2006). Before we talk about the positive ways to cope with stress, let's look at some typically unsuccessful ways of dealing with a stressful problem:

- Repress it so you won't have to think about it.
- Take it out on other people when you feel angry or depressed.
- Keep your feelings to yourself.
- Tell yourself the problem will go away.
- Refuse to believe what is happening.
- Try to reduce tension by drinking and eating more.

Fortunately, there are successful coping strategies as well.

See Stress as a Challenge Rather Than a Threat Consider how first-year students may view stress differently. Antonio sees an upcoming test as stressful; Anna sees it as a challenge. Greta views a D on a paper as a disaster; Dion views the same grade as a challenge to improve his writing. To some extent, stress depends on how we interpret events.

To cope successfully, it helps to (1) see the circumstances as a challenge to overcome rather than an overwhelming, threatening stress and (2) have good coping resources such as friends, family, a mentor, and the counseling center at your college (Blonna 2007).

DILBERT: ©Scott Adams/Dist. by United Features Syndicate, Inc.

Develop an Optimistic Outlook and Think Positively Do you look on the positive side of things or the negative? How important is it to be optimistic? In one study, college students were initially identified as optimists or pessimists (Peterson and Stunkard 1986). Then their health was monitored over the next year. The pessimists had twice as many infections and doctors' visits as the optimists did. A more recent study also found that students who were optimistic at the beginning of their first semester of college had less stress and depression and more social support over the course of the semester (Brisette, Scheier, and Carver 2002).

How can you develop a more optimistic outlook? One way is to use positive thinking to challenge self-defeating thoughts (Greenberg 2007). This strategy helps you avoid ruminating and wallowing in self-pity when bad things happen. Another good strategy is to dispute your negative thoughts. Pessimists tend to use absolute, all-encompassing terms to describe their defeats. They often use words like *never* and *always*. If this sounds like you, talk back to these negative thoughts in a self-confident, positive way that will get rid of self-blame and negative feelings.

Thinking positively helps to put you in a good mood and improves your self-esteem. It also gives you the sense that you're controlling your environment rather than letting it control you. Thinking positively improves your ability to learn. A negative outlook increases your chances of getting angry, feeling guilty, and magnifying your mistakes.

Talk positively to yourself. It can help you reach your full potential. Monitor your self-talk, because unchallenged negative thinking has a way of becoming a self-fulfilling prophecy. That is, if you tell yourself you can't do something well, you won't. How can you monitor your self-talk? At random times during the day, ask yourself, "What am I saying to myself right now?" Potentially stressful moments are excellent times to examine your self-talk. You also can ask friends to give you feedback on your negative or positive attitudes.

© 2000 Tom Cheney, from cartoonbank.com. All rights reserved.

Seek Emotional Support In stressful times, family members, friends, classmates, and coworkers can help by reassuring you that you're a valuable person who is loved. Knowing that others care about you can give you the confidence to tackle stressful circumstances.

Consider Juan, who was laid off from three jobs in three years. By all accounts he should be depressed. Yet he says he is a happy person. When asked his secret in the face of adversity and stress, Juan says it stems from the support of a wonderful family and great friends.

Recognize the potential support in your own life. Learn how to draw on these resources in times of stress. Sometimes you can improve your ability to cope by joining community groups, interest groups, or informal social groups that meet regularly (Taylor 2006).

Relax We usually think of relaxation as unwinding in front of the TV, taking a quiet walk in the evening, and so forth. These activities can be relaxing. However, a different form of relaxation can also help college students cope with anxiety and stress. It's called *deep relaxation*.

Try the following to attain a deeply relaxed state (Davis, Eshelman, and McKay 2000):

1. In a quiet place, either lie down on a couch or bed or sit in a comfortable chair with your head supported.
2. Get into a comfortable position and relax. Clench your right fist tighter and tighter for about five seconds. Now relax it. Feel the looseness in your right hand. Repeat the procedure with your left hand. Then do it with both hands. When you release the tension, let it go instantly. Allow your muscles to become limp.
3. Bend your elbows and tense your biceps as hard as you can. After a few seconds, relax and straighten out your arms. Go through the procedure again. Tighten your biceps as hard as you can for a few seconds and then relax them. As with your biceps, do each of the following procedures twice.
4. Turn your attention to your head. Wrinkle your forehead as tightly as you can, then relax it. Next, frown and notice the strain it produces. Close your eyes now. Squint them as hard as you can. Notice the tension. Now relax your eyes. Let them stay closed gently and comfortably. Now clench your jaw and bite hard. Notice the tension throughout your jaw. Relax your jaw.
5. Shrug your shoulders. Keep the tension as you hunch your head down between your shoulders. Then relax your shoulders.
6. Breathe in and fill your lungs completely. Hold your breath for a few seconds. Now exhale and let your chest become loose. Repeat this four or five times. Tighten your stomach for several seconds. Now relax it.
7. Tighten your buttocks and thighs. Flex your thighs by pressing your heels down as hard as you can. Relax and feel the difference. Next, curl your toes downward, making your calf muscles tight. Then relax. Now bend your toes toward your face, creating tension in your shins. Relax again. To avoid muscle cramping, don't over-tighten your toes.

The time to relax is when you don't have any.

Sydney J. Harris
Twentieth-century American newspaper writer

Some students have limited success when they first try deep relaxation. With practice, though, it usually works. Initially you may need twenty to thirty minutes to reach a deeply relaxed state, but eventually many students can become deeply relaxed in two to three minutes. The resources section on this book's website provides further information about deep relaxation. *Note:* If you have high blood pressure and are taking medication for it, do not try the deep relaxation exercise, because it could lower your blood pressure too far.

Write about Your Stress Writing about your stress not only provides a release of pent-up tension but also can stimulate you to think about ways to cope more effectively with the stress (Pennebaker 2001). Some further strategies for writing about your stress appear in "Build Competence: Writing about Stress." Also, the Journal activity "Write about Your Stress" on page 299 gives you an opportunity to use writing as a coping strategy.

BUILD COMPETENCE

Writing about Stress

Here are some recommended strategies for writing about stress (Pennebaker 1997):

- *What to Write.* You don't need to write about the biggest trauma in your life. Write about issues that currently bother you and preoccupy your thinking. Write about things that you may not be telling others out of fear of embarrassment or punishment. Write as objectively as you can about an experience that troubled you. Express your emotions and write as deeply as you can about your feelings.
- *How to Write.* Just start and keep writing. If you get stuck, go back and repeat what you were writing before you got stuck.
- *When and Where to Write.* Write when you feel like it. Write when you feel ready to pursue writing on an emotional level. Find a place where you won't be interrupted or distracted.
- *What to Expect.* Writing about your stress is not a cure-all. It is not a substitute for tackling problems that may keep you sad, angry, or frustrated. However, writing about stress can help you see things from a better perspective. You may feel sad or depressed for several hours after writing about your stress, but most people report that they feel relieved, happier, and more content over time when they write about their stress.

Tackle Depression

Depression is all too common among college students. In one study, depression was linked with poor academic performance (Haines, Norris, and Kashy 1996). Consider Cassandra, who was depressed for several months. Nothing seemed to cheer her up. Cassandra's depression began when the person she planned to marry broke off their relationship. Her emotional state worsened until she didn't feel like getting out of bed most mornings. She started missing many classes and got behind in all of them. One of her friends noticed how sad she was and got Cassandra to go to the counseling center at her college.

Each of us feels blue or down in the dumps some of the time. These brief bouts of sad feelings or discontent with the way our life is going are normal. If sad feelings last for only a few hours, a few days, or a few weeks, you won't be classified as depressed. But if the sad feelings linger for a month or more, and you feel deeply unhappy and demoralized, you probably are in a state of depression. A person with depression often has the following symptoms:

- changes in sleep patterns
- changes in appetite
- decreased energy
- feelings of worthlessness
- difficulty concentrating
- feelings of guilt

Depression is so widespread that it's called the "common cold" of mental disorders (Nolen-Hoeksema 2007). More than 250,000 people in the United States are hospitalized every year for depression. Students, professors, and laborers get depressed. No one is immune to it, not even great writers such as Anne Sexton and Ernest Hemingway, or famous statesmen such as Abraham Lincoln and Winston Churchill.

A man's lifetime risk of having depression is 10 percent. A woman's lifetime risk is much greater—almost 25 percent. Many people with depression suffer unnecessarily, because depression can be treated effectively.

Increasing numbers of college students are taking antidepressants, drugs that are designed to reduce depression. Researchers have found that antidepressant drugs work best when combined with psychotherapy (Oltmanns and Emery 2007). Furthermore, nondrug treatments, such as regular exercise, also have shown positive benefits in reducing depression (Lane, Crone-Grant, and Lane 2002). To think further about depression and other health issues, complete the Journal activity "Become a Movie Producer" on page 300.

Understand Suicide

The rate of suicide in the United States has tripled since the 1950s. Each year about twenty-five thousand people in this country take their own lives. As many as two out of every three college students say they have thought about suicide on at least one occasion. Immediate and highly stressful circumstances can produce suicidal thoughts. These include the loss of a partner, a spouse, or a job; flunking out of school; and unwanted pregnancy. In many cases, suicide or its attempt has multiple causes.

Consider Brian, who just flunked two of his college courses. When the grades came in, his father harshly criticized Brian and told him he had not put enough effort into his classes. This past week, Brian's girlfriend broke off their long-standing relationship. He became depressed and began to think about putting an end to his life. If you know someone like Brian, what can you do? Some guidelines are offered in "Build Competence: What to Do When Someone Is Thinking about Suicide."

What to Do When Someone Is Thinking about Suicide

- **Stay calm.** In most cases, there is no rush. Sit and listen, *really* listen, to what the person is saying. Be understanding, and emotionally support the person's feelings.
- **Deal directly with the topic of suicide.** Most people have mixed feelings about death and are open to help. Don't be afraid to ask or talk directly about suicide.
- **Encourage problem solving and positive actions.** Remember that the person in the crisis is not thinking clearly. Encourage the person to refrain from making any serious, irreversible decisions while in the crisis. Talk about the alternatives that might create hope for the future.
- **Get help.** Although you want to help, don't take full responsibility by being the sole counselor. Seek out resources, such as your college counseling center, for help. Do this even if it means breaking confidence. Let the troubled person know that you're so concerned that you're willing to get help beyond what you can offer.
- **Emphasize getting through it.** Say that the suicide crisis is temporary. Pain that feels unbearable can be survived.

Seek Help for Mental Health Problems

When should you seek professional help? There is no easy answer to this question. However, as a rule, seek psychological help:

- if you're psychologically distressed
- when you feel helpless and overwhelmed
- if your life is seriously disrupted by your problems

Various mental health professionals can help students. They include clinical psychologists, counselors, social workers, and psychiatrists. Clinical psychologists, counselors, and social workers use psychotherapeutic strategies to help students, but they do not prescribe drugs. Psychiatrists are medical doctors who often prescribe drugs in treating students' emotional problems. They also can conduct psychotherapy.

The counseling or health center at your college is a good place to go if you think that you have a mental health problem. The center will probably have staff to help you or will refer you to a mental health professional in the community. Figure 10.2 shows some reasons college students have sought counseling. In addition, the Journal activity "Visit the Health and Counseling Centers" on page 299 will help you prepare in advance in case you ever need these services.

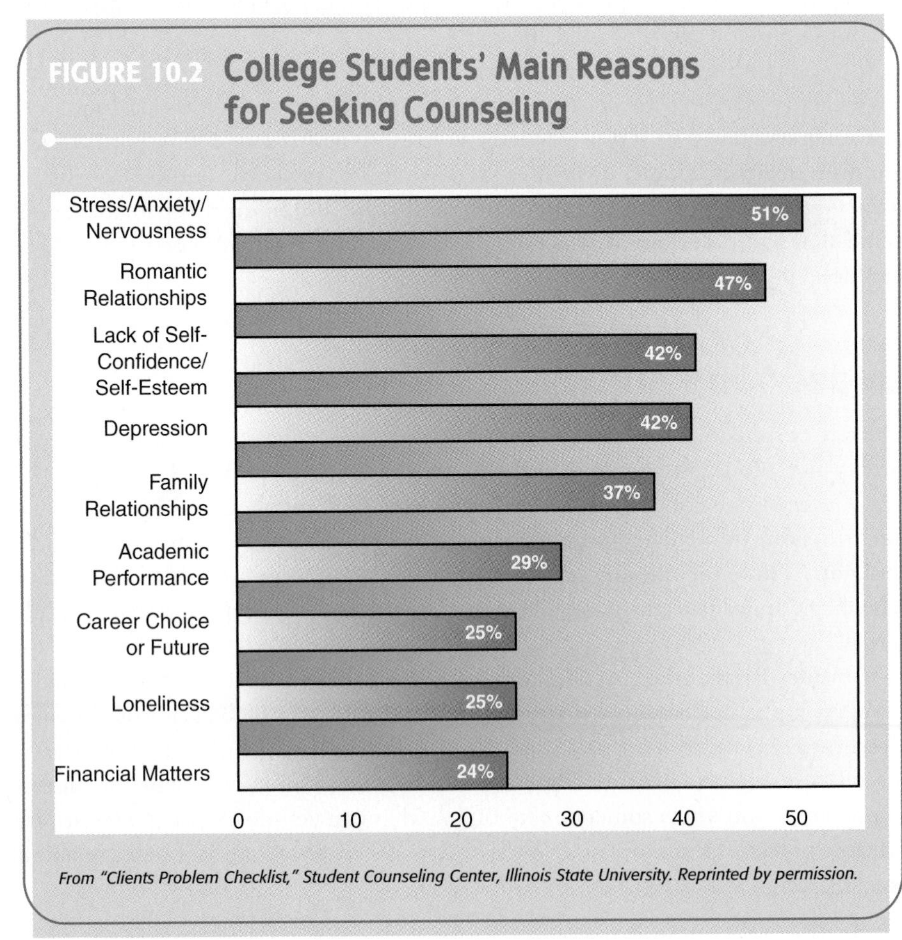

From "Clients Problem Checklist," Student Counseling Center, Illinois State University. Reprinted by permission.

Some students may not admit their problems or seek help for them because they fear others will think they are weak. It takes courage to face your problems. Instead of a weakness, consider it a strength to admit that you have a problem and are willing to seek help for it. You'll be doing something about a problem that stands between you and your goals.

Making changes can be hard. Be patient and allow some time for professional help to work. Part of the success of therapy involves developing a positive relationship with the therapist, so it may take several sessions for you to notice a change. Also, if you do seek professional help, continue to evaluate how much it is benefiting you. Not all therapists and therapies are alike. If you become dissatisfied, ask to be referred to someone else.

More information about mental health professionals is provided in the resource section on the website for this book. Also, the Journal activity "Increase Awareness of Your Health Behaviors" on page 300 will help you further assess the status of your physical and mental health.

It is hard to make people miserable when they feel worthy of themselves.

Abraham Lincoln
Nineteenth-century U.S. president

Summary Strategies for Mastering College

Value and Practice Physical and Mental Skills to Get You in Shape to Reach Your Academic Goals

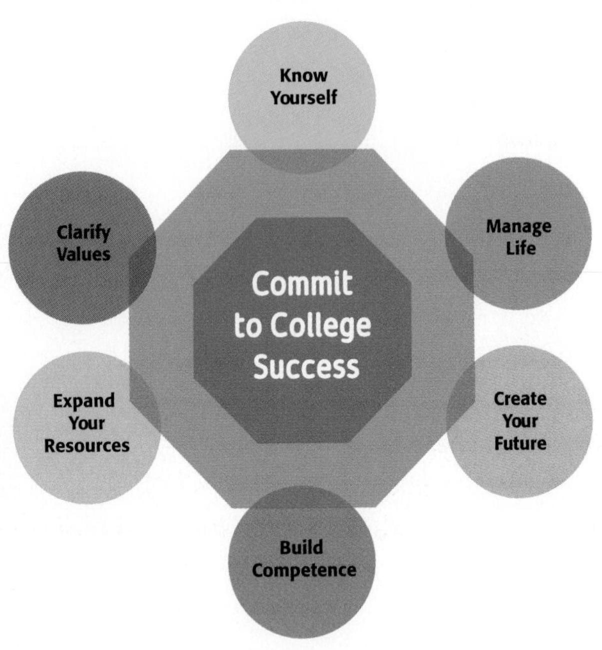

Focus on the Six Strategies for Success above as you read each chapter to learn how to apply these strategies to your own success.

1 Value Health and Adopt a Healthy Lifestyle

- Learn to control an important aspect of your health—your lifestyle.
- Evaluate your health habits to improve them.
- Avoid common risks to college students.

2 Pursue and Maintain Physical Health

- Develop healthy behaviors and address problems.
- Exercise regularly. It will help your physical and mental health.
- Get enough sleep, which for most college students means eight hours or more each night to maximize alertness and productivity the next day.
- Eat right, which means eating a variety of foods, maintaining a healthy weight, and not going on extreme, unhealthy diets. Watch out for the "freshman 15," and avoid anorexia nervosa and bulimia.
- Don't smoke. Smoking is difficult to quit once started. Seek help from the health center of your college if you have a smoking problem.
- Don't take drugs. Alcohol abuse is a major problem on college campuses, and it can seriously undermine success. If you have a substance abuse problem, admit it and listen to what others are saying about you. Seek help for your problem, and use the resources on the website for this book.
- Make the right sexual decisions. Increase your understanding of sexually transmitted diseases and protect yourself against them by assessing your and your partner's risk status, obtaining prior medical exams, using condoms, and avoiding sex with multiple partners. Protect yourself against unwanted pregnancy by abstaining from sex or by using effective contraceptive methods.

3 Safeguard Your Mental Health

- Cope with stress. Some strategies include perceiving stress as a challenge rather than a threat, establishing an optimistic outlook and thinking positively, seeking emotional support, and learning how to engage in deep relaxation.
- Know if you are experiencing depression and your resources for help.
- Know what to do when someone is contemplating suicide.
- Seek help for mental health problems at the counseling or health center at your college. Know that making changes can be hard. Be patient and allow some time for professional help to work.

Review Questions

1. List three strategies you can implement to exercise, sleep, and eat better.

   Exercise strategies:

   1. ______
   2. ______
   3. ______

   Sleep strategies:

   1. ______
   2. ______
   3. ______

   Nutrition strategies:

   1. ______
   2. ______
   3. ______

2. If a person has a drug problem, what are some effective strategies for kicking the habit? List a few ways drug use can negatively impact your success in college.

   Strategies: ______

   Negative effects: ______

3. What can you do to protect yourself from sexually transmitted diseases and unwanted pregnancy?

   Strategies for avoiding STDs: ______

   Strategies for avoiding pregnancy: ______

4. List three effective ways of coping with stress.

   1. ______
   2. ______
   3. ______

5. How can you tell if you have a mental health problem? If you think you have one, what should you do?

Know Yourself

SELF-ASSESSMENT 1

Is Your Lifestyle Good for Your Health?

Your lifestyle includes many components: the ways you work, relax, communicate, and perform other activities. The following assessment is designed to help you explore your lifestyle choices and determine whether they are affecting you positively or negatively. Your responses will help you understand the impact of your lifestyle on your health.

Directions: Respond to each of the statements with one of the following designations: 5—definitely true; 4—mostly true; 3—not sure; 2—mostly false; 1—definitely false.

Write the number that corresponds to your answer in the blank at the left.

_____ I am doing well in school.
_____ I am enjoying myself, not feeling bored or angry.
_____ I have satisfying relationships with other people.
_____ I express my emotions when I want to.
_____ I use my leisure time well and enjoy it.
_____ I am satisfied with my sexual relationships.
_____ I am satisfied with what I accomplish during the day.
_____ I am having fun.
_____ I am making use of the talents I have.
_____ I feel physically well and full of vitality.
_____ I am developing my skills and abilities.
_____ I am contributing to society.
_____ I am helpful to other people.
_____ I have a sense of freedom and adventure in my life.
_____ I feel joy or pleasure on most days.
_____ I feel that my body is fit enough to meet the demands made upon it.
_____ I feel rested and full of energy.
_____ I am able to relax most of the day.
_____ I enjoy a good night's sleep most nights.
_____ I usually go to bed feeling happy and satisfied about the day.

Scoring: Add up the numbers in your answers.

If your score was 90 to 100, you are making lifestyle choices that promote good health. Your lifestyle is making a very positive contribution to your health.

If your score was 80 to 89, you are doing well in many areas. Many of your lifestyle choices are healthful ones. Look at the statements that you marked with a 1, 2, or 3 for areas that need improvement.

If your score was 61 to 79, there are a number of aspects of your lifestyle that could use improvement. Statements to which you responded 1, 2, or 3 indicate areas where you could do better. Your lifestyle choices may be negatively affecting your physical, emotional, intellectual, social, or spiritual health.

If your score was 60 or below, your lifestyle puts your health at high risk. Carefully review your responses, focusing on statements that you marked with a 1 or 2, and decide what you can do now to make better lifestyle choices. Altering your lifestyle will help you preserve your health.

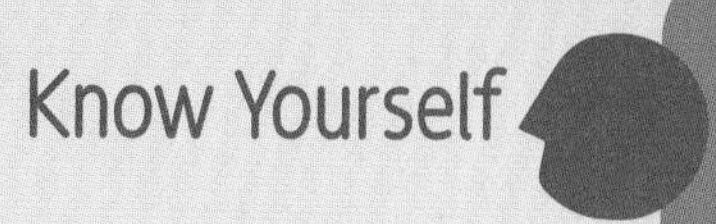

SELF-ASSESSMENT 2

Do I Abuse Drugs?

Check Yes or No to the right of each question below.

	Yes	No
I have gotten into financial problems because of using drugs.		
Using alcohol or other drugs has made my college life unhappy at times.		
Drinking alcohol or taking other drugs has been a factor in my losing a job.		
Drinking alcohol or taking other drugs has interfered with my preparation for exams.		
Drinking alcohol or taking drugs is jeopardizing my academic performance.		
My ambition is not as strong since I started drinking a lot or taking drugs.		
Drinking or taking other drugs has caused me to have difficulty sleeping.		
I have felt remorse after drinking or using other drugs.		
I crave a drink or other drugs at a definite time of the day.		
I want a drink or another drug the next morning.		
I have had a complete or partial loss of memory as a result of drinking or using other drugs.		
Drinking or using other drugs is affecting my reputation.		
I have been in a hospital or institution because of drinking or taking other drugs.		

College students who responded Yes to these items from the Rutgers Collegiate Abuse Screening Test were more likely to be substance abusers than those who answered No. If you responded Yes even to just one of the thirteen items on this drug-abuse screening test, you're probably a substance abuser. If you responded Yes to any items, go to your college health or counseling center for help with your problem.

SELF-ASSESSMENT 3

My Sexual Attitudes

Indicate your reaction to each statement below by choosing a number from 1 to 5 according to the following scale. (The letters to the left of each question will help you interpret your responses.)

Agree Strongly	Agree Somewhat	Cannot Decide	Disagree Somewhat	Disagree Strongly
5	4	3	2	1

(P) _______ Premarital intercourse between consenting adults is acceptable.
(C) _______ Sexual intercourse is a kind of communication.
(O) _______ Oral sex can provide more effective sexual stimulation than does intercourse.
(H) _______ Homosexuals should be eligible for jobs where they may serve as role models for children.
(M) _______ Masturbation is acceptable when the objective is simply to attain sensory enjoyment.
(O) _______ Oral sex should be viewed as an acceptable form of sex play.
(C) _______ Communication barriers are the key factors in sexual problems.
(H) _______ Homosexuality should be regarded as a personal inclination or choice.
(M) _______ Relieving tension by masturbating is healthy.
(O) _______ Women should be as willing as men to participate in oral sex.
(P) _______ Women should experience sexual intercourse before marriage.
(P) _______ Many couples live together because the partners have a strong sexual need for each other.
(C) _______ The basis of sexual communication is touching.
(P) _______ Men should experience sexual intercourse before marriage.
(M) _______ Masturbation should be encouraged in certain circumstances.
(H) _______ Homosexual practices are acceptable between consenting adults.

Now total your responses for each letter category listed to the left of each question and find your grand total.

	Total	Category	Liberal	Undecided	Traditional
(C)	_______	Sexual communication	15–12	11–7	6–3
(H)	_______	Homosexuality	15–12	11–7	6–3
(M)	_______	Masturbation	15–12	11–7	6–3
(O)	_______	Oral sex	15–12	11–7	6–3
(P)	_______	Premarital intercourse	20–12	15–9	6–4
	_______	Grand total	80–60	59–37	36–16

Questions:
In which categories do you have the most extreme opinions, positive or negative?
Do any of your scores reveal an attitude that you might not have expected in yourself?
Would you be able to cope with sexual matters better if any of your expressed attitudes changed? Which ones?

Think about your sexual *behaviors* and sexual *attitudes*:
Do you consciously make decisions about your sexual behaviors?
Would it be better if you did?
Are your decisions about sexual behaviors ever inconsistent with your attitudes?

Your Journal

REFLECT

1. Think about Your Diet

Do you think you have a healthy diet? Let's find out. For one week, keep track of everything you eat, and the times you eat meals and snack. Record this information in a food journal. At the end of the week, review your data. How healthy was your diet? Were there particular days or times when you tended to eat more sweets? List your healthy eating habits and your unhealthy habits below. Then think of ways you can replace unhealthy habits with healthy ones.

Healthy habits: ______________________________

Unhealthy habits: ______________________________

Replacement strategies: ______________________________

2. Examine Your Coping Style

This is good time to take stock of your coping style. Think about how you tend to cope with stress. Examine your life in the last few months. When stressful circumstances have come up, how have you handled them in general?

- Did you appraise them as harmful, threatening, or challenging?

  ____

- Did you repress the stress, or did you consciously make an effort to solve your problems?

  ____

- Did you refuse to believe what was happening or accept the circumstances?

  ____

- Did you try to reduce the stress by eating and drinking more?

  ____

DO

1. Visit the Health and Counseling Centers

Where are the health and counseling centers at your college? Record their addresses below. Stop by and find out what services and materials are available. Describe these services below. Ask for copies of any health or mental health brochures that interest you.

Health center address: ______________ Phone no. and/or e-mail address: ______________

Counseling center address: ______________ Phone no. and/or e-mail address: ______________

Available services: ______________________________

Available materials: ______________________________

2. Write about Your Stress

Follow the advice given in "Build Competence: Writing about Stress," and, over the next four days, write about your deepest emotions and thoughts pertaining to the most upsetting experience in your life. Did this writing exercise make you feel better or worse about this experience? Why?

____

____

Your Journal

THINK CRITICALLY

1. Evaluate Your Sleep

Critically evaluate your sleep habits. Do you have trouble falling asleep or remaining asleep for the entire night? How often do you feel well rested when you wake up? Keep a sleep journal for one week. Record your eating and drinking habits each evening, the time you go to bed, any difficulties sleeping throughout the night, and the time you wake. Do you see any patterns that might be impacting your ability to get a good night's sleep?

____

____

____

2. Increase Awareness of Your Health Behaviors

Go back and review all of the self-assessments you completed for this chapter. What did you learn about your own health behaviors? Did you make any resolutions regarding changing any unhealthy behaviors? Too many people are not aware that they engage in unhealthy behaviors and that these behaviors can have serious consequences. For example, they may not be aware that they are stressed or depressed. How can we help people become more aware of the behaviors that are particularly unhealthy, or their problems that they don't seem to acknowledge? What thinking strategies would you recommend to someone for becoming more aware of these behaviors and problems?

____

____

____

CREATE

1. Become a Movie Producer

Imagine that you're a screenwriter with a major studio. Your task is to create a movie on a college student's health problems, such as drug abuse, anorexia nervosa, or depression. Describe the movie by writing a short treatment of it. Give it a title.

Health issue: ______________________________

Your movie concept: ______________________________

Your movie title: ______________________________

2. Promoting Safe Sex

What type of campaign do you think would be most effective in promoting safer sex on your campus? How do you think you could best reach the most students who are at risk? Come up with a slogan for your campaign and write it down below.

Your safe sex slogan: ______________________________

Campaign strategy: ______________________________

11 Be a Great Money Manager

© Ariel Skelley/CORBIS

KNOW YOURSELF

Money plays a very important role in college success. Knowing how to manage your finances is key to achieving many of your current and future goals. To get an idea of your financial know-how, read the following list and place a check mark next to only the items that apply to you.

- When I spend money, I consider whether or not it's a wise purchase.
- I know what financial success means to me.
- I can accurately describe my regular monthly expenses.
- I know where I would get money in the event of an emergency.
- I organize my spending effectively by using a budget.
- I recognize the demands of succeeding in college and have planned my work schedule accordingly.
- I can describe various financial aid resources at my disposal.
- I am aware of how to establish good credit.
- I avoid unwise use of credit cards.
- I have a plan in case I get into debt.

As you read about Reed Hastings, think about the ways that cutting even small costs can make a difference in your quality of life—both in college and in the long run.

CHAPTER OUTLINE

Take Control of Your Finances

Look to the Future
Recognize Income and Acknowledge Expenses
Budget for Success
Plan to Save

Find the Right Place for Your Money

Open a Bank Account
Manage Your Accounts

Explore Financial Resources

Get a Job
Pursue Financial Aid

Understand Credit

Know the Basics
Know the Myths
Avoid Problems with Credit Cards

Say Good-Bye to Debt

Reduce Your Expenses
Pay It Off Sooner
Consider Friends and Family
Recognize the Incredible Value of School

Images of College Success

Reed Hastings

One night when Reed Hastings had to fork over forty dollars in late fee charges for *Apollo 13* at the video store, it occurred to him that his life could be better. Not only were chronic late charges an annoyance, but they could build up over time and prove costly in the long run. Hastings reasoned that if he were hassled by such minor annoyance, other people probably were as well, and he began looking for a better way (Hopkins 2006).

The better way was *Netflix,* a video delivery service Hastings founded that registers over 125,000 new subscribers every month, proving that others were also interested in avoiding late video fees that eroded their budgets. The system Hastings devised provides a rating system for its options and uses an algorithm to recommend movies that the consumer might like based on other rentals. Hastings patented the delivery model and became a major force not only in entertainment distribution but in Hollywood as well. Films that don't do well at the box office, such as *Whale Rider,* have made a recovery in home distribution through *Netflix*.

Hastings was born in Boston and grew up in Boston and Washington, DC. He was an award-winning mathematics major at Bowdoin College who joined the Peace Corps and reported that he "absolutely loved" working in Swaziland from 1983–85. Hastings then completed a master's degree in computer science at Stanford in 1988, settling in the Silicon Valley, which he described as "nirvana." By 1990 he had founded Pure Software, one of the 50 biggest software companies in the world. When it went public, Hastings's career as an entrepreneur took off.

Since his smashing success in both the software and video distribution industries, Hastings has turned his attention to other political and social concerns. He is a tireless advocate for establishing charter schools as a way of improving the quality of public education. He recently assumed the role of president of the California State Board of Education and has become heavily involved in the state's politics, where many suggest his future looks especially bright.

© Fred Brouser/Reuters/CORBIS

Reed Hastings transformed an irritating late charge on a video rental into the impressive video empire of *Netflix*.

As you read, think about the Six Strategies for Success listed to the left and how this chapter can help you maximize success in these important areas. For example, when you take control of your finances, you not only give yourself peace of mind and free yourself up to focus on your academic goals but you lay the foundation for a financially successful future.

Take Control of Your Finances

Money is a concern for many college students. In a national survey of first-year college students, more than half were concerned about financing college and one in five students had major concerns (Sax and others 2000). Nothing will disconnect you from college faster than running out of money. College students can quickly get into debt by simply spending more money than they have. Credit cards and student loans can quickly pile on responsibilities that have long-lasting effects. A *Money* magazine article (Malhotra 2002) estimates that the average student loan debt upon graduation from a private school registers a whopping $18,000, with public school debt lagging only slightly behind at $16,700. What are some important ways to maximize your control over money concerns so your energies can be freed for academic success?

Look to the Future

You've probably already thought about your earning potential after graduation. Having your degree will give you the opportunity to get a good-paying job, most likely making more money than you ever have before. But what are you going to do with your money? What will you spend it on? How much will you save? Will you have significant debts? Certainly you can't answer all of these questions now, but your values regarding money will help guide you in your planning. Self-Assessment 1, "Where Does the Money Rank?" on page 326 can help you identify and prioritize these values.

Your Financial Values Remember from Chapter 1 that being aware of what's important to you is the foundation that guides your motivation and directs your goals. You may also realize that while your fundamental values will remain the same, your financial circumstances will not. Depending on whether you have more or less money to work with, your opportunities for experiencing life as you value it may change. Thus you not only want to consider how to be financially savvy now but in the future. Developing the habit of using your values to guide your financial plans will make you a better money manager, which could mean the difference between financial security and difficulty.

> ***You cannot prevent the birds of sorrow from flying over your head, but you can prevent them from building nests in your hair.***
>
> Chinese proverb

Where to Start For many students, college marks the start of financial independence and the first time they are faced with their own decisions regarding money. For students starting college later in life, college expenses compete with existing financial burdens. Whatever your circumstance, we hope you came prepared to take on this responsibility. Using the Journal activity "The Money in My Past" on page 329, think back to the money lessons you learned at home and how these experiences have shaped your financial values. This will help you identify what you still need to learn about basic money management.

Sound financial management also entails thinking about your future. Your career exploration has probably included consideration of potential salaries. Will you strive for merely a comfortable life or a posh one? Your decision can energize the pursuit of your degree, but it can also serve as a motivator for becoming financially savvy to produce the financial outcome you desire. If you can't manage your money now, it is not likely you'll do any better when you have more to spend. As you work toward the goal of earning your degree, you also should work toward a financial goal for after graduation as well. Take some time to explore your vision of financial success with the Journal activity "Define Financial Success" on page 330.

Post-graduation debt may be a factor. If you take advantage of any loans during your college years, you will be expected to begin paying them back after graduation. Being aware that you have to incorporate this burden into your financial planning can help direct your budgeting efforts now.

Recognize Income and Acknowledge Expenses

The place to start when managing money is to create a budget—a record of how much is coming in versus how much is going out.

Count It All Most of your income is obvious, such as work paychecks and family money or other sources. But be sure not to overlook additional resources such as predictable special-occasion checks, cash from selling textbooks back at the end of the semester, money returned from loans to friends, and additional income from summer jobs. Accurately predicting your annual income stream is a very important aspect of financial planning. See "Create Your Future: Learn the Role of Money" for what can happen when your predictions are inaccurate.

"There's nothing wrong with your personal finance software. You just don't have any money."

Know Where It Goes Some expenses are easy to anticipate and track. Regular payments for goods and services such as rent, car payments, and your cable bill generally have concrete records for easy reference and tallying. These are considered fixed expenses because the amount is fairly predictable (or "fixed") each month.

Anticipating and tracking variable expenses is more difficult. For example, "entertainment" costs such as attending a concert, going out to dinner with friends, or buying a CD or DVD are more elusive and most likely vary from month to month. You may experience a month or two in which you do more socializing and go out to various functions quite a bit. When college demands increase, you may find yourself eating at home and watching television for an occasional diversion rather than going out and spending. Check out "Build Competence: Following the Money Trail," for ideas on how to keep track of multiple and varied expenditures.

Be Honest with Yourself Begin by acknowledging not just all the ways in which you spend your money but how much you spend. Not owning up to your bad money habits will result in nagging feelings of guilt, frustration, and the sense you are doing less than your best. Recognizing your spending tendencies will enable you to understand better where your money is going and where it will likely go in the future. This awareness should enable you to recognize your power in taking control of the situation. Take Self-Assessment 2, "Are You a Compulsive Spender?" on page 327 to see if you show signs of problematic spending.

Budget for Success

Once you have identified all your sources of income and can acknowledge your expenses, you can create a budget. Your budget should not be simply a static presentation of income versus expenses, but rather a *tool* for assessing where you stand financially. More important, it can help you recognize where you need to make changes to meet your monetary goals. For example, if you discover a great deal of your money is going toward eating out, you can plan to start eating in more often. Or, if you are spending money regularly to repair your car, you might decide to ride the bus or join a car pool. In an extreme case, it may be worthwhile to put your money into a newer, more reliable vehicle.

In college, financial success should be marked by your ability to take the course load you want and have enough time to study and do well in your classes, all the while having as little stress stemming from money worries as possible. In Self-Assessment 3, "Your Money and You," on page 328, you can assess your current financial functioning and whether or not you should be concerned. Also see "Manage Life: Stay Connected" for good suggestions on cutting communications costs.

Choosing a Budget Time Frame There are many ways to approach budgeting. One consideration is the time frame of the budget. Do you want to manage your money on a monthly basis, look ahead six months, or plan for an entire year? When you first begin to make a budget or when you have a major financial change in your life, you may want to work on a monthly basis. This strategy will enable you to focus in more closely on the short-term flow of your money and make adjustments accordingly. Once you've established a routine income and expense cycle, setting goals and planning for longer periods may be more efficient.

The Proactive Budget You also can choose to approach budgeting proactively or reactively.

CREATE YOUR FUTURE

Learn the Role of Money

José had always been careful with his money. His mom worked two jobs to make ends meet, and he had chipped in whatever he could from part-time and summer jobs for as long as he could remember. College was a stretch, but with loans and a part-time job at the local pub he was making it work.

His roommate was a different story. Alan never seemed to worry about money, eating out, buying expensive computer and stereo equipment, and practically living on his cell phone, until the day his credit card was rejected and he realized he had overdrawn his bank account. How could this have happened?

Alan panicked, having no idea how to deal with his debt. José, on the other hand, had lots of good ideas. He helped Alan pick up some shifts at the bar where he worked and arrange a plan to pay off his bank and credit card company in small monthly installments that would leave enough to live on—in a much less luxurious manner. This experience and his business major led José to consider a career in financial planning. He researched internships at the career counseling office and landed a position with Morgan Stanley for the summer. It was mainly clerical, but it allowed him to continue bartending at night and get his foot in the door toward a full-time position after graduation.

Meanwhile, Alan's experience made him realize the importance of finding a career that would allow for the standard of living he preferred; he also recognized that in the future he would have to avoid the debt problems he encountered in college. It was a good lesson to learn in college, while his debt was manageable, rather than later, when it could more negatively impact his long-term credit history.

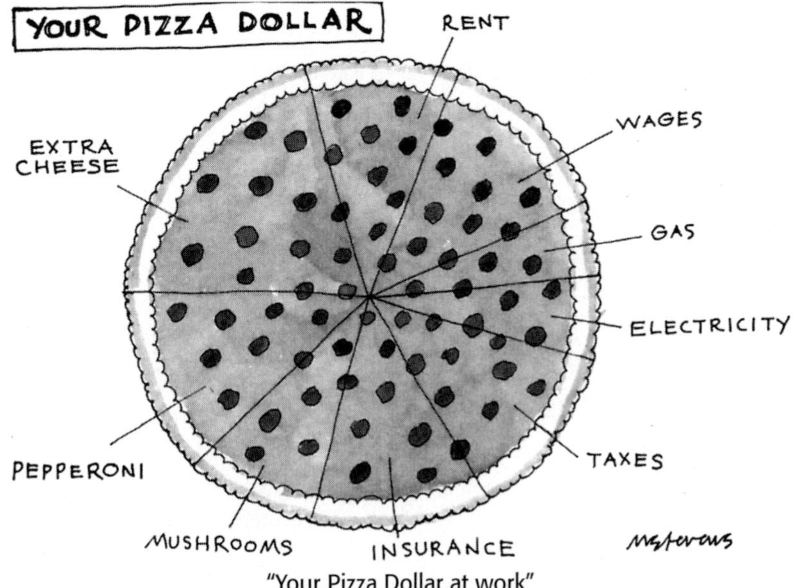

"Your Pizza Dollar at work"

BUILD COMPETENCE

Following the Money Trail

A budget is only useful if it is accurate. Keeping track of all that you spend can be challenging, particularly when you are spending cash, but it is essential for your financial success. Here are a few suggestions to help you identify where your money is going:

- **Use your checkbook register.** When depositing money and writing checks, make it a habit to immediately record the date and transaction in the register.
- **Record the source of deposit.** When making a deposit, note in your checkbook register the source of the income, such as scholarship money, work paycheck, allowance from parents, and so on.
- **Categorize check purchases.** Along with the amount spent and where, record in your checkbook register the *type* of expense, such as food, entertainment, toiletries, gifts, and so on.
- **Keep ATM receipts.** After making a cash withdrawal from an ATM, save the receipt in your wallet or purse and transfer it to a special envelope at home. Use the receipts to identify cash flow from your account.
- **Keep a receipt envelope in your purse or car.** When spending cash for *anything,* keep your receipts. Make it easy by keeping an envelope handy so that you can collect them in one place to use later when budgeting.
- **Note expense category on receipts.** Not all receipts clearly identify the purchases. Quickly jot down what kind of expense it was prior to filing it in your envelope.
- **Keep a categorized file.** Once you get a few minutes at home, transfer the receipts you've collected to an accordion file labeled with your expense categories.
- **File all bills.** When you receive any kind of bill in the mail, from utilities to credit cards, file the statements for future reference.

When you are ready to do your budget, you will find you have clear records of all of your income and, particularly, all of your expenses. Keeping receipts allows you to account for cash purchases, which are hardest to track.

Proactive budgeting involves anticipating your upcoming expenses and making sure they do not exceed your projected income. In this case, you set limits on what you will spend in each expense category in order to stay within your budget.

The Reactive Budget Reactive budgeting involves looking back at what you have earned and what you have spent over a period of time. You already know whether your expenses exceed your income and you can see exactly where your money went. You can then decide what to do with any extra money (save, invest, add it to next month's income) or decide how to offset a negative balance (where to cut back in next month's expenditures). Effective budgeting will actually involve a combination of both planning ahead and looking back. The most important task is recognizing your spending limit and sticking to it!

Your Debt-to-Income Ratio An important figure to be aware of is your debt-to-income ratio. This number can give you an idea of whether you should be concerned about your level of expenditures relative to your level of income. Figure 11.1 provides an example of an actual budget you can use to practice what you have learned. It also demonstrates how to calculate your debt-to-income ratio, and indicates what each result means. Take some time to evaluate your current budget and figure your debt-to-income percentage, to have a greater awareness of your risk for future debt.

Plan to Save

In addition to your monthly expenses, you should budget to save at least a little money each month. There will be both planned and unplanned reasons for you to use money from savings. When you commit to saving money regularly, you will be better equipped to deal with unforeseen circumstances, as well as enable yourself to enjoy unexpected opportunities in the future. In addition, starting good habits about saving now will produce satisfying long-term gains because your savings will have a longer time frame in which to accrue interest.

Expect Emergencies Everyone encounters unexpected events that involve unanticipated expenditures. Given the inevitability of such emergencies, it is important for you to figure out, in advance, how you plan to deal with them. Keep in mind that the farewell concert tour of your favorite recording artist may feel like an unexpected must, but you may be the only one who considers it an emergency. Is being the only one not going on the spring break road trip due to lack of funds an emergency? Probably not. These kinds of expenses should serve as a motivator for you to establish a savings plan, but don't plan to use "emergency" funds. The Journal activity "In Case of Emergency" on page 329 will help you prepare in advance for unexpected expenditures.

The only way not to think about money is to have a great deal of it.

Edith Wharton
American novelist

Anticipate Enjoyment One wise move toward becoming a great money manager is identifying something you want in the future and taking steps to afford it. Whether

FIGURE 11.1 My Monthly Budget

Fill in your budget plan for the next month in the **Planned** column. Then monitor your income and expenses in the next month. A good monitoring strategy is to keep track of all your expenses in a small notebook each day. Keep a running tab of all your expenses for the next month. At the end of the month, write down your actual income and expenses in the **Actual** column.

	Planned	Actual
Income and expenses for the next month		
Family	$ ______	$ ______
Savings	$ ______	$ ______
Financial aid	$ ______	$ ______
Work	$ ______	$ ______
Total Income for the next month:	$ ______	$ ______
Fixed expenses for the next month		
Tuition and fees	$ ______	$ ______
Books	$ ______	$ ______
Supplies	$ ______	$ ______
Housing	$ ______	$ ______
Child care	$ ______	$ ______
Total fixed expenses for the next month:	$ ______	$ ______
Variable expenses for the next month		
Food (at home or prepaid at university cafeteria)	$ ______	$ ______
Food (snacks, lunches, and other meals out)	$ ______	$ ______
Transportation	$ ______	$ ______
Utilities	$ ______	$ ______
Clothing	$ ______	$ ______
Laundry/dry cleaning	$ ______	$ ______
Entertainment	$ ______	$ ______
Hair care/beauty treatments	$ ______	$ ______
Miscellaneous	$ ______	$ ______
Total variable expenses for the next month:	$ ______	$ ______

Add up your total fixed and variable monthly expenses, then subtract this total from your total monthly income. This determines whether your balance at the end of the next month will be positive or negative.

How to Calculate Your Debt-to-Income Ratio

Step One

Add up your total monthly expenditures:

- Rent $150.00
- Car payment $165.00
- Insurance $105.00
- Credit card $ 80.00

Total Monthly Payments: $500.00

Step Two

Divide the total by your income*

$$\frac{\$500.00}{\$2500.00} = 20\%$$

Result

Under 15%	Relax
15–20%	Be cautious
Over 20%	Danger

* Use net pay, after taxes, for income from work paychecks.

> ***If you can eat it, wear it, or drink it, it is not an emergency.***
> Kim Rebel
> *Credit counselor*

you want to take your date to the fanciest restaurant in town, sign up to study abroad, or own a new car, putting money away to accomplish personal goals shows signs of a mature financial thinker. It also puts a positive spin on saving. When you have enjoyable experiences to look forward to, it is much easier to allot money for savings.

Of course, don't plan on using all your savings at once—you still need to have an emergency reserve. However, if you can anticipate the cost of your future goals, you can determine how long it will take to reach them based on how much you budget for savings each month. You may even be surprised at what you are willing to cut back on in order to reach your goal sooner!

MANAGE LIFE

Stay Connected

Most college students take refuge in staying connected to friends and family, but some communication choices can make mincemeat of your budget. Plan wisely how best to stay in touch.

Prepaid phone cards help you make long-distance connections and are available for purchase in numerous drug and grocery stores. Phone cards can cost as little as one dollar or as much as fifty dollars and higher and link purchase price to a set amount of calling minutes. Typically, phone cards offer some of the cheapest phone charges per minute available. Consider buying one card per month for your long distance calls. When you have used up the time, no more calls can originate from your end until the next month.

Cell phones offer monthly plans that can support both local and long distance phone connections. Many models offer other features such as text messaging and video capture. Choose a plan that offers a set monthly charge that is within your budget. Shop around for the best deal, offering the most free minutes per monthly charge. If you find a good deal, consider using a cell phone exclusively and eliminating the monthly payment for a land line. Be sure to clarify if long-distance calls are included in the free minutes or if they involve an additional charge.
Many cell phones inform you of the length of each call to help you keep track of your free minutes used. If you can't get a good deal with free long-distance calls, reconsider whether or not you really need a cell phone. If it is not in your budget, don't have a cell phone simply to be trendy or slightly easier to reach.

Personal data assistants (PDAs) offer more sophisticated ways to stay connected. A good PDA not only provides phone line access but it also facilitates sending and receiving e-mail, video capture and transmission, electronic calendar management, and a host of other handheld features. However, PDAs are very expensive. The unit itself typically can run between three hundred dollars and five hundred dollars, and there are also costly monthly charges that require a long-term commitment. If you can afford it, a PDA can be a great resource. If not, think twice before signing on to a long-term commitment for a fancy device that, although fun, will leave you strapped.

Learn Ways to Save Saving money is all about making choices. How you choose to spend your money ultimately determines how much you have to save. Although it is often a difficult process, saving plays a big role in successful financial planning. You can do many things on a larger scale to save money, such as having additional roommates to share the rent, foregoing cable television, and using public transportation or a bike instead of having a car. These daily sacrifices will lead to a huge payoff in the future. Think about what you might be willing to give up to save money by completing the Journal activity "Simplifying My Life" on page 329.

Smaller-scale options for saving money abound. At first glance such things as clipping coupons and shopping at discount stores may seem trivial, but the money you save can add up quickly. Borrowing from Reed Hastings's experience with late video fees, think about the number of dollars that simply erode from your control because you failed to pay attention to and act on financial arrangements at the right time. Check out "Expand Resources: Beyond Coupons" for many great ideas to get you started in strategies that have a better pay-off.

Be an entrepreneur. There may be some opportunities that you can exploit to expand available funds. For example, faculty may recruit "house sitters" for specific periods of time or look for competent students to perform child care. Or you may look to other avenues to be entrepreneurial. For example, some clever college students have established a thriving cookie delivery business that delivers treats to studying students as late as 3 a.m. Consider how you might be able to solve some needs of your peers on a larger scale and you may be able to generate some interesting opportunities. Next, consider how your entrepreneurial success might shape your future by completing the Journal activity "My Money-Making Dream" on page 330.

Find the Right Place for Your Money

Financial options abound. Although you can invest in goofy strategies for building your financial base, such as playing the lottery or investing in high-risk opportunities, consider the advantages associated with specific financial services. With so many financial institutions available for you to choose from, it is important to be aware of what they offer and how they work.

© Owaki-Kulla/CORBIS

If an emergency occurs, are you financially prepared for it? Make a plan now in case you find yourself facing unexpected expenses.

Open a Bank Account

Chances are good that you already have experience in managing a bank account, but you may not be aware of how widely services can vary among banks. Most banks have a website so that you may gather the information online. Some will even enable you to apply for an account online, without having to visit the actual bank. Specifically check for student banking services. There are often reduced and waived fees for student accounts, and the minimum amount required to open the account, as well as the minimum daily balance, may be significantly lower for students. See "Build Competence: Banking Basics" for a list of things you should inquire about before opening an account.

Choose Checking, Savings, or Both The two primary types of bank accounts are checking and savings accounts. Checking accounts enable you to draw money regularly through the use of checks. One of the primary issues you need to research prior to choosing a bank and opening a checking account are the fees. There can be monthly maintenance fees, a charge for your checks, and a fee for processing each check you write. Some banks do waive some or all of these fees if you open a savings account in addition to your checking account, or if you are a student.

A savings account exists for the primary purpose of putting money in, and rarely, if ever, taking it out. Establishing a savings account gives you a safe place to put away money, where you won't be tempted to touch it. It can also earn a small amount of interest and grow over time.

Money market accounts are a more sophisticated type of savings account. You will have to keep a higher balance, but some of these accounts offer the benefit of overdraft protection. This means that should you write more checks than you have money for in your checking account, the bank will cover it without charging you a fee or returning the check to the recipient.

Whichever type of account you choose to open, there is likely to be a minimum initial amount required for deposit. This is typically lower for checking accounts, with some student accounts requiring a deposit as little as a ten to twenty-five dollars. Savings accounts tend to require at least a one-hundred-dollar initial deposit, and money market accounts usually require around one thousand dollars. You should plan to bring cash, a check, or a money order with you when you go to open your accounts.

> ***The safest way to double your money is to fold it over and put it in your pocket.***
> Kin Hubbard
> *American humorist*

EXPAND YOUR RESOURCES

Beyond Coupons

Clipping coupons is a great way to save money, but there are many other savings opportunities that are available to students. To help you save money, consider the following:

- **Exploit good deals:**
  - Pay attention to on-campus events offering free food and entertainment.
  - Look in the local newspaper for restaurants offering "two-for-one" dinners or student bargain meals. Movie theaters may also have discounted movie times or student discounts.
  - Take advantage of campus resources that are free: tutoring, computer labs with printers, and seminars on job opportunities on campus.
  - For leisure reading, don't forget about the campus or public library. Read their books, magazines, and newspapers instead of buying them yourself. Libraries also offer computer use and Internet access, which may be a life-saver if other campus facilities are busy.

Continued on next page

- Check on the web for discount travel options for students.
- Use the college gym rather than joining a health club.
- Use grocery store coupons to stock up on easy-to-make meals rather than ordering out. All of those pizzas add up.
- Consider a food co-op to make and share meals with others, including other students, who have a similar need to save time and money.

- **Establish a Savings File:**
  - Clip only coupons that you realistically need, to avoid losing time and money.
  - Coupons and fliers for discounts and bargains are useless if you forget about them, so design a system you can manage easily.
  - Keep an accordion envelope labeled with categories, such as "food," "drugstore," "school supplies," "entertainment," and so on.
  - Keep the file in a highly visible, easily accessible place in your dorm or apartment.
  - When you find coupons or receive fliers, file them, highlighting the expiration date.
  - Discard those that have expired so that your file doesn't overflow and become neglected.
  - Check the file on a regular basis.
- **Pursue other sources of discounts:**
  - Your campus newspaper.
  - Fliers posted around the dorm or the student union.
  - Signs posted on stores, theaters, and restaurants.
  - Entertainment coupon books (some must be purchased, but it might be worthwhile to go in on one with your friends or roommates).

Take Advantage of Additional Services It is very common for banks to offer additional services to their customers. Most accounts entitle you to an automatic teller machine (ATM) card, which enables you to withdraw cash at numerous locations. Any branch of your bank will have an ATM, as will branches of other banks. ATMs also are located in grocery stores, convenience stores, some movie theaters, and even fast food restaurants! Inquire about the fees associated with making withdrawals, however. In some cases, banks will charge you to take out cash, if not at their branch locations then at other banks and additional locations. On top of your own bank's fees, you may be charged a fee by the bank where you withdrew the money. Research such charges before you open your account, as some banks offer free ATM use for students.

Debit cards, sometimes called *check cards*, look like credit cards but function like checks. When you make a purchase, the amount is automatically deducted from your checking account. Some check cards double as an ATM card. Debit or check cards offer a safer means to make purchases than carrying around lots of cash. They also may be used for automatic bill payment, which allows you simply to have your monthly bills deducted from your checking account automatically.

The drawback of a check card is that you need to be very diligent in recording your purchases and cash withdrawals as you make them. These items will be noted on your bank statement, but if you don't keep track of how much is deducted on a regular basis, you may spend more money than you have in your account.

Manage Your Accounts

Once you've placed your money in the bank, it is important that you keep organized records and stay on top of managing where the money goes.

> ***I figure you have the same chance of winning the lottery, whether you play or not.***
> Fran Liebowitz
> *American writer*

Balance Your Checkbook A major benefit of having a checking account is that it makes keeping track of your money quite easy. With each checkbook comes a check register—a table for you to fill in all of your deposits and expenditures. Get in the habit of using your check register at the time you make deposits and write checks. Don't wait to record the information when you get home, since you are quite likely to forget. As soon as you sign and hand over a check, note the date, amount, recipient, and purchase in your register. Keeping a current record will enable you to always know how much money is available to you in your account.

Once a month you will receive a statement from your financial institution. It will note any deposits, with the dates and amounts, along with a list of checks, and the dates you wrote them, to whom, and for how much. Also included will be any fees you've incurred or payment for new checks, as well as ATM withdrawals and payments with your check card. You can then reconcile this information with your check register.

> ***Money and success don't change people; they merely amplify what's already there.***
> Will Smith
> *American actor*

The total amount indicated in your register should match that shown on your statement, with the exception of outstanding checks. Sometimes you will have written checks that are not listed on your bank statement. This is because either you wrote them after the ending date on your statement (too late for the bank to include them on that month's record), or because the recipient of the check has not yet cashed it—(it is still *outstanding*).

Also, be sure to note which deposits have been recorded by the bank on your statement. If you just put money into your account, it, too, will not be reflected on your statement. As you note the items shown on your statement in your register, you can then add the outstanding deposits and checks to the total to know exactly how much money exists in your account.

Remember, banks make mistakes! This is why it is crucial that you keep careful records of your income and expenditures. If you can't seem to reconcile your account after a couple of tries, call to speak with someone at your bank. If you don't resolve discrepancies as soon as you discover them, you are at risk for bouncing checks and being overdrawn.

BUILD COMPETENCE

Banking Basics

When opening a bank account of any kind, inquire about the following:

- Is there a minimum amount required to open the account?
- Must you keep a minimum balance in the account? If so, what are the penalties for going below the minimum balance?
- Do they offer any special deals for college students?
- What do they charge for a box of checks?
- What is their fee for processing each check you write?
- What happens if you bounce a check? Do they cover it and charge you a fee, or do they return it to whom it was written?
- Do they offer an ATM card? What are the fees for using it at your bank and its branches? What is your bank's fee for using it at other banks' ATMs?
- Do they offer a debit card? What fees and conditions apply?
- Do they offer online banking? Can you conduct transactions or just check your balance?

Keeping Track of Savings If you are serious about saving, you will want to open a separate savings account. This way, you will be less tempted to dip into that money for regular monthly expenses. The best plan for saving is to commit to doing it on a regular basis. Some banks even offer the option of having a certain dollar amount automatically transferred from your checking account to your savings account each month. As it is deducted monthly from checking, you simply note it in your budget and it becomes part of your financial plan. And, because you don't have to make the effort to deposit it each month, you are more likely to see your savings grow.

Just like your checking account, you will note transactions in your savings account in a register. (Your withdrawals should be few and far between.) Your savings account statements will list both deposits and withdrawals along with any interest you have earned. Most savings accounts accrue interest. The rate is generally fairly low, but the income is there nevertheless. Be sure and note it in your register.

Invest for the Future If you have some substantial savings and would like the opportunity for your money to actually grow beyond your monthly deposits, consider investing it. There are numerous investment options and certain ones, such as mutual funds, can enable a small regular investment in savings to yield dramatic results over a long period of time. For example, if you invested \$100 in an opportunity that yielded 4 percent return, after twenty years the value of the investment would be \$220.50. On the other hand, if you regularly deposited \$100 investment per month to build your nest egg at the same rate of return, the long-term value would be dramatic. In twenty years, your long-term investment would grow to approximately \$36,500. Over a forty-year period, your gain would exceed \$117,000.

These are investments designed for long-term financial gain. If you would like to get a head start on saving for a house, starting your own business, or early retirement, consider contacting a financial planner to find out what it takes.

Although it may not be fun, it's important to reconcile your checkbook records with your bank statement regularly, in order to maximize financial security.

Explore Financial Resources

Whatever your situation, it makes good financial sense to research your financial aid opportunities. There are many types of financial aid; you simply need to know where to look and what to look for. The best place to start is at your campus's financial aid office. The Journal activity "It Can't Hurt" on page 329 will get you thinking about how financial aid might benefit you and what steps you can take to obtain some extra money.

Before you go, make an appointment to meet with one of the staff financial aid advisers. Don't consider it a one-time visit. Map out a plan for funding your education in its entirety and expect to meet with your financial aid adviser prior to each semester. If you develop this relationship, your adviser will be more likely to keep abreast of your situation and alert you to any new options that arise, and you can feel good knowing someone is always working on your behalf.

Get a Job

A recent national study found that 74 percent of full-time college students worked while attending college (King and Bannon 2002), and 84 percent of those students said that they work simply to meet college expenses. In that same national survey, students who worked more than twenty-five hours a week said that working interfered with their academic achievement (King and Bannon 2002). Sixty-three percent of those students, however, reported having no choice but to work that much to pay for their education (see Figure 11.2).

With money in your pocket, you are wise and you are handsome and you sing well, too.
Yiddish proverb

It's true that it takes a lot of money to get a college education, but it also takes a lot of studying and hard work. Although many students find it necessary to work in order to pay for college, that same effort to earn the required fees may hinder one's progress toward actually earning the degree itself.

This situation can lead to very difficult and frustrating outcomes. Students who work long hours are more at risk for failing and dropping courses, at which point it is too late to get their money back. In addition to having lost those fees, they will most likely have to register—and pay for—those courses *again* in order to graduate. Thus, although working more hours earns you more money, you actually end up losing both money and time when work interferes with your success in school.

It makes much more sense to work less and pass your courses the first time around.

However, if working means the difference between staying in school and dropping out completely, by all means, get a job. There are many options available for you to pursue, so take the time to investigate what will work best with your needs and goals. See "Manage Life: Work and School: Finding a Balance" for things to consider when working during college.

Investigate Work-Study Programs and Internships Work-study programs offer opportunities to work either on campus or in the community, earning at least minimum wage or more, depending on the kind of work and required skills for the job. These programs are funded by either the federal government, your academic institution, or both and are based on financial need. Your income is monthly, paid *after* work is completed, and the number of hours you work each week is limited, in recognition of the fact that substantial time is required for schoolwork for you to be successful.

Work-study programs focus on employing students either in community service positions or on campus, often in areas related to your course of study. Students who work on campus have the opportunity to become more connected with school, as they frequently see and interact with faculty and staff, meet more peers, and sometimes have additional access to campus resources. They also benefit from having no commute time between going to class and going to work.

You can find out about work-study positions through your campus financial aid office or career services center. If you do not qualify for work-study, there still may be part-time employment opportunities on campus. Check career services, the campus newspaper, or your institution's website for listings.

If you have declared a major, you may want to find out if there are any paying internships or co-ops available in your related field. Often local companies will hire students on a part-time basis to help them learn about possible future careers and to connect the company with potential future employees. Internships can be a great choice of jobs, not only due to the valuable experience that you will gain working in your chosen field but because company employers are often sensitive to the needs of students. Because they want you to do well in school, they are likely to work around exam and paper due dates, midterms, and finals. Summer internships are also a great opportunity to work more hours, gain experience, and make more money to put away for the upcoming semester. You will learn more about internships and co-op opportunities in the next chapter.

FIGURE 11.2 Relation of Hours Worked Per Week in College to Grades

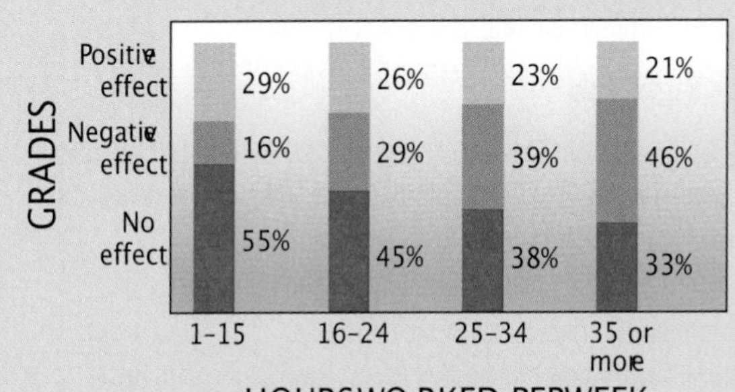

Look for Jobs with Light Work Loads Some jobs require that you be physically present, but they don't necessarily involve constant effort and may allow time to do some schoolwork.

If you enjoy children, you might consider offering your services as a babysitter or part-time nanny. Although child care involves a high degree of responsibility and attentiveness to the children, they may nap or play in their rooms by themselves, giving you the chance to read, review, or outline ideas for a paper.

Working as a student tour guide or a helper in the library reference room also may provide the same study opportunities. Whereas your focus on the responsibilities of your work must be first and foremost, some jobs offer limited "breaks" from the flow of demands, freeing you to spend some time on school tasks.

Be Your Own Boss If you have a talent to share with others, use it to your advantage to make money. If you play a musical instrument, or competitive tennis, or have an artistic flair, consider giving private lessons. You may be an excellent typist or have a great deal of computer know-how. These are also skills that are highly in demand.

If you wish to pursue your own "business," make sure you research competitive fees for your time and expertise (for example, are music lessons going for ten dollars or twenty dollars an hour? Do typists charge by the page or the hour?). You will also need to advertise. It doesn't require a great deal of money, and in many cases you can do it for free. Check out the local bargain newspaper, campus newspaper, or student union

Choose a job that allows flexibility in scheduling to accommodate periods in the semester where your academic load will be heavy.

Work and School: Finding a Balance

If you need or choose to work during your college career, it is important to strike a balance between time spent at your job and the necessary commitment to succeed academically.

Find the Right Job

- Try to get a part-time job on campus. This way you can be close to your classes, obtain easy access to on-campus resources, and have regular contact with faculty, staff, and peers.
- Seek out a job that allows flexibility in scheduling, to work around times of great academic demands.
- Submit your midterm and final exam dates, along with other important due dates, to your employer as soon as possible.
- Talk to people on and around campus to find an employer who is sympathetic to students' needs and offers flexible scheduling.
- Look for a job in which you have periods of time for reading and studying, such as babysitting, manning a switchboard, and so on; or market your skills and be your own boss.

Master Time Management

- Get your monthly work schedule as soon as possible, then plan your classes and study time around work times. Be sure and schedule some down time for rest and leisure activities.
- Break down assignments, papers, and studying into small tasks to do between classes, breaks at work, and shorter periods of time available at home.
- Make the best use of your time at school. If classes are spread out, use the time in between to review, read, study, visit the library, or work in the computer lab.
- Use your commute time between home, school, and work to listen to recordings of lectures or notes you've put on tape.
- If you must have a heavy workload, take fewer classes and get good grades.

Choose the Right Classes

- Talk to other students or research instructor evaluations to find courses that fit your learning needs. For example, look for classes that have fewer regular assignment demands; those offering more frequent, but less intensive, exams; or those requiring more reading as opposed to writing.
- Identify professors who are understanding toward students who work; they should be willing to be flexible with assignment deadlines and demands.

bulletin boards to find out what it takes to present your service. You may even consider creating a website highlighting your skills, work availability, and fees. Not only can you make good money from your own knowledge and skills but when you are your own boss, you can pick and choose when and how much you work.

Be Assertive in Seeking Your Ideal Job Jobs will not just come to you; you must seek them out, especially if you are looking for something different from traditional food service or retail store employment. Those jobs are popular but may not allow you the freedom and time to succeed in school. Many jobs, and particularly internships, are not advertised publicly.

You can often secure an internship by speaking with professors in your major and declaring your need and interest. News about job availability around campus may simply travel by word of mouth, so if you are interested, talk to people in different positions in various departments. If you have other ideas of where you might like to work, pick up the phone and call or visit the location in person. You will learn more about the power of networking in Chapter 12.

Communicate your sincerity in finding a job that fits with your schedule as a student.

Often employers respect and appreciate students and feel that students are responsible and reliable workers. Use your motivation to find a balance, between earning the money you need and doing well in school, to discover and land the right job for you.

Pursue Financial Aid

At this point you have probably already explored what opportunities might be available through financial aid. If you are lucky, you received solid counseling from the financial aid specialists on your campus. Skilled counselors can instruct you regarding the vast array of financial aid that exists for students of all nationalities, religions, majors, ages, and talents. There is aid money specifically designated for women; disabled students; international students; students planning to attend law school, business school, and graduate school; and gay and lesbian students. Review the breadth of the base of your financial counseling. If you think the counseling was not as thorough as it might have been, schedule a return visit and ask for more assistance from someone who will look carefully at all your opportunities.

Scholarships Scholarships are a form of *gift aid*—monetary awards that the student does not need to pay back. Money for scholarships can be provided by any number of groups, organizations, or schools. They are usually awarded on the basis of academic merit or particular talent or skill, such as athletics or music, but not always. Some take into account financial need, others do not. Many are awarded to the most qualified students meeting certain eligibility requirements, such as membership in a particular organization (Future Business Leaders of America, Debate Club, Girl Scouts/ Boy Scouts), participation in a group (church, band, thespians), or children of parents who work for a certain business or are members of a civic group (Kiwanis, Shriners).

Scholarships may be awarded on a one-time basis or may be available for renewal each semester based on performance in school and continued participation in a designated group or major. The application process may be highly involved, with many requiring students to write an essay about themselves, to obtain letters of recommendation, and even to go through a personal interview. Although somewhat time-consuming, putting together scholarship applications can be very rewarding. See "Build Competence: Show Scholarship Savvy" for pointers on putting together a winning scholarship application. Keep in mind that even if you don't receive a scholarship the first time you apply, you may be chosen the next time around. Be persistent.

Grants Another form of gift aid is grants. Unlike many scholarships, grants are awarded on the basis of financial need. The most common grant is the federal Pell Grant, and the amount available to students each year is based on the funding allotted by Congress. For example, the awards for 2004–2005 ranged from four hundred dollars to a little over four thousand dollars.

The amount given to each student is determined by a combination of factors, including whether the student is full-time or part-time (both are eligible for aid), the cost of attending school, and how much money the student's family is able to contribute to the student's education. The government uses a specific formula to calculate this figure, based on information the student provides in the *Free Application for Federal Student Aid* (FAFSA). There are no academic requirements or GPA minimums necessary to receive a Pell Grant; however, certain schools are not considered eligible.

For students with exceptional financial need (as determined by the federal government's lowest expected-family-contribution calculation) there is the *Federal Supplemental Education Opportunity Grant* (FSEOG). Students awarded a Pell Grant have priority to receive an FSEOG but are not guaranteed the aid. Contributing factors in determining funding from this grant are the level of need, funding and financial aid policies of the school the student attends, and the date the student applies for the grant. Applications and information regarding both grants can be found at your institution's financial aid office.

Loans In addition to gift aid, loans are available to help pay for your college education. The largest source of loan money comes from the federal government. Government loans are very appealing because they offer many ideal conditions for borrowing money. The interest rates are low, there are less

BUILD COMPETENCE

Show Scholarship Savvy

If you thought there was an opportunity to secure assistance, you probably have already completed scholarship applications. However, scholarships can become available to you based on your performance or other emerging opportunities. Keep your scholarship application skills viable. You never know when an opportunity will come along.

- **Research.** There are more scholarships available than most students are aware of. Spending time investigating a variety of scholarship websites and publications will increase your chances of finding a list of scholarships that are a good match for you.
- **Organize.** Scholarship applications have numerous parts and requirements for documents. Create a separate folder for each application, attach a checklist of steps required, and file by the deadline date.
- **Provide support.**
  Transcript
  Standardized test scores
  Financial aid forms such as the FAFSA

Continued on next page

Parents' financial information, including tax returns
One or more essays
One or more letters of recommendation
Proof of eligibility (such as group membership credentials)

- **Follow instructions.** One extremely easy way for scholarship screeners to eliminate potential recipients is to discover errors in their application. Be honest in your responses and make sure that you are actually eligible.
  Include all required documents but no additional items. Also follow the specified length requirements for any essays. Do not exceed them, as more is *not* better in scholarship applications.
- **Proofread.** All applications should be completed in ink or typed. Regardless of whether you use your computer's *spell check* option, visually proofread your answers and essays to insure accurate presentation of information.
- **Make copies.** Prior to sending in your application, make a copy of the completed application, along with any accompanying documents, essays, and letters.
- **Beat the deadline.** If at all possible, send your application in well ahead of the deadline. It will not make you more eligible for the scholarship, but you are assured that it will make it there on time. Consider sending it by certified mail.
- **Follow up.** After allowing ample time for your application to arrive at its destination, follow up with a phone call to confirm its receipt. Also consider writing a thank-you note for the opportunity to be considered as a scholarship recipient.
- **Watch your pocket.** Some scholarship screening businesses may promise to find you a bonanza of unallocated money in scholarships. Be careful. You are likely to be better off with the advice of a good financial counselor.

stringent credit requirements, and repayment may be deferred, and/or spread over a longer period of time.

The first step in acquiring a federal loan is to fill out an FAFSA form, mentioned in the previous section. As is stated in its name, obtaining the form and submitting it is *free*, and it can even be done on the Internet. States and schools also may use the information on your FAFSA form to determine eligibility for other aid programs such as grants and scholarships. The FAFSA requires that students and their parents provide extensive information on family occupations and income, as well as tax return materials. An online copy of the FAFSA can be obtained at www.fafsa.ed.gov, and information to help you fill out the form, along with frequently asked questions, can be found at www.ed.gov/studentaid.

The Stafford Loan is the name of the federal loan for students and takes two forms.

The *Federal Family Education Loan Program* (FFELP) involves obtaining the loan through private lenders, but with a guarantee against default by the federal government.

The *Federal Direct Student Loan Program* (FDSLP) involves loans provided directly from the government, but administered by "direct lending schools," which give the money directly to students and their parents. A Stafford loan may be either subsidized or unsubsidized.

The former involves the government paying the interest for the duration of your time in school, and requires demonstration of financial need. Unsubsidized Stafford loans require you to pay the interest; however, they allow you to defer payments until after graduation. Financial need is not a qualifying factor in obtaining an unsubsidized loan, but the amount you may borrow will vary depending on whether you are still a dependent of your parents or are financially independent.

The Perkins loan program is designed for students with exceptional financial need. It is a campus-based program; thus, the amount awarded is determined by your school's financial aid office. Perkins loans have extremely favorable terms if you qualify. They are subsidized by the federal government while you are in school, as well as during a nine-month grace period; the interest rate is then 5 percent and they allow you ten years to repay them. Perkins loans also may be used to supplement other loan-based income that does not completely meet your financial needs.

Debt n. An ingenious substitute for the chain and whip of the slave-driver.
Ambrose Bierce
American writer

Another loan option is the PLUS program *(Parental Loans for Undergraduate Students),* which is federally sponsored and enables parents to borrow up to the full cost of their child's education (less the amount of other aid received). Private loans are also available through banks, credit unions, and savings and loans. The conditions of eligibility, interest, and repayment for private loans vary by institution, so you need to research these carefully before pursuing any particular one.

Under certain circumstances, the federal government may cancel all or part of your loan repayment. Known as *loan forgiveness programs*, participation in AmeriCorps, Peace Corps, VISTA (Volunteers in Service to America), the National Defense Education Act, and others, will qualify you for partial or complete loan forgiveness. To find out more about these programs and the financial potential they offer, talk with a financial aid adviser, or contact each organization directly.

Understand Credit

Our society provides tremendous opportunities for spending money that we don't have. With credit, we can buy a house, a car, go shopping, and even get an education. Credit can be a wonderful option when used correctly, but it also can be the cause of serious, long-lasting problems if abused and misunderstood. When weighing your financial options, you need to consider credit carefully.

Know the Basics

Before you can determine if credit is the right option for you, and in order to implement it correctly, you need to be familiar with the basic terms and concepts. Figure 11.3 provides a list of important definitions.

Establish Good Credit Establishing a good credit history is important for most college students. Many utility companies require a credit check before assigning an account. Further in the future, you might need to lease a car or get a mortgage. These and another installment plan buying options are all dependent on a good credit history. There are several things you should know about establishing credit:

1. Successfully handling a checking or savings account at a bank or credit union is a good means of establishing credit.
2. Creditors look for stability. If possible, remain with the same employer and maintain your place of residence for at least a year prior to applying for any major form of credit.

FIGURE 11.3 Common Credit Terms

Character = The willingness of a potential borrower to repay the debt as determined by his credit history.

Cosigner = A person who, by his signature on a contract, guarantees payment of a debt and is liable for the debt if the original signer defaults.

Credit = A trust that goods and services received now will be paid for in the future.

Credit History = A continuing record of a borroweris debt commitments and how well these have been honored.

Credit Rating = A record of an individual's past credit behavior; rating system assigned by the credit grantor to reflect past credit behavior. Each credit grantor establishes its own criteria for extending credit.

Debtor = A person who receives credit and promises to repay.

Default = Failure to meet payment or to fulfill an obligation.

Finance Charge = The amount charged for the use of the credit services.

Interest = Amount paid for the use of credit over a period of time, expressed as a percentage.

Line of Credit = The dollar amount a lender is making available to a borrower, which may or may not be borrowed.

Overdraft = A check written for an amount exceeding the balance in the signer's account.

Principle = The amount to be paid on the original amount borrowed, not on the interest amount added to the loan.

Repossession = Act of reclaiming property pledged as collateral purchased on credit; for payment that is past due.

3. Utilities such as your electric, cable, and phone bill are considered part of your credit history, particularly when you are just beginning to establish credit. Pay them on time!
4. Having someone cosign on a loan may help, but be sure that person himself has a good credit history. If your partner defaults on his payments, you will be responsible for the remaining balance.
5. If you do take out a small loan, be sure to make regular, timely payments.
6. Application for credit of any kind will be noted on your credit report as an *inquiry.* Numerous inquiries may cause denial of future credit.
7. If you do use a credit card, pay all your bills on time and in full if possible.
8. Prospective employers and current employers both have the right to look at your credit report. Consider what it might tell them if it is problematic.

   Remember that using credit comes with a great deal of responsibility. It is important that before you take on any major financial obligation you are fully aware of the terms and conditions under which you must operate.

Know the Myths

You not only need to know the basics about credit, you need to avoid the myths that surround credit as well. These include the following:

1. *If you check your credit rating, it will drop your score.* Actually, you should know your credit rating, and your informal inquiry should not influence your number.
2. *If you close an old account or pay off a past negative balance, it will automatically improve your credit rating.* Wrong! Credit ratings reflect past action, so the effects of bad credit strategies will linger even if you change your ways.
3. *If you cosign for a loan, you aren't really responsible for it.* This strategy can leave you holding the bag.

Avoid Problems with Credit Cards

College students are a major draw for credit card companies. You may find you have already been pre-approved for several credit cards and can begin charging purchases at any time. Although you shouldn't be discouraged from having a credit card, they need to be accompanied by words of caution. Keep in mind that the average credit card debt for college students is $2,748 (Tyler 2001)! Surely you don't want this to be you.

Calculate the Costs of Credit Credit cards are often offered to students along with several "perks." These may include everything from free hats and T-shirts to very low interest rates and deferred annual fees. What may look enticing in the beginning can catch up with you very quickly.

How many inquiries do you want to have on your credit report simply to collect some free stuff with bank logos on it? If you decide that you need a credit card, make sure you shop around. Interest rates, or annual percentage rates (APRs), can range from as little as 8.99 percent to more than 20 percent! And annual fees are also variable. They may vary based on the balance on your card—the less you owe, the higher the interest rate and vice versa. Even if the company offers a low introductory rate, these usually only last six months, at which point the interest rate can skyrocket.

Many companies have credit cards designed specifically for students. They often have no annual fee but tend to have higher interest rates (15 percent to 20.9 percent).

Some cards offer additional benefits, such as frequent flyer miles, systems for earning points toward free merchandise and dining, annual rebates of 1 to 2 percent of your total yearly expenditures, access to low-interest student loans, and consumer protection so that you won't be responsible for unauthorized purchases.

No matter what "good deal" you may find on a credit card, don't assume it will keep you out of trouble. You are still responsible for charging only what you can afford and making timely payments.

Pay the Balance Every Month Although most credit cards enable you to keep a balance on your card (called *revolving* credit) and only require that you pay a minimum balance each month, the best and safest way to use a credit card is to charge only what you know you can completely pay off when the bill arrives (*open* credit accounts, such as American Express, require that you do this) (CCCS 2000).

What happens if you pay only the minimum? Let's explore a concrete example (Barrett 2003). Suppose you succumb to the temptation of a spring break vacation and charge your thousand-dollar trip. However, when you return, you can only manage to make the minimum payment. At prevailing interest rates, it could take more than fifteen years to pay off your one week of fun. The original thousand-dollar expense will cost closer to twenty-four hundred dollars when your account is settled.

When you pay your bill in its entirety, you know you are not incurring any debt with your card. Despite the initial appeal of simply paying the minimum, this approach to paying credit card bills will cost you significantly more money. If you continually pay only the minimum, it will take years to completely clear your debt. As one student put it, "Who wants to pay interest on a meal eaten a month ago?" (Tyler 2001). For an eye-opening analysis of this phenomenon, read "Clarify Values: The $2,000 Afternoon."

Only pay less than the entire balance if you know that you'll be able to cover your current expense *and* the remaining balance next month. Or you should commit to not using the card at all for the next month in order to only have the remaining balance to pay. However, don't forget to calculate the interest that will accrue on the amount that's not yet paid off—you'll owe that, too. For a look at the effects of compounded interest, see Figure 11.4.

Be sure and make your payments on time. Having a credit card is a fundamental means of establishing credit, so use it in such a way as to ensure you are establishing *good* credit. Mail your payments in order to allow plenty of time for them to reach their destination, and try not to take advantage of the grace period if you are given one. Late payments are one more way of spending more money than is necessary, and in some cases they are noted on your credit report.

One of the benefits of using a credit card is that it provides itemized records of your purchases. Your monthly statements will be very useful for assessing your budget and categorizing your expenditures. Also, keep them on file for future reference for tax purposes and budget planning.

CLARIFY VALUES

The $2000 Afternoon

Susan was so excited when her new credit card arrived in the mail! This was her first one, and she had a credit limit of $1,000. Susan and her roommate decided to go shopping and break in her card. She "took advantage" of numerous sales, but, with all the new clothes she bought (along with the fancy lunch she treated her roommate to), Susan reached her credit limit by the end of the afternoon.

Susan was shocked at how quick and easy it had been to spend so much money and vowed never to use the card again.

She wasn't really worried about affording all her purchases, though, because she knew she could easily make the $20 minimum payment each month. Susan might have thought twice about her shopping spree, however, if she realized that with her 19.9 percent annual interest rate and paying only the minimum payment, it was going to take her eight and a half *years* to pay off her afternoon of fun! Not only that, but her original expense of $1,000 will have doubled, and those same (now outdated) clothes will have cost her $2,000 in extra interest!

Of course, this is assuming Susan never charged with the card again. If she had made additional purchases even after paying her first bill, she would have incurred an over-the-limit fee, because, out of her $20 payment, only $3.50 would have gone toward paying off her principal balance ($16.50 was required to cover the interest). Thus begins a cycle that becomes increasingly harder to break. See below.

Balance	$1,000.00	New balance	$ 996.50
Interest	+16.50	New charge	30.00
Payment	–20.00	Over-the-limit fee	+25.00
New balance	**$ 996.50**	Adjusted balance	**$1,051.50**

FIGURE 12.4 Be Cautious about Compounding

Before you take on the responsibilities of choosing and using a credit card, it is important for you to be aware of the significant impact the interest will have on the price you ultimately pay for things. Investigate the rate at which your interest *compounds*–monthly, weekly, or daily. There is a big difference between interest added to your existing balance once at the end of the year, and interest that is calculated monthly based on your remaining balance, and *added to that balance* each month.

Take a look at the following scenario in which the individual charged $500 and is only paying the minimum requirement of $10 a month. If the individual never charges another thing for the rest of the year, despite putting $120 toward paying off the principal balance, hardly a dent was made. The calculations are based on a 17 percent APR–a very common interest rate for student credit cards–which has a monthly rate of 1.42 percent.

	Month 1	Month 2	Month 3	Month 4	Month 5	Month 6	Month 7	Month 8	Month 9	Month 10	Month 11	Month 12
Unpaid Balance	$500.00	$ 497.10	$494.16	$491.18	$488.15	$485.08	$481.97	$478.81	$475.61	$472.36	$469.07	$465.73
Interest	$ 7.10	$ 7.06	$ 7.02	$ 6.97	$ 6.93	$ 6.89	$ 6.84	$ 6.80	$ 6.75	$ 6.71	$ 6.66	$ 6.61
Minimum Monthly Payment	$ 10.00	$ 10.00	$ 10.00	$ 10.00	$ 10.00	$ 10.00	$ 10.00	$ 10.00	$ 10.00	$ 10.00	$ 10.00	$ 10.00
Balance Due	$ 497.10	$494.16	$491.18	$488.15	$485.08	$481.97	$478.81	$475.61	$472.36	$469.07	$465.73	$472.34

After an entire year, $472.34 is still owed on the initial $500 charge! Out of the $120 paid, only $27.66 went toward paying the principal, while $92.34 was spent on the interest alone.

Imagine if you had charged that money for a spring break trip–the memories might be fading, but you can't afford to go this year, since you're still paying for *last* year. Maybe you purchased new clothes, but they don't fit anymore. You'll still be paying for them whether or not you're still wearing them.

You can continue to calculate this scenario and others at http://www.bankrate.com.

I make myself rich by making my wants few.

Henry David Thoreau
American author

Use Credit Only in Emergencies If you decide you need a credit card for emergency situations only, remember that all of this information still applies. First, be sure to define what a true emergency is, as discussed earlier in this chapter. If you begin to define "emergency" as any situation in which you are without cash or your checkbook, you'd better be careful. All that using the card does is relieve you of having to pay the full cash amount at the time of the emergency. You will still receive a bill within a month for anything charged on your card, and you will be responsible for making the payments. Of course, you can pay off the bill in monthly increments if you need to, but you will be charged interest; and if you have any other purchases on the card, you will have a larger balance on which the finance charges will be based.

For financial safety's sake, an emergency should be defined as a circumstance in which you do not have the cash for something you *absolutely cannot do without.* These would be such things as medical assistance; safe, reliable transportation; food; and required school supplies. In a true emergency, you will have *no other means* for obtaining what it is that you need. Always consider your options in situations—have you been to the health center to see a doctor? Can you use public transportation? Are there computers available to you on campus? Do they have printers? Are there articles or books on reserve at the library?

Define your needs stringently and be willing to use other resources if you want to limit credit card use. Assess your credit card characteristics by completing the Journal activity "A Question of Credit" on page 330.

Say Goodbye to Debt

Sometimes debt is unavoidable. What's important to understand is how to get out of debt as quickly as possible. When you recover from a negative balance, you can get your budget back on track and begin repairing your credit history. In some cases, creditors actually applaud your documented recuperation from being in debt.

Reduce Your Expenses

The first place to start when you discover that you're in debt is to reduce your expenses. Most of us live fairly luxurious lives—even in college. It is the norm now for college students to have their own personal computers, elaborate entertainment systems, cars, and money for first-rate entertainment, such as sporting events and rock concerts. If you find yourself in financial trouble, you need to look at ways to cut your spending.

Spending less can take many forms. Certainly eliminating true luxuries like expensive concert tickets and frequent dining out is one way to save money. But to really get serious about cutting costs, you need to review your basic living expenses:

- *Where you live.* Could you move to a cheaper place? Get an additional roommate (or two)? Move home?
- *Utilities.* Do you like to take long, hot showers? Crank the air-conditioning up in the summer? Leave lights on when you go out? Pay attention to your utility use. Shower quickly, turn off all the lights, and spend much of the summer indoors—somewhere like the library.
- *Transportation.* Could you sell your car and take the bus? Ride a bike? Carpool with others and split the cost for gas? Not owning a car will also eliminate your insurance bill.
- *Food.* Do you eat out a lot? Even fast food costs add up. Start grocery shopping and find quick and easy recipes in the library or online. Don't forget to cut coupons.
- *Television.* Are you paying for cable or a satellite dish? Do you have premium channels? This is a big luxury, particularly if you're a student and watching TV should be kept to a minimum. Stick with the basic channels and rent an occasional movie.
- *Telephone.* Monthly landlines can be expensive with multiple surcharges and taxes. Consider looking for a good cell phone deal and *only* using that.
- *Computer.* Does your school have computer labs? Can you get a school computer account, giving you access to e-mail and the Internet? If so, you don't need your own computer. If you have one, sell it and cancel your account with your Internet service provider.
- *Entertainment.* Redefine what you do for fun. Check out books from the campus or public library to read (or use their Internet services). Go to the park for a picnic. Hike. Ride a bike. Play board games and card games with friends. Go to free on-campus events.

Getting out of debt requires a number of sacrifices, but who knows? You may find you actually enjoy your new, simplified lifestyle.

© The Image Bank/Getty Images

What are your spending habits like?

If you find yourself in debt, there are several options to consider. First, investigate your financial aid options. If you can secure a student loan, or even qualify for some scholarships or grants, that will free up money you would have used for tuition and books; you can apply that money to paying off your debts. If your debts are substantial, you may want to investigate consolidating all of your loans to make your management task easier. Remember, student loans won't have to be paid off until you have a permanent job, and they typically have very low interest rates.

Pay It Off Sooner

To get a handle on outstanding accounts, try to make even slightly larger payments on your smallest bills. This will help you pay them off at a faster rate, at which point you can then do the same thing with your larger ones. When you make a larger than required payment, the extra money is applied to the principal balance rather than the interest. Once your principal sum is paid, your balance is zero.

Begin making purchases with cash only. This will force you to reduce your buying to things you really need, as opposed to unnecessary luxuries. You also can keep immediate track of where your money is going, and when it's gone, it's gone.

Consider Friends and Family

Seek other resources. You may really want to be independent and make it on your own, but it's wiser to ask for help before you get yourself in too much debt. Ask your parents or a close relative to loan you some money to get your finances under control. They may be willing to do so for a low interest rate or none at all. You may want to make it official by drawing up a contract for repayment terms and conditions. Although you will still owe money, family and friends want to see you reach your goals, and thus they are likely to be supportive and understanding.

Recognize the Incredible Value of School

The majority of students who drop out of college have a GPA of 2.5 or above (Boyer Commission Report 1998)! Obviously they aren't leaving because they can't do the work but because they feel they can't afford it. This demonstrates how critical it is to learn to budget effectively, understand credit, and take advantage of financial aid resources. See "Manage Life: When Disaster Strikes, Don't Drop Out" for some important considerations.

When you become a great money manager, you free yourself to focus on your education. Earning your degree is one of the most valuable things you can do for yourself. It is a guaranteed investment of both time and money. What you learn throughout your college experience—knowledge in a particular field of study; skills of time management; effective listening, writing, and speaking; dedication; commitment; and responsibility—you will have forever. Your academic accomplishments are only the beginning, as they will propel you toward growth in all areas of your life. It is this growth and your multitude of abilities that will open the door of opportunity, enabling you to reach your goals.

When Disaster Strikes, Don't Drop Out

If at any point you realize that your financial problems have reached a serious level, consider all of your options before you consider leaving school.

- **Specify your problems.** Begin by mapping out all of your debts and to whom they're owed. By visualizing your financial demands, you can create a plan to begin eliminating them.
- **Tally your resources.** Now make a list of your income possibilities that you can put toward your debts. Also note any ideas for increasing your income, such as financial aid options or working extra hours.

Continued on next page

The sacrifices you may be required to make when you are in college will be difficult, and for most students, a lack of money is one of the main reasons that sacrifices must be made. But talk to people who have graduated and landed a professional job, and they will tell you it was all worth it. Careful budgeting and money management may seem tiresome and unnecessary, but doing so will insure your education and guarantee increased earning power after college. Now complete the Journal activity "Imagine That!" to explore your values regarding money.

- **Identify ways to cut back.** List all of the ways that you could reduce the expenses in your life. Don't hold back. Consider all the things that contribute to your living and entertainment expenses. Add up the money you will save if you cut out cable TV, stop eating out, and get a roommate. Now act on your options.
- **Approach your creditors.** Go down your list of who you owe money to and begin to speak with each creditor. Be honest in telling them your circumstances, and see if they are willing to work with you to defer your payments over a longer period of time. Go to them with a specific plan and amount of money which you are certain you could pay on a weekly or monthly basis. An earnest approach and sincerity about wanting to remain in school will help.
- **Seek credit counseling.** Credit counseling services can be found in most major cities, but your school's financial aid office also may provide this service. People there can help you put together a workable plan for paying off your debts and may serve as liaisons between you and your creditors.
- **Talk to your family.** It is likely that your family members want to see you succeed and graduate. You may want to be independent, and your parents may have told you that you're on your own, but in times of crisis they may be the key to staying in school. They may simply give you money to help out, or they may offer you a no-interest or low-interest loan. It doesn't hurt to ask. That's what families are for.
- **Reduce your course load.** If your situation requires that you either spend less on school or work significantly more hours in order to catch up financially, consider dropping at least some classes.
- **Commit to recovery.** Once you have devised your plan and put it in motion, commit to seeing it through. Know that it is possible to get yourself out of debt, even if it takes awhile.
- **Keep your goals in sight.** Nothing should motivate you more than realizing you are making progress toward your future goals. As long as you remain in school, you are getting closer to graduation with every semester.

Do not quit! Hundreds of times I have watched people throw in the towel at the one-yard line while someone else comes along and makes a fortune by just going that extra yard.

E. Joseph Cossman
Entrepreneur

Summary Strategies for Mastering College

Understand Your Financial Values to Manage Your Money for College and Future Success

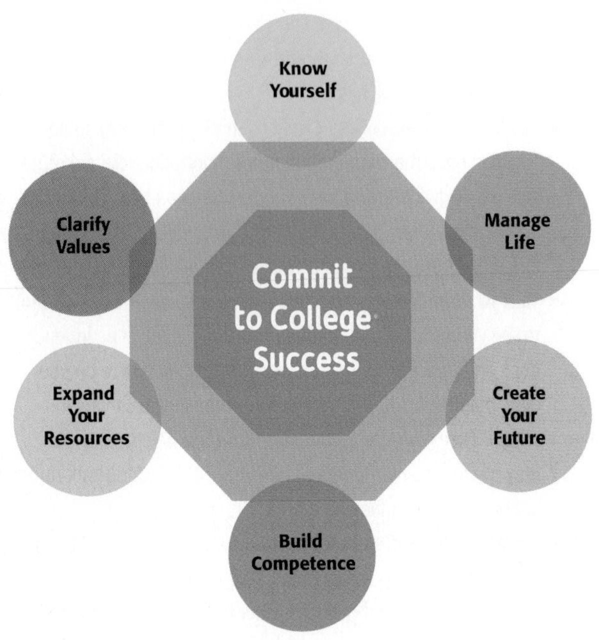

Focus on the Six Strategies for Success above as you read each chapter to learn how to apply these strategies to your own success.

1 Take Control of Your Finances

- Recognize the importance of learning effective money management now.
- Count all your income, know where it goes, and be honest with yourself.
- Create and use a budget to manage your money.
- Figure out a way to start or maintain a savings plan.
- Establish a source of money for unexpected expenses.

2 Find the Right Place for Your Money

- Open a bank account for either checking, savings, or both.
- Learn how to balance your checkbook, keep track of savings, and even invest money for your future.

3 Explore Financial Resources

- Get a job, but work with caution so as not to disrupt your school success.
- Pursue financial aid with the assistance of an on-campus financial aid adviser.
- Learn about the various scholarship, grant, and loan options available to you.

4 Understand Credit

- Establish good credit by learning what's important in a good credit history.
- Avoid problems with credit cards by knowing how credit cards work and your financial responsibilities when you charge.
- Don't be fooled by the myths that can harm your credit.

5 Say Good-Bye to Debt

- Reassess what you spend each month and reduce your expenses.
- Pay bills off sooner by allotting more money for smaller accounts.
- Use cash only to keep spending in check.
- Consider friends and family to help you through difficult times.
- Recognize the incredible value of school and that your education is the best investment.

Review Questions

1. Why is it important to look to the future for motivation to become a good money manager *now*? List three actions you can take now to improve your financial future.

1. __________

2. __________

3. __________

2. Describe a few of the factors to consider when creating a budget and how a budget can be considered a *tool* for assessing your finances.

3. What are some types of financial aid, and why might everyone benefit from exploring these options?

4. What are some advantages of checking and savings accounts? Can you think of any disadvantages?

5. Describe at least three important things to know in order to establish good credit.

1. __________

2. __________

3. __________

6. Explain debt-to-income ratio and why it is important. How should you use this information to evaluate your budget on a regular basis?

SELF-ASSESSMENT 1

Where Does Money Rank?

Rank the following life values in order of importance to you.

____comfortable life
____ job success
____community service/volunteer activities
____large investment portfolio
____culture (movies, theater, and so on)
____new home or condo
____earning a lot of money
____prestige/social recognition
____education/knowledge
____recreation
____excitement/stimulation
____reducing or eliminating debt
____family activities
____religion
____family vacation
____security
____friends
____sense of accomplishment
____happiness/contentment
____shopping/spending money
____health
____starting/maintaining own business
____image/personal appearance
____top-of-the-line products and services
____independence/autonomy

Evaluate your priorities. What aspects of life do you value the most? How much money is required to obtain the things you value? How might you manage your money in order to live your life according to what you value the most? For a more in-depth look at your specific financial goals, also complete Self-Assessment 2 on your CD-ROM.

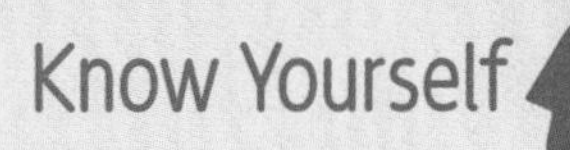

SELF-ASSESSMENT 2

Are You a Compulsive Spender?

Place a checkmark by those statements that apply to you.

____It takes 20 percent or more of my income to pay my debts.
____I spend more when I am depressed and/or angry.
____I am nearing (or at) the limit on lines of credit.
____I make only minimum payments on revolving charges and loans.
____I am charging food/groceries because I lack cash.
____I frequently pay late charges on bills.
____I tap into my savings to pay current bills.
____I have an insufficient or nonexistent savings cushion.
____I would be in immediate financial difficulty if I lost my job.
____I am being threatened with repossession or having earnings garnished.
____I work overtime to make ends meet.
____I have no idea how much I owe.
____I worry about money frequently and feel hopeless and depressed.

If you have checked five or more of the statements, your problem may be due to your spending habits. Begin by examining exactly what you are spending money on, and for those things that are not absolute necessities, be honest with yourself as to why you are spending the money. In some cases, low self-esteem can not only result from poor money management but also may be the cause of it, resulting in problematic spending tendencies.

SELF-ASSESSMENT 3

Your Money and You

Check the column that best represents you for each statement.

	Never	Sometimes	Often	Always
I tend to be late in paying bills; I shuffle them around, paying some this month and others next month.				
I am unsure where my money goes.				
I am at the maximum limit on my bank credit cards.				
I pay only the minimum amount due each month on my charge accounts.				
Some of my creditors have started sending me reminders about overdue payments.				
I frequently have checks bounce or frequently use the overdraft loan feature on my checking account.				
I don't discuss money with my family because I feel uncomfortable or am afraid it will start an argument.				
I've had to borrow money from parents or other close relatives just to meet basic living expenses.				
My financial situation makes me feel depressed and/or affects my performance at school.				

Give yourself one point for each "Never" answer, two points for each "Sometimes" answer, three points for each "Often" answer, and four points for each "Always" answer. Add up your total number of points and divide by nine. The higher your score, the more concerned you should be about your situation.

Total:

From http://www.answerdesk.orst.edu. Reprinted with permission. 1997, Oregon State University

Your Journal

REFLECT

1. The Money in My Past

Think about your experiences with money in the past—earning it, spending it, getting an allowance.

- What lessons did you learn from your family about money? What did you learn from observing their financial management?

- What lessons from your past do you think will be helpful as you become increasingly financially independent?

2. Simplifying My Life

List some examples of things you have become accustomed to having that you really don't need but simply enjoy having as a convenience or little "extra"? How much could you save if you didn't have them?

DO

1. In Case of Emergency

Brainstorm about some emergency situations you might encounter in the coming year such as car problems, doctor visits during flu season, or a family emergency requiring a trip home. List these situations below. Then talk with family members, friends, or your boss to find out to what extent they are willing to help you out in an emergency situation. Adjust your spending to live within your resources.

2. It Can't Hurt

With all of the different kinds of financial aid available to students, you may be surprised to find that there are options that appeal to you and that would alleviate some of your money concerns. Visit your school's financial aid office and speak with a financial aid adviser to investigate. What are some questions you should prepare?

Your Journal

THINK CRITICALLY

1. Define Financial Success

Financial success means something different to everyone. By examining your values, you will be able to define financial success for yourself. Begin with your dreams (and dream big!). What is your financial ideal for the future? Don't feel like you have to use a dollar amount; however, identify what it is you would like to be able to do and use your money for. Do you see those dreams as a reality based on your career path? If not, what might you more realistically be able to expect in terms of "financial success"?

2. A Question of Credit

You've heard many warnings about credit cards for college students, but credit cards also can offer several benefits. Using them appropriately and responsibly is truly a matter of awareness and self-control. What do you find challenging or tempting about having credit cards? What have you done to overcome these challenges and temptations?

CREATE

1. My Money-Making Dream

- If you could be an entrepreneur doing anything you want, what would it be?
- Does it relate to your current career goals? If so, how?
- What can you do now to help make this dream a reality?

2. Imagine That!

Suppose you are one of those very rare individuals who manages to win the lottery. (The odds are not very favorable. It has sometimes been estimated that it is more likely you will be struck by lightning twice when on horseback!) However, if you inherited sudden wealth, what would you do with that resource? Describe five actions you would take if you didn't have to worry about money. Then examine what those actions communicate about your values. How does your imaginary wealthy existence compare to the real values you express in your routine financial decisions?

12 Explore Careers

© Bob Daemmrich/PhotoEdit

KNOW YOURSELF

Concentrate on identifying careers that fit with your values and interests. The time you spend exploring careers will help anchor your college work and your success after college. To evaluate where you are now in your career exploration, place a checkmark next to only those items that apply to you.

- I have begun to explore career options and know of at least one that matches with my values.
- I know what my skills are and how they will help me in a career.
- I know my personality and how it might connect with careers.
- I have ideas about work experiences during college that might help me with my long-term goals.
- I have studied the *Occupational Outlook Handbook.*
- I have talked with a career counselor.
- I have set career goals and planned how to reach them.
- I have networked about careers and job possibilities.
- I know how to land a great job after college.

As you read about Giselle Fernandez, think about how her part-time work in college provided her with an important context for deciding what career path she wanted to follow.

CHAPTER OUTLINE

Evaluate Yourself

Choose Career Options That Match Your Values
Assess Your Skills
Link Your Personality and Career Choice

Acquire Positive Work Experiences During College

Explore Relevant Part-Time and Summer Jobs
Do an Internship or a Co-op
Engage in Service Learning

Become Knowledgeable about Careers

Explore the Occupational Outlook Handbook
Select Several Careers, Not Just One
Network
See a Career Counselor
Scope Out Internet Resources

Set Career Goals

Land a Great Job

Know What Employers Want
Research the Job
Network Some More
Create a Résumé and Write Letters
Knock 'Em Dead in a Job Interview

Images of College Success

Giselle Fernandez

Born in Mexico, raised and educated mainly in California, Giselle Fernandez pursues a genuine passion for journalism. She currently is co-anchor of Los Angeles television station KTLA's morning news show and has earned five Emmy awards for her journalistic efforts. She was the first reporter in twenty years to interview in English Cuban dictator Fidel Castro. Giselle also has her own interview program on the Si TV cable network titled *Café Olé* and heads up her own production company, *Skinny Hippo Productions*, at which she develops programs for cable network TV.

When Giselle decided on a career in politics, she wanted to be near the nation's capital so she applied to Goucher College in Baltimore and received a partial scholarship. She enrolled there and chose a major in international relations. When she was at Goucher, she was awarded an internship to work with a U.S. senator. This experience led her to become disillusioned with Washington politics and motivated her to look for a different career path.

Giselle transferred to Sacramento State University and changed her major to journalism. There she worked for the college newspaper, the *Sacramento Hornet*, and for a magazine, *Executive Place.* She covered news events at the California state capitol in Sacramento. When Giselle went to the state capitol to cover a story, she remembers seeing TV reporters seeming to have more fun than she was as a newspaper reporter and magazine writer. After graduating from Sacramento State University with a major in journalism and a minor in international relations, she embarked on a career as a TV reporter.

Today, Giselle Fernandez is one of the leading Latinas in broadcast journalism. She also actively lectures on subjects of Latina empowerment, health, and fitness, and is active in raising money and awareness for breast cancer research, education, and treatment.

GISELLE FERNANDEZ, a leading Latina broadcast journalist, whose internship and part-time jobs during college helped to shape her career path.

As you read, think about the Six Strategies for Success listed to the left and how this chapter can help you maximize success in these important areas. For example, linking your values with your career goals will help motivate you through college, and knowing yourself will put you on the right track to finding a career that you will enjoy.

Evaluate Yourself

Making the right career choice is a critical step in the journey of life. This is a good time to get motivated to consider several different career paths and evaluate your values, interests, abilities, and skills. As you read this chapter, think about how your career interests and goals align with the courses you are taking and your college major, as well as your general interests. The Journal activity "Collect Inspirations," on page 351 can also help with this process.

Choose Career Options That Match Your Values

An important first step in choosing career options is to know your values. Knowing what you value most—what is important to you in life—will help you refine your career search and choice.

Some people want to pursue a career in which they help others. Some desire a career that is prestigious. Others seek one in which they will make a lot of money. Yet others want one that will give them plenty of time for leisure and family interests. Complete Self-Assessment 1, "My Values and My Career Pursuits," on page 348 to examine your values in relation to your career pursuits.

Clarifying your values helps you zero in on the careers that will likely be the most meaningful and rewarding to you. Once you've decided on a career, you need to set goals, plan how to reach them, and monitor your progress, one of the important strategies for success listed previously. When your values, career choice, and career goals are established and aligned, your internal motivation to think and learn will be strengthened.

> ***Whatever you can do, or dream you can, begin it. Boldness has genius, power, and magic.***
> Johann Wolfgang von Goethe
> *Nineteenth-century German playwright and novelist*

Assess Your Skills

Skills include both your academic and personal strengths. We develop some skills easily while others are more difficult to learn. Honestly evaluating your areas of strength and weakness will help you a great deal in realistically appraising majors and careers.

SCANS Skills The U.S. Department of Labor issues reports created by the Secretary's Commission on Achieving Necessary Skills (SCANS). The SCANS reports describe skills and personal qualities that will benefit individuals as they enter the workforce. It focuses on four types of skills and personal qualities (basic, thinking, personal, and people). You have already studied about and completed exercises related to many of these skills and personal qualities in this book. As you read, consider which skills represent areas of strength or weakness for you.

Basic Skills. Basic skills include:

- ***Reading***
  Identify basic facts.
  Locate information in books/manuals.
  Find meanings of unknown words.
  Judge accuracy of reports.
  Use computers to find information.
- ***Writing***
  Write ideas completely and accurately in letters and reports, with proper grammar, spelling, and punctuation.
  Use computers to communicate information.
- ***Mathematics***
  Use numbers, fractions, and percentages to solve problems.
  Use tables, graphs, and charts.
  Use computers to enter, retrieve, change, and compute numerical information.
- ***Speaking***
  Speak clearly.
  Select language, tone of voice, and gestures appropriate to an audience.
- ***Listening***
  Listen carefully to what a person says, noting tone of voice and body language.
  Respond in a way that indicates an understanding of what is said.

Thinking Skills. Thinking skills include:

- ***Creative Thinking***
  Use imagination freely, combining information in innovative ways. Make connections between ideas that seem unrelated.
- ***Problem Solving***
  Recognize problems.
  Identify why a problem is a problem.
  Create and implement solutions to problems.
  Observe to see how effective a solution is.
  Revise as necessary.
- ***Decision Making***
  Identify goals.
  Generate alternatives and gather information about them.
  Weigh pros and cons.
  Choose the best alternative.
  Plan how to carry out your choice.

- ***Visualization***
  Imagine building an object or system by studying a blueprint or drawing.

Personal Qualities. Personal qualities include:

- ***Self-Esteem***
  Understand how beliefs affect how a person feels and acts.
  Listen and identify irrational or harmful beliefs that you may have.
  Know how to change these negative beliefs when they occur.
- ***Self-Management***
  Assess one's own knowledge and skills accurately.
  Set specific and realistic personal goals.
  Monitor progress toward goals.
- ***Responsibility***
  Work hard to reach goals, even if a task is unpleasant.
  Do quality work.
  Have a high standard of attendance, honesty, energy, and optimism.

People Skills. People skills include:

- ***Social***
  Show understanding, friendliness, and respect for others' feelings.
  Be assertive when appropriate.
  Take an interest in what people say and why they think and behave the way they do.
- ***Negotiation***
  Identify common goals among different people.
  Clearly present your position.
  Understand your group's position and the other group's position.
  Examine possible options.
  Make reasonable compromises.
- ***Leadership***
  Communicate thoughts and feelings to justify a position.
  Encourage or convince.
  Make positive use of rules or values.
  Demonstrate the ability to get others to believe in and trust you because of your competence and honesty.
- ***Teamwork***
  Contribute your ideas to the group in a positive manner.
  Do your own share of the work.
  Encourage team members.
  Resolve differences for the benefit of the team.
  Responsibly challenge existing procedures, policies, or authorities.

Additional Skills The National Association of College Employers conducted a survey of its members. The employers ranked oral communication, interpersonal relations, and teamwork as the three most important skills of a prospective job candidate (Collins 1996). All of these skills involve communicating effectively. Complete the Journal activity "How Good Are Your Communication Skills?" on page 351 to evaluate your skills in this area. Employers also value candidates with the following abilities:

- speaking skills
- leadership skills
- interpersonal skills

- proficiency in field of study
- analytical skills
- writing skills
- teamwork skills
- computer skills
- flexibility

Self-Management Skills Self-management skills were described earlier as important personal qualities. Many people think of work-related skills as engineering, writing, speaking, and computer skills, to name a few. These skills are important in many jobs. However, self-management skills are also extremely important to career success (Farr 1999). By completing Self-Assessment 2, "My Self-Management Skills" on page 349 you can evaluate your strengths in this area.

The skills and qualities you checked off in Self-Assessment 2 are among the most important things a prospective employer should learn about you. They have to do with your ability to be a competent worker in many different situations and to adapt to challenging tasks. Even so, most job seekers don't understand how important they are and don't mention them during interviews. Don't make this mistake.

Link Your Personality and Career Choice

Recall that we introduced two personality scales in Chapter 4, The Myers-Briggs Type Indicator (MBTI) and the Big Five Personality Theory. These two approaches to evaluating personality styles are especially relevant to learning styles. The MBTI was not designed as a career assessment tool, but it is often used alongside interest and aptitude assessments to provide career direction. If you are interested in taking the Myers-Briggs test as part of determining your fit with various careers, contact the career counseling center at your college.

The Big Five personality traits (openness, conscientiousness, extraversion, agreeableness, and neuroticism/emotional instability) have not been widely used to direct career choice. However, the Big Five typology has been used to assess work and nonwork environments that affect career change, work performance, and job satisfaction (Day and Schleicher 2006).

One of the most commonly used systems for examining the link between personality style and career choice was developed by John Holland (1997). Holland believes that there are six basic personality types: realistic, investigative, artistic, social, enterprising, and conventional. Following is a description of each, linked with some appropriate careers:

- *Realistic.* People who have athletic or have mechanical ability, prefer to work with objects, machines, tools, plants or animals, or to be outdoors. They often are less social, have difficulty in demanding situations, and prefer to work alone. This personality type matches up best with jobs in labor, farming, truck driving, construction, engineering, and being a pilot.
- *Investigative.* People who like to observe, learn, investigate, analyze, evaluate, or solve problems. They are interested in ideas more than people, are rather indifferent to social relationships, are troubled by emotional situations, and are often aloof and intelligent. This personality type matches up with scientific, intellectually oriented professions.
- *Artistic.* People who have artistic, innovative, or intuitional abilities and like to work in unstructured situations using their imagination and creativity. They enjoy working with ideas and materials that allow them to express themselves in innovative ways. They value nonconformity, freedom, and ambiguity. Sometimes

they have difficulty in social relationships. Not many jobs match up with the artistic type. Consequently, some artistic individuals work in jobs that are second and third choices and express their artistic interests through hobbies and leisure.

- *Social.* People who like to work with other people to enlighten, inform, help, train, or cure them, or are skilled with words. They tend to have a helping orientation and like doing social things more than engaging in intellectual tasks. This personality type matches up with jobs in teaching, social work, and counseling.
- *Enterprising.* People who like to work with people, influencing, persuading, performing, leading or managing for organizational goals or economic gain. They may try to dominate others to reach their goals and are often good at persuading others to do tasks. The enterprising type matches up with jobs in sales, management, and politics.
- *Conventional.* People who like to work with data, have clerical or numerical ability, carry out tasks in detail or follow through on others' instructions. They function best in well-structured situations and are skilled at working with details. The conventional type matches up with jobs in accounting, banking, and secretarial work.

Rules for Taking Career Tests

Richard Bolles (2006), author of the popular book *What Color Is Your Parachute?,* offered these rules for taking career tests:

1. There is no one career test that always gives better results than others. One career test may work well for you, another one for your best friend.
2. You should take several tests, not just one. You likely will obtain a better picture of your career interests from as many as three or more tests rather than just one.
3. Consult your intuition. You likely know more about yourself than a test does. Treat no test outcome as "gospel." If the test results seem just dead wrong to you, evaluate yourself apart from the test and use your intuition as part of figuring out your career interests.
4. You are never finished with a test until you have done some good, hard thinking about yourself. Career tests can be fun, but just reading the results is not enough. You also need to think deeply about what makes you different from everyone else, what makes you (like your fingerprints) unique. This deeper inquiry about yourself can help you to find the careers that are likely best for you.

Most people are a combination of two or three types and this is taken into account in matching up a person's type with careers in Holland's system.

When taking a test to find out the best careers for you, you should keep in mind a few cautions, described in "Build Competence: Rules for Taking Career Tests."

Acquire Positive Work Experiences During College

As discussed in Chapter 11, students can participate in part-time or summer work, internships, and cooperative education (co-op) programs relevant to their fields of study. This experience can be critical in helping you obtain the job you want when you graduate. Many of today's employers expect job candidates to have this type of experience.

Explore Relevant Part-Time and Summer Jobs

College students benefit more when their jobs are on campus rather than off. This apparently keeps students more in touch with campus life and it takes them less time to commute to their job. Also, on-campus jobs are more likely to be linked with academic pursuits. A good strategy for finding out about on-campus jobs is to go to the financial aid office at your college and ask for a list of available part-time positions. See whether any of them will help you develop skills for a future career.

Most departments on a college campus hire student assistants, usually to perform specialized duties such as website design, data input, or clerical work. If you are interested in a major and career in psychology or biology, you might want to go to these departments and ask if any student assistant jobs are available.

With advance planning, summer jobs can provide good opportunities not only to earn money but also to obtain experiences relevant to your major and career interests. Obtaining this type of summer job can give you a glimpse of the day-to-day workings of a career you might be interested in and provide a better sense of whether this is the type of life work you want to do. Even if you don't find a part-time or summer position that is relevant to your career interests, most jobs allow you to demonstrate work-related skills and a work ethic that any prospective employer will find attractive.

Do an Internship or a Co-op

Many college students wonder: How do I figure out what I want to do? How do I get a job without experience? How do I get experience without a job? What if I spend four years studying in a particular major and it turns out I don't like it? Internships and co-op experiences can help you answer these questions. These are jobs in the real world that are linked to your academic and career interests.

Internships Most internships are part-time jobs that last for about three to six months, although some last longer. The only time that they might be full-time is in the summer and when you aren't taking classes. Some internships pay a little money, but most don't include a salary. Nonetheless, they can significantly help you down the road when you begin looking for full-time employment and a career after college. One study found that students who served in internships during college were 15 percent more likely to find employment after graduation, and 70 percent said that they were better prepared for the workplace because of this internship experience (Knouse, Tanner, and Harris 1999).

Co-ops Co-ops pay a salary and typically last more than a year. Many co-op programs offer academic credit, and a typical student makes eight thousand dollars a year. In four-year colleges, you may not be able to pursue a co-op experience until your junior year, whereas in two-year colleges the co-op experience may be available to both first- and second-year students.

In a national survey of employers, almost 60 percent said their entry-level college hires had co-op or internship experience (Collins 1996). More than a thousand colleges in the United States offer co-op (cooperative education) programs.

Co-ops and internships let you test your career objectives and can help you identify your talents and acquire valuable skills that you may need in a future career. Before seeking a particular co-op or internship, ask yourself these questions:

- What type of work do I want to do?
- In what field?
- In what type of organization do I want to work?
- What skills do I want to gain from the work experience?

For some strategies in obtaining an internship experience, see "Expand Your Resources: Get an Internship Experience."

Engage in Service Learning

A wide range of life experiences during college may also help you explore your values related to careers. One example is *service learning*, which is engaging in activities that promote social responsibility and service to the community (Hart, Atkins, and Donnelly 2006). In service learning, you might tutor, help older adults, volunteer in a hospital, assist in a day care center, or clean up a vacant lot to make a play area. One college student worked as a reading tutor for students from low-income backgrounds with reading skills well below their grade levels. An especially rewarding moment came when one young girl told her, "I want to learn to read like you so I can go to college when I grow up."

There are some signs that U.S. college students are shifting toward a stronger interest in the welfare of society. For example, the percentage of college freshmen who said they were strongly interested in participating in community action programs in the coming year increased from 18 percent in 1990 to 25.6 percent in 2005 (Pryor and others 2005).

Why should you participate in service learning during your college years? Researchers have found that when students participate in service learning (Benson others 2006; Reinders and Youniss 2006):

- Their grades improve, they become more motivated, and they set more goals.
- Their self-esteem improves.
- They become less self-centered.
- They increasingly reflect on society's moral order and social concerns.

To think further about your work experiences and skills, complete the Journal activity "My Work Skills" on page 350.

Become Knowledgeable about Careers

Career exploration involves investigating the world of work and becoming knowledgeable about different careers. Think about what type of work you are likely to find rewarding and satisfying. This involves exploring different job opportunities while still in college as well as conducting research to gather information from many sources about different fields, industries, and companies.

Get an Internship Experience

Here are some recommendations for internship opportunities:

- Check with your academic adviser or the campus career center to find out about the internship opportunities that are available.
- Attend job fairs. Employers often use job fairs to identify students for co-op or internship experiences.
- Contact the chamber of commerce in the city where you are attending college or in the city where you will be living next summer.
- Network. Talk with friends, family, instructors, professionals in the field in which you are interested, and others. Let them know that you want to obtain an internship experience.
- If a particular company interests you, contact the company to see if it has internships that are available.
- The Internet has sites that can be helpful. The following site lists many internships: http://www.internjobs.com.
- Explore *Internships* (Fishberg and others 2005), a book that lists more than forty thousand internships. If it is not available on your campus, call 1-800-338-3282 to find out where it can be located.

Explore the Occupational Outlook Handbook

As you explore the type of work you are likely to enjoy and in which you can succeed, it is important to be knowledgeable about different fields and companies. Occupations may have many job openings one year but few another year, as economic conditions change. Thus, it is critical to keep up with the occupational outlook in various fields. An excellent source for doing this is the *Occupational Outlook Handbook*, which is revised every two years. Based on the 2006–2007 edition, service industries are expected to provide the most new jobs, with professional and related occupations projected to increase the most. Computer and health care occupations are expected to produce the most new jobs through 2014.

Projected job growth varies widely by educational requirements. Jobs that require a college degree are expected to grow the fastest. Education is essential to getting a high-paying job (*Occupational Outlook Handbook* 2006–2007).

You can access the *Occupational Outlook Handbook* online at http://www.bls.gov/oco/home.htm. The handbook provides excellent information about what workers do on the

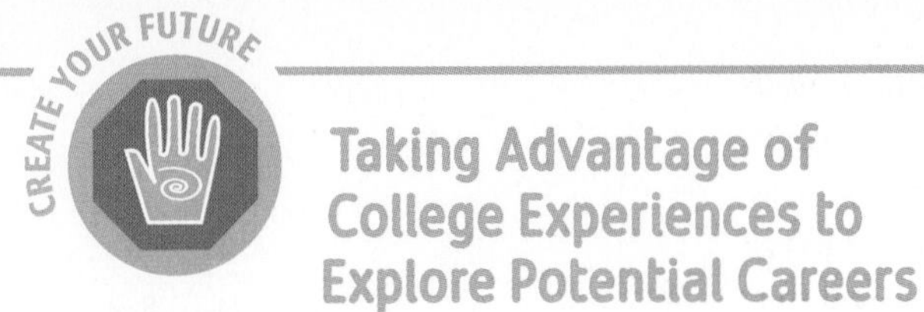

Taking Advantage of College Experiences to Explore Potential Careers

Karen was shocked when her first semester books and supplies wiped out her spending money for the entire term. She checked the college newspaper for part-time jobs, thinking that a position on campus would be more convenient and maybe even provide a chance to get some studying done. She lucked into a job at the college library based on her experience using the Internet and her organizational skills–she had done some filing and clerical work in high school.

Although she was able to get some studying done while things were quiet, she was generally busy helping students do Internet searches for research materials and find journals and articles online. This helped build on her skills in this area and motivated her to take some courses in web design. When the time came to think about a long-term career, she began researching technology opportunities at some of the larger companies in the area, eventually landing a job as an assistant in the Internet support group of a local healthcare firm. Her hands-on experience and a solid reference from her supervisor in the campus library were instrumental to her success.

Tamika was an English major who loved her courses and writing assignments but had no idea how this could lead to any type of career. She approached the chair of the English department, who suggested she consider the area of publishing. She then went to the campus career resource center, which had a list of alumni who were involved in this industry. With phone numbers and e-mail addresses in hand, she contacted a half-dozen resources and lined up a few informational interviews.

Most of this networking was conducted over the phone, as her contacts lived and worked all over the country, but the contacts were still incredibly helpful in teaching Tamika about the publishing industry and suggesting various entry-level career paths. Most important, she learned about an internship program with an educational publisher in her general geographic area and secured a nonpaying internship in the company's marketing department for the summer before her senior year. Although she had to waitress at night to make ends meet, it was worth it for the experience she gained and the contacts she made in the office. She felt confident that she would be seriously considered for a full-time position after graduation and knew what it would take to make herself a top candidate.

job, working conditions, training and education needed for various jobs, and expected job prospects in a wide range of occupations. Libraries are also good sources for finding out more about careers. You might want to ask a librarian at your college or university to help you with your career information search.

Select Several Careers, Not Just One

When initially seeking the right career, it's good to have several in mind rather than just one. In a recent national survey of first-year college students, only 14 percent believed that they were likely to change their major field of interest (Pryor and others 2005). In reality, far more students will. Thus, it pays to be knowledgeable about more than just one career field. It also pays to develop a wide variety of general skills, such as communication, that will serve you well in various fields.

Network

Networking is making contact and exchanging information with other people. Check with people you know—your family, friends, people in the community, and alumni—about career information.

They might be able to answer your questions themselves or put you in touch with people who can. For example, most college career centers have the names of alumni on file who are willing to talk with students about careers and their work. Networking can lead to meeting someone who can answer your questions about a specific career or company. This is an effective way to learn about the type of training necessary for a particular position, how to enter the field, and what employees like and don't like about their jobs. See the Journal activity "Your Network" on page 351.

See a Career Counselor

You might want to talk with a career counselor at your college. This professional is trained to help you discover your strengths and weaknesses, evaluate your values and goals, and help you figure out what type of career is best for you. The counselor will not tell you what to do. You might be asked to take an interest inventory, which the counselor can interpret to help you explore various career options. To think further about seeing a career counselor, complete the Journal activity "Visit Your College's Career Center" on page 350.

Scope Out Internet Resources

The dramatic growth of websites has made instantly available almost countless resources for job possibilities and careers. Most companies, professional societies, academic institutions, and government agencies maintain Internet sites that highlight their latest information and activities.

The range of career information on the Internet tends to overlap with what is available through libraries, career centers, and guidance offices. However, no single network or resource is likely to contain all of the information you're searching for, so explore different sources. As in a library search, look through various lists by field or discipline or by using keywords. Table 12.1 describes some of the leading computer-aided occupation searches. For example, Guidance Information System (GIS) contains information that links careers with interests, physical demands, work conditions, lifestyle, salary, employment potential, and education/training.

Be sure to scan the resources on the website for this book. You'll find some helpful books and web links that explore many aspects of careers. To think further about careers, complete the Journal activity "Why Do People Choose Particular Careers?" on page 351.

Set Career Goals

From your self-evaluation and increased knowledge of careers, a picture should begin to emerge about the kind of work you would like to do and where you want to do it. Once you have decided on one or more careers that you would like to pursue, it is helpful to think about some long-term and short-term goals. It is important that you be able to articulate these goals to employers and interviewers. The kind of information you should think about incorporating in your career goal setting includes (OCS Basics, 2004):

- major career field target
- preferred type of work, including the ideas or issues you would like to pursue
- income requirements
- geographical requirements (city, rural, mobility, near home, climate, and so on)
- special needs (training, management development, advancement opportunities, career flexibility, entrepreneurial opportunity, and so on)
- industry preferences (manufacturing, government, communications, nonprofit, high tech, products, services, and so on)

You can think further about your career goals by completing the Journal activity "My Ideal Job," on page 350.

Land a Great Job

A career-oriented position may not be the only job you are thinking about for the future. You also might be looking for a part-time campus job, a job between terms, or one for next summer. As with exploring potential careers, finding the right job involves doing your homework and becoming as knowledgeable as you can about jobs in which you have an interest. Keep in mind that a part-time campus job may help you gain an interesting full-time job after you graduate. (See "Create Your Future: Taking Advantage of College Experiences to Explore Potential Careers.") Among the most important things for you to do in your job search are:

1. know what employers want
2. research the job
3. network
4. create a résumé and write various letters
5. prepare for a job interview

TABLE 12.1 Widely Used Computer-Guided Career Systems

System	Publisher
Career Information System	Career Information System National Office, Eugene, Oregon
Career Visions	Wisconsin Career Information System, Madison, WI
Career Ways	Wisconsin Career Information System, Madison, WI
Choices	Careerware: ISM Systems Corp., Ottawa, Ontario (Canada)
Modular C-Lect	Chronicle Press, Moravia, NY
COIN	COIN Educational Products, Toledo, OH
Discover	American College Testing, Hunt Valley, MD
Guidance Information System	Riverside Publishing, Chicago, IL
SIGI Plus	Educational Testing Service, Princeton, NJ

Note: To learn more about any of these systems, type in the title of the system or the publisher on an Internet search engine like Google.

From Lee E. Isaacson & Duane Brown. Career Information, Career Counseling, and Career Development, *7th Ed. Published by Allyn & Bacon, Boston, MA. Copyright © 2000 by Pearson Education. Adapted by permission of the publisher.*

Know What Employers Want

In the national survey of employers of college students mentioned earlier in the chapter, employers said that first-year students need to be already thinking about the career they want to pursue (Collins 1996). Graduation and job hunting are only a few years away. Much of what employers look for in top job candidates (such as relevant experience) takes time to acquire. The employers especially recommend that first-year students focus on obtaining:

- work-related experience
- good grades
- computer skills
- leadership positions
- participation in campus or extracurricular activities

Research the Job

Research the type of job that you want, identifying the skills and experience necessary to perform it. Determine both the general requirements of the job and the day-to-day tasks and responsibilities. Brainstorm about a potential employer's needs, attitudes, and goals. Also research the company or employer in general. If you can determine the company's philosophy, you will be able to determine more accurately how you might contribute to the company and whether it is a good match for you.

The more you know about the job, the stronger a candidate you will become. Check out ads in newspapers and use web resources related to your interests and skills. If you are looking outside your geographic area, arrange to receive any newspapers that include job listings in your area of interest, or read them on the web. Two websites stand out for their benefits in a job search. *The Riley Guide* (http://www.rileyguide.com) has an online tutorial that takes you through a series of steps on how to use the Internet in a job search. *The Job Hunter's Bible* (http://www.jobhuntersbible.com) is also a valuable job-hunting resource (Bolles 2006).

Network Some More

Earlier in the chapter, we described networking as a valuable tool for learning more about careers. It also is valuable in a job search and is especially helpful in finding out about non-publicized job openings. When you network, you can ask for suggestions of people that you might contact for information about job or internship possibilities. The personal contact gained through networking can enhance your chance of getting a job; by networking you have a much better shot of getting hired than you would if you had submitted an anonymous application. "Expand Your Resources: Networking Strategies" provides some strategies for effective networking.

> EXPAND YOUR RESOURCES
>
> ### Networking Strategies
>
> These are some good strategies for networking effectively (OCS Basics 2004):
>
> - *Use a wide net.* People you can network with: everybody. This includes professors, guest speakers, people in line at the coffee shop, your parents, their friends, neighbors, high school teachers, tutors, lab supervisors, alumni of your high school and college, and staff members of community organizations.
> - *Network wherever you go.*
> - *Be well prepared.* Be able to clearly spell out as much you know about what you are looking for in a job.
> - *Always be professional, courteous, and considerate.*
> - *Be gracious.* Write a thank-you letter when people take the time to meet with you.
> - *Give back.* Know enough about the people you meet in networking to keep their needs in mind. You may be able to pass along ideas, articles, and contacts that will interest them.

Create a Résumé and Write Letters

To land a great job, you are going to need a good résumé. You also need to know how to write a variety of letters.

Résumé A résumé is a clear and concise description of your interests, skills, experiences, and responsibilities in work, service, extracurricular, and academic settings. There are a number of different styles for résumés, and no particular one is considered universally the best. Use white paper, a font size of ten to twelve points, and black type. There should be no errors—misspelled words, grammatical errors, typos—whatsoever in your résumé. Also, your résumé must be an accurate reflection of your job history and accomplishments. Lies on your résumé will catch up with you.

Three types of résumés are most commonly used (OCS Basics 2004):

1. *Chronological.* This is the most common format, which describes your experiences in reverse chronological order, beginning with your most recent experiences.
2. *Functional.* This highlights your marketable skills by organizing your accomplishments by skill or career area. This format may be the best choice if you have limited work experience related to the job for which you are applying.
3. *Achievement.* This format highlights prior work or academic accomplishments. Use it as an alternative to the first two formats when your accomplishments are centered on a particular skill or experience category.

Most résumés include the following parts (Writers Workshop 2006):

- NAME: Centered and boldface font.
- ADDRESS: Present and permanent. May include your phone number and/or e-mail address.
- JOB OBJECTIVE: This likely will be different for each job you apply for. It summarizes your reason for submitting a résumé (the position you desire) and your qualifications. The rest of your résumé should relate to and support your job objective.

"I threw in a couple of paragraphs about my love life to make my resume interesting."

- EDUCATIONAL RECORD: Begin with your most recent education (college you are now attending) and list all schools attended and degrees earned since high school. Indicate your major and areas of specialization. You may want to include your GPA if you have a B average or better. You might list distinctions and honors, such as the dean's list or scholarships, or you can save these for a separate category, "Awards and Honors."
- EMPLOYMENT HISTORY: List the dates, job title, and organization involved in each job you have held. Do not disclose salary information. This section is organized in reverse chronological order, that is, you begin with the most recent job and conclude with your first.

  Remember that in this section you can include volunteer jobs or working with a professor on a project if these experiences are relevant. Alternatively, these could be placed under "Educational Record" if they are academic or under "Special Skills" or "Activities." Be sure to include a brief description of your work on each job, the tasks you performed, the skills you acquired, any special responsibilities or projects, and promotions or achievements.
- SPECIAL SKILLS: List any skills that are relevant to the job you want but are not mentioned elsewhere on the résumé. For example, list expertise with specific software packages or fluency in foreign languages.
- PROFESSIONAL AFFILIATIONS/ACTIVITIES: List your membership in any professional organizations and any active role or office you have held. Do not include personal interests or leisure activities.
- HONORS AND AWARDS: List any honors you have earned or awards you have received since high school. If you have two honors or less, delete this section and include the information with the "Professional Affiliations" section or under an "Honors and Activities" heading.
- REFERENCES: Don't include references on your résumé unless they are specifically requested. State "References available upon request," and take a typed list of two to four references with you to any job interview (list name, title, organization, relationship, address, and phone number).

For further strategies in writing résumés, see "Build Competence: Résumé-Writing Guidelines." To think further about your résumé, also complete the Journal activity "Current and Future Résumé" on page 350.

Letters Letters provide a great opportunity to communicate in a personal and professional manner. They give you an opportunity to stand out in a crowd. One important rule of thumb is to never use a form letter. Always tailor each letter individually to the person you are writing. Letters should always be addressed to an individual by name and include the person's title and address. If you don't know this information, call or consult the company's website. Among the different types of letters that you might need to write are employment inquiry letters, cover letters, and thank-you letters (OCS Basics 2004).

Employment Inquiry Letter You can write an employment inquiry letter if you have identified a specific organization for which you would like to work. You are not asking for a job but for advice and information.

Introduce yourself and concisely explain why you are writing. Then, demonstrate that you have researched the company, highlight your relevant experience, and clarify why you think you are well qualified for this type of work. Finally, express your interest in obtaining advice from this person, and state that you will call at a specific time, usually in about one week, to arrange a time to meet.

Cover Letter A second type of important job letter is a cover letter that introduces you to a potential employer. You should never send a résumé to a potential employer without a cover letter. The cover letter briefly describes your qualifications, motivation, and interest in the job. Don't just repeat information in the résumé but come up with fresh phrases and sentences related to your experiences, skills, and the job you want.

Thank-You Letters Also get in the habit of writing thank-you letters to the people related to your job search within twenty-four hours of meeting them. This might be done after an informational meeting with someone you have networked with and should always follow a job interview. It might be tempting to follow up with an e-mail as it tends to be more efficient. However, a more formal letter sent through "snail mail" is much more impressive and memorable. Don't cut corners here.

BUILD COMPETENCE

Résumé-Writing Guidelines

Some good strategies for writing good résumés include (Writers Workshop 2006):

- *Do a self-evaluation.* Jot down all your significant experiences, including jobs, course projects, internships, volunteer work, or extracurricular activities. Analyze your experiences in terms of skills that most resemble those needed in your desired career.
- *Write.* After you have determined which experiences are most relevant to the job you want, write short descriptive phrases for each job activity. Use action verbs such as *prepared, monitored, organized, directed*, and *developed*. Emphasize skills by writing phrases such as "designed new techniques for . . . ." Use bullets with short sentences rather than lengthy paragraphs. Whenever possible, give specific evidence to illustrate your skills, such as "Designed new techniques for computer processing, saving the company $50,000 over a one-year period." Decide which of the three résumé styles that we described best suits your needs, then write a draft of your résumé on a word processor.
- *Revise.* Let your draft sit for a day or two, then critically reexamine it. Get other people to look at your résumé, and see what they think about it. Based on these critical analyses, revise the résumé.
- *Print.* When you have written a draft you like, print out an error-free copy on a quality printer and have it photocopied onto good paper. Your final résumé should be only one or two pages. If it is longer, be suspicious of irrelevant or unnecessary material. If your résumé is two pages, make sure the most important information is on the front page.

Knock 'Em Dead in a Job Interview

A key step in getting the job you want is to perform well in an interview. Following are some strategies for success (Yate 2006):

- *Be prepared.* Interviewers ask for detailed examples of your past experience. They figure you'll do as well on the new job as the old one, so the examples you give can seal your fate.
- *Know your résumé.* Résumés are important. Employers use them to decide whether they want to interview you in the first place and will often ask questions about what they contain. Organize your résumé, write it clearly, and avoid jargon.
- *Don't wing the interview.* Do your homework. Find out as much about your prospective employer as possible. What does the company do? How successful is it? Employers are impressed by applicants who have taken the time to learn about their organization. This is true whether you are interviewing for a part-time job at your college library or for a full-time job in a large company after you graduate.
- *Anticipate what questions you'll be asked.* Do some practice interviews. Typical interview questions include "What is your greatest strength?" "What interests you the most about this job?" "Why should I hire you?" Also be prepared for some zingers. For example, how would you respond to "Tell me something you're not very proud of" or "Describe a situation where your idea was criticized"? These are examples of questions some interviewers ask to catch you off guard and to see how you handle the situation.
- *Ask appropriate job-related questions.* Review the job's requirements with the interviewer.
- *Keep your cool.* Always leave in the same polite way you entered.
- *Decide whether you want the job.* If so, ask for it. Tell the interviewer that you're excited about the job and that you can do it competently. If it isn't offered on the spot, ask when the two of you can talk again.
- *Follow up.* Immediately after the interview, send your follow-up letter. Keep it short, less than one page. Mail it within twenty-four hours of the interview. If the decision is going to be made in the next few days, consider hand delivering the letter. If you do not hear anything within five days, call the organization to ask about the status of the job.

Summary Strategies for Mastering College

Explore Careers and Jobs and Link Them to Your Values to Motivate Yourself Through College

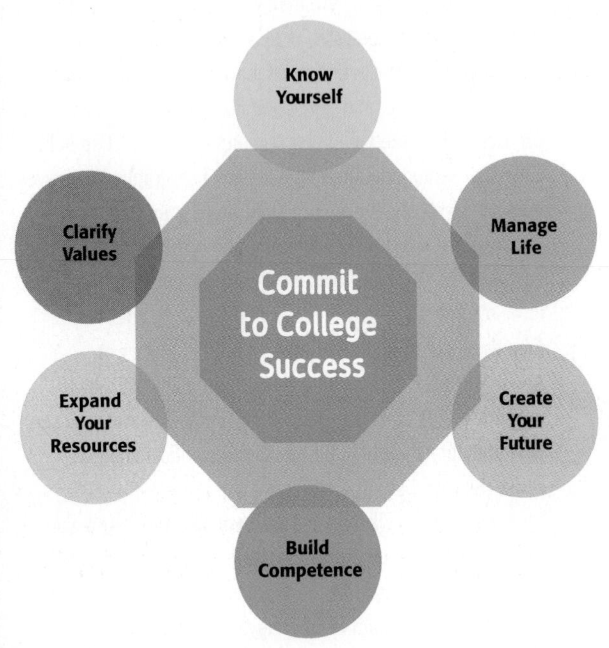

Focus on the Six Strategies for Success above as you read each chapter to learn how to apply these strategies to your own success.

1 Evaluate Yourself

- Choose career options that match your values.
- Assess your academic and personal strengths as well as your communication skills.
- Evaluate your self-management skills.
- Link your personality and career choice, considering Holland's system.

2 Acquire Positive Work Experiences During College

- Explore relevant part-time and summer jobs to make money and obtain relevant work experience.
- Consider an internship or a co-op position to gain valuable experience and explore different careers.
- Engage in service learning to improve your motivation, grades, and self-esteem.

3 Become Knowledgeable about Careers

- Explore the *Occupational Outlook Handbook* to assess career opportunities.
- Consider several careers and develop general skills.
- Network to learn more about career options.
- See a career counselor to explore your strengths and weaknesses and assess your interests.
- Scope out Internet resources to learn more about various companies and positions.

4 Set Career Goals

- Know your short- and long-term goals for a career.
- Understand how to articulate your goals to a potential employer.

5 Land a Great Job

- Know what employers want and focus on obtaining those skills.
- Research the type of job you want.
- Network some more to find out about all possible job opportunities.
- Learn how to create a résumé organized chronologically, functionally, or based on achievements.
- Know how to write an appropriate employment inquiry letter, cover letter, and thank-you letter.
- Knock 'em dead in a job interview by being prepared, anticipating questions, asking appropriate questions, and following up.

Review Questions

1. List a few important aspects of evaluating the career(s) you want to pursue.

2. What are some of the most effective ways to acquire work experience while you are still in college?

3. Describe some advantages of networking and using the Internet to explore career opportunities.

4. List three strategies for creating a strong résumé. Which one do you think will work best for you?
   1. ______
   2. ______
   3. ______

5. Describe three types of letters that are part of the career-exploration process. List a few aspects of each.
   1. ______
   2. ______
   3. ______

Know Yourself

SELF-ASSESSMENT 1

My Values and My Career Pursuits

Place a checkmark next to those values you consider important in a career.

____ work with people I like

____ feel powerful

____ have peace of mind

____ make a lot of money

____ be happy

____ have self-respect

____ contribute to the welfare of others

____ not have to work long hours

____ be mentally challenged

____ be self-fulfilled

____ have opportunities for advancement

____ work in a setting where moral values are emphasized

____ have plenty of time for leisure pursuits

____ have plenty of time to spend with family

____ work in a good geographical location

____ be creative

____ work where physical and mental health are important

____ other: ____

____ other: ____

____ other: ____

As you explore careers, keep the values you checked off in mind. How do those values match the careers you've thought about pursuing? Explain.

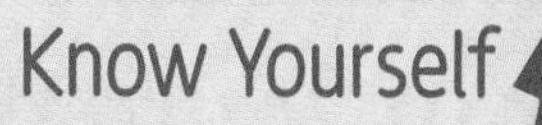

SELF-ASSESSMENT 2

My Self-Management Skills

To explore your self-management skills, place a checkmark next to any skills and qualities that you believe you have.

____ accept supervision
____ complete assignments
____ get along with coworkers
____ learn quickly
____ get things done on time
____ take pride in work
____ good attendance
____ sense of humor
____ hard working
____ honest
____ productive
____ punctual
____ able to coordinate
____ ambitious
____ assertive
____ cheerful
____ conscientious
____ creative
____ dependable
____ eager
____ energetic
____ flexible
____ well-organized
____ friendly
____ helpful
____ humble
____ imaginative
____ intelligent
____ loyal
____ mature
____ motivated
____ open-minded
____ optimistic
____ patient
____ persistent
____ responsible
____ self-confident
____ sincere
____ trustworthy
____ other: ______________________________
____ other: ______________________________
____ other: ______________________________

Now go back through the list and select your five strongest self-management skills. Number them 1–5. Are there any items you did not place a check mark next to that you think would help you in the careers you might pursue? If so, what can you do to develop these self-management skills and qualities? Make sure to mention these strengths in future interviews.

From J. M. Farr, *America's Top Jobs for College Graduates*, 3rd ed., (Indianapolis, IN: JIST Works, 1999): 365–6.

Your Journal

REFLECT

1. My Ideal Job

If you have not done so yet, complete **Self-Assessments 1** and **2** before you do this exercise.

- Write down your ideal occupation choice.

____

- Describe the degree you'll need for your ideal job, such as an AA, BA, MA, or PhD. How many years will this take?

____

- On a scale of 1 to 10, estimate your chances of obtaining your ideal job.

Poor 1 2 3 4 5 6 7 8 9 10 Excellent

- What can you do now to increase your chances of obtaining this career?

____

2. My Work Skills

List all of the work experiences you have had so far.

____

Are any of these related to any careers that might interest you? Why or why not?

____

What kind of career-related or general work skills have you demonstrated in these jobs that might be attractive to a potential employer?

____

DO

1. Current and Future Résumé

Based on what you have read in this chapter, begin creating or updating your résumé. List your education, work experience, high school or college campus organizations, and extracurricular activities. List any honors or awards you have achieved. Then write down what you would like your résumé to look like when you apply for your first job after college. How do the two differ?

____

2. Visit Your College's Career Center

Visit the career center at your college. Write down the relevant contact information for future reference.

____

What materials and services are available for your career search?

____

Consider making an appointment with a career counselor. List a few questions you would like to discuss.

____

Your Journal

THINK CRITICALLY

1. Why Do People Choose Particular Careers?

Consider your opinions about different careers. For example:

- Are some people born to be engineers or nurses? Why or why not?
- Did your parents shape your career interests?
- Do your teachers influence your career interests?
- What kind of an impact can mentors have on a career choice?
- Are economic factors important to you?
- What values are most important and why?

---

2. How Good Are Your Communication Skills?

Among the skills that employers want college graduates to have, communication skills are the most important. Honestly examine your communication skills. Rate yourself from 1 to 5 on the following:

	Weak				*Strong*
Speaking skills	1	2	3	4	5
Interpersonal skills	1	2	3	4	5
Teamwork skills	1	2	3	4	5
Writing skills	1	2	3	4	5
Listening skills	1	2	3	4	5

- What are your strengths and weaknesses?
- Find out how important each of these skills is for the job you want to pursue when you graduate from college.
- What can you do now to start improving your areas of weakness?

CREATE

1. Collect Inspirations

Many creative people write down daily impressions, events, and feelings on index cards or in notebooks. These notes can be the raw material from which creative ideas spring.

Some artists tear out dozens of interesting images from magazines and newspapers, put them in boxes, and then return to them for creative inspirations. Start keeping a special box to store your impressions, feelings, and images related to your career interests and dreams. Come back to them from time to time for inspiration.

2. Your Network

Brainstorm for ten minutes about all of the individuals you know who could serve as a career network. This includes family, friends, employers, teachers, and mentors. Write down each name, followed by a sentence or two about how each person might be able to aid your job search. Then write down contact information for each individual. Try to talk with one of these people each week to start building your network now.

References

A

Alberti, R., and Emmons, M. (1995). *Your perfect right* (7th ed.). San Luis Obispo, CA: Impact.

Alverno College. (1995). *Writing and speaking criteria.* Milwaukee, WI: Alverno Productions.

American Pregnancy Association. (2006). *Effective contraception.* Irving, TX: American Pregnancy Association.

American Psychological Association. (2002). *Controlling anger—before it controls you.* Retrieved from http://www.apa.org/pubinfo/anger.html.

Anderson, L. W., and Krathwohl, D. R. (Eds.). (2001). *A taxonomy for learning, teaching, and assessment: A revision of Bloom's taxonomy of educational objectives.* New York: Longman.

Appleby, D. (1997, February). *The seven wonders of the advising world.* Invited address at the Southeastern Teachers of Psychology Conference, Kennesaw State University, Marietta, GA.

Arnett, J. J. (2006). Emerging adulthood: Understanding the new way of coming of age. In J. J. Arnett and J. L. Tanner (Eds.), *Emerging adulthood in America.* Mahwah, NJ: Erlbaum.

Athanasou, J. A. and Olabisi, O. (2002). Male and female differences in self-report cheating. *Practical Assessment, Research and Evaluation, 8* (5). Retrieved May 21, 2006 from http://PAREonline.net/getvn.asp?v=8&n=5.

Austin, A. (1993). *What matters in college: Four critical years revisited.* San Francisco: Josset-Bass.

B

Bailey, C. (1991). *The new fit or fat* (Rev. ed.). Boston: Houghton Mifflin.

Bandura, A. (2006). Going global with social cognitive theory: From prospect to paydirt. In S. I. Donaldson, D. E. Burger, and K. Pezdek (Eds.), *The rise of applied psychology.* Mahwah, NJ: Erlbaum.

Barrett, J. (2003). Excessive Credit Card Use Causes Student Debt Woes, retrieved from http://www.youngmoney.com/credit_debt/get_out_of_debt/021007_03/.

Baumrind, D. (1991). Parenting styles and adolescent development. In J. Brooks-Gunn, R. Lerner, and A. C. Petersen (Eds.), *The encyclopedia of adolescence.* New York: Garland.

Baxter Magolda, M. B. (1992). *Knowing and reasoning in college.* San Francisco: Jossey-Bass.

Beck, J. (2002). Beck therapy approach. In M. Hersen and W. H. Sledge (Eds.), *Encyclopedia of psychotherapy.* San Diego, CA: Academic Press.

Benson, P. L., Scales, P. C., Hamilton, S. F., and Sesman, A. (2006). Positive youth development: Theory, research, and applications. In W. Damon and R. Lerner (Eds.), *Handbook of child psychology* (6th ed.). New York: Wiley.

Bjork, R. A. (1994). Memory and metamemory considerations in the training of human beings. In J. Metcalfe and A. Shimamura (Eds.), *Metacognition: Knowing about knowing.* Cambridge, MA: MIT Press.

Blonna, R., and Paterson, W. (2007). *Coping with stress in a changing world* (4th ed.). New York: McGraw-Hill.

Bloom, B. S., Englehart, M. D., Furst, E. J., and Krathwohl, D. R. (1956). *Taxonomy of educational objectives: Cognitive domain.* New York: David McKay.

Bolles, R. N. (2006). *What color is your parachute?* Berkeley, CA: Ten Speed Press.

Bourne, E. J. (1995). *The anxiety and phobia workbook* (2nd ed.). Oakland, CA: New Harbinger Publications.

Bransford, J. D., and Stein, B. S. (1984). *The ideal problem solver.* New York: Freeman.

Brisette, I., Scheier, M. F., and Carver, C. S. (2002). The role of optimism in social network development, coping, and psychological adjustment during a life transition. *Journal of Personality and Social Psychology, 82,* 102–111.

Brown, F. C., and Buboltz, W. C., Jr. (2002). Applying sleep research to university students: Recommendations for developing a student sleep education program. *Journal of College Student Development, 43,* 411–416.

Brown, F. C., Buboltz, W. C., Jr., and Soper, B. (2001). Prevalence of delayed sleep phase syndrome in university students. *College Student Journal, 35,* 472–476.

Browne, M. N., and Keeley, S. M. (1990). *Asking the right questions: A guide to critical thinking* (3rd ed.). Englewood Cliffs, NJ: Prentice Hall.

C

Cacioppo, J. T. (2002). Emotion and health. In R. J. Davidson, K. R. Sherer, and H. H. Goldsmith (Eds.), *Handbook of affective sciences.* New York: Oxford University Press.

Callahan, D. (2004). The cheating culture. Why more Americans are doing wrong to get ahead. New York: Harcourt Brace.

Canfield, J., and Hansen, N. V. (1995). *The Aladdin factor.* New York: Berkeley.

Carroll, J. L. (2007). *Human sexuality* (2nd ed.). Belmont, CA: Wadsworth.

Carsakdon, M. A. (1999). Consequences of insufficient sleep for adolescents: Links between sleep and emotional regulation. In Wahlstrom, K. L., *Adolescent sleep needs and school starting times.* Bloomington, IN: Phi Delta Kappa Educational Foundation.

Carskadon, M. A. (2006, April). *Adolescent sleep: The perfect storm.* Paper presented at the meeting of the Society for Research on Adolescence, San Francisco.

Cizek, G. J. (1999). *Cheating on tests: How to do it, detect it and prevent it.* Mahwah, NJ: Lawrence Erlbaum.

Clark, M. R. (2005). Negotiating the freshman year: Challenges and strategies among first-year college students. *Journal of College Student Development, 46,* 296–316.

CNET Tech. (2002). *When games stop being fun.* Retrieved from http://news.com.com/2100-1040-881673.html.

Collins, M. (1996, Winter). The job outlook for '96 grads. *Journal of Career Planning,* 51–54.

Courtenay, W. H., McCreary, D. R., and Merighi, J. R. (2002). Gender and ethnic differences in health beliefs and behaviors. *Journal of Health Psychology, 7,* 219–231.

Covey, S. R. (1989). *The seven habits of highly effective people.* New York: Simon and Schuster.

Covey, S. R., Merrill, A. R., and Merrill, R. R. (1994). *First things first.* New York: Simon and Schuster.

Crooks, R., and Bauer, K. (2002). *Our sexuality* (8th ed.). Pacific Grove, CA: Brooks/Cole.

Crooks, R. L., and Bauer, K. (2005). *Our sexuality* (9th ed.). Belmont, CA: Wadsworth.

Csikszentmihalyi, M. (1995). *Creativity.* New York: HarperCollins.

Csikszentmihalyi, M. (1997). *Finding flow.* New York: Basic Books.

Cutrona, C. E. (1982). Transition to college: Loneliness and the process of social adjustment. In L. A. Peplau and D. Perlman (Eds.), *Loneliness: A sourcebook of current theory, research, and therapy.* New York: Wiley.

D

Davis, M., Eshelman, E. R., and McKay, M. (2000). *The relaxation and stress reduction workbook* (5th ed.). Oakland, CA: New Harbinger Publications.

Day, D. V., and Schleicher, D. J. (2006). Self-monitoring at work: A motive-based perspective. *Journal of Personality, 74,* 685–713.

DeFleur, M. L., Kearning, P., Plax, T., and DeFleur, M. H. (2005). *Fundamentals of human communication* (3rd ed.). New York: McGraw-Hill.

Dement, W. C., and Vaughn, C. (2000). *The promise of sleep.* New York: Dell.

DeVito, J. (2004). *Interpersonal communication workbook* (10th ed.). Upper Saddle River, NJ: Prentice Hall.

Diener, E., and Seligman, M. E. P. (2002). Very happy people. *Psychological Science, 13,* 81–84.

Dweck, C. (2006. *Mindset. The new psychology success.* New York: Random House.

E

Economos, C. (2001). Unpublished manuscript: *Tufts longitudinal health study.* Medford, MA: Center on Nutrition Communication.

Elliott, M. (1999). *Time, work, and meaning.* Unpublished doctoral dissertation, Pacifica Graduate Institute.

Encyclopedia of psychotherapy. San Diego, CA: Academic Press.

Epstein, R. L. (2000). *The pocket guide to critical thinking.* Belmont, CA: Wadsworth.

F

Farr, J. M. (1999). *America's top jobs for college graduates.* Indianapolis, IN: JIST Works.

Fishberg, M. T., Lin, A., Skibiki, I., Able, M., Sullivan, A., Oram, F. A., Heinz, C., and Wagner, A. (2005). *Internships.* Princeton, NJ: Peterson's.

Folkman, S., and Moskowitz, J. T. (2004). Coping: Pitfalls and promises. *Annual Review of Psychology.*

Frank, S. (1996). *The everything study book.* Avon, MA: Adams Media.

Fulghum, R. (1997). Pay attention. In R. Carlson and B. Shield (Eds.), *Handbook for the soul.* Boston: Little, Brown.

G

Gardner, H. (1989). *Frames of mind.* New York: Basic Books.

Gardner, H. (1999a). *The disciplined mind.* New York: Simon and Schuster.

Gardner, H. (1999b). *Intelligence reframed: Multiple intelligences for the 21st century.* New York: Basic Books.

Garner, P. W., and Estep, K. M. (2001). Empathy and emotional expressivity. In J. Worell (Ed.), *Encyclopedia of women and gender.* San Diego, CA: Academic Press.

Gewertz, K. (2000). *Harvard University Gazette.* Retrieved from http://www.news.harvard.edu/gazette/2000/06.08/ellison.html.

Glater, J. (2006, May 18). Colleges chase as cheats shift to higher tech. *New York Times. Retrieved from* http://www.nytimes.com/2006/05/18/education/18cheating.html?pagewanted=2andei=5090anden=78a072a6881a89f8andex=1305604800andpartner=rssuserland&emc=rss.

Goldberg, H. (1980). *The new male.* New York: Signet.

Goleman, D., Kaufmann, P., and Ray, M. (1992). *The creative spirit.* New York: Plume.

Gordon, T. (1970). *Parent effectiveness training.* New York: McGraw-Hill.

Gottman, J., and Silver, N. (1999). *The seven principles for making marriages work.* New York: Crown.

Greenberg, J. S. (2007). *Comprehensive stress management* (9th ed.). New York: McGraw-Hill.

Grynbaum, Michael M. (2004, June 10). Mark E. Zuckerberg '06: The whiz behind thefacebook.com. *The Harvard Crimson.*

H

Haag, S., and Perry, J. T. (2003). *Internet Explorer 6.0.* New York: McGraw-Hill.

Hahn, D. B., Payne, W. A., and Lucas, E. B. (2007). *Focus on health* (8th ed.). New York: McGraw-Hill.

Haines, M. E., Norris, M. P., and Kashy, D. A. (1996). The effects of depressed mood on academic performance in college students. *Journal of College Student Development, 37,* 519–526.

Halberg, E., Halberg, K., and Sauer, L. (2000). *Success factors index.* Auburn, CA: Ombudsman Press.

Halonen, J. S., and Gray, C. (2001). *The critical thinking companion for introductory psychology.* New York: Worth Publishers.

Halpern, D. F. (1997). *Critical thinking across the curriculum.* Mahwah, NJ: Erlbaum.

Hamm, M. (2004). Winners never quit! New York: HarperCollins.

Hansen, R. S., and Hansen, K. (1997). *Write your way to a higher GPA.* Berkeley, CA: Ten Speed Press.

Harbin, C. E. (1995). *Your transfer planner.* Belmont, CA: Wadsworth.

Harris, R. A. (2001). *The plagiarism handbook: Strategies for preventing, detecting, and dealing with plagiarism.* Los Angeles: Pyrczak Publishing.

Hart, D., Atkins, R., and Donnelly, T. M. (2006). Community service and moral development. In M. Killen and J. Smetana (Eds.), *Handbook of moral development.* Mahwah, NJ: Erlbaum.

Hasher, L., Chung, C., May, C. P., and Foong, N. (2001). Age, time of testing, and proactive interference. *Canadian Journal of Experimental Psychology, 56,* 200–207.

Higbee, K. L. (2001). *Your memory: How it works and how to improve it.* (2nd ed.). New York: Marlowe and Company.

Hillman, R. (1999). *Delivering dynamic presentations: Using your voice and body for impact.* Needham Heights, NJ: Allyn and Bacon.

Hofstetter, F. T. (2003). *Internet literacy.* New York: McGraw-Hill.

Holland, J. (1997). *Making vocational choices.* Lutz, FL: Psychological Assessment Resources.

Hopkins, J. (2004, April 23). 'Charismatic' founder keeps Netflix adapting. *USA Today,* Retrieved from http://www.usatoday.com/tech/products/services/2006-04-23-netflix-ceo_x.htm?POE=TECISVA.

Horvitz, L. A. (2006). *Meg Whitman.* New York: Ferguson.

Howatt, W. A. (1999). Journaling to self-evaluation: A tool for adult learners. *International Journal of Reality Therapy, 18,* 32–34.

Hurtado, S., Dey, E. L., and Trevino, J. G. (1994). *Exclusion or self-segregation? Interaction across racial/ethnic groups on college campuses.* Paper presented at the meeting of the American Educational Research Association, New York.

Hyde, J. S., and DeLamater, J. D. (2006). *Understanding human sexuality* (9th ed.). New York: McGraw-Hill.

I

International Reading Association, Inc. (1994). Reading Strategies, *Journal of Reading, 38.*

J

Jandt, F. E. (2004). *An introduction to intercultural communication.* Thousand Oaks, CA: Sage.

Jendrick, M. P. (1992). Students' reactions to academic dishonesty. *Journal of College Student Development, 33,* 260–273.

Johnston, L. D., O'Malley, P. M., Bachman, J. G., and Schulenberg, J. E. (2006). *Monitoring the Future: National results on adolescent drug use.* Bethesda, MD: National Institute of Drug Abuse.

Jonassen, D. H., and Grabowski, B. L. (1993). *Handbook of individual differences, learning, and instruction.* Mahwah, NJ: Erlbaum.

K

Kagan, J. (1965). Reflection-impulsivity and reading development in primary grade children. *Child Development, 36,* 609–628.

Kaplan, R. M., and Saccuzzo, D. P. (1993). *Psychological testing: Principles, applications, and issues* (3rd ed.). Pacific Grove, CA: Brooks/Cole.

Kappes, S. (2001). *The truth about Janeane Garofalo.* Retrieved from http://people.aol.com/people/features/celebrityspotlight/0,10950,169561,00.html.

Karlin, S. (2006, May 3). Young inventors of the world unite. IEEE *Spectrum Online.* Retrieved from http://www.spectrum.ieee.org/careers/careerstemplate.jsp?Articleid=i030104.

Keith-Spiegel, P. (1992, October). *Ethics in shades of pale gray.* Paper presented at the Mid-America Conference for Teachers of Psychology, Evansville, IN.

Keller, P. A., and Heyman, S. R. (1987). *Innovations in clinical practice.* Sarasota, FL: Professional Resource Exchange.

Kierwa, K. A. (1987). Note-taking and review: The research and its implications. *Instructional Science, 19,* 394–397.

King, T., and Bannon, E. (2002, April). *At what cost? The price that working students pay for a college education.* Washington, DC: U.S. Department of Education, State Public Interest Research Groups' Higher Education Project.

Knouse, S., Tanner, J., and Harris, E. (1999). The relation of college internships, college performance, and subsequent job opportunity. *Journal of Employment Counseling, 36,* 35–43.

Kroger, J. (2006). *Identity development: Adolescence through adulthood.* Thousand Oaks, CA: Sage.

L

Lakein, A. (1973). *How to get control of your time and your life.* New York: Signet.

Lane, A. M., Crone-Grant, D., and Lane, H. (2002). Mood changes following exercise. *Perceptual and Motor Skills, 94,* 732–734.

Lerner, J. W. (2006). *Learning disabilities and related disorders: Characteristics and teaching strategies.* Boston: Houghton Mifflin.

Levine, M. (2003). *The myth of laziness.* New York: Simon and Schuster.

Levinger, E. E. (1949). *Albert Einstein.* New York: Julian Messner.

Loftus, E. F. (1980). *Memory.* Reading, MA: Addison-Wesley.

Loftus, E. F. (1993). The reality of repressed memories. *American Psychologist, 48,* 518–537.

Loftus, E. F. (2003, March). Our changeable memories: Legal and practical implications: Nature Review. *Neuroscience, 4,* 231–234.

Lorayne, H., and Lucas, J. (1996). *The memory book.* New York: Ballantine.

M

Maas, J. (1999). *Power sleep: The revolutionary program that prepares your mind for peak performance.* New York: HarperPerennial.

MacKenzie, A. (1997). *The time trap* (3rd ed.). New York: American Management Association.

Malhotra, S. (2002). *Five ways to dump student debt early.* Retrieved from www.money.cnn.com/2002/08/08/pf/college/q_payoffloans/index.htm.

Marcus, A., Mullins, L. C., Brackett, K. P., Tang, Z., Allen, A. M., and Pruett, D. W. (2003). Perceptions of racism on campus. *College Student Journal, 37,* 611–617.

Martin, G. L., and Pear, J. P. (2006). *Behavior modification* (8th ed.). Upper Saddle River, NJ: Prentice Hall.

Matlin, M. (1998). *Cognitive psychology* (3rd ed.). New York: Harcourt Brace.

McCabe, D. L., Trevino, L. K., and Butterfield, K. D. Cheating in academic institutions: A decade of research. *Ethics and Behavior, 11,* 219–232.

McKowen, C. (1996). *Get your A out of college: Mastering the hidden rules of the game.* Los Altos, CA: Crisp Publications.

McNally, D. (1990). *Even eagles need a push.* New York: Dell.

McWhorter, K. T. (2000). *Study and critical thinking skills in college* (4th ed.). New York: Longman.

Mercer, C. D., and Mercer, A. R. *Teaching students with learning problems* (7th ed.). Upper Saddle River, NJ: Pearson.

Michael, R. T., Gagnon, J. H., Laumann, E. O., and Kolata, G. (1994). *Sex in America.* Boston: Little, Brown.

Miller, G. A. (1956). The magical number seven, plus or minus two: Some limits on our capacity for information processing. *Psychological Review, 48,* 337–442.

Miller, J. B. (1986). *Toward a new psychology of women* (2nd ed.). Boston: Beacon Press.

Missimer, C. (2005). *Good arguments: An introduction to critical thinking* (4th ed.). Upper Saddle River, NJ: Pearson Prentice Hall.

Mrosko, T. (2002). *Keys to successful networking.* Retrieved from http://www.iwritesite.com/keys.html.

Murphy, M. C. (1996). Stressors on the college campus: A comparison of 1985 and 1993. *Journal of College Student Development, 37,* 20–28.

N

Narvaez, D. (2006). Integrative ethical education. In M. Killen and J. Smetana (Eds.), *Handbook of moral development.* Mahwah, NJ: Erlbaum.

National Center for Health Statistics (2006). *Obesity.* Atlanta: Centers for Disease Control and Prevention.

Newman, E. (1976). *A civil tongue.* Indianapolis: Bobbs-Merrill.

Nichols, R. B. (1961, March). Do we know how to listen? Practical helps in a modern age. *Speech Teacher, 10,* 22.

Nieman, D. C. (2007). *Exercise testing and prescription* (6th ed.). New York: McGraw-Hill.

Nilson, L. B. (2006, July 2). *Getting students to do the reading.* 31st Annual Improving University Teaching Conference, Dunedin, New Zealand.

Nolen-Hoeksema, S. (2007). *Abnormal psychology* (4th ed.). New York: McGraw-Hill.

O

Occupational Outlook Handbook. (2006–2007). Washington, DC: U.S. Bureau of Labor Statistics.

OCS Basics. (2002). *Job search basics.* Cambridge, MA: Office of Career Services. Retrieved from http://www.ocs.fas.harvard.edu/basics.

OCS Basics. (2004). *Career development.* Cambridge, MA: Office of Career Services, Harvard University.

Oltmanns, T. F., and Emery, R. E. (2007). *Abnormal psychology* (5th ed.). Upper Saddle River, NJ: Prentice Hall.

P

Packham, G., Jones, P., Miller, C., and Thomas, B. (2004). E-learning and retention: Key factors influencing student withdrawal. *Education and Training, 46,* 335–342.

Pauk, W. (2000). *Essential study strategies.* Clearwater, FL: H and H Publishing.

Peck, M. S. (1978). *The road less traveled.* New York: Touchstone.

Peck, M. S. (1997). *The road less traveled and beyond: Spiritual growth in an age of anxiety.* New York: Simon and Schuster.

Pennebaker, J. W. (1997). *Opening up* (Rev. ed.). New York: Avon.

Pennebaker, J. W. (2001). Dealing with a traumatic experience immediately after it occurs. *Advances in Mind-Body Medicine, 17,* 160–162.

Perkins, D. N. (1984, September). Creativity by design. *Educational Leadership,* pp. 18–25.

Peterson, C., and Stunkard, A. J. (1986). *Personal control and health promotion.* Unpublished manuscript, Department of Psychology, University of Michigan, Ann Arbor.

Porter, B. F. (2002). The voice of reason: Fundamentals of critical thinking. New York: Oxford.

Potter, W. J. (2005). Becoming a strategic thinker: Developing skills for success. Upper Saddle River, NJ: Pearson Prentice Hall.

Pryor, J. H., Hurtado, S., Saenz, V. B., Lindholm, J. A., Korn, W. S., and Mahoney, K. M. (2005). *The American freshman: National norms for fall 2005.* Los Angeles: Higher Education Research Institute, UCLA.

R

Raimes, A. (2002). *A brief handbook* (3rd ed.). Boston: Houghton Mifflin.

Ratcliff, J. L., Johnson, D. K., and Gaff, J. G. (2004). *Changing general education curriculum.* San Francisco: Jossey-Bass.

Reinders, H., and Youniss, J. (2006). School-based required community service and civic development in adolescence. *Applied Developmental Science, 10,* 2–12.

Rosen, L. J. (2006). *The academic writer's handbook.* New York: Pearson Longman.

S

Sax, L. J., Astin, A. W., Korn, W. S., and Mahoney, K. M. (2000). *The American freshman: National norms for fall 2000.* Los Angeles: Higher Education Research Institute, UCLA.

Sax, L. J., Lindholm, J. A., Astin, A. W., Korn, W. S., and Mahoney, K. M. (2001). *The American freshman: National norms for fall 2001.* Los Angeles: Higher Education Research Institute, UCLA.

Schaffzin, N. R. (1998). *The Princeton Review: Reading smart: Advanced techniques for improved reading.* New York: Random House.

Sears, D. O., Peplau, L. A., and Taylor, S. E. (2003). *Social psychology* (11th ed.). Upper Saddle River, NJ: Prentice Hall.

Shaver, P. R., Belsky, J., and Brennan, K. A. (2000). Comparing measures of adult attachment: An examination of interview and self-report methods. *Personal Relationships, 7,* 25–43.

Sher, K. J., Wood, P. K., and Gotham, H. J. (1996). The course of psychological distress in college: A prospective high-risk study. *Journal of College Student Development, 37,* 42–51.

Skinner, K. (1997). *The MSE Oracle System.* Dallas, TX: Southern Methodist University.

Sternberg, R. J. (1988). *The triangle of love.* New York: Basic Books.

Sternberg, R. J., and Lubart, T. I. (1995). *Defying the crowd: Cultivating creativity in a culture of conformity.* New York: Free Press.

Strong, R. W., Silver, H. F., Perini, M. J., and Tuculescu, G. M. (2002). *Reading for academic success.* Thousand Oaks, CA: Corwin Press.

Swartz, R. (2001). Thinking about decisions. In A. L. Costa (Ed.). *Developing minds: A resource book for teaching thinking.* Alexandria, VA: Association for Supervision and Curriculum Development.

Swift, A. (2006, May 6). [Personal communication].

T

Tannen, D. (1990). *You just don't understand!* New York: Ballantine.

Tavris, C. (1989). *Anger: The misunderstood emotion* (2nd ed.). New York: Touchstone.

Tavris, C. (1992). *The mismeasure of woman.* New York: Touchstone.

Taylor, S. E. (2003). *Health psychology* (5th ed.). New York: McGraw-Hill.

Taylor, S. E. (2006). *Health psychology* (6th ed.). New York: McGraw-Hill.

Teague, M. L., Mackenzie, S. L. C., and Rosenthal, D. M. (2007). *Your health today.* New York: McGraw-Hill.

Tulving, E. (1972). Episode and semantic memory. In E. Tulving and W. Donaldson (Eds)., *Origins of memory.* San Diego: Academic Press.

Tyler, S. (2001). *Been there, should've done that: More tips for making the most of college* (2nd ed.). Michigan: Front Porch Press.

U

University of Illinois Counseling Center. (1984). *Overcoming procrastination.* Urbana-Champaign, IL: Department of Student Affairs.

U.S. Bureau of Labor Statistics. (2003). Washington, DC: U.S. Department of Labor.

V

Von Oech, Roger. (1990). A whack on the side of the head: How you can be more creative. New York: Warner.

W

Walters, A. (1994). Using visual media to reduce homophobia: A classroom demonstration. *Journal of Sex Education and Therapy, 20,* 92–100.

Wechsler, H., Lee, J. E., Kuo, M., Seibring, M., Nelson, T. F., and Lee, H. (2002). Trends in college binge drinking during a period of increased prevention efforts: Findings from Harvard School of Public Health College Alcohol Study surveys: 1993–2001. *Journal of American College Health, 50,* 203–217.

West, T. (2003). Secret of the super successful...They're dyslexic. *Thalamus, 21,* 48–52.

Whimbey, A., and Lochhead, J. (1991). *Problem solving and comprehension.* Mahwah, NJ: Erlbaum.

Whiteside, K. (2003, September 23). Rejuvenated Hamm still a reluctant star. *USA Today.* Retrieved from www.usatoday.com/sports/soccer/national/2003-09-02-ham_x.htm.

Whitley, B. E., Jr., and Keith-Spiegel, P. (2002). *Academic dishonesty: An educator's guide.* Mahwah, NJ: Erlbaum.

Winston, S. (1995). *Stephanie Winston's best organizing tips.* New York: Simon and Schuster.

Writers Workshop. (2002). *Writing resumes.* Urbana-Champaign, IL: Center for Writing Studies, University of Illinois. Retrieved from http://www.english.uiuc.edu/.

Writers Workshop. (2006). *Writing resumes.* Urbana-Champaign, IL: Center for Writing Studies, University of Illinois. Retrieved from www.english.uiuc.edu/ on July 2, 2006.

Wuest, D. A., and Bucher, C. A. (2006). *Foundations of physical education, exercise science, and sport* (15th ed.). New York: McGraw-Hill.

Y

Yager, J. (1999). *Creative time management for the new millennium* (2nd ed.). Stamford, CT: Hannacroix Books.

Yate, M. (2006). *Knock 'em dead.* Boston: Adams Media.

Z

Zeidner, M. (1995). Adaptive coping with test situations: A review of the literature. *Educational Psychologist, 30,* 123–133.

Zeurcher-White, E. (1997). *Treating panic disorder and agoraphobia: A step-by-step clinical guide.* Oakland, CA: New Harbinger Publications.

Zucker, R. A., and others. (2006). Predicting risky drinking outcomes longitudinally: What kind of advance notice can we get? *Alcoholism: Clinical and Experimental Research, 30,* 243–252.

Credits

Photo Credits

Prologue, page x: © Royalty-Free/CORBIS
Prologue, page x: © Theo Westenberger
Prologue, page x: © Bill Aron/PhotoEdit
Prologue, page x: © Christine Kennedy/DK Stock/Getty
Chapter 1, page 1: © Chuck Savage/CORBIS
Chapter 1, page 2: © 2005 AFP/Getty Images
Chapter 1, page 7: © Royalty-Free/CORBIS
Chapter 1, page 17: © Stewart Cohen/Index Stock Imagery
Chapter 1, page 20: Courtesy of Rob Grauer
Chapter 2, page 31: © John Henley/CORBIS
Chapter 2, page 32: © 2006 Getty Images
Chapter 2, page 47: © David Young-Wolff/Getty Images
Chapter 2, page 50: © Bill Losh/Getty Images
Chapter 2, page 52: © Jim Ruymen/Reuters/CORBIS
Chapter 3, page 61: © PhotoDisk Red/Getty Images
Chapter 3, page 62: credits TK
Chapter 3, page 68: © John Coletti Photography
Chapter 3, page 69: PalmOne is a trademark of PalmOne, Inc.
Chapter 3, page 69: © Najlah Feanny/CORBIS
Chapter 4, page 89: © David Young-Wolff/PhotoEdit
Chapter 4, page 90: © T. Mendoza/L.A. Daily News/CORBIS
Chapter 4, page 105: © Dennis McDonald/PhotoEdit
Chapter 4, page 107: © Bill Aron/PhotoEdit
Chapter 5, page 119: © Digital Vision/Getty Images
Chapter 5, page 120: Courtesy of Anne Swift Enterprises, Inc.
Chapter 5, page 123: © Royalty-Free/CORBIS
Chapter 5, page 127: John Coletti Photography
Chapter 6, page 149: © Gary Conner/PhotoEdit
Chapter 6, page 150: © 2006 Getty Images News
Chapter 6, page 153: © Colin Young-Wolff/PhotoEdit
Chapter 6, page 168: © Digital Vision/Getty Images
Chapter 7, page 185: © John Henley/CORBIS
Chapter 7, page 186: © Pace Gregory/CORBIS SYGMA
Chapter 7, page 188: © Kelly-Mooney Photography/CORBIS
Chapter 7, page 198 (upper left): © Daniel Acker/Bloomburg News/Landov
Chapter 7, page 198 (upper right): © Frank Trapper/CORBIS
Chapter 7, page 198 (bottom left): © Ethan Miller/Reuters/Landov
Chapter 7, page 198 (bottom right): © Fred Prouser/Reuters/Landov
Chapter 8, page 213: © Royalty-Free/CORBIS
Chapter 8, page 214: © Bettmann/CORBIS
Chapter 8, page 219: © David Young-Wolff/PhotoEdit
Chapter 9, page 241: © DesignPics, Inc./IndexOpen
Chapter 9, page 242: © Reuters/CORBIS
Chapter 9, page 244: © Jeff Greenberg/PhotoEdit
Chapter 9, page 246: © John Henley/CORBIS
Chapter 9, page 248: © JP Lafont/Sygma/CORBIS
Chapter 9, page 257: © Richard Hutchings/CORBIS
Chapter 9, page 262: © Noel Henderson/Photographer's Choice/Getty Image

Chapter 10, page 273: © Kathrine Wessel/CORBIS
Chapter 10, page 274: © C.J. Gunther
Chapter 10, page 284: © Paula A. Scully
Chapter 10, page 286: © Casey Cohen/PhotoEdit
Chapter 11, page 301: © Ariel Skelley/CORBIS
Chapter 11, page 302: © Fred Brouser/Reuters/CORBIS
Chapter 11, page 309: © Owaki-Kulla/CORBIS
Chapter 11, page 311: © Royalty-Free/CORBIS
Chapter 11, page 313: © Mo Wilson/Photofusion Picture Library/Alamy
Chapter 11, page 322: © The Image Bank/Getty Images
Chapter 12, page 331: © Bob Daemmrich/PhotoEdit
Chapter 12, page 332: Copyright © 2003 NBC News

Cartoon Credits

Chapter 1, page 11: © Herald Carl Bakken
Chapter 1, page 12–14: © Mickey Choate. University of Texas at Dallas, Career Center. Reprinted by permission.
Chapter 2, page 35: PEANUTS reprinted by permission of United Feature Syndicate, Inc.
Chapter 2, page 40: Copyright 2002 by Randy Glasbergen. www.glasbergen.com
Chapter 2, page 44: Copyright 2004 by Randy Glasbergen. www.glasbergen.com
Chapter 2, page 45: © Ralph Hagen. Reproduced by permission of www.CartoonStock.com.
Chapter 3, page 65: © 2000 Charles Barsotti, from cartoonbank.com. All Rights Reserved.
Chapter 3, page 77: © 2001 Ron Therien. Reproduced with permission of www.CartoonStock.com.
Chapter 3 page 80: © Mike Baldwin. Reproduced by permission of www.CartoonStock.com.
Chapter 4, page 90: © 2003 Sidney Harris. Reproduced by permission of ScienceCartoonsPlus.com.
Chapter 4, page 106: © *The New Yorker Collection* 1999, Danny Shanahan from cartoonbank.com. All rights reserved.
Chapter 5, page 123: © Carole Cable. Used with permission of the cartoonist.
Chapter 5, page 124: © 1997 by Scott Adams, Inc./Dist. by UFS, Inc.
Chapter 5, page 130: © Sidney Harrris. Reproduced by permission of ScienceCartoonsPlus.com.
Chapter 5, page 136: © *The New Yorker Collection* 1990, Eric Teitelbaum, from cartoonbank.com. All rights reserved.
Chapter 6, page 155: Reprinted by permission of Vivian Scott Hixson.
Chapter 6, page 162: © Arnie Levin. Published in *The New Yorker* March 11, 1996. All rights reserved. Reproduced by permission of cartoonbank.com.
Chapter 6, page 169: © Ed Fisher. Published in *The New Yorker* January 26, 1998. All rights reserved. Reproduced by permission of cartoonbank.com.
Chapter 6, page 171: © Arnie Levin. Published in *The New Yorker* September 13, 1993. All rights reserved. Reproduced by permission of cartoonbank.com.
Chapter 6, page 173: © Gahan Wilson
Chapter 7, page 195: © *The New Yorker Collection* 1986, J.B. Handelsman from cartoonbank.com. All Rights Reserved.
Chapter 7, page 203: © 2003 by Sidney Harris. Reproduced by permission of ScienceCartoonsPlus.com.
Chapter 8, page 216: © *The New Yorker Collection* 1991, Mike Twohy from cartoonbank.com. All Rights Reserved.
Chapter 8, page 221: © Herald Carl Bakken
Chapter 8, page 226: PEANUTS reprinted by permission of United Features Syndicate Inc.
Chapter 8, page 231: © *The New Yorker Collection* 1990, Danny Shanahan, from cartoonbank.com. All Rights Reserved.
Chapter 9, page 254: PEANUTS reprinted by permission of United Feature Syndicate, Inc.
Chapter 9, page 255: © W.B. Park. Published in *The New Yorker* June 22, 1998. All rights reserved. Reproduced by permission of cartoonbank.com.
Chapter 9, page 265: © 2004 Leo Cullum, from cartoonbank.com. All Rights Reserved.
Chapter 10, page 289: © 2002 Tom Cheney from cartoonbank.com. All Rights Reserved.
Chapter 10, page 289: DILBERT: © Scott Adams/Dist. by United Feature Syndicate, Inc.
Chapter 11, page 304: © Ted Goff. All Rights reserved. Reproduced by permission of cartoonbank.com.
Chapter 11, page 305: © Mick Stevens. Published in *The New Yorker* June 8, 1992. All Rights reserved. Reproduced by permission of cartoonbank.com.
Chapter 11, page 315: © *The New Yorker Collection* 1986 Warren Miller from cartoonbank.com. All Rights Reserved.
Chapter 11, page 321: © Robert Mankoff. Published in *The New Yorker* May 6, 2002. All Rights reserved. Reproduced by permission of cartoonbank.com.
Chapter 12, page 343: © Engleman/Rothco Cartoons, Inc.

Text Credits

Chapter 1, page 19: Mick O'Leary, *The Online 100*, 1995.
Chapter 2, page 39: After data presented by Ed Diener and Martin E.P. Seligman, "Very Happy People," *Psychological Science* 13, 81–84. Copyright © 2002 by Blackwell Publishing. Reprinted by permission of the publisher.
Chapter 4, page 105: Drew C. Appleby, "Faculty and staff perceptions of irritating behaviors in the college classroom," from *Journal of Staff, Program, and Organizational Development*, 8, pp. 41–46. Copyright © 1990. Reprinted with permission of New Forum Press.
Chapter 4, page 110: Adapted from *Looking At Type And Careers* by Charles R. Martin. Used by permission of the Center for Applications of Psychological Type, Inc.
Chapter 4, page 115: From *The Barsch Learning Style Inventory* by Jeffrey R. Barsch, Ph.D. Copyright 1996 by Academic Therapy Publications, Novato, CA. Reprinted with permission of the publisher. All Rights Reserved.
Chapter 5, page 125. From V. R. Ruggiero, *Beyond Feelings: A Guide to Critical Thinking*, 4th Edition. Copyright © 1995 by Mayfield Publishing Company.
Chapter 5, page 124: From Browne, M. Neil; Keeley, Stuart M., *Asking the Right Questions: A Guide to Critical Thinking*, 7th Edition. Copyright © 2004, p. 13. Adapted by permission of Pearson Education, Inc., Upper Saddle River, NJ.
Chapter 5, page 137. Derived from Roger Van Oech, *A Whack on the Side of the Head: How You Can Be More Creative*. Copyright © 1998 by Roger Van Oech. Reprinted with permission of Warner Books, Inc.
Chapter 5, page 138: From Diane Halpern, *Critical Thinking Across the Curriculum*. Copyright © 1997 by Lawrence Erlbaum Associates, Inc. Reprinted by permission of the publisher.
Chapter 6, page 185: Adapted from Miholic, V. (1994). "An inventory to pique students' metacognitive awareness of reading strategies." *Journal of Reading*, 38 (2), 84–87. Copyright 1994 by the International Reading Association. Reprinted with permission. All Rights Reserved.
Chapter 7, page 190: Wilbert J. McKeachie, *Teaching Tips*, Eleventh Edition. Copyright © 2002 by D.C. Heath and Company. Used with permission of Houghton Mifflin Company.
Chapter 7, page 200: From *Episodic and Semantic Memory in Organization of Memory*. E. Tulving & W. Donaldson (Eds.) Copyright © 1972 by Academic Press. Reprinted by permission of the publisher.
Chapter 8, page 217: Astin, Alexander W., *What Matters in College?: Four Critical Years Revisited*. Copyright © 1993 by Jossey-Bass Inc. Reprinted by permission of John Wiley & Sons, Inc.
Chapter 8, page 233: Adapted from Academic Dishonesty by Bernard E., Jr. Whitley and Patricia Keith-Spiegel. Copyright © 2002 by Lawrence Erlbaum Associates, Inc. Reprinted by permission of the publisher.
Chapter 9, page 268: Adapted from *Criteria for Effective Writing*. Copyright © Alverno College. Reprinted by permission of Alverno College Productions.
Chapter 10, page 283: From *Adolescence*, Ninth Edition by John Santrock. Copyright © 2003 McGraw-Hill Companies, Inc. Reprinted by permission of the publisher.
Chapter 10, page 284: H. Wechsler, A. Davenport, G. Dowdall, B. Moeykens and S. Castillo, "Health and Behavioral Consequences of Binge Drinking in College" from *Journal of the American Medical Association*, Vol. 272, No. 21, December 7, 1994. Copyright © 1994 by the American Medical Association. All rights reserved.
Chapter 10, page 292: From "Clients Problem Checklist," Student Counseling Center, Illinois State University. Reprinted by permission.
Chapter 10, page 296: Adapted from R. Allen & S. Linde, Lifeagain, p. 25-26. Copyright © 1981 by Human Resources Institute, LLC., www.healthyculture.com. Reprinted by permission.
Chapter 10, page 297: Reprinted with permission from Journal of Studies on Alcohol, vol 54, pp. 522-527, 1993. Copyright © 1993 by Alcohol Research Documentation, Inc. Rutgers Center of Alcohol Studies, Piscataway, NJ 08854. The RCASST is to be only used as part of a complete assessment battery since more research needs to be done with this instrument.
Chapter 10, page 298: "My Sexual Attitudes," adapted from Robert F. Valois "The Valois Sexual Attitude Questionaire," page 52–54, *Wellness R.S.V.P.*, First Edition, 1981, Benjamin/Cummings Publishing Company, Inc, Menlo Park, CA, copyright © 1992 by Valois, Kammermann & Associates and the authors. Used with permission of Valois, Kammermann & Associates and the authors.
Chapter 11, page 313: King, T., & Bannon, E. "At what cost? The Price that working students pay for a college education" Copyright © 2002 by The State PIRGs' Higher Education Project. www.uspirg.org. All rights reserved. Reprinted by permission.
Chapter 11, page 326: Barbara O'Neill, *Saving on a Shoestring: How to Cut Expenses, Reduce Debt, and Stash More Cash*. © Copyright 2006 Kaplan Publishing. All rights reserved. Reprinted with permission.
Chapter 11, page 327: © 2002 Baptist Memorial Health Care Corporation.
Chapter 12, pages 336–337: Reproduced by special permission from the Publisher, Psychological Assessment Resources, Inc., 16204 North Florida Avenue, Lutz, Florida 33549, from Making Vocational Choices, Third Edition, Copyright © 1973, 1985, 1992, 1997 by Psychological Assessment Resources, Inc. Further reproduction is prohibited without permission from PAR, Inc.
Chapter 12, page 342: From Lee E. Isaacson, Duane Brown. *Career Information, Career Counseling, and Career Development*, 7e. Published by Allyn and Bacon, Boston, MA. Copyright © 2000 by Pearson Education. Adapted by permission of the publisher.

Index

A

AA degrees, 12
Abbreviations in notes, 161–162
ABC method, 74–75
ABI/INFORM database, 19
Abstinence, 286
Academic advisers. *See* Counselors and advisers
Academic Index, 19
Academic integrity pledge, 105
Academic support services, 3–4
Academic values, xxvi
Accidental plagiarism, 259
Accounting majors, skills for, 12
Accuracy in problem solving, 134
Achievement
  of goals, xxxi
  résumés, 343
Acquaintance rape. *See* Date rape
Acronyms and memorizing, 203
Acting on best strategy, 133
Action plans, 67
Active listening in class, 153–154
Active reading, 167–168
Adams, Scott, 137
Addictions. *See also* Alcohol; Drugs
  computer addiction, 20–21
Advertising, questioning, 128
Advisers. *See* Counselors and advisers
Advising, 35
Aerobic exercise, 277
Aggression and communication, 36
Agreeableness in personality model, 96–97
Al-Anon, 282
Alberti, R., 37
Alcohol, 5, 283
  avoiding, 280–281
  binge drinking, 284
  Greek organizations and, 6
  overdrinking, 282
  self-assessment of, 297
  sleep problems and, 278
Alcoholics Anonymous, 282
Allen, R., 296
Altman, Jeff, 173
Alumnus as mentor, 104
Ambivalent attachment, 38–39
American Psychological Association style manual, 250, 254
Americans with Disability Act, 198
AmeriCorps, 316
Amphetamines, 281, 283
Anaerobic exercise, 277
Analysis in Bloom's Taxonomy, 190
Analytic reading, 168
Anderson, L. W., 190
Anger, controlling, 36
Annual percentage rates (APRs), 318
Anorexia nervosa, 280
Answering machines, 64
Anticipating class material, 152
Antidepressants, 291
Antivirus protection, 17
Anxiety
  and science/math improvement, 193
  test anxiety, 221–222
Apostrophes, 255
Appleby, D., 217
Application in Bloom's Taxonomy, 190
Architecture majors, skills for, 12
Arguments, 128–129
  faulty arguments, 130
  in first drafts, 251–252
  lingo in, 131–132
Arnett, J. J., xxx
Artists
  creativity and, 95
  personality, artistic, 336–337
Assertiveness
  and communication, 37
  with roommates, 46
  working on, 37
Assignments, finishing, 152
Associated Press database, 19
Associate of arts (AA) degrees, 12
Associate of science (AS) degrees, 12
Associations and memorizing, 202

Assumptions in reasoning, 131
Astin, A. W., 6, 73, 79, 187, 217
Athanasou, J. A., 230
Atkins, R., 338
Atlases, 249
ATMs (automatic teller machines)
 receipts, keeping, 306
 using, 310
Attachment styles, 38–39
Attention
 memorizing and, 201
 to speaker, 33
Attitudes
 about diversity, 52
 and lecturers, 154–155
 and memorizing, 202
 and reading, 163–164
 sexual attitudes, assessment of, 298
 stress and, 289
 for tests, 216
Atwood, Margaret, 192
Audience
 speaking to, 262, 264
 writing for, 250–251
Auditory learners, 92–93
 matching skills to instructors, 94
 tests, studying for, 218
Authoritative parents, 44
Avoidant attachment, 38–39

B

Babysitting jobs, 313
Bachar, K., 40
Bachelard, Gaston, 195
Baez, Joan, xxx
Baha, Allah, 48
Bailey, Covert, 279
Baker, Russell, 132
Balancing checkbooks, 310–311
Baldwin, James, 275
Balfour, Arthur James, 167
Bandura, A., xxxi
Bank accounts, 309–311. *See also* Checking accounts; Savings accounts
 basic information for, 311
 managing, 310–311
 summary strategies, 324
 types of, 309–310
Bannon, E., 312, 313
Barbiturates, 281, 283
Barrett, J., 319
Barrie, James M., 203
Barron's Profiles of American Colleges, 15
Barsch, Jeffrey R., 115
Basic skills, 334
Bauer, K., 285
Baumrind, Diana, 44
Baxter Magolda, M. B., 205
Behaviors and instructors, 105
Belsky, J., 38
Bennett, M.E., 297
Benson, P. L., 339
Bewildering lecturers, 154
Bias
 confirmation bias, 138
 hindsight bias, 138
 and reasoning, 131
Bierce, Ambrose, 316
Big Five Personality Theory, 336
Bills
 credit and, 318
 filing, 306
Binge drinking, 284
Biological rhythms
 self-assessment of, 208
 studying and, 189
 time management and, 76
Biology major, skills for, 13
BIOSIS, 19
Bisexual students, 51–52
Blackberries, 69
Blended programs, 19
Blogs, 94
Blonna, R., 288
Bloom, Benjamin, 190
Bloom's Taxonomy, 190–191
Bodily-kinesthetic intelligence, 92
 career choices for, 108
Body of first draft, 251–252
Bolado de Espinosa, Ana, 46–47, 50
Bolles, Richard, 337, 343
Bombeck, Erma, 104
Books in Print, 19
Boolean searches, 125
Boredom, tackling, xxix–xxx
Boundaries with instructors, 106
Bourne, E. J., 37, 56
Brainstorming
 job search, 342
 for writing topics, 247

Bransford, J. D., 132–133
Breaks and reading, 164
Breathing
  and anxiety, 222
  and speaking, 263
Brennan, K. A., 38
Brisette, I., 289
Britannica Online, 19
Brown, Duane, 342
Brown, F. C., 278
Browne, M. N., 124
Bruner, Jerome, 132
Buboltz, W. C., Jr., 278
Bucher, C. A., 277
Buckley Amendment, 106
Budgets
  for communication expenses, 308
  establishing, 305–306
  monthly budget plan, 307
Bulimia, 280
Business majors, skills for, 13
Butterfield, K. D., 230, 231

C

Cacioppo, J. T., 41
Café Ole, 332
Caffeine, 280–281
  sleep problems and, 278
  and test anxiety, 222
Calendar term planners, 69–71
Callahan, David, 230
Camus, Albert, 46
Cancer, 276
Canfield, J., 3
Capturing. *See* Connecting
Career Information System, 342
Careers. *See also* Employment
  counselors, 340
  future, planning for, xxxi–xxxii
  goals, setting, 341
  intelligent career choices, 108
  job search tips, 341
  Myers-Briggs Type Inventory (MBTI) and, 109–110
  Occupational Outlook Handbook, 339–340
  personality and, 336–337
  researching job search, 342–343
  résumés, creating, 343–344
  service learning and, 338–339
  skills and, 333–336
  summary strategies for, 346
  tests, 337
  time management skills, 65
  values and, 333, 348
Career Visions, 342
Career Ways, 342
Carpooling
  studying while, 188
  time management, 80–81
Carskadon, M. A., 189, 278
Carter, Angela, 169
Carver, C. S., 289
Carver, George Washington, 157
Casual sex, 40
Categories and mindfulness, 134
Cause-and-effect patterns in lectures, 155
Cell phones, 308
  smart cell phones, 69
Central ideas, listening for, 34
Certificates, 12
Cervical caps, 287
Challenging yourself, xxii
Characteristics
  of creative thinkers, 136
  of problem solvers, 133–134
Charts for literary reading, 170
Cheating, 230–233
  consequences of, 232
  excuses for, 233
  understanding, 231
The Cheating Culture (Callahan), 230
Check cards, 310
Checking accounts, 309
  balancing checkbook, 310–311
  categorizing check purchases, 306
  registers, using, 306
Chemistry major, skills for, 13
Child care
  facilities, 44
  jobs, 313
Children
  caring for, 44–45
  time management with, 80
Children's Defense Fund, xxii
Choate, Mickey, 12–14
Choices, 342
Cholesterol, 279
Chronological résumés, 343
Chunking information, 199–200

Churchill, Winston, 263, 291
Cigarette smoking, 280
Citations
  for Internet resources, 249
  plagiarism, avoiding, 260, 261
  of reference sources, 248–249
A Civil Tongue (Newman), 253
Cizek, G. J., 230–231
Claims
  acceptance of, 127
  questioning claims, 128
  reasoning and, 127–129
Clarification
  of tests, 223
  of values, xxv–xxvi
Clark, Karen Kaiser, xxiv
Clark, M. R., 99
Classes. *See also* Lectures; Online classes
  anticipating material, 152
  assignments, finishing, 152
  commitment to, 151–152
  distractions, minimizing, 152–153
  employment and, 79
  general education classes, 9
  listening in, 153–154
  missing classes, 152
  online classes, 18–19
  selection of, 10
  timeliness for, 152
Classroom assistance, 8
Clues, listening for, 155
Cocaine, 281–283
Cocaine Anonymous, 282
COIN, 342
Collaboration for science/math improvement, 193
College catalogs, 9
College Success Factors Index (Halberg, Halberg & Sauer), xxv
Collins, M., 335, 338
The Color Purple, 32
Commitment
  choosing commitments, 6
  dramatizing commitments, 77
  to health care, 288
  to lectures, 151–152
  procrastination and, 78
  to reading goals, 163–166
  to science and math, 193
  to setting goals, xxvii
  summary strategies for, 178
Common sense
  and safety issues, 5
  time management and, 63
Communication. *See also* Listening skills; Writing
  barriers, avoiding, 34–35
  budgeting for, 308
  conflict resolution and, 36–38
  effective communication, 33–38
  negotiating, 37–38
  nonverbal communication, 36
  with parents, 42–43
  with partners, 43–44
  practicing skills, 35
  with roommates, 46
  skills, 335–336
  strategies for, 245
  summary strategies for, 54
Community connections, 7
Commuting
  studying while, 188
  time management, 80–81
Comparison patterns in lectures, 154
Compensation and learning disabilities, 199
Competence
  building, xxvi–xxviii
  summary strategies for, xxxiv
  thinking and, xxviii
Completion dates for goals, xxvii
Compounding interest, 320
Compromises, 38
Compulsive spender checklist, 327
Computer engineering major, skills for, 13
Computers. *See also* Internet
  addiction, avoiding, 20–21
  career searches and, 340–341, 342
  expenses, reducing, 321
  games, 20, 21
  online education, 18–19
  procrastination and, 77
  registration, 10
  strategies for success with, 22
  technological facility, 98
  word-processing programs, 17–18
  working with, 16–21
Concentration
  in classes, 152–154
  on reading, 165–166
  summary strategies for, 178
  and tests, 223
Concept maps, 160, 161

and memorizing, 204
for reading notes, 173
Conclusions
in arguments, 128–129
in first draft, 252
taking time for, 132
Condoms, 286
Confirmation bias, 138
Conflict resolution, 36–37
Confusion
lecturers, confusing, 154
and notetaking, 156–157
reading and, 163–164
Connecting
creativity and, 139
in literary reading, 170
to reading, 166–169
summary strategies for, 178
Conscientiousness in personality model, 95
Consumers, 122, 123
Content
mastering, xxxii
teachers, content-centered, 102
Context, mindfulness and, 134
Conventional personality, 337
Cooperation and assertiveness, 37
Co-ops and careers, 338
Copies of work, keeping, 106
Coping, xxxi
Core courses, 9
Cornell method, 158–160
for reading notes, 173, 175
Cossman, E. Joseph, 323
Counselors and advisers
career counselors, 340
contacting, 8
credit counseling, 323
four/five-year plans, creating, 15
help from, 3–4
learning disabilities, help with, 197–198
loneliness, help for, 41–42
mapping academic path with, 8
mental health counseling, seeking, 292–293
personal concerns, counseling for, 4
for returning-students, xxiv
strategies for success with, 22
Counterarguments, 129
Coupons, clipping, 308, 309
Courtenay, W. H., 276
Cover letters, 344–345
Cover page with writing, 256
Covey, Stephen, xxv, 74–76
Coward, Noel, 258
Cox, S. G., 298
Cramming
avoiding, 215
cram cards, 203
strategic cramming, 219–220
Creative thinking, xxxiii, 95, 136–139
in Bloom's Taxonomy, 190
detailed assignments and, 100
flow, discovering, 138–139
fostering, 137–138
mental locks, breaking, 136–137
self-assessment for, 145
skills, 334
summary strategies for, 140
Creative writing, 245
Credit
approaching creditors, 323
common terms, list of, 317
compulsive spender checklist, 327
counseling, 323
in emergencies, 320–321
good credit, establishing, 317–318
myths about, 318
problems, avoiding, 318–321
reports, 318
summary strategies, 324
Credit cards, 318–321
balance, paying off, 319
compounding interest, 320
Criteria for questions, 124
Critical thinking, xxxiii, 94–95, 121–126
and criticisms, 123–124
and Internet, 124–126
questions and, 122–123
self-assessment for, 142–143
summary strategies for, 140
Criticism
and communication, 35
critical thinking and, 123–124
Crone-Grant, D., 291
Crooks, R. L., 285
Csikszentmihalyi, Mihaly, 138–139
Cues for tests, 217–218
Culture, 7
diversity, appreciating, 46–53
Curiosity, 122–123

Cursing, 36
Cut-and-paste Internet strategies, 176
Cutrona, C. E., 41
Cutting classes. *See* Skipping classes
Cycle patterns in lectures, 155

D

Daily plans, 67
  ABC method, 74–75
  creating, 74–76
  priorities, setting, 74
  summary strategies for, 82
Dance major, skills for, 13
Dashes in writing, 255
Databases, 19
  in libraries, 248
Date rape, 40–41
  alcohol use and, 282
Dating, 39–40
Davis, M., 64, 65, 289
Day, D. V., 336
Deadlines
  instructors and, 103
  and procrastination, 78
  for writing, 257
Debit cards, 310
Debt, 303. *See also* Credit
  expenses, reducing, 321–322
  -to-income ratio, 306
  summary strategies, 324
Deceiving yourself, 77
Decision making
  bad decisions, pull toward, 138
  factors in, 136
  fuzzy thinking, clarifying, 135
  narrow thinking, expanding, 135
  skills, 334
  snap decisions, avoiding, 135
  sprawling thinking, containing, 135
  summary strategies for, 140
Declarative memory, 200
Decoding messages, 33
Deductive reasoning, 129–131
Deep learning, 99
Deep relaxation, 289–290
Defining problem, 132–133
DeFleur, M. L., 36
DeLamater, J. D., 285
Delivery of speeches. *See* Speaking
Dement, W. C., 278
Dempsey, Patrick, 198
Depo-Provera, 287
Deposit source, recording, 306
Depressants, 281, 283
Depression, 290–291
Descriptive writing, 244–245
Detailed assignments, 100
Diaphragm, breathing from, 222
Diaphragms (contraceptive), 287
Dictionaries, 164–165, 249
Diener, E., xxv, 38, 39
Dietary Guidelines for Americans, 279
Dieting, 279–280
Direct lending schools, 316
Disabled students
  assistance for, 7–8
  rights of, 198
Disciplines, mastering, 191–195
Discover, 342
Dismissiveness, 38
Disorganized lecturers, 155
Dissertation Abstracts, 19
Distinctive students, 103
Distractions
  minimizing, 152–153
  to reading, 165–166
Diversity
  appreciation for, 46–53
  relationships and, 52–53
  summary strategies for, 54
Division of tasks, 78
Doing, learning by, 94
Donnelly, T. M., 338
Double majors, 11
Doyle, Arthur Conan, 134
Dramatizing commitments, 77
Dreams and values, xxv
Drinking. *See* Alcohol
Dropping out, 322–323
Drugs, 5
  avoiding, 280–281
  list of, 283
  reasons for using, 281–282
  self-assessment on use of, 297
  sleep problems and, 278
  and test anxiety, 222
Dweck, C., 134
Dyslexia, 196

E

Earhart, Amelia, 137
Eating disorders, 280
Eating habits, 6, 278–280
Economic Literature Index, 19
Economics major, skills for, 13
Economos, C., 278
Ecstasy, 281
Edelman, Marian Wright, xxii
Editing writing, 253–255
Education for All Handicapped Children Act of 1975, 198
Effort
  learning styles and, 99–101
  maximizing, xxix
80-20 principle, 64–65
Einstein, Albert, 213–214
Electives, 9
Electronic planners, 68
Elliott, M., xxvii
Ellison, Brooke, 273–274
E-mail, 16, 17
  commuter directory for, 80
  to counselors and advisers, 8
  instructors, connecting with, 103
  with parents, 42–43
  as time waster, 64
Emergencies
  credit in, 320–321
  money management and, 306
  and tests, 222–223
Emergency contraception, 286
Emerson, Ralph Waldo, 36
Emery, R. E., 291
Emmons, M., 37
Emotional support, xxxi
Employment, 337–338. *See also* Careers
  balancing college and, 79, 314
  careers and work experiences, 337–339
  credit and, 318
  and finances, 312–314
  inquiry letters, 344
  job interviews, 345
  letters in job search, 344–345
  on-campus jobs, 79
  summary strategies for, 346
Encoding messages, 33
English major, skills for, 13
Enmeshed parents, 42
Enterprising personality, 337
Entertainment expenses, reducing, 321
Enthusiasm, 4
Environment
  creative thinking and, 138
  exploring, 22
Episodic memory, 200
ERIC, 19
Eshelman, E. R., 64, 65, 289
Essay tests, 218–219
  decoding questions, 227
  master strategies, 226–228
  tips for writing, 228
Estep, K. M., 39
Ethics. *See also* Integrity
  academic integrity pledge, 105
  instructors and, 104
Ethnicity, 47–49
Ethnocentrism, 48
Evaluation in Bloom's Taxonomy, 190
Even Eagles Need a Push (McNally), xxvii
EverQuest game, 21
Examinations. *See* Tests
Examples
  lectures, patterns in, 154–155
  supporting judgment with, 124
Exclamation marks, 255
Exercise
  and health, 277
  sleep and, 278
  time for, 6
Expanding resources, xxx
Expectations for tests, 217
Expenses, acknowledging, 304–305
Experimental learning preferences self-assessment, 116
Expert evidence and claims, 127
Exploring approaches to problem, 133
Expository writing, 244
Expulsion, risk for, xxvi
Extracurricular activities, 6–7
Extraversion
  in five factor personality model, 96
  in Myers-Briggs Type Inventory (MBTI), 97

F

Facebook.com, 17, 42, 62
Faculty. *See* Instructors

FAFSA (Free Application for Federal Student Aid), 315–316
Family. *See also* Children
  connecting with, 42–43
  financial help from, 322, 323
  study time and, 219
Family Educational Right to Privacy Act, 106
Family Education Responsibility and Privacy Act (FERPA), 43
Farr, J. M., 349
Fast-talking lecturers, 154
Fats in diet, 279
Fearfulness, 38
Federal Direct Student Loan Program (FDSLP), 316
Federal Family Education Loan Program (FFELP), 316
Federal Supplemental Education Opportunity Grants (FSEOGs), 315
Feedback, 215
  assertiveness and, 37
  in communication, 245
  listening and, 34
  on notes, 162
  on writing, 257
Feelings and assertiveness, 37
Fernandez, Giselle, 331–332
Fidgeting, 36
Fill-in-the-blank test strategies, 225
Finance major, skills for, 13
Finances. *See* Money management
Financial aid, 79, 314–316
First drafts, 250–252
Fishberg, M. T., 339
Five factor personality model, 95–97
Five-year plans, creating, 15
Fixed expenses, 304
Flexibility
  creative thinking and, 137
  options, 111
Flow, discovering, 138–139
Focus
  cramming and, 219–220
  and memorizing, 202
Follow-through, 37
Food expenses, reducing, 321
Ford, Henry, 218
Foreign language study skills, 194–195
Formal outlines, 250
Four/five year plans
  assessing, 26
  creating, 15
Frank, S., 167, 203
Frankl, Viktor, 186
Franklin, Benjamin, 76
Franklin Covey planner, 68
Fraternities, 6
Free writing, 246
Freshman 15, 279
Fried, SuEllen, 265
Friends
  and attachment, 38–39
  financial help from, 322
  instructors, friendships with, 106
  for international students, 49
  partners, friendships with, 44
  returning-students and, xxiv
Fruits in diet, 279
Functional résumés, 343
Future, creating, xxxi–xxxii
Fuzzy thinking, clarifying, 135

G

Gaff, J. G., 121
Gandhi, Indira, 196
Gardner, Howard, 91–92, 191
Garner, P. W., 39
Garofalo, Janeane, 185–186, 187
Gay and lesbian students, 51–52
Gender issues
  insights into, 49–51
  self-improvement strategies, 51
  sexual harassment, 50
General education classes, 9
Geology major, skills for, 13
Gerrold, David, 93
Ghandi, Mahatma, 228
Gift aid, 314
Gilman, Caroline, 135
Gingrich, Newt, 197
Glass ceiling, 49
Glater, J., 230
Goals, xxvii–xxviii
  career goals, 341
  creativity and, 139
  for reading, 165
  revisiting, 66–67
  summary strategies for, 82
  time management goals, 66
  for writing, 244

Goethe, Johann Wolfgang von, 333
Goldberg, H., 51
Goldberg, Whoopi, 198
Google, 16
Gordon, Ruth, 262
Gordon, T., 35
Gotham, H. J., 288
Gottman, J., 44
Government major, skills for, 14
GPA (grade point average)
  dropping out and, 322
  targeting, 231
  in traditional grading system, 229–230
Grabowski, B. L., 94, 100
Grades. *See also* GPA (grade point average)
  challenging grades, 229
  changes in, 217
  cheating and, 230–233
  curves for, 229–231
  holistic grading, 257
  negotiating grade changes, 229
  pass-fail systems, 230
  summary strategies for, 234
  traditional grades, 229–230
Graduate programs, 11
Grammar
  ten top violations of, 256
  in writing, 254
Grants, 315
Graphics packages, 19–20
Gray, C., 126
Greek organizations, 6
Greenberg, J. S., 289
Grimes, Martha, 262
Groups. *See also* Study groups
  developing work skills, 100
  obstacles, overcoming, 196
Growth mindset, 134
Guessing on multiple-choice test items, 224
Guidance Information System (GIS), 341, 342

H

Hahn, D. B., 276
Halberg, E., xxv, 42
Halberg, K., xxv
Hallucinogens, 283
Hallucinogens, avoiding, 281
Halonen, J. S., 126
Halpern, Diane F., 121, 138–139
Hamm, Garrett, 90
Hamm, Mia, 89–90, 93
Hansen, K., 246
Hansen, N. V., 3
Hansen, R. S., 246
Happiness in college, xxv
Harassment, sexual, 50
Harbin, C. E., 15
Harris, E., 338
Harris, R. A., 259
Harris, Sydney, J., 290
Hart, D., 338
Hasher, L., 76
Hastings, Reed, 301–302, 308
Health issues. *See also* Mental health; Sexual health; Sleep
  access to care, 5
  attention, seeking, 276
  developing healthy behaviors, 276
  eating habits, 278–280
  medical attention, seeking, 276
  obesity and, 278
  protecting, 216
  risks to students, 276
  self-assessment of lifestyle, 296
  self-control program for, 288
  summary strategies, 294
  valuing health, 275–276
Hearing impairments, 7–8
Helicopter parents, 42
Hemingway, Ernest, 291
Heraclites, 232
Heyman, S. R., 78
Higbee, K. L., 201
Higher-order thinking skills, 190
Highlighted notes, 174
High school, transition from, xxiii–xxiv
Hill, Napoleon, xxvii
Hindsight bias, 138
Historical Abstracts, 19
History
  major, skills for, 14
  reading in, 171
HIV/AIDS, 285
  condoms and, 286
Holistic grading, 257
Holland, John, 336–337
Home, studying at, 189
Homonyms, 255
Homosexual students, 51–52

Hopkins, J., 302
Horvitz, L. A., 2
Howatt, W. A., xxvii, xxxiii
Hubbard, Kin, 309
Humanities, studying for, 191–192
Humanities Abstracts, 19
Humor
  counselors and advisers, 4
  in essay tests answers, 228
Hunches, 225
Huxley, Thomas Henry, 188
Hyde, J. S., 285

I

Iacocca, Lee, 71
Identifying problem, 132
Imagination. *See also* Creative thinking
  in literary reading, 170
  taking charge of, 139
Immature behaviors, 105
Important tasks/activities, 74–76
Impromptu speeches, 262
Impulsive students, 100
Inattentive behaviors, 105
Income, recognizing, 304–305
Inductive reasoning, 129–131
Inferences, 126–127
Informal outlines, 250
Information avoiders, 122, 123
Inge, William R., 223
Insomnia, 278
Instant messaging, 17
Instructions for tests, 223
Instructors. *See also* Tests
  boundaries, respecting, 106
  complaints to, 107
  connections with, 103–104
  content-centered teachers, 102
  cues from, 125
  distinctive students, 103
  first impressions and, 102–103
  matching skills to, 94
  mismatches, resolving, 105–106
  problem solving with, 104–107
  reconciling learning styles with, 101–102
  relationships with, 45
  rights as student and, 106–107
  student-centered teachers, 102
  summary strategies for relationships with, 112
  wrong side, getting on, 105
Integrity, 230, 232–233. *See also* Cheating; Moral character
  participation with, xxvi
  in writing, 258–260
Intelligence profile, 91–92
  self-assessment, 114
Interference and memory, 201, 202
Internal control, establishing, xxix
International students, 48–49
Internet. *See also* Online classes
  age of data on, 125
  best data, finding, 125–126
  bookmarking resources, 177
  Boolean searches, 125
  career resources, 340–341, 342
  career search on, 343
  critical thinking and, 124–126
  evaluating information on, 18
  exploration of, 16–17
  Google, 16
  internship information, 339
  locating information on, 124–125
  loneliness and relations on, 42
  Occupational Outlook Handbook, 339–340
  online education, 18–19
  procrastination and, 77
  reading strategies, 176–177
  recording information from, 176–177
  registration tips, 10
  research on, 249
  and science reading, 171–172
  technological facility, 98
Internships, 312–313
  careers and, 338
  recommendations for, 339
Internships (Fishberg and others), 339
Interpersonal intelligence, 92
  career choices for, 108
Interpretations and inferences, 126–127
Interviews, job, 345
Intrapersonal intelligence, 92
  career choices for, 108
Introduction in first drafts, 251
Investigative personality, 336
Involvement
  becoming involved, xxix–xxx
  learning styles and, 100
  in lectures, 156

loneliness and, 41
and networking, 46
Isaacson, Lee E., 342
Isolation, avoiding, 41
IUDs (intrauterine devices), 287

J

Jandt, F. E., 48
Jendrick, M. P., 231
The Job Hunter's Bible, 343
Job interviews, 345
Jobs. *See* Employment
Johnson, D. K., 121
Johnston, L. D., 281
Jonassen, D. H., 94, 100
Journalism major, skills for, 14
Journals, xxxiii
environment, exploration of, 28–29
reflective learners and, 94
writing for, 245
Joyner, Florence Griffith, 219
Judging/perceiving in Myers-Briggs Type Inventory (MBTI), 97

K

Kagan, J., 94
Kaplan, R. M., 221
Kapor, Mitchell, 178
Karlin, S., 120
Keeley, S. M., 124
Keirsey Temperament scale, 97
Keith-Spiegel, P., 231
Keller, P. A., 78
Kerr, Clark, 109
Key word searches, 16
Kinesthetic learning, 93
King, Martin Luther, Jr., 53
King, T., 312, 313
Kingsolver, Barbara, 202
Kissinger, Henry, 71
Knouse, S., 338
Knowledge, 53
self-knowledge, xxx–xxxi
Kolb, David, 94
Koss, M., 40
Krathwohl, D. R., 190
Kroger, J., xxx

L

Lab reports, writing, 245
Lakein, Alan, 74
Lane, A. M., 291
Lane, H., 291
Language. *See also* Grammar; Vocabulary
foreign language study skills, 194–195
misleading use of, 128
Leadership skills, 335
Learning differences, 196
Learning disabilities
accommodation requests, 199
compensation for, 199
evaluating issues, 197–198
rights of students with, 198
self-assessment of, 209
study skills and, 196–199
study skills specialists and, 4
summary strategies for, 206
Learning Portfolio, xxxiii
Learning styles, 89–90. *See also* Creative thinking; Critical thinking
doing, learning by, 94
effort and, 99–101
experiential learning preferences, 93–95
intelligence profile and, 91–92
majors and, 96, 107–111
personality and, 95–98
reconciling learning styles with instructors, 101–102
reflective learners, 94
right mix, finding, 109
sensory preferences, 92–93
strategic thinking about, 98–101
summary strategies for, 112
technological facility, 98
Lectures. *See also* Classes; Notes and notetaking
clues, listening for, 155
commitment to, 151–152
connecting ideas, 155, 156–157
content-centered teachers, 102
difficult lecturers, 154–155
key ideas, capturing, 154–156
patterns of information in, 154–155
sixth sense, developing, 155–156
summary strategies for, 178
taping lectures, 162
Legal issues, 43
Leno, Jay, 198

Lerner, J. W., 196
Letters in job search, 344–345
Levine, M., 196
Levinger, E. E., 214
Levy, M., 298
Library
  careers, researching, 341
  disabled students, services for, 8
  exploration of, 4–5
  research and, 248–249
  research databases, 19
Liebowitz, Fran, 310
Lincoln, Abraham, 291, 293
Lindbergh, Anne Morrow, 244
Linde, S., 296
Lingo in arguments, 131–132
Listening skills, 34
  basic skills, 334
  in class, 153–154
  loneliness, avoiding, 41–42
  and networking, 46
Listing patterns in lectures, 154
Listservs, 16
Literature
  reading, 170–171
  study skills for, 191–192
Little Sisters program, 32
Loans. *See also* Debt
  credit and, 318
  forgiveness programs, 316
  government loans, 315–316
Lochhead, J., 133
Loftus, Elizabeth, 128, 201
Logical arguing, 35
Logical-mathematical intelligence, 91
  career choices for, 108
Lombardi, Vincent T., 152
Loneliness, 39
  dealing with, 41–42
  self-assessment, 57
Long-term memory, 200–201
Looking back on problem, 133
Lorayne, H., 203
Lose-lose negotiation strategy, 37
Lower-order thinking skills, 190
LSD, 281, 283
Lubart, T. I., 137
Lucas, E. B., 276
Lucas, J., 203
Lunelle injection, 287

M

Maas, J., 189, 278
Mackenzie, A., 63
Mackenzie, S. L. C., 276
Majors, 10–12
  creative degree options, 11
  double majors, 11
  four/five-year plans, creating, 15
  learning styles and, 96, 107–111
  skills and, 12–15
  summary strategies for choosing, 112
Malhotra, S., 303
Managing your life, xxviii–xxx
  summary strategies for, xxxiv
Manipulation and communication, 36–37
Mannerisms in speaking, 264
Man's Search for Meaning (Frankl), 186
Marcus, A., 48
Marijuana, 281, 283
Marketing major, skills for, 14
Martin, G. L., 288
Mathematics
  basic skills, 334
  improving skills, 193
  major, skills for, 14
  study skills for, 192–193
Matlin, M., 202
McCabe, D. L., 230, 231
McCreary, D. R., 276
McKay, M., 64, 65, 289
McKeachie, Wilbert J., 190
McLaughlin, Mignon, 280
McNally, D., xxvii
McWhorter, K. T., 218
Mead, Margaret, 7, 47
The Measure of Our Success (Edelman), xxii
Mechanical engineering major, skills for, 14
Media
  claims, support for, 128
  in speeches, 263
Medical issues. *See* Health issues
Medline, 19
Memory
  biological rhythms and, 76
  in Bloom's Taxonomy, 190
  decay, 201
  evaluating progress, 205
  improving, 199–205
  long-term memory, 200–201

principles for memorizing, 201–202
reconstructed memories, 128
self-assessment of, 210
short-term memory, 199–200
sleep needs and, 189
strategies for improving, 202–205
summary strategies for, 206
Men, issues for, 51
Mental health
depression, 290–291
help, seeking, 292–293
suicide, 291–292
summary strategies, 294
Mentors, 9
instructors as, 104
for international students, 49
Mercer, A. R., 196–197
Mercer, C. D., 196–197
Merighi, J. R., 276
Merrill, A. R., xxv
Merrill, R. R., xxv
Method of loci system, 203
Microsoft PowerPoint, 19–20
Miholic, V., 181
Miller, G. A., 200
Miller, Jean Baker, 50
Milne, A. A., 246
Mindfulness, 134
Minor delays, 77
Miracles Happen (Ellison & Ellison), 274
Mismatch with instructor, 105–106
Mismeasure of Woman (Tavris), 49–50
Missimer, C., 131–132
Mnemonics, 202
examples of, 204
Modern Language Association style manual, 250, 254
Modular C-Lect, 342
Money magazine, 303
Money management. *See also* Bank accounts; Budgets; Debt
compulsive spender checklist, 327
control, taking, 303–308
credit, understanding, 317–321
debt-to-income ratio, 306
expenses, acknowledging, 304–305
financial aid, 314–316
future, thinking about, 303–304
honesty and, 305
income, recognizing, 304–305
investments, 311
jobs and finances, 312–314
proactive budgeting, 305–306
ranking money, 326
reactive budgeting, 306
role of money, 305
savings plans, 306, 308
self-assessment, 328
summary strategies, 324
values, financial, 303
Money market accounts, 309
Moral character, 230–233
self-assessment of, 238
summary strategies for, 234
Moralizing, 35
Morning after pills, 286
Motivation
creative thinking and, 138
for exercise, 277
Motor/mobility impairments, 7–8
Mrosko, T., 46
Multiple-choice test strategies, 224–225
Multiple intelligences theory, 91–92
Murphy, M. C., 288
Musical intelligence, 92
career choices for, 108
Music major, skills for, 14
Mutual funds, 311
Myers, Joyce A., 97–98, 250
Myers-Briggs Type Inventory (MBTI), 97–98
career choices and, 336
career links and, 109–110

N

Name-calling and communication, 35
Naps, 278
Narrow thinking, expanding, 135
Narvaez, D., xxvi
National Association of College Employers, 335–336
National Defense Education Act, 316
Naturalistic intelligence, 92
career choices for, 108
Natural science
reading in, 171–172
study skills for, 192–193
Negative feedback, 34

Negotiating, 37–38
  skills, 335
Netflix, 302
Networking, 46
  for careers, 340
  with instructors, 104
  for internships, 339
  strategies for, 343
Neuroticism in personality model, 96–97
Newman, Edwin, 253
Nexus, 19
Nichols, R. B., 153
Nicotine, 281
  gum/patches, 280
Nilson, L. B., 163
911 calls, 5
Noise
  reducing, 152
  studying and, 188
Nolen-Hoeksema, S., 291
Nontraditional students, 52–53
Nonverbal communication, 36
Norplant, 287
Notes and notetaking. *See also* Reading
  abbreviations in notes, 161–162
  auditing personal style, 180
  borrowing notes, 153
  concept maps, 160, 161
  confusion, noting, 156
  connecting ideas, 156
  Cornell method, 158–160
  details to main point, relating, 155
  energy-saving tips, 156
  erasing mistakes, 160
  feedback on notes, 162
  identification of class, 160
  key ideas
    capturing, 154–156
    reducing, 160
  main point, relating details to, 155
  master strategies, 160–162
  organizing materials, 162
  outlining method, 158, 173
  question technique, 160
  reducing key ideas, 160
  reviewing notes, 162
  sixth sense, developing, 155–156
  style, developing, 157
  summary method, 157
  summary strategies for, 178
  taping lectures, 162
  topics, finding, 245
  unknown words, noting, 156

O

Obesity, 278–279
Objective tests, 218
Observations, 133–134
Occupational Outlook Handbook, xxxii, 339–340
OCEAN personality model, 95–97
Office hours of instructors, 103
Off-task pressures, reducing, 152–153
O'Leary, Mitch, 19
Oltmanns, T. F., 291
O'Neill, Barbara, 326
One-upping, 35
Online classes, 18–19
  assessing value of, 27
  learning styles and, 101
Open credit accounts, 319
Openness
  in five factor personality model, 95
  with partners, 43
Opiates, 283
Opinion pieces on Internet, 125
Opportunities
  for communication, 245
  creating, xxii
Optimism and stress, 289
Optional tasks, 74–75
Oral contraception, 286
Ordering, 35
Organization
  in first drafts, 251–252
  memorizing and, 201–202
  of notes, 162
  and procrastination, 78
  for tests, 221
O'Rourke, P. J., 165
Ortho Evra patches, 286–287
Outlines
  for essay tests, 226
  as notetaking method, 158, 160
  for reading notes, 173
  of speeches, 262
  for writing, 250
Overcommitting yourself, 6
Overconfidence, 138

and test-taking, 224
Overinvestment, 138
Overlearning, 203–205
Overusing words in writing, 253
Overweight, 278–279

P

Pacing
reading, 169, 215
studying, 216
Packam, G., 101
Palm Pilots, 69
Pandit, Vijaya Lakshmi, 215
Panic attacks, 222
Paper-and-pencil planners, 68
Paraphrasing
citations for, 260
in notes, 156
plagiarism, avoiding, 261
speakers, 33
Parents. *See* Family
Pareto, Vilfredo, 64–65
Partial learning, 203–205
Participation in college, xxvi
Partners. *See* Spouses and partners
Part-time employment. *See* Employment
Pass-fail systems, 230
Passivity, communication and, 37
Paterson, W., 288
Patience
international students and, 49
and networking, 46
Patterns
in lectures, 154–155
listening and, 34
Pauk, W., 160, 225
Payne, W. A., 276
PDAs (personal data assistants), 308
Peace Corps, 316
Pear, J. P., 288
Peck, M. Scott, xxix, 153
Pekins Loan, 316
Pell Grants, 315
Pennebaker, James W., xxxiii, 290
People skills, xxxii, 335
Peplau, L. A., 48
Perkins, D. N., 136
Persistence
motivation and, xxix
problem solving and, 134
for science/math improvement, 193
Personal concerns, counseling for, 4
Personal experience
claims, acceptance of, 127
with diverse others, 53
topics, finding, 245
Personality. *See also* Myers-Briggs Type Inventory (MBTI)
career choice and, 336–337
five factor personality model, 95–97
Holland's personality types, 336–337
instructors and, 45
Keirsey Temperament scale, 97
learning styles and, 95–98
self-assessment, 56
Personalizing text, 172–173
Personal plans, xxvii
Perspectives
critical thinking perspectives, 121
on diversity, 53
Persuasive writing, 244
Peterson, C., 289
Peterson's National College Data Bank, 15
Phi Beta Kappa, 229
Phil Kappa Phi, 229
Philosopher's Index, 19
Phone cards, 308
Physical health. *See* Health issues
Physical impairments, 7–8
Plagiarism, 258–259
assessing risk factors for, 269
citations for avoiding, 260
preventing, 261
Planning. *See also* Daily plans; Four/five year plans; Term plans; Weekly plans
for careers, xxxi–xxxii
for study, 187–190
for writing, 250
PLUS (Parental Loans for Undergraduate Students) program, 316
Poole, Mary, 282
Porter, B. F., 129–130
Positive self-talk
and procrastination, 78
and stress, 289
and test anxiety, 222
Potter, W. J., 122, 123
PowerPoint presentations, 19–20, 262, 263, 264
Pregnancy, 286–287

Prejudice, 47–49
Premises, 128–129
  in faulty arguments, 130
Prepaid phone cards, 308
Preparation
  for job interviews, 345
  for writing, 243–247
Prerequisite courses, 9
Presentation software, 19–20
Previewing reading material, 166
Primary sources
  in libraries, 248–249
  reading, 169–170
Printing résumés, 345
Problem solving, 132–134
  characteristics for, 133–134
  IDEAL method, 132–133
  with instructors, 104–107
  lectures, patterns in, 154–155
  mindfulness and, 134
  self-assessment for, 144
  skills, 334
  summary strategies for, 140
Procedural memory, 200
Procedural tests, 219
Procrastination, 76–78
  overcoming, 78
  self-assessment of, 86
  summary strategies for, 82
  types of, 77–78
  and writing, 258
Products, claims about, 128
Professional information processing, 177
  summary strategies for, 178
Professional networks, 46
Professional summaries, 220
Professors. *See* Instructors
Progress toward goals, xxvii–xxviii
Promiscuity, 285–286
PROMT database, 19
Proofreading
  essay tests answers, 227
  final draft of writing, 256–257
  scholarship applications, 316
Proust, Marcel, 5
Pryor, J. H., xxixv, 49, 339, 340
Pseudolistening, 34
Psychiatric help, seeking, 292–293
Psychoactive drugs. *See* Drugs
PsychoInfo/PsychLit database, 19
Psychology major, skills for, 14
Psychotherapy, 291
Public speaking. *See* Speaking
Punctuation in writing, 255
Pure Software, 302
Purpose of speech, 261–262

Q

Qualifying terms in true/false tests, 225
Quality of research sources, 248
Questions
  claims, questioning, 128
  counselors and advisers, help from, 3–4
  critical thinking and, 122–123
  improving analytical skills with, 124
  in job interviews, 345
  for library exploration, 5
  as notetaking technique, 160
  to tedious lecturers, 155
  unwelcome questions, 123
  and writing topics, 247
Quotation marks, 255
Quotations
  books of, 250
  citations for, 260
  plagiarism, avoiding, 261

R

Racial prejudice, 48
Rape, 40–41. *See also* Date rape
Rapport with instructors, 45
Ratcliff, J. L., 121
Rational Recovery Systems, 282
Reactance, 138–139
Reactive budgeting, 306
Reading
  active reading, 167–168
  analytic reading, 168
  basic skills, 334
  commitment to, 163–170
  concentration for, 165–166
  concept mapping, 173
  connecting to, 166
  Cornell method for notes, 158–160
  in different disciplines, 170–172
  habits, 165

history, reading for, 171
importance of, 163
Internet, strategies for, 176–177
levels of effort, 166–167
multiple-choice test items, 224
notetaking
methods for, 172–173
summary strategies for, 178
tips for, 173–176
outlining while, 173
pacing, 169, 215
plan for, 165
previewing material, 166
primary sources, 169
professional reading strategies, 177
reader profile, creating, 181
reviewing after, 169
in sciences, 171–172
secondary sources, 169
skimming, 166
speed
increasing, 165
self-assessment of, 182
summarizing while, 173
summary reading, 170
summary strategies for, 178
on writing topic, 247
Realistic personality, 336
Reasoning, 126–132
arguments, forming, 128–129
assumptions, checking, 131
bias and, 131
and claims, 127–129
counterarguments, 129
deductive reasoning, 129–131
inductive reasoning, 129–131
inferences, 126–127
refinement of, 129–130
summary strategies for, 140
Rebel, Kim, 308
Reconstructed memories, 128, 201
Reeve, Christopher, 274
References
gathering sources, 248
for tests, 221
writing references, 249–250
Reflecting in journal, xxxiii
Reflective learners, 94
mistakes and, 100
Registration. *See also* Classes
counselors and advisers, contacting, 8
disabled students, assistance for, 8
for reasonable course load, 10
suggestions for, 10
Rehearsing speeches, 262
Reinders, H., 339
Reinhold, Ross, 110
Relationships. *See also* Friends; Spouses and partners
attachment styles, 38–39
dating relationships, 39–40
developing, 38–42
with diverse others, 52–53
with instructors, 45
positive relationships summary strategies, 54
sexual threats, 40–41
and social life, 39–40
summary strategies for, 54
time management and, 79–80
Relatives as mentors, 104
Relaxation
deep relaxation, 289–290
sleep and, 278
and test-taking, 223
Religious life, 7
Remedies
for foreign language study, 194
humanities, studying, 192
sciences, studying for, 193
for social sciences, 194
Remembering. *See* Memory
Rereading writing, 252
Research, 248–249
databases, 19
on Internet, 249
Internet research, 16–17
in job search, 342–343
library research, 248–249
on scholarships, 315
sources, gathering, 248
streams, 246
Resident advisers (RAs), 45
Resources
examining, xxix
expanding, xxx
for foreign language study, 194
humanities, studying, 192
sciences, studying for, 194
for social sciences, 194

Respect
for diverse others, 53
for instructors, 104
for roommates, 46
for speakers, 33
Responsibility
self-esteem and, xxxi
self-responsibility, xxix
skills, 335
Restatements, asking for, 154
Résumés, 343–344
in job interviews, 345
writing guidelines, 343–344, 345
Returning-student strategies, xxiv
Reuters database, 19
Reviewing
reading, 169
time for, 189
Revisions
of first drafts, 252–253
of résumés, 345
of writing, 252–253
Revisiting goals and values, 66–67
Revolving credit accounts, 319
Rewards
procrastination, overcoming, 78
for studying, 216
Rhymes and memory, 202–203
Rice, Condoleezza, 150, 166
Rights as student, 106–107
assertiveness and, 37
of learning disabled students, 198
The Riley Guide, 342–343
Risks, 100–101
creative thinking and, 138
of disciplines, 191
for foreign language study, 194
humanities, studying, 192
sciences, studying for, 193
for social sciences, 193–194
The Road Less Traveled (Peck), xxix
Roommates
dealing with, 45
problems, fixing, 46
Rosen, L. J., 176
Rosenthal, D. M., 276
Rowling, J. K., 241–242, 243, 245
Rubrics, 257
Rules
of disciplines, 191
for foreign language study, 194
humanities, studying, 191–192
sciences, studying for, 192–193
for social sciences, 193
Rush process, 6
Russell, D., 57

S

Saccuzzo, D. P., 221
Safety issues, 5
Salt in diet, 279
Santrock, John, 283
Saturated fats, 279
Sauer, L., xxv
Savings accounts, 309
tracking, 311
Savings files, 310
Savings plans, 306, 308
Sax, L. J., 303
SCANS (Secretary's Commission on Achieving Necessary Skills), 334–336
Schaffzin, N. R., 169, 170
Scheier, M. F., 289
Schleicher, D. J., 336
Scholarships, 314, 315–316
Schwab, Charles, 198
Sciences. *See also* Natural science; Social sciences
improving skills, 193
studying for, 192–193
Search engines, 16
Searching the Internet, 124–125
Sears, D. O., 48
Secondary sources
in libraries, 248–249
reading, 169
Second impulses, going with, 139
Secure attachment, 38
Security personnel, 5
Seductive behavior, 50
Self-confidence, 138
Self-contracts, 65
Self-efficacy, xxxi
Self-employment, 313–314
Self-esteem, xxx–xxxi
health and, 275
partners and, 43
skills, 335
time management and, 65
Self-knowledge, xxx–xxxi

Self-management skills, 335, 336
  assessment of, 349
Self-responsibility, xxix
Seligman, M. E. P., xxv, 38, 39
Sellar, W. C., 229
Semantic memory, 200
Semester plans. *See* Term plans
Semicolons, 255
Senders of communication, 33
Seneca, 64
Sensing/intuiting in Myers-Briggs Type Inventory (MBTI), 97
Sensory preferences, 92–93
  self-assessment, 115
Sequence patterns in lectures, 155
Service learning, 338–339
Service learning opportunities, 7
Set time, 74
The Seven Habits of Highly Effective People: Powerful Lessons in Personal Change (Covey), xxv
Sexism, 49
Sexton, Ann, 291
Sexual bribery, 50
Sexual harassment, 50
Sexual health, 284–287
  pregnancy, 286–287
  self-assessment of attitudes, 298
  sexually transmitted infections (STIs), 285–286
Sexually transmitted infections (STIs), 285–286
  risk factors for, 285
Sexual orientation, 51–52
Sexual threats, 40–41
Shakespeare, William, 78
Shaver, P. R., 38
Shaw, George Bernard, 121
Sher, K. J., 288
Short-answer test strategies, 226
Short-term memory, 199–200
Sidney, Philip, 6
SIGI Plus, 342
Signal words in lectures, 154
Silver, N., 44
Situational cues and memorizing, 205
Skimming, 166
  and cramming, 219
Skinny Hippo Productions, 332
Skipping classes, 152
  costs of, xxvi
  before tests, 218
Sleep, 277–278
  depression and, 291
  overcoming desire for, 191
  problems with, 278
  studying and, 189
  tests and, 221
  time management and, 76
Smart cell phones, 69
Smith, Will, 310
Smoking, 280
Snap decisions, avoiding, 135
Social life, 39–40
Social needs, 216
Social personality, 337
Social sciences
  reading in, 171–172
  study skills for, 193–194
Social skills, 335
Social work major, skills for, 14
Sociological Abstracts, 19
Sociology major, skills for, 14
Sodium, use of, 279
Software, word-processing programs, 17–18
Songs and memorizing, 203
Soper, B., 278
Sororities, 6
Spam blockers, 17
Spatial intelligence, 92
  career choices for, 108
Speaking, 243, 262–263
  audience, engaging, 262
  basic skills, 334
  delivery, 262–263
    problems with, 264–265
  evaluating speeches, 264
  finishing speeches, 263
  message, building, 262
  opportunities for, 261
  questions after speech, 264
  rehearsing speeches, 262
  second chances for, 265
  strengths/weaknesses, evaluating, 270
  summary strategies for, 266
  writing speeches, 261–262
Special status, achieving, 215
Speeches. *See* Speaking
Speed. *See* Reading
Spelling, 255
Spermicides, 287
Spiritual/existential intelligence, 92

Spiritual life, 7
Spouses and partners
  communication with, 44
  relating to, 43–44
  time management and, 79–80
Sprawling thinking, containing, 135
Spreadsheets, 19
St. Vincent Millay, Edna, 42
Stafford Loan, 316
Stark, R., 174
Statistical sources, 248
Stein, B. S., 132–133
Stereotypes, 47–49
  avoiding, 53
  racial prejudice and, 48
Sternberg, R. J., 43, 137
Stimulants, 281, 283
Strategists, 122
Stress
  attitude and, 289
  coping with, 288–290
  friends and, 39
  sleep problems and, 278
  time management and, 63–64, 65
  writing about, 290
Strong, R. W., 122, 154
Student-centered teachers, 102
Student leaders as mentors, 104
Student loans. *See* Debt
Student rights, 106–107
Study groups, 195–196
  obstacles, overcoming, 196
  problems and solutions for, 197
  summary strategies for, 206
Studying, xxxii. *See also* Cramming; Study groups
  best available space, finding, 188
  Bloom's Taxonomy, 190–191
  conditions for studying, 188
  for foreign languages, 194–195
  learning disabilities and, 196–199
  material for study, 189–191
  places for, 187–188
  planning for, 187–191
  review, time for, 189
  for sciences, 192–193
  for social sciences, 193–194
  strategy for, 218
  summary strategies for, 206
  test anxiety and, 221
  time for, 80, 188–189, 219
  timetable for, 220
Study skills specialists, 4
Stunkard, A. J., 289
Style
  notetaking style, developing, 157
  writing style, refining, 253–254
Style manuals, 250
Style sheets, 254
Subgoals, xxvii, xxviii
Sugars, use of, 279
Suicide, 291–292
Summarizing
  in essay tests, 227
  as notetaking method, 157
  for reading notes, 173
  speakers, 33
Summer jobs, 337–338
Supplies for tests, 221
Support groups, 4
  for international students, 49
  and stress, 289
  for test anxiety, 222
  time management and, 65
Surface learning, 99
Surprises, maximizing, 138–139
Swift, Anne, 120, 122, 133
Swift, Jonathan, 131, 253
Swiss cheese time, 74
Syllabus, using, 103–104
Szent-Györgyi, Albert, 248

T

Tactile learners, 93
  content-centered teachers and, 102
  matching skills to instructors, 94
  tests, studying for, 218
Tannen, D., 44
Tanner, J., 338
Taping lectures, 162
Tavris, Carol, 36, 49–50
Taylor, S. E., 48, 278, 288, 289
Teachers. *See* Instructors
Teague, M. L., 276
Teamwork skills, 335
Technology, 98
  cheating and, 230
  mindfulness and, 134

in notetaking process, 157
in speeches, 264
Tedious lecturers, 155
Telephones. *See also* Cell phones
commuter telephone directory, 80
counselors and advisers, calls to, 8
directories, 3
reducing expenses, 321
as time waster, 64
Television expenses, reducing, 321
Term papers, downloading, 17
Term plans, 67
creating, 69–71
summary strategies for, 82
Test anxiety, 221–222
self-assessment of, 236
Tests. *See also* Grades; Test anxiety; specific types
attitudes about, 216
career tests, 337
cheating, 230–233
cues from instructors, 217–219
disabled students, testing, 8
emergencies, handling, 222–223
essay tests, 218–219
expectations about, 217
general test-taking strategies, 223–225
long term planning, 216
objective tests, 218
procedural tests, 219
reviewing work, 228–229
self-assessment for, 237
short term planning, 216–219
summary strategies for, 234
Textbooks, study aids in, 219
Thank-you letters, 345
Theater major, skills for, 14
Theft, protecting against, 5
Themes
in essay tests, 226–227
listening and, 34
in literary reading, 169
Thesauruses, 139, 249
Thesis, developing, 247
Thinking, 334–335. *See also* Creative thinking; Critical thinking
future, thinking about, 303–304
fuzzy thinking, clarifying, 135
higher-order thinking skills, 190
lower-order thinking skills, 190
in Myers-Briggs Type Inventory (MBTI), 97
narrow thinking, expanding, 135
sprawling thinking, containing, 135
Thoreau, Henry David, 320
Threatening, 35
Thurber, James, 221
Time management, xxx
action plans, 67
balancing life responsibilities, 78–81
benefits of, 65–66
budget time frame, 305
children, caring for, 44
creativity and, 139
80-20 principle, 64–65
misconceptions, 63–64
procrastination, 76–78
and relationships, 78–81
set time, 74
study time, 80, 188–189, 219
summary strategies for, 82
Swiss cheese time, 74
term planners, 69–71
test anxiety and, 222
time matrix, 75–76
tools for, 67–69
wasters of time, 74
weekly plans, 71–74
Time matrix, 75–76
Titles for writing, 255–256
Tolerance, 51–52
Topics
narrowing topic, 246–247
support groups, topic-specific, 4
for writing, 245–247
Tranquilizers, 281, 283
Transcriptions, 160
Transfer credits, 15–16
Transitioning to college, xxiii–xxiv
summary strategies for, xxxiv
Transportation expenses, reducing, 321
Tree diagrams. *See* Concept maps
Treos, 69
Trevino, L. K., 230, 231
True/false test strategies, 225
The Truth about Cats and Dogs, 186
Tubal ligation, 287
Tulving, E., 200
Tutoring center, 3
Twain, Mark, 126
Tyler, S., 319

U

Underestimating work involved, 77
Understanding in Bloom's Taxonomy, 190
Unknown words, noting, 156
Unwelcome questions, 123
Urbanlegends.com, 125
Urgent activities, 75–76
Utilities
  and credit history, 318
  reducing cost of, 321

V

Validity of claims, 127
Valois, R. F., 298
Values
  careers and, 333, 348
  of children, 44
  clarifying, xxv–xxvi
  revisiting, 66
  self-assessment of, xxxvi, 84
  summary strategies for, xxxiv, 82
Van Oech, Roger, 137
Vasectomy, 287
Vaughn, C., 278
Vegetables in diet, 279
Verbal-linguistic intelligence, 91
  career choices for, 108
VISTA (Volunteers in Service to America), 316
Visual impairments, 7–8
Visualization
  and memorizing, 203
  skills, 334
Visual learners, 93
  content-centered teachers and, 102
  matching skills to instructors, 94
  tests, studying for, 218
Viswanathan, Kaavya, 259
Vital tasks, 74–75
Vocabulary
  building, 164
  in science reading, 171
  word attack skills, 164
Voice
  for delivery of speech, 263
  for writing, 258

W

Waiting lists for classes, 10
Walker, Alice, 67
Walters, A., 52
Ward, William A., 100
Websites. *See* Internet
Wechsler, H., 282
Weekly plans, 67
  creating, 71–74
  evaluating, 74
  self-assessment of, 85
  study time, allocating, 73
  summary strategies for, 82
Weight issues, 278–280
West, T., 196
Wharton, Edith, 306
What Color Is Your Parachute (Bolles), 337
Whimbey, A., 133
Whitley, B. E., Jr., 231
Whitman, Meg, 2
Wikipedia, 126
Winfrey, Oprah, 32
Win-lose negotiation strategy, 37
Winston, S., 67
Win-win negotiation strategy, 37–38
Wishing, 128
Women. *See* Gender issues
Wood, P. K., 288
Wooden, John, 111
Woolf, Virginia, 154
Word attack skills, 164
Word processors, 256
  software, 17–18
Work. *See* Employment
Work habits. *See* Studying
Working thesis, developing, 247
Work-study programs, 79, 312–313
World Wide Web (WWW). *See* Internet
Wright, Stephen, 170
Writer's block, 258
Writing, 243–244. *See also* Research
  basic skills, 334
  editing, 253–255
  feedback, learning from, 257
  first drafts, 250–252
  goals, clarifying, 244
  grammar in, 254
  integrity in, 258–260
  length, determining, 252–253

narrowing topic, 246–247
outlines, 250
overuse of words in, 253
plagiarism, 259–260
plan for, 250
preparation for, 244–247
procrastination, avoiding, 258
professional product, producing, 256
proofreading, 256–257
punctuation in, 255
purpose, defining, 244–245
refining style, 253–254
résumés, guidelines for, 343–344, 345
revisions of, 252–253
routines, establishing, 249–250
rules, following, 254
speeches, 261–262
spelling in, 255
strengths/weaknesses, evaluating, 268
on stress, 290
summary strategies for, 266
thesis development, 247
timetable for, 251
titles, choosing, 255–256
topics for, 245–247
voice for, 258
Wuest, D. A., 277

Y

Yager, J., 64
Youniss, J., 339

Z

Zeidner, M., 221
Zeno of Citum, 34
Zoning out and reading, 163
Zucker, R. A., 281
Zuckerberg, Mark, 62